THE KLEIN FAMILY EDITION

THE WORLD THAT WAS *America*

1900-1945

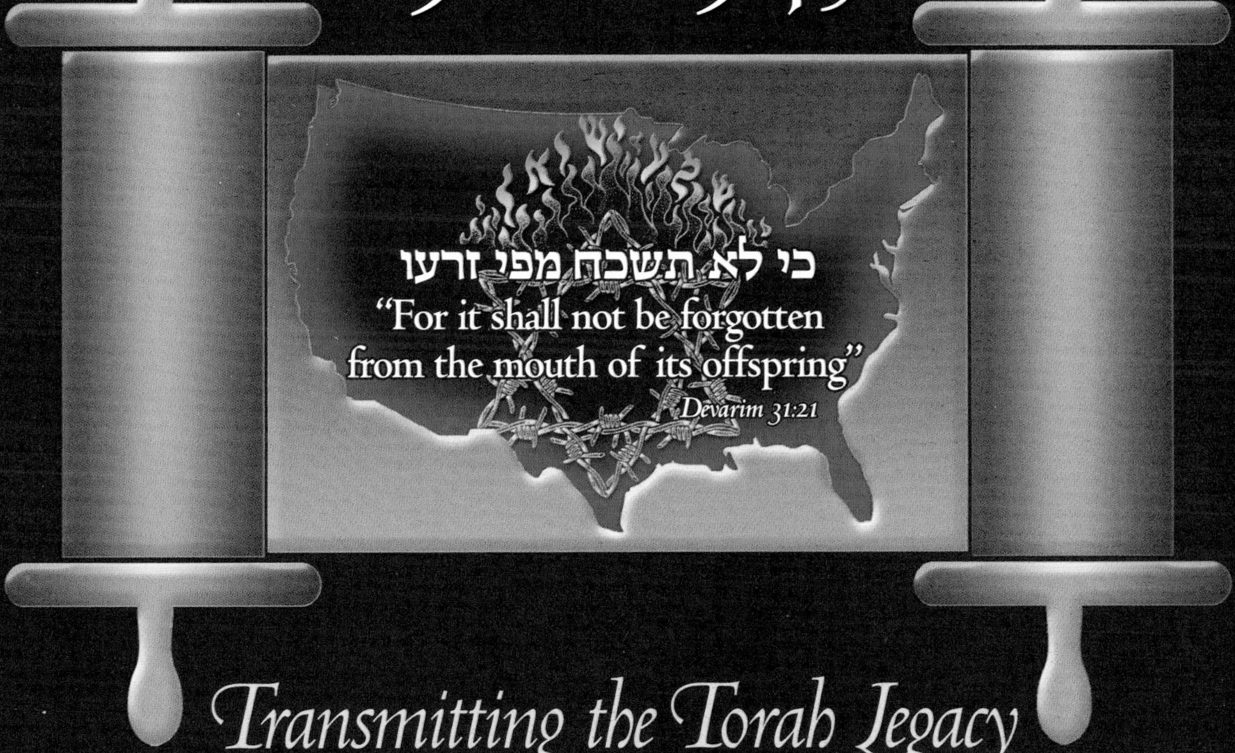

כי לא תשכח מפי זרעו

"For it shall not be forgotten
from the mouth of its offspring"

Devarim 31:21

*Transmitting the Torah Legacy
to America*

THE KLEIN FAMILY EDITION

THE WORLD THAT WAS

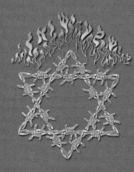

PUBLISHED BY
THE LIVING MEMORIAL
A PROJECT OF
THE HEBREW ACADEMY OF CLEVELAND

THE SHAAR PRESS

America
1900-1945

Transmitting the Torah Legacy to America

BY RABBI A. LEIB SCHEINBAUM

We thank the many families, students and friends of the individuals presented in this volume for their assistance in making available to us many of the pictures that enhance this book.

We also thank the following for providing us with photos for this project:
Agudath Israel Archives; Rabbi Amos Bunim; C.I.S. Publications; Ezras Torah; Feldheim Publishers; Betzalel Fixler; Mr. Betzalel Kahn; Herman Landau; Magen David Yeshiva; Orthodox Union; Sephardic Center, Sheila Shwekey; Rabbi Pinchas Stolper; Torah Umesorah; M.D. Yarmish; Yeshiva University Archives, Young Israel

The publisher has made every effort to determine and locate the owners of the additional photos used in this publication. Please notify The Living Memorial in case of accidental omission.

Published by the **Living Memorial** in conjunction with the **Hebrew Academy of Cleveland** and Distributed by **MESORAH PUBLICATIONS, LTD.**
4401 Second Avenue / Brooklyn, NY 11232 / (718) 921-9000 / www.artscroll.com

Distributed in Israel by SIFRIATI / A GITLER
6 Hayarkon Street / Bnei Brak 51127 / Israel

Distributed in Europe by LEHMANNS
Unit E, Viking Business Park, Rolling Mill Road / Jarrow, Tyne and Wear, NE32 3DP / ENGLAND

Distributed in Australia and New Zealand by GOLDS WORLD OF JUDAICA
3-13 William Street / Balaclava, Melbourne 3183, Victoria / Australia

Distributed in South Africa by KOLLEL BOOKSHOP
Shop 8A Norwood Hypermarket / Norwood 2196 / Johannesburg, South Africa

Designed and produced by:
Kenneth Fixler / KF Graphics
Cleveland, Ohio 44106 / 216.421.8520 / www.kfgraphics.com

Cover design by:
Hershy Feuerwerker, Brooklyn, NY

ISBN: (HARDCOVER) 1-57819-360-5

Printed in the United States of America by Edison Lithograhing and Printing Corp.
Custom bound by Sefercraft, Inc. / 4401 Second Avenue / Brooklyn, NY 11232

This volume is dedicated to the memory of our parents

Naftali Herzka and Rivka Klein

ר' נפתלי הערצקא בן ר' מנחם משה ז"ל

נפטר ט' אייר תשס"ג

רבקה בת ר' יונה ע"ה

נפטרה ד' אייר תשנ"ט

They were Holocaust survivors who never forgot their roots or the values
and traditions of their childhood. Imbuing their family with these ideals,
they ensured the perpetuation of the mesorah of their forebears.

Courage, mesiras nefesh, and deep abiding faith were the noble attributes
which personified our parents. Family was their greatest joy and primary concern.
Their children, grandchildren and great-grandchildren are the beneficiaries
of their vision and hope – a legacy that will endure forever.

and

To the memory of our brother

Yona Klein

ר' יונה בן ר' נפתלי הערצקא ז"ל

who was taken from our midst in the prime of his life.
The imprint that he made remains forever engraved in the hearts and minds
of his family, who follow in his and their grandparents' noble ways.

Mendy and Ita Klein and Family

אשרי תמימי דרך ההלכים בתורת ד'

"Praiseworthy are those whose way is perfect, who walk with the Torah of Hashem".
(Psalms 119:1)

In loving memory of our dear aunts

פייגע בת ר' מנחם משה ע"ה   רחל בת ר' מנחם משה ע"ה

Weisner   Zelczer

Each of their lives was a narrative attesting to their unfailing emunah in Hashem and
boundless chesed to others. The vicissitudes of life which they confronted were their stepping
stones to a greater and deeper realization of Hashem's true beneficence.
May their memory serve as a blessing and inspiration to their families.

Mendy and Ita Klein and family

• •

In loving memory of our great-grandparents
Mr. and Mrs. Yitzchok Feigenbaum ז"ל
true baalei chesed and pillars of the Cleveland Jewish Community -
whose vision, magnanimity, commitment and fervor helped lay the foundation
of the Telshe Yeshiva and Hebrew Academy of Cleveland
and

In Honor of and profound gratitude to
Rabbi and Mrs. Nochum Zev Dessler שליט"א
pioneers of Torah chinuch in Cleveland - whose mesiras nefesh,
determination and steadfastness established Cleveland as a premier makom Torah.

Together, they were a force that overcame the apathy and challenges confronting
the Torah community in the specter of the Holocaust. Their outstanding legacy
endures and thrives in the thousands of Torah-committed Jews, who are
the realization of their vision.

וכל מי שעוסקים בצרכי צבור באמונה הקב"ה ישלם שכרם

Leo and Sylvia Feigenbaum
Chicago, Illinois

In Appreciation

We are grateful to all those whose generous support and encouragement helped make this ambitious project a reality. We especially recognize and pay tribute to Morry and Judy Weiss, who launched this project with love, awe and conviction. Following in the noble tradition of the patriarch of their family, Mr. Irving I. Stone, they have become legends in the fields of Torah education and philanthropy. No project is too great, no endeavor too small, if it will enhance the study of Torah; if it effects a stronger, more vibrant Am Yisrael, they stand at the vanguard with encouragement and support.

We are also indebted to Leonard Stern and the Stern Family Foundation, for investing in our vision at a time when the project was yet in its infancy. Richard and Amelia Bernstein; Max Fisher; and Sam and Arie Halpern assisted in sponsoring The Living Memorial's education programs.

Dr. Joseph and Faye Geliebter are devoted to preserving the memory of the Kedoshim. To this end, they sponsored The World That Was: Poland. Their efforts on behalf of Torah chinuch are exemplary and notable. Sidney and Phyllis Reisman, sponsors of The World That Was: Hungary/Romania, have demonstrated throughout the years unparalleled commitment to the furtherance of Jewish education throughout the world. Their ongoing friendship has been especially valuable and meaningful. Hershel and Helly Ostreicher, interviewees and sponsors of the Hungary / Romania volume, are Holocaust survivors, who triumphed over adversity and transformed the challenges they encountered into opportunities to help rebuild Torah in America.

We acknowledge the involvement and assistance of George and Adele Klein who continue to carry the torch ignited by his father – as one of the vanguards who built Torah in America. We pray that Hashem grant them the ability to continue their noble endeavors on behalf of Klal Yisrael. We applaud the generosity of Leo and Sylvia Feigenbaum who continue to support the ideals of the Living Memorial. Leo, an alumnus of the Hebrew Academy, truly brings honor to his alma mater.

Mendy and Ita Klein have redefined the standards for chesed and philanthropy. Their devotion to Torah chinuch and its disemination knows no bounds. As sponsors of this volume, they have once again demonstrated their commitment to remembering the world of their parents, "The World That Was".

With profound gratitude, The Living Memorial acknowledges the support and encouragement of the Conference On Material Claims Against Germany. The Claims Conference has been at the forefront of the struggle for justice for the survivors of the Holocaust throughout the world. Their assistance has empowered the survivors to live their lives with a measure of dignity, and to assume their rightful place as productive members of society. Their grants to institutions that research and document the Holocaust and its imprint upon the Jewish People, ensures that future generations will never forget the past. Their magnanimous endowments to The Living Memorial has enabled us to do our work and provide meaningful books that have impacted upon the hearts and minds of its readers.

✺ TABLE OF CONTENTS

Relief and Rescue from the European Inferno

Vaad Hatzala

Transmitting the Legacy – Torah Visionaries

Diversity in Pioneering Torah

⚈ **PREFACE**

זכרתי לך חסד נעוריך. . .לכתך אחרי במדבר בארץ לא זרועה

"I will remember the kindness of your youth… When you
followed Me in the wilderness in a land that was not sown."

(Yirmiyahu 2:2)

t was approximately two hundred years ago, when the Vilna Gaon's
primary disciple, Rabbi Chaim Volozhin, who at the time was
laying the cornerstone for his preeminent yeshiva in Volozhin,
called attention to the potential sanctuary for Torah that lay across the ocean.
This haven for Jewry would be the last stop in their exile.   Rav Chaim shed tears
– tears that were mistaken as tears of joy, but were really tears of grief. "No," said
Rav Chaim. "I cry out of sadness. Were Volozhin to be the last station for Torah's
wanderings before the advent of Moshiach, I would cry for joy. Unfortunately, the
Torah is destined to wander further, to the wilds of America, before Moshiach
Tzidkeinu arrives and who can tell how many thousands of Jews will be lost to our
people in America."

How prophetic were his words! The Torah did "wander" to America where
it was in galus, exile.   For years it was relegated to antiquity, ignored and
repudiated – exiled, with no one who could or would liberate it. Today, we are
blessed with yeshivos, kollelim; Bais Yaakov girls' schools, chadorim and day
schools of every persuasion.   Torah Umesorah now has 600 day schools in its
directory, in just about every state in the Union.   Covering the entire spectrum of
Orthodoxy – running the gamut from right to left – these schools are home to
some 180,000 Jewish boys and girls in elementary through high school.   There are
approximately 90 yeshivos gedolos, catering to students of various backgrounds
and academic proficiencies.

Yes, we are truly blessed in America – and it is not over! Kollelim and yeshivos are constantly opening. Day schools are in the planning stage in communities
where they were only a dream – or a nightmare. Yeshivos are reaching out as high
schools are being established throughout the country.   It is a Kiddush Hashem.
Moshiach is coming. But, it was not always like this.

Let us go back and examine America's Torah renaissance – its greatness, its
pioneers and architects of Torah; those who had the vision and stood at the
vanguard, forging the way for us, so that we could avail ourselves of their toil and
devotion to the spiritual needs of Klal Yisrael. Sixty five years ago, there was very
little indeed, in terms of Torah education. There were a few yeshivos in New York,
and Baltimore was still a fledgling community. It was the roshei yeshiva, embers
from the fires of the Holocaust, who came here with fiery dedication to rebuild
what the Nazis had destroyed. The Torah that we enjoy in America is European

*Let us go back
and examine
America's Torah
renaissance –
its greatness,
its pioneers and
architects of
Torah; those
who stood at
the vanguard,
forging the way
for us.*

Torah, rescued, transplanted, nurtured, and flourishing. But, in every sense of the word – it is European.

The roshei yeshiva came here with a mission – to build Torah. But, they could not have succeeded alone. There were certain rabbonim and baalei batim, dedicated lay people, who understood the supremacy of Torah and its significance to the Jewish People. Their commitment and support facilitated the establishment of yeshivos. There were also talmidim, students, who had a thirst for their birthright that had heretofore been denied them. They wanted to learn Torah, to plumb its profundities like their counterparts had done in Europe. Together, they created a nucleus, a team that would succeed in creating the greatest renaissance of Torah since the times of Ezra HaSofer.

The best team effort will not succeed unless it is blessed with Siyata D'Shmaya, Divine assistance. They were blessed with unprecedented Siyata D'Shmaya. Why? Perhaps, the words of Rabbi Eliyahu Eliezer Dessler in his preface to the Michtav M'Eliyahu sums it up best:

> "One who works for Tikun Olam, the betterment of the world, merits Siyata D'Shmaya, if he does so faithfully, with sincerity, in search of the emes, truth. He will also succeed in his endeavor, because whoever is needed for the benefit of the world will succeed, even if he is not really fit for this work. If there is no one else to engage in this endeavor besides him, he will merit Divine assistance.

> "In this impoverished generation of ours, rebuilding Torah is of critical importance. Even though we are not worthy or fitting for this awesome task, it is incumbent on us to put ourselves into the thick of the responsibility and with this we will merit Siyata D'Shmaya."

Today, we, enjoy the fruits of this Siyata D'Shmaya. People ask me what motivated the effort to put together such a history. There is no question that while most people will see its overriding significance and need, as always, there will be detractors who will feel, "why get involved in history?" There is invariably the possibility of omitting someone who rightfully deserves to be included, or even omitting a significant aspect of a person's life story. For this I apologize. I spoke to many people in the "know" and after detailing comprehensive "criteria" for inclusion in this volume, we have prepared fifty-two biographical sketches. These individuals, many of them Holocaust survivors, were foremost advocates in transmitting the legacy and building Torah in America. The biographies are not intended to be detailed or comprehensive accounts of their lives, nor do we necessarily subscribe to their personal philosophy or hashkafa, rather, they are a brief overview of the individual and his contribution.

Preceding the individual biographical sketches is a description of the spiritual landscape of America in the first half of the twentieth century. It includes a detailed account of the structuring of Orthodoxy and the vital contributions of the three major Orthodox Jewish organizations of that period – the Orthodox Union, Young Israel, and Zeirei Agudath Israel.

As part of the spiritual landscape, we also discuss Torah education in America, its genesis and further development; the story of the yeshiva movement; girls' schools; and Torah Umesorah and the nascent Day School movement.

The Torah that we enjoy in America is European Torah, rescued, transplanted, nurtured, and flourishing. But, in every sense of the word – it is European... Indeed, we stand on their shoulders. They sacrificed, persevered, and labored so that we can enjoy and thrive in the spiritual oasis that America has become.

The Vaad Hatzala (Rescue Committee), and its notable accomplishments are studied in depth. This organization was instrumental in rescuing Jews from the Holocaust inferno, many of whom became the spiritual lay leaders and *roshei yeshiva* in America.

Following the biographical sketches are three first person accounts of Torah visionaries in America during the 1940s. They represent a cross-section of Torah activists. All were students together in the same class in Mesivta Torah Vodaath, where they imbibed from their *rebbeim* the *hashkafah* that would shape their lives.

Each in his own way was instrumental in developing Jewish communities and Torah education in America. Their priorities and values were shaped by the Holocaust era. These trailblazers include a pulpit Rabbi, a Torah Umesorah pioneer, and one of the first flagship day school principals.

The last section of this volume presents vanguards of Torah in America. These gentlemen were primary lay leaders and champions for Orthodoxy and Torah education of their generation. They were involved in relief and rescue work during the war and demonstrated by thought and deed that no sacrifice was too great, if it was on behalf of their people. Their knowledge, self-sacrifice and unfailing dedication enabled Torah life and Torah institutions to be built and flourish in America.

In a sense, this volume in "The World That Was" series might better be entitled, "The World That Was Becoming," because the book ends with 1945, which was a launching pad for explosive growth. Even the greatest optimists in 1945 could not have predicted the tremendous proliferation of Torah institutions and communities that have flourished and inspired countless Jews across America. And, in the familiar cliché, the best is yet to come.

If the primary focus of this book extended beyond 1945, it most likely would devote extensive chapters to Rabbi Aharon Kotler and the Satmar Rav, Rabbi Yoel Teitelbaum, who respectively were the spiritual dynamos who inspired, led, and shepherded the growth of the yeshiva and *Chassidic* worlds. No doubt it would devote an extensive chapter to Rabbi Eliyahu Meir Bloch, the Telshe *Rosh HaYeshiva*, whose charismatic and visionary leadership was tragically cut short at too young an age. However, this volume concentrates on a period of Jewish history when there was no substantive Jewish history, but only a **hope** for the future of Torah in America.

Getting back to why I undertook to prepare and edit a volume of this magnitude. I was motivated by a number of reasons. First, there is a lesson to be derived from the power of the *yachid*, individual. The people included in this volume were individuals who refused to accept negativity, did not succumb to apathy, and overcame challenges with resolution and fortitude. Second, there is a sense of *hakoras hatov*, gratitude and appreciation that we owe them. We are their beneficiaries, as we reap and benefit from the fruits of their accomplishments. Perhaps, they would not "fit" in today's milieu for various reasons. But, theirs was **a very different time with a different set of values.** All too often, we judge people by our standards and our perspective, ignoring the

We must not view history myopically... Great care has been taken not to rewrite history to fit our present image. Rather, we must ratify history by remaining true to the facts – both positive and negative.

fact that their challenges were much different than ours. Indeed, we stand on their shoulders. They sacrificed, persevered, and labored so that we can enjoy and thrive in the spiritual oasis that America has become.

We must not view history myopically. Our view of the events of the past should and must be seen through the prism of the past. We should not permit ourselves **to rewrite history to fit our present image. Rather, we must ratify history by remaining true to the facts – both positive and negative.**

This volume will forever impact on the hearts and minds of its readers – both young and old. It will offer them new insights into the challenges confronting our people in the first half of the twentieth century, and develop a deeper appreciation of the Holocaust survivors. They built Torah in America, thereby deleting the word "final" from the Final Solution. Their response to tragedy was to rebuild. Our mandate is to **continue** their work and transform Rav Chaim's tears of sadness into joy.

Acknowledgments

It takes many dedicated individuals to produce a book of this scope and magnitude. From its very genesis to the moment of completion, when the realization of a dream finally comes to fruition, there is but one focus in mind: to produce a volume that is true to historical fact and that presents a Torah-oriented perspective of the development of Torah in America.

Horav Nochum Zev Dessler, שליט״א, Dean, Hebrew Academy of Cleveland, was our spiritual mentor. A scion of the Lithuanian *Mussar* dynasty, he "lives" the "world that was." One of the true pioneers of Torah in America, he inspired much of our work.

We are grateful to **Horav Shmuel Kamenetsky**, שליט״א, who has provided guidance, advice and encouragement from the inception of this project. Aware of his many responsibilities, both public and private, we are especially gratified that he considers the Living Memorial to be a priority and that he made the time to review the book.

The Hebrew Academy of Cleveland spearheaded this project and has set the standard for Torah-oriented curriculum. We are grateful to **Rabbi Simcha Z. Dessler**, its Educational Director, during whose tenure this project saw fruition. His expertise in Jewish education has been of great assistance to us. **Rabbi Eli Dessler**, Financial Director of the Hebrew Academy, has gone beyond the call of duty in his support of this project. His dedication to the Hebrew Academy and its staff is unsurpassed. **Ivan Soclof**, President of the Hebrew Academy, has been a guiding force in the realization of this curriculum. His propensity for detail maintained our perspective in achieving our goal. He has always been a firm believer that the Hebrew Academy's mandate extends beyond Cleveland. It is because of his vision, and that of his predecessors, that the Hebrew Academy has become a world-class Torah institution.

Our previous volumes, authored by **Rabbi Yitzchak Kasnett** have received incredible response from teacher, student and layman alike. The deeply moving first-person accounts of *mesiras nefesh*, total dedication to the point of self-sacrifice, are meaningful and inspiring. It is our most heartfelt prayer that these volumes serve as a tribute to the spiritual and moral greatness of the Orthodox Jews of Eastern Europe, while inspiring our children to emulate such levels of spiritual purity. Rabbi Kasnett prepared the Student Guide for this volume in his usual proficient and innovative manner.

The success of this project can be attributed to many people. First, we are grateful to **Morry Weiss** whose brainchild it was to provide a Holocaust-oriented curriculum for the Yeshiva Day School student so that the "world that was" – the world of his parents – would never be forgotten. He gave up much of his personal time and attention, despite his heavy schedule. He has been both parent and friend to this project throughout its development.

Harry M. Brown, president of the Living Memorial, has been a pillar of strength and encouragement. His belief in the project's success, and his sense of obligation to the Holocaust victims spurred us on while he helped us overcome the challenges in our path.

Mrs. Arlene Jaffe is our Director of Development. Her ongoing commitment to this project has been a source of inspiration and encouragement.

Kenny Fixler of KF Graphics, himself the child of Holocaust survivors, was personally inspired by the experiences and feelings of that era. His creative talents are evident on each page. The compelling logo of the Living Memorial was magnificently designed by him and is a true manifestation of our mission. He has been a partner throughout the design and production of this volume.

The administration and staff at the Hebrew Academy have been incredible in their patience with the author and invaluable in their devotion to the project. **Rabbi Malkiel Hefter** has always been there for me, whether with technical or moral support. **Mr. Michael Wojdak** has spent many hours refining the manuscript. **Mrs. Hadassah Rivkah Kutoff** typed most of the original manuscript.

I am grateful to the many people who wrote, researched, edited and made suggestions; and to the *talmidim* and family members who provided information, anecdotes and pictures for the biographical vignettes. Special gratitude to **Rabbi Amos Bunim, Rabbi Dovid Eliezri, Rabbi Reuven Gerson, Mordechai Gottlieb, Rabbi Mordechai Kamenetsky, Rabbi Moshe Kolodny, Rabbi Hillel Yarmove, Rabbi Shalom Ziskind, Dr. Rivkah Blau, Rebbetzin Malkah David** and **Mrs. Hildee Weiss**.

We would like to express our sincere appreciation to **Rabbi Meir Zlotowitz** and **Rabbi Nosson Scherman** of Mesorah Publications for their efforts on our behalf in disseminating these volumes to Jewish communities throughout the world.

We are grateful to **Avrohom Biderman** for his valuable input and direction in shepherding this volume to production.

We are grateful to **Torah Umesorah**, the National Society for Hebrew Day Schools, and its Director, **Rabbi Joshua Fishman**, for their advice, support and encouragement throughout this endeavor.

A special acknowledgment to Mrs. Ethel Gottlieb who is the editor par-excellence, collaborator and writer for much of this volume. A part of herself has gone into this project. She has given life to the words as she helped produce a book that will be accepted by laymen and students throughout the panorama of Judaism. She wrote and researched many of the historical chapters as well as some biographies and other sections. Her expert advice and abilities developed during years of editing many works of Jewish literature, has greatly enriched my writing experience. Her patience and counsel were unflagging and she shares in every aspect of this volume.

Last but not least, are the unsung heroes – my family, and most important my wife, **Neny**. Producing a book of this magnitude while juggling other projects and responsibilities takes the total devotion and support of an *Eishes Chayil* par excellence. She exemplifies the proverbial woman of valor in the true essence of the word. As the consummate life companion, she has been the reason for whatever success I have achieved. Together, may we merit to see the spiritual values of "the world that was" manifest in our own children and grandchildren, and that the love of Torah, its study and dissemination, be the hallmarks of our home.

We pray to Hashem that our work will truly serve as a *"Living Memorial"* to the victims of the Holocaust.

Rabbi A. Leib Scheinbaum
National Director, The Living Memorial
Iyar 5764, May 2004

Rabbi CHAIM P. SCHEINBERG
Rosh Hayeshiva "TORAH ORE"
and Morah Hora'ah of Kiryat Mattersdorf

הרב חיים פינחס שיינברג
ראש ישיבת "תורה אור"
ומורה הוראה דקרית מטרסדורף

בס"ד ו' אייר תשס"ד

זכור ימות עולם בינו שנות דור ודור
הנה מודעת זאת בקרב אחינו בני ישראל החרדים לדבר ה' שבעזה"י ובחסדיו המרובים אשר הבטיח לנו בתורתו הק' "כי לא תשכח מפי זרעו" קם בארצה"ב דור דעה של מבקשי ה'. נתרבו ספסלי בתי המדרש, אלפים בני תורה ממיתים עצמם באהלה של תורה, ורבבות משפחות מדקדקים בקלה כחמורה בכל חלקי השו"ע כאבותנו ואבות אבותנו מדור דור.

אולם כאשר נתגדלתי משחר טל ילדותי במדינה זו עיני ראו ולא זר השממה הרוחנית הנוראה שהיתה כאן וגם זכיתי לראות איך שהצדיקים מועטים שהקב"ה שותלן בכל דור מסרו נפשם לנטוע מחדש עולם של תורה ויר"ש. אשרי עין ראתה זאת! כמעט שזכינו לקיים הנבואה "הקטן יהי' לאלף והצעיר לגוי עצום".

כאשר הביאו לפני הספר החשוב שמטרתו לחנך לצעירי התלמידים ההסטורי' של עולם התורה באמריקא ע"כ אמרתי שדבר גדול וטוב עושים הרבנים הנכבדים עוסקים במלאכת הקדש להגיד לדור החדש מעשה הצדיקים שמהם ועל ידם נבנה עולם חדש זה.

החותם לכבוד התורה ועמליה,
חיים פינחס שיינברג

[illegible]

רחוב פנים מאירות 2, ירושלים, ת.ד. 6979, טל. 537-1513 (02), ישראל
2 Panim Meirot St., Jerusalem, P.O.B. 6979, Tel. (02) 537-1513, Israel

TORAH UMESORAH
תורה ומסורה

The National Society for
Hebrew Day Schools

COMMITTING
GENERATIONS
TO TORAH

It is with great pleasure that Torah Umesorah proffers its expressions of congratulations to the Hebrew Academy of Cleveland, and to Rabbi Avraham Leib Scheinbaum, for this monumental publication, "The World That Was: America".

In the 1930's and 40's, the prevalent belief amongst American Jewry was that there was no hope for a thriving, vibrant Orthodox Jewish way of life in North America. There was great apathy for the Torah and mitzvos, which many claimed was relegated to the shtetlach of Europe, and could not gain footing in the new "goldeneh medinah." Many felt that the future of Judaism in America would be in the camps of the reform and conservative.

There was, however, a truly great Gadol, with visionary foresight, who felt otherwise. The Founder of Torah Umesorah, Rav Shraga Feivel Mendlowitz zt"l, knew that the future of Yiddishkeit lay in the age-old traditions of the Torah. And he acted; against great odds, he persevered, even when many others thought it was an impossibility. He founded Day Schools, Yeshivos, Chassidic communities. And he imbued within his hundreds of talmidim - in Yeshiva Torah Vodaath, Beis Medrash Elyon, and Aish Dos - a burning desire to be "marbitz Torah"; to continue spreading the bright flame of Torah that he ignited on these shores.

Today, Torah communities, Day Schools, Yeshivos and many Torah institutions are flourishing even in the most remote locations throughout the continent.

"The World That Was: America" beautifully depicts the story of the transformation of America into a fortress of Torah. It is a celebration of the magnificent world of Yiddishkeit that we enjoy today, made possible only by the sweat, toil and perseverance of Rav Shraga Feivel, and many other great Gedolim, Rabbonim and Roshei Yeshiva, who paved the way for us and our children to live a Torah life.

I commend the Hebrew Academy of Cleveland for producing this, and many other such magnificent publications. The Hebrew Academy has always served as a benchmark for Day Schools, exemplifying excellence in chinuch. This volume, so ably prepared by the eminent mechanech and writer, Rabbi Aryeh Leib Sheinbaum, is a beautifully illustrated, highly readable masterpiece. It is true "Kiddush Shem Shomayim", and a must-read for us, our children, and our children's children.

160 BROADWAY, 4th Fl.

NEW YORK, NY 10038

TEL: (212) 227-1000

FAX: (212) 406-6934

E-mail: umesorah @ aol.com

Sincerely,

Joshua Fishman

Rabbi Joshua Fishman
Executive Vice President

A Monthly Magazine of Jewish Thought and Opinion

1 Rosh Chodesh Adar I, 5763 / February 3, 2003

Anyone who experienced the last 65 years of Jewish life in America – especially if he or she had contact with members of preceding generations – was personal witness to the ongoing miracle of the transformation of the American spiritual wasteland into a blossoming Torah landscape.

All Jewish children should know the inspiring thrust and the sparkling details of this miracle, especially since they are not only beneficiary to its legacy, they are living the miracle as it continues to unfold.

Capturing this story and conveying it to our children through the written word may be a formidable challenge, but it is also a matter of great value and urgency. They should be aware of the phenomenal times in which we are living and the myriad factors of *Hashgacha* that have brought – and are bringing – it about.

It is thus with great excitement that I greet the publication of *The World That Was: America*, masterfully prepared and edited by the veteran *mechanech* Rabbi A. Leib Scheinbaum. As is well-known, Rabbi Scheinbaum has been writing and disseminating *Peninim* on the weekly *Sedra*, bringing timeless insights into the Torah's timeless wisdom to tens of thousands of families over the past thirteen years. In his expert hands, we can be certain that our youth will be led through tumultuous yet extraordinarily productive decades that witnessed the awakening of Jewish America to the call of Torah, and its continual renaissance and development, reaching for unforeseen heights… heights that may be beyond our limited vision, but which we are yet destined to scale.

This work offers our schools and their charges an opportunity to plumb the depths of Divine *Hashgacha*, as they are stimulated to appreciate, and hopefully emulate, the achievements of the leaders of the pioneering generations, and are thus prepared to measure up with *mesiras nefesh* to the resultant challenges yet to be met.

Nisson Wolpin

Rabbi Nisson Wolpin

42 Broadway • 14th floor • New York, NY 10004 • 212-797-9000 • fax 646-254-1600

Building the future on the foundations of the past, the Hebrew Academy of Cleveland's Living Memorial Project has published a Holocaust series to sensitize contemporary youth with an awe and appreciation for the glorious world that was. The Torah world will welcome the addition of this volume entitled, *The World That Was: America* which documents the historic transplant of Torah to America.

My grandfather, *Rav Eliyahu Eliezer Dessler, זצ"ל* clearly perceived his immediate family's miraculous survival from the destruction of the Holocaust as a Divine mission with a sense of urgency, stating: "Our obligation is to rebuild what was destroyed and to restore what was lost." Indeed, despite the trials and tribulations, the tragedies and atrocities that confronted scores of sacred Jews during the darkest moments of Jewish history, they remained steadfast in their faith, determined against all odds to do just that – to build. In fact, they transformed the spiritual landscape of America.

We stand on the shoulders of those giants who are the true architects and pioneers of Torah on these shores. With dedication and perseverance, they planted and nurtured seeds, laid foundations and left an enduring legacy for our generation. They taught us that there are worlds to be conquered and seas to be navigated. As we carry with us their message of hope and inspiration, their story must be told.

I am humbled to represent a nationally acclaimed *mosad* which continues to leave an indelible imprint upon Jewish life across the globe and has undertaken yet another monumental project. I applaud my colleague, Rabbi A. Leib Scheinbaum for preparing and editing this outstanding publication. A dynamic *mechanech* and prolific writer, Rabbi Scheinbaum has once again transformed dream to reality inspiring Jews the worldover with the beauty of our heritage.

Sincerely,

Rabbi Simcha Dessler
Educational Director

Phil and Mary Edlis Elementary School • Beatrice J. Stone Yavne High School • Jacob Sapirstein Campus

"A People Survives As Long As It Transmits Its Heritage From One Generation To The Next"

THE WORLD THAT WAS *America*

1900-1945

⤳ The Spiritual Landscape of America

A FOREWORD

In order to fully grasp the uphill battle that confronted those who had the courage and fortitude to attempt to build Torah in America, one must understand the circumstances that prevailed from the beginning to the middle of the twentieth century. 1881-1914 were the years of the Great Immigration. The masses of Jews streaming to the United States were broken refugees fleeing the pogroms and massacres of Eastern Europe, as well as the abject poverty and persecution of *shtetel* life.

The contrast between the *shtetel* and a city in America was tremendous. Various communal/social institutions (administered by the *Kehillah*), together with the strong family unit, helped preserve *Yiddishkeit* in the *shtetel*. Although many were not learned, they were religiously observant. Not only that, but each community had a *rav* who was a *talmid chacham* who had profound influence on the community. The *Kehillah* institutions and the leadership of community rabbis were sorely lacking in America during that period.

The masses of Jews streaming to the United States (1881-1914) were broken refugees fleeing the pogroms and massacres of Eastern Europe, as well as the abject poverty and persecution of shtetel life

Leaving Europe was a great spiritual risk and a challenge, as well. It was not uncommon for an immigrant arriving at these shores to be greeted with the following words: "Young man, you have just landed in the great city of New York, where many opportunities are open before you. But you must forget about your G-d and your religion and especially about the Sabbath and the dietary laws. You must work every day, including the Sabbath, and eat whatever you can get, for G-d has been left on the other side of the ocean." (A six-day workweek was the norm until the 1940s. Indeed, the only *shomer Shabbos* retail chain was Barton's Bonbonniere, owned by Stephen Klein and Herbert Tenzer, whose 65 stores were closed on Shabbos.)

Apparently, economic preservation and spiritual survival were not compatible in America – or so the refugees were informed. Indeed, many immigrants succumbed to leaving G-d on the "other side of the ocean." But there were some who refused to sell their "birthright" for a "bowl of red lentils." That was not why they had fled the dangers and uncertainties of Europe.

Immigrants streaming into the country at the turn of the century

They had not left Europe's threat of *physical* harm to risk *spiritual* extinction in America. They suffered great hardship and constant ridicule, even from their own people – but they remained steadfast in upholding the Torah because of their trust in G-d, as well as their dedication and determination. They certainly did not forget about G-d; they did not leave Him in Europe. He was here in America and they would see to it that His Name would be sanctified.

The European newcomer was generally poverty stricken, and would toil long backbreaking hours under the most inhumane conditions in order to eke out a meager livelihood. The immigrants had dreamed of a better life in the "*Goldeneh Medinah*" – the "golden country" of America. They arrived thinking that the streets were "paved with gold," but the cold reality of the cobblestones quickly dispelled this notion. In the end, they would be content if their children would be "real" Americans, in every sense. There were, however, tens of thousands of observant Jews – from rabbis to laborers – who tried to maintain their commitment to Torah in hundreds of communities across America. Their laudable *mesiras nefesh* was, nevertheless, often insufficient to influence their children. Unfortunately, at the time, American society was antagonistic to Shabbos and *kashrus* observance, as well as Jewish education.

Processing immigrants at Ellis Island

Orthodox Jewish immigrants had not left Europe's threat of physical harm to risk spiritual extinction in America. Suffering great hardship and constant ridicule, even from their own people, they remained steadfast in upholding the Torah because of their trust in G-d.

Slowly, Orthodox Jewry addressed the situation, and ultimately three vital organizations were founded who stood at the vanguard, entered the breach and established a stronghold for Orthodoxy in that turbulent era.

Many of the Jewish immigrants felt that a traditional Jewish lifestyle was antithetical to succeeding – financially or socially – in America. Consequently, those offering a solution to this "problem" were able to make inroads.

Not only outside forces challenged *Yiddishkeit,* but there were anti-religious forces *within* the Jewish community that had to be contended with. The non-Orthodox and secular movements offered these Jews a means of assimilating into American society. They were viewed as modern and American. In addition, the Yiddish newspaper, *The Forward*, and various Socialist organizations which were anti-religious, had a great influence on this segment of the community. Finally, in the 1920s, two Orthodox newspapers – *Yiddish Tageblatt* and *Der Morgen Journal* – were established and counterattacked *The Forward*. It was not enough, however; far more was needed.

A salesman trying to earn a living

There were always Orthodox rabbis and laymen who attempted to battle against these forces. Since they were greatly outnumbered, and generally operated independently, they did not succeed in reaching a large portion of the community. Fortunately, there were capable and determined individuals who realized that a different sort of action was necessary – an organized group with strong leadership and common goals to give Orthodoxy a voice. Slowly, Orthodox Jewry addressed the situation, and ultimately three vital organizations were founded – the Orthodox Union, Young Israel and Zeirei Agudath Israel – who stood at the vanguard, entered the breach and established a stronghold for Orthodoxy in that turbulent era.

Working in a New York sweatshop

The American Jewish Community at the Turn of the Century

Structuring Orthodoxy

Organized "Movements"

⇜ Part 1: The Orthodox Union

(UNION OF ORTHODOX JEWISH CONGREGATIONS OF AMERICA)[1]

A MOVEMENT IS BORN

Shortly before the turn of the twentieth century, Reverend Dr. Henry Pereira Mendes of Congregation Shearith Israel, Rabbi of the prestigious Spanish and Portuguese Synagogue in New York City, was at the forefront of a movement to organize the Orthodox congregations in America. He recognized that previous attempts to establish such an organization (i.e., the Association of American Orthodox Hebrew Congregations that appointed Rabbi Jacob Joseph* as Chief Rabbi of New York) had failed, due to reasons that he hoped to remedy. Dr. Mendes (a medical doctor) understood that such an organization had to include a larger membership, reflecting the diverse makeup of the Orthodox Jewish community. It could not be limited to *shuls* of Eastern European origin (as was the Association of American Orthodox Hebrew Congregations), but had to include Ashkenazic and Sephardic congregations, as well as Eastern and Western European Jews. The need existed for an Orthodox congregational organization which would be based on Torah and Halachah, in order to bring unity and leadership to the various Orthodox factions.

The primary issues of the day were Jewish education, Shabbos observance, *kashrus*, divorce, conversions, and Christian proselytizing, in addition to other matters relating to Jewish life in America.

On June 8, 1898, representatives of approximately 50 synagogues from the United States and Canada met at Shearith Israel, under Dr. Mendes's leadership, to establish a union of Orthodox synagogues. The delegates represented a cross section of Jewish life in America. The name, Orthodox Jewish Congregations Union of America, was chosen and a constitution was adopted. The Declaration of Principles stated:

> *Shortly before the turn of the 20th century, the need existed for an Orthodox congregational organization which would be based on Torah and Halachah, in order to bring unity and leadership to the various Orthodox factions.*

---

1. Adapted from **The Orthodox Union Story**, Saul Bernstein, Jason Aronson Inc., Northvale, N.J., 1997

* Refer to the biography of Rabbi Jacob Joseph, pg. 174

This conference of delegates from Jewish congregations in the United States and the Dominion of Canada is convened to advance the interests of positive Biblical, rabbinical, traditional, and historical Judaism, and we affirm our adherence to the authoritative interpretation of our Rabbis as contained in the Talmud and Codes (Shulchan Aruch, etc.).

We are assembled not as a synod, and therefore we have no legislative authority to decide religious questions, but as a representative body which by organization and cooperation will endeavor to advance the interests of Judaism in America...

We affirm our belief in the existence of G-d, His Revelation to Israel, the coming of the Messiah, and the Thirteen Principles of Faith (as declared by) of Maimonides.[2]

At the sixth convention of the Orthodox Union (June 29, 1913) the purposes guiding the formation of the Orthodox Union were summarized as:

To speak with authority in the name of (the fold of) Orthodox Judaism and to defend the rights of Orthodox Jews as citizens...It was also established to protest whenever necessary against secular-based Judaism.[3]

Dr. Mendes was elected president of the newly formed Orthodox Union and was to serve in that capacity for 15

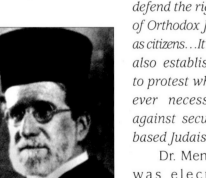

Reverend Dr. Henry Pereira Mendes, Rabbi of the Spanish and Portuguese Synagogue

Congregation Shearith Israel, the Spanish and Portuguese Synagogue in New York City

years, until ill health forced him to step down. Rabbi Bernard Drachman succeeded him.

ACTIVITIES

From the outset, action was taken to address certain vital issues facing the Jewish communities. The negative influences of the society in which the young generation lived had to be countered. At the top of the Orthodox Union's agenda were campaigns designed to meet the needs of the Jewish children and young people. The public schools of that era flagrantly Christianized their curriculum, and the vast majority of Jewish children who

From the outset, action was taken to address certain vital issues facing the Jewish communities. The negative influences of the society on the young generation had to be countered.

2. Orthodox Union Constitution, Founding Convention, June 1898

3. Reports of the Sixth Convention (June 29, 1913), Forward

Rabbi Bernard Drachman

To combat the dangers of assimilation and Christian proselytizing the Orthodox Union established after-school classes, clubs and study circles to teach the young about their Jewish religion and heritage.

attended these schools (since there was only one yeshiva at that time) were exposed to insidious teachings at a most vulnerable time in their lives. In addition, Christian missionaries also attempted to ensnare Jewish children, knowing that they were often unsupervised while their parents worked. To combat these dangers Dr. Mendes spoke out publicly, often in the press, to alert the community at large to the prevailing crisis. After-school classes were set up in various synagogues to teach Hebrew reading, Jewish history, Jewish laws and customs, and *Chumash*. The volunteer teachers were chosen from among those who could best influence the children religiously. Clubs and study circles were also established in several places where children and young people could go *"...during their leisure hours and find their recreation in an atmosphere that is truly Jewish, rather than be drawn to the [de-Judaizing, assimilationist-sponsored] centers and settlement houses as sole alternatives to the poolrooms, dance halls or the streets."*[4]

Another accomplishment of note regarding the early activities of the Orthodox Union was in the area of Shabbos observance. As has been previously mentioned, the Jewish immigrants of that period were faced with a desperate situation – to work on Shabbos or lose their jobs. Thousands upon thousands succumbed and transgressed this sacred *mitzvah*. The Orthodox Union set up a special division to address this critical problem – the Jewish Sabbath Association. Rabbi Bernard Drachman was the chairman (eventually this division became an autonomous organization, called the Jewish Sabbath Alliance). They convinced businesses and factories to close on Shabbos, conducted classes to educate the community about Shabbos and helped find employment for *shomer Shabbos* people. 1500 jobs were obtained for Shabbos observers in 1907 alone, as reported by Rabbi Drachman.

Over time, the Orthodox Union achieved several other important accomplishments for Shabbos observers: privileges for *shomer Shabbos* college students were obtained, the Bar exam was transferred from Shabbos and leaves of absence on *Yom Tov* were arranged for Jewish municipal workers.* At the time of the Spanish-American War, the Orthodox Union requested that the War Department grant furloughs to Jewish officers and soldiers for observance of Jewish holidays. In 1904, in response to a letter from Dr. Mendes, President Theodore Roosevelt ordered that "commanding officers be authorized to permit Jewish soldiers to be absent for services on Jewish holy days.[5]

4. Report, 1907, to Orthodox Union by Albert Lucas, an OU Officer, regarding the religious classes conducted under his direction at various New York synagogues.

* It should be noted that Edward S. Silver, D.A. of Brooklyn, judge of Surrogate Court, President of National Council of Young Israel, and the first Orthodox Jew to hold a major political position was instrumental in negotiating that the Bar Exam and municipal work exams not be given on Shabbos.

5. **An Old Faith in the New World**, David & Tamar de Sola Pool, Columbia University Press, N.Y., 1955

This presidential order was followed by an official regulation from the War Department granting such leave to Jewish officers and soldiers.

Additionally, in its first decade-and-a-half, the Orthodox Union mobilized aid for victims of Russian persecutions, including the Kishinev Pogrom, and on behalf of communities suffering from outbreaks in Romania and Morocco, as well as officially protesting discrimination against Jews in some Latin American countries.

At the Orthodox Union's Convention in 1913, the following range of notable activities was submitted in the official report:

During the 15 years [the Union] has been in existence it has been occupied with the following subjects: Russian persecutions; immigration laws that hinder Jews coming to America; the passport question; International and Labor arbitration; Kashruth, Shechitah, Milah, Gittin, etc; Organization of a Sabbath Society.

The establishment of Orthodox Jewish religious schools; schools for physically handicapped and deaf and dumb Jewish children; Jewish school books; the defense of Judaism against misrepresentation by Secular Jews or Christians; Jewish rights in public schools; conversionists' activities; college exams on our Holy Days; government employees and Holy Day observance; aiding our co-religionists in Russia, Romania, Turkey, Cuba, Haiti, Central America, etc.

It is truly remarkable how much was accomplished during this early period, despite limited funds and no professional staff. Only because of the hard work and devotion of the Union's officers and dedicated volunteers did their plans succeed.

Once the organization was established and its achievements became known, many more congregations joined the Orthodox Union. It was recognized as a central force within the nationwide Jewish community, even among the non-affiliated synagogues. One persistent problem, however, was the attitude among both the affiliated and non-affiliated congregations that the Orthodox Union was obligated to provide the Orthodox Jewish community's needs. This would have been acceptable if at the same time this sense of obligation was shared together with the workload. No one was turned away, but it took a long time before there was joint cooperation and participation. This limited the organization's *total* effectiveness, until an equitable solution to this dilemma was achieved.

HATZALAS NEFASHOS

The Central Relief Committee (CRC), set up in 1914 during World War I, was considered the crowning achievement of Dr. Mendes's administration. This organization mobilized a large-scale relief campaign on behalf of the millions of Jews who were suffering in the war zones of Eastern Europe and the *Yishuv* – the Jewish settlement in *Eretz Yisrael*, then under Turkish rule. Other organizations, including the Agudas HaRabbonim, cooperated with the Orthodox Union and joined the C.R.C. A widespread fundraising campaign was initiated in several cities. Rabbi Drachman and Mr. Morris Engelman, both officers of the Orthodox Union, went on a five-week crosscountry fundraising drive. Subsequently, two others–Albert Lucas and Dr. Masliansky–embarked on a similar venture. Thousands of people were inspired to give to this noble cause. Mr. Engelman was very creative and devised several unique and successful fundraising projects (war relief stamp; a cantorial concert

It is truly remarkable how much was accomplished during this early period in many areas – Jewish education, Shabbos observance, kashrus, divorce and conversions - despite limited funds and no professional staff.

The Central Relief Committee (CRC), set up in 1914 during World War I, was considered the crowning achievement of Dr. Mendes's administration. It mobilized a large-scale relief campaign for millions of Jews suffering in the war zones of Eastern Europe and the Yishuv.

tour and Jewish Relief Day) raising hundreds of thousands of dollars. The money was channeled to the *rabbanim* and community leaders in Eastern Europe to provide food and other necessities to the victims of the war and pogroms, as well as to the yeshivos. Non-Orthodox groups also formed committees to help in the relief effort. Eventually, the groups joined together to establish the Jewish Joint Distribution Committee (J.D.C. or "Joint"). It was headed by Rabbi Dr. Leo Jung, rabbi of the Manhattan Jewish Center*, and has continued to play an important role in Jewish life ever since. The Central Relief Committee, however, continued to channel aid *directly* to the yeshivos, and fundraising within Orthodox Jewish channels remained under the

UOJCA-sponsored Central Relief Committee. The great service rendered by this organization cannot be overstated. One can only imagine what they would have achieved had they not been forced to cease fiscal operation (in the 1930s and 40s) because of circumstances beyond their control (they ceased operating in 1950). The Orthodox Union was involved in relief and rescue work during World War II through the Vaad Hatzala.

During World War I and World War II the Orthodox Union worked valiantly to address the religious needs of the thousands of Jews in the Armed Forces. To facilitate religious observance, kosher food. *sefarim and siddurim* were provided. Eventually, an Armed Forces Division was established within the

OU Regional Convention, Sept. 1962, Seattle, WA. Seated at the table, Torah Umesorah's Leadership (L-R, 2nd from left): Moses Feuerstein, Rabbi Binyomin Goldenberg, Rabbi Dr. Joseph Kaminetsky and (standing behind Rabbi Goldenberg): Rabbi Pinchas Stolper, Executive Vice President of the O.U.

---

* Refer to the biography of Rabbi Dr. Leo Jung, pg. 176

Orthodox Union, and by the time of the Korean War (1950-53) they were able to provide ongoing and invaluable services to Jewish troops serving in the military.

ADDRESSING AMERICAN ORTHODOXY'S NEEDS

Adapting to the changing conditions of Jewish life in America, an idea was advanced to provide women with their own role in Jewish affairs. In 1923, the Women's Branch of the UOJCA was formed. They undertook several projects over the course of their existence to help the Jewish community in the areas of education, practical guidance and programming for the *shul* sisterhoods. One of their earliest projects was raising the necessary funds to provide a dormitory for students attending Yeshiva College, founded in the mid-1920s. They also established and maintained the Hebrew Teachers Training School for Girls (1928-1954). This school trained thousands of young women as teachers. Its graduates were accomplished professionals who made noteworthy contributions in this vital area.

The extremely difficult problems plaguing the *kashrus* field, and specifically, *hechsheirim,* had initially prevented the Orthodox Union from becoming too involved. (Until that time the *kashrus* field was chaotic – there was a lack of integrity in the provision and production of kosher meat and poultry; corruption was wide-spread.)* This changed in 1924, following the passage (in 1915 and 1920) of strict laws in New York State regarding fraudulent representation of kosher food. It was finally recognized that legislative measures were the best means of remedy-

Secretary of Defense Dick Cheney receives Orthodox Union Medal of Freedom at Orthodox Union National Dinner, May 5, 1991 at the New York Hilton for his courageous leadership during the Persian Gulf crisis and Operation Desert Storm. (L-R): Sheldon Rudoff, president of Orthodox Union, Rabbi Pinchas Stolper, Executive Vice President, Secretary Dick Cheney, and, presenting the award, Dr. Mandell I. Ganchrow, Chairman, Orthodox Union Institute for Public Affairs

ing the situation. Several other states adopted similar laws after a unanimous Supreme Court decision upheld the legislation.

Additional motivation resulted from the revolutionary developments taking place then in the processing and marketing of convenient new food products. The kosher consumer was confused as to the kosher status of all these products – the manufacturers' and advertisers' claims were often unsupported or endorsed by those with questionable status. Clearly there was a need for reliable supervision and certification, and so was born the OU symbol of *kashrus* – a trusted name in the kosher food industry to this very day.

The subsequent development of the Orthodox Union's *kashrus* service is without parallel. It certainly was

There was great need for reliable supervision and certification of the kosher food industry. In the mid-1920s the trusted O.U. symbol for kashrus was born.

---

* Refer to the biographies of Rabbi Jacob Joseph and Rabbi Hillel Klein, pgs. 174, 206

*Rabbi Pinchas Stolper making Havdalah at an
NCSY convention, 1966*

lets were published as early as 1925. These publications addressed those subjects that were of interest to the Jewish community – Jewish beliefs, practices and concepts. They were distributed to synagogues across the United States and Canada. To the present day, the Orthodox Union continues to produce informative and substantive publications – books, booklets, periodicals, newsletters, etc.

Regional and national conventions were held to plan projects and events, as well as evaluate what had been accomplished. These conventions also gave the delegates a sense of shared purpose and friendship.

In the mid-1920s, the need for

never envisioned at the time of its inception to become such a powerful force in Jewish religious life.

In the years between the world wars there were additional projects. A series of popular educational book-

NCSY Israel Seminar, 1995

youth organizations for Jewish Orthodox high school boys and girls was apparent. Habonim was established for boys and Habanoth for the girls. These two organizations functioned successfully for ten years. Eventually, the Orthodox Union achieved enormous success in its work with Jewish teenagers with the formation in 1954 of NCSY (National Conference of Synagogue Youth).

July 26, 1934, marked the first national radio broadcast under Orthodox Jewish auspices. Broadcasting from NBC Studios in New York, the program

*NCSY Convention, 1964. (L-R): A young (Rabbi) Shalom Strajcher,
and (Rabbi) Yehuda Cheplowitz, unidentified,
Rabbi Wasserman, Rabbi Pinchas Stolper*

The NCSY Miracle

In 1959, years before anyone thought a *Teshuvah* movement was possible in America, the leadership of the Orthodox Union enlisted Rabbi Pinchas Stolper, a *talmid* of Rav Yitzchak Hutner, *zt"l,* to create a youth movement for its 1,000 affiliated synagogues that would break the rapid spiral of decline in America's great "out of town" and recapture Jewish youth for Torah.

In 1959, it was considered ludicrously impossible that an educational, Orthodox youth organization stressing Torah values such as modesty, Shabbos observance and Torah learning would appeal to American Jewish teenagers coming from non-observant or minimally-observant backgrounds. Ten years later, Rabbi Stolper would write that "in its unique ability to sink grass roots in America's great backyard, NCSY has demonstrated that American Jewish youth is in search of Torah."

What is NCSY?

Is it 800 young people gathered at a National Convention from nearly every community in North America reaffirming their loyalty to Torah; or is it the private awakening of a fifteen-year-old who has decided to keep his or her first Shabbos?

Is it over three hundred regional and district seminars, Summer Camps, Israel Programs, Shabbatons, Conclaves and Leader's Institutes attended by over 35,000 each year; or is it a sixteen year old who has made a secret pledge to become an observant Jew?

Is it the thousands of letters between teenagers and the young yeshiva advisors they met at an educational event carrying messages of hope and strength to a generation that is prepared to declare its loyalty to Torah living; or is it a seventeen-year-old girl who has refused a non-Jewish date because NCSY offered an alternative to a life filled with dead ends?

NCSY is this and more

Functioning in thirty-seven American states and five Canadian provinces, NCSY has grown into one of the largest and most active Jewish youth movements in the world with an organizational structure encompassing 465 chapters in twelve regions, with 26,600 inspired members, hundreds of dedicated volunteers on every level, and scores of thousands of alumni from coast-to-coast, increasing numbers of whom have decided to keep Shabbos, learn in yeshiva and become leaders of American Jewry.

NCSY has tapped the unique human resources of the Yeshiva movement to infuse spiritual and intellectual direction into a vast nationwide program of Jewish re-discovery. This has resulted in an astounding Jewish renaissance among scores of thousands of alienated youth.

The young "*ba'al teshuvah*" is no longer a rarity. Regained for their people and faith, thousands have moved on from the NCSY experience to yeshivos. Many serve today as rabbis, day school principals, teachers, youth leaders, and *roshei yeshiva*, with tremendous impact on both the youth and adult community. The significance of this phenomenon must be measured in historic terms.

From Vancouver to Miami... from Montreal to Los Angeles... NCSY has transformed communities, restored hope, rekindled the fervor of young people from committed homes, and reached out to those who never tasted the deep wellsprings of our tradition.

---

presented various noted personalities who spoke on important issues of the day. Their broadcast also included a religious musical program offered by well-known cantors. The radio program was important to its listeners and helped energize them and revive their spirits and faith which had suffered as a result of the Depression. It should be noted that many Jewish people were victims of the Depression and therefore were unemployed, so morale was low. The program offered them much needed encouragement. The importance of Jewish education was frequently discussed as well. Overall, the broadcast had an important impact on the Jewish community.

As the oldest Orthodox Jewish organization in America, the Orthodox Union has been at the forefront of all efforts aimed at the improvement of Jewish religious life and the perpetuation of Orthodox Judaism in America.

The Orthodox Union has been at the forefront of all efforts aimed at the improvement of Jewish religious life and the perpetuation of Orthodox Judaism in America.

ᝫ Part 2: Young Israel*

THE HISTORICAL SETTING FOR THE FOUNDING OF A MOVEMENT

Confronting Challenges

In contemporary America, living a *complete* Torah-observant life is considered quite common in the Orthodox Jewish community. However, America at the dawn of the twentieth century was a disappointing, harsh, and often dangerous place for a Torah-true Jew. There were strong negative feelings about immigrating to America expressed by many European rabbis and leaders. They were very anxious about the spiritual wasteland that was the American landscape at that time.

One man who confronted this crisis directly was Rabbi Jacob David Willowsky, the Rabbi of Slutzk, Lithuania. Known by the acronym *Ridvaz*, he came to the United States in the latter part of the nineteenth century. His purpose was to earn enough money to publish his profound commentary on the Talmud *Yerushalmi* (the Jerusalem Talmud). Consequently, when Chicago's rabbinate and laity invited him to address their community's inadequate halachic standards, notably in *kashrus*, the

Ridvaz accepted. For three difficult years, he turned his dynamic personality toward strengthening their Jewish institutions and reforming *kashrus* supervision and other breaches of Halachah. Despite his best efforts, like Rabbi Jacob Joseph in New York City, the *Ridvaz* was constantly thwarted by apathetic Jews, or even more troubling, by those who would gain through unethical practices. He was very upset and expressed compassion for those Jews who were truly *moser nefesh* to observe Halachah. Eventually, the *Ridvaz* realized that he could not combat the heretics in a land antithetical to Torah. Heartbroken, he left for Safed, Palestine in 1905.

However, before leaving America, the *Ridvaz* wrote *Nimukei Ridvaz*, which depicts the great pitfalls facing American Jews at that time. It also includes a scathing attack on American Jewish life: "When the Jews were exiled," he wrote, "some found refuge in America, where they met with affluence. Yet the very essence of this country precludes adherence to Torah. Laws requiring com-

> *America at the dawn of the twentieth century was a disappointing, harsh, and often dangerous place for a Torah-true Jew. European rabbis and leaders were very anxious about the spiritual wasteland that was the American landscape at that time.*

---

* The material for this section is adapted from **A Fire in His Soul**, Amos Bunim, Feldheim Publishers, 1989

pulsory education, for example, enforce the commingling of all cultures. As a minority, how can we Jews prevent our children from emulating the secular culture, antithetical to our sacred tradition? Some hire tutors, which is a disastrous failure since these lessons are conducted after a long day at regular school. Not only is the child's energy spent, but he also resents staying indoors while his non-Jewish friends are free to play outside.

"Furthermore," the *Ridvaz* wrote, "it is most difficult for one to observe the sanctity of Shabbos when enticed by the momentary gain of double pay. This transgression is compounded when those who work on Shabbos observe Sunday as their day of rest, dressing in their Shabbos clothes and thus elevating Sunday while denigrating their own holy day. This is equal to absolute idolatry.

"Many individuals of questionable repute take advantage of our state of transition. They pose as rabbis and dress in rabbinic garb, preach sermons and present certificates of ordination, which cannot be traced. These charlatans have become the purveyors of America's *Yiddishkeit*. Similarly, many have become so-called kosher butchers, befriended by these so-called rabbis who agree to certify the *kashrus* of their meats. Together, they have fattened their purses by selling non-kosher meat to fellow Jews. Then there are so-called *shochtim* who received certification even though they are men of evil character.

"The observant Jew is therefore faced with an impossible dilemma: Who can he trust, since every store displays a sign proclaiming 'Kosher Meat' in its window?

"Similar conditions prevail in the areas of marriage and circumcision.

The only religious functionaries available to perform marriages or issue divorces are these same *shochtim* and *mohelim*, who do so indiscriminately despite a woeful lack of knowledge in these areas. At worst, they encourage *Kohanim* to marry divorcees, or permit women to remarry without first obtaining a *get*.

"Who can tell," the *Ridvaz* concluded, "whether some day, with G-d's will, Torah will find a haven on these shores? And who will know in future generations what America was like at the time of the *Ridvaz*? Ultimately, however, one cannot condemn the Jewish people, descendants of the saintly Patriarchs. There still are honest Jews whose religion burns strongly within them, who are untainted and truly deserving of the World to Come."

It did not take long for religious visionaries to see, as had the *Ridvaz*, that many influences in American society posed an alarming threat to Torah Judaism: social, philosophical and religious. The young pioneers of Orthodoxy in America remembered (or knew of) the economic hardships and the endless pogroms they had suffered at the hands of their gentile neighbors in Europe. Like many Jews, these visionaries had a strong desire to correct these and other social and spiritual problems.

The greatest tragedy was the abandonment of Torah Judaism. Many young Orthodox pioneers witnessed how their contemporaries from very religious homes deviated from Jewish life: dating non-Jewish women, eating non-kosher food, desecrating Shabbos,

Rabbi Jacob David Willowsky

The young pioneers of Orthodoxy in America remembered (or knew of) the economic hardships and the endless pogroms they had suffered at the hands of their gentile neighbors in Europe. They desired to rectify the social and spiritual problems.

*Rabbi Meir Shapiro,
Lubliner Rav*

*The greatest
tragedy was the
abandonment
of Torah
Judaism.
The Orthodox
vanguard vowed
to fight against
assimilation
with the
greatest
dedication.
They created a
movement to
address
these issues.*

and calamitously marrying non-Jews, which meant the end of that family's Jewish lineage. This Orthodox vanguard vowed to fight against assimilation with the greatest dedication. Though the motivation may have varied from person to person, this handful of young activists would soon create a movement that, at that time, could only be considered ludicrous to the rank and file Jewish population of America in the 1920s.

Two major obstacles stood in the way of their quest. The first was the Socialist Party's increasingly vehement anti-religious campaign. The Socialists – and the more radical Bundists – portrayed Torah life as an enemy of progress, unscientific, and an obstacle to mankind's redemption. The Young Socialist League sponsored cellar clubs with social dancing as the main attraction. The most defiant attack on Torah, however, was the annual Yom Kippur Ball. For many of those surrounded by hardships and subjected to anti-religious propaganda, the Socialists seemed to provide a meaningful response.

America itself was the second obstacle. Religious Jews were simply overwhelmed by the many hardships and the secularism and materialism of this country. Overwrought by culture shock, many abandoned the fight for *Yiddishkeit*.

This problem persisted and was acknowledged by important Torah personalities of the time. Rabbi Meir Shapiro, the Lubliner Rav, renowned for his Torah scholarship, for founding Yeshivas Chachmei Lublin and instituting the *Daf Yomi*, visited America in

1928 to raise funds for his yeshiva. He was guest of honor at a meeting of Jewish leaders. In turn, he honored a colleague by requesting that Rabbi Shraga Feivel Mendlowitz*, subsequent founder of the Torah Umesorah Day School movement, be seated next to him. The other attendees were surprised at the high honor accorded Rabbi Mendlowitz, who was not well known at that time. Rabbi Shapiro said, "Any person who can stay in America and try to build Torah has the greatest place in *Olam Haba* and I would be privileged to sit alongside him there."

The language barrier was one of American Jewry's greatest challenges. English had become the primary language of the younger Jews, but was a foreign tongue to their parents and rabbis. Furthermore, Torah education was sorely lacking. At the turn of the century there were only three day schools in New York – Eitz Chaim (1886), Rabbi Jacob Joseph School (1903), and, in East New York, Yeshiva Toras Chaim (1927, East New York). Formal Jewish learning was chaotic and disorganized at best, and young American Jews attended public schools as was mandated. As America's Torah life dissipated, and young Jews moved away from *Yiddishkeit*, those hopeful of building a Torah-true community despaired of the future.

YOUNG ISRAEL IS ESTABLISHED

Perhaps they despaired, but they did not give in. As early as 1911, Max Grablowsky, Joshua Horowitz and Benjamin Koenigsberg founded an organization to save American Jewish youth. The immediate catalyst was the

---

* Refer to the biography of Rabbi Shraga Feivel Mendlowitz, pg. 244

news that Stephen Wise, America's foremost secular Zionist leader, planned to open a branch of his Free Synagogue on the Lower East Side of Manhattan. Wise offered American Jews something they could not find in the *shtiblach* of their parents – astute discussions of Jewish topics in English. However, the three men had heard Wise and knew that what he said, and

Lower East Side of Manhattan

did, perverted Torah Judaism; his ideas and practices were heretical to *Yiddishkeit*. After one of his Shabbos lectures, they were astonished when a church-style collection plate was passed around on a day when handling money was forbidden!

Resolved to create a viable American Orthodox alternative to Wise's movement, Grablowsky, Horowitz and Koenigsberg approached Dr. Judah Magnes at the recently established New York *Kehillah*. Based on the traditional European models, the *Kehillah* was a broad-based New York City

communal organization devoted to improving *kashrus* standards, religious education, living conditions, and more. Dr. Magnes had founded the *Kehillah* in 1908 and served as its president until 1922. He was sympathetic to the three young men. Frequently, he attended a Lower East Side *shtibel* on Shabbos. But Dr. Magnes had another agenda as well, for he realized how important the English language and American life style were to these young Jews. He felt he could attract them to the Conservative movement – an enticing blend of old world and new, of *Yiddishkeit* and Americanism. Without hesitation, Magnes offered the three young men the Second Avenue *Kehillah* offices for meetings.

At that time, the lines between Orthodoxy and Conservatism were particularly blurred in the eyes of the general public, since the founders of the Conservative Jewish Theological Seminary (JTS) in 1886 were themselves of Orthodox background. Graduates of JTS were the only Jewish leaders who spoke English, and consequently they attracted many Jews.

The fledgling organization grew, and by 1912 there were fifteen young men and women. They called themselves the Hebrew Circle, and Benjamin Koenigsberg gave them use of his new law office. Magnes helped the members select a new name, Young Israel, and worked with them to organize a series of Friday night lectures in English.

The Kalvarier Synagogue (known as the Pike Street Shul) was one of the Lower East Side's most imposing buildings and was chosen as the best

Benjamin Koenigsberg

The new organization – Young Israel – organized a series of Friday night lectures on Torah subjects, in English, to attract young Jewish people. This was a novel idea at that time, in 1912.

THE YOUNG ISRAEL PROGRAM

TRADITIONAL JUDAISM
To perpetuate traditional Judaism in America.

AMERICANISM
To instill in the hearts of American Jewish youth a love for Americanism and for the principles of democracy.

YOUTH CLUBS
To provide clubs for our young boys and girls in the environment free of radical and destructive influences, and based on morality, rectitude and sanctity.

EMPLOYMENT
To solve the problems of vocational guidance and employment for observant and religious youth.

VETERANS
To aid in the religious and economic rehabilitation of returning veterans.

LEADERSHIP
To prepare young boys and girls for future participation and leadership in community affairs.

PALESTINE
To promulgate a love for Eretz Yisroel and a desire to build it as a Jewish Homeland in accordance with the laws and spirit of the Torah.

EDUCATION
To educate our youth and our adults in the heritage and culture of the Jewish people and to introduce them to the vast treasures of wisdom and righteousness based on our Torah and developed by our sages.

SYNAGOGUE
To bring Jewish youth back to the Synagogue.

PHILANTHROPY
To participate in all charitable and philanthropic enterprises regardless of sect, religion, or race.

CIVIC PRIDE
To unite the Jewish youth of America for the purpose of participation in civic endeavors.

The original Young Israel Mission Statement

In all likelihood without Young Israel thousands of Jewish youth might never have remained Torah observant, a fact many of us today tend to forget.

location to inaugurate the Young Israel series. At first, the *shul's* trustees were skeptical; English simply was not spoken in a synagogue. In fact, they only permitted Dr. Magnes to speak on that first Friday night after he agreed to return the following day and deliver the same speech in Yiddish! It turned out that the trustees had worried needlessly about attracting people, because the Magnes lecture was an astounding success. The public's thirst to hear an English speaker on a Torah subject was so great that more than 5,000 people jammed the synagogue. The overflow crowd had to be controlled by mounted police.

That first Young Israel lecture series featured the eminent Orthodox rabbi, Dr. Joseph H. Hertz, later Chief Rabbi of Great Britain. Many of the Conservative leaders of the time were also invited as guest lecturers, thus creating an extremely tenuous situation.

Mr. Irving Bunim[*], one of America's staunchest activists for Torah causes, and a few others realized that the neophyte Young Israel organization lectures were not bringing Torah to those who were unable to discern between authentic Torah Judaism and its antithesis. They grasped what few understood at the time: the authenticity of Torah must be eternally maintained without any revisions.

They chose what seemed the most viable option – to enter the Young Israel movement and to work from *within* to transform it. This decision benefited the activists by forcing them to develop their talents and hone their own Torah scholarship in order to capture the Jewish youth through compelling Torah lectures in English. Irving Bunim, for example, chose the homiletic *Pirkei Avos* (*Ethics of the Fathers*) as his text, because he felt it would be readily understood by the general public. He also utilized extensively the *Malbim's* commentary, because that great scholar's philosophy related so well to the contemporary scene. Mr. Bunim was truly the catalyst that helped change the future of American Orthodox Jewry. All it took was will, and he and his dedicated compatriots possessed it in quantity.

---

[*] Refer to the biography of Mr. Irving Bunim, pg. 394

BROADENING THE SCOPE

Young Israel had limited its activities to lectures and forums at its inception in 1912. The leadership quickly came to the realization that it needed a synagogue of its own to overcome the religious apathy that was prevalent. They planned to include a synagogue service for youth, an unheard-of practice at that time. Well aware that the young congregants felt like outcasts at services dominated by older Europeans, because they received few *aliyos* or chances to lead the services, they hoped to change the format. The older generation believed that a young man was not an important synagogue participant until he was married. The Young Israel members felt this stance was too inflexible.

Furthermore, many of the younger generation also objected to the sale of honors to the wealthy, and to services completely devoid of melodies and congregational participation. The youth, torn between their parents' worldview and their own, devised a solution which, despite its shortcomings, helped save a generation of Orthodox Jewish youth. In all likelihood, without Young Israel thousands of Jewish youth might never have remained Torah observant, a fact many of us today tend to forget.

A turning point occurred in the summer of 1913. A few young men who were walking on East Broadway were asked to join a storefront *minyan*. One old man asked them to attend the *minyan* once a week. They agreed on the condition that they be permitted to lead the services twice a month. When it was their turn, they introduced melodies into the service. News of the new *minyan* spread quickly, and within three months the storefront was so crowded that they moved to the second floor of the Educational Alliance building.

The original name of this *minyan* was the Model Synagogue Organization, but soon after they adopted Young Israel, the name of their forum organization. For five years (1913-18), there were two conflicting sides within Young Israel, often split along ideological lines. The more liberal members desired better cultural and social programs, while the more Orthodox members wanted improved synagogue services. Finally, in 1918, a truce was reached, and the two groups merged.

It was an uneasy alliance. Young Israel had too many dissimilar interests, and there were many who were aware that its more liberal faction threatened the growth of authentic Torah Judaism. Many feared that this faction would undermine the Young Israel movement. Since men such as Judah Magnes, Israel Friedlander and Mordechai Kaplan served as top advisors, Young Israel could easily have strayed from traditional Orthodoxy. Moreover, because the older rabbis withheld their recognition of Young Israel, it seemed only natural for the fledgling movement to gravitate toward the Conservatives, who welcomed this traditionally oriented organization for young Jews.

Those who feared that this change in

Rabbi Joseph Hertz, Chief Rabbi of the British Commonwealth, 1913-1946

The leadership quickly realized that it needed a synagogue of its own to overcome the religious apathy that was prevalent. They instituted greater participation of the young, and melodies in the service.

direction would come about witnessed its actualization; following the Model Synagogue's truce in 1918, just after World War I, the Conservatives in fact made greater inroads into Young Israel.

As early as 1920, Irving Bunim and his allies felt that this alliance could not work. At this juncture, Irving Bunim became Young Israel's strongest and most vocal opponent of any form of Judaism that was not wholly dedicated to Torah dictate: He fought fervently to prevent any non-Orthodox groups from seizing control of the movement. He chose two methods of sustaining Young Israel as an authentic Torah movement. First, he convinced his antagonists that endless infighting was senseless and they should ask Rabbi Dr. Dov (Bernard) Revel[*], president of Yeshivas Rabbeinu Yitzchak Elchanan (which later became Yeshiva University), to mediate the conflict. Dr. Revel, a noted Talmudic scholar and Torah leader, saw the danger inherent in Young Israel's non-Orthodox faction. He supported the Orthodox position so vigorously, that eventually the secularists who sought to undermine the Torah objective were all but banished from Young Israel.

Secondly, Mr. Bunim used networking to create an Orthodox stronghold in Young Israel. A respected leader, he had important allies among a dedicated group of distinguished, influential Jews. Together, they inserted new requirements into the Young Israel charter to ensure its Orthodox integrity: all branches had to have Shabbos and holiday services, regular Torah learning, youth programs, *mechitzos* (partitions separating men and women) where they *davened,* and *shomer Shabbos* officers. It was a major victory and, more importantly, it

categorically defined Young Israel as an Orthodox organization.

The movement developed quickly throughout Greater New York. At first, each Young Israel operated independently. In 1922, a Council of Young Israel was formed to centralize activities and plan a nationwide expansion program. Within two years, all Young Israel organizations had joined the Council. In 1926, the Council (then called the Council of Young Israel and Young Israel Synagogue Organization) was incorporated and given a charter by the New York State Legislature. Only a group that possessed a charter from the Council could call itself Young Israel.

During this period, Young Israel established Orthodox synagogues, Torah-learning opportunities, and even social welfare programs. Its first annual convention was in 1924, and within a year it created the Employment Bureau for Sabbath Observers. The Bureau found jobs for more than five hundred *shomer Shabbos* men and women. Eventually, Young Israel provided vocational training and then helped their trainees find placement. The organization also had its own monthly publication, the *Council Chronicle,* later renamed the *Young Israel Viewpoint.* A network of youth programs was created. In the late 1920s, Young Israel had more than two dozen affiliates, a full-time professional staff and Wall Street offices.

By the 1930s, Young Israel had branches in New England, the Midwest, Canada and Palestine. These new affiliates were soon hosting the movement's annual conventions. The Young Israel annual convention was the most inspiring, uplifting, and encouraging

As the movement developed, a council was formed to centralize activities and plan a nationwide expansion program. Young Israel established Orthodox shuls, Torah-learning, and social welfare programs.

[*] Refer to the biography of Rabbi Dr. Dov Revel, pg. 256

medium and motivating force for preserving and strengthening the spirit and commitment of young Jewish men and women.

In 1935, the Council instituted its Rotating College, under whose auspices Torah scholars lectured at various Young Israel centers in Greater New York. Shortly thereafter, Young Israel established correspondence courses in *Chumash, Mishnah*, laws and customs, and current events.

Young Israel's main focus was on the young, educated Jewish men and women. Even as early as 1926, the Council offered adult education lectures, forums on *taharas hamishpachah* (laws of family purity), community meetings, *shiurim* and Shabbos classes. This movement proved that Orthodoxy was compatible with American life. It was the first organization to serve *ba'alei teshuvah*, particularly on college campuses where it funded kosher kitchens. It is critical to realize that Young Israel and its leadership literally saved an entire generation of Jewish youth. This inspired group of dedicated Orthodox activists lived a Torah-true life while bringing fellow Jews back to Torah.

THE LEADERSHIP ISSUE

The decades between the World Wars were difficult for many Orthodox rabbis. Although scholarly, they were unappreciated. Unable to speak English, they earned little and often supplemented meager salaries as *kashrus* supervisors. These rabbis felt threatened by this upstart, English-speaking Orthodox movement, and did not hesitate to make their feelings known. They considered Young Israel an institution for non-observant Jews, one with which no observant Jew should associate.

National Council of Young Israel Dinner, Astor Hotel, 1938. (L-R): Arthur LeVine, Rabbi Dr. David Stern (spiritual leader of the National Council of Young Israel), Irving M. Bunim, Israel Upbin, Isidore (Iggy) Klein

Early on, Young Israel members were vilified as "*Amerikanisher shkotzim*" (American defilers). Even in 1934, the movement was denounced from the podium of the Agudas HaRabbonim convention. The Orthodox leaders of Young Israel worked tirelessly to convince people that the slurs were untrue.

Some feel Young Israel exacerbated the situation because of its early negative attitude toward rabbis. There were exceptions. One rabbi, Dr. David S. Stern, a Torah scholar who was also secularly knowledgeable, was vital to the Young Israel movement. Rabbi Stern taught mathematics at Columbia University and Yitzchak Elchanan Talmudic Academy High School; he later served as principal of Yeshiva Torah Vodaath. Every Shabbos afternoon, for over forty years, Rabbi Stern walked across the Williamsburg Bridge to the Lower East Side. There he taught *Chumash*, holiday observance, and *Pirkei Avos* to Young Israel congregants. His impact on the Young Israel congregants was enormous. Many acknowledged becoming *shomrei Shabbos* because of his lectures.

Young Israel's main focus was on the young, educated Jewish men and women. They proved that Orthodoxy was compatible with American life.

Young Israel's "Children's Hour"

It was not until the late 1930s that any Young Israel congregation retained the services of a rabbi. Few English-speaking rabbis were available. By necessity, lay leaders developed talents for teaching and leading services. As they grew in Torah, they presented its eternal message in a framework of American life. During its first decades, Young Israel provided extensive lay training that has rarely been duplicated. The message proclaimed by the early Young Israel leaders was constant: If you do not have true Torah values, then your children will acculturate, then assimilate, and be lost forever.

> *The message proclaimed by the early Young Israel leaders was constant: If you do not have true Torah values, then your children will acculturate, then assimilate, and be lost forever.*

SUSTAINING ORTHODOXY

In 1925, the problem of the Socialist dances still continued. To combat them, three Young Israel activists–Benzion Weberman (later a prominent orthodox lay leader), Beryl Koenigsberg (the future lay chairman of secular studies at the Rabbi Jacob Joseph School) and Irving Bunim–devised a new strategy. They did not boycott the Friday night balls, as they had previously done. Instead, they went to them, stood outside, and confronted those from observant homes who had been lured there. The three would convince them to leave and attend Young Israel services the following morning. The strategy worked.

Underlying these courageous efforts was an enduring optimism about the future of American Jewry. One early ally who gave them strength and en-

couragement was Gedaliah Bublick, a graduate of the Mirrer Yeshiva and editor of the Orthodox *Yiddishe Tageblatt* (*The Jewish Daily Page*), America's highly popular Yiddish newspaper, and *Der Morgen Journal* (*The Morning Paper*). He authored *Min Hameitzar* (*From the Depths*), a collection of essays published in 1923, and served as president of American Mizrachi.

He was concerned about assimilation. "It's a battle between Harvard and Volozhin," Bublick wrote. "If Harvard wins, Judaism has no hope in America." There would be no change, he insisted, unless something revolutionary happened.

Bublick's words complemented the ideology of Young Israel, and he fought for the honor and dignity of *Klal Yisrael* in America. He would neither compromise on Torah issues or back down from a fight.

Advertisement for a Yiddish play held on Rosh Hashanah

Rabbi Alexander Linchner

BATTLING TO PRESERVE ORTHODOXY

The battle to preserve Orthodoxy continued on many fronts. Although Young Israel charters mandated a kosher *mechitzah*, this requirement caused some dissent during the movement's early years.

Other battles ensued. When members of the Young Israel movement set out to build the first *mikveh* in Brooklyn's East New York section, they quickly discovered that before construction could begin, they would have to educate virtually the entire Jewish community about the crucial *mitzvah* of *taharas hamishpachah*. They soon realized that the community's ignorance was coupled with antagonism. The spiritual leader of Agudas Achim Bnei Yaakov Synagogue, Rabbi Alexander (Sender) Linchner, (son-in-law of Rabbi Shraga Feivel Mendlowitz of Yeshiva Torah Vodaath and later the head of Jerusalem's Boys' Town), enlisted the aid of several knowledgeable Jews who could properly present the concepts of *taharas hamishpachah*. First, he

> *The battle to preserve Orthodoxy continued on many fronts. They had to contend with both ignorance and antagonism. Adult education was crucial, especially in the area of mitzvah observance.*

Bublick also took on the secular Stephen S. Wise, who was considered America's most prominent spokesman for American Jewry. Battle lines were drawn in 1925, when Wise delivered a sermon urging his fellow Jews to accept the Christian messiah as both a co-religionist and a teacher equal to those in the *Mishnah*.[1]

Orthodoxy was infuriated. The Agudas HaRabbonim put a *cherem* (ban of excommunication) on Wise. In *Der Morgen Journal*, Bublick charged Wise with "near apostasy and betrayal of Judaism." The *Yiddishe Tageblatt* said that Wise was sending "the younger generation to the baptismal font." Young Israel protested vehemently. Although Wise responded that "Bublick's opinion is not public opinion," he admitted shortly before he died that his own position had been wrong.

Young Israel Officers' Meeting, Hotel Martinique, June, 1933

---

1. Op. cit., **A Fire in His Soul**, pg. 36

National Council of Young Israel Annual Dinner at the Astor Hotel, March 1951. (L-R, upper dais): Hon. Edward S. Silver, Mayor Robert F. Wagner, (unidentified), Dr. Samson R. Weiss, Arthur LeVine, (L-R, lower dais): Rabbi Aharon Kotler, Rabbi Avrohom Jofen, Rabbi Yaakov Y. Ruderman

The organization maintained an active voice in Jewish affairs and emphasized that Torah was the one fixed point in the eternal life of the Jewish People.

recruited Rabbi Leo Jung* of Manhattan's Jewish Center, and then, convinced that an eloquent lay speaker would help his cause, he enlisted Irving Bunim. As the time for the *mikveh* construction drew near, Mr. Bunim walked one Shabbos from synagogue to synagogue teaching *taharas hamishpachah* around the clock. Gently, he convinced the community to build, support and, above all, use the *mikveh*.

EXPANDING THE BORDERS

In the 1920s and '30s, New York City was considered the sole repository of Orthodoxy in North America. Everyone thought there could never be a *mechitzah* west of the Hudson River, but the members of the movement thought otherwise. If Young Israel could thrive all over New York, it was reasoned that it could grow all over the continent. After all, what had started with a single *minyan* in 1913 had quickly grown to four, when some members

moved from Manhattan's Lower East Side to the Williamsburg, Boro Park and East New York sections of Brooklyn. In 1928, the Williamsburg Young Israel, with five hundred members, had its own building, an old mansion on Bedford Avenue and Rodney Street.

While others predicted a dismal Jewish future, members of the Young Israel movement seized upon demographic changes in Jewish settlement to help Young Israel centers flourish in cities like Boston, Cleveland, Detroit, Chicago, and St. Louis. They were so successful that by 1926, Young Israel had built branches in twenty American cities and one in Jerusalem, with a membership totaling five thousand.

Across the country, the Young Israel activists found that Jews had an enormous thirst for a Torah message delivered in English. They were contacted by lay leaders, pleading that they help them organize and raise funds.

Jews in isolated communities all over the Midwest flocked to the conventions. The encouragement and learning they received there inspired them to cling to a Torah way of life. In short, Young Israel left an indelible, eternal imprint on these families. Indeed, many of the sons and grandsons of the original Young Israel families now learn Torah in *kollelim*. These younger generations are precious seeds that the early activists of Young Israel helped sow.

In the late 1930s, the Young Israel movement rescinded their charter and agreed to retain pulpit rabbis, without which the movement would eventually stagnate. The first campaign began at Young Israel of Flatbush (Brooklyn), one of the stronger bastions opposing the rabbinate. In 1939, after years of infighting,

---

* Refer to the biography of Rabbi Leo Jung, pg. 176

the congregation acquiesced, retaining a noted scholar, Rabbi Solomon J. Scharfman, who had received *semichah* at the *Chofetz Chaim* Yeshiva. It was a revolutionary move that paved the way for other Young Israel congregations.

The early years of Young Israel were full of conflict and self-assertion for young Orthodox Jews. The organization maintained an active voice in Jewish affairs and emphasized that Torah was the one fixed point in the eternal life of the Jewish People; it should not be made subservient to political or party goals, no matter how laudable. Jewish education was the most essential factor of all.

ERETZ YISRAEL

Palestine was always of great importance to Young Israel; thousands of dollars were raised for the *Yishuv* (the Jewish community in Palestine) in *Eretz Yisrael* in the 1920s and 30s. In 1940, for example, Rabbi Isaac Herzog, the Chief Rabbi of Palestine, came to the United States to raise money for the European-style yeshivos in *Eretz Yisrael* which were in dire financial straits. Rabbi Herzog was desperate; the *Yishuv* had flatly refused to acknowledge such Yiddish-speaking yeshivos, supporting instead only Hebrew-speaking schools. In the United States, too, virtually the entire organized Jewish community ignored him, except for Young Israel. Rabbi Herzog was invited to be a guest speaker at the Young Israel Annual Dinner in March, 1941. By the time he returned to Palestine the following July, he had raised a substantial sum, all due to Young Israel.

National Council of Young Israel Reception for Rabbi Isaac Herzog, Chief Rabbi of Palestine, March 1941. (L-R, seated): Irving M. Bunim, Julius Lifschitz, Rabbi Isaac Herzog, Joseph Schechter. (L-R, standing): David Berman, Elijah Stein, Rabbi Dr. Samson Raphael Weiss, Pinchas Iseson

CONCLUSION

Virtually from its inception, Young Israel's motto was a passage from the Prophet *Malachi* (3:24): "And He shall turn the heart of the fathers to the children, and the heart of the children to their fathers." The early pioneers of Young Israel gave life to that philosophy, reuniting generations of young Americans with their ancestors' heritage. Its efforts helped an emerging American Orthodoxy define itself, formulate its own goals, and become closer to Torah.

The pioneers of Young Israel gave life to the philosophy of reuniting generations of young Americans with their ancestors' heritage. Its efforts helped an emerging American Orthodoxy define itself and become closer to Torah.

❧ Part 3: Zeirei Agudath Israel (Z.A.I.)

THE EARLY YEARS

The numerous challenges facing Jewish immigrants who came to America during the war years precipitated a generation gap. The tensions between parents and children took various forms. Unfortunately, many young immigrants were drawn to American society and culture at the expense of religious observances, which they viewed as an impediment. The parents were ill-prepared to counter the dangers and influences of the outside society, especially since this had been less of a problem in the European *shtetlach*. Further compounding the situation was the limited availability of Jewish religious education. In addition, those youth who did attend *shuls* and *shtiblach* were not included in leading the services or receiving honors. These conditions alienated them and set them apart even more. Clearly something had to be done –

new organizations and leadership were desperately needed to save the youth.

Those young Jews who were either foreign-born or first-generation Americans – in their late teens or 20's – and remained observant, joined together in groups. One such group that had been formed to strengthen *Yiddishkeit* among the youth was *Bachurei Chemed*, organized in 1917, by Reb Shea Gold, on the Lower East Side of New York. A delegation of Agudath Israel came to America in 1921, led by Rabbi Meir Don Plotzky, the Ostrover Rav, a foremost leader of Polish Jewry. They urged *Bachurei Chemed* to affiliate with Agudah, thus setting them apart from other groups because they would be part of a world organization. The membership was divided – those who wanted to form a new group left *Bachurei Chemed* and thus established the first Zeirei Agudath Israel in America.

In America at that time, Agudath Israel was unpopular because of its position regarding political Zionism. Most American Orthodox Jews joined Mizrachi, the religious Zionist movement. Agudah refused to recognize political secular Zionism as a representative of the Jewish People, and opposed Mizrachi as well. The differing ideologies split religious Jews into opposing camps.

The purpose of the newly-founded Zeirei was not ideological or political. The young men simply wanted a place where those who shared their views and ideals could join together to *daven* and learn *Gemara*. The Lower East Side branch met in the basement of the Gorlitzer Chevra on Lewis Street. Primarily, the original members were European born and Yiddish was their first language. The majority of them worked full time, then attended night high school, after which they came to their Zeirei "home" to learn *Gemara* at 9 p.m. These young men were highly

The Agudath Israel delegation upon their arrival in America. (L-R): Rabbi Asher Spitzer, Rabbi Dr. Meir Hildesheimer, Rabbi Meir Don Plotzky, Rabbi Joseph Lev and Dr. Nathan Birnbaum

committed and demonstrated great *mesiras nefesh* (self-sacrifice) – despite facing ridicule and the difficulties of keeping kosher and holding a job because of Shabbos observance. They became close friends and supported one another.

Within a few years other branches of Zeirei opened in Williamsburg, Brownsville, Boro Park, and the Bronx. Williamsburg differed from the Lower East Side. It was considered a step up for those immigrants who needed larger accommodations than they had on the Lower East Side. It was a more Americanized neighborhood, predominately Italian and Irish. Into the 1930s there were few *shomer Shabbos* stores. English could be heard more often than not and many of the young people attended college.

In 1923, the first Zeirei was established in Williamsburg on Marcy Ave. Like the East Side branch, they considered their affiliation with Agudath Israel as non-political. Though more Americanized, they viewed themselves as removed from Young Israel and considered themselves "*frummer*" (more

Rabbi Shea Gold

The purpose of the newly-founded Zeirei was not ideological or political. The young men simply wanted a place where those who shared their views and ideals could join together to daven and learn Gemara.

A 1930s Williamsburg Bnos trip. Mrs. Mandel is in the back row on the left. The girls are, the Wilhelm sisters: Claire (Gerwirtz) (middle row on left), Leah (Herskowitz)(sitting), and Channah (Belsky) (on Mrs. Mandel's left), fourth girl is unidentified

BNOS IS BORN

It is very important to note that the need for such groups for girls was even greater than for boys. Religious education for girls was almost non-existent then. The first Bais Yaakov elementary school did not open in America until 1937, and there was no high school until the mid 1940s. There were only Talmud Torah type schools, which were limited in scope, and public school attendance was mandatory. At that time the only school available for girls in Williamsburg was the Beth Jacob Hebrew School, which was an afternoon Talmud Torah, founded by Rabbi Shraga Feivel Mendlowitz and Reb Binyomin Wilhelm.* On the Lower East Side there was only the National Hebrew School.

Nothing comparable to Zeirei existed for girls until 1930. Mrs. Frume Leah Mandel saw a need and organized groups for 16 to 18-year-olds in Brownsville. Two years later, she moved to Williamsburg and started groups there. To attract girls from the entire spectrum of Orthodox families the groups were originally called Bnos Bais Yaakov.

In 1932, when Mrs. Mandel originally organized Bnos chapters in Williamsburg, she started with the older girls. Eventually, these girls became the leaders for the newly established younger girls' groups. At first, they only met on Shabbos. The program was then extended to one or two additional times during the week, for activities such as drama or arts and crafts. On Sundays, outings to parks, boating, or hikes were organized. Twice a year, the Bnos chapters sponsored a *tzedakah* campaign to raise money for a yeshiva or another cause.

Religious education for girls was almost non-existent then. Consequently, the need for girls' groups similar to Zeirei was essential – Bnos is born.

religious). They felt that the Young Israel programs were geared more toward communal development, while their activities focused on learning. However, many Zeirei members also *davened* in Young Israel *minyanim* at times, because of geographical considerations. They acknowledged the positive influences of Young Israel on the English-speaking young Jews who would not have fit into Zeirei. Many Zeirei members also attended Young Israel forums and lectures. In 1930, the Marcy Ave. Zeirei joined another branch and relocated to Rodney St., closer to the center of Jewish Williamsburg.

*Refer to the biography of Reb Shraga Feivel Mendlowitz, pg. 244, and the biography of Reb Binyomin Wilhelm, pg. 342

The Lower East Side also had active Bnos chapters and sponsored Torah study classes – *Chumash* and *Rashi, Pirkei Avos*, and Jewish laws and customs. These classes were especially significant, because in most cases it was the only learning opportunity available to the girls. Bnos played a vital role then, more so than decades later, because it offered a religious environment for girls who attended public schools and were susceptible to peer pressure. The Bnos groups helped reinforce the values taught to the girls at home, in a warm and friendly environment. Strong friendships were formed and the girls helped each other in many ways.

At that time it was difficult for *frum* young men and women to meet. Zeirei organized special social events where young people could socialize in a religious group setting. They sponsored *Melaveh Malkahs*, forums and a Z.A.I. boat ride. Many *shidduchim* resulted from these joint programs.[1]

EVOLVING INTO A NATIONAL ORGANIZATION

In 1938, five branches of Zeirei Agudath Israel joined together into a loose confederation called the Interbranch Council. Each chapter (including Williamsburg) in the Council retained its independence. In essence, the only common project sponsored by the Council was a bi-annual *tzedakah* campaign. The crucial ingredient that was lacking to transform Zeirei into a national organization was dynamic leadership.

In the early 1930s Young Israel was

Committee of Zeirei Agudath Israel of America, 1927. (L-R): Nathan Horowitz, Joseph Fogel, Charles Fogel, Abba Gliecher, Fishel Eichenthal, Joseph Wienrib, Hirschel Berliner

a more dynamic organization than Z.A.I. It was larger and expanding beyond New York. Young Israel helped preserve Orthodoxy in many communities outside New York. Nevertheless, it was lacking certain important elements that were essential to address the challenges of that period. Agudah could offer international organization affiliation and the leadership of *gedolim*.

An atypical Zeirei member was the catalyst who transformed Z.A.I. into a more enterprising and vigorous national organization. A newcomer to Zeirei, Mike Tress[*] joined the Williamsburg *minyan* in search of more meaningful *Yiddishkeit*. The basic ideals of Agudah appealed to him. Primarily, it was their principle that all Jews should be united and dedicated to the preservation of Torah and its teachings. He was English speaking, modern in appearance, and college educated, but eager to expand his Torah learning. Rabbi Gedaliah Schorr[**], a brilliant young *talmid chacham*, gave a

> *Bnos groups helped reinforce the values taught to the girls at home, in a warm and friendly environment. Strong friendships were formed and the girls helped each other in many ways.*

---

[1] Rosenblum, Yonason, **They Called Him Mike**, Mesorah Publications, New York, 1995, pg. 59
[*] Refer to the biography of Elimelech "Mike" Tress, pg. 324
[**] Refer to the biography of Rabbi Gedaliah Schorr, pg. 278

Rabbi Gedaliah Schorr with Mike Tress

The crucial ingredient that was lacking to transform Zeirei into a national organization was dynamic leadership. Enter Mike Tress, who transformed Z.A.I. into a vigorous and enterprising organization.

nightly *Daf Yomi shiur* at the Rodney Street Zeirei and was considered their unofficial *rav*. Despite his youth, Reb Gedaliah was respected and looked up to by all the members. Mike Tress was immediately inspired by him and attended as many of his *shiurim* as possible. The two became extremely close and Rabbi Schorr was a major personality who greatly influenced him for the rest of his life. Mike Tress' attributes, especially his friendliness, kind heart and leadership abilities, were quickly recognized. In a short time, he was elected president of the Williamsburg Zeirei and things began to happen.

Mike Tress decided to expand the scope of Zeirei and his first project was a *Shemiras Shabbos* Campaign. The objective was to close down the Jewish-

owned stores on Lee Ave. on Shabbos. Rallies were held on Thursday nights for over a year, discussing the importance of *shemiras Shabbos*. The campaign succeeded beyond their expectations – more than half the stores closed. A second campaign was launched to arouse public protest against hiring non-religious *chazzanim* to attract crowds, as was the practice in many synagogues.

These campaigns increased the community's awareness of Zeirei. New members were attracted and Zeirei members were injected with a sense of commitment and purpose: they realized that they could make an important difference. Additionally, the campaigns demonstrated Mike Tress's organizational genius. He understood that in order to expand Z.A.I., it would have to center its programs around the youth. Until then, Zeirei was only

LOYALTY vs. TREASON!
A STUDY IN CONTRAST

PLEASE TAKE NOTICE!!

THIS STORE WILL BE CLOSED ◇ ◇ SUNDAY ALL DAY!!

We Value Your Patronage And Ask You to Cooperate With Us! Please Do Your Shopping ON SATURDAY

We appeal to you to help us maintain business hours! Thank You!

The picture at the left is that of **the** poster displayed by the Shabbos observing grocerymen, which proclaims in Hebrew: "Remember The Shabbos Day To Keep It Holy!" At the right is the placard displayed by the "Sunday observing" Jewish grocerymen, which brazenly advises: "Do Your Shopping On Saturday!"

Advertisement for Shemiras Shabbos campaign

geared for young men in their teens and 20s. Pirchei groups were formed for 8-year-olds and up, as well as Bnos groups for girls of that age. Shabbos groups were arranged. A game room was set up in the Williamsburg branch. Stories and singing were included as part of the program.

In the late 30s and early 40s new chapters were formed. Mike Tress traveled to each one to speak at *Melaveh Malkahs*. He had a special rapport with the young and they were enthralled by his stories of *gedolim*. American youth finally had an organization where they could find companionship with their own, as well as learn important Torah values, Jewish history, and respect for *talmidei chachamim* and appreciation for their roles. Membership gave them a sense of belonging, and the singing and dancing also helped them develop *ruach* – the special spirit and joy associated with being a Jew. The importance of Torah learning was emphasized and Torah study classes were organized. Activities were arranged between the young Pirchei members and the older Zeirei members. This engendered a sense of being part of a larger movement. Involving the youth

Mike Tress (in center) on a Zeirei boat ride, June 1933

in these programs, as well as the special *tzedakah* drives sponsored by the organization, instilled self esteem and pride in being Jewish.

Outside places such as Williamsburg, the importance of Pirchei and Bnos cannot be stressed enough. For the many who did not attend yeshivos, it was the one place where they could meet other Jewish peers in a religious environment and learn about their heritage in an enjoyable manner. The dangerous and negative influences of the public schools were counteracted by these programs. It kept them out of trouble and gave them a new focus.

American youth finally had an organization where they could find companionship with their own, as well as learn important Torah values, Jewish history, and respect for talmidei chachamim and appreciation for their roles.

A group of Zeirei members (standing L-R): Moshe Sandhaus, Rabbi Avrohom Pam, Rabbi Anshel Fink, Yitzchok Mendelowitz, Robert Krane. (Seated L-R): Moe Fensterheim, Frank Newman, Berel Belsky, Rabbi Heshy Leiman, Rabbi Gedaliah Schorr, Rabbi Alexander Linchner

616 Bedford Avenue

By the mid-1930s, Torah Vodaath was firmly ensconced in Williamsburg, attracting many religious families. Outreach efforts, which are so popular today, were first practiced by some Zeirei members and yeshiva *bachurim* who went on out-of-town recruiting trips. Also, through the encouragement of Pirchei, many boys eventually went to yeshiva who otherwise would not have attended.

RESCUE AND RELIEF ACTIVITIES

Between 1933 and 1941, there was a flood of German and Austrian refugees who escaped Europe. Zeirei became involved in the all-important task of relief and rescue work. At first, the Rodney St. location became makeshift living space for many refugees. It soon became apparent that more space was needed. Money was raised to purchase a three-story building on Bedford Avenue. The new building would serve as headquarters for Zeirei activities and as a refugee home.

In 1939, the move into the new building marked a milestone for the Zeirei of Williamsburg. For the next six years, they focused most of their efforts on rescuing the Jews of Europe. They

Zeirei became involved in the all-important task of relief and rescue work. One division that was immediately set up was the Refugee and Immigration Division. Their task was securing immigration visas.

Preparing food packages to send to Jerusalem, Israel 1948

(L-R): Mike Tress and Louis J. Septimus inspecting packages destined for Europe

An advertisement to help raise money for European Jewry

called themselves the Agudath Israel Youth Council of America for purposes of this critical work. One division that was immediately set up was the Refugee and Immigration Division. Their task was securing immigration visas and learning the many complicated details involved in the process. The president, Mike Tress, established an important network of connections with people in Washington, D.C. to expedite the visa process.

During this period the accomplishments of the Youth Council were nothing short of amazing. In addition to the Refugee and Immigration Division, a Jewish Serviceman's Welfare Bureau was established. Its function was to help meet the special needs of Orthodox Jewish soldiers, specifically to obtain kosher food. The Youth Council also started to publish two monthly newspapers – *Orthodox Youth* (which eventually became the *Orthodox Tribune*) and

Rabbi Joshua Silbermintz, director of Pirchei Agudath Israel, at Siyum Mishnayos

The young idealistic volunteers of Z.A.I. learned what it meant to work and be committed to the Klal.

Zeirei Agudath Israel outing, 1942

The basic ideology was to understand and perceive themselves as part of Klal Yisrael and, therefore, responsible for their brethren. Coupled with this philosophy was the view that Torah must govern every aspect of life, and leadership should come from those who are most learned.

Darkeinu for the young people.

The Pirchei and Bnos members were not lost in the shuffle; during this period Camp Agudah and Camp Bnos were established. Also, the National Councils of Pirchei and Bnos were instituted. Regular chapter activities continued, although they too did their part to help the relief effort.

It should be noted that all these extraordinary accomplishments were achieved by young, idealistic *volunteers* (in their teens and 20s). At a relatively young age, they learned what it meant to work and be committed to the *klal*. Above all, they were involved in the critical work of *hatzalas nefashos* – saving Jewish lives.

The Bedford Ave. building also served as the refugee home to hundreds of young men, between 1939-1942. The Youth Council not only provided housing (usually short-term), but also arranged meals (at Torah Vodaath or Goldenberg's Restaurant) and helped them find employment. In addition, medical and dental services, as well as clothing, were provided for those in need. The majority of immigrants were families. Bnos organized fundraisers to

provide them with their basic necessities. The Youth Council managed to arrange living quarters for 150 families. To meet all these expenses Pirchei and Bnos organized fundraisers. When immigration to the U.S. was cut off, money was raised to supply food to the Jews in the European ghettos, or for other relief work.

During this period, Gershon Kranzler was hired to try to form a national organization from the many different chapters. The ideologies of Agudath Israel had not been an issue for the American branch of Zeirei, but that was to change. The basic ideology which drove all the Zeirei, Pirchei, and Bnos activities during the war years is what inspired the American young

FOOD FOR THE JEWISH CHILDREN OF EUROPE, Inc.

Auspices of
AGUDATH ISRAEL YOUTH COUNCIL

(L-R): Rabbi Moshe Sherer, Lester Udell, and Mike Tress

Camp Agudah in Highmount, New York, 1951

people to accomplish all that they did – it was to understand and perceive themselves as part of *Klal Yisrael* and, therefore, responsible for their brethren. Coupled with this philosophy was the view that Torah must govern *every* aspect of life, and leadership should come from those who are most learned. These principles would also be the basis for the formation of a national organization for Zeirei, and eventually for Pirchei and Bnos.

The new Zeirei publication, *Orthodox Youth*. was widely used to convey this message. The members received positive reinforcement for their vital role in all the relief activities in which they engaged. The articles also stressed the international scope of the organization. This helped create a sense of unity with Jews all over the world. By the 1940s, there were national summer conventions, banquets and midwinter conferences. All of these events provided a united sense of purpose and commitment. The Youth Council remained at the forefront of American rescue efforts of European Jewry. At the time, it was considered their most vital mission. Eventually, Agudah became a driving force and spokesman representing the interests of American Orthodoxy.

Torah Chinuch in America

Historical Background

Jewish education at the turn of the 20th century consisted of small *chadarim* and makeshift Hebrew schools, taught by unprofessional *melamdim*, teachers who were, for the most part, far from qualified for this line of work. There were also a few Talmud Torahs, afternoon schools, that provided a limited Jewish education. These schools met in the afternoon, four to five times per week, for sessions of two or three hours. Included in the curriculum was Hebrew prayers, *Chumash* and *Rashi, Mishnah* and *Gemara. Bar Mitzvah* preparation was also offered. Yiddish was the predominant language of instruction, but by the 1920s English replaced it. Since these studies followed a full day of public school, most children found attendance at such a school to be laborious and irrelevant to their life in America. These young Jews were certainly more Americanized than their parents. Attending public school (which was compulsory) helped them develop their English language skills and exposed them to American culture. These factors widened the gap between the generations and tensions mounted. Furthermore, many of the youth regarded religious observance as nothing more than rituals. They wanted to "fit in" with their American school friends and being observant was viewed as an impediment. Most of these students did not continue their Jewish studies beyond *bar mitzvah.*

The immigrants lacked time and money, and therefore, they delayed establishing yeshivos. They were ill prepared for the dangers of the outside world and its influence on their children. This deplorable state of affairs could only be remedied by the establishment of yeshivos, and subsequently the Day School.

❧ Yeshivos and Their Beginnings

Eitz Chaim Yeshiva and RIETS[1]

1886-Eitz Chaim, the first elementary Hebrew school, was founded. 1896 - Yeshivas Rabbeinu Yitzchok Elchanan was established. Its ruach and curriculum closely resembled an Eastern European yeshiva.

The first elementary Hebrew school to be founded was the Eitz Chaim Yeshiva, established in 1886.

In 1888, Rabbi Jacob Joseph[2], known as the *Maggid* of Vilna and founder of yeshivos in Lithuania, arrived in America to serve as Chief Rabbi of New York City. He supported and strengthened the Eitz Chaim Yeshiva. In 1896, Yeshivas Rabbeinu Yitzchok Elchanan (later known as RIETS) was set up in New York's Lower East Side by a group of men interested in providing a better and more advanced form of education for Jewish youth. It was named in memory of the great Kovno sage Rabbi Yitzchok Elchanan Spector. The *ruach*, spirit, of this yeshiva and its curriculum closely resembled that of an Eastern European yeshiva.

While today we may take the emergence of a yeshiva for granted, we must consider the bleak horizon upon which the light of Torah was beginning to shine. The Jewish community was far from homogeneous. There were the Americanized Jews of Sephardic descent on one hand, and then there were the assimilated German Jews who had become accustomed to the American lifestyle. The last thing they wanted was for their Eastern European

Rabbi Yitzchok Elchanan Spector, The Kovno Rav

Rabbi Isaac Elchanan Theological Seminary, 136 Henry Street (1904-15)

1. Refer to the biographies of Rabbi Dovid Lifshitz, pg. 236, Rabbi Dr. Dov Revel, pg. 256, and Rabbi Dr. Yosef Soloveitchik, pg. 302

2. Refer to the biography of Rabbi Jacob Joseph, pg. 174

brethren to bring the European *shtetl* to America. Besides, not all the European Jews who came to America were observant. On the contrary, because of all the "isms" that permeated society in Russia and Poland, there was only a minority who did not subscribe to Socialism, Comm-unism, Secularism or Anarchism. Torah observance was certainly not in vogue.

Yet against this backdrop, the first American yeshiva was founded. The first *rebbeim* were of Lithuanian descent. The yeshiva's goal was to study *Torah lishmah* (Torah for its own sake) which was the standard of the European yeshivos of old, as set forth by the father of the yeshiva movement, Rabbi Chaim Volozhiner. The yeshiva's curriculum soon changed and expanded to include secular studies, to better prepare the yeshiva graduate for a career in rabbinics, in a growing American society.

In 1915, Eitz Chaim and RIETS merged. Eitz Chaim focused upon educating elementary and high school students in both religious and secular subjects. RIETS became the advanced yeshiva, or *Beis Medrash*. It was their perspective that the yeshiva produce a student who was knowledgeable both in Talmud and secular erudition. Rabbi Dr. Bernard Revel was asked to serve as President of the school. A man well versed both in Torah and secular studies, Dr. Revel sought to mold the seminary in his image and make the yeshiva an American institution, rather than a replica of the traditional Lithuanian yeshiva.

In 1928, Yeshiva College, a four-year Liberal Arts School, was established and merged with RIETS. Dr. Revel succeeded in convincing a segment of the Orthodox community of the importance of instruction in both

Yeshiva University today

Torah and secular studies. The subject was contentious, to say the least.

To raise the level of Torah studies, Dr. Revel sought to interest and draw some of the greatest Torah scholars to serve as *Roshei Yeshiva*. In 1922, he succeeded in attracting Rabbi Shlomo Polatchek, the "Meitcheter *Ilui*," from Europe. One of the foremost students of Rabbi Chaim Soloveitchik, his erudition in Torah was exemplary. In 1929, Rabbi Moshe Soloveitchik of Brisk and Warsaw joined the faculty of RIETS. He was well received by the students who were impressed by his brilliance. Rabbi Soloveitchik was a demanding teacher who was able to motivate his students to seek a greater understanding of the profundities of Torah. Rabbi Shimon Shkop, *Rosh HaYeshiva* of Yeshivas Shaar HaTorah in Grodno, also was a faculty member for a period of time. While there was always a presence of great Torah scholars at RIETS, there remained continued opposition to its integration of secular studies into the curriculum.

Yeshivas Rabbi Yitzchok Elchanan's curriculum soon changed and expanded to include secular studies, to better prepare the yeshiva graduate for a career in rabbinics, in a growing American society.

Rabbi Jacob Joseph Yeshiva[3]

Rabbi Jacob Joseph Building, Lower East Side

RJJ's unique dual education program set the pattern for the yeshivos and day schools that followed.

Rabbi Shmuel Yitzchak Andron

Shortly after the establishment of RIETS (1896), the Rabbi Jacob Joseph Yeshiva (RJJ) was founded in 1903. Named after the great *Maggid* of Vilna and Chief Rabbi of New York City, Rabbi Jacob Joseph, it opened its doors on the Lower East Side of New York. What made RJJ unique was its dual education program which set the pattern for the hundreds of yeshivos and Hebrew day schools which have since been established in this country. Priority was given to religious studies, while the importance of secular studies was emphasized. By 1910, there were almost 500 students enrolled in the school. In 1920, the Yeshiva made an unsuccessful attempt to open a yeshiva high school. Despite a serious reversal in enrollment as a result of the Great Depression, RJJ was one of the few yeshivos

to survive. With the resurgence of religious Jewry in this country as a result of the influx of Holocaust survivors, the yeshiva entered a period of great advancement and expansion.

Its enrollment included students from outlying areas, as its high school and *Beis Medrash* grew in stature. In 1941, Rabbi Mendel Kravitz, a refugee from the Holocaust survivor and brilliant Talmudic lecturer, joined the yeshiva as *Rosh HaYeshiva*. With the decline in Jewish population of the Lower East Side, RJJ again suffered a serious setback in enrollment. Nevertheless, the

RJJ class, 1939

yeshiva has persevered and been restored to its former illustrious position. With campuses in Staten Island, New York and Edison, New Jersey, the vision of Rabbi Samuel Andron, its founder and first president, as well as that of Julius Dukas and Joseph Golding, who also helped shape the yeshiva and served as president, has been blessed with success.

---

3. Refer to the biographies of Mr. Irving Bunim, pg. 394, and Rabbi Mendel Kravitz, pg. 216

Mesivta Yeshiva Rabbi Chaim Berlin[4]

Yeshiva Rabbi Chaim Berlin, Stone Avenue

The oldest yeshiva in Brooklyn, Yeshiva Rabbi Chaim Berlin, actually began as the Yeshiva Tiferes Bachurim in a storefront in Brownsville in 1904. It acquired its permanent name in 1910. In the first several decades of the twentieth century, Brownsville became home to the largest and densest Jewish population in the United States. The yeshiva came to be the place where the precious spirit of Torah was kept alive for the many Jewish families of the community. It served as an elementary school until 1939, when an advanced yeshiva was established under the dynamic leadership of Rabbi Yitzchok Hutner. The *Rosh HaYeshiva* emphasized the majesty of Torah and the majesty of man, lessons imparted to him by his revered *Rebbe*, Rabbi Nosson Tzvi Finkel, the *Alter* of Slobodka.

With the establishment of the yeshiva, Rabbi Hutner set as his goal to produce "*derhoibene talmidei chachamim,*" Torah scholars of the highest caliber, both scholastically and spiritually. Because of the small number of students, they were availed an unprecedented opportunity for scholarship and spiritual growth. Rabbi Hutner was the dominant force and quintessential role model for influencing and shaping the *hashkafos*, Torah perspective and philosophical outlook of his students.

In 1957, the Kollel Gur Arye was founded, the name reflecting the *Rosh HaYeshiva's* particular affinity for the

Yeshiva Rabbi Chaim Berlin, the oldest yeshiva in Brooklyn (1904), kept the spirit of Torah alive for the Jewish families of Brownsville - then the largest in the U.S.

Yeshiva Rabbi Chaim Berlin, Prospect Place

---

4. Refer to the biography of Rabbi Yitzchok Hutner, pg. 164

Yeshiva Rabbi Chaim Berlin Bais Medrash — today

teachings of the *Maharal* of Prague. In 1979, Rabbi Hutner realized a life-long dream by establishing a yeshiva and *kollel* named Pachad Yitzchok in Yerushalayim.

Mesivtha Tifereth Jerusalem[5]

Mesivtha Tifereth Jerusalem, 145 East Broadway, on Manhattan's Lower East Side

Mesivtha Tifereth Jerusalem opened its doors in 1907. The yeshiva moved several times, until it finally settled into its present location in the Lower East Side of New York. Various departments were gradually added and in 1929, the Mesivta-High School was started, thus providing students with the opportunity to continue their Jewish education. In 1937, the Rabbinical Seminary was founded. Under the direction of its *Rosh HaYeshiva*, Rabbi Moshe Feinstein, who joined the yeshiva in 1938, the yeshiva became famous. In June 1944, the first group of sixteen men were ordained as

rabbis. Reb Moshe guided the yeshiva and formulated policy. His many *talmidim,* who became *rabbanim* and *roshei yeshiva* have always remembered the teachings and love and respect of their revered *rebbe,* as they serve in *kehillos* across the country carrying on the legacy of their venerable *rosh yeshiva.*

Mesivtha Tifereth Jerusalem in Staten Island

5. Refer to the biography of Rabbi Moshe Feinstein, pg. 120

Mesivta Torah Vodaath[6]

Mesivta Torah Vodaath was founded in the Williamsburg section of Brooklyn in 1917. Originally established as an elementary school by a group of highly dedicated people, it formed its high school in 1926. In 1921, the Mesivta engaged Rabbi Shraga Feivel Mendlowitz as principal. He was a charismatic and innovative leader who reorganized the yeshiva's educational component. Indeed, he prepared a curriculum that satisfied and challenged both the traditional and modern students. The success of the high school was due to his educational talents, his warm relationship with the students, and his overall leadership abilities.

Rabbi Dovid Leibowitz was invited to be *Rosh HaYeshiva*. He held this position for six years, and then left to found his own yeshiva named for his uncle, the *Chofetz Chaim*. After his departure, Rabbi Shlomo Heiman, who had origi-

Mesivta Torah Vodaath in Williamsburg, N.Y.

nally been *Rosh Yeshiva* in the Vilna Yeshiva (popularly called Remailles), assumed the position of *Rosh HaYeshiva*. He remained at this position until his untimely death in 1944.

Reb Shraga Feivel Mendlowitz left his imprimatur on Mesivta Torah Vodaath. At his urging, the yeshiva adopted as its primary goal to produce laymen well versed in Torah knowledge, who would be respected leaders of their respective communities. Together, the *Rosh HaYeshiva*, Rabbi Heiman and Reb Shraga Feivel Mendlowitz produced a generation of *rabbanim* and *askanim*, rabbis and lay leaders, who were the backbone of Orthodoxy in America.

Present Yeshiva building in Flatbush, N.Y.

> *Mesivta Torah Vodaath produced a generation of rabbonim and askanim, rabbis and lay leaders, who were the backbone of Orthodoxy in America.*

---

6. Refer to the biographies of Rabbi Shlomo Heiman, pg. 156, Rabbi Yaakov Kamenetsky, pg. 186, Rabbi Dovid Leibowitz, pg. 220, Rabbi S.F. Mendlowitz, pg. 244, Rabbi Gedaliah Schorr, pg. 278, and Reb Binyomin Wilhelm, pg. 342

Beis Medrash LeRabbonim[7]

Rabbi Yehuda Levenberg

The first yeshiva founded in America which was completely patterned after the European yeshivos was Beis Medrash LeRabbonim.

The first yeshiva founded in America which was completely patterned after the European yeshivos was Beis Medrash LeRabbonim. Under the direction of Rabbi Yehuda Levenberg, it was first established in New Haven, Connecticut, in 1923. His goal was to build a yeshiva whose principles would follow the Volozhiner *derech*, (approach) – of *Torah lishmah*, Torah study for its own sake, and the *mussar*, ethical behavioral approach to Torah and *mitzvos*, which was the hallmark of his alma mater, the Slobodka Yeshiva. He appointed as *Rosh HaYeshiva* Rabbi Moshe Don Scheinkopf, a brilliant scholar who later became *rav* in Waterbury, Connecticut. In keeping with the yeshiva's identification as a *mussar* yeshiva, he brought a *mashgiach*, ethical mentor, from Slutzk, Poland, Rabbi Sheftel Kramer, to supervise the daily spiritual and ethical development of the student body. The yeshiva was also concerned with the overall development of its students, providing them with the opportunity to learn the English language and training them to become spiritual leaders with the ability to inspire and lead the next generation. A number of great Torah scholars, including Rabbi Moshe Feinstein and Rabbi Yaakov Yitzchok Ruderman, taught there for short periods.

In 1930, the yeshiva moved to Cleveland, Ohio. Unfortunately, the move did not prove to be a successful one, due to a number of political / communal and internal problems. The severity of these problems undermined Rabbi Levenberg's ability to fully immerse himself in the yeshiva as in the past, and eventually led to the yeshiva's untimely closing in the late 1930s.

New Haven Yeshiva, Roshei Yeshiva and student body

7. Refer to the biography of Rabbi Yehuda Levenberg, pg. 224

Hebrew Theological College (Chicago)[8]

New York was not the only city where people realized the need for an advanced yeshiva education. In 1922, the Midwest followed suit as the Hebrew Theological College (H.T.C.) Bet Medrash LeTorah was established in Chicago. It was the result of a merger between Yeshivath Etz Chaim, founded in 1899 with 34 students, and Yeshiva Beth Hamedrash LeRabbonim which came into existence in 1918. Under the merger agreement, Etz Chaim was to become the preparatory department of H.T.C. The old Beth Medrash LeRabbonim would become the rabbinical department. Similar to RIETS, H.T.C. also offered secular studies as part of the curriculum. A new division, a teacher's institute for women, was established as well.

Rabbi Chaim Zvi Rubinstein, Rosh Yeshiva

Rabbi Nisson Yablonsky Rosh Yeshiva

Rabbi Chaim Korb Rosh Yeshiva

Rabbi Saul Silber became H.T.C.'s president and primary spokesman and mentor for 24 years. The yeshiva had many great scholars as *Roshei Yeshiva,* among whom were Rabbi Nisson Yablonsky, formerly the *Dayan* of Slabodka, who came in 1922, and Rabbi Chaim Zvi Rubinstein, who is referred to as the "father of the Yeshiva." Over the years, the yeshiva has produced many scholars and lay leaders who have left their mark on the American Jewish community.

Hebrew Theological College of Chicago was established in 1922. Over the years, it has produced many scholars and lay leaders who have left their mark on the American Jewish

West Side Building of H.T.C.

Hebrew Theological College, Skokie, Illinois, today

---

8. Refer to the biography of Rabbi Saul Silber, pg. 294

Yeshivas Ner Israel[9]

Yeshivas Ner Israel's first building

In 1933, Rabbi Yaakov Yitzchok Ruderman founded Yeshivas Ner Israel in Baltimore, Maryland. Five years later, he forged a legendary partnership with Rabbi Neuberger, benefiting both the Yeshiva and the greater Jewish community.

In 1933, Rabbi Yaakov Yitzchok Ruderman founded Yeshivas Ner Israel in Baltimore, Maryland. He arrived in America in 1931, from the Slobodka Yeshiva, where he had been a *talmid* of the *Alter* of Slobodka, to become a *rebbe* in the New Haven Yeshiva. He accepted the position of rabbi of Tiferes Yisroel Shul in Baltimore with the understanding that he could use the facilities for a yeshiva. The yeshiva opened with just five students. There were a few staunch supporters of the yeshiva, but for the most part people were unreceptive, even hostile.

In 1938, a young immigrant, Rabbi Naftoli Neuberger, arrived at Ner Israel from the Mirrer Yeshiva. He volunteered to help the *Rosh Yeshiva,* and thus was forged a legendary partnership, benefiting not only the yeshiva but the greater Jewish community. Rabbi Ruderman became his mentor to whom he always turned for guidance and sage advice. The *Rosh Yeshiva* recognized the young man's talents and gave him the necessary latitude to implement his ideas. Rabbi Neuberger's broad vision encompassed erecting a building for the yeshiva (1941) at a time of nationwide rationing – an amazing feat. He also helped arrange for several hundred refugees to emigrate to the U.S. during the War years.

Rabbi Naftoli Neuberger

9. Refer to the biography of Rabbi Yaakov Yitzchok Ruderman, pg. 266

The yeshiva grew steadily but slowly in the early years. Rabbi Ruderman firmly held on to his dream that this yeshiva would become a great Torah center. By 1943, it had its own building with space for over one hundred *talmidim*. During the postwar years the yeshiva flourished, necessitating an extension to be built in 1949. Between 1954 and 1957 the yeshiva continued to grow, and established a high school.

In the early 1960s Rabbi Ruderman established the *Kollel* for which he personally raised the funds. The *Kollel's* existence created a new pattern for *yungerleit*, young married men, to settle in Baltimore. Consequently, the Torah community of Baltimore has become one of the finest and largest in North America.

The *Rosh HaYeshiva* constantly focused on making his *talmidim* aware of the breadth and inter-relationship of the Torah. He stressed the centrality of Torah to living. He felt that whatever a *talmid* would be in the future, it was essential that he learn constantly. Rabbi Dovid Kronglas, who came from the Mirrer Yeshiva via Shanghai, Japan, was the *Mashgiach* of the Yeshiva. Reb Dovid infused his *talmidim* with great devotion to Torah and *yiras Shamayim*.

During the 1960s, the yeshiva, now with over 250 *talmidim*, had to move because the neighborhood had changed and was no longer suitable. In 1969, Yeshivas Ner Yisroel moved to its current campus in Pikesville, Maryland. This campus created an opportunity for a complete Torah community where

Current Ner Israel Campus, Pikesville, Maryland

faculty and students learn and live together.

Rabbi Neuberger pioneered the first matriculation agreement between a yeshiva and a secular college, initially to address the needs of Torah Umesorah for qualified educators with graduate degrees. This important step granted yeshivos the recognition they deserved as places that provide quality education, and paved the way for other similar programs. Rabbi Neuberger also played a central and active role in rescuing and helping Iranian Jews during the Shah's regime. He arranged a program at Ner Israel that saved many young men from losing their Jewish identity. Similar programs were implemented for South and Central American young Jewish men. Today Ner Israel has grown and developed into a major *yeshiva gedolah* with over 650 *talmidim* in its high school, *bais medrash*, and *Kollel*.

The Rosh HaYeshiva constantly focused on making his talmidim aware of the breadth and inter-relationship of the Torah. He stressed the centrality of Torah to living.

Rabbinical Seminary of America
Yeshiva Chofetz Chaim [10]

Original Building of Rabbinical Seminary of America, 135 South Ninth St., Brooklyn, N.Y.

Yeshiva Chofetz Chaim's goal was to provide the young men of America with a yeshiva that would follow in the traditions of scholarship, piety, and atmosphere of Slobodka.

Rabbi Dovid Leibowitz originally held the position of *Rosh HaYeshiva* of Mesivta Torah Vodaath for six years. In 1933, he left to start his own yeshiva, the Rabbinical Seminary of America, Yeshiva *Chofetz Chaim*, named after his uncle, Rabbi Yisrael Meir Kagan, better known as the *Chofetz Chaim*. The Yeshiva's goal was to provide the young men of America with a yeshiva that would follow in the traditions of scholarship, piety, and atmosphere of Slobodka.

The yeshiva quickly outgrew its first quarters. By 1940, it had already celebrated three *Chag HaSemichah* programs ordaining nineteen rabbis, who would take positions of distinction in the American Jewish community.

The *semichah* off-ered by the yeshiva was unique in that it only conferred the title of *Yoreh Yoreh, Yadin Yadin*, the highest degree of ordination.

Focusing on an educational philosophy emphasizing the development of strong analytical skills in conjunction with character refinement, the Yeshiva gained national recognition as its enrollment began to grow.

In 1941, with the untimely passing of Rabbi Dovid Leibowitz, the mantle of leadership was passed to his son and spiritual successor, Rabbi A. Henoch Leibowitz. In 1945, Kollel Ner-Dovid Rabbinical Graduate Institute opened as the first Post-Graduate Kollel for advanced Talmudic studies in America. Adhering to his sainted father's educational philosophy, the yeshiva grew under Reb Henach's stewardship and set up branches throughout the country.

Current Rabbinical Seminary of America building

---

10. Refer to the biography of Rabbi Dovid Leibowitz, pg. 220

Telshe Yeshiva[11]

The war years saw further growth in the yeshiva movement as the European *roshei yeshiva*, miraculously saved from the fires of the Holocaust, came to these shores with the hopes of rebuilding their lives and the holy *mekomos haTorah*, the yeshivos of Europe. In 1941, Rabbis Eliyahu Meir Bloch and Chaim Mordechai Katz, after a long and arduous journey, came to Cleveland, Ohio, and re-established the famed Telshe Yeshiva. They were helped by Dr. Bernard Revel, President of Yeshiva University, who was himself a *"Telzer talmid."* Indeed, Dr. Revel was instrumental through his contacts with various diplomatic channels in rescuing many Torah scholars.

Rebuilding a European yeshiva in a new country would be difficult enough, even if the builders themselves were not foreigners. Rabbi Bloch and Rabbi Katz, like so many other *roshei yeshiva*, were not deterred by the obstacles and challenges that they confronted. With determination, fortitude and courage they paved the way, charting the course of Torah for future generations.

In developing Telshe Yeshiva, the *Roshei HaYeshiva* modeled the *derech halimud* (method of Torah studies) on the curriculum and methodology that distinguished Telshe in Europe. There was a *Telzer derech*, a characteristic way of learning Torah, since the yeshiva's inception some sixty years earlier. Telshe was noted for its analytical approach to Torah study. They emphasized dialectic reasoning as a method for a clear comprehension of the subject matter and subsequent halachic application. *Mussar* (ethical discourse) was considered an integral part of Jewish study.

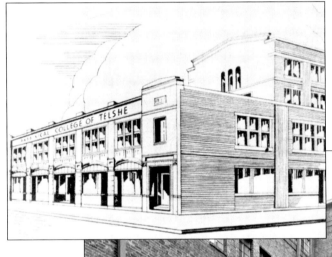

In developing Telshe Yeshiva, the Roshei HaYeshiva modeled the derech halimud, method of Torah studies, on the curriculum and methodology that distinguished Telshe in Europe.

Telshe Yeshiva's original building on East 105th Street, Cleveland, Ohio

11. Refer to the biographies of Rabbi E.M. Bloch, pg. 110, and Rabbi C.M. Katz, pg. 200, as well as the interview with Rabbi N.Z. Dessler, pg. 350

Telshe Yeshiva Bais Medrash, Wickliffe, Ohio

They did not stop with establishing an advanced yeshiva. They also founded and maintained an elementary school and a high school, The Hebrew Academy of Cleveland. As in Europe, they saw to it that an educational system was established for educating girls — Yavne High School. The famed Telzer *seder* – order, structure – and exacting schedule which was the trademark of Telshe was incorporated into the yeshiva's constitution. Strict discipline coupled with demanding respect for the yeshiva's faculty and leadership were all vital components in the training of a *ben Torah*. Indeed, the *Telzer talmid* acutely felt that he was part of a *mesorah*, a long chain of tradition.

Beth Medrash Govoha, or the Lakewood Yeshiva, would revolutionize Torah education in this country. The man responsible for the creation of what would become the largest yeshiva in America was Rabbi Aharon Kotler.

Beth Medrash Govoha[12]

Beth Medrash Govoha, or the Lakewood Yeshiva, would revolutionize Torah education in this country. The man responsible for the creation of what would become the largest yeshiva in America, a yeshiva that has given birth to a community unprecedented in Jewish history, was Rabbi Aharon Kotler. "Reb Aharon," as he was affec-

tionately and respectfully called, was the catalyst for successfully bringing the concept of *Torah lishmah*, Torah study purely for its own sake, to these shores. He was intent on producing Torah scholarship of the highest caliber. He did not believe that his yeshiva would thrive in a large city. It had to be removed from the centers of com-

12. Refer to the biography of Rabbi Aharon Kotler, pg. 210

The first home of Beth Medrash Govoha

After some time, he agreed to teach a class. Thus was born the beginnings of "Lakewood."

Reb Aharon's concept of a yeshiva focusing solely on *Torah lishmah* was truly novel. Indeed, it would be the only yeshiva of its kind, as all the others were oriented toward producing rabbis, teachers and laymen. He sought to produce scholars of the highest caliber who would devote their lives to immersing themselves in the sea of Torah. Reb Aharon, whose quintessential quality was his uncompromising integrity, once told a group of would-be supporters, "I do not seek to mislead you. There is a need for *roshei yeshiva* in this country – and Lakewood will produce them. There is a need for rabbis and teachers to function in various capacities – and Lakewood will produce them. There is a need for laymen who

Reb Aharon was the catalyst for successfully bringing the concept of Torah lishmah, Torah study purely for its own sake, to these shores.

merce so that its students could delve into the profundities of Torah, undisturbed and undistracted. Reb Aharon was a *gadol* in Europe. His commitment to *Klal Yisrael* was without bounds; his support of Torah law and tradition was uncompromising; his love for his people was unparalleled. He spearheaded the Vaad Hatzala, Rescue Committee, for those who survived the Nazi horror. He was indefatigable in his fight to save Jewish lives from physical and spiritual extinction.

"Lakewood," as Beth Medrash Govoha is commonly referred to, was ultimately established in Lakewood, New Jersey in 1943 – close enough to New York, but not part of the sprawling urban center. Its origin was the White Plains Kollel, a *beis medrash* composed primarily of European scholars, under the aegis of Rabbi Hillel Bishko who turned to Reb Aharon to lead their group.

Beth Medrash Govoha Campus in Lakewood, New Jersey

are adept and scholarly – and Lakewood will produce them. However, this is not Lakewood's goal. The *raison d'etre* of Lakewood is *"limud ha'Torah lishmah,"* to learn and study Torah for its sake, for its own value. It is with this under- standing and for this purpose, that I ask for your support." It took time, but Reb Aharon's goal was realized in Lakewood, and eventually it became the central approach to Torah study in the yeshiva world.

The Post-War Years

It would be appropriate to say that the "American" Torah perspective that we enjoy today has been influenced and inspired by the "European" Torah perspective.

The post-war period ushered in a new era for the growth of Torah in America. Between 1947 and 1951, thousands of Orthodox immigrants, survivors from the flames of Europe, came to America. These were people who if not for the Holocaust would never have emigrated to this country. They were secure and content with the level of spirituality that was the stan- dard in Europe. America posed prob- lems. It would have to change, and change it did. Most of the day schools and advanced yeshivos, as well as the spiritual climate which we enjoy today, is a result of the impact of these survivors.

Numerous yeshivos were estab- lished in the years following World War II. The Mirrer Yeshiva[13] and Beis HaTalmud Rabbinical College were established in 1946 and 1949 respec- tively. Many yeshiva day schools were established as the seeds of Torah were planted. While this thesis records pri- marily the Lithuanian-"style" yeshivos established in America, the story of the Chassidic yeshivos founded by the great *Admorim* also deserves to be noted.

Bobov[14], Klausenberg[15], Lubavitch[16], Satmar[17], Munkacs, Gur, Pupa, Vien – just to mention a few – all inspired their respective students as they were instructed in Torah and Chassidus.

The intellectual and spiritual loss incurred as a consequence of the trag- ic deaths of the thousands upon thou- sands of erudite scholars who perished during the Holocaust is incalculable Those survivors who came to America were only a sampling of the great citadels of Torah that shone in Europe. Yet it was these scholars who revived and gave strength and succor to those interested in building Torah *chinuch* in America. They brought their scholar- ship and culture, imbuing the American spiritual landscape with an entirely new outlook. It would be appropriate to say that the "American" Torah perspective that we enjoy today has been influenced and inspired by the "European" Torah perspective. Indeed, the world that was – Europe – inspired the world that *is* – America.

13. Refer to the biographies of Rabbi Yechezkel Levenstein, pg. 230, and Rabbi Avraham Kalmanowitz, pg. 182
14. Refer to the biography of Rabbi Shlomo Halberstam, pg. 146
15. Refer to the biography of Rabbi Yekusiel Yehudah Halberstam, pg. 152
16. Refer to the biography of Rabbi Yosef Yitzchak Schneerson, pg. 272
17. Refer to the biography of Rabbi Yoel Teitelbaum, pg. 312

Eitz Chaim Yeshiva and RIETS

Rabbi Jacob Joseph Yeshiva

Mesivtha Tifereth Jerusalem

Mesivta Yeshiva Rabbi Chaim Berlin

Mesivta Torah Vodaath

Hebrew Theological College (Chicago)

Yeshiva Ner Israel

Telshe Yeshiva

Rabbinical Seminary of America Yeshiva Chofetz Chaim

Beth Medrash Govoha

≈ Chinuch HaBanos
The Development of Jewish Education for Girls in America

BAIS YAAKOV MOVEMENT

While the nascent yeshiva movement was struggling to establish itself as a viable alternative to the educational systems that were in vogue at the time, education for girls was almost totally non-existent. Even parents who would send their sons to a *cheder* (primary school) were reluctant to send their daughters to a new all-girls school. Moreover, the financial yoke that came

Bais Yaakov
of Williamsburg,
November 29, 1953

with supporting a Jewish day school was something most people refused to accept when it concerned girls. In the 1920s, the only Hebrew schools for girls were afternoon Talmud Torahs and Sunday schools which were co-ed, and boys' *bar-mitzvah* classes which some girls would join. These schools focused on Jewish culture, as opposed to Jewish religion. Thus, those

girls who hailed from devout, pious families had no option but to study privately at home.

In Europe, the dynamic Frau Sarah Schenirer took the country by storm as she founded the first Bais Yaakov School. This school was the forerunner of a movement to educate Jewish girls *al taharas hakodesh*, with purity and holiness. Inspired by Sarah Schenirer,

Reb Binyamin Wilhelm[*], a prominent lay-leader who founded Mesivta Torah Vodaath, together with his brother-in-law Benzion Weberman and the venerable Torah activist Rabbi Shraga Feivel Mendlowitz, and other community leaders founded the Beth Jacob

In the 1920s, the only Hebrew schools for girls were afternoon Talmud Torahs and Sunday schools which were co-ed. Girls who hailed from devout, pious families had no option but to study privately at home.

---

* Refer to biography of Reb Binyamin Wilhelm, pg. 342

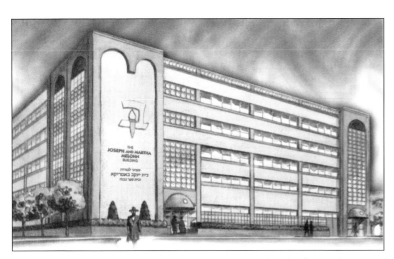

Beth Jacob Teachers Seminary & High School of America
Boro Park, N.Y.

Hebrew School for Girls in 1925, This was the first all-girls afternoon school.

In 1929, a small group of lay people, under the direction of Rabbi Mordechai Gimpel Wolk, opened an all-girls elementary school, in Brooklyn, the Shulamith School. Their High School opened in 1980. The Shulamith group agreed in principle with Sarah Schenirer's conclusions that girls needed Jewish education, especially in America with its stronger secularized society. They also adhered to the belief that these classes should be held separately – non-coeducational. They differed, however, in their religious Zionist ideology. Nonetheless, they continued to participate in all Bais Yaakov activities, much the same as those schools which are not in the metropolitan New York area and do not carry the Bais Yaakov name, but are Bais Yaakov-oriented.

In 1937, two Bais-Yaakov-type elementary day schools were established in Williamsburg – Bais Sarah and Bais Rochel. After the first one (it is unclear which one began first) failed,

the second started shortly thereafter in 1941. The second school also was unsuccessful and was soon followed by the establishment of Beth Jacob of Williamsburg. Rabbi Avrohom Newhouse*, a recent émigré from Holocaust-torn Europe, was the founding principal. This Bais Yaakov grew and blossomed for many years under Rabbi Newhouse's leadership.

The Bais Yaakov movement itself experienced considerable growth in the 1940s. By 1945, there were eleven schools, and as of 1946, there were fourteen. For the most part, these were elementary schools. There were two high-school branches. Most of these schools closed during their early years of operation due to a lack of funds. Beth Jacob of Williamsburg opened in 1941, with 20 students, and by 1944 had a student population of 200 students. These schools, primarily served their neighborhoods. In 1945, there were two Beth Jacob Schools in East New York and two in Washington Heights. A third school opened in Washington Heights in 1946. One of the issues at the time, as well as today, was whether these schools were servicing varied populations, or if, in fact, they were competing for students and resources. While most of these schools offered parochial school, kindergarten and Talmud Torah classes, Beth Jacob of Williamsburg also offered "Fundamentals of Judaism" classes at night.

The Bais Yaakov movement came to America and experienced considerable growth in the 1940s. These schools primarily served their neighborhoods. Most of them closed during their early years due to a lack of funds.

---

* Refer to biography of Rabbi Avrohom Newhouse, pg. 252

Sarah Schenirer

BAIS YAAKOV HIGH SCHOOL AND TEACHERS SEMINARY

When *Rebbetzin* Vichna Kaplan* arrived on these shores in 1937, there was as yet no religious school for girls of high-school age. This dynamic woman, the prize student of Sarah Schenirer, began her first class with seven teenage girls in her small apartment at 134 South 9th Street in Williamsburg. In order to help the fledgling school, her husband, Rabbi Boruch Kaplan, left his position as *Maggid Shiur* (lecturer) in Mesivta Torah Vodaath, to assume the financial administrative responsibilities of Bais Yaakov. In the seventh year of the school's existence, Rabbi and *Rebbetzin* Kaplan formally opened a full-day high school in January 1944.

Many of the early teachers were themselves students of Sara Schneier. The dedicated principal of the school for over half a century continues to be Rabbi Uri Hellman, an esteemed student of Rabbi Dr. Joseph Breuer.

The concept of Bais Yaakov for girls should not be taken as a matter of course. It took blood, sweat, and tears of love and devotion to *Klal Yisrael* and *chinuch habanos* (Torah education for girls) to start the growth of a movement that together with the yeshiva movement saved American Orthodoxy.

Today, specialized Torah schools exclusively for girls exist in almost every major Jewish community. While they do not all bear the name "Bais Yaakov" – either because they were established independent of the Bais Yaakov system, or because, due to variations in philosophy, they have assumed names of their own – each one adheres to the basic premise of Torah *chinuch* for girls.

Rabbi Uri Hellman

---

* Refer to the biography of *Rebbetzin* Vichna Kaplan, pg. 196

Following is a sampling of such schools. Yavne Seminary, in Cleveland, Ohio founded by the Telshe *Roshei Ha-Yeshiva*. Yavne, originally established in Telshe, Lithuania after World War I, was an innovator in the field of education for girls. Not only did teachers and students speak Hebrew in all classes – including secular courses such as physics and algebra, as well as *Chumash* and Halachah – they even corresponded with each other in Hebrew. The students were exposed to the full gamut of Jewish religious studies on the highest level, plus five languages and such secular courses as mathematics, science, geography, history, crafts, drawing, singing, and exercise. The Yavne High School, a division of the Hebrew Academy of Cleveland, also founded by Telshe, maintains a high standard of educational balance adhering to the traditional philosophy of its founders. Rika Breuer, in New York's Washington Heights neighborhood, is a part of the Adath Jeshurun educational system adhering to the philosophy of Horav S. R. Hirsch. In addition, in Brooklyn, there were Sarah Schenirer High School founded by Rabbi Nachman Bulman. Central Yeshiva High School for Girls, founded by Stephen Klein,* where Dr. Isaac Lewin, the son of Rabbi

Dr. Isaac Lewin

Aharon Lewin, the Rav of Raizow, Poland, served as principal. He was also Agudath Israel's representative to the United Nations. Esther Schonfeld High School was originally located in the lower East Side and later relocated to Brooklyn. There were also various chassidic schools: Bais Sarah, Karlin Stolin; Bais Rivkah, Lubavitch; Bais Rochel, Satmar; Bnos Tzion, of Bobov. There is no question that the fledgling school that began a little over half a century ago has spurred a movement that has inspired and changed the spiritual landscape of this country.

Today, specialized Torah schools exclusively for girls exist in almost every major Jewish community. They have inspired and changed the spiritual landscape of this country.

---

* Refer to the biography of Mr. Stephen Klein, pg. 410

Torah Umesorah

THE NATIONAL SOCIETY FOR HEBREW DAY SCHOOLS
Historical Background

At the dawn of the twenty-first century the following statement might seem strange – "If Judaism was to survive in America (1940s) it could not and would not happen without Jewish schools." To us, living in twenty-first century America, where there are hundreds of day schools and yeshivos from coast to coast, this comment is incomprehensible. However, in the 1930s and 1940s Jewish assimilation was accelerating at an alarming rate. Something had to be done to stem the tide of acculturation and bring Jews back to Torah – the synagogues could not do this alone.

In the early 1940s, Rabbi Shraga Feivel Mendlowitz[*] recognized the fact that Jewish schools were the linchpin necessary to sustain the American Jewish community and rekindle the light of Torah that had been partially extinguished. His vision and mission was to build an Orthodox Jewish day school in every major Jewish community in America. He was not deterred by the reality that other than a handful of places (New York, Baltimore, Chicago, and Cleveland), America was a spiritual wasteland. His efforts planted the seeds for the emergence of Torah Umesorah – the National Society for Hebrew Day Schools. It seemed an impossible dream, but this great man and those he chose to work with him dared to dream and helped revolutionize Torah *chinuch* in America.

> *"If Judaism was to survive in America (1940s) it could not and would not happen without Jewish schools."* Rabbi Shraga Feivel Mendlowitz's vision and mission was to build an Orthodox Jewish day school in every major Jewish community in America.

---

[*] Refer to the biography of Rabbi Shraga Feivel Mendlowitz, pg. 244

TORAH UMESORAH –
THE EARLY YEARS

Torah Umesorah was organized in June 1944, at a public dinner at the Waldorf Astoria Hotel. Indeed, it was more than an organization; it was an idea, a mission to save the Torah in this country. Reb Shraga Feivel had a dream – a dream with a vision for *Klal Yisrael.* He was spurred by a famous passage in the *Yalkut Shimoni,* one that he would often quote: "The 72,000 inhabitants of Givat Binyamin – why were they killed?

"It was the duty of the *Sanhedrin,* the High Court, to gird their loins with ropes of iron, to lift up their cloaks, and make the rounds of every village and town in *Eretz Yisrael.* From Lochish to Eglon, from there they were to travel to Chevron and on to Beth El, and finally to Yerushalayim, with one goal – to teach Torah to Jewish children. This was their mission. This was their duty. But they did not do so. Instead, the moment they entered the land, each hurried to his vineyard and to his olive field, and exclaimed, 'I am at peace – why should I worry?'" Reb Shraga Feivel's dream was to ensure that Torah would be disseminated throughout America.

When Torah Umesorah began, the prevailing mode of Jewish education was the afternoon Talmud Torah, and only a few Hebrew day schools existed. The teachers were for the most part untrained educators, and many were Europeans who could not relate to American children. Parents feared that Jewish schools would limit their children's chance of becoming successful Americans. Many Jewish community

(L-R): Rabbi Binyomin Goldenberg, Rabbi Alexander Gross, Rabbi Dr. Joseph Kaminetsky

leaders (with some exceptions) did little to dispel this notion – they even advocated the American public schools as fortresses of religious freedom and democracy. The myth that a Jewish school education would hold the child back from mainstream American life had to be eliminated.

Housed in the same building as the Vaad Hatzala and Agudas HaRabbonim, Torah Umesorah opened shop in downtown Manhattan with a small staff of four committed, selfless and energetic men, who each headed a department: Rabbi Bernard Goldenberg,[*] Publicity and Public Relations; Rabbi Alexander S. Gross, Founding New Schools; and Dr. Joseph Kaminetsky[**], who began as Educational Director and assumed the position of National Director following the death, in 1948, of Rabbi Shraga Feivel Mendlowitz. Reb Shraga Feivel, although never taking a titular position, was the founder, heart and soul, and inspiration of Torah Umesorah. Obviously, with such a limited staff, each man had to wear many hats. Not only that, but funds were

The myth that a Jewish school education would hold the child back from mainstream American life had to be eliminated.

* Refer to the biography of Rabbi Binyomin Goldenberg, pg. 364
** Refer to the biography of Dr. Joseph Kaminetsky, pg. 192

(L-R): Rabbi Aharon Kotler, Rabbi Reuven Grozovsky, and Rabbi Yitzchak Hutner at a Torah Umesorah Dinner

A small staff of four committed, selfless and energetic men each headed a department of Torah Umesorah. Each man had to wear many hats. Undaunted, they began their work.

meager and there was little public support. Undaunted, they began their work. In those early days, there were three basic impetuses and goals for the founding of day schools:

1. To restore to the American mindset the concept of a *ben Torah*, or *talmid chacham*. The greatest curse of American Jewry at the time was *am ha'artzus*, ignorance of the basic Jewish texts, concepts and ideas of Judaism. Illiteracy led to non-observance, indifference and apathy.

2. To provide a sufficient number of knowledgeable and intelligent leaders for the Jewish communities, since direction and leadership were sorely lacking in many places at that time. The early pioneers traveled the country in an attempt to assure the Jewish community that they would provide them with students, scholars and "saints."

3. They understood that to best reach the parents, they had to go through the children. They rode the trains and buses bearing in mind the prophet Malachi's refrain, indicating that Eliyahu *HaNavi* would *"restore the hearts of the fathers through their children."* They were convinced that the *"pintele Yid,"* spark of Jewishness, within every Jew could be awakened and restored to its original brilliant flame.

In a nationwide outreach effort, staff members traveled throughout the country in an attempt to fight Torah illiteracy. Torah Umesorah's first slogan was, "A *yeshiva ketana* in every major Jewish community across America." This concept was foreign to the average Jew in America. The incomprehensible reports of the Holocaust shocked them, igniting their desire to maintain Jewish institutions (i.e. synagogues, Talmud Torahs) and identify with Jewish ideals. However, regarding Jewish education it was an uphill battle. Nevertheless, the handful of dedicated men at the forefront of Torah Umesorah were not to be deterred. In those early days, with limited resources but working tirelessly, devotedly and with great *mesiras nefesh*, self-sacrifice, they succeeded in building 8 to 12 day schools each year.

RABBINICAL ADMINISTRATIVE BOARD

A Rabbinical Administrative Board was set up by Torah Umesorah, comprised of the greatest Torah authorities in America at the time – Rabbi Moshe Feinstein, Rabbi Reuven Grozovsky, Rabbi Yitzchok Hutner, Rabbi Yaakov Kamenetsky, Rabbi Aharon Kotler and Rabbi Yaakov Yitzchok Ruderman – who served as the policy-makers of Torah Umesorah, as well as advising and bringing their own special qualities to the organization. Their primary function was to ensure that the organization and its schools operated according to the *Shulchan Aruch*, the Code of Jewish Law. Many difficult and sensitive issues had to be addressed in the formative years and this unparalleled group of *gedolim* was more than equal to the task. Among the challenges confronting them was the problem of children with non-Jewish mothers and

*Rabbi Simcha Wasserman, with many of the participants in the first Aish Dos program.
(R-L, front row): Rabbi Meyer Lubin, Rabbi Moshe Wolfson, Rabbi Berel Schwartz,
Rabbi Wasserman, Zissel Walkenfeld, Rabbi Shmuel Mendlowitz, Rabbi Sholom Goldstein.
(second row): Meyer Strassfeld, Rabbi Yisroel Spinner, Rabbi Moshe Weitman,
Rabbi Shlomo Weinberger, Rabbi Heshie Mashinsky, Yitzchak Schwinder, Rabbi Avrahom Abba
Friedman. (top row): Rabbi Abish Mendlowitz, Rabbi Eliyahu Moshe Shisgal,
Lennie Kestenbaum, Rabbi Milton Terebelo, Rabbi Mendel Eller*

Jewish fathers and the issue of separate boys' and girls' classes. Bridges were built between the yeshiva world and the disparate communities nationwide where day schools were being established.

TORAH UMESORAH'S AGENDA

The Torah Umesorah staff went to the various communities to lay the groundwork – meetings were held, plans were drawn up, and opponents and skeptics had to be convinced of the need to build and support a day school. Once progress was achieved, Torah Umesorah helped the community establish the actual school, provided the teachers and curricula, and assisted with finances. They would also go from house to house canvassing for students.

The typical day school in the early years was primarily an outreach institution. The vast majority of the student body did not come from *shomer Shabbos*, observant, or kosher homes. To ensure local support and not alienate prospective parents and supporters, great care and sensitivity had to be exercised not to antagonize them by imposing stringent standards at the outset. Such action would have been counterproductive. The Rabbinic Board used great wisdom and discretion when addressing sensitive issues. They entrusted and involved the local *posek*, *rav* and halachic arbiter, who was familiar with the specific circumstances and knew those concerned, to help formulate policy. Matters were decided on a case by case basis.

Torah Umesorah staff went to the various communities to lay the groundwork – meetings were held, plans were drawn up, and opponents and skeptics had to be convinced of the need to build and support a day school.

Joseph Shapiro

To ensure local support in the early years, and not alienate prospective parents and supporters, great care and sensitivity had to be exercised not to antagonize them by imposing stringent standards at the outset.

AISH DOS

At the inception of Torah Umesorah, Reb Shraga Feivel set up the *Aish Dos* Institute to prepare idealistic educators for the day school movement. The plan was to prepare them to handle their outreach mission, as well as train them as educators. The program was led by Rabbi Simcha Wasserman* and Dr. Samson Raphael Weiss, the original director. Unfortunately, due to a lack of funds, the *Aish Dos* program closed in its second year. Reb Shraga Feivel was not well at this time, but he did manage to begin the day school campaign without *Aish Dos*. Besides enlisting some of his own *talmidim,* he also put together a group of Torah-true lay leaders, who were also men of means, to help the fledgling organization. Reb Shraga Feivel chose Samuel Feuerstein** of Brookline, MA., to serve as president of Torah Umesorah, a position he held until his death in 1983. Others included Irving and Amos Bunim***, Moses Feuerstein, Anshel Fink, Harry and Sam Herskowitz, Stephen Klein****, Frank Newman, Ira and Joseph Rosenzweig and Joseph Shapiro.

NATIONAL CONFERENCE OF YESHIVA PRINCIPALS

In the early years of Torah Umesorah, the National Conference of Yeshiva Principals was founded. The principals of the various day schools would meet in symposia, pedagogical workshops, curriculum conferences and a national convention to design and establish the guiding principles of Torah Umesorah. The annual national convention was attended by the *Roshei Yeshiva* who would address the principals. The first such event was held in 1947, at the Hebrew Academy of Cleveland in Cleveland Hts., Ohio, generously sponsored by the Spero Family Foundation. The principals were inspired and energized by these events. The organization evolved over time and promoted intensive contact between principals. This was especially beneficial to new principals.

INFRASTRUCTURE OF TORAH UMESORAH

The major departments of Torah Umesorah were School Organization, Education, and Publications. Besides the National Conference of Yeshiva Principals, a National Association of Hebrew Day School PTA's was established in May of 1948 to organize the various PTA's and inspire the communities about day school education. The National PTA sponsored a series of

National Conference of Yeshiva Principals Convention, Minneapolis, MN. (L-R back row): Unknown, Rabbi Meir Belsky, Rabbi N.Z. Dessler, Rabbi Chaim Tzvi Katz, Rabbi Joseph Elias, (L-R front row): Rabbi M. Pick, Rabbi Shalom Rephun, Rabbi Meir Eisemann

---

* Refer to the biography of Rabbi Simcha Wasserman, pg. 334
** Refer to the biography of Samuel Feuerstein, pg. 72
*** Refer to the biography of Irving Bunim, pg. 394
**** Refer to the biography of Stephen Klein, pg. 410

lectures on the weekly *parashah*. They also published a magazine – *The Jewish Parent* – with articles on Jewish education, book reviews and columns by leading educators. Their programs were well received by the various communities.

The School Organization Department founded new day schools by carefully researching which communities had the potential for the establishment of a day school. Once this was determined, Torah Umesorah did whatever was necessary to ensure the existence of such a school. In concert with this task was composing and designing the essential promotional materials. This literature was intended to convince its readers of the many advantages of a day school education. Rabbi Goldenberg ably directed this department for many years.

The Education Department had the responsibility of supervising the educational programs in the day schools and the placement of teachers and principals. Originally, this department was dynamically led by Dr. J. Kaminetsky. Eventually, a separate placement department was set up.

The Publications Department was founded to provide the schools with Torah educational texts and other curricular materials. The Spero Foundation helped underwrite the costs of Torah Umesorah Publications in its early years. They set up a revolving fund (1959-60) to help *Olomeinu*, and Earl Spero remained involved in *Olomeinu* affairs until his death. Rabbi Yaakov Fruchter was, and continues as the Department's talented director. He also serves as editor of the popular *Olomeinu* magazine, which helped to

Torah Umesorah Dinner, 1970

popularize the Torah Umesorah name. Today, *Olomeinu* is the most popular children's magazine in the English Jewish world, with a circulation of over 20,000 and an estimated readership of over 75,000.

CONCLUSION

Those individuals who worked tirelessly and with great *mesiras nefesh* on behalf of Torah Umesorah saw the dream of Reb Shraga Feivel Mendlowitz become a reality. This organization helped link the leadership of the *roshei yeshiva* with lay leaders, such as Irving Bunim, Samuel Feuerstein, and Stephen Klein, who devoted their lives to building and disseminating Torah on these shores. They prevailed, challenged by the charge of Reb Shraga Feivel to build an Orthodox Jewish day school in every major Jewish community in America. Sixty-plus years later the accomplishments of Torah Umesorah are nothing short of remarkable. Above all, they have ensured the growth and survival of the American Jewish community through the establishment of more than 600 Torah schools in America and Canada. We are forever indebted to them.

Those individuals who worked tirelessly and with great mesiras nefesh on behalf of Torah Umesorah saw the dream of Reb Shraga Feivel Mendlowitz become a reality – 600 Torah schools in the U.S. and Canada.

SPERO FAMILY FOUNDATION

The Spero family of Cleveland, Ohio, is renowned for their philanthropy and for spearheading many innovative projects to foster Torah growth in America, beginning in the 1940s. The four brothers, Leon, Ben and Herb of Cleveland, and Earl, who was then living in New York, established the Spero Foundation during World War II. They personally sought out and then addressed the specific areas in the Jewish community that needed their support.

Leon Spero

Leon Spero was the oldest of the brothers. His likeable demeanor and serene disposition were important qualities in the founding and early work of the Spero Foundation. His unfortunate passing in 1946 deprived his brothers of an invaluable asset in their charitable efforts. Yet he remained an inspiration to them.

Ben Spero

Ben Spero was a quiet, unassuming individual who preferred to remain behind the scenes. He strongly supported his brothers' ideas and the Foundation's activities with his solid business acumen and by pledging financial resources. His commitment to all worthy *tzedakah* projects and to many individuals was well known throughout the Torah world.

Earl Spero was the New York connection of the Spero Foundation. Based in the Williamsburg section of Brooklyn, he became a well-known link between the Young Israel (where he was a *baal tefillah* for half a century) and the Chassidic communities. He devoted his creative talents to the preparation and publication of the popular and informative Spero Foundation publications. He also designed and manufactured the portable Spero *succah*.

Earl Spero

Herbert Spero, though much younger than his brothers, brought to the Spero Foundation an energy and "*chutzpah*" to think big. Sharing with his brothers a complete respect and devotion to *Roshei Yeshivos*, he served as the first President of Telshe Yeshiva and was a primary founder of the Hebrew Academy of Cleveland. His commitment went far beyond financial support; he literally involved himself on a day-to-day basis in the building of these Torah institutions, with the moral and financial support of his brother, Ben.

Herbert Spero

The Spero brothers' achievements are many, and their contribution to the development and strengthening of American Orthodoxy is impressive indeed.

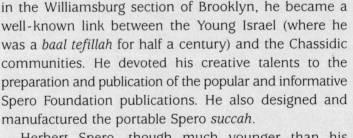

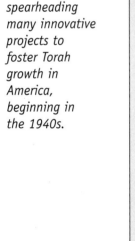

The Spero family of Cleveland, Ohio, is renowned for their philanthropy and for spearheading many innovative projects to foster Torah growth in America, beginning in the 1940s.

AMONG THEIR UNDERTAKINGS:

- Ben and Herb Spero were instrumental in bringing the Telshe Yeshiva and the Hebrew Academy of Cleveland to Cleveland and were mainstays of the Yeshiva throughout their lives.

- Earl Spero was actively involved in the Parents Association of Mesivta Torah Vodaath. He organized fundraising bazaars and door-to-door campaigns to solicit funds for the yeshiva. Torah Vodaath also benefited from the untiring service and devotion of Samuel Dropkin, Ben Spero's *mechutan* who served as treasurer from 1931 to 1963.

- A series of *Jewish Pocket Books* was published on various areas of Jewish thought, under the auspices of Agudath Israel.

- *Benchers* and *Zemiros* booklets, as well as pocket-size *Minchah/Maariv Siddurim* were prepared and printed by them.

- The Speros financed the preparation, publication, and distribution of original booklets for *Chevra Kadisha* and *Bikur Cholim* groups to dis tribute to mourners and the sick, respectively.

- Paperback *siddurim* were published for distribution in refugee camps and surviving European *shuls*, at Vaad Hatzala's request. A special message of hope was included in the volume.

- The publication of out-of-print *mussar* classics (i.e. *Orchos Tzaddikim* and *Derech Hashem*) for yeshivos, and individual *Gemara* chapters for use in Orthodox summer camps, was sponsored by the Speros.

- A *Taharas Ha'mishpachah* booklet – the laws, as well as a directory of U.S. *mikvaos*–was printed and distributed throughout the country.

- A set of architectural plans for the construction of a kosher *mikvah* was designed by the Foundation and made available to any Jewish community that desired it.

- They sponsored a series of biographies of well-known Jewish personalities, under the auspices of Torah Umesorah, in addition to their involvement in *Olomeinu*.

- The design, manufacture and distribution of the first prefabricated *succah*, complete with bamboo poles for *s'chach* and electric lights, was initiated and maintained by Earl Spero.

- A modern fully-equipped printing shop was set up by the Foundation in the heart of Yerushalayim in the early 50s to address their printing and publishing needs. The Speros stipulated that any profits should be used to purchase *challos* for Jerusalem's needy.

- Ben Spero set up a *gemach*, interest-free loan fund, to yeshivos, in his wife's memory, under the aegis of Torah Umesorah.

The Speros have stood at the vanguard of Torah and its dissemination to the Jewish masses, whether it was through their support of Telshe Yeshiva, Hebrew Academy of Cleveland, Torah Vodaath, Orthodox Union, Young Israel, Agudath Israel, or Torah Umesorah. The American Orthodox Jewish community has been enriched by their breadth of vision and myriad accomplishments.

The American Orthodox Jewish community has been enriched by their breadth of vision and myriad accomplishments.

CORRESPONDENCE AND PROGRAM FOR FIRST TORAH UMESORAH NATIONAL CONVENTION HELD IN CLEVELAND, OHIO IN 1947

DEDEPARTMENT OF EDUCATION
TORAH UMESORAH

132 NASSAU STREET NEW YORK 7, N.Y.
CORTLANDT 7-2738

DR. JOSEPH KAMINETSKY
Director
January 29, 1947

Dear Colleagues,

During the past few months I have had an opportunity to visit a number of yeshivot ketanot along the Eastern coast, as well as in New York City and its environs. Everywhere I noticed genuine enthusiasm and some very fine work being done in the field. Many principals and executives also expressed a real desire to "get together" to discuss the problems we have in common and to work out some coordinated plans for the more effective functioning of the all-day Jewish school in America.

The Spero Foundation of Cleveland and New York, which has already done yeoman work in disseminating traditional Jewish classics and genuine Jewish educational literature, has suggested to us that such a Conference be called in Cleveland, Ohio, at their expense – i.e. they would take care of the housing and boarding of all delegates. The only expense to the school sending representatives would be the train or plane fare to Cleveland.

Accordingly, in cooperation with the Spero Foundation, we have set a date of <u>Friday, March 14th, through Sunday, March 16th,</u> (the Shabbat Parah weekend) for this Conference which will be attended, we trust, by the spiritual leaders, principals, executive directors, head-teachers and lay-leaders of the yeshivot ketanot throughout the country. (This invitation is being sent to all yeshivot, irrespective of their affiliation with Torah Umesorah or any other national body.)

The general scope of the Conference will include discussion of the following major areas of interest:

1) The Place of the All-Day School in the American Scene, its need, its compatability with Americanism, its endeavors to achieve a genuine religious orientation for our children.

2) The Teaching Program – the course of study, methods of teaching, coordinating the Hebrew and secular programs, teacher-training, in-service training and staff relationships.

3) Public Relations – "Propaganda" for the Day School, fiscal administration, pupil enrollment, parent-teacher work, the lay-board of the school and the like.

4) National Coordination – teachers seminars, summer courses, "model" curricula, certification of teachers and related matters.

The program for the Conference is now being drawn up. Suggestions by you are earnestly solicited. Our plan is to have, besides a number of main addresses by leading personalities, papers read or short talks delivered by the people working in the field, and general discussion by all delegates.

We hope that you will make every effort to have the key-people in your school, besides yourself, participate in this Educational Conference. In a few days, letters inviting the participants in the program will be sent out; and we will then send you a copy of the tentative program.

Meanwhile, please discuss this Conference with your people and send to the list of your delegates to our office as soon as possible. The names of these delegates, you will understand, will have to be certified by the head of the institution.

Many thanks, beforehand, for your fine cooperation. We look forward to your early favorable reply.

Sincerely yours,

Dr. Joseph Kaminetsky

DEPARTMENT OF EDUCATION
TORAH UMESORAH

132 NASSAU STREET NEW YORK 7, N.Y.
CORTLANDT 7-2738

DR. JOSEPH KAMINETSKY
Director

Dear Colleague:

The following is an important Memorandum on the "Conference on Yeshiva Education." Please read it carefully.

I. Change of Date:

The response to our proposed "Conference on Yeshiva Education" to be held in Cleveland, Ohio, has been most encouraging. As a matter of fact, most of the people who have been invited to participate in the program have asked for more time to prepare their papers.

Accordingly, we have decided to postpone the Conference until after Passover, please G-d. The new date is the week-end of April 25th – 27th. The place is the same:

Cleveland, Ohio — to make it possible for the people in the West and Mid-West to attend the sessions and help make this a real national conference.

Arrangements are the same too: The Spero Foundation will provide housing and meals for all delegates. The only expense to the school sending representatives will be the train or plane fare to Cleveland.

II. Tentative Program: . . . .

The tentative program for the Conference follows (the new date may allow for an additional session on Friday):

Friday Evening:
Addresses by leading Roshei Yeshiva on the general theme: "The Need of The Hour – Yeshiva Education."

Saturday Afternoon:
Addresses by leading religious educators and men in the field on the general themes:
1) "Compatibility with the American Scene"
2) "A Religious Orientation for Our Children"

Saturday Evening:
Theme: "The Teaching Program"
Presentation of papers, not exceeding 15 minutes, on the following:
1) Planning the Course of Study (3 papers by 3 principals)
2) Teaching Chumash and Related Subjects
3) The Kindergarten – Its Organization and Program
4) Coordination of the Hebrew and Secular Programs
5) Teacher – Principal Relationships
6) Teacher-Training
7) In-Service Training and Teacher Growth
8) Text-books for our Schools Discussion

Sunday Morning:
A) 9:00-10:00 - Visit to the new
Hebrew Academy Building
in Cleveland.
B) 10:00 to 12:00 – Meeting of
Committees – Three Committees
to be formed:
1. On curriculum and general
course of study
2. On teachers, their background
and training, certification, etc.
3. Executive Administration of
Yeshivot Ketanot . . .

Sunday Afternoon:
Theme: "The Externa of Yeshiva Education"
Presentation of papers, not exceeding 15
minutes on the following:
1. Harnessing Public Opinion
2. Fiscal Administration of the
Yeshivot Part I: Fund-raising,
Part II: Budgeting, etc.
3. Pupil Enrollment, Tuition fees,
Transportation etc.
4. Canvassing Techniques
5. Building the Out-of-Town Yeshiva
6. A Plan to Sell the Yeshiva Idea
7. The Parent-Teacher Association
8. The Lay Board of the Yeshiva
9. National Coordination

Discussion
Reports of Committees
Summation of Conference...........
(Roster of people participating in
the program is incomplete at
present; hence the omission of
all names.)

III. Your Suggestions and Cooperation:
Any suggestions re: the above are
earnestly solicited and will be more
than welcome.
Please discuss this Conference with
your people and send on the list of your
delegates to our office as soon as
possible. The names of these delegates,
you understand, will have to be certified
by the head of the institution.

Many thanks, beforehand, for your
fine cooperation. We look forward to your
early favorable reply.

Sincerely yours,
Dr. Joseph Kaminetsky

CONFERENCE ON YESHIVA EDUCATION
5 - 7 Iyar (April 25-27th) Cleveland, Ohio

Conference Headquarters

New York – Torah Umesorah – 132 Nassau St.,
N.Y.7, N.Y. Cortlandt 7-2738

Cleveland – Hebrew Academy of Cleveland –
1860 S. Taylor Rd. Cleveland, Ohio 44118

Registration of Delegates – Friday,
April 25th, 1947 – 10:00 A.M.

Opening Session – 12:00 noon – Friday

Chairman –   Moses I. Feuerstein,
Chairman, Organizations Committee,
Torah Umesorah

Address of Welcome – Louis Schreiber,
President, Hebrew Academy of Cleveland

Greetings – Herbert Spero, Chairman,
Bldg. Comm. Hebrew Academy of
Cleveland
- Rabbi Louis Engelberg – for
Rabbinical Council of
America & UOJCA
- Rabbi Leon Machlis – for
Egud HaRabbonim of America

Purpose of Conference – Rabbi Aharon
Kotler, Chairman, Rabbinical
Administrative Board, Torah Umesorah

Organization of Conference – Dr. Joseph

Kaminetsky, Director, Dept. of Education, Torah Umesorah
Appointment of Committees.

Meetings of Committees, Friday, 2:00-4:30 P.M.

1. General Resolutions – Rabbi David Lifshitz, Rosh Yeshiva, Yeshivath Rabbenu Isaac Elchanan, New York City

2. Curriculum and General Course of Study – Chairman, Gershon Kranzler, Principal, Yeshivath Zichron Moshe, Bronx, N.Y.

3. Teacher-Training and Certification – Chairman, Dr. Markus Elias, Principal, Hebrew Teachers Training School for Girls, New York City

4. Executive Administration of Yeshivoth – Chairman, Rabbi Samuel Prero, Director, Federated Torah Fund, New York City

5. Building New Yeshivos – Rabbi Morris Pickholz, Principal, Hebrew Day School, Providence, Rhode Island

Friday evening – Kabbalos Shabbos at Telsher Yeshiva. 706 E. 105th St. Cleveland

Shabbos Seudah – Telsher Yeshiva

Mesibas Lel Shabbos – Rabbi Moses Rothenberg, Dean, Yeshivath Chachmey Lublin, Detroit, Mich. – Chairman

Greetings – Rabbi Ch. Mordecai Katz – Dean, Telsher Yeshiva, Cleveland, Ohio

Irving Bunim, National Council of Young Israel, New York City

Addresses on "Yeshiva Education – The Need of the Hour"
- Rabbi Reuven Grozovsky, Rosh Yeshiva, Mesivta Torah Vodaath, Bklyn, N.Y.
- Rabbi Elijah M. Bloch, President, Telsher Yeshiva, Cleveland, Ohio

Saturday morning –

Tefilah Betzibbur – Telsher Yeshiva–8:00 A.M.

Sermon – Rabbi Jacob Lessin, Menahel Ruchoni, Yeshivath Rabbenu Isaac Elchanan, New York City

Saturday afternoon – Shabbos Seudah – Telsher Yeshiva

Mesibas Shabbos – Saturday afternoon – 3:30 P.M.
Rabbi Mordechai Gifter, Rosh Yeshiva, Telsher Yeshiva, Cleveland – Chairman

Address – "What the Yeshivah Ketanah Can Do for the American Child" Rabbi Oscar Z. Fasman, President, Hebrew Theological College, Chicago, Chicago, Ill.

Address – "Spreading the Idea of the Yeshiva Ketanah" Rabbi David Lifshitz, Rosh Yeshiva, Yeshiva Rabbenu Isaac Elchanan New York City

Sholosh Seudos – 5:30 or so:

Reception for Delegates by the Hanhalah of Telsher Yeshiva

"Davar Halachah"– Rabbi E.M. Bloch, Telsher Yeshiva – Rabbi Mendel Zaks, Rosh Yeshiva, Yeshivath Rabbenu Isaac Elchanan

Session – Saturday Evening – 8:00 at Telsher Yeshiva

Theme: "Planning the Program of the Yeshivah Ketanah"

Chairman – Dr. Joseph Kaminetsky, Director, Dept. of Education, Torah Umesorah

1. The Course of Study –

    A) The Intensive Ivrit B'Ivrit Curriculum – Rabbi I. Levin, Principal Hebrew Day School, Trenton, N.J.
    B) The Eight Year Course – Rabbi Eli Schwartz, Principal, Yeshivas Toras Emes, Brooklyn, N.Y.
    C) "The Departmental System" – Rabbi N. W. Dessler, Principal, Hebrew Academy, Cleveland, Ohio

2. Coordination of the Hebrew and Secular Programs – Dr. Harold Leiman, Yeshivos Superintendent of Schools, Brooklyn, N.Y.

3. Teaching Chumash and Beginning the Study of Gemarah – Rabbi Judah Davis, Principal, Yeshiva of Brighton, Brooklyn, N.Y.

4. Religious Training in the Yeshiva – Rabbi Avigdor Miller, Menahel Ruchoni, Mesifta Chaim Berlin, Brooklyn, N.Y.

5. Text-Books for our Schools –

    a) Dr. Hugo Mandelbaum, Principal, Yeshiva Beth Yehuda Day School, Detroit, Mich.
    b) Dr. Jechiel Lichtenstein, Instructor in Bible, Brooklyn Branch, Yeshivath Rabbenu Isaac Elchanan, Bklyn, N.Y.

6. "The Language Problem in the Yeshivah Ketanah" – Rabbi Joseph Baumol, Spiritual Leader, Yeshiva of Crown Heights, Brooklyn, N.Y.

7. "Extending the Yeshivah Ketanah Into a Mesivta" – Rabbi Yehudah L. Kagan, Dean, Yeshiva Rabbi Israel Salanter, Bronx, N.Y.

Discussion

Sunday Morning –
Tefilah and Breakfast at Hebrew Academy Building – 1860 South Taylor Road, Cleveland Heights, Ohio

9:00 a.m. – Tour of our new building of the Hebrew Academy of Cleveland

Session – 10:00 a.m.

Theme: "Teachers for our Schools and School Organization" – Rabbi Alexander Gross, Director, Department of School Organization, Torah Umesorah Chairman

1. Teacher-Training – Rabbi Joseph Elias, Principal, Bes Hamidrash Le' Mechanchim, Mesivta Torah Vodaath, New York City.

2. In-Service Training and Teacher Growth – Dr. Wm. W. Brickman, Instructor, School of Education, New York University, New York City

3. Teacher-Principal Relationships – Dr. David S. Stern, Principal, Yeshiva Torah Vodaath, Brooklyn, N.Y.

4. The Out-of-Town Yeshiva – Rabbi Max J. Wohlgelernter, President, Yeshivath Beth Yehuda – Detroit, Michigan

5. Canvassing Techniques – Shubert Spero, Brooklyn, N.Y.

6. Pupil Enrollment – Rabbi Dovid Pruzansky, Executive Director, Hebrew Academy of Washington, D.C.

Discussion

Lunch

(Special Session of Roshei HaYeshiva and Board of Directors of Torah Umesorah)

Sunday afternoon Sessions – 1:30 P.M.

Section A

Theme: "The Externa of Education" Chairman, – Rabbi Bernard Goldenberg, Director, Dept. of Public Relations Torah Umesorah

1. Greetings: – National Council Beth Jacob – Rabbi Abraham Newhouse & Beth Jacob Seminary – Rabbi David Brisman

2. Harnessing Public Opinion – David Eidelsberg, Feature-writer, Jewish Morning Journal, New York City

3. The Lay Board of the Yeshiva Ketanah – Moses I. Feuerstein, Chairman, Organizations Committee, Torah Umesorah; Brookline, Mass.

4. The Parent Teachers Association – Rabbi Meilech Silber, Principal, Yeshiva of Eastern Parkway, Brooklyn, N.Y.

5. Fiscal Administration of the Yeshiva Ketanah – Rabbi Samuel Prero, Director, Federated Torah Fund, N.Y.C.

6. Planning the Fund Campaign – Samuel L. Usadi, National Field Director, Torah Umesorah, New York City

Section B

Theme: "Extension of Torah Education" Chairman – Rabbi Nahum Schulman – Chairman, Board of Education, Torah Academy, Minneapolis, Minn.

1. Building the Yeshiva Ketanah in the South and West – Rabbi Tibor Stern, Spiritual Leader of Federated Orthodox Congs., Kansas City, Mo.

2. Torah Education in South America – Maximo Yagupsky, General Director, Vaad Hachinuch Haroshi B'Argentina, South America

3. Torah Education in the DP Camps and Liberated Communities of Europe – Rabbi Samuel Shechter, former educational representative of Vaad Hatzalah in Europe, Brooklyn, N.Y.

Discussion

Sunday afternoon 5:00 P.M. – Closing Session

1. Report of Committees – by the Committee Chairman

2. General Resolutions – Rabbi David Lifshitz

3. Closing Address – Rabbi Aharon Kotler

SAMUEL C. FEUERSTEIN

A notable individual who bridged the worlds of commerce, Torah commitment and philanthropy was Samuel C. Feuerstein of Malden and Brookline, Massachusetts.

A man who valued the importance of Torah education, Sam Feuerstein was chosen by Rabbi Shraga Feivel Mendlowitz to serve as Torah Umesorah's first National President, a position he held for almost 40 years. Under his dynamic tenure the fledgling organization achieved solid direction and prestige. Dr. Joseph Kaminetsky, longtime National Director of Torah Umesorah, said, "The aristocratic mien of Mr. Samuel Feuerstein, especially in his younger years, galvanized our annual dinners...his deep interest in the movement continued throughout the years, with his son, Moe, carrying out his ideas and ideals. His daughter Irma (Feuerstein Horowitz) was part of the team; her concerns and interests were not only for the National P.T.A. but for the movement as a whole." Torah Umesorah was a "family business" as much as his textile business. Sam Feuerstein, the family patriarch, had indeed inculcated his children with the same zeal and commitment to Torah education as he possessed. The Feuersteins were also among the largest contributors to Torah Umesorah from its inception. The eminent Rabbinical Administrative Board of Torah Umesorah depended on them to help implement their policies; an indication of the *gedolim's* confidence in their abilities.

In keeping with Sam Feuerstein's tremendous support and commitment to Torah *Chinuch*, he was also involved in Chinuch Atzmai for several years.

Moses (Moe) Feuerstein, has not only followed in his father's footsteps but has set his own course, creating footprints of his own. At a time when Orthodoxy in America was overshadowed in leadership and resources by the deviation movements, Moe Feuerstein helped fill the void by accepting the presidency of the Orthodox Union (1954-66).

(L-R): Rabbi Aharon Kotler, Mr. Samuel Feuerstein, Dr. Leo Jung, Rabbi S.R. Weiss

A notable individual who bridged the worlds of commerce, Torah commitment and philanthropy was Samuel C. Feuerstein.

Samuel Feuerstein speaking

His tenure marked a turning point for the organization. A gifted leader and spokesman, Moe Feuerstein, an American-born, yeshiva-educated young man, possessed great *kavod haTorah*, respect for Torah and its leaders. He firmly believed that in his quest to develop programs and set policies for the Orthodox Union, he had to defer to the guidelines established by the *gedolim* of that time. This view was far from widespread or popular in the early 1950s. However, he did consult with various Torah leaders before making important decisions – including Rabbi Aharon Kotler and Rabbi Joseph B. Soloveitchik. He was committed to developing cooperation between the *gedolim* and the Orthodox lay leadership. An indication of his success is that during his tenure, *roshei yeshiva* regularly participated in Orthodox Union conventions.

Moe Feuerstein asserted the viability of the Orthodox *shul* in American Jewish life through the many educational, synagogue and youth programs and projects he instituted. The Orthodox Union's voice also gained strength and effectiveness in the communities, as well as governmental and legislative issues of Jewish concern – i.e., *shechitah* and Federal aid to parochial schools.

He has further contributed to American Orthodoxy through his active involvement as chairman of the Executive Committee of Torah Umesorah, helping to build and mold that organization for 35 years.

In both capacities he was the unifier, linking the worlds of the *shul* and the day school. Moe Feuerstein has always tried to unite the various forces of Torah in America and has succeeded in great measure.

The selfless mission of this father and son has successfully developed and strengthened Torah in America and we are their fortunate beneficiaries.

Moe Feuerstein, a gifted leader and spokesman, was the unifier, linking the worlds of the shul and day school, as President of the O.U. and chairman of Torah Umesorah.

(L-R): Samuel Feuerstein, Rabbi Dr. Joseph Soloveitchik, Moe Feuerstein

FOOD for JERUSALEM
AUSPICES:
AGUDATH ISRAEL YOUTH COUNCIL
OF AMERICA
113 WEST 42ND ST., N.Y.C.
מזון לירושלים על ידי צעירי אגודת ישראל

Relief and Rescue from the European Inferno

The Story of the VAAD HATZALA

≈ **Vaad Hatzala**

No history of this era would be complete without studying the vital role played by the Vaad Hatzala. Among its notable accomplishments was the rescue of those individuals who became the religious leaders and *roshei yeshiva* in America.

HISTORICAL BACKGROUND

Following the terrible events of *Kristallnacht* (Nov. 1938), there was no doubt as to the Nazis' intentions. Ten months later, when Germany invaded Poland, the lives of 3.5 million Jews were endangered. A German-Soviet pact (Ribbentrop-Molotov Treaty) maintained Lithuania's independence and returned Vilna to Lithuania after nineteen years of Polish rule.

Many Jews fled to Vilna, which became the center of rescue and relief efforts in the region. Several yeshivos relocated there, including Mir, Europe's oldest yeshiva. Conditions were terrible – food and housing shortages, scarcity of work permits and severe cold. The actual escape across the border was difficult and dangerous. Nevertheless, ten thousand refugees came, including 2650 yeshiva *talmidim* and *rabbanim*, from the fall of 1939 until June 1940, when the Soviets annexed Lithuania.

Vilna sustained its own refugee aid committee, supported by the European and American Hebrew Immigrant Aid Society (HIAS) and the American Joint Distribution Committee (Joint). Under the leadership of the *gadol hador*, Rabbi Chaim Ozer Grodzenski (who passed away in August 1940), Vilna assumed the overwhelming task of helping the refugees in all areas – food, housing, documentation and even crossing the border. The yeshivos managed to persevere as a result of the help they received.

Rabbi Chaim Ozer Grodzenski

Although the Joint continued to provide relief, their resources were severely taxed in trying to meet the needs of so many refugees. Furthermore, they were unable or unwilling to address the unique problems of the yeshivos. As early as 1933, Rabbi Grodzenski wrote to Rabbis Eliezer Silver[*] and Yehuda Leib Seltzer complaining about the Joint's weak support and its attending consequences.

VAAD HATZALA IS ESTABLISHED

In desperation, the yeshivos turned to the Agudas HaRabbonim in the fall of 1939. A two-day conference was convened by them (Nov. 13-14) to address the crisis. Hundreds attended, and this gathering was a turning point for all relief and rescue work during the war and post-war years. Could the various disparate groups unite to raise money and save the *rabbanim* and *talmidim* in Vilna?

They were well aware of the extreme and present danger faced by the *yeshivaleit*, since they were easily recognizable as Jews and considered by the Soviets to be anti-communists. In addition, they were the first ones subject to disease and starvation. Hence, this group needed a special support organization to come to their aid.

The conference was divided on how to proceed. One group felt that each yeshiva should continue to raise its own funds. A second faction maintained that Orthodox groups should work with the Joint or Ezras Torah, international fundraising organizations that also supported yeshivos. The third group, with Rabbi Eliezer Silver as their spokesman, suggested creating an entirely new organization called Vaad Hatzala (The Rescue Committee), which would be more Torah-oriented than the Joint, and more vocal and political than Ezras Torah – a change in approach seemed necessary.

The conference supported Rabbi Silver, and the Vaad immediately opened offices at 673 Broadway. Originally called the Emergency Committee for War-Torn Yeshivoth (and later the Emergency Committee for Relief, Rehabilitation and Reconstruction), the Vaad functioned as an independent arm of the Agudas HaRabbonim.

From the beginning, the Vaad was a delicate alliance of dissimilar groups, and their differences would ultimately lead to its dissolution in the post-war years. Setting partisanship aside, they all worked together for a common goal.

The enormous task of sustaining the refugees in Vilna soon became overwhelming. It was clear that a new organization was needed to aid the yeshivos who were at greater risk than any other group.

---

*Refer to the biography of Rabbi Eliezer Silver, pg. 296

Rabbi Bernard Levinthal

Rabbi Yechiel Mordechai Gordon

was led by a presidium of five: Rabbis Eliezer Silver, Israel Rosenberg, Bernard Levinthal, Yechiel Mordechai Gordon and Jacob Levinson, with Rabbi Jacob Karlinsky serving as executive director. Eventually, the Vaad encompassed the entire spectrum of the Torah community (including all *roshei yeshiva*, Orthodox congregational *rabbanim*, important organizations such as Mizrachi, the Orthodox Union, Agudath Israel, Young Israel, and the overall lay community), and top leadership came initially from the Agudas HaRabbonim, supported by Rabbi Herbert S. Goldstein of the Rabbinical Council of America, Elimelech "Mike" Tress** of Agudath Israel, and Irving Bunim**, officially representing Young Israel.

Things were disorganized at first. Finally, it was decided to merge each individual yeshiva's efforts and become one organization. Rabbi Avraham Kalmanowitz**, *Rosh HaYeshiva* of the Mirrer Yeshiva's American branch, a *gadol* and true *moser nefesh*, joined

A conference was convened by the Agudas HaRabbonim in New York to address the crisis. The disparate groups united behind the plan to create a new organization – the Vaad Hatzala

Its initial aims were clearly stated in letters written by Rabbi Simcha Wasserman* (December 17 and 19, 1939), to Abraham Horowitz of the Central Relief Committee, a group formed by Rabbi Israel Rosenberg** with other American *rabbanim* after the First World War to aid yeshivos. Rabbi Wasserman wrote that although the Joint had greatly helped the yeshivos, it was "overburdened." Consequently, the Vaad Hatzala would carry out "a one-time campaign" during the winter of 1939-40 for the relief, rescue and reestablishment of the war-torn yeshivos, which Rabbi Wasserman rightly called "the greatest Torah centers in the Jewish world...Their existence [means] preserving the Torah."[1]

Initially, the Vaad

Rabbi Israel Rosenberg

Rabbi Herbert S. Goldstein

---

* Refer to the biography of Rabbi Simcha Wasserman, pg. 334

** Refer to the biographies of Rabbi Israel Rosenberg, pg. 260; Mike Tress, pg. 324; Irving Bunim, pg. 394; Rabbi Avraham Kalmanowitz, pg. 182.

1. Vaad Hatzala Collection, Yeshiva University Archives 1985, CRC 318/1-6, Rabbi Simcha Wasserman's Letters.

Rabbi Silver as the impetus behind the Vaad. Rabbi Kalmanowitz's involvement and his efforts had a strong impact on the Orthodox Jewish community and increased their support.

Several laymen provided important services, notably Irving Bunim, Menashe Stein (the first Finance Committee chairman), Stephen Klein* (a major rescue activist, who together with the Sternbuchs tried to rescue children from the camps during the war and served as chairman of the Immigration Division in the post-war period), and Mike Tress (who headed Agudath Israel's rescue division). They all worked tirelessly for the Vaad – fundraising, processing visas and affidavits, and securing the assistance of government officials.

Rabbi Silver gave the Vaad their initial direction. Indirectly, Reb Chaim Ozer was also a driving force – his 1939 plea for emergency aid mobilized the Vaad during its initial four years. Its first focus was providing relief and rescue for the Eastern European yeshivos. In April 1941, Rabbi Aharon Kotler** arrived in America and quickly joined the leadership of the Vaad. Rabbi Kotler imbued the Vaad with the additional focus and energy that it sorely needed. At his insistence, the various Orthodox Jewish organizations set their own political agendas aside to work together within Vaad Hatzala. The advantage was that the new organization would have greater resources and political clout.

MISSION TO VILNA

Vilna's Jews were temporarily unharmed in 1939, but conditions there were terrible. Rabbi Silver proposed that the Vaad should send a representative to Vilna, to meet with the great Torah leaders and determine the best course of action for relief and rescue, and perhaps bring the yeshivos to America or *Eretz Yisrael*. He chose fellow-Cincinnatian Samuel Schmidt, a Kovno-born, non-observant Jew, who left America in February 1940, and traveled throughout Lithuania. Dr. Schmidt sent weekly reports, describing the enormous dedication and suffering of the refugees, especially the *yeshiva-leit*. He was greatly affected by the personality of Reb Chaim Ozer, who accorded him respect as well.

Schmidt reported his impressions of the situation, distributed Vaad funds, and when he returned spoke with the Vaad leadership. He stressed the importance of saving the yeshivos. He conveyed a message from the dying Reb Chaim Ozer, requesting that the Vaad

Initially, Rabbis Kalmanowitz and Silver were the impetus behind the Vaad. Several laymen provided important services. Rabbi Kotler's arrival in 1941, imbued the Vaad with additional focus and energy.

Dr. Samuel M. Schmidt

---

* Refer to the biography of Stephen Klein, pg. 410

** Refer to the biography of Rabbi Aharon Kotler, pg. 210

and the American rabbis redouble their efforts to rescue the yeshivos and support Torah.

DIFFERING IDEOLOGIES

Even as late as mid-1940, there were those who remained complacent – despite everything, the yeshivos had survived. The Vaad leaders, however, knew that in Lithuania nothing was stable at that time. Their response was to act upon Schmidt's report with alacrity and do whatever was necessary to save the yeshivos. Whatever they achieved would be valuable. However, there was a shortage of visas.

Furthermore, the Joint was the only group with sufficient resources to arrange such a massive emigration, but because of the Joint's ideology, it would never use any means to help the refugees that were not strictly legal. They also were opposed to singling out just one group for rescue. The Joint was reluctant to bring several thousand foreign-looking yeshiva students into America, because they had no real means of support and they feared an anti-Semitic backlash.

The Jewish Labor Committee and the American Federation of Labor convinced President Roosevelt to issue emergency visitors' visas to endangered leaders in Occupied France and Lithuania. The Vaad requested 2,654 for its own purposes, hoping to bring *roshei yeshiva* and yeshiva students to America. The Joint felt that that was too great a number. Stephen Wise, the voice of secular Judaism, sided with the Joint's suggestion to bring over 300 or 500 Vilna scholars – a workable number according to them. Wise also did not feel that the President should be pressured to issue additional visas. Finally, only 2,600 visas were issued to all groups and the Torah group received just 500. Unfortunately, by the time the majority of the visas arrived in Europe it was too late to help.

As was mentioned, the Joint absolutely refused to do anything extralegal, including sending illegal cables. That does not diminish their outstanding record of aiding Jews, however. Alternatively, the Vaad maintained that the *mitzvah* of *hatzalas nefashos* (saving lives) takes precedence over *everything* else – superseding even the Torah's other commandments and prohibitions. When Jewish lives were at stake they were prepared to do whatever was necessary. The Vaad simply employed discretionary measures to funnel funds through Switzerland, Sweden and Uraguay. The Joint would never support such a policy. Throughout the war, the Vaad took courageous action to save Jewish lives and was not afraid to be non-conformist.

The Vaad's first fundraising campaign to support the Torah scholars and yeshivos trapped in Lithuania lasted for two years. In the third year, the funds raised enabled 1,064 yeshiva students, family members, and teachers to escape to Japan through the Soviet Union. Additionally, they supported 512 of those refugees who found refuge in Shanghai. The Vaad sustained the yeshiva population in China, and worked diligently to secure safe havens for them in other countries, including America, Belgium, Great Britain, Holland and Norway (to name several).

Vaad Hatzala accomplished miracles for the endangered and stranded Jews of Europe, because it had totally dedicated men fighting for its cause. Their abilities and motives notwithstanding, they could not change immigration quotas, issue visas, or create

---

The Vaad maintained that the Torah mitzvah of hatzalas nefashos, saving lives, takes precedence over everything else – superseding even the Torah's other commandments and prohibitions. When Jewish lives were at stake they were prepared to do whatever was necessary.

Jewish havens. They could provide funds, apply pressure and offer refuge, but could *not* guarantee results. Like every organization, the Vaad knew they could not operate in a vacuum. They understood that others could help in ways they could not. At times, help comes from unexpected sources. For Vilna's stranded yeshiva students, it came from an unanticipated place: Curaçao.

CURAÇAO AND JAPANESE VISAS

In 1940, Curaçao surprisingly became a key element in the struggle to save the *talmidei chachamim* of Europe. For centuries, Jews had lived on the small Caribbean island, which boasted the oldest synagogue and Jewish cemetery in the Western Hemisphere. Nathan Gutwirth, a Dutch national, Telshe Yeshiva student and refugee in Lithuania, certainly did not have Curacao in mind when he went to see Dutch Ambassador Dekker, hoping to leave war-torn Europe.

Dekker authorized the Dutch "Consul" in Kovno, Jan Zwartendijk, to issue visas to Curaçao. From July 23 - August 31, 1940, between 1200 - 1400 visas to Curaçao

Dutch "consul" in Kovno, Jan Zwartendijk

were issued to Polish refugees in Lithuania holding valid passports.

The next problem was finding an exit route and securing transit visas to reach there. The best option was via the Far East (most of Western Europe was Nazi-occupied). They would have to travel across the Soviet Union through Japan, thus necessitating a Japanese transit visa.

The Japanese Consul in Kovno, Sempo Sugihara, agreed to help (despite orders to the contrary from the Japanese Foreign Ministry). Approximately 3500 visas were issued.

Moshe Zupnik, a Mir *talmid,* served as a travel agent. He worked with Sugihara's assistant – a German named Goetke who hated Nazi anti-Semitism – stamping these Japanese transit visas (issued because of the invalid Dutch visas to Curaçao). The authorities accepted only 2,000 of the 3500 visas, and 816 of them were eventually used by the various Vilna yeshiva groups. Their hopes for escape rekindled, the

Sempo Sugihara

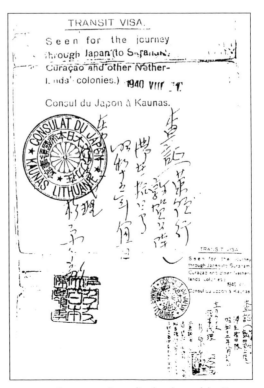

Japanese transit visa issued in Kovno by Sempo Sugihara

The problems of obtaining visas and finding Jewish havens were serious. Help came from unexpected sources – the Dutch Consul Zwartendijk and Japanese Consul Sugihara in Kovno.

Rabbi Shimon Sholom Kalish, the Amshenover Rebbe

Miraculously, the $50,000 necessary for the trans-Siberian trip to save the rebbeim and talmidim was raised in New York in one day!

Dr. Zerach Warhaftig

yeshiva community was ecstatic. They were not worried about the Dutch or Japanese authorities, but many were afraid to travel through Siberia, remembering Russian brutality during and after World War I. Only because Rabbi Shimon Sholom Kalish, the Amshenover *Rebbe*, Rabbi Leib Mallin of the Mirrer Yeshiva, and Dr. Zerach Warhaftig, a prominent Mizrachi leader, pressured them, did the hesitant ones agree to try to use the visas.

To their great surprise, the Soviet officials granted permission to the yeshiva representatives who approached them to cross Siberia and leave the Soviet Union. To their dismay, however, the price for the trans-Siberian trip fluctuated between $170 and $240, pre-paid in American dollars to *Intourist*, the official Soviet tourist agency. How would they ever pay for this? In November 1940, they received an ultimatum – either pay the group's full fare or face one of two consequences: permanent residency under Soviet control, or deportation to German-occupied Poland. The options were fraught with danger. Choosing to go to Poland meant immediate exile to Siberia for treason. Hoping the money would materialize seemed unrealistic. However, they had not bargained on the dedication and determination of men like Rabbi Silver, Rabbi Kalmanowitz, and Irving Bunim, who would do anything to save Jewish lives.

HATZALAS NEFASHOS SUPERSEDES SHABBOS

The *roshei yeshiva* who had escaped to Vilna cabled Rabbi Shlomo Heiman. They informed him of the dire need to *immediately* raise $50,000, to help the *rebbeim* and *talmidim* from the various yeshivos escape imminent death at the hands of the Russians, if the visas and the permits for the trans-Siberian trip from Vilna to Vladivostok could not be purchased. Many *gedolim*, including Rabbi Aharon Kotler, had escaped to the Vilna area. At this time, their lives were endangered. Despite months of work on an escape plan, the Vaad was unsuccessful. Now, it appeared that there was a viable solution. All that was necessary was the cash.

The *gedolim* in America – Rabbi Moshe Feinstein, Rabbi Shlomo Heiman and Rabbi Shraga Feivel Mendlowitz – considered this a matter of *pikuach nefesh* (a life and death situation), and as such it superseded even Shabbos. Consequently, on a Shabbos in November 1940, Rabbi Sender Linchner, Rabbi Boruch Kaplan and Irving Bunim traveled by taxi throughout the Flatbush section of Brooklyn raising money, because time was of the essence. With the help of the Almighty, they were successful in raising $45,000 and the Joint released the money – adding the $5,000 deficit – to Vilna. Miraculously, the *rebbeim* and *talmidim* were rescued!

Among the rescued *gedolim* were the Amshenover *Rebbe*, Rabbi Shimon Sholom Kalish; Rabbi Zalman Sorotzkin, the Lutzker *Rav;* Rabbi Eliezer Yehuda Finkel, *Rosh HaYeshiva* of the Mirrer Yeshiva and the son of the famed Rabbi Nosson Tzvi Finkel (the *Alter* of Slobodka), who went to Palestine; the Modzitzer *Rebbe*; Rabbi Reuven Grozovsky, the Kaminetzer *Rosh Yeshiva*; Rabbi Avraham Jofen, the Novardoker *Rosh Yeshiva* who came to the United States; and Rabbi Yechezkel Levenstein, *mashgiach* of the Mirrer Yeshiva who went to Shanghai.

Rabbi Eliezer Yehuda Finkel

The *gedolim* who reached America infused Vaad Hatzala with greater drive, dedication and purpose than anyone could have imagined. They complemented the strong leadership of Rabbis Eliezer Silver and Avraham Kalmanowitz, two scholars who had learned at the great European yeshivos and, therefore, could relate to the anguish of European Jewry.

THE THREE MIRACLES

The difficult journey across the Soviet Union proved even more harrowing because of weather conditions. They finally arrived in Kobe, Japan almost six days later than scheduled. However, after all this, they found out that there was no way to reach Curaco or elsewhere! Setzuso Kotsuji, a Japanese Bible scholar, managed to convince the authorities to extend their visas that were about to expire. Many refugees remained in Kobe throughout the War and were well treated by its citizens. Others went to Shanghai, including the entire contigent of the Mirrer Yeshiva. The entire rescue operation was nothing less than miraculous – a clear demonstration of Divine intervention.

First of all, Jan Zwartendijk, the purported Dutch Consul in Kovno who had granted all the Curacaoan visas, was *not* the consul, but rather the local representative for Phillips, Holland's largest corporation. He certainly did not have the authority to issue visas.

The real consul – an avowed Nazi sympathizer – had left Kovno only a few weeks before.

The purported Japanese Consul, Sempo Sugihara, whom the Mirrer Yeshiva called an "Angel of Salvation," was also not a consul. Actually, he was a spy sent by the Imperial government to see when and if the Germans might invade the Soviet Union, although his cover story was that he was Kovno's first commercial attaché from Japan. (Sugihara may have been discovered by the Soviets, because after they annexed Lithuanania, they forced him to close the Consulate by the end of August 1940.)

The final miracle was Goetke, Sugihara's German assistant, who although an ardent Nazi was opposed to the terrible persecution of Jews. A practical person, he told Moshe Zupnik who worked with him that one never knows how things will turn out,

The entire rescue operation to Japan was a clear demonstration of Divine intervention.

Rabbi Herbert S. Goldstein and Rabbi Zalman Sorotzkin, Chairman of the Moetzes Gedolei HaTorah in Eretz Yisrael

and he should remember all the help he gave to the Jewish cause.

DIVINE PROVIDENCE

Nevertheless, the reasons for certain events cannot be explained logically and must be viewed as Divine Providence intervening. After all, how else can the sudden change in Soviet policy be accounted for? Also, why did Japan allow thousands of Jews to enter their country – including 2000 with invalid visas from Lithuania? No other country was willing to accept more than a minimal number of refugees during that period. It cannot be explained other than that it was *Yad Hashem* (the hand of G-d).

Initially, there were Vaad activists who thought the early reports from Japan regarding the Jewish refugees were only propaganda, to make a favorable impression on the United States. Otherwise, they could not conceive that an ally of Nazi Germany and a strict militaristic regime would demonstrate such a profoundly pro-Jewish policy. Yet such was the case.

Japan's policy was publicly announced as of March 1939. Jewish refugees arrived in great numbers to Shanghai. The Germans ultimately brought great pressure on Japan to change their Jewish immigration policy. Not until 1943 did the Japanese capitulate, but all they did was create a sort of ghetto in Shanghai. The Jews still remained autonomous, but their movement was restricted, except for the yeshiva community who received a special collective pass. Foreign Minister Yasuke Matsuoka, who helped create the 1940 Tripartite Pact linking Japan, Italy, and Nazi Germany, guaranteed Jewish safety. How ironic!

The Germans relentlessly contin-

Yad Hashem, the hand of G-d, is the only way to explain certain events throughout the war.

ued to pressure Japan to change their policy. Finally, the Japanese convened top-ranking military and Shinto leaders to interview major representatives of the Jewish community, including the Amshenover *Rebbe* and Rabbi Moshe Shatzkes, the Lomzer *Rav*. Leo Hanin of JEWCOM, (Jewish Committee of Kobe, Japan) was not permitted into the interrogation room. He worried that the European rabbis would not understand the Japanese mindset, nor communicate effectively.

His fears were unfounded. After the meeting, the Amshenover *Rebbe* told him not to worry, that all was well. When asked why the Germans hate the Jews, he replied, "The Germans hate us because they consider us Orientals too." Men of such caliber had insight into the psyche of all types of people, regardless of their differences.

As a result of all these events the European yeshivos were not entirely lost and Torah learning continued. It injected the Vaad Hatzala with much-needed strength to continue its vital work.

At this point, America had still not entered the war, and the major Nazi death camps were not opened yet. The Vaad struggled to consider all events from a Torah viewpoint and, consequently, argued with the more secular American Jewish groups over what course of action should be followed regarding European Jewry. As atrocities in Europe escalated, the Vaad increased its efforts to save the trapped Jews. The Vaad's role became more global and they were now regarded as an important rescue agency.

RABBI KOTLER'S LEADERSHIP

In October 1941, the Vaad held a meeting to discuss its composition. Stephen Klein suggested a formal board of directors, a select committee, and a paid executive director. "A real organization should be created," the minutes read, "with an active office, as can be found in every other distribution agency."[2] Once Rabbi Kotler became involved in the Vaad, he became the spiritual, political and philosophical guide of the organization.

Rabbi Kotler constantly raised funds for the Vaad and avoided even the slightest appearance of personal gain. He was amazingly astute concerning American institutional politics. After being denied access to President Roosevelt, he launched a six-month telephone campaign from his own home, drafting the support of a broad spectrum of Jewish groups to alert their elected officials about events in Europe, and to propose workable solutions for refugees. Rabbi Kotler organized his own network of friendly congressmen, and turned to them more frequently as the situation deteriorated. Attaining support of the broad Jewish community was very difficult. What sustained the dedicated workers was the fact that they were fulfilling the great *mitzvah* of *hatzalas nefashos*, saving endangered lives.

RESCUE AGENCY

The Vaad, under the leadership of Rabbi Kotler, became experts at various means of helping stranded Jews wherever they might be. Diplomatic cables were employed to transfer funds to Switzerland for dispersal around the world, notably to the yeshivos in Shanghai. Lifesaving food and clothing packages were sent to Lithuania and Siberia. Numerous visa applications and affidavits were filled out to help get Jews out of Europe. Anything that could be done to save lives was done.

Generally, the Vaad worked alone, but occasionally joined forces with Agudath Israel and the Irgun, led by Hillel Kook who had come to America from Palestine, initially to raise funds for the Jewish army. The Agudah, under the leadership of Moreinu Yaakov Rosenheim and Mike Tress, set up a very successful emergency visa and employment affidavit agency (see Zeirei Chapter). The Irgun launched an Emergency Committee to Save the Jewish People of Europe. The "Bergson Group" (informal name of the Irgun faction) succeeded more than any other Jewish group in piercing the "conspiracy of silence" that surrounded the Holocaust. (Peter Bergson was Hillel Kook's English name that he used for his group's public information campaigns.)

Recognizing the importance of working with mainstream organizations like the Joint and American Jewish Congress, the Vaad tried to maintain relationships with them. Realistically speaking, Rabbi Kotler was not well known in the American Jewish community, but Stephen Wise was. Considered the most influential leader of American acculturated Jews, he had a close personal relationship with President Roosevelt. A major objective was to change the restrictive American immigration laws, as well as the American government's inertia in responding to the Nazi atrocities. The Vaad hoped that these established groups would give more money for relief and rescue efforts and extend their own services to the victims. Their influential contacts were also invaluable to the rescue effort.

Rabbi Kotler dispelled the misconception prevalent among American Jews that a Torah scholar was unworldly,

Once Rabbi Kotler became involved in the Vaad, he became the spiritual, political and philosophical guide of the organization.

2. Vaad Hatzala Collection, Yeshiva University Archives, 1985, VH 1-1

Hillel Kook

Hillel Kook (a.k.a. Peter Bergson) (1915-2001)

One man can make a difference, despite claims to the contrary. Hillel Kook, a heroic personality who emerged during the Holocaust years, was one of these men. Undaunted by an antagonistic American Jewish establishment, an anti-Semitic United States State Department, and an apathetic American President, Hillel Kook was prepared to do whatever was necessary to save European Jewry.

Originally, Hillel Kook, the nephew of the Chief Rabbi of Palestine, Avraham Yitzchak HaKohen Kook, was a Revisionist Zionist and a leader of the Irgun. He adopted the name Peter Bergson when he came to the United States from Palestine in the early days of World War II, to raise funds for an independent Jewish army that would fight alongside the Allies for Jewish causes, including the establishment of a Jewish state.[1] However, when the reports of Hitler's Final Solution for the Jews was confirmed in 1942, he and his group (known as the Bergson Boys) concentrated all their efforts and energies on rescue work.

Kook launched an extensive public information campaign about the catastrophe in Europe and the Allies' failure to respond. He placed full-page ads, written by the well-known author Ben Hecht and Pierre Van Paasen, in major U.S. newspapers such as the *New York Post* and the *Washington Post*. One such ad (March 1943) read: "For Sale To Humanity: 70,000 Romanian Jews, Guaranteed Human Beings, at $50 apiece" – it was an appeal to ransom Romanian Jews! The purpose was not only to shock the reader, but to point out that rescue was indeed possible. He also sent cables to high government officials worldwide to take action.

The Emergency Committee to Save the Jewish People of Europe, which he established in 1943, organized rallies and pageants that toured the United States to arouse public opinion for large-scale rescue.

When the Bergsonites, aided by such Hollywood talent as Ben Hecht, Kurt Weill, Edward G. Robinson, and Paul Muni, mounted a pageant entitled, "We Will Never Die," which drew 40,000 viewers to Madison Square Garden, and 60,000 more in five cities around the country, mainstream Jewish organizations orchestrated a campaign to dissuade sponsoring committees from presenting the pageant in other cities. This despite the fact that the pageant had proven itself to be the most successful instrument to date in arousing the American public to the plight of European Jews.[2]

The behavior on the part of the mainstream Jewish establishment was precipitated because "the leading Zionist organizations were so fearful of the growing influence of the Revisionist Zionist group led by Peter Bergson that they sought to stymie all the Bergsonites' efforts to arouse American public opinion for large-scale rescue."[3] Nevertheless, the Bergson group attracted a sizable following in the general public, and even in Congress. The establishment Jewish organizations attacked them bitterly and claimed that they were divisive and "unauthorized" to work for rescue. This did not deter Peter Bergson and his group, and they continued their work to raise funds for rescue.[4]

In October 1943, Bergson initiated and organized most of the details of the Rabbis' March on Washington, D.C. in cooperation with the Agudas HaRabbonim to protest the Roosevelt administration's inaction and indifference to European Jewry's imperilment. Four hundred Orthodox Rabbis participated; Rabbi Avrohom Kalmanowitz, Rabbi Eliezer Silver and Peter Bergson led the March. It is important to note that the rabbis' active participation in this event was something that had never happened before. However, they all felt that the critical situation called for drastic measures.

Vice-President Henry Wallace met them, together with a Congressional delegation. Unfortunately, the planned meeting of five rabbis with President Roosevelt never took place. At the recommendation of his trusted Jewish advisors, Roosevelt was elsewhere on "pressing business" and did not meet with the rabbis. Notwithstanding this snub by the President, the March was a success since it precipitated important changes in policy. The most dramatic outcome was the establishment, at last, of the War Refugee Board in January 1944. The Vaad Hatzala and Bergson share the credit for its creation.

Sadly, though, all the foot dragging had dire consequences – millions of Jews had already been murdered. Hillel Kook / Peter Bergson was not afraid to break "the conspiracy of silence" which surrounded the genocide that was raging in Europe. He was both tireless and relentless in his crusade, dedicated to the salvation of European Jewry. He brought these qualities to bear in aiding the establishment of the State of Israel. Personal glory or accolades were not in his lexicon – he was a man who made a difference because he knew what was important and had the ability to do something about it.

1. David S. Wyman, **The Abandonment of the Jews: America and the Holocaust** 1941-1945, New York, 1984, pg. 84
2. Ibid., pgs. 90-92
3. Ibid.
4. Berel Wein, **Triumph of Survival**, Shaar Press, N.Y., 1990, pg. 374

and incapable of comprehending or handling contemporary issues. However, he made it crystal clear that Torah **eternally** governs *all* phases of Jewish life — a fact that will **never** change. In the area of *hatzalah* he insisted that a rescue agent must adhere to spiritual values and possess sensitivity regarding every Jew's fate.

Alternatively, the assimilated secular Jews remained fearful of anti-Semitism and did whatever they could to prevent it. Consequently, to avoid even the appearance of dual loyalty, they greatly limited their Jewish activity. Acculturated Jews were a step above them, in that they retained Jewish interests. In their desire to be accepted by American society, they adopted American culture as their own and disliked Eastern European Jews whom they perceived as a threat to their goal of fitting in. They, too, feared anti-Semitism, as well as the possibility of a great influx of European Jews. These groups never made *hatzalah* a priority.

ACCOMPLISHMENTS

The Vaad activists were loyal and even patriotic to America, but their overriding allegiance was to Torah. They fought against American apathy and the misguided fears and infighting of the greater Jewish community, as well as their aversion to *Ostjuden* (East European Jews), and their focus on Palestine as a haven rather than America. Demonstrating continual courage and perseverance, the Vaad would not succumb to hopelessness.

The funds raised by the Vaad were used for visas, food and clothing. (At the time, Agudath Israel was the only other organization sending food packages to help combat the widespread starvation and disease rampant in the Polish ghettos.) Despite limited resources, the Vaad developed unique channels for sending food and clothing to *rebbeim* and *talmidim* trapped in Siberia. As reports later verified, and contrary to what the Joint Distribution Committee and others claimed, only the Vaad shipments reached Siberia, literally making the difference between life and death.

Although exact figures are impossible to obtain, records suggest that more than 5,500 Torah scholars in the Soviet Union, Shanghai and Japan received monthly supplies from the Vaad. Renee Reichman, matriarch of Toronto's great industrial and philanthropic family, who emigrated from Vienna to Morocco, sent out nearly four thousand packages every week, many through the Red Cross, to Hungarian Jews in Auschwitz and Birkenau.

Rabbi Kotler felt that relief and rescue work must be attempted, no matter how small the chance of success. Halachah, he said, dictates *hatzalah* at any cost.

The Vaad activists were loyal and even patriotic to America, but their overriding allegiance was to Torah. They fought against American apathy and the misguided fears and infighting of the greater Jewish community.

Agudath Israel's volunteers preparing packages for shipment

Unloading food in Munich, Germany, for the survivors, 1946

Rabbi Kotler said that "thousands of heart-rending cries for help are far more important and authoritative" than British policy, misguided Jewish loyalties, or any other consideration.[3] Regrettably, the mistrust between the variant segments of the American Jewish population never ended – even after the war. Yet Rabbi Kotler decreed that, despite these differences, the Vaad must work with all Jewish factions. Everything possible must be done to help the Jews in Europe and ultimately unite all Israel. Unfortunately, most American Jews did not subscribe to the Vaad's Torah view of *hatzalah* and felt that it threatened the status of Jews in America.

Despite this strife, the Vaad worked ceaselessly to obtain any papers – legal and discretionary – that could get Jews out of Nazi Europe. Their specialty was securing affidavits and visas for the limited number of immigrants the Vaad helped, despite State Department restrictions.

OVERCOMING THE INFORMATION GAP

The Vaad and other Torah activists provided ongoing accurate information concerning the worsening Holocaust during the early years of the war. Unfortunately, a lot of the data coming from Europe was unreliable; consequently, even the most poignant stories were overlooked.

Rabbi Kotler felt that relief and rescue work must be attempted, no matter how small the chance of success. Halachah, he said, dictates hatzalah at any cost.

However, even these actions were difficult to achieve. The Vaad also faced intense political pressure from other Jewish groups to stop these relief efforts. Great Britain objected, citing its blockade of Germany and German-occupied countries. Nevertheless, many fought or disregarded the blockade, citing humanitarian concerns. However, by summer 1941, almost every American Jewish group had joined the boycott – except for those Torah activists who maintained that Jewish lives superseded British policy.

The Vaad's position evoked strong disapproval. Dr. Joseph Tenen- baum, chairman of the Joint Boycott Council, attacked all their relief activities and called it a breach of Jewish unity behind the Allied war effort.

The Vaad Hatzala was not deterred by this criticism. Their shipments abroad continued without interruption.

---

3. The Goldberg Commission Report, Chapter 2, pg. 31

A month after the *Einsatzgruppen* (German mobile killing squads) began their murderous work along the Eastern Front, reports of mass killings began to leak out in July 1941. But it was not until June 10, 1942, when two men in London, Shmuel Zygielbojm (representing Poland's Jewish Labor Bund) and Zionist Dr. Ignacy Schwarzbart, forcefully documented the massacres, that the Allies could no longer ignore what was happening.

Nevertheless, many, especially America's State Department, remained skeptical about these charges of genocide. Finally, in August 1942, World Jewish Congress representative Gerhart Riegner, a German refugee living in Switzerland, received detailed, incontrovertible evidence delineating the Nazi plan for murdering all of Europe's Jews. He immediately turned over the information to the American Consul in Geneva, requesting that it be sent to Stephen Wise for review and dissemination. Instead, the consul sent Riegner's data to the State Department for verification. When Wise finally received the information, he neither shared it with other Jews nor made it public. He delayed further by giving it instead to American officials to be processed and sent through official channels to President Roosevelt.

Were it not for Yitzchak Sternbuch, information of Nazi genocide might never have reached the public. He released similar information in September to the Agudath Israel's New York offices. A Jew who had escaped from Auschwitz to Switzerland reported to him not only about the deportation and murder of a hundred thousand Jews from Warsaw, but also the unfath-omable news that their bodies had been reduced to soap and fertilizer. Sternbuch warned that the same fate would certainly befall every Jew in Occupied Europe, and he ended his cable to World Agudath Israel President (Moreinu) Jacob Rosenheim by urging: "Do whatever you can to cause an American reaction to halt these persecutions."[4]

The entire Vaad was mobilized by the horrifying news. Everyone rushed to raise money and put pressure on key individuals in Congress and the State Department to stop the genocide. By the end of the day, Rabbi Kotler, Irving Bunim, Stephen Klein, and Jacob Rosenheim had contacted virtually every American Jewish leader – Stephen Wise; Abba Hillel Silver, prominent Reform rabbi and ardent Zionist; Nachum Goldmann, head of the World Jewish Congress; and others to inform them of the mass murders in Poland. Rosenheim sent a cable to the

Although the Vaad and other Torah activists provided ongoing accurate information concerning the worsening Holocaust during the early years of the war, and in 1941 of Nazi genocide, the reports were received with skepticism.

Mr. Yitzhak Sternbuch, Dr. Isaac Lewin and Mrs. Sterbuch with rescued children at the Villa Raphael in Aix-les-Bains

4. David Wyman, **The Abandonment of the Jews**, New York, 1984, pg. 45

Moreinu Jacob Rosenheim

Were it not for Yitzchak Sternbuch, information of Nazi genocide might never have reached the public. The entire Vaad was mobilized by the horrifying news and immediately raised money and pressured key government individuals to help.

President on September 4, briefing him about events in Europe and asking him to help stop the massacres. "I dare in the name of Orthodox Jews all over the world," Rosenheim wrote, "to propose for consideration the arrangement by American initiative of a joint intervention of all the neutral states in Europe and America expressing their moral indignation."[5]

Despite Rosenheim's forceful cable, Roosevelt never bothered to respond, and did nothing whatsoever to help European Jewry until December 1942 – four months after the data was verified – and more than a year after early reports were received.

American Jewish leaders were more responsive than the President. The Vaad activists promptly met with Wise, who at first placed little credence in the Sternbuch cable. Rabbi Kotler, Rabbi Kalmanowitz and others greatly pressured him and they finally agreed on several points. In return for a promise from the Vaad and Agudah that they would not disseminate the Riegner and Sternbuch reports until the State Department could confirm them, Wise agreed to call a meeting of thirty-four major American Jewish organizations to discuss cooperative rescue activi-

ties. That meeting (September 6, 1942), produced a new group – the Temporary Committee.

When the State Department finally confirmed the Vaad's harrowing reports, in late November, Wise publicly announced the Nazi murder of more than two million Jews. He requested a meeting with Roosevelt after extreme pressure was brought by all Jewish groups. But instead of asking for a discussion of relief and rescue efforts, he requested from Roosevelt words of solace and hope to millions of Jews who mourn – "an expression of the conscience of the American people." This was politics, not substance.

Historian David Wyman, in discussing Wise's infatuation with President Roosevelt writes,

"After about 1935, Wise was unable to be critical of, or even objective about, the President. He was convinced that FDR was personally anxious to help the persecuted European Jews in the 1930s, that he wanted to do everything possible to rescue Jews during the Holocaust years, and that he

(L-R): Rabbi Rubenstein, chief Rabbi of Paris; Mr. Levi, Mrs. Recha Sternbuch, Dr. Lewin. Standing: Mr. Yitzchak Sternbuch, in Aix-les-Bains, 1947

5. Agudath Israel Archives, September 1942

fully, though quietly, supported the Zionist movement. These assessments were wide of the mark and should have been recognized as such at the time. In retrospect, in view of Wise's position as the foremost Jewish leader, his total trust in Roosevelt was not an asset to American or European Jews."[6]

Five Temporary Committee representatives, including Wise, were granted a twenty-minute meeting with the President on December 8, 1942. The meeting produced no tangible relief whatsoever. Wise decided the Temporary Committee had served its purpose and disbanded it after the meeting. (In March 1943, it was revived as the Joint Emergency Committee on European Jewish Affairs.)

As a result of extreme pressure from many sources, on December 17, the Allies issued an official declaration condemning German atrocities against the Jews. This declaration formed the basis of the "crimes against humanity" charges brought at the post-war Nuremberg Trials. The Vaad activists were gratified by these words of support. It was a hollow victory, however, because none of the humanitarian sentiments elicited any tangible action. The genocide in Europe continued while the Allies refused to even provide safe havens to those few Jews fortunate enough to escape.

The Vaad continued to seek Jewish unity despite the disbandment of the Temporary Committee. It cooperated with anyone or any group which could possibly help, regardless of their religious philosophy. Once, Rabbi Kotler was criticized for working with the secular Stephen Wise. His reaction was

emphatic: "I would work with the Pope," he answered with characteristic fire, "if it would save even the fingernail of one Jewish child!"[7]

The Vaad leadership recognized that so much more would be achieved if it pooled resources with others. Still, first and foremost was the Torah command of saving lives. Although the activists persevered in trying to recruit the help of various government officials, they did not always succeed. A notable exception was Secretary of the Treasury, Henry Morgenthau, a secular Jew.

Much to their surprise, not only did he agree to a meeting but was visibly moved by what he learned. Morgenthau demanded a meeting with President Roosevelt, threatening to resign if his request was denied! This was a complete turnabout from his earlier reactions to Jewish issues when he had barely said anything.

Morgenthau's meeting with Roosevelt did not result in immediate changes in Allied policy. Nonetheless, it was a great victory for the Vaad. It laid the foundation for the creation of the War Refugee Board, which helped provide relief and rescue for thousands of Jews during and after the war. Of greater importance, Morgenthau became a major Washington contact and proved to be extremely helpful during and after the war, most notably with overseas fund transfers. He championed the Vaad's agenda in the Roosevelt Administration.

BROADENING THE SCOPE

As conditions in Europe deteriorated, the Vaad gradually broadened its range of activities. Following their successful

As a result of extreme pressure from many sources, on December 17, the Allies issued an official declaration condemning German atrocities against the Jews. It was a hollow victory, however, because none of the humanitarian sentiments elicited any tangible action.

---

6. Op.cit., David Wyman, pg. 69

7. Beth Medrash Govoha Archives, *Kesavim U'Michtavim of Rabbi Aharon Kotler*

Henry Morgenthau, Secretary of the Treasury

In 1943, when Hitler's Final Solution claimed thousands of Jewish lives daily, Vaad Hatzala's rescue and relief work increased proportionately.

meeting with Morgenthau, the Vaad expanded its operations as determined by events and contacts. Eventually, when it became apparent that the Allies and the secular American Jewish groups would not initiate relief or rescue programs, they continued their relief activities in Europe, Siberia, Kobe and Shanghai independently.

VAAD REDOUBLES ITS EFFORTS

In 1943, when Hitler's Final Solution claimed thousands of Jewish lives daily, Vaad Hatzala's rescue and relief work increased proportionately.

Rabbi Kotler continued to plead for unity in the Orthodox camp – rivalries were set aside and efforts were intensified. The Vaad was prepared to work with whoever could help. Unfortunately, only a small number of refugees were granted visas by the State Department. Most upsetting was the discrimination against Torah scholars by the American Jewish Congress and Stephen Wise of the Joint, who effectively controlled American Emergency Visitors' Visas to America and Palestine. This group only received 6% of available visas. Their opposition was based primarily on the presumption that Torah observant Jews were the least able to integrate into American society. Nonetheless, the Vaad continued to collaborate with the Joint and others who could aid in their rescue and relief mission.

Where Vaad Hatzala parted ways with American mainstream Jewish groups was regarding tactics and agenda. They favored unconventional and even extralegal means, if necessary –

based on the Torah precept that saving lives supersedes legal considerations. They knew without a doubt that relief and rescue efforts could not be postponed until after the war. Such was the philosophy of other factions (and Roosevelt's policy), but by then it would be too late!

With the failure of the Biltmore Conference (May 1942, in New York, calling for a post-war Zionist solution in Palestine) to take immediate action in response to the destruction of European Jewry, the disbanded Emergency Committee was re-established in March 1943, to include all Jewish organizations involved in European Jewish affairs. Meanwhile, reports of genocide turned public opinion against the Allies. Consequently, Britain called for the Bermuda Conference in April 1943, to offer solutions for endangered Jews. (This Conference rubber-stamped Allied inaction regarding any type of rescue work.) Citing military considerations, Wise and the Emergency Committee delegation were refused admission to the Conference. This sent a clear message that the Allies were not prepared to help the Jews.

Naturally, the Vaad was upset, but more so by the apathy of Washington. Many Jewish organizations did demonstrate. Wise continued to defend Roosevelt. Wise's successor, Abba Hillel Silver, advocated Jewish nationhood after the war – a plan presented by him at the American Jewish Conference at the Waldorf Astoria Hotel in New York, in August 1943.

This American Jewish and Allied reaction was viewed by the Vaad as tragic. Therefore, under the leadership of Irving Bunim and Stephen Klein, they broadened their base of operation by working with oversees activists in

Chief Rabbi Isaac Herzog accompanied by young yeshiva students at Vaad Hatzala Yeshiva, Prague, 1946

Switzerland, England, Slovakia, Turkey and Palestine, by the end of 1943. The Vaad also launched a more aggressive fundraising campaign in America. In addition, they forged more alliances with important government officials in Washington. Through sheer determination and intellect, tempered with respect, they succeeded despite their lack of political power.

RABBIS' MARCH ON WASHINGTON

A major event organized by Peter Bergson, leader of the Emergency Committee to Save Jewish People of Europe, was the Rabbis' March on Washington, on October 6, 1943. More than 400 rabbis participated. Representatives from all the rescue organizations met with Vice-President Wallace and presented him with a petition detailing events in Europe. President Roosevelt had agreed to meet with them but canceled at the last minute. Nevertheless, the March resulted in

several policy changes: two congressional rescue resolutions were introduced and the State Department sent a letter stating that all points in the petition would be considered.

Rabbi Nathan Baruch, Director of American Vaad Hatzala in Munich, Germany, bidding farewell to Secretary of State James F. Byrnes after a conference to discuss the needs of the "displaced persons" in Germany

Where Vaad Hatzala parted ways with American mainstream Jewish groups was regarding tactics and agenda. They favored unconventional and even extralegal means, if necessary – based on the Torah precept that saving lives supersedes legal considerations.

Union of Orthodox Rabbis of the U.S. and Canada march to Washington on behalf of Nazi-persecuted European Jewry. (R-L, front row): Jewish War Veteran Commandant, Rabbi B. L. Leventhal; Vice-President of Agudas HaRabbonim, Rabbi Israel Rosenberg; Co-President of Agudas HaRabbonim, Rabbi Eliezer Silver; Co-President of the Agudas HaRabbonim, Rabbi Abraham Kalmanowitz; Jewish War Veteran Commandant, Rabbi Reuven Levovitz; Rabbi Pesach Levovitz (representing Mesivta Tifereth Jerusalem); Rabbi Nathan Baruch (representing Mesivta Torah Vodaath)

CREATION OF WAR REFUGEE BOARD

Eventually, when public pressure became too great to ignore, Congress finally took action. On January 16, 1944, Morgenthau led a delegation to the President and he agreed to establish a Rescue Commission immediately. The War Refugee Board (WRB) was created on January 22. This was considered a public relations coup for Roosevelt, but in essence this Commission was powerless because they lacked government funds and cooperation. Even so, it could serve as the official venue for Vaad Hatzala to channel funds to the Sternbuchs (a couple renowned for their rescue activities beginning in 1938).

Consequently, two vital results were achieved:
(1) Thousands of Jews were rescued, and
(2) Distribution of vital relief services was carried out.

THE MUSY NEGOTIATIONS

Conditions in Europe had become so desperate that the Vaad was prepared to back a daring plan – to negotiate with the Nazis to ransom Jewish prisoners.

Two major developments in 1944 catalyzed this:

Through sheer determination and intellect, tempered with respect, they succeeded despite their lack of political power.

Rabbis' March: Surging up the stairs of the Senate building, the Rabbis are given a sober welcome by Vice-President Wallace and Senate leaders, while Washingtonians and servicemen pause to watch.

(a) Hungary was annexed by Germany, bringing three-quarters of a million more Jews under Nazi control; and (b) The Sternbuchs (in Switzerland) conceived a rescue plan to mediate negotiations with Himmler, with the intention of ransoming Europe's remaining Jews. This extremely ambitious plan became known as the Musy Negotiations.

BACKGROUND

When Adolf Eichmann became head of operations in Hungary, everyone's worst fears were realized – three-quarters of a million Jews were deported to death camps. In response, Jews staged protest rallies worldwide. The War Refugee Board was lobbied and besieged by memoranda, asking the American government to warn Hungary that they would be held responsible for war crimes if they collaborated with the Nazis. It was re-quested that agents be dispatched to Hungary, whose mission was to pay gentiles to hide Jews and when possible help them escape to Turkey or other neutral places.

The Vaad had its own agents (non-Jews) for similar rescue actions, and to provide relief money and bribe border guards when possible. An underground network was formed linking the spies and Orthodox rescue leaders to one central control – the Sternbuchs. In rescue work since 1938, when German and Austrian Jews were first endangered by the Nazis, they were in constant touch with Rabbi Michoel Ber Weissmandl[*], a man of great vision and the Slovakian *Rosh HaYeshiva* who was the first one to call for the ransom of all European Jews.

In 1942, by bribing Nazi agent Dieter Wisliceny with $50,000 to stop all Jewish deportations from Slovakia, Rabbi Weissmandl and his multi-party Working Group saved the Slovakian Jews for two years. Again using Wisliceny in 1943, Rabbi Weissmandl initiated his Europe Plan to ransom Jews. When the Nazis took over Hungary, in 1944, it was Rabbi Weissmandl who called for restarting ransom negotiations to save as many Jews as possible. The Vaad completely supported this strategy.

As the War turned against the Nazis, they were willing to consider several ransom plans that were presented. The Musy Negotiations was the boldest plan of all. In what turned out to be a prelude to the Musy Negotiations, the Vaad sent $300,000 to the Sternbuchs, between July and September 1944, some of which was transferred to Rabbi Weissmandl. He used these funds to bribe Slovakian officials to shelter 1800 Hungarian Jews.

Conditions in Europe had become so desperate that the Vaad was prepared to back a daring plan – to negotiate with the Nazis to ransom Jewish prisoners.

(L-R, front): Rabbi Jacob Herzog, Moshe Shapiro, Rabbi Eliyahu Botchko, Chief Rabbi Herzog, Rabbi S.P. Wohlgelernter, Herman Landau, Dr. Shaul Weingort, (back row): Rabbi Zev Gold, Mr. Ellinson Mizrachi Shaliach from Eretz Yisrael

---

[*] Refer to the biography of Rabbi Michoel Ber Weissmandl, pg. 338

Musy train's arrival in Montreux, Switzerland, in February 1945. Herman Landau (top right) greets concentration camp inmates released from Theresienstadt

As the War turned against the Nazis they were willing to consider several ransom plans that were presented. The Musy Negotiations was the boldest plan of all.

MUSY – THE NEGOTIATOR

The former president of Switzerland, Jean-Marie Musy, a pro-Nazi, was the Vaad's intermediary with SS Chief Heinrich Himmler. The plan (named for Musy) was to ransom the 600,000 Jews who remained under the Nazis. It was an audacious plan and almost succeeded.

In early November 1944, Musy met with Himmler after he was recruited by Mrs. Sternbuch, who had learned that he had served as an intermediary in rescuing a Jewish couple from a concentration camp. Another vital aspect in the Sternbuchs' decision to use Musy as the negotiator was his extraordinary access to Himmler and his willingness to go to Berlin. The initial offer was one million Swiss francs ($250,000) for 600,000 Jews. Himmler preferred trucks. However, later that month, he made a counteroffer of 20

million francs ($5 million) for 300,000 Jews. The Sternbuchs turned to the War Refugee Board representative in Switzerland, Roswell McClelland, for the money and were turned down, as expected. They also wrote to Stephen Klein to assist in negotiations with the U.S. government to obtain funds.

Via their secret Polish diplomatic cable, the Sternbuchs informed the Vaad of Himmler's terms: For twenty months, they would pay $250,000 monthly and 300,000 Jews would be released (approximately $17 per person). The Vaad accepted the terms and began raising the enormous sum.

It was an overwhelming task, but on December 5, 1944, the Vaad sent $107,000 to the Sternbuchs. There were those who did not want to contribute, because they did not want to give money to Nazis. On the other hand, there were others who sacrificed all they had in order to help. The money sent via the WRB was identified as money for expenses incidental to the release of the first group of 15,000 Jews – not ransom. (At that point the WRB did not know of the Musy Negotiations – they learned of it in late January 1945.) In mid-January, an additional $150,000 was sent ensuring the ongoing negotiations and establishing a line of credit.

Already by the next day (December 6), the Vaad was informed by the Sternbuchs that 1368 Jews had arrived in Switzerland by train from Bergen-Belsen – the Musy Negotiations were evolving positively.

Musy met again with Himmler in January 1945, wanting assurance that the negotiations were authentic. Evidence was sent by the Vaad attesting to the fact that "Rabbi Dr." Sternbuch was their sole representative. At this time,

Displaced persons arriving from Theresienstadt concentration camp

Musy pointed out to Himmler that since the Allies were continuing to make progress in the War his demands were unreasonable. Not only that, but since the people he represented could not access all their assets, $5 million was not a reasonable or feasible amount. Himmler countered with a two-part demand: (a) $1.25 million, to be placed in a Swiss bank. In return 1200 Jews would be released weekly. As a sign of good faith, 1210 Jews were released from Theresienstadt on February 5, 1945. (b) In exchange for the $3.75-million reduction, he wanted the influential Jews to create favorable world-wide media reports about the Nazis. This demand was made with a view to the post-war years and the need to reshape negative world opinion.

Sternbuch had to act immediately. He first went to the WRB and McClelland in an attempt to influence American policy. Aware that McClelland was opposed to ransom and other questionable tactics, he told him about the need for "necessary gratuities" for border crossings, camp accommodations, Musy's fee, etc. McClelland did approve of such expenses.

The Vaad was faced with the tremendous task of raising $1 million in a very short time. The only option was to ask other Jewish groups for help. On principle, the Joint would not be a party to ransom. The Joint proposed a different plan: the money would be deposited in Switzerland and used to purchase non-military equipment for Germany. Secondly, the concentration camp inmates were to remain in the camps under the supervision of the Red Cross until the War ended.

The Vaad and Sternbuch were par-

The money sent via the WRB was identified as money for expenses incidental to the release of the first group of 15,000 Jews – not ransom.

ticularly upset with the second aspect of the Joint plan. They knew how horrendous conditions were in the camps and they wanted the immediate release of the inmates.

Meanwhile, Saly Mayer – the Joint's Swiss representative who was anti-religious and adverse to making waves with the U.S. government – was meeting separately with the Nazis.

Sternbuch was concerned that Himmler would be confused by the multiple offers and might halt negotiations. Consequently, he approached Rudolph Kastner, the Budapest representative of the Jewish Agency, and begged him to join forces with him. Sternbuch was prepared to support the Joint plan only on the condition that Saly Mayer would insist on the immediate release of Jewish inmates. Mayer was only prepared to pay the Red Cross to administer the camps.

Himmler decided that Musy's plan was the best option – $1.25 million and an improved image for Germany.

After the arrival of the Theresienstadt train (February 1945) saving 1210 Jews, which was preceded by the Bergen-Belsen Train which saved 318 Jews, in August 1944, and 1368 Jews in December 1944, the major New York papers carried the story. Irving Bunim traveled to Washington to obtain permission from the WRB to send the articles and pictures to Sternbuch.

The cash was still needed – Sternbuch and the Vaad raised $63,000 (1/4 million Swiss francs). They were $937,000 short of the $1 million needed. Only the Joint had such an enormous sum at their disposal, and to save Jewish lives the Vaad would do whatever was necessary – so, reluctantly, the Vaad approached them. A meeting was arranged.

It was a difficult meeting – from

The Vaad was faced with the tremendous task of raising $1 million in a very short time. The only option was to ask other Jewish groups for help.

the outset the Vaad knew that their most powerful argument of *hatzalas nefashos* would have no impact on the Joint. Not only that, but Saly Mayer had informed the New York Joint that they could not trust Sternbuch. The basic difference between them was that the Joint followed government protocol while the Vaad placed Torah Law first – especially in the critical area of *hatzalah*. Only after the Vaad threatened to reveal the Joint's refusal to support the rescue plan to its major Orthodox donors did the Joint agree to the loan. They did make one condition, which they felt the Vaad could never meet – the U.S. government must grant a license to the Vaad to transfer the money to Switzerland and through their agents to Himmler.

The Vaad accepted the condition. A meeting with Mr. Morgenthau was arranged (February 1945). At first he refused, but then reconsidered and agreed to help.

In March 1945, the Vaad representatives returned to Morgenthau for a follow-up. He told them that the license would be issued, but the release and distribution of the funds in Switzerland would require Sternbuch's and McClelland's signatures. Such a resolution was untenable, since it meant WRB supervision and thus no ransom would be allowed.

An alternative solution was offered. Because humanitarian considerations were at issue, allowances should be made for incidental and legitimate expenses – i.e. transport costs, gratuities to Swiss and German authorities etc. – not ransom. Morgenthau agreed to this, and it was arranged.

The Vaad hoped that Sternbuch would be resourceful with this arrangement. In addition, a subsequent publicity campaign had to be generated.

These follow-up stories were more difficult to place – but the publicity campaign succeeded in the end. The articles were translated and forwarded to Switzerland. Musy sent them to Himmler in the hope of gaining further releases of Jewish inmates.

Unfortunately, Saly Mayer continued to object to the Vaad's approach. To exacerbate the matter, Nathan Schwalb, head of PALCOR, the Zionist news agency and a friend of Mayer, published negative reports about the Musy Negotiations. These reports were shown to Hitler, who became so infuriated that he ordered a stop to further releases. In effect, this ended the Musy Negotiations and the fate of thousands of Jews was sealed.

As can be imagined, the Sternbuchs and the Vaad were shocked and appalled by what had happened. Sternbuch attempted to reopen negotiations and prevailed upon Musy to make additional trips to Berlin. Musy did manage to obtain several life-saving concessions from Himmler. Also, with William O'Dwyer's (the new WRB Chief) help, Rabbi Kalmanowitz sent Red Cross ambulances, disguised as U.S. army trucks, filled with relief supplies. These "last-minute" efforts saved 100,000 concentration camp inmates. Naturally, the Vaad was grateful for these achievements.

However, the Vaad was heartbroken that overall the Musy Negotiations had failed in its objective.

POST-WAR YEARS

With War's end the Vaad's focus and energies were directed towards the thousands of survivors. Although officially there was peace, the political conditions had not improved that much – anti-Semitism was still prevalent in many Eastern European governments and countries.

The primary challenges of providing for the refugees' physical and spiritual well-being, as well as re-building the destroyed Torah centers and yeshivos, were overwhelming. Enormous sums were required to meet the many needs of the survivors and it was no easy task to raise these funds in secularized America.

Unfortunately, there were influential individuals from other Jewish groups who objected to the Vaad's approach. Ultimately, the Musy Negotiotions ended, sealing the fate of thousands of Jews.

(L-R): Rabbi Aviezer Burstein and Rabbi Nathan Baruch inspecting stored clothing for distribution to survivors

Vaad Hatzala conference in Montreux, 1946. (L-R): Rabbi S.P. Wohlgelernter, Rabbi Eliyahu Botchko, Rabbi Zev Gold, Rabbi Chizkiyahu Mishkowsky, Chief Rabbi Herzog, Mr. Shertok and Agudah delegates

With War's end, the Vaad's focus and energies were directed towards the thousands of survivors. The primary challenges of providing for the refugees' physical and spiritual well-being, as well as rebuilding the destroyed Torah centers and yeshivos, were overwhelming.

Most American Jews and some of the other organizations involved in relief and rescue work could not understand or appreciate the *spiritual* needs of the Orthodox Jewish survivors.

The task before them was infinite and interminable. Vaad Hatzala was fortunate to have several dedicated and tireless workers at home and abroad who possessed the necessary *mesiras nefesh* to undertake the mission. Among them were Stephen Klein, Herbert Tenzer, Irving Bunim, Rabbis Eliezer Silver, Nathan Baruch, Solomon Rosenberg, Solomon Wohlgelernter, Zerach Warhaftig, Simcha Wasserman, Messrs. Charles Ullman and Maurice Enright, each contributing in his own unique way. The invaluable information sent to the New York Vaad by the European activists (the Sternbuchs in Switzerland, Rabbis Victor Vorhand in Austria, Isaac Levi in Iran, Manfred Danzig in Italy, Aron Milevsky in Uruguay, Dr. Solomon Schonfeld in England, Wolf Jacobson in Sweden, Dr. Yaakov Griffel in Turkey and Mrs. Renee Reichman in Morocco), provided them with an accurate assessment of the refugees' needs and whereabouts.

The hardships faced by the survivors were daunting, and unfortunately the conditions in the DP camps were terrible. The refugees lived in crowded apartments shared by several families (often four families in one room!). There was no privacy and limited gainful employment. To say the least, it was depressing. The limited food rations provided offered minimal sustenance. Most lacked such basic necessities as proper clothing and shoes. However, Vaad Chairman of Immigration, Stephen Klein, who spent several months traveling and working in many European countries directing the activities in the DP camps laying the groundwork for its operations, and Rabbi Nathan Baruch, Director of Vaad Operations in Germany (1946-48), both reported about the amazing spirit of cooperation among the DPs that they witnessed. The survivors willingly shared the little they had. Upon his return to America, Stephen Klein embarked on a major public relations campaign, to raise American Jewish awareness of the situation of the refugees in Europe with the refugees. Many were inspired to donate money to this vital cause.

Vaad Hatzala sent vital food and clothing packages. Most places had Exchange Centers where various items,

Mrs. Renee and Eva Reichman

which were all worth points, could be exchanged for what a person needed. A valuable commodity that could be easily traded was cigarettes. William O'Dwyer, of the War Refugee Board, helped the survivors by sending fifteen Vaad Hatzala trucks filled with food – camouflaged as Red Cross vans – into several camps, with General Eisenhower's approval.

Rabbi Dr. Solomon Schonfeld

Rabbi Aron Milevsky

Rabbi Dr. Yaakov Griffel

The plight of the Orthodox Jewish refugees was even more desperate because of their adherence to kashrus. The Vaad tried to ensure that these survivors received kosher food. To further alleviate the problem, the Vaad set up kosher kitchens in many of the DP camps.

Religious schools for children were established by the Vaad in the DP camps. In addition to religious studies, general studies and various trades were taught so the students could become self-supporting.

The Vaad set up seminaries to train teachers to work in Hebrew and religious schools in Europe, South America and the United States, where there were shortages of trained teachers.

In order to encourage and strengthen religious life in the DP camps, *sifrei torah, tefillin, siddurim, talleisim, chumashim,* and *gemaras* were provided by the Vaad. They also built *mikvaos* and sent *shochtim*. With survivors marrying and beginning new families, the need arose for trained *mohelim*, and they too were provided.

All of these activities were essential, but cost money. Fundraising was as great, if not more so, than during the War years.

Conditions in DP camps were terrible – crowded, limited food, clothing and employment. Vaad Hatzala sent vital food and clothing packages, as did the WRB.

Vaad Hatzala Conference in Montreux, 1946.
(L-R): Yitzchak Sternbuch, Herman Landau, Recha Sternbuch,
Rabbi S.P. Wohlgelernter, Rabbi Eliyahyu Botchko

Captain Aharon Beker to the left of Rabbi Isaac Herzog, at ruins of Warsaw Ghetto, July 1946

RESCUE CHILDREN, INC.

To alleviate the plight of Orthodox Jewish refugees, the Vaad set up kosher kitchens in many DP camps. Religious schools, trade schools, general studies programs and teacher training were organized.

One of the most serious and heart-wrenching problems of the post-war years were the thousands of Jewish children, who had survived the War and now were orphaned. There were at least 15,000 children hidden in non-Jewish homes, monasteries and cloisters! These children represented the future generations of Jews and it was imperative that they be found and liberated so as not to be lost forever. Failure was not an option! Additionally, it became known that many non-Jewish guardians of thousands of Jewish children were demanding ransom for their release.

To address this situation, Rescue Children was established in 1946 (as well as other similar organizations). Beginning as a Vaad Hatzala initiative, it quickly became a semi-autonomous organization. Herbert Tenzer, a New York lawyer, later elected to Congress, was the Chairman. Stephen Klein, who extended his business partnership with Herbert Tenzer to become partners in rescue, and Charles Ullman were among

the board members, and Rabbi William Novick served as executive director. Their mission was nothing less than to save thousands of surviving Jewish children. They would: "a) Establish Orthodox Jewish children's centers in Europe; to provide adequate housing and shelter, food and clothing, medical and dental care, secular and religious education for Jewish War orphans in Europe. b) Voluntarily assist and aid in the continued maintenance and care of children's centers already in existence in Europe... c) Voluntarily assist in location of relatives of European war orphans with a view of reuniting them with members of their own families. d) Spend net funds... for sole benefit of European War orphans. e) Solicit, collect and otherwise raise funds for carrying out charitable and philanthropic purposes."[8]

A notable individual involved in the rescue of hundreds of Jewish children from churches and convents was Aharon Beker. He had joined the Polish Army from Russia to fight the Nazis. He came to Berlin with the Red Army and by war's end was appointed Jewish Chaplain of the Polish Army. In this capacity, and as a captain of the Polish Army, he met many Jewish survivors of the Holocaust. In 1946, Aharon Beker

Mrs. Sternbuch with Chief Rabbi Herzog and Jewish children from Poland who were rescued with her help

8. Certificate of Incorporation of Rescue Children, Inc. July 24, 1946.

accompanied the famous mission led by Chief Rabbi Isaac Herzog to Poland. Hundreds of Jewish children (including 200 from the Agudath Israel institution in Poland) left Poland, through Czechoslovakia, for France as a result of their efforts.

Rescue Children worked with four Orthodox groups – Agudath Israel, Poalei Agudah, Mizrachi and Poalei Mizrachi to establish fifteen children's homes called *Kibbutzim* in France and Belgium. They also set up yeshivos in several cities.

Fundraising initiatives, conceived by Mr. Tenzer, included Adopt-A-Child whereby people sponsored and supported these children. The sponsor was provided with a picture and biographical information of the child. Using his many contacts, Mr. Tenzer obtained much needed publicity and donations for Rescue Children, including food, clothing, and toys. Dan Parker, sports columnist for the *N.Y. Daily Mirror*, wrote an article about the physical fitness needs of the children in Rescue Children's homes. Hundreds of gifts poured in as a result. In Europe, agents of Rescue Children searched for Jewish children, sometimes going door-to-door. Often, a redemption fee (ransom) was necessary to secure a child's release.

Over a two-year period (1946-48), 2100 children were housed, fed, clothed, educated, and reunited with immediate family, relatives, or placed with adoptive families or schools in Palestine. In 1948, the Joint took over and assumed all expenses of Rescue Children.

Children studying in Vaad-sponsored yeshivos

VISA PROCUREMENT

Vaad Hatzala's original agenda was not forgotten. The Vaad continued to work tirelessly to obtain visas to the United States and Palestine for surviving Torah scholars and yeshiva students. The situation of the *bnei Torah* was particularly dangerous; it was unsafe for them to remain under Russian governance. To compound matters, the visa procurement process was lengthy and much red tape was involved. Undaunted, the Vaad did all that was necessary and eventually helped streamline the process.

Rabbi Eliezer Silver, Chairman of the Vaad, spent three months as the Vaad's representative traveling throughout Europe. This dynamic individual did the work of several men and brought hope to the survivors, especially the Torah scholars. He wore a surplus American Army uniform and moved about freely, distributing money to build yeshivos, *mikvaos*, and kosher kitchens. He also located children who had been in hiding throughout the war.

Rabbi Silver did experience some awkward moments. Once, an Allied soldier saluted him, and he did not

Rescue Children, Inc. was established to save thousands of Jewish children who had survived the War. Children's homes were set up and relatives were sought to care for them. Their every need was addressed.

*Vaad-Hatzala sponsored Beis Yesomim
(girls' orphanage) in Prague, 1946*

not believe him and were prepared to detain him.

Distressed, Rabbi Silver pointed to the telephone and ordered, "Call Senator Taft. Tell him Silver's here!" The officials looked at each other, unaware that the diminutive angry man enjoyed a personal and political friendship with the powerful Ohio Senator Robert Taft.

After lengthy delays, the exasperated American Occupation official finally reached Senator Taft's Washington office. "What?" Taft shouted when he

The Vaad continued to work tirelessly to obtain visas to the United States and Palestine for surviving Torah scholars and yeshiva students. Although much red tape was involved, they persevered and streamlined the process.

return the salute, causing the soldier to doubt his credentials. When Occupation officials asked to see his military identification – after all, he was a man in uniform – Rabbi Silver stared defiantly and proclaimed, "I don't need papers. I am the Chief Rabbi of the United States and Canada!" (spoken with his characteristic accent). Understandably, the American authorities did

Students of Yeshivas Bnei Akiva

Vaad-sponsored orphanage dedicated in honor of Mrs. Sternbuch

learned whom they were holding. The Senator knew that if his friend remained in the Occupation office much longer, the Rabbi – not the army – would be running Germany. He quickly vouched for Rabbi Silver's mission and credentials. "Get rid of him," he added, laughing, "as soon as possible."

Rabbi Silver left Germany, and quickly

1946, at the boat as Stephen Klein was leaving on a mission to Europe. (L-R): Eli Klein, Isaac Klein, Martin Klein, Irving Bunim, Stephen Klein, Rabbi Solomon Fishoff, Rabbi Shabse Frankel, Rabbi Shimon Kornitzer, Menashe Stein

The Vaad representatives who traveled to Europe, post-war, to help the refugees were devoted and tireless in their monumental efforts — they brought hope to the survivors.

traveled to Poland, where conditions were worse than anyone had expected. He wired New York asking the Vaad for additional funds: "*Talmidei chachamim* lying in the streets, living in unsanitary conditions... Everybody naked, poor and heartbroken... Great work must be done immediately to help Jews and bring our youth back to Torah. If you do not send immediate help to me and Sternbuch, the whole rescue effort will break down." Rabbi Silver ended his cable with the following words: "I will borrow great sums [on] your account," he wrote, "because I cannot see Jews dying before our eyes."[9]

"He is living on Torah, not food," Rabbi Emanuel Rackman, then a U.S. Army chaplain, wrote in August 1946, to Rabbi Silver's son, David. "And he is lecturing beyond the capacity of any five humans half his age. I was inspired... by his enterprise and locomotion."

Rabbi Nathan Baruch was also an example of an outstanding Vaad activist during the post-war years. For two years

(1946-48), he was Director of Vaad Operations in Germany. His devoted and tireless efforts aided thousands of Jews to resume religious life despite the desperate post-war conditions. He continued his efforts on the survivors' behalf after his return to the States, by fundraising and speaking to various Jewish organizations.

In America, the Vaad obtained thousands of visas and also found supporters who were willing to post bonds for temporary visas. These bonds, at a cost of $600 per person, assured the government that the individual would leave and not become a public charge when their visa expired.

As chairman of Vaad Hatzala's Immigration Department, Stephen Klein, who traveled to Europe

Rabbi Nathan Baruch (c.) Munich, Germany

9. Rakefet-Rothkoff, **The Silver Era in American Orthodox Jewry:** *Rabbi Eliezer Silver and His Generation*; N.Y., 1981, pg. 234

(L-R): Rabbi Aviezer Burstein, Rabbi Nathan Baruch speaking with a survivor, Munich, 1947

"the righteous and benevolent gentiles of the world."

The Vaad attempted, once again, to bring the Mirrer Yeshiva out of Shanghai, this time to America. Conditions were unstable in China, and it was crucial that the Yeshiva leave before it was too late. The main problem was refugee quotas – 512 visas were needed by the Yeshiva! Rabbi Kotler, Rabbi Kalmanowitz, Mr. Bunim, and Stephen Klein went to Under Secretary Acheson to plead their case. After explaining to him the importance of these Torah scholars to the American Jews and why

Motivated by a sense of responsibility to Klal Yisrael, the Vaad helped rebuild and support the essential institutions of Jewish religious life in post-war Europe.

as a captain in UNRRA, was an energetic and determined leader, who secured visas and issued and guaranteed affidavits for thousands of Jews. Despite the difficulties encountered, he and the other activists involved in this area were successful. They managed to secure the all-important support and aid of the State Department, especially that of Under Secretary of State Dean Acheson, who was instrumental in instituting a new policy that expedited the visa processing. Although in past meetings with government officials, the Vaad representation had to use all their powers of persuasion – and even then it would often require several attempts – Mr. Acheson proved himself to be truly one of the *chasidei umos ha'olam –*

Conference at Vaad Hatzala headquarters in Munich. (L-R): Rabbi Nathan Baruch, Stephen Klein, Rabbi Israel Rosenberg, Herman Landau and Rabbi Aviezer Burstein

Rabbi S.P. Wohlgelernter, Rav of Cong. Bikur Cholim in Seattle

they were needed in the United States, Secretary Acheson agreed to help. Imagine the Vaad representatives' pleasant surprise when he informed them that the quota restrictions and required physical entry examinations would all be rescinded and their visas expedited! Mr. Bunim told Secretary Acheson, "Your name will be engraved in gold letters in Jewish history."

Arrival at Vaad Hatzala conference, Montreux, Switzerland. (L-R): Rabbi Z. Gold, Chief-Rabbi Herzog, Moshe Shapiro, Herman Landau

pitals and kosher kitchens. The Vaad reprinted and distributed thirty thousand copies of six Talmudic tractates, revitalizing the *Daf Yomi* program.

CONCLUSION

In the post-war years, several Orthodox Jewish organizations were involved in the critical work of *hatzalas nefashos*. Each group had its own agendas and goals, which did not necessarily coincide with the others. This undermined the global efforts of Vaad Hatzala and fragmented Orthodoxy's achievements in this arena. The efforts of those who tried to maintain unity failed. In 1948, Vaad Hatzala effectively closed down, although a skeletal staff was maintained through 1954.

Vaad Hatzala, which originally was founded to aid the Eastern European yeshivos during the War, eventually metamorphosed into an international relief and rescue organization based on Torah precepts. They raised tremendous funds to provide crucial food and clothing to their brethren during and after the war; obtained visas and guaranteed affidavits; amended immigration policies; and helped rebuild and support the essential institutions of Jewish religious life in post-war Europe – yeshivos, kashrus, *mikvaos, sefarim,* etc. The noble, dedicated, and selfless efforts and achievements of Vaad Hatzala will forever stand as the paradigm of *hatzalas nefashos* at its zenith.

Subsequently, the Vaad commissioned a scroll of honor – like a *megillah* – to present to Secretary Acheson, recording how much he had helped the Jewish People, and his name was indeed inscribed in gold. This gift moved him tremendously and he offered to assist them further. Secretary Acheson's initiatives engendered the help of other State Department officials.

OTHER POST-WAR ACHIEVEMENTS

Rabbi Wohlgelernter wrote, "If our work fails, we shall never be able to justify our very existence before G-d and Israel." The Vaad did not fail! They achieved notable successes in several crucial areas of Jewish religious life. Motivated by a sense of responsibility to *Klal Yisrael,* they helped to rebuild and support (as of 1948) thirteen yeshivos throughout liberated Europe, including 61 elementary schools (yeshivos *ketanos*) and Talmud Torahs, and sixteen Bais Yaakov girls' schools. They also rebuilt *mikvaos* and supported hos-

The noble, dedicated, and selfless efforts and achievements of Vaad Hatzala will forever stand as the paradigm of hatzalas nefashos at its zenith.

Transmitting the Legacy

Biographical Vignettes of Torah Visionaries In America

The vision necessary to build Torah in America was manifest in those individuals who through thought and action transmited the legacy of Torah, each in his own inimitable manner. A visionary is an idealist who has a dream but is **not** a dreamer. He is a doer, who takes the initiative and actualizes his conception and vision by recognizing the possibilities and implementing them — not for himself, but for others. The rabbinic and lay leaders who were the foremost advocates in transmitting the legacy and building Torah in America were "visionaries" and "master builders." Many of them were Holocaust survivors and as they rebuilt their personal lives, they also committed themselves, *b'lev va'nefesh* (heart and soul), to laying the foundation of Torah and *Yiddishkeit* in this country. Most of the premier yeshivos, Bais Yaakovs, day schools, *shuls*, and *kehillos* were established by these individuals, through *mesiras nefesh* (self-sacrifice) and relentless efforts. We are ennobled by their deeds and are the fortunate recipients of the fruits of their labor, which serve as their legacy.

Although this volume focuses on rabbis and lay leaders, this in no way is meant to exclude or diminish the role played by the women. The wives of these great men were the paradigms of the true *eizer k'negdo* (helpmate) and *eishes chayil* (woman of valor). Not only were they partners to their husbands in a personal sense, but they encouraged, enabled and worked alongside them in their *avodas hakodesh*, holy endeavors. Since modesty requires that a righteous Jewish woman minimize her being in the public eye, they remained in the background. Nevertheless, they were *actively* involved in nurturing and growing the seeds of Torah Judaism in the inhospitable land that was the America of the first half of the 20th century. We are forever indebted to these selfless and talented women for their many contributions.

These vignettes are not intended to be detailed or comprehensive accounts of the person's life, nor do we necessarily subscribe to their personal ideology, rather they are <u>historical, biographical sketches</u> – an overview of the individual, his era, and his contributions.

✒ Rabbi Eliyahu Meir Bloch

1894-1955

"**R**abbi Bloch, this is the last *Ketzos* to be sold in America." These words of defeat were spoken by the salesman in a *sefarim* (book) store in New York. (He was referring to the *Ketzos HaChoshen*, an analytical work on gemara which, contrary to his dire prediction, is studied today in yeshivos throughout the world.) It reflected the overall attitude of Orthodox Jewry in America during the pre-war years. Even erudite sages despaired of raising their own children as observant Jews. Undaunted, Reb Eliyahu Meir threw himself into the challenge of build- ing Torah, by establishing a real yeshiva on American soil, a yeshiva that would not com-promise the timeless standards achieved by the Lithuanian yeshivos. Motivated by the words of Yonasan to Dovid *HaMelech*, "Go, for Hashem has sent you," Reb Eliyahu Meir felt that he had been saved from the destruction of Europe to fulfill a mission – to transplant Torah from Telshe to America. For the rest of his life, he would set aside his own personal loss of family and the destruction of the yeshiva in Europe and work tirelessly to raise the level of Torah scholarship in America.

Born and educated in Telshe, Lithuania, his father was Rabbi Yosef Leib Bloch, *Rav* of Telshe, Lithuania, and *Rosh HaYeshiva* of the Telshe Yeshiva. Reb Eliyahu Meir married the daughter of Reb Avraham Moshe Kaplan, a *talmid chacham*, merchant, and pillar of the Memel community. Reb Eliyahu Meir spent eight years in Memel, learning and delivering *shiurim*. His father then summoned him back to Telshe. For twelve years (until the outbreak of World War II), he served as a *Rosh Yeshiva* of Telshe, wrote, and was active in Agudath Israel. During the war years, he came to America with his brother-in-law, Rabbi Chaim Mordechai Katz.

Reb Eliyahu Meir Bloch charted his own course. Instead of remaining in the bustling Jewish metropolis of New York, as others did, he headed to the Midwest. Many thought his plan would fail and he would be forced to return to New York. Cleveland was chosen as the new site for the Telshe Yeshiva; a strange choice, as Cleveland was the seat and

Reb Eliyahu Meir felt that he had been saved from the destruction of Europe to fulfill a mission – to transplant Torah from Telshe to America.

hotbed of secular Judaism.

Surprisingly, when Reb Eliyahu Meir and his brother-in-law, Rabbi Chaim Mordechai Katz, opened the yeshiva, the Orthodox community experienced a resurgence and renewed self-esteem. Not that the yeshiva was large and imposing – it only consisted of a handful of European refugees – but the dignified personality of Reb Eliyahu Meir provided them with a leader and a sense of pride. It did not take long before the yeshiva began to attract local, American-born students.

The students recall their initial feelings: here were two "old world" rabbis, who were probably not in tune with American teenagers. However, it did not take long before they realized that not only was Reb Eliyahu Meir in touch with the American psychology – he was way ahead of it. He understood their strengths and weaknesses, and with patience and determination, he molded their personalities into that of a "yeshiva man."

A young Rabbi Eliyahu Meir Bloch

A man of immense energy, he would "tease" the *bachurim,* saying, "Some get old (i.e., himself) and some are born old," as he out-danced the *bachurim* at a *simcha* or on *Yom Tov.* He had little in this world to be happy

He understood his students' strengths and weaknesses, and with patience and determination, he molded their personalities into that of a "yeshiva man."

Rabbi Eliyahu Meir Bloch at the Purim Seudah at his home

about – the wife of his youth and their four children were killed during the war. The Telshe Yeshiva built by his father and grandfather was destroyed, and now he was the head of what could hardly be called a yeshiva. But he had a mission, and nothing would stand in the way of accomplishing his goal.

Rabbi Eliyahu Meir Bloch

Reb Eliyahu Meir tailored the yeshiva's program to the real needs of the *bachurim* – up to and including football. He interested himself in their growth, but he never gave in to their weaknesses. When a *bachur* did something that was not in consonance with the yeshiva's spirit, Reb Eliyahu Meir declared that he would sooner close the yeshiva than compromise on its standards. He trained the students not only in learning Torah, but also the appropriate respect for Torah. For example, when the need arose for *davening* in a public place arose, Reb Eliyahu Meir did not hide in an unobtrusive spot as if embarrassed, or allow the *bachurim* to do so; rather, he demanded that they *daven* in the open, with pride.

Reb Eliyahu Meir saw to it that a day school was opened in Cleveland. The Hebrew Academy of Cleveland was established and developed into a flagship day school for Torah Umesorah, placing at its helm one of the students of the yeshiva, Rabbi N.Z. Dessler. A *kollel* and a seminary for training teachers was also opened under the auspices of the yeshiva. Reb Eliyahu Meir was asked why he kept his students in yeshiva for so many years – five in *kollel* – when they were needed in the outside world. His answer was that an army needs infantry and also artillery – his students are the artillery of the Torah world. One well-trained student can effect greater impact on a community than an entire battalion of infantrymen.

Rabbi Eliyahu Meir Bloch leading the singing at the Purim Seudah

Rabbi Eliyahu Meir Bloch making the "kinyan" with a chassan, Yechezkel Merzel, prior to his chupah

So it was – the graduates of the early years served as *rebbeim* and teachers in dozens of communities in America, Canada, and even South Africa.

Within a few years, the yeshiva outgrew its premises and a large building was purchased on 105th Street. The dedication ceremony of the "Telzer" Yeshiva breathed new life into the spirit of the Orthodox community. All who participated were strengthened with the knowledge that Torah centers were once again blossoming, promulgating a Torah study rejuvenation.

The Yeshiva High School, or Mechina, as it was called, included a complete secular department. There were those who were opposed to a yeshiva allowing any secular studies to be offered under its aegis. Reb Eliyahu Meir disagreed. He felt that if the yeshiva provided a complete high school program, then all of the subjects that were taught must come under the yeshiva's authority and meet its standards. A first-class government-approved secular program was thus

created. Not only did the yeshiva encourage the learning of the necessary subjects, but the *Rosh HaYeshiva* demanded excellence. Studies at the college level were not encouraged by the *Rosh HaYeshiva*, but he did not scorn those who left the yeshiva. Rather, he built upon a relationship of mutual respect and nurtured a lifelong bond with a *talmid,* in order that, in the future, he would always turn to his *rebbeim* for guidance.

Reb Eliyahu Meir did not believe that his yeshiva should be reclusive. When Torah Umesorah made an urgent appeal to help save the day school in Minneapolis, MN, it was Reb Eliyahu Meir who answered their call. Notwithstanding the distance from Cleveland, he chose a group of students to help rehabilitate the faltering

> *He built upon a relationship of mutual respect and nurtured a lifelong bond with a talmid, so that, in the future, he would always turn to his rebbeim for guidance.*

Rabbi Eliyahu Meir Bloch speaking at an Agudath Israel function

(L-R): Rabbi Dr. Shlomo Slonim, Rabbi Eliyahu Meir Bloch, Rabbi Nosson Tzvi Baron

---

school. This function of the yeshiva was an outgrowth of the yeshiva's role in disseminating Torah as it once existed in Lita/Lithuania. During those years, the students toiled in *chinuch* without remuneration for their efforts. However, they did receive something greater – the tremendous satisfaction from the fruits of their labor. Students from Minneapolis eventually joined the yeshiva and developed into true *bnei Torah*.

The same commitment established yeshivos in South Africa and Montreal. Reb Eliyahu Meir inspired his students to feel a real sense of obligation to ensure the continuity of Torah study in the community at large. His own example served as the prime motivator as they strove to emulate him.

It was this sense of responsibility that motivated him to align himself with Agudath Israel of America. To Reb Eliyahu Meir there existed only one goal and one endeavor – building Torah. When Agudah business would require him to leave the yeshiva, he was able to concentrate and give his complete attention to the cause at hand. On his return, he would immediately resume his learning and his *shiur* – no break and no time for relaxation.

Rabbi Eliyahu Meir Bloch dancing at the Purim Seudah. Behind him (L-R): Rabbi Michoel Raitzik, Rabbi Naftoli Silberberg

In the center (L-R): Telzer Rav, Rabbi Avrohom Yitzchok Bloch, Rabbi Zalman Bloch, Menahel Ruchani of the Yeshiva, accompanied by students of the Yeshiva, bidding farewell to Rabbi Eliyahu Meir Bloch on his journey to America.

Rabbi Aharon Kotler, his colleague in the Agudah, recalled that with Reb Eliyahu Meir there was no vacillating. He was firm and resolute in his opinion. Yet when the majority of the *gedolim* voted against him, their position became his position. To Reb Eliyahu Meir, *daas Torah* of the *gedolim* was law. So too, in the yeshiva – the decision of the *hanhalah* was carried out unanimously, as if it were the opinion of *all* the members, without other consideration. Legions of *talmidim* and dedicated alumni continue in his footsteps. This is his legacy. To that salesman of long ago, Reb Eliyahu Meir's response is, No! There will be more *Ketzoses* and more *sefarim* sold and learned in America – and so it is.

Legions of talmidim and dedicated alumni continue in his footsteps. This is his legacy.

(L-R seated): Rabbi Eliyahu Meir Bloch, Rabbi Avraham Turin, Rabbi Nachum Zev Dessler, Rabbi Nosson Tzvi Baron, Rabbi Gavriel Ginsberg, Rabbi Yechezkel Munk, at a Seudah at the Rosh HaYeshiva's home.

Rabbi Dr. Joseph Breuer *1882-1980*

The Talmud tells us (in *Kiddushin* 30a): "The Holy One, blessed is He, said to Israel, 'My children, I created the evil inclination, but I [also] created the Torah as an antidote to it, and if you occupy yourselves in the Torah, you won't be given over to its power.'" Germany is a land which historically has seen the evil inclination exalted as its crowned head, so to speak – but it has also witnessed the antidote to the incarnate evil represented so infamously by Austrian, Prussian, and German villains. In reality, men of the stature of Rabbi Samson Raphael Hirsch, and his son-in-law, Rabbi Salomon Breuer, were more than just antidotes to the *yetzer hara* (the evil inclination) Indeed, they embodied the necessary curative and restorative powers that succeeded in fending off the winds of Reform and assimilation in their native Germany, by constructing a vibrant, active *kehillah* that thwarted the designs of the most malicious enemies of Torah-loyal Judaism. Rabbi Joseph Breuer of Frankfurt (the son of Rabbi Salomon Breuer), scion of Rabbi Hirsch and chief promulgator of his philosophical legacy, brought the Hirschian *weltanschauung,* world-view, to the shores of the United States, where he transplanted the Frankfurt *kehillah.* He both encouraged and nurtured its astonishing growth into a model of Orthodox communal activism.

Born in Papa, Hungary in 1882, to Rabbi Salomon Breuer and his wife, Sophie Hirsch Breuer (Rabbi Hirsch's youngest daughter), Rabbi Joseph Breuer was imbued with the Hirschian philosophy of *Torah im Derech Eretz,* Torah combined with its implementation in every permissible facet and activity of the outside world. Two years after his illustrious grandfather's death, in 1888, in Frankfurt, Germany, the Salomon Breuers moved from Papa, where Rabbi Breuer was the rabbi, to Frankfurt, where he succeeded his late father-in-law. In that city, Rabbi Salomon Breuer set up a *yeshiva gedolah*; in fact, he was his son's *rebbe muvhak* (principal instructor). In 1903, Joseph received *semichah* from his beloved father and from the *dayan* of Budapest, Rabbi Koppel Reich.

Rabbi Dr. Salomon Breuer

Rabbi S.R. Hirsch

Rabbi Koppel Reich

He also earned his Ph.D in philosophy and political economy in 1905, having studied these subjects at the universities of Giessen and Strasbourg.

After he returned to Frankfurt, Rabbi Joseph Breuer taught in the Realschule, the highschool division of his father's yeshiva. It is interesting to note that he taught both Talmud and *Tanach*, for in future years he achieved considerable fame for his scholarly work, particularly in the area of *Nevi'im* and *Kesuvim*. He also taught German history. Indeed, Rabbi Breuer saw no inconsistency in this curriculum. Hirschian philosophy mandates that one imbue everything he undertakes with holiness. Accordingly, one can approach history in such a manner as to witness the *yad Hashem*, G-d's power, clearly, almost palpably – *if*, of course, he is trained to approach the subject from the proper Torah perspective.

In 1938, Nazi Germany had become the locus of the government-sanctioned horror known as *Kristallnacht*. In his late fifties and clearly sensing the magnitude of the approaching debacle, Rabbi Breuer fled the country. After a short stay in Antwerp, Belgium, he left Europe permanently for the United States, where he was destined to set up a *kehillah* in Washington Heights, New York. Beginning his tenure as rabbi of Congregation K'hal Adath Jeshurun, Rabbi Breuer's influence spread throughout the entire Washington Heights community. And just as he had done in the original paradigm – the Frankfurt *kehillah* – he succeeded in welding his community into one all-embracing unit that provided for the needs of its members, literally from cradle to grave.

However, it is essential to any discussion of Rabbi Breuer's legacy to expound upon the connection between this monolithic community and the Hirschian philosophy that energized it.

Torah im Derech Eretz, the Hirschian synthesis of Torah with the ways of this world, could not have meant for Rabbi Breuer that it was fine to be a "Jew in your tent, but a man abroad," as was the "common wisdom" shared by assimilationist Jews at the turn of the twentieth

He succeeded in welding his community into one all-embracing unit that provided for the needs of its members, literally from cradle to grave.

Rabbi Dr. Joseph Breuer - age 22

Rabbi Breuer with his class in the Hirsch Realschule

abundance of women's *shiurim* which they attend, but also in the multitude of ways in which they actively involve themselves in *kehillah* work. Such is genuine *Torah im Derech Eretz!*

One final point about the Hirschian world-view that Rabbi Breuer espoused his whole life and which he subsequently exported to the United States: As was true of his grandfather and his father before him, he was unyielding when it came to compromising those sacred values which he held dear. Whether it was setting strict standards in *kashrus* for his butchers and for his supervisory agency, the K'hal Adath Jeshurun (KAJ); or opposing membership in groups that were not 100-percent committed to Torah ideals; or demanding a thorough knowledge of *Tanach,* at a time when most other rabbis and educators downplayed such knowledge; or his insistence upon thoroughly ethical behavior in one's business dealings – Rabbi Breuer consistently acknowledged that there existed no "gray area," no room for concessions and trade-offs. Accordingly,

As was true of his grandfather and his father before him, he was unyielding when it came to compromising those sacred values which he held dear.

century. Quite the contrary! The above quoted gemara states that Hashem told Israel that if they but **occupy themselves** in the Torah, they will be saved from the machinations of the evil inclination. "Occupying oneself" can have more than one denotation. Indeed, learning Torah is the highest of all "occupations." But *kehillah* work – performing acts of *chesed* for one's fellow Jews at every step along life's way – is also a Torah "occupation." Acting upright and conscientious in one's business dealings constitutes a Torah "occupation" as well. Being a good Jew thus comprised all these "occupations" –that is to say, being *oseik b'divrei Torah* (occupying oneself with the words of Torah) Women also play an essential role in the Hirschian *weltanschauung,* not just in the

The Frankfurt Yeshiva

(R-L): Rabbi Dr. Joseph Breuer and
Rabbi Shimon Schwab

Rabbi Shlomo Wolbe

he saw to it that his *kehillah* remained unaligned with any group that even smacked of compromise with non-Torah-loyal ideals.

When he was in his seventies, he brought his former student, Rabbi Shimon Schwab, the man who was eventually to succeed him as head of the Washington Heights *kehillah*, into the community's rabbinate. Rabbi Breuer lived to be almost 100 years old. When he passed away in 1980, his funeral cortege was in essence a potpourri of Jews of all types and backgrounds – a genuine testimony to the effect that Rabbi Breuer had on his fellow Jews both in the United States and abroad. In eulogizing him, Rabbi Shlomo Wolbe, the *mashgiach* of Be'er

Rabbi Shimon Schwab

Rabbi Dr. Joseph Breuer officiating
at a wedding

Yaakov in Israel and a former student of his, declared that the greatness of men like Rabbi Joseph Breuer and his father, Rabbi Salomon Breuer, is that it "...transcended community. They belonged to *Klal Yisrael*, so they were honored by *Klal Yisrael*, all of it." His life serves as a reminder of what one man, who truly occupies himself with Torah in all its aspects, can accomplish.

His life serves as a reminder of what one man, who truly occupies himself with Torah in all its aspects, can accomplish.

❧ Rabbi Moshe Feinstein

1895-1986

His entire life was marked by unswerving dedication to the Torah and to *Klal Yisrael*. His home was the address for thousands of people seeking personal advice and answers to complicated halachic questions. He greeted everyone with a smile, a countenance that reflected total immersion in the sea of Torah. Indeed, as one *gadol* said, when Reb Moshe spoke, one could see that the *Shechinah* was communicating to us through his mouth.

Rabbi Moshe Feinstein, the *posek* (halachic arbiter) and final halachic authority for American Jewry for over fifty years, was born to Rabbi Dovid and Faya Gittel Feinstein on the seventh of *Adar*, 1895, in the small town of Uzda, near Minsk. Moshe *Rabbeinu*, the quintessential leader of the Jewish People, was born and died on the seventh of *Adar*. Hence, his parents, hoping their son would follow in Moshe *Rabbeinu's* footsteps, named him Moshe.

Reb Moshe, as he was fondly called by all, began his Torah education in his hometown of Uzda. His first teacher was his father, the rabbi of Uzda. Recognized as a child prodigy, he was sent after his *bar mitzvah* to the yeshiva in Slutzk. He studied under Rabbi Isser Zalman Meltzer, and later he moved to Shklov, where he became a close student of Rabbi Pesach Pruskin from whom he received his *semichah* (rabbinical ordination) at the young age of 21.

In 1921, Reb Moshe commenced his career as a community rabbi in the small city of Luban. It was here that he began his prolific career as an author par excellence. He wrote copious notes on all aspects of Torah. When he decided to leave Russia, as a result of religious persecution, he mailed his novellae to America. Reb Moshe set sail with his family for America in 1937.

Reb Moshe's fame preceded him. The editor of the popular Torah journal "*HaPardes*" rallied the rabbis and Torah scholars of New York to come out en masse to greet the "Lion who has ascended from Babylon," a Talmudic reference to the arrival of a scholar of

Rabbi Mordechai Gifter with Rabbi Moshe Feinstein

Rav Isser Zalman Meltzer, as a young man

stature of *psak* (halachic decisions,) in America. His responsum, entitled *Igros Moshe*, one of the foremost collections of responsa in the modern era, cover every aspect of life, including complicated scientific and medical issues. With self-confidence borne of his erudite knowledge, he tackled every question posed to him. His opinion in these matters became the reference point for much of the halachic debate that would follow.

As a leading *posek*, he felt a responsibility to the many post-Holocaust *agunos*, survivors of the Holocaust whose husbands were

Reb Moshe's name became synonymous with diligence in Torah study – pure, uninterrupted Torah study.

note. Being a man of integrity, Reb Moshe went to Toledo, Ohio to serve as the rabbi, because he had signed a government form stating that he would be employed as a rabbi upon his arrival in America. Only after he had kept his word did he return to New York. His next position was as Talmudic lecturer at the Yeshiva of New Haven, which was at that time located in Cleveland, Ohio, under the direction of Rabbi Yehuda Levenberg.

Rabbi Pesach Pruskin

In 1938, Reb Moshe returned to New York, to head Mesivtha Tiferes Jerusalem. He remained in this position until his passing. Under his direction, the yeshiva flourished. Reb Moshe trained his students in practical halachos, an area in which he received worldwide fame. "Reb Moshe says," became a watchword in the world of Halachah. Indeed, it was Reb Moshe who elevated the

Rabbi Moshe Feinstein with Rabbi Aharon Kotler

Rabbi Moshe Feinstein with son Rabbi David Feinstein

Rabbi Moshe Feinstein with son Rabbi Reuven Feinstein

Mesivtha Tifereth Jerusalem in Staten Island

Despite all his fame as a talmid chacham he was not a "cold intellectual." Indeed, he was famous for his caring and sensitivity.

missing. Reb Moshe worked tirelessly to find a *heter* (authoritative permission) for them to be able to remarry. Literally thousands of *agunos* received his attention and were granted permission to remarry. Once, a lady appeared before him claiming that a certain great rabbi had permitted her to remarry, and now her husband has reappeared. Reb Moshe was not convinced of her story. In uncharacteristic harshness, he challenged her. Finally, she admitted that her story was fabricated. When pressed to explain, Reb Moshe said that the rabbi quoted was a famous *posek,* and it was impossible that he could have erred in Halachah.

Such was his clarity of vision and faith in the ability of the rabbinate.

Reb Moshe initiated a rabbinical ordination program, which included his own students and also students from other yeshivos. The examination for ordination was not difficult. Reb Moshe felt that with time and experience, all serious students would develop the necessary skills and experience

Rabbi Moshe Feinstein with his first talmidim in Tifereth Jerusalem

Mesivtha Tifereth Jerusalem, 145 East Broadway on Manhattan's Lower East Side

Skolyer Rebbe with Rabbi Moshe Feinstein

to fulfill the task. Reb Moshe's name became synonymous with diligence in Torah study – pure, uninterrupted Torah study. Yet he would constantly urge yeshiva students to take time out from their own studies to reach out and help others. He would often quote the story of *Rav* Preida, who reviewed a passage in the Torah with his student four hundred times, so that the latter would be able to understand it. Reb Moshe was very firm in his commitment to the dissemination of Torah knowledge throughout America and the world. He was not an insular scholar; he was a man with a mission – one mission, with which he imbued his students.

Reb Moshe's discourses on Talmud also achieved fame. Meticulously prepared, his Talmudic lectures were as highly regarded by him as his halachic renderings, and as such he published them in a series called *Dibros Moshe*. The scope and breadth of his *shiurim* (lectures) left many unable to fathom the greatness of their author. Despite all his fame as a *talmid chacham*, he was not a "cold intellectual." Indeed, he was famous for his caring, sensitivity.

Reb Moshe's sterling character made as great an impression on the Torah world as his exceptional contribution to Talmudic literature. His humility was legend. Once, while *davening Maariv* during a wedding, Reb Moshe prayed a very long *Shemoneh Esrei*, delaying all the participants in the *minyan*. His son asked him why he had inconvenienced them. In honest surprise, Reb Moshe replied that, since he was not in his yeshiva, it had never crossed his mind that they would wait for him.

A man of integrity, his advice was sought in all matters, communal and private. His greatness notwithstanding, he refused to behave in a manner different from the community, forego-ing his personal preferences for the

He was patient and open-minded in listening to disputes... his humility was legend.

Mr. Irving Stone, prominent Cleveland Philanthropist, being greeted by Rabbi Moshe Feinstein. (L-R): Irving Stone, Rabbi Yisroel Edelman, Rabbi Reuven Feinstein, Rebbetzin Feinstein is in the background.

One cannot define Reb Moshe's relationship to Torah without the use of superlatives.

Rabbi Moshe Feinstein lighting the menorah

Rabbi Moshe Feinstein

local custom. Reb Moshe was affable to all who sought his counsel; he gave of his time and showed great interest when addressing their problems, successes, and decisions. He was patient and open-minded in listening to disputes. Indeed, even those who chose to differ with him were treated

with respect; a respect that was not always reciprocated. Reb Moshe was appointed Chairman of the Moetzes Gedolei HaTorah, Council of Torah Sages, of Agudath Israel. For many years he served as the president of the Union of American Orthodox Rabbis of the United States and Canada, and also served as a member of the Rabbinical Administration Board of Torah Umesorah.

One cannot define Reb Moshe's relationship to Torah without the use of superlatives. Yet, if one were to choose

Rabbi Yaakov Kamenetsky with Rabbi Moshe Feinstein

(L-R): Rabbi Avraham Pam, Rabbi Mordechai Tendler, Rabbi Moshe Sherer, Rabbi Moshe Feinstein

Rabbi Moshe Feinstein writing notes in a sefer.

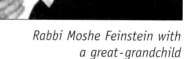

Rabbi Moshe Feinstein with a great-grandchild

a phrase, two words, which define the essence of this remarkable *gadol*, it would be – *eved Hashem* (servant of Hashem). Like his namesake, Moshe *Rabbeinu*, Reb Moshe was the consummate servant, devoted totally, committed unequivocally, to Hashem. His life's story is the personification of one whose entire essence is suffused with Torah. Reb Moshe was a *gadol b'Yisrael* whose greatness in Torah was tempered with a gentility of the soul.

Torah was his life force and it refined every aspect of his personality. His exemplary character left an indelible imprint on his generation. His passing, in 1986, left the Torah world bereft of a giant of Torah and *middos*.

...if one were to choose a phrase, two words, which define the essence of this remarkable gadol, it would be - eved Hashem, servant of Hashem.

Rabbi Moshe Feinstein

Philipp Feldheim

1901-1990

Where was one likely to meet Jews from all backgrounds – *roshei yeshiva, rabbanim, talmidim*, laymen, observant and non-observant – in the Lower East Side of the 1940s? At Feldheim's Bookstore, where one was enveloped by *sefarim* and Jewish books. Presiding over the seeming chaos was Philipp Feldheim, with a smiling face and listening ear. Noted for his *chesed* and *emes*, he was also an astute and experienced businessman, who pioneered a revolutionary concept in Jewish publishing in America-English-language *sefarim*. Who was this man of vision?

Born in Vienna, Austria in 1901, his father, Reb Tzvi Mordechai, was an esteemed member of the famous Schiff Shul and followed the *minhagim* (customs) of the *Chasam Sofer*, which was common among Jewry of Central Europe. Mr. Feldheim was in the textile business, printing designs on fabrics. Reb Tzvi Mordechai valued having personal relationships with *gedolim*, and among others he became close with the Altshtadter Rav. He sought the *Rav's* counsel on a regular basis. The Feldheim sons were sent away to various yeshivos. Philipp learned in Shuran, Serdahel and Galanta. In Galanta, he learned under the tutelage of Rabbi Yosef Zvi Dushinsky, whose scholarship and saintliness had a profound impact on the young Philipp, lasting all his life.

He returned to Vienna and worked in the family business. Philipp continued his learning with the *Rav* of the Schiff Shul, Rabbi Yeshaya Feurst. Already at a young age, he was interested in communal affairs. He was active in Agudath Israel and attended the Second Knessiah Gedolah of Agudah in Vienna, in 1923. At that time, it was his *zechus* (privilege) to attend to the needs of Rabbi Moshe Mordechai Epstein, *Rosh Yeshiva* of Slobodka, who was attending the convention. In 1930 he married, and the young couple settled in Vienna.

In the late 1930s Nazi domination intensified in Austria. November 10, 1938, *Kristallnacht,* marked a turning point in the lives of countless Jews, Philipp

Noted for his chesed and emes, he was also an astute and experienced businessman, who pioneered a revolutionary concept in Jewish publishing in America – English – language sefarim.

Feldheim among them. He was arrested on that fateful night and after his release, 12 days later, resolved to leave Austria. He managed to arrange for his immediate family to leave Vienna – sending his parents to his sister in London. On September 1,1939 – the day Poland was invaded by Germany – Philipp Feldheim, his wife and three children sailed for America from Rotterdam. They arrived in Hoboken, New Jersey on *erev* Rosh Hashanah. He had 30 dollars in his pocket.

The Feldheims settled in Williamsburg. Mr. Feldheim's efforts to find employment in the textile industry were unsuccessful, because he refused to work on Shabbos, as was expected in those days. The need for *parnasah* (a livelihood) led him to the *sefarim* business. From his apartment, Mr. Feldheim sold the small amount of *sefarim* he received from family in Europe. After a while, the European publishers (mainly in Warsaw, Vienna, Vilna and Budapest) shipped directly to him. Through word-of-mouth, the fledgling business developed and eventually outgrew the confines of the apartment. A basement was rented on Hester Street, with the help of friends, and the business expanded.

At that time in America, the publication of *sefarim* was negligible, and therefore Europe was the main supplier. As the war intensified the shipments from Europe stopped.

Like his father, Philipp Felheim fostered relationships with *talmidei chachamim,* and through his business he met several. Among them was Rabbi Shraga Feivel Mendlowitz, *menahel* of Torah Vodaath, who encouraged him to start his own publishing business. His first venture was

the publication of the essential *Rishonim* needed by yeshiva and rabbinical students – *Shita Mekubetzes*, *Rashba* and *Chiddushei HaRan*. Mr. Feldheim also was involved in the printing of the *Shulsinger Shas* – the first *Shas* printed in America.

Despite his personal struggles, Mr. Feldheim still involved himself in the needs of his *Kehillah* (community). He founded the Vienna *Kehillah*, Adas Yereim, in Williamsburg in 1941, together with a small group of other *baalei batim*. Initially, they used the Feldheim apartment. He maintained his connection to Adas Yereim throughout his life.

In 1950, the Feldheims moved to Washington Heights and Rabbi Joseph Breuer, founder of Khal Adas Yeshurun, became his *rav*, mentor and beloved friend. Mr. Feldheim became active in the *Kehillah* and was a member of the Board of Trustees, in keeping with the importance he attached to *klal* work.

Rabbi Breuer encouraged Mr. Feldheim

There was a great need in America at this time for sefarim in English. Philipp Feldheim undertook this challenge, publishing translations of works on Chumash, classics of hashkafah, etc., and commissioning works he felt addressed the Jewish community's needs and interests.

*Mr. Philipp Feldheim
as a young bachur*

The Feldheim family. (Back row, L-R): Yitzchak Feldheim, Mrs. Feldheim, Philipp Feldheim. (Front row, L-R): Yaakov Feldheim and sister, Eva (the future Mrs. Hollander)

He opened vistas of knowledge to countless people, making Torah and Yiddishkeit accessible to them.

to publish *sefarim* in English, following the tradition of Rabbi Samson Raphael Hirsch, who felt it was important to translate and write *sefarim* in the language of the country. In Europe, *Chumash*, Talmud, *Midrash*, and the works of Rabbi Hirsch and Rabbi Elie Munk were all available in German. There was a great need in America at this time for *sefarim* in English. "There was certainly a crying need for such *sefarim*, and this was really the beginning ... the very earliest awakening of what later became the *Baal Teshuvah* Movement... the first gropings for light in the darkness," said Mr. Feldheim, in an interview on the eve of his 88th birthday.

Philipp Feldheim undertook this challenge and published English transla-

tions (from German) of the writings of Rabbi S. R. Hirsch and Rabbi Elie Munk. As the demand for such books increased, he had classics like the *Mesilas Yesharim (Path of the Just)* and *Shaarei Teshuvah (Gates of Repentance)* translated into English. Mr. Feldheim broadened the parameters of Jewish publishing by commissioning works he felt addressed the needs and interests of the Jewish community. Because of his many contacts, he became aware of possible books and would encourage those whose potential he recognized – e.g., Irving Bunim's *Ethics From Sinai*. In addition to publishing, Feldheim Publishers became involved in the distribution of *sefarim* and Jewish books across the United States, Israel and Europe, including some not published by Feldheim.

Not all of the books were commercially successful. However, if Mr. Feldheim felt the book made a contribution, even a limited one, he considered it his

Original site of Feldheim's Book Store, 45 East Broadway, 1949

obligation to do what he could. He did not view his work as merely selling, rather he looked upon it as a sacred mission to help *all* Jews grow in Torah learning. Over the years, the business evolved into a major publishing enterprise, centered in Spring Valley, New York and Israel. Mr. Feldheim remained involved in the business until his mid-80's. In the interview he gave on the eve of his 88th birthday, he said the following about the changes in the business he had built: "...regardless of all the technology...we still strive to publish titles that reflect good taste, modesty...books that uphold true Jewish ideals."

Although there are many English language publishers of *sefarim* and books of Jewish literature today, Philipp Feldheim was the pioneer. This generous man of *chesed* and *emes* bridged "the world that was" to "the world that is." He opened vistas of knowledge to countless people, making Torah and *Yiddishkeit* accessible to them.

Although there are many English – language publishers of sefarim and books of Jewish literature today, Philipp Feldheim was the pioneer.

FOLLOWING FELDHEIM'S LEAD

Today's flourishing world of English-language Torah literature adds luster to the Feldheim legacy as the pioneer in the field. Among the many English-language Torah publishers today, the most prominent is ArtScroll/Mesorah. Its first book, *Megillas Esther*, was originally intended to be its only book. **Rabbi Meir Zlotowitz** conceived of it as a memorial to a dear friend who had suddenly passed away in his sleep. At the time, 1976, Rabbi Zlotowitz was a creator of brochures and illuminated scrolls to be used as awards (hence the origin of the name ArtScroll). He asked **Rabbi Nosson Scherman**, a friend who was *menahel* of Yeshiva Karlin Stolin, to help with the editing and to write an introduction, which he called an "overview." **Reb Sheah Brander**, a graphics genius who worked for ArtScroll, was involved in the design of the *sefer*.

None of the collaborators were prepared for the response. After the initial surprise that a book of *Tanach* could be presented so beautifully and accurately, and that English could be co-opted as a language of Torah, there was an avalanche of requests for more such *sefarim*. Rabbis Zlotowitz and Scherman continued working part-time to produce the other four *Megillos*. The Telshe *Rosh Yeshiva*, Rabbi Mordechai Gifter reached out to express his support and offered to read galleys and offer comments, which he did for over two years. The two authors left their professions and decided to devote their full time – actually time-and-a-half and double-time – to the newly born ArtScroll Series.

As the years flew by, ArtScroll/Mesorah published the Yad Avraham *Mishnah* Series and many books of *Tanach*, the first of a succession of revolutions in Jewish life. The ArtScroll *Siddur* and *Machzorim* and the Stone *Chumash* became the staples of the English-speaking world, and brought legions of English-speaking Jews closer to Torah learning, life, and observance.

The crown jewel of what has been called the "ArtScroll Revolution" is undoubtedly the Schottenstein Edition of *Talmud Bavli*. The idea for the project was originally suggested by Rabbi Yaakov Kamenetsky about six years before the work actually began. The 73-volume English edition was initiated with *Maseches Makkos* in 1990, and is scheduled for completion in conjunction with the *Siyum Daf Yomi*, in March 2005. The ArtScroll/Schottenstein *Talmud* has spawned a huge increase of people who are returning to, or starting, the study of *Gemara*. This phenomenon is especially apparent in the astounding growth of *Daf Yomi* groups.

More than 800 titles after the first *Megillas Esther* rolled off the press, ArtScroll/Mesorah is still making history. Rabbi Moshe Feinstein called it "a yeshiva without walls." Rabbi Yaakov Kamenetsky said "it is the greatest English-language *harbatzas Torah* undertaking in history" – and these statements were made when ArtScroll/Mesorah was in its relative infancy. Rabbi Yosef Shalom Eliyashiv says of the people producing the works, "they have *siyata diShemaya* (Heavenly assistance)."

Philipp Feldheim surely looks down with pride at the work he pioneered.

Rabbi Mordechai Shlomo Friedman *1891-1971*

THE BOYANER REBBE

The youngest son of the famous Boyaner *Rebbe*, Reb Yitzchok, was named Mordechai Shlomo; Mordechai after his grandfather, Reb Mordechai of Chernobyl, and Shlomo after his uncle, Reb Shlomo of Sadigera. His mother, Rebbetzin Malka, was the daughter of the Rachmastrivker Rebbe. He was born on 13 *Tishrei,* 1891. The young Mordechai Shlomo was very dear to his father.

The *Rebbe,* Reb Yitzchok, set aside special time for each of his four sons; quality time dedicated to discussing with them issues of Torah and *Chassidus.* Mordechai Shlomo's time was always on Shabbos; the *Rebbe* explained that since it was a special pleasure for him to speak with his young son, he therefore reserved Shabbos as their designated time.

Even as a young child, Reb Mordechai Shlomo was extremely sensitive to others. He would literally weep at

seeing another Jew suffer. He was also a very diligent student and spent long hours poring over his learning. At the age of 17, he married Chava Sarah, the daughter of Reb Yisroel Shalom of Mezibuz. She was to be his life-partner in all of his charitable and spiritual endeavors. With the outbreak of the First World War the family fled Boyan for Vienna.

After his father's passing in 1917, he and his brothers led the Boyan community. In 1925, Reb Mordechai Shlomo received a request from his father's *chassidim* in New York to be their *Rebbe.* At first, the *Rebbe* considered disregarding their request, but his uncle, the famous Chortkover *Rebbe,* advised him to go: "In America, you will not only help the floundering community, but also help strengthen the failing *Yiddishkeit* of the American community." This persuasive argument characterized the *Rebbe* – responsibility

The Rebbe's Shul in Boyan

to others could not be shrugged off. His move to America paved the way for many who survived the war to follow him, and helped transplant the European lifestyle to which they had been accustomed to America.

He was extremely pained by the losses that *Klal Yisrael* suffered during the war. He would say, "The *goyim* are holding parades to mark their victory. We, however, have lost the war, we have lost everything." Nevertheless, pain did not stop him and despair was

alien to him. He would personally greet survivors at the docks and help them resettle in America.

True, the America of 1927 was hardly a hospitable or fertile place for the development of a *chassidic* sect, but the *Rebbe* was undaunted. He opened a *shtibel* on East Broadway, in the Lower East Side of New York, and remained there for 40 years. As the population shifted, he was advised to relocate his *shtibel*, but he refused. The Boyaner *Rebbe* once explained

He was extremely pained by the losses that Klal Yisrael suffered during the war. Nevertheless, despair was alien to him. The Rebbe was undaunted.

Rabbi Moshe Feinstein with Boyaner Rebbe

Boyaner Rebbe visiting the Boyaner Yeshiva in Eretz Yisrael

that the proposed new location already had *shtiblach* from other *rebbeim* and he did not want to encroach on their territory and possibly take away some of their followers. Such was his sensitivity.

His heart overflowed with love for his fellow Jews, and this soon attracted young people to his *shtibel*. Gone were the days when *shtiblach* were the domain of the old. In fact, the local Police Department, who suspected him of brainwashing his young followers, monitored his actions. The *Rebbe* encouraged *bachurim* to learn, even those not affiliated with the Boyaner community. He would travel to Torah Vodaath to talk in learning and test the *bachurim*. Only when students began to attend his *tisch* did he discontinue his visits, for fear that people would say he was attempting to recruit new *chassidim*. When visiting Philadelphia, he would always go to the Yeshiva to spend time with the *Roshei Yeshiva* and the *bachurim*.

The Boyaner *Rebbe's* address was the place for all matters of charity and kindness. Beggars and *meshulachim* would come to him for advice and help, as well as a check. Often, the

Rebbe would pave the way for others. Once, Rabbi Aharon Kotler approached the *Rebbe* for aid in collecting money for Chinuch Atzmai, but the *Rebbe* was not able to help him. A few days later, Reb Aharon went to an affluent Jew, who gave him an unexpectedly large donation. To Reb Aharon's surprise, the man explained that the Boyaner *Rebbe* had already approached him about the matter.

Reb Mordechai Shlomo's noble bearing and purity of character endeared him to all. His greatness in Torah bridged the gap between all the different sectors of the Jewish community, both in America and Israel. He unstintingly gave of himself to others, serving their spiritual and physical needs. His love for others was so intense that even when hospitalized, he refused to deny entrance to those who felt they needed him. "If *Yidden* need me, I must make myself available to them," he said.

Among fellow *admorim* he was recognized as a *gadol*, and they appointed him the *Nasi* of the *Agudas Ha-Admorim*. The Boyaner *Rebbe* utilized his position to help other *chassidic*

Boyaner Rebbe with Rabbi Eliezer Silver

rebbeim who had survived the war, to reestablish themselves in America and to acclimate themselves to the American landscape. He truly fulfilled the expectations of the *gedolim* of the previous generation who foresaw his greatness. The *Chazon Ish,* after speaking in learning with the *Rebbe,* exclaimed that he was a true *lamdan.* The great leaders of American Jewry, Rabbi Silver and Rabbi Kotler held the *Rebbe's* advice in high regard. Rabbi Moshe Feinstein would make a special visit to the *Rebbe* on *erev Rosh Hashanah* to receive his blessings for the New Year.

With the founding of the American branch of Agudath Israel in 1939, the *Rebbe* was elected vice-president. He viewed the Agudah as a vehicle for *ahavas Yisrael,* love of fellow Jews. The *Rebbe* also served for many years as a senior member of the *Moetzes Gedolei HaTorah.* He would contribute not only time and effort to the Agudah, but also

money. It was most appropriate, given his involvement in communal affairs, that he became president of *Vaad HaEzra,* an organization that sent money and aid to Europe. The *Rebbe* personally knocked on doors and raised astronomical sums of money for this vital cause.

From his *beis medrash* in New York, his influence spread far and wide. He visited *Eretz Yisrael* on numerous occasions, each time bringing spiritual elevation to the many *chassidim* aligned with the Rizhin-Boyan dynasties. He was also instrumental in the building of the Rizhin Yeshiva in Jerusalem and Bnei Brak, leading the flourishing communities of the Boyaner *chassidim* with dedication and selflessness. Today's various Boyaner and Rizhin institutions and communities, which are thriving in *Eretz Yisrael,* exist in great measure due to the untiring efforts of the Boyaner *Rebbe,* Reb Mordechai Shlomo Friedman.

In *Adar,* the very month that he began to lead the community of Boyan, on the fifth of the month, the *Rebbe* passed away. He was laid to rest on Har HaZeisim in Jerusalem. Presently, his grandson Rabbi Nochum Dov Brayer is the Rebbe of the Boyaner *chassidim.*

The Rebbe's noble bearing and purity of character endeared him to all. His greatness in Torah bridged the gap between all the different sectors of the Jewish community in America and Israel.

Boyaner Rebbe visiting the Boyaner Yeshiva in Eretz Yisrael

⤳ Rabbi Reuven Grozovsky *1896-1958*

In 1944, Mesivta Torah Vodaath in New York City lost its great *Rosh HaYeshiva*, Rabbi Shlomo Heiman. What sort of man would be chosen to take his place, and how would his personality influence and contribute to the already respected reputation of the yeshiva? Rabbi Reuven Grozovsky, the highly revered son-in-law and companion of the saintly Rabbi Boruch Ber Lebowitz, famed head of the European yeshiva known as Knesses Bais Yitzchak, was the ideal choice to be Rabbi Heiman's successor. And indeed, his effect on American Jewry may best be gauged by his profound influence on his *talmidim,* both at Mesivta Torah Vodaath and at Bais Medrash Elyon in Monsey, New York. Additionally, his work on the Vaad Hatzala culminated, among other things, in his rescuing 110 members of the old Kaminetz Yeshiva, eighty of whom were brought to these shores, subsequently becoming members of the Kaminetz Kollel in New York's Lower East Side. Rabbi Grozovsky was a man who was *kulo Torah*, his entire essence was completely defined by Torah, and his *hasmadah*, diligence was

exceptional. His legacy lies in his fierce determination to make Torah foremost, not merely in his own life but also in the lives of his fellow Jews.

Born in 1896 in Minsk, where his father Rav Shamshon was the leading *dayan* of the city. Reb Reuven (as he was known to his many students) studied in Slobodka under the *Levush Mordechai* (Rabbi Moshe Mordechai Epstein) and under the *Alter (Elder)* of Slobodka, Rabbi Nosson Zvi Finkel. In 1919, he married Rabbi Boruch Ber Lebowitz's daughter, and he later accompanied his illustrious father-in-law to Kaminetz. Reb Reuven undertook the financial burden of the yeshiva in Kaminetz. In addition, he delivered a weekly *shiur,* investing numerous hours to prepare for it. Rabbi Grozovsky spent several hours each day in the yeshiva, talking in learning and keeping a close eye on everyone and everything. He also counseled *talmidim* when he felt they needed *mussar*. While in Slobodka, he directly influenced and guided three of the greatest *gedolim* of the century: Rabbi Yaakov Kamenetsky, Rabbi Aharon Kotler, and Rabbi Yaakov Ruderman – all three of whom were largely responsible for transforming American Orthodoxy,

(L-R): Rabbi Reuven Grozovsky, Rabbi Shraga Feivel Mendlowitz

by changing its focus from centering basically on laymen's interests and desires to concentrating on the learning and teaching of Torah as benchmarks of an accomplished Jewry.

In this regard, it is important to note that Rabbi Grozovsky became chairman of the Rabbinical Advisory Council of Torah Umesorah, the well-known national organization for day school education, which had been the brainchild of Rabbi Shraga Feivel Mendlowitz. He thus became an ardent advocate for Torah education throughout the United States. Perhaps most typical of his attitude on this subject is a remark which he made in Providence, Rhode Island, at the "kick-off campaign" for a new day school: "There's a long-standing rule in the Torah, that saving lives assumes a higher priority over everything else. Without Torah study, the children of this community are being buried alive....If, as a result of this meeting, we save but one child, we will be worthy of being blessed with the light of the Torah." This remark was indicative of his ongoing campaign to save Jews from the trends of the times, whether in Russia or the United States. Reb Reuven was a very private and humble person. Consequently, there are many hidden facets to this great man and our ability to know him. Only by examining his deeds and words as a *rosh yeshiva* and communal leader can we attain a bit of an understanding and appreciation of this Torah giant. Reb Reuven lived very simply and was constantly available to serve his illustrious father-in-law, with whom he shared a house. His overriding focus in preparing his *shiurim* was always for the *talmidim*, and ensuring their understanding was his priority. Reb Reuven, taking a cue from his father-in-law, believed that it was important to know what *not* to say, if it does not explain

He was able to implement the Torah weltanschauung, world view, that the old-world institutions had embodied in previous decades, through his carefully crafted shiurim.

(L-R): Rabbi Reuven Grozovsky, Rabbi Yaakov Kamenetsky, and Rabbi Aharon Kotler

> The needs of
> the Klal were
> of paramount
> importance
> to him.
> Reb Reuven
> was unafraid to
> stand up and
> speak out if
> he felt that
> kavod haTorah
> was at stake.

anything – "Whatever doesn't add, detracts from your major thesis and can only spoil your presentation." His *shiurim*, therefore, were penetrating and detailed, weighing all sides of an issue. Reb Reuven's analytical approach to learning did not change when he came to Torah Vodaath, after serving as *Rosh Yeshiva* in Kaminetz for almost 20 years.

Reb Reuven's role as the head of the *Moetzes Gedolei HaTorah* (the Council of Torah Sages of the Agudath Israel) was a pivotal one. Rabbi Aharon Kotler, the great *Rosh HaYeshiva* of Beth Medrash Govoha in Lakewood, New Jersey, depended heavily on him, as did other great Torah leaders. When refugee children who arrived in Palestine were forced into Israeli leftist, atheistic *kibbutzim* against their will, it was Reb Reuven who eloquently protested this outrage at a mass meeting in New York. Indeed, at Rabbi Grozovsky's prompting, the Zeirei

Agudath Israel, Agudath Israel's youth organization, refused to allow the press to misrepresent the Torah viewpoint on any issue, for he had encouraged them to write letters of protest and explanation to the media.

The needs of the *Klal* were of paramount importance to him. Reb Reuven was unafraid to stand up and speak out if he felt that *kavod haTorah* was at stake. The story is told that, in Vilna, after World War I, Reb Reuven organized a demonstration against a Jewish football team who were *mechallel Shabbos*. He was detained by the police for this action. The *Chofetz Chaim* wrote to him after this incident: "I envy your merit of suffering for the glory of Heaven."

In 1951, a mass meeting was organized in New York to protest the placement of refugee children in irreligious *kibbutzim* in *Eretz Yisrael*, therby robbing them of their heritage. Reb Reuven delivered an impassioned speech, vehemently protesting this action: "Can one love a seducer of young innocent lives? Corrupting a child is even worse than murdering him!" His words were greeted by applause. However, Reb Reuven silenced them, "It is time for *kinos* (lamentations), not applause!"

Reb Reuven is known for the anthology of his lectures, entitled *Chiddushei Reb Reuven (Novellae of Reb Reuven)* which was published posthumously in 1958, and *Ba'ayos Hazeman (Problems of the Era),* which reflects contemporary situations as seen from his Torah-oriented viewpoint. Rabbi Reuven Grozovsky is best remembered as a lion among Torah scholars, and also as a precious link to the Slobodka/ Kaminetz styles of learning Torah. He was able to implement the Torah *weltanschauung* (world view) that these old-world institutions had embodied in previous decades, through his carefully crafted *shiurim* which he delivered at Mesivta Torah Vodaath and Beis Medrash Elyon. Consequently, his leadership in the Torah world has made a profound difference in American yeshiva pedagogy to this very day, as well as our concepts and activities on behalf of *Klal Yisrael*.

His leadership in the Torah world has made a profound difference in American yeshiva pedagogy to this very day, as well as our concepts and activities on behalf of Klal Yisrael.

Rabbi Levi Yitzchok Grunwald 1894-1980

ZEHLEMER RAV

The individual responsible for elevating and enforcing the *kashrus* standards of *shechitah* in America in the early 1940s was Rabbi Levi Yitzchok Grunwald, the Zehlemer *Rav*. A great *talmid chacham* and man of warmth, compassion, and humility, he impacted on the lives of countless Jews.

Born in Chust, Czechoslovakia (now Russia), Rabbi Levi Yitzchok Grunwald was a son of the famed *"Arugas Habosem,"* Rabbi Moshe Grunwald, who led a well-known yeshiva in Chust. The young Levi Yitzchok learned with his father until his passing and then studied in the Chust Yeshiva.

After intense diligent study, he received *semichah* from three foremost *rabbanim* – Rabbi Shmuel Rosenberg, the Unsdorfer Rav (author of *Be'er Shmuel*); Rabbi Mordechai Leib Winkler, Rav of Mad (author of *Levushei Mordechai)*; and Rabbi Shmuel Engel, Radomishel Rav (author of *Sh'eilos U'Teshuvos Maharosh*). He was married to his oldest brother's daughter, after his father passed away and left him an orphan at age 17.

Subsequently, Rabbi Grunwald served with distinction in three *kehillos* – Paya, Visk and Orshiva – where he was accorded great respect. In 1932, the *kehillah* of Zehlem engaged him. In addition to leading the community, Rabbi Grunwald also served as *Rosh HaYeshiva* until the *Anschluss* – the annexation of Austria by the German Reich in March 1938.

The Jews of Austria were the very first victims of Nazi tyranny outside of Germany. The city of "Zehlem", a Yiddish designation for *"Deutschkreutz,"* was one of the *"Sheva Kehillos"* in Austria – seven communities located near one another, all adhering to strict Jewish religious life.

All the Jews of Zehlem were expelled as soon as the Germans entered in March 1938. After taking refuge in Vienna for one half-year, the Zehlemer *Rav* succeeded in reaching the United States, settling in Williamsburg. To his dismay, he found the state of *Yiddishkeit* in America to be deplorable.

A great talmid chacham and man of warmth, compassion, and humility, he impacted on the lives of countless Jews.

The Zehlemer *Rav's* first priority, even before he established himself, was to obtain affidavits and other necessary papers to save as many Jews as possible from Europe and bring them to the United States. Among those people whom he provided with papers was Yosef Rosenberger, who later became well known for spearheading the *"Shatnez"* Laboratory[*].

Rabbi Levi Yitzchok Grunwald

The next endeavor of the Zehlemer *Rav*, in 1944, was the establishment of *"Chalav Yisrael,"* heretofore almost unknown in America. This venture enabled every Jew to purchase dairy products that were produced under the *Rav's* reliable supervision.

Furthermore, the *Rav* set to work on instituting *"glatt kosher" shechitah*, which had been a virtually unknown entity in America at that time (1944). After exerting extreme effort and suffering great hardship – since he was threatened by the establishment – he finally succeeded in surmounting all obstacles and recruited an eminent *shochet*, thus establishing Zehlemer *Shechitah* in America. The *Rav* himself had a *"kabalah"* on *shechitah*, and he personally accompanied the *shochet* to the slaughterhouse to institute the procedure.

The Zehlemer *Rav* was also a *sofer* (scribe) and a highly qualified *mohel*; as such, he circumcised literally thousands of children during his lifetime. He refused to accept any remuneration for his services from refugees.

The Zehlemer *Rav* considered his crowning achievement to be the founding of the first chassidic yeshiva in Williamsburg (1944). It became the prototype for all other yeshivos of its kind, which were later established by other *rebbes* and leaders of rabbinic dynasties.

The Yeshiva and Mesivta Arugath Habosem constituted a new concept on the American scene. The *talmidim*, students, were not permitted to have a *"tchupp"* (shock of hair) and were required to have a *"shiur peyos"* (the halachically prescribed length for sidelocks).

The standard of learning was on a high level, and even the English Department produced accomplished students. The *Rav* made it a rule to administer an oral test to the *talmidim* on a weekly basis.

After the War, in 1946, there was a sizable influx of *talmidim* to the yeshiva from the DP camps – survivors of the Holocaust. The *Rav* helped them rebuild their lives and gave them the *chizuk*, encouragement, and support they needed.

The Yeshiva and Mesivta flourished and graduated

The Zehlemer Rav was responsible for elevating and enforcing the kashrus standards of shechitah in America in the early 1940s.

Rabbi Levi Yitzchok Grunwald dancing with a chassan

---

[*] Refer to the biography of Yosef Rosenberger, pg. 263

thousands of students, who not only distinguised themselves in Torah and *yiras Shamayim*, but also conducted themselves with dignity and nobility of character.

There are many stories told about the Zehlemer *Rav's* acts of *chesed*, including the following:

Once, a poor Jew in Zehlem came to the *Rav* and complained bitterly that the heavy snowfall during the winter had

Rabbi Levi Yitzchok Grunwald

caused his roof to cave in. He was left, literally, without a roof over his head. The Zehlemer *Rav*, whose personal resources were very limited, went immediately to another room, and after consulting the *Rebbitzen* he gave the poor Jew a precious piece of jewelry, an inheritance and of great sentimental value. He advised the man to sell it and hire the workman to repair his roof.

His charitable deeds were boundless. A *talmid chacham* who had recently emigrated from *Eretz Yisrael* visited the *Rav* in Williamsburg. It was bitterly cold and the visitor only had a light coat. The *Rav* told him to try on his new, fur-lined winter coat that had been presented to him just a few weeks earlier by one of his wealthier admirers. It was a perfect fit and the *Rav* told the visitor to keep the coat.

On another occasion, the Zehlemer *Rav* was approached by a man who pleaded for a blessing on behalf of a needy Jew who was ill. The *Rav* asked for the name and address of the sick individual. Immediately, the *Rav* closed his *gemara*, went to pay the sick person

a *bikur cholim* visit and left a very substantial sum of money on his table. He returned a few times and on each occasion helped the impoverished Jew. (This story was related by Rabbi Yisroel Shurin, a son-in-law of Rav Yaakov Kamenetsky, *Rosh Yeshiva* of Mesivta Torah Vodaath, and reprinted in *Olomeinu*, published by Torah Umesorah.)

In addition to leading his *kehillah* and Yeshiva, as well as supervising the *kashrus* operation, the Zehlemer *Rav* wrote many responsa on all four parts of the *Shulchan Aruch*, replies to halachic questions, and approbations. Moreover, he compiled a great number of *chiddushei Torah*,

Rabbi Levi Yitzchok Grunwald davening

Yeshiva and Mesivta Arugath Habosem was considered his crowning achievement. The students distinguished themselves in Torah, yiras Shamayim and nobility of character.

The Zehlemer Rav (center); looking on in background, Rabbi Shraga Feivel Mendlowitz, Menahel of Mesivta Torah Vodaath, and (on the right) Rabbi Reuven Grozovsky, Rosh Yeshiva of Mesivta Torah Vodaath

Zehlemer Rav as mesader kiddushin at a chasunah; looking on are Kopyczinitzer Rebbe (c.) and Rabbi Aharon Kotler(l.)

More than 30,000 people participated at his funeral; it was the largest *levaya* ever seen in Williamsburg.

The entire media, including *The New York Times*, reported the sad event. It is remarkable that *Time Magazine* emphasized that the "Zehlem Rabbi Grunwald touched the lives of all observant American Jews by requiring enforcement of the most rigorous standards of the preparation of kosher food."

Zehlem had been one of the first Jewish communities in Europe to be destroyed. On the other hand, it was one of the first to be transplanted and reestablished in the United States. This was due to the *mesiras nefesh* and untiring efforts of the Zehlemer *Rav*, Rabbi Levi Yitzchok Grunwald.

novellae on Torah, Shabbos, *Moadim, Mikvaos, Hagaddah*, etc., that were printed posthumously.

The Zehlemer *Rav* was also an accomplished orator, an excellent *baal tefillah*, gifted *baal korei* and flawless *baal tokeia*, as well as a recognized *posek*.

He was an exceptionally charitable person, who contributed large sums to needy Torah scholars. The *Rav* did not confine his *tzedakah* to the *aniyim* of America; he sent astronomical amounts to the destitute in *Eretz Yisrael* as well.

Above all, the Zehlemer *Rav* was an extremely humble man who did not even permit the mention of the title *Rav* on his *matzeivah* (headstone), but only his name.

To the profound sorrow of all who knew him, the Zehlemer *Rav* passed away on 27 *Nissan*, 5740 (1980), at the age of 86.

Zehlemer Rav as mesader kiddushin at a Chasunah. Standing next to the Chassan (L-R): Novominsker Rebbe, Rabbi Aharon Kotler, Rabbi Moshe Feinstein. Back row center, young Rabbi Yaakov Perlow, present Novominsker Rebbe

≈ Rabbi Chaim Meir Hager

1881-1972

VIZHNITZER REBBE

Vizhnitz, a name that resonates with history, glory, and tradition. A hub of chassidic culture and a dynasty of great *rebbeim*, it was almost destroyed by the horrors of the Second World War. However, from the brink of the abyss it was saved by the Vizhnitzer *Rebbe*, Reb Chaim Meir Hager.

Reb Chaim Meir was the second son of the third *Rebbe* of the Vizhnitz dynasty, Rabbi Yisroel Hager, himself a scion of the Kossov dynasty. At the age of twenty-two, Reb Chaim Meir was appointed *Rav* of Villchovitz. His young age did not hinder his ability to lead the community. The great love he had for every Jew and his perceptive personality endeared him to everyone. Reb Chaim Meir was also a pivotal figure in Agudath Israel in Romania and served on the *Moetzes Gedolei HaTorah*. He attended all the *Knessiah Gedolah* gatherings. Many *gedolei Yisrael* would seek his sage advice and counsel.

With the passing of his father, most of the Vizhnitzer *chassidim* turned to him to serve as the successor of the late *Rebbe*. It was a wise choice, and for the following five years he led his flock. It was his shining personality that ensured that the flame of Vizhnitz was not extinguished. It did not merely flicker and burn, but flared into a bright flame. His court in Europe spiritually energized the entire region.

But the war brought all this to an abrupt halt. Miraculously, the *Rebbe* survived. The *Rebbe's* leadership and organizational abilities were challenged, indeed, when the Romanian Jews were deported in 1941 to Transnistria (a death camp in the Ukraine, administered jointly by the Germans and the Romanians from July 1941 to March 1944).

The Rebbe and his brothers, Reb Boruch and Reb Eliezer, threw themselves, heart and soul, into the rescue operation of helping to alleviate

Vizhnitzer Rebbe with his entourage

the suffering in Transnistria. With every fiber in their bodies, they overcame every obstacle in their way. They moved mountains, at great personal sacrifice, and established a rescue apparatus that saved thousands of Jewish souls from certain death.

No time was spent in despair: the work of rebuilding had to begin immediately. Within a short time, the *Rebbe* gathered around him a group of survivors, thirsty for spirituality. He changed their lives, taking broken despondent refugees on the road to nowhere and turning them into confident and optimistic *chassidim*. It did not take the *Rebbe* long to realize that Europe would no longer yield the harvest of holiness that it had

in the past. Consequently, the *Rebbe* set his sights on the Holy Land.

Although the *Rebbe* settled in *Eretz Yisrael,* his influence was powerfully felt in America. The *Rebbe's* second son, Reb Mordechai, was placed in charge of the American community. The growth of this community was augmented with the opening of communal schools and yeshivos. The *ahavas Yisrael* of the *Rebbe* also emanated from his son to the many who counted themselves as *chassidim* of the Vizhnitz tradition.

The ultimate highlight in the lives of the Vizhnitzer *chassidim* in America was a visit by Reb Chaim Meir. He would come from *Eretz Yisrael* to raise funds for the growing Vizhnitz com-

Although the Rebbe settled in Eretz Yisrael, his influence was powerfully felt in America. The burgeoning Vizhnitz community was united by the all-encompassing personality of the great Rebbe.

Vizhnitzer Rebbe as mesader kiddushin at a wedding

Greeting the Vizhnitzer Rebbe on his arrival in America

munity in Israel and also to inspire his *chassidim* in America. The burgeoning Vizhnitz community was united by the all-encompassing personality of the great *Rebbe*.

The *Rebbe* visited America three times: in 1949, 1954 and 1957. These visits planted the seeds of Vizhnitzer *chassidus* in America. These seeds produced the beautiful fruits that are seen today: yeshivos, Talmud Torahs, *chadarim*, girls' schools and *shuls*, in Monsey, Boro Park, Williamsburg, the Catskill Mountains and Montreal.

If the *Rebbe's* visits were the highlight, then the *Rebbe's tisch* marked the zenith of his presence. The *shtibel* on Ross Street in Williamsburg would be packed to the rafters. Not only Vizhnitzer *chassidim* attended, but all those who sought spiritual uplift. The *Rebbe's* entrance was greeted with a hush. Then the *Rebbe* would welcome the Shabbos and all the assembled with a beautiful *niggun*. Through the night, the *tisch* would draw on the spiritual

essence of all the participants. Time was immaterial. The songs forged the large gathering into a single entity.

The *Rebbe* would then share his *shirayim* with the assemblage. Everyone was included, even those who were not *chassidim*. Afterwards, the *Rebbe* discussed the Torah reading of the week. During the meal, spontaneous dancing would take place. It was then that the *Rebbe* displayed his tremendous love for each *chassid*. As he stood in the center of the dancing swirls of *chassidim*, he would recognize old friends, or thank someone for a long-forgotten favor – the *Rebbe* never seemed to forget a face, a person, or a favor.

When the first group of people left, the tables would be reset with fruit and *kugel*. This *tisch* was especially for the younger people. Each student would be given the opportunity to say a *dvar Torah,* and the *Rebbe* would listen and comment. This *tisch* would continue late into the night. Still later, after more *niggunim* and dancing, the final *tisch*

Vizhnitzer Rebbe dancing at a wedding, 1955

was set. Now the *Rebbe* turned his full attention to the *bachurim*. He would encourage them, infusing them with *emunah* and *bitachon* to be resolute in their commitment to Torah and

chassidus on the American continent.

Although the *Rebbe* lived in *Eretz Yisrael*, his constant involvement in the lives and structure of the American community made him the spiritual link between them and the glorious past of Vizhnitz. His leadership continued until his passing on *Shabbos HaGadol*, 1972. His son, the *Rebbe*, Reb Mordechai, continues the great traditions of Vizhnitz in his leadership of the growing community of Vizhnitzer *chassidim* in America.

The impact of Vizhnitz *chassidus* on the remnants of Romanian/Hungarian Jewry is impressive. Founded by the *Rebbe*, *zl*, Reb Chaim Meir, and nurtured under the dynamic and loving leadership of his son, the *Rebbe, shlita,* Reb Mordechai, Vizhnitz *chassidus* has blossomed from a tender sapling in a tiny room on Division Avenue in Williamsburg, to a fortress of Torah encompassing the major Jewish communities on the East Coast and Montreal.

Reb Mordechai Hager,
The Monsey-Vizhnitz Rebbe

His constant involvement in the lives and structure of the American community made him the spiritual link between them and the glorious past of Vizhnitz.

Rabbi Shlomo Halberstam *1908-2000*

BOBOVER REBBE

He took the broken shards of Galician Jewry, shattered after Hitler's cataclysmic Holocaust destroyed everything that was dear to them, and rebuilt their lives.

They stood there, heads bent in sorrow, tears streaming down their faces. Some wailed, others cried; everyone was brokenhearted. It was as if their father had been taken from them. But, indeed, he was their father – the Bobover *Rebbe*. Rabbi Shlomo Halberstam was more than a *rebbe* to his *chassidim*, he was their loving father. He took the broken shards of Galician Jewry, shattered after Hitler's cataclysmic Holocaust destroyed everything that was precious to them, and rebuilt their lives. He gave them hope; he gave them courage; he gave their lives purpose.

The *Rebbe* had also suffered, losing everything that was precious and dear to him. The fires of the Holocaust claimed his father, Rav Benzion, his first wife and two young children, and much of his extended family. Yet he did not falter.

He did not waiver in his commitment to his *chassidim*, in his responsibility towards *Klal Yisrael*. He was the anchor upon which hundreds of traumatized and embittered Jews relied. Had it not been for his superhuman efforts on behalf of the remnants of Galician Jewry, Hitler's toll would have reached greater proportions.

The *Rebbe* arrived on these shores with a mission to rebuild Bobover *chassidus*, first in America and then beyond. Fully aware that unless the focus was placed on the children there would be no hope for a future, he began to build a yeshiva. "My sole purpose for existence is to further Torah learning. I can only dedicate the rest of my life to reclaiming for future generations that which has been destroyed."

These were not mere words; this was his mission. Today, more than half

Rabbi Benzion Halberstam,
father of Rabbi Shlomo Halberstam

a century after those words were uttered, the Bobover *kehillah,* headquartered in the Boro Park section of Brooklyn, spans the world. Thousands of young people are enrolled in *chadarim,* yeshivos, *kollelim* and schools for girls. All this was accomplished because the *Rebbe* refused to succumb to depression and despair. He triumphed where Hitler sought to destroy. He would not let Amalek succeed in his diabolical plan to destroy *Am Yisrael.* How true is the statement: "He saved Galician Jewry."

The Bobover *Rebbe* was a scion of an illustrious lineage traced back to the *Divrei Chaim,* Rav Chaim Sanzer. His *yichus* served as a springboard for his mission in life. He had inherited from his father, grandfather, and great-grandfather a love for *Klal Yisrael,* a responsibility to serve them, and bring them closer to Hashem *Yisbarach.* His life, from birth through his captivity in war-torn Europe, and his

last illness, was replete with miracles. It was as if Hashem wanted the *Rebbe* to continue his mission in this world. His parents had two daughters before him and for six years they did not have another child. On one occasion, his mother asked her famous uncle, the Gorlitzer *Rebbe,* for a blessing that she have a son. The Gorlitzer asked her to contribute an enormous sum to *tzedakah.* She borrowed the money and presented it to her uncle, who promptly distributed the entire amount to the poor. A year later the future Bobover *Rebbe* was born.

Shlomo was a bright, perceptive child. By the time he reached *bar mitzvah* he was famous for his brilliance and leadership capabilities. He traveled to study Torah and *chassidus* from the wellsprings of Torah of the Bluzhever *Rebbe* and Harav Itzikel Stutchiner. He married and continued his studies, soon becoming an accomplished *talmid chacham.* In 1931, his father decided to leave Bobov for five years and move to Tshebin.

In his absence, Rav Shlomo became the *"yinger rav,"* the young *rav* of the community. Even when his father returned, the young *rav* continued on as *posek* and *Rosh HaYeshiva.* He became famous for his leadership abilities as opportunities arose for him

> *All this was accomplished because the Rebbe refused to succumb to depression and despair. He triumphed where Hitler sought to destroy.*

Three generations of Bobov –
(L-R): Young boy is the present Bobover Rebbe, Rabbi Naftali Halberstam. Behind him is his father, Rabbi Shlomo Halberstam, and in front, his grandfather, Rabbi Benzion Halberstam

*The last home of the Bobover Rebbe,
Rabbi Benzion Halberstam, in Lemberg*

Every time he was spared, he considered it a sign from Heaven that he must renew and redouble his efforts on behalf of Klal Yisrael.

to manifest his unique qualities.

With the outbreak of World War II, a new chapter, albeit a tragic one, began for the Bobover Rebbe. In 1939, the *Kedushas Tzion*, the Bobover *Rebbe's* father, gathered his family and left his beloved Bobov for the last time. They went to Lemberg, hoping their lives would be spared. The *churban* (destruction) of Europe had begun.

In 1941, *Rav* Bentzion was killed, *al Kiddush Hashem,* by a gang of bloodthirsty Ukrainian hoodlums. Rav Shlomo was now the leader of the Bobover *chassidim*. The *Rebbe's mesiras nefesh* on behalf of all the Jews is legend. His devotion to Jewish children was exceptional. Miracle after miracle catalyzed the *Rebbe's* survival and his ability to continue his rescue work. One would think that, after being saved from the executioner's death grip, the *Rebbe* would refrain from taking chances. But, no - this was not the Bobover *Rebbe*. Every time he was spared, he considered it a sign from Heaven that he must renew and redouble his efforts on behalf of *Klal Yisrael*.

They finally reached Hungary, where they thought they would have a respite from their persecution. Their reprieve, however, was short-lived. The Nazis invaded Hungary in March

of 1944, and that country and its Jewish population became their latest *korbanos*. It was in Hungary that the *Rebbe* was separated from his wife and two younger children, who were tragically sent away to Auschwitz. The *Rebbe* was devastated, but he did not succumb to his despair and continued working. He was on a mission – to help *Klal Yisrael*. This goal transcended his personal pain. He and his son, *Rav* Naftali, disguised themselves as gentiles and escaped to Bucharest, Romania, where they were eventually liberated.

The war's end marked the *Rebbe's* beginning in global relief and rescue work. He traveled everywhere, giving hope and encouragement to the shattered remnants of the war. He battled an indifferent secular Jewish bureaucracy to give more financial aid to sustain the survivors, rallying help from any possible source he could.

*Bobover Rebbe, Rabbi Shlomo Halberstam,
with his son, Naftali Halberstam,
the present Bobover Rebbe.*

Bobover Rebbe dancing with his chassidim

On *Taanis Esther* 1947, the *Rebbe* arrived in New York to begin a new chapter in his life and in the annals of Bobover *chassidus*. A year later, the *Rebbe* married the daughter of the Tomashover *Rebbe*. Together, they had six children; one son, Rav Bentzion, the present *"Rav HaTza'ir,"* and five daughters, each married to *talmidei chachamim* of repute. It did not take long for the fledgling Bobover *chassidus* to outgrow their quarters in

The war's end marked the Rebbe's beginning in global relief and rescue work. He traveled everywhere, giving hope and encouragement to the shattered remnants of the war.

Bobover Rebbe at an "Upsherin."

Bobover Rebbe giving a berachah to his son-in-law before his chupah

the West Side of New York. They moved to Crown Heights, to an area that would permit them to expand.

The yeshiva he started with four students began to grow under the *Rebbe's* direction. Everything was children-oriented. They were the future. The *rebbeim* had to be paid on time. Every single Thursday night there had to be money to pay the *rebbeim*. If funds were deficient, the *Rebbe* would personally go out and raise the necessary money.

Bobov finally moved to their present world headquarters in Boro Park in 1967. The yeshiva continues to grow and expand at an incredible rate.

He was rebbe, father, and even mother to so many. He transcended the ambiguities and pettiness of this world.

Bobover Rebbe, zl, giving Chanukah gelt to Rabbi Naftali Halberstam, the present Bobover Rebbe

Branches exist throughout the world, all maintaining that special flavor that makes Bobov unique. The *Rebbe* is no longer here, but his impact is felt and evident in the fruits of his timeless labor. He was *rebbe*, father, and even a mother to so many. He transcended the ambiguities and pettiness of this world.

Bobover Rebbe putting tefillin on a bar mitzvah boy

Bobover Rebbe dancing with a chassan, 1970

The Bobover *Rebbe* lived and breathed *Klal Yisrael.* As an "*ohev shalom v'rodef shalom*," he abhorred *machlokes*, distancing himself from any sort of controversy. His life encompassed a devotion to *Klal Yisrael*, collectively and individually; a commitment to Torah study and its dissemination; and *mesiras nefesh* for *shalom*, harmony and unity among Jews. While many great people possess one or two of these attributes, the Bobover *Rebbe* embodied all three – to their fullest extent.

His life encompassed a devotion to Klal Yisrael, collectively and individually; a commitment to Torah study, and mesiras nefesh for shalom.

Bobover Rebbe dancing at a mitzvah tantz

(L-R): Moshe Brunner, son of Reb Zalman Brunner, who was a distinguished lay leader and builder of the Bobov community; present Bobover Rebbe, Rabbi Naftali Halberstam; Rabbi Benzion Halberstam,"Rav HaTza'ir"

Rabbi Yekusiel Yehudah Halberstam *1905-1994*

THE SANZ-KLAUSENBERGER REBBE

Responsibility to the *klal* and love for his fellow-Jew were hallmarks of the late Sanz-Klausenberger *Rebbe,* Rabbi Yekusiel Yehudah Halberstam. Overcoming personal tragedy and irreplaceable loss, he was able to be both a spiritual giant and creative communal builder for his people. These were not distinct separate roles, rather they were one and the same. The common denominator creating this unity of roles was the power of Torah, which shaped the very essence and persona of the *Rebbe* and enabled him to cope with all the vicissitudes of life.

The Sanz-Klausenberger *Rebbe* was born in 1905 (4 *Shevat,* 5665). His father was the *Rav* of Rudnik in Galicia. His great-grandfather, who greatly impacted on him and influenced his *derech hachaim* (way of life), was the great sage and *tzaddik* Rabbi Chaim Halberstam, the Sanzer *Rav,* known as the *Divrei Chaim.*

Already as a young child, the *Rebbe* was recognized as having been blessed with unique talents. Primarily, what was most evident was his remarkable *hasmadah* (diligence) in learning Torah and his extreme devotion in *davening* – often to the point of exhaustion.

Tragically, when he was only 13 years old, he was orphaned from his father. The young *bachur* delivered a three hour *hesped* (eulogy), replete with quoted sources from *Shas* and *Midrash*, which astounded the many great *rabbanim* who were privileged to hear it.

To advance his learning, at age 16, he left home and traveled to several cities throughout Europe – studying in Brisk and with various chassidic *rebbeim,* including the Belzer *Rav,* Bendiner *Rav,* Radimisheler *Rav* and Munkaczer *Rav.*

Both the Ostrovtzer *Rav* and the Radimisheler *Rav* granted him *semichah,* (ordination) and blessed him. Rabbi Meir Arik also gave him *semichah.*

Klausenberger Rebbe as a young man

Soon, Rabbi Halberstam became well known as a brilliant scholar.

He married the daughter of the Sigheter *Rav*, Rabbi Chaim Tzvi Teitelbaum. After his marriage, he assumed the responsibilities of his father's *kehillah* in Rudnik. Later, he became the *Rav* in Klausenberg. Wherever he was, the *Rebbe* was absorbed in Torah learning and *davening*. Teaching by example was his creed.

The *Rebbe's mesiras nefesh* during the Holocaust years is legendary. No matter how horrific conditions were in the deportation camp, concentration camps (Auschwitz, Dachau, Mildorf) and D.P. camps, he never transgressed any *mitzvos*. The *Rebbe* learned various *masechtos,* tractates of Talmud, from memory, even while doing slave labor. Not only that, but he *davened* daily, maintaining a regular schedule. Miraculously, the *Rebbe* managed, at great risk, to keep a pair of *tefillin,* which he shared with many others. The *Rebbe* also provided his fellow-Jews with

encouragement and moral support and tried to reassure them.

After the War, when many survivors were in DP camps, the *Rebbe* did not abandon them; he never thought about his own needs. Despite suffering extreme personal loss (his wife and eleven children were murdered), the *Rebbe* did not cry, for fear that others would think that he was being critical of the *darkei Hashem* (the ways of Hashem). Because of his own tragic losses, the *Rebbe* understood the survivors' needs and was concerned with restoring their *emunah*. He worked tirelessly to provide them with basic religious necessities – kosher kitchens, *tefillin*, and printing presses for *sefarim*, Torah literature necessary for learning. The *Rebbe* also founded the first yeshivos established after the Holocaust. He arranged marriages among the survivors and even provided *sheitels* (wigs) for the women. The *Rebbe* traveled to America to raise funds for all these endeavors and then returned to Germany.

In 1947, the *Rebbe* and a group of his followers emigrated to the United

The Rebbe's mesiras nefesh during the Holocaust years is legendary. The Rebbe also provided his fellow-Jews with encouragement and moral support and tried to reasure them.

Klausenberger Rebbe shortly after the war

Klausenberger Rebbe being greeted in Bilgurai, Galicia 1938

Wherever he was, the Rebbe was absorbed in Torah learning and davening. Teaching by example was his creed. He considered it his supreme duty to rebuild, beginning with the establishment of shuls and yeshivos.

States and settled in Williamsburg. He considered it his supreme duty to rebuild, beginning with the establishment of shuls and yeshivos. Among the survivors at that time (late 1940s), it was unheard of for young men to learn full time – they worked. The *Rebbe* wanted to change this and established *chadarim* and several girls' schools. He also set up the first Torah-oriented pre-school program for non-American children, so they would not waste their precious early years. The Klausenberg *kehillah* established a yeshiva, *beis medrash, kollel* and old age home over the next several years.

The *Rebbe* did not limit his activities to his *kehillah*. He also fought against the powerful secular Jewish organizations whose policies did not foster *Yiddishkeit*, especially for the new immigrants. The *Rebbe* spoke publicly about these

issues and those affecting Jews in Europe and Israel. He was not afraid to say what was necessary – his was a solitary yet powerful voice. The *Rebbe's mussar* (admonition) stemmed from his limitless love for every Jew.

In keeping with the *Rebbe's* wide-ranging involvements, his *chassidim* were the first survivor group to establish a complete community in *Eretz Yisrael* (1956) – Kiryat Sanz in the Netanya area, a resort town. It is the only major city in *Eretz Yisrael* where there is harmony between *dati'im and chiloni'im*, observant and secular Jews.

Klausenberger Rebbe visiting the medical center in Kiryat Sanz, Israel, to his right is Rabbi Meir Eisemann, director of the Laniado-Kiryat Sanz hospital

For over a decade, the *Rebbe* observed with keen interest how the *roshei yeshiva* of American yeshivos inspired young American *bachurim,* students to study Torah with *hasmadah* (diligence) and sincerity. He felt, however, that they could accomplish even more. He strongly believed that one must acquire knowledge and understanding of the entire *Shas* and commentaries before writing *chiddushim* (Torah novellae). Consequently, he implemented his own learning system by setting up a program in Kiryat Sanz, which he personally taught. The *Rebbe* also established two programs, the *Shas Kollel* and *Mifal HaShas*. These required the learning of 70 and 30 *blatt* (folios) of Talmud a month, respectively, and the successful completion of a written test following which generous stipends were awarded. These programs set higher standards for the quantity and quality of learning.

For those who could not go to *Eretz Yisrael,* the *Rebbe* established a yeshiva and community in Union City, NJ, offering the same opportunities as in *Eretz Yisrael.* Rabbi Yaakov Kamenetsky said, "The Klausenberger *Rebbe* is the greatest *marbitz Torah* (disseminator of Torah) in our generation; and since my lifetime spans three generations, I can say that he is the greatest in the past three generations."

In 1960, the *Rebbe* moved to *Eretz Yisrael* and prevailed, after lengthy negotiations, in obtaining licensure for the erection of a hospital in Kiryat Sanz. Recognizing the importance of the nursing staff – he viewed them as the "heart" of the hospital – the *Rebbe* gave *shiurim* to a select group of students. The Laniado Hospital Nursing School in

Klausenberger Rebbe

Kiryat Sanz is the only nursing school in Israel in which Torah subjects are an integral part of the curriculum. Every graduate has been licensed as a registered nurse.

Although the *Rebbe* suffered severe physical pain and had cardiac problems, he did not complain and willingly accepted his condition. He *davened* for the ability "to welcome trials and tribulations, adversity and challenge." It is noteworthy that the *Rebbe* did not suffer pain while he was learning Torah – such was the power of his learning with *kavanah* (total concentration).

The Klausenberger *Rebbe's* legacy is outstanding – his tireless efforts and accomplishments for *Klal Yisrael* exemplify *Torah, avodah* and *gemilus chasodim.*

The Klausenberger Rebbe's legacy is outstanding – his tireless efforts and accomplishments for Klal Yisrael exemplify Torah, avodah and gemilus chasadim.

Rabbi Shlomo Heiman

1888-1944

The insignificant village of Paritz, a suburb of Minsk, achieved eternal fame through one of its sons, Rabbi Shlomo Heiman. He was born in 1888, to his distinguished parents, Rabbi and Mrs. Michel Heiman. After receiving his early education in the Yeshiva of Halusk, Shlomo transferred to the Slobodka Yeshiva. It was in Slobodka that he became the *talmid muvhak* of Reb Boruch Ber Leibowitz. As a student in Slobodka, his tremendous capacity as a teacher of Torah was already recognized. Other students would present their *chiddushim* and questions to him for his critique and insight. Even his *rebbe*, Reb Boruch Ber, would review his *shiur* with him before delivering it in the Yeshiva. Reb Shlomo also spent time in the Radin Yeshiva, in close proximity to the *Chofetz Chaim*.

He married the daughter of a local rabbi in 1917. Immediately after his wedding, he became *rosh mesivta* (dean) in Krimentchug. Unfortunately, he was compelled to flee in order to avoid Bolshevik agitators. At the behest of the *Chofetz Chaim*, he remained for some time in Smilowitz, disseminating Torah there under very trying conditions. In 1922 or 1923, he acceded to the request of the celebrated *Rosh Yeshiva*, Rabbi Elchonon Wasserman, to become *rosh mesivta* in Baranowitz. In the summer of 1927, Rabbi Chaim Ozer Grodzenski invited him to become *Rosh Yeshiva* of Remailles Yeshiva in Vilna.

His final station on his journey as a leader of *Klal Yisrael* was Brooklyn, New York, where he was invited in the mid-1930s by Rabbi Shraga Feivel Mendlowitz to become *Rosh HaYeshiva* of Yeshiva and Mesivta Torah Vodaath, a position which he held until his untimely death in 1944.

It was not without a struggle that Reb Shlomo came to America. The Remailles Yeshiva attempted to retain their premier *Rosh Yeshiva*. Reb Shlomo's *shiur* attracted the elite of the Yeshiva world. His clarity of explanation and ability to introduce novel ideas in a simple and coherent manner, made him an educator par-excellence. Reb Shraga Feivel knew that for the struggling American yeshiva world, a man of Reb Shlomo's caliber was not a luxury, he was an imperative. Reb Shlomo was quick to adapt to the American yeshiva students, cloaking his brilliance in simplicity, tailored to the level of his new charges. On Shabbos afternoons, he would gather together with *bachurim* (yeshiva students) and *baalei batim*, in the home of Reb Shraga Feivel to deliver *divrei Torah* insights on the *parasha*. The spectacle of so many people assembled to learn Torah, and the ensuing procession to *Minchah* that followed, left a deep impression on those who witnessed it.

Rabbi Shlomo Heiman at the Mesivta Torah Vodaath dedication

Reb Shlomo was a master educator. His influence, in subtle ways, impressed his students in a manner that lasted a lifetime. During a *shiur* one *bachur* demonstrated amazing depth

Rabbi Boruch Ber Leibowitz

and understanding. After a few exchanges between the *rebbe* and student, Reb Shlomo commented, "You must have *davened* well this morning." It was the beginning of a new awareness for his *talmidim* of the inter-relationship between *tefillah* and Torah, a lesson that lasted a lifetime. Perhaps his greatest influence on his students was achieved by example. Reb Shlomo's sterling personality and his unwavering adherence to *emes* were exemplary. Like the famous Rabbi Akiva Eiger, whom he constantly quoted, he was never ashamed to admit that he did not know the answer to a question, infrequent though such a circumstance might have been. Indeed, he **lived** the Talmudic dictum, "Train your tongue to say, 'I do not know,' lest you become a liar and be tripped up by your own words" (*Derech Eretz Zuta*, chapter 3; *Berachos* 4a). Owing to this allegiance to truth, Rabbi Heiman was able to make the keen distinctions between authentic Torah concepts and specious ones.

Moreover, his unswerving dedication to and veneration of his *rebbe muvhak*, primary teacher, Rabbi Boruch Ber Leibowitz, was certainly reciprocated by that famed scholar, as the letter that he sent to Rabbi Heiman on the occasion of the latter's appointment to the position of *Rosh HaYeshiva* of Torah Vodaath clearly indicates: "All my mother's labor pains were worth undergoing, in light of my having produced a

His influence, in subtle ways, impressed his students in a manner that lasted a lifetime. Reb Shlomo's sterling personality and his unwavering adherence to emes, truth were exemplary.

Rabbi Shlomo Heiman speaking; to his left is the Stoliner Rebbe.

"The sweetness of his smile, the warmth of his heart were boundless...To strangers who often came to pay their respects, and even to servants, he was always kind and considerate."

student like you!" That special love was similarly reflected in the emotions that Rabbi Heiman's own students felt for him. In an article in the *Orthodox Tribune*, one of Rabbi Heiman's *talmidim muvhakim* (faithful and outstanding students) paid tribute to this great *Rosh Yeshiva*: "The sweetness of his smile, the warmth of his heart were boundless.... To strangers who often came to pay their respects, and even to servants, he was always kind and considerate." Indeed, even as he approached his demise, his concern for his life's helpmate, his beloved *Rebbetzin*, superseded his own critical, extremely painful condition.

A *talmid* related the following incident which gives us some insight into the type of *gadol* Rabbi Heiman was: A terrible blizzard struck New York and only four or five students managed to come to yeshiva that day. Rabbi Heiman delivered his *shiur* with his usual exuberance, exerting himself so that his voice filled the far corners of the *beis medrash*. After the *shiur*, one *talmid* approached him and inquired why the *rosh yeshiva* had taxed his energies to such an extent when so few *talmidim* were present. Rabbi Heiman replied, "You must understand, I was not speaking only to you, but to your children and all the generations to come. I had to make sure that they could hear me."

Although Reb Shlomo primarily concentrated his efforts on the Yeshiva and his students, he did not shy away from participating in national Jewish issues. He was a regular and popular speaker at Orthodox organizational banquets and special occasions. He saw to it that the Torah journals of that time dedicated space not only to the writings of the *rabbanim* and *Roshei Yeshiva*, but also to the young budding scholars. He was in constant contact with many of the American *gedolim* and together they planned ways to strengthen the Orthodox position in America. All this did not minimize his strong feelings and fidelity to his *rebbeim* back in Europe, to whom he continued to turn for counsel.

Unfortunately, his life was marked by physical weakness and great suffering. Although it did not prevent him from teaching, it did prevent him from committing much of his Torah legacy to writing. After undergoing intensive surgery, the doctors predicted that his chronic ulcers would be cured. His joy was boundless and he made a festive meal in the Yeshiva dining room to express his gratitude to Hashem. But it was not to be. The disease, unnoticed by the doctors, had spread to his liver and his condition deteriorated. Until his final stay in the hospital he continued, on a limited

(R-L seated): Rabbi Shraga Feivel Mendlowitz, Rabbi Shlomo Heiman and Mr. J.A. Samuel

should prepare two chairs for them. Who were these guests? One was the famous scholar Rabbi Akiva Eiger (1761-1837), whose method of preparing Torah studies he rigorously followed, and the other was the great Rabbi Chaim Ozer Grodzenski, who had ordained him – both of these *gedolim* had made the study of Torah paramount while they were alive. Indeed, Rabbi Shlomo Heiman's life was an enduring legacy of Torah. In turn, Yeshiva Torah Vodaath and its thousands of students constitute the *Rosh HaYeshiva's* ongoing legacy for our generation and for generations to come.

scale, to teach and inspire. As always, his sensitivity to his wife was exemplary and served as a paragon for his students.

As his end drew near, he told the students who were present at his demise that important guests were coming to his bedside, and that they

Indeed, Rabbi Shlomo Heiman's life was an enduring legacy of Torah.

Rabbi Yosef Eliyahu Henkin

1881~1973

Rarely does an individual emerge who even without the backing of an institution still impacts on the future of so many. This man did not head a famous yeshiva or institution – he **was** an institution. Rabbi Henkin headed the Ezras Torah Charity Organization. It was not only a distribution center that gave money and assistance to destitute *talmidei chachamim*, it was "a heart." Rabbi Henkin personally carried in his heart the pain and suffering of all those supported by Ezras Torah. Thousands were helped by him, but no one knew their identities.

Rabbi Henkin was born in 1881 to the *Rosh HaYeshiva* of Klimonovitz in Bylorussia. By his early teens, he had mastered many of the intricate areas of *Shas*. At 15 he entered the Yeshiva of Karelitz, where he remained for a short time. He then presented himself to Rabbi Isser Zalman Meltzer, the *Rosh Ha-Yeshiva* in Slutzk, for an entrance exam. The request was preposterous, as he was years younger than the other students. Moreover, he requested to be tested on two of the most difficult tractates – *Shabbos* and *Eruvin*. To Rabbi Meltzer's surprise, the young Yosef Eliyahu excelled; Rav Isser Zalman is said to have exclaimed, "The *bachur* knows it better than me!"

On his way to becoming a premier *posek* in America, he received *semichah* from Rabbi Isser Zalman Meltzer, Rabbi Yaakov Dovid Willowsky (the *Ridvaz*), Rabbi Baruch Ber Lebowitz, and Rabbi Yechiel Mechel Epstein (the *Aruch HaShulchan*). Afterwards, he served as *Rav* in numerous cities in Europe, but due to government persecution he fled to America. Rabbi Henkin held the position of *Rav* of Congregation Anshei Shtutsen in New York for a short time.

In 1925, he became the director of Ezras Torah (founded 1915). It was in this capacity that he impacted the broader American community. The mission of Ezras Torah was to raise and distribute money to needy *talmidei chachamim*, and at the time, to aid those who were forced to flee Europe during the difficult post-World War I years.

> It was not only a distribution center that gave money and assistance to destitute talmidei chachamim, it was "a heart." Rabbi Henkin personally carried in his heart the pain and suffering of all those supported by Ezras Torah.

Rabbi Yosef Eliyahu Henkin with Rabbi Moshe A. Margolin

His stature as a communal leader reached great heights. The responsibility of caring for hundreds of *talmidei chachamim* devolved on him. He raised funds and distributed them with immense sensitivity. Rabbi Henkin never revealed the identities of the recipients to anyone besides the IRS. He supported an army of *talmidei chachamim,* not only physically but emotionally as well. He felt their pain and shared their happiness as if it was his own.

The needs of the *klal* transcended his personal needs. His salary was meager by any standard, but he refused to take a raise, preferring to dispense the extra funds to the needy. When the directors of Ezras Torah voted to grant him a raise, he threatened to resign! Rabbi Henkin was integrity personified – he kept a logbook in which he noted any minutes that he was involved in personal affairs during Ezras Torah hours, and these minutes were made up to the organization. It is no wonder that he was so successful in his endeavors for others.

Benevolence was not the only area in which he impacted the American Jewish community. Rabbi Henkin was the consummate *posek*. He was fluent in all areas of Talmudic law. Moreover, with his brilliant acumen, he was able to apply his vast erudition to questions relevant to the modern era. His stature demonstrated to the community the preeminence of the *talmid chacham*. After he blazed the trail, future *poskim* were able to hold sway over the community in halachic areas.

It was Rabbi Henkin who formulated the correct spelling of American names and cities necessary for *gittin* and other religious documents. Under his guidance, the famed Ezras Torah calendar, which delineates the proper order and customs for prayer, was formulated. This calendar has become the standard for thousands of synagogues. His opinion was, and still is, sought after and accepted within all branches of practical halachos. A small portion of his halachic responsa were collected and published in two volumes.

Rabbi Henkin never sat on a dais and never led a famous yeshiva or community. His standing was generated by his personal merit and by his influence on the community. His impact was made by his very presence, a presence that is still felt today.

> *The needs of the klal transcended his personal needs.*
> *His salary was meager by any standard, but he refused to take a raise, preferring to dispense the extra funds to the needy.*

(L-R): Rabbi Moshe Feinstein speaking with Rabbi Henkin

Rabbi Pinchas Dovid Horowitz 1876-1941

THE BOSTONER REBBE

In 1916, the first American chassidic court was established in Boston ... For twenty years this unassuming man toiled, never compromising the religious ideals with which he had been raised.

Boston – a true American city, the birthplace of the American Revolution – is also the seat of the first American-grown chassidic Court. The Bostoner *Rebbe*, Rabbi Pinchas Dovid Horowitz, was born in Jerusalem to a third-generation Jerusalem family. This family traced its roots to the *Chozeh* of Lublin and the Rebbe Reb Shmelke of Nikolsburgh, two outstanding names in the chassidic world. Pinchas Dovid studied in Jerusalem and Tzefas until 1913. By then, he was proficient in Jewish wisdom, in both Talmud and *Kabbalah*. It was certainly not part of his life-plan to go to America.

The famed Lelover *Rebbe*, Rabbi Dovid Biederman, Reb Pinchas Dovid's uncle, encouraged him to move to America and establish a chassidic community. For years, Pinchas Dovid avoided acting upon this advice. In 1913, he left for Galicia to resolve a financial dispute involving the chassidic community in Jerusalem and some Galician benefactors. In 1914, Pinchas Dovid found himself in the middle of war-torn Europe. He attempted to return to Jerusalem, only to be arrested in Greece for returning to Turkish-held territories. The Chief Rabbi of Salonika interceded on his behalf and succeeded in procuring a visa to America for him. And so, in 1914, alone, Rabbi Pinchas Dovid arrived in New York.

He became involved with the Brownsville Jewish community, but soon found himself inspired by his uncle's wish that he establish a chassidic court. In 1916, he moved to Boston, joined by a small group of idealistic followers. With this move, the American court of Bostoner *chassidim* was established. Rabbi Pinchas Dovid Horowitz became the first Bostoner *Rebbe*. In 1920, his wife and son Moshe joined him. After purchasing a building in Boston's West End, the *Rebbe* established a small congregation, Machzikei Torah, and also the New England *Chassidic* Court. For twenty years this unassuming man toiled, never compromising the religious ideals with which he had been raised. The Bostoner community helped new immigrants, finding them jobs and

The present Bostoner Rebbe, Rabbi Levi Yitzchak Horowitz, reciting Tehillim at his father's grave.

providing the families with social aid. He was involved with their every need, and soon developed a working relationship with the prestigious medical institutions in Boston. This relationship was to flourish in later years with his son's involvement in the community. The community grew around the *Rebbe*. Unlike other chassidic *rebbeim*, the *Rebbe* did not demand that his *chassidim* don the distinctive chassidic garb. Against the background of compromise, the *Rebbe* stood out as a bulwark. He personally adhered to the customs of chassidic Jerusalem. He only ate meat if he personally supervised the *shechitah*, and sheltered his entire family from the secular world. Rabbi Pinchas Dovid did not impose his *chumros* (stringencies) on his *chassidim*, but he did encourage them to take pride in their *Yiddishkeit* and not look for the easy way out.

The *Rebbe* yearned for Jerusalem and attempted to return. In 1929, the Arab riots and unrest, coupled with the Depression in America, made it impossible for him to go. In 1934, Rabbi Pinchas David and his family returned to Israel and celebrated the *bar mitzvah* of their son, Levi Yitzchak (the present Bostoner *Rebbe*).

The *Rebbe* realized that the only way to stem the tide of "Americanization" of the immigrant children was to provide for their Jewish education. Although the number of students in his yeshiva grew to one hundred and fifty students, overall the public school system affected the children's commitment to *Yiddishkeit*. He tried to convince the *rabbanim* of Boston to open a full-fledged day school, where students would study Torah and secular subjects in a Jewish atmosphere, but he argued to no avail. Years later, when Rabbi Joseph B. Soloveitchik moved to Boston, the *Rebbe* realized that the university-educated Rabbi Soloveitchik could attract lay support. With the *Rebbe's* encouragment, Maimonides School opened in 1937.

With the demographic changes in the West End of Boston, the old and almost blind *Rebbe* had to make the difficult decision to move. The neighborhood had deteriorated and the *chassidim* no longer felt safe. Consequently, in 1939, the ailing *Rebbe*, sadly left Boston for Williamsburg and established the Bostoner dynasty in New York. He passed away two years later, in 1941.

His legacy was continued by his two sons. The oldest, Reb Moshe, was the Bostoner *Rebbe* of Brooklyn for many years (he passed away in 1982). His second son, Reb Levi Yitzchak, returned to Brookline, Massachusetts in 1944 and successfully rebuilt his father's court. The Bostoner *chassidim* remain to this day a dynamic and vibrant chassidic sect with communities in Boston, New York, Switzerland and Australia. Har Nof, Jerusalem is also a major stronghold of Bostoner *chassidim*.

Rabbi Pinchas Dovid Horowitz with his young son, the present Bostoner Rebbe, Rabbi Levi Yitzchak Horowitz

Elizabeth Peabody House, ca. 1915, the first Chassidic Center in Boston's West End

Rabbi Yitzchak Hutner

1906-1980

Where did the world of chassidic inspiration and Lithuanian intellect blend? What type of personality encompassed these very different interests and profundities in one synthesized harmony of brilliance, intellect, passion and warmth? Rabbi Yitzchak Hutner, *Rosh HaYeshiva* of Mesivta Rabbi Chaim Berlin, was this unique individual. Indeed, his interests spanned the entire range of the human experience. His personality incorporated a kaleidoscope of facets, each independently brilliant and beautiful in their synthesis. Yet as exceptional as he was, he had the ability to transmit his perspective to his students who, in turn, integrated it into their being.

Rabbi Hutner was born in Warsaw in 1906. At the young age of fifteen he entered the famous Slobodka Yeshiva. The great pedagogue, Rabbi Nosson Tzvi Finkel, the *Alter* of Slobodka, recognized the young Yitzchak's potential and took a special interest in him.

It was the *Alter* who implanted in him the seeds that flourished into the great educator par excellence that he became.

In 1925, Rabbi Hutner traveled to *Eretz Yisrael* and studied in the Chevron branch of Slobodka for four years. In addition to his yeshiva learning, he developed relationships with the full gamut of Torah sages living in *Eretz Yisrael* at the time. These included the *Saba Kadisha* (Rabbi Sholom Eliezer Alfandari), Rabbi Avrohom Aharon Burstein, Rabbi Yosef Chaim Sonnenfeld, Rabbi Isser Zalman Meltzer, and Rabbi Avrohom Yitzchak Kook. He absorbed the Torah and character traits they each had to offer, incorporating aspects of each *gadol* into his own personality. In early 1929, he returned to Europe for a short while, but soon went back to *Eretz Yisrael*. During his short stay in Europe he published his first volume of novellae, entitled *Toras HaNazir* which received enthusiastic approbations from the leading Torah leaders of the day.

His interests spanned the entire range of the human experience...as exceptional as he was, he had the ability to transmit his perspective to his students who, in turn, integrated it into their being.

Rabbi Yitzchak Hutner

educator, *rebbe*, and *Rosh HaYeshiva* par excellence with his position as principal of the Rabbi Jacob Joseph Yeshiva. Two years later, he founded the Mesivta Rabbi Chaim Berlin and became its *Rosh HaYeshiva*. It was through his association with the yeshiva that his fame spread throughout the world.

Under his leadership, the yeshiva prospered and took its place among the great Talmudic institutions. It was not only in quality that the yeshiva grew but also in diversity – a *bais hamedrash*/high school and a *kollel*, Gur Aryeh, were established. With his personality, *gadlus baTorah*, wide-ranging knowledge and pedagogic skills, Rabbi Hutner was able to attract and inspire an equally broad range of students. Many of his students gained fame in the Torah world. Each student attempted to emulate a facet of his great *rebbe* and mentor. Using his superior instructional skills, learned at

The impact of his philosophies overflowed to the Torah world, leaving his unique imprimatur on the thought process of many.

Rabbi Hutner married in Warsaw and continued his studies in Palestine until he immigrated to America in 1934. Upon his arrival, he took upon himself the project of completing his work on the *Pirush Rabbeinu Hillel Al HaSafra*. He began his life's work as

Chinuch Atzmai Dinner, New York Hilton, December 1964. (L-R): Rabbi Simcha Elberg, prominent leader of Agudas HaRabbonim, Rabbi Yitzchak Hutner, Rabbi Moshe Feinstein and Rabbi Avrohom Jofen

the feet of his mentor, he was able to personalize his attention to each student. Rabbi Hutner's famous *"ma'amorim,"* immortalized in the multi-volume work *Pachad Yitzchak,* left a deep impression on the minds and hearts of his students. The impact of his philosophies overflowed to the Torah world, leaving his unique imprimatur on the thought process of many. Strong bonds were forged between Rabbi Hutner and his students, who remained dedicated to their *rebbe* and to following his path, even after his passing.

Rabbi Yitzchak Hutner and Rabbi Eliezer Silver

At a meeting of the Moetzes Gedolei HaTorah attended by (L-R): Rabbi Nachum Perlow (Novominsker Rebbe), Rabbi Moshe Horowitz (Bostoner Rebbe), Rabbi Moshe Feinstein, Rabbi Yitzchak Hutner, Rabbi Yaakov Yitzchak Ruderman, Rabbi Boruch Sorotzkin

ough perception of Torah. Emphasizing concentration and in-depth analysis, he sought perfection in understanding and thoroughness in knowledge. He had a natural disdain for the superficial and artificial, and he recoiled from the grandiose and pretentious. He was genuine and he sought that quality in everyone and everything. Broad-minded by nature, his genius enabled him to maintain his profundity in any area of interest to him.

He did not seek acclaim, maintaining a low profile as he built the foundation of Torah that would ultimately generate high visibility for his yeshiva

While many of his contemporaries focused upon spreading Torah to the masses, reaching out to the spiritual wasteland that was America in those days, Rabbi Hutner devoted his energies to developing his students qualitatively. He saw his *talmidim* as the standard-bearers of a more thor-

Rabbi Moshe Feinstein with Rabbi Yitzchak Hutner

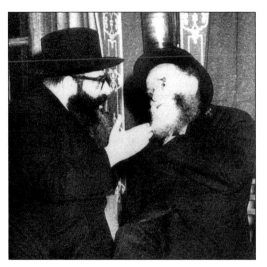

Rabbi Hutner with Rabbi Aharon Kotler

Rabbi Yisrael Zev Gustman and Rabbi Hutner

and students. He built a solid fortress of Torah-rooted scholars, who would one day impact on Torah in America. His reputation brought hundreds to the yeshiva to hear, to listen, to be inspired. This was the only podium he ever graced – his yeshiva. His style of speech and vernacular were poetic, adding an aesthetic quality to his *divrei Torah*.

Rabbi Hutner was a man of principle who did not shy away from confrontation. His advice was sought by many, particularly in the area of communal issues. He was fearless. He took issue with the attitude in vogue at the time, that Talmud study should be augmented by secular

studies. Rabbi Hutner did allow, however, select individuals to pursue a university education.

His vision of Orthodoxy was that it remain pure and unadulterated. He refused to sanction Orthodox

> *He built a solid fortress of Torah-rooted scholars, who would one day impact on Torah in America.*

(R-L): Rabbi Yitzchak Hutner his son-in-law Rabbi Yonason David, Rabbi Aharon Schechter

Novominsker Rebbe and Rabbi Yitzchak Hutner

Mesivta Bais Hamedrash

(L-R): Rabbi Yitzchak Hutner, Rabbi Moshe Feinstein, Rabbi Yaakov Yitzchok Ruderman

(L-R): Rabbi Aharon Kotler, Rabbi Reuven Grozovsky, and Rabbi Yitzchak Hutner at a Torah Umesorah dinner

> *His personality and sagacious advice left an indelible imprint.*

involvement in any organization that allowed secular Judaism to participate equally. He felt that doing so was in part legitimizing an approach to Judaism that was not Torah-oriented. This could never be. It was either Torah or it was not Judaism. His crystal-clear perception was sought after at the highest levels. He was invited to serve on the *Moetzes Gedolei HaTorah*, Council of Torah Sages. Here too, his personality and sagacious advice left an indelible imprint.

His life's achievements were many. In addition to his *sefarim* were his outstanding *shiurim* and *ma'amorim*, lec-

tures to thousands of students whose minds were honed by his penetrating analysis and artistic delivery. His mastery of the works of *Maharal* was unparalleled, rendering this great master's works accessible to those who had the resolve to plumb its depths. The teachings and customs of the *Vilna Gaon*, the profound insights of the *Ishbitzer* and Rav Tzadok *HaKohen*, the *chassidic* thoughts of Kotzk and Ger, all became lucid, comprehensible and valued in his *bais medrash*. The philosophical insights of the great *mussar gaonim* of Slobodka, Kelm, and Novardok were infused with renewed life as their perceptions became

Rabbi Yitzchak Hutner and Rabbi Yaakov Kamenetsky

Rabbi Yitzchak Hutner and Rabbi Moshe Feinstein dancing together at a simcha

His students are a reflection of their great rebbe, exemplifying stature in Torah, dignity, and a striving for further spiritual growth and perfection.

profound truths that were not merely spoken, but lived. His magnum opus, the *Pachad Yitzchak*, a collection of his *maamorim* continue to inspire the serious student who is able to fathom its profundities. But his greatest achievement was the *makom Torah* that he established that continues to carry on his legacy.

In 1975, he fulfilled his life's dream of opening a yeshiva in *Eretz Yisrael*. Yeshivas Pachad Yitzchak in Yerushalayim became his second home, as he trav-eled between America and Israel, teaching and inspiring students in his own unique manner, on both sides of the Atlantic Ocean. Rabbi Hutner's students are a reflection of their great *rebbe*, exemplifying stature in Torah, dignity, and a striving for further spiritual growth and perfection. They are the greatest tribute to the dynamic spirit bequeathed by their mentor. It is through them and his scholarly works that his inspiration remains vibrant to this very day.

Rabbi Avrohom Jofen *1887-1970*

Driven by total honesty and dedication to Hashem, Rabbi Jofen helped Torah's voice be heard in his role as Rosh Yeshiva of the Novardok Yeshiva and leader of the Novardok Torah Network.

Novardok – a word that is synonymous with total dedication to Hashem. In Europe, the Novardok Torah Network included over seventy schools and yeshivos. The entire network was under the constant guidance of the founder, Rabbi Yosef Yoizel Horowitz (1850-1920), popularly known as the *Alter mi*Novardok. The yeshivos founded by the Novardok Yeshiva were incorporated into a network known as Yeshivas Beis Yosef. Many famous people counted themselves among the alumni of Novardok. The list includes Rabbi Avrohom Jofen. He was also the son-in-law and successor of Rabbi Horowitz, and leading exponent of the Novardok school of *mussar*.

Rabbi Jofen was born in 1887, in a small village near Pinsk. His parents encouraged him in his studies, and he was very successful. In due time, he continued his studies in the Yeshiva at Slutzk and other great yeshivos. He came to the attention of the sharp-eyed *Rosh HaYeshiva* of Novardok, who brought him to his yeshiva. There he blossomed into a *talmid chacham* in his own right. He was eventually installed as a teacher in the yeshiva. When the *Rosh Yeshiva* sought a husband for his daughter in 1913, Reb Avrohom was chosen.

The Novardok Institutes continued to flourish in Poland after they escaped the persecutions of the communist regime in Russia. The main center of the Novardok Network was established in Bialystok. Reb Avrohom became an ardent follower of the *Alter's* approach to *mussar*, and was subsequently appointed *Rosh Yeshiva*, assisting his father-in-law in administering the various branches of the school. Upon the latter's passing, Reb Avrohom ascended to the leadership of the yeshiva and the Novardok Torah Network.

In the late thirties, the yeshiva in Bialystok dedicated a new building. Although much effort had been expended to build it, Reb Avrohom perceived the dangers of the approaching Germans. Reb Avrohom selflessly divided all of the yeshiva's money among the students and encouraged them to make their way to America.

The students refused to leave without him. Together, they traveled to Vilna.

Chinuch Atzmai Dinner, June 1963. (L-R): Rabbi Moshe Feinstein, Rabbi Avrohom Jofen, Rabbi Avraham Kalmanowitz, and Rabbi Chaim Mordechai Katz

Through his efforts the yeshiva remained a cohesive unit and continued to function according to its usual schedule. They traveled through Siberia, Japan and Shanghai, until they finally reached America.

Rabbi Avrohom Jofen

Shortly after his arrival in New York, he dedicated the Beis Yosef Yeshiva, named for his illustrious father-in-law. The new yeshiva continued along the hallowed paths of its European predecessors. The yeshiva's educational focus and goals were on leading non-materialistic lives, finding satisfaction in learning, and character development through the study and practice of *mussar*. [It should be noted that the *mussar* yeshiva of Lithuania was the prototype of the contemporary yeshiva. All the major yeshivos (Slobodka, Mir, Telshe, Kelm, Novardok, Kletzk) were products of this movement and their leaders its disciples.] Although far removed from the indulgent lifestyle of America, the yeshiva held its own. Reb Avrohom was not satisfied with the spiritual attainments of the fledgling yeshiva. He longed for the spirituality that had been destroyed in Europe, and refused to accept the illusion that Torah, in its European

The yeshiva's educational focus and goals were on leading non-materialistic lives, finding satisfaction in learning, and character development through the study and practice of mussar.

(L-R): Rabbi Moshe Feinstein, Rabbi Avrohom Jofen

Driven by total honesty and dedication to Hashem, he helped Torah's voice be heard. Faithful to the traditions of the Alter, he opened many more branches of the Novardok Network.

sense, had been transplanted in America.

Nevertheless, disappointment did not cause him to abandon the Torah world. He toiled together with the other *roshei yeshiva*, first in the Vaad Hatzala and then in the Agudath Israel. As a member of the Council of Sages his impact was felt on the American scene. Driven by total honesty and dedication to Hashem, he helped Torah's voice be heard. Faithful to the traditions of the *Alter*, he opened many more branches of the Novardok Network. In Israel, France, and England, schools were established, and Rabbi Jofen was their final authority and leader.

Rabbi Jofen was a man of impeccable spiritual character. Indeed, as the following episode demonstrates, Rabbi Jofen "lived" what he taught. This incident occurred several decades ago at the marriage of Rabbi Jofen's granddaughter. As one can imagine, there were numerous Torah personalities of great distinction at this wedding. Hence, there was some

"competition" for the various *berachos* and honorariums during the marriage ceremony. Rabbi Jofen undertook to organize the proceedings and to give honor where he felt it was due. Everything seemed to make sense, until an individual of very little renown was summoned to the *chupah* and asked to recite a *berachah*. What seemed even more strange was that no one, not even the bride or groom, had any idea who he was.

Rabbi Jofen was "not available" for comment, and refused to explain his choice. It was not until Rabbi Jofen left this world and was called to take his rightful place in the Heavenly Yeshiva that the mystery surrounding this rabbi was cleared up by Rebbetzin Jofen.

A number of years before their granddaughter's wedding, they were invited to the wedding of a certain rabbi's daughter. Not knowing either set of parents or the young couple, Rabbi Jofen apologized for not being able to attend the ceremony. The rabbi called and implored Rabbi

Jofen to reconsider and grace his daughter's *simchah*. Finally, Rabbi Jofen relented and agreed to attend.

The wedding was held quite some distance from the Jofen home, and since no travel arrangements had been made, the elderly couple used public transportation. Two subway trains and one bus later, they arrived. The rabbi, upon noticing Rabbi Jofen, greeted him warmly.

Surprisingly, Rabbi Jofen was neither publicly recognized nor given any honor during the ceremony. After the wedding, Rabbi Jofen and his wife trudged home on the bus and two subways.

The *Rebbetzin* continued, "You see, the *mussar* of Novardok preaches that one must repay a slight with a favor, a slap with a kiss: *Tachas hakpadah, hatavah* – instead of taking revenge, act graciously; in return for disdain, respond with generosity."

Thus, when Rabbi Jofen's own granddaughter was married, he invited the same unknown rabbi, who had years earlier acted improperly to him, to

attend his *simchah*. Moreover, he bestowed upon him the honor of reciting a blessing under the *chupah*! This was the unique character of Rabbi Jofen.

He published his own works: *Derech Eisan*, lectures on *Masechtos Chullin* and *Bava Metzia*, and his ethical discourses, entitled *Sefer HaMussar VeHadaas*, and also the writings of his great father-in-law. Notwithstanding all of these achievements, he felt that he was not ascending the heights of spirituality. He longed for an atmosphere removed from the hustle and bustle of New York. He felt that the materialism and secular pursuits of America were inhibiting the growth of Torah. It may have been for this reason that, in 1964, he left for *Eretz Yisrael*. The institutions that he had founded continued functioning after he left. His students and family upheld the vision that he demanded of them.

The purity and quality of the Novardok lifestyle has made an indelible mark on American Torah life.

The purity and quality of the Novardok lifestyle has made an indelible mark on American Torah life.

Rabbi Jacob Joseph 1843-1902

The famous *Maggid* of Vilna, Rabbi Jacob Joseph, accepted the position as the first Chief Rabbi of New York in 1888. At the time of his appointment, he was serving as the *dayan* of Vilna and the de facto *Rav* of the city. His dynamic and effective preaching had earned him the title of "*Maggid* of Vilna."

Rabbi Joseph, born in 1843, in Krozhe, a province of Kovno, studied in the Volozhin Yeshiva where he was known as "*Rav* Yaakov *Charif*," because of his sharp and keen mind. He later became one of the foremost *talmidim* of Rabbi Yisrael Salanter, the founder of the *Mussar* movement, in his Kovno Yeshiva.

This multitalented individual, in addition to being a great *talmid chacham* and speaker, was also a man of sterling character. Rabbi Joseph had several misgivings about coming to America. He was aware that there were problems and that, by and large, the less religious Eastern European Jews had been the ones to emigrate. Nevertheless, financial considerations were a major issue and, consequently, he accepted the position in order to support his family.

The Association of American Orthodox Hebrew Congregations – led by the oldest and most prominent Polish-Russian congregation in New York, Beth Hamedrash Hagadol on the Lower East Side – was comprised of approximately 30 congregations. They were thrilled when Rabbi Joseph accepted the position. Their goal was to have one central rabbinic authority, who would bring order to the chaotic conditions that existed in the field of *kashrus*, as well as expand Jewish education and devise programs to halt *chilul Shabbos*.

Rabbi Joseph certainly possessed the credentials to meet these challenges. Unfortunately, he was confronted with problems that he never imagined. Despite his valiant efforts and the positive changes he managed to institute in the kosher meat and poultry industry, it was a losing battle. He was opposed by corrupt and greedy businessmen, as well as unscrupulous butchers. For every step forward, he was forced to take many more steps backwards. Nonetheless, he did achieve some notable accomplishments – a sufficient number of qualified *shochtim* were hired, irremovable seals ("*plumba*") identifying kosher birds were introduced, and *mashgichim* were hired to check the slaughterhouses.

The first yeshiva founded in New York on the Lower East Side, in 1866, was Eitz Chaim. It expanded from an elementary school to include a high school, teaching both Jewish and secular subjects. Rabbi Joseph took an active role in the yeshiva.

He tried to bring structure to Jewish religious life, but he never completed this undertaking. The greatest obstacles to success were the active opposition of some people and groups, and the apathy of others. Rabbi Joseph also had to contend with attacks and quarrels from anti-religious factions and Socialist and atheistic Yiddish newspapers and journalists. Such constant conflict, opposition, and struggle doomed the Chief Rabbinate and the Association. Eventually, the Association could not financially maintain the office of Chief Rabbi. The butchers then assumed the responsibility of paying Rabbi Joseph, in essence rendering him a *mashgiach*.

Throughout all these tribulations, Rabbi Joseph maintained his dignity. He would not permit his supporters to stoop to the level of his attackers by responding in kind.

In 1895, the butchers discontinued paying Rabbi Joseph's salary and the congregations of the Association could not assume the responsibility. Shortly thereafter, he suffered a stroke which incapacitated him for the last years of his life.

Rabbi Joseph was only 59 years old when he passed away. His funeral was one of the largest in New York. How ironic that in death he was accorded greater respect than in life! The ill-fated attempt to establish a chief rabbinate in New York died with him.

His legacy is memorialized to this very day by the renowned Rabbi Jacob Joseph Yeshiva (R.J.J.), established in his memory – first located in the Lower East Side and now with branches in Staten Island, New York and Edison, New Jersey.

Throughout all these tribulations Rabbi Joseph maintained his dignity. He would not permit his supporters to stoop to the level of his attackers by responding in kind.

❧ Rabbi Dr. Leo Jung *1892-1987*

A well-known Jewish personality of the twentieth century came to America as a young man from Europe. His impact on the American Jewish scene, as well as his valiant efforts and achievements on behalf of his brethren in Israel, Europe, and North Africa are legendary. Rabbi Dr. Leo (Eliyahu) Jung was this man – a leading rabbi in New York for over six decades – and his legacy is notable.

He was born in 1892, in Ungarish Brod (Hungary), where his father, Rabbi Meir Tzvi Jung, was a rabbi and also founded a Jewish trade school. Later, the family moved to London where Rabbi Meir Jung again served as a rabbi and established a Jewish trade school. Young Leo began his yeshiva education in Eperjes, Czechoslovakia, at the yeshiva of his maternal grandfather, Rabbi Jacob Silberman. From there he went to the yeshiva in Hundsdorf for about a year. Then he learned in the Hildesheimer Rabbinical Seminary in Berlin, Germany for three years. At the same time, he attended the University of Vienna and University of Berlin for two years. Due to the outbreak of World War I, he returned to London (where his parents lived) for several years. In London, he attended the University of London, then Cambridge University, eventually receiving a PhD from the University of London. While in London, he received *semichah* from Rabbi Mordechai Schwartz and Rabbi Avraham Kook. In 1920, he traveled back to Berlin to receive *semichah* from Rabbi Dovid Hoffman.

During his years in London (1914-1919), aside from his studies, he was very involved in communal work. Rabbi Jung served as director of the Sinai League, an organization which promoted the study of Jewish law and history among young Jewish immigrants. He was also the editor of a Jewish journal, *The Sinaist*, written by his father, and he contributed many articles as well.

In 1919, Knesset Israel, a *shul* in Cleveland, Ohio, offered the position of rabbi to Rabbi Meir Tzvi Jung, who decided to send his son instead. Rabbi Leo Jung agreed to assume the position. Soon after, in 1922, he was offered the rabbinical post at The Jewish Center in New York City, and he accepted – serving the congregation for over sixty years.

The Jewish Center was an Orthodox *shul*, with a mostly upper-middle class membership. Many of the members were immigrants, who had been in America for a number of years. Their children found it difficult to relate to the ways of their parents, and European Jewry in general. At that time, most Orthodox *shuls* were geared toward the older European immigrants who spoke Yiddish. Consequently, the rabbis who were primarily immigrants themselves spoke in Yiddish, a language many younger people did not understand. These children attended public schools, and had only a rudimentary Jewish education, if any. Rabbi Dr. Jung undertook the task of establishing a more "modern" American Orthodoxy, recognizing that the future of Orthodoxy depended on the children, not the parents. The philosophy of *Torah im Derech Eretz*, of combining the best of American culture and Jewish tradition,

was not considered a contradiction to him, but rather, as he said, "a combination of modern method applied to ancient scholarship." He stressed morality and, particularly, *mitzvos* which pertained to man and his fellow man – the Jew as an upstanding citizen and a kind, compassionate individual. With his knowledge of Torah and science, Rabbi Jung was able to explain many concepts and ideas that were previously unknown to his listeners.

His sermons, delivered in English, were aimed at the personal, moral and practical. Rabbi Jung stressed personal growth and improvement of every Jew. He felt that decorum was an absolute necessity during *davening* and expected absolute quiet in the *shul*. He also instituted a lot of congregational singing, as well as verse by verse recitation of certain passages, sometimes led by him, and other times led by the congregants. All these practices

Rabbi Avraham Kook

His sermons, delivered in English, were aimed at the personal, moral and practical. Rabbi Jung stressed personal growth and improvement of every Jew.

THE JUNIOR CITIZEN

PUBLISHED FOR THE PARENTS AND CHILDREN OF OUR
JEWISH EDUCATIONAL INSTITUTIONS

| No. 1 | COMMITTEE ON ORTHODOX JEWISH EDUCATION OF THE WEST SIDE | September, 1946 |

ADVISORY COMMITTEE — C.O.J.E.W.S.

RABBI HERBERT S. GOLDSTEIN
West Side Institutional Synagogue

RABBI JACOB HOFFMAN
Congregation Ohab Zedek

RABBI LEO JUNG
Jewish Center

RABBI D. DE SOLA POOL
Spanish and Portuguese Synagogue

Rabbi Leo Jung and representatives of the American Biblical Encyclopedia Society, shown presenting President Harry S. Truman with the first English Edition of Torah Shleimah at the White House on January 9, 1953. The author is the scholar of renown Rabbi Menahem M. Kasher. (L-R): Mr. Jacob H. Arond, Rabbi Leo Jung, President Harry S. Truman, Dr. John Meyers, Judge Walter H. Maloney and Mr. Alex A. Bernstein.

Rabbi Jung did not just encourage women of his congregation to volunteer and perform acts of chesed, but was a living example of these attributes.

were aimed at greater participation by the membership. The *shul* had a boys-only day school, which taught both Judaic and secular studies. The school lasted until the 1930s, and subsequently an afternoon and Sunday school program was established.

During the 1920s, society viewed the woman's role as that of a mother and homemaker. Most of the women of The Jewish Center were wives of well-to-do individuals, and, with ample domestic help, these women had a great deal of leisure time. Rabbi Jung encouraged them to volunteer in communal affairs, especially to be involved in taking care of the poor and needy. He also emphasized the importance of the mother's role in child-rearing, referring to women as "the power behind the throne." He stressed

that mothers are essential for the moral education of their children.

Rabbi Jung did not just encourage the women of his congregation to volunteer and perform acts of *chesed*, but was a living example of these attributes. He was involved in many communal and global organizations. Not only did he become a board member or serve on an executive committee for an organization, but he personally became an active participant – distributing funds, traveling to the areas which he was helping support, and forging close personal relationships with many of the people he aided. Following is only a

Betrothal of Miss Irma Rothschild of Zurich to Rabbi Jung Announced

The betrothal of Miss Irma Rothschild of Zurich, Switzerland, to Rabbi Leo Jung, spiritual leader of Knesseth Israel congregation, has been announced.

Miss Rothschild is the daughter of Mr. and Mrs. Berthold Rothschild of Zurich. She is active in Jewish educational circles in Zurich and is a leader in Agudath Israel movements. Miss Rothschild is attending the University of Zurich at the present time.

The marriage of Miss Rothschild and Rabbi Jung will take place early in the coming year.

small sampling of his various organizational involvement.

The Joint Distribution Committee was an independent organization whose aim was to rescue, relieve, and rehabilitate Jewish communities throughout the world. In 1926, Rabbi Jung joined the Cultural Religious Commissions of the Joint and became the chair in 1941. This committee distributed funds to institutions and programs of Jewish culture and learning throughout the world.

Rabbi Leo Jung

During World War II, he also chaired the Cultural Affairs Committee. After the war, this committee distributed funds to help institutions in Palestine and Europe. It also rescued Torah scrolls, *sefarim*, and other religious articles. Rabbi Jung traveled to the different regions to help determine the needs of a particular community, as well as to show his concern. He would collect large quantities of clothing from his congregants to send the communities. He helped establish and distribute funds to yeshivos in Israel, and also established vocational schools.

Rabbi Jung personally raised funds and visited yeshivos in North Africa (Morocco, Algeria, and Tunisia). He was also very involved with the Bais Yaakov movement in Europe and Palestine. He not only raised money for the schools but visited them, and maintained correspondences with students and teachers for many years. During World War II, he sent food

packages to the Bais Yaakovs in Europe. In 1942, he received a heartrending letter from a Bais Yaakov in Warsaw, in which a student explained the decision made by her and her ninety-two classmates to commit suicide rather than be forced by Nazi soldiers to sin. Their only request was that Rabbi Jung say *Kaddish* for them. Rabbi Jung translated that letter into English and it was printed in *The New York Times*. After the War, Rabbi Jung remained involved in the Bais Yaakov movement in Europe, Israel, and America.

Throughout the War, he worked tirelessly to convince his congregants to sign affidavits in order to rescue victims of the Nazis, or for Jews who had escaped Europe and were stranded in some foreign country. He wrote personal letters and made house calls, to persuade his congregants to provide

From the outset, Rabbi Jung was actively involved in many organizations. He helped Vaad Hatzala in many ways and personally collected 1,200 affidavits, which rescued over 9,000 Jews.

A Bais Yaakov class in Cracow, 1932

(L-R): Rabbi Dr. Samson R. Weiss, Rabbi Dr. Leo Jung, Samuel Feuerstein, Rabbi Aharon Kotler

room and board for the refugees. He personally collected 1,200 affidavits, which led to the rescue of over 9,000 Jews. Rabbi Jung himself trained Mike Tress of the Zeirei Agudah, and his staff, how to complete affidavits. He helped the Vaad Hatzala in many ways, including raising funds to cover the transportation costs for those who obtained American visas.

Agudath Israel honored Rabbi Jung's devotion to Israel and Jewish education by naming their girls' village Kfar Eliyahu, in recognition of all of his accomplishments. This girls' village housed a junior high, high school, and a Teachers College for Orthodox Jewish girls. The girls mainly came from poor neighbohoods that did not offer an

adequate Torah education. Kfar Eliyahu combined Jewish education with a secular education. Rabbi Jung raised money for the girls' village, and the proceeds of the *sefarim* he wrote helped support it.

He helped establish and raised funds for yeshivos and vocational schools in Israel and North Africa. He raised money for Bais Yaakovs and visited them in Europe during the war. He continued to be involved in the movement in Europe, U.S., and Israel.

New York University

Presentation, Citation and Investiture of

Leo Jung

with the Honorary Degree of

Doctor of Humane Letters

Leo Jung: Born in Moravia and nurtured in England where his home environment was saturated with learning and culture, he was inevitably predestined for eminent spiritual leadership. His academic prowess is hall-marked by degrees from Cambridge and London Universities and a doctorate of Divinity, honoris causa, from Yeshiva University, the last a fitting token of appreciation of his years of academic service, remembered chiefly by his students for fervid impartation of the moral teachings of the Hebrew Prophets. His is the unique distinction of being the only American rabbi to share in the monumental translation of the Soncino Talmud into English. Serving since 1922 as rabbi of the first Synagogue Center in America, his allied interests over the years have encompassed the presidency of the Jewish Academy of Arts and Sciences, the role of counsellor to our own University Jewish Culture Foundation, and service as aid to the War Department in 1949 in a survey of conditions of the Far Eastern Command. For interpreting brilliantly Jewish heritage to the English-speaking world, for outstanding contributions to Jewish life and letters, and for distinguished leadership to the community. he is now presented for the doctorate of Humane Letters, honoris causa.

Chairman, Department of Hebrew Culture and Education

Leo Jung: Through your scholarly attainments and services both at home and abroad you have nurtured most effectively the heritage of religious and cultural traditions which had its advent in this country three hundred years ago. In testimony of our sense of the significance of the anniversary we gladly tender you our academic honors.

Dated April 3, 1955

Chancellor

Keren Yaldeinu was an organization founded to combat the missionary organizations, which tried to attract young Jewish children in Israel. It sponsored youth centers and clubs for underprivileged youths throughout Israel. Rabbi Jung was an honorary national co-chairman and spoke frequently at their fundraisers in America.

Rabbi Jung was involved in education in New York as well. He taught Jewish ethics at Yeshiva College and Stern College for women (Yeshiva University) for many years. He chaired the New York State Department of Agriculture and Markets Advisory Board on Kosher Law Enforce- ment for thirty years. He and his wife worked tirelessly for the Rabbonim Aid Society, which helped rabbis, especially victims of the Holocaust, and widows of rabbis who were in need. This Aid Society continued operation through the 1980s.

Rabbi Jung organized the Rabbinical Council of the Union of Orthodox Jewish Congregations of America in 1925, to provide English-speaking rabbis with an organization that would discuss issues facing American rabbis. They met monthly, and Rabbi Jung often corresponded

(L-R): Rabbi Jung, Charles Bendheim, Max Stern

with the other rabbis. Rabbi Jung chaired the *Bris Milah* Board of New York, which established with Mt. Sinai Hospital a *Bris Milah* School, that trained people to become *mohelim*. He also served on the Rabbinical Administrative Board of Torah Umesorah.

Rabbi Jung passed away at the age of 95. He lived a long and fruitful life, filled with Torah and *mitzvos*. He utilized the many talents he was blessed with for the sake of *Klal Yisrael*. He affected many people with his eloquence, stature, and intellect. Rabbi Jung saved thousands of Jews during and after World War II. In truth, it can be said that he helped save a generation of Jews, who without him may have lost their Jewish identity. For all these things, we are truly indebted to him.

He lived a long and fruitful life, filled with Torah and mitzvos. He utilized the many talents he was blessed with for the sake of Klal Yisrael.

Rabbi Avraham Kalmanowitz 1891-1964

The Mirrer Yeshiva is one of the best-known institutions of its kind in the world today. Such a reputation was not acquired overnight – it needed the guiding hand, the inspiration, and exceptional *mesiras nefesh* of a man of genius. That man was Rabbi Avraham Kalmanowitz. What distinguished Rabbi Kalmanowitz from most of his contemporaries was his ability to meld within his character the personality of a distinguished *rav* with that of a dedicated *rosh hayeshiva*. Owing to his ability to carry out both functions, he was able to withstand the yeshiva's arduous transplant from Mir to the United States by way of Vilna; Keidan; Kobe, Japan; and Shanghai, China. This indeed is a testament to his greatness.

Born in Delyatitz, Byelorussia, to a distinguished rabbinical family, he demonstrated his brilliance in Torah scholarship at a very young age. Indeed, shortly after his *bar mitzvah,* he prepared a manuscript of commentary on the Talmud, which, although not published, received the encouraging approbation of several leading Talmudic scholars. This commentary earned him an enviable reputation as an exceptional student of Talmud and future *gadol baTorah*. Rabbi Kalmanowitz received *semichah* from a number of leading rabbinic scholars, including Rabbi Moshe Mordechai Epstein, Rabbi Raphael Shapiro and Rabbi Eliezer Rabinowitz. In 1913, he became *Rav* of the town of Rakov, and much later (1929), of the city of Tiktin. Not coincidentally, he founded yeshivos in both places. But it was in the area of leadership where Rabbi Kalmanowitz was to make his greatest impression. A devoted protégé of Rabbi Chaim Ozer Grodzenski, he was the latter's partner in establishing a *kollel* (Ateres Tzvi) in Vilna. Furthermore, he was a dynamic member of the *Moetzes Gedolei HaTorah* (the Council of Torah Sages) of Poland's Agudath Israel, emerging as one of the outstanding rabbinic leaders of Eastern European Orthodoxy.

It was his appointment as honorary president of the Mirrer Yeshiva, however, that proved to be the compass for his subsequent life's work. In 1941,

Rabbi Kalmanowitz and his family traveled to America, where he would become instrumental in saving the *b'nei hayeshiva*, the members of the yeshiva community, from extermination at the hands of the Nazi murderers. Despite America's entrance into the war as an implacable enemy of the Japanese – a result of their bombing Pearl Harbor – Rabbi Kalmanowitz was able to arrange that money be sent to assist the Mirrer *b'nei hayeshiva*, who had escaped to and were living in Japan. He also helped some of the Mirrer students find refuge in Siberia and Shanghai, until they could obtain visas to emigrate to America. Moreover, as one of the primary leaders of the Vaad Hatzala, he played a vital role in

Early photo of Mirrer Yeshiva, Brooklyn, N.Y. Rabbi Kalmanowitz is standing in the center of the Bais Hamedrash.

Rabbi Kalmanowitz making a passionate plea on behalf of Vaad Hatzala

saving as many European Jews as possible. Indeed, Joseph J. Schwartz, chairman of the European executive council of the Joint Distribution Committee, averred that in the Vaad Hatzala "there was a rabbi (Kalmanowitz) with a long white beard, who, when he cried, even the State Department listened." Rabbi Kalmanowitz also prevailed upon other government officials to help Europe's Jews and the Mirrer Yeshiva. Procrastination and negativity were not part

of his lexicon, as the following episodes illustrate:

Rabbi Kalmanowitz even moved those who were initially opposed to rescue, such as Congressman Emanuel Celler. It was too late when Celler himself realizated that he was a member of a government that was unwilling to work to save Jews; it was too late when he grasped that he was a liberal Democrat who had placed too much faith in his President. In his memoir he recalled:

He also helped some of the Mirrer students find refuge in Siberia and Shanghai, until they could obtain visas to emigrate to America.

The Mirrer Yeshiva learning in the Bais Aharon Synagogue in Shanghai, China. First row far left is Rabbi Yechezkel Levinstein, second from right is Rabbi Chaim Shmuelevitz.

It would be difficult to overstate Rabbi Kalmanowitz's influence on Congressman Celler, who became the prime mover in transferring the Shanghai yeshiva to the U.S. after the war, although space on ships was limited.

Rabbi Kalmanowitz greeting Secretary of the Treasury Mr. Henry Morgenthau.

"It is difficult to describe the sense of helplessness and frustration which seized one when streams of letters poured in from constituents asking for help for a sister, brother, mother, child, caught in the Nazi terror. There is one day, which is marked out from all others during this period... Into my office came an old rabbi... everything about him, his hat which he didn't remove, his long black coat and patriarchal beard, the veined hands clutching a cane, these stand before me, even to this day. Trembling and enfeebled, he had traveled from Brooklyn to Washington to talk to his Congressman. Not once did he seem conscious of his tears as he pleaded, 'Don't you see; can't you see; won't you see that there are millions – millions – being killed? Can't we save some of them? Can't you, Mr. Congressman, do something?'

"Do something!" I had talked and written to President Roosevelt... The President's response was not very encouraging, and that of the rest of the bureaucracy was not much better...

"I tried to tell the rabbi that I, too, was convinced that these officials of the State and Treasury Department wanted to do something. I believed this. But the rabbi kept interrupting, striking his cane on the floor of the office. 'If six million cattle had been slaughtered,' he cried, 'there would have been greater interest. A way would have been found. These are people,' he said. 'People.'

"I dreamed about him that night. The old rabbi stood on a rock in the ocean, and hordes of people fought through the water to get to that rock. And the people turned into cattle and back again to people. I was on shore, held by a rope, which somebody was pulling back."

It is not easy to overstate Rabbi Kalmanowitz's appeal, for, influenced by this great *Rosh Yeshiva*, Congressman Celler became the prime mover in the successful transfer of the Shanghai yeshiva after the war, at a time when Allied transports were busy transporting troops home across the Pacific and space on board ship was at a premium.

Another time, when Rabbi Kalmanowitz went to Washington to plead for the Mirrer Yeshiva, he arrived in the office of John Pehle, head of the War Refugee Board, late in the day and just as Pehle was preparing to leave. "Don't worry, Rabbi," Pehle said, "I'll take it up with my boss [Treasury Secretary Morgenthau] the first thing in the morning. So why don't you sleep on it?"

"Sleep on it?" the white-bearded rabbi bristled. "Who can sleep at a time like this? I'll wait here until the morning."

Then Rabbi Kalmanowitz quietly settled into a chair next to Pehle's desk and began reading his ever-present *sefer*.

"But, Rabbi," Pehle protested, not knowing how to remove the elderly man, "you'll be disturbing the cleaning ladies."

"Don't worry," Rabbi Kalmanowitz answered tranquilly, "I won't get in their way." Then he sat back, obviously ready to spend the night if necessary.

Pehle then understood the lesson the rabbi was teaching; rescue was not ordinary business. "O.K., Rabbi," he said a bit sheepishly, "you win. Let's go to Mr. Morgenthau right now and settle the matter."*

After the Holocaust, Rabbi Kalmanowitz traveled to Germany via Czechoslovakia, in order to provide whatever aid he could to his fellow Jews who had survived the war. The following episode underscores Rabbi Kalmanowitz's overwhelming devotion to *Klal Yisrael*:

While staying at the home of a friend in Baltimore, MD, one evening Rabbi Kalmanowitz told his host, that he would be leaving the following morning to keep an appointment in Washington D.C. During the night, a heavy snowfall covered the streets and taxi cabs were not running. At four A.M., the host heard Rabbi Kalmanowitz leaving the house.

"Where are you going at such an early hour?" he asked.

"Since taxis are not running I'm walking to the station," Rabbi Kalmanowitz replied. "I cannot miss the appointment. Our children are freezing in Siberia, and starving in Shanghai, and we are sleeping in comfort!"

The host later added, "It was only

Rabbi Kalmanowitz greeting newly arrived Moroccan students

then that I noticed that he did not even have galoshes on his feet!"

His efforts on behalf of the Sephardic communities of North Africa and the Middle East were exemplary. Traveling to Morocco, Tunisia, and Algiers, he assisted in the formation of Jewish religious schools for Sephardic children, specifically, the Otzar HaTorah network of schools in Morocco. Later on, he helped to establish a Jewish school in Tehran, Iran.

Brooklyn's Mirrer Yeshiva is a lasting tribute to this great *Rav* and *Rosh HaYeshiva*, for he was one of the major forces in the redeployment of the original Mirrer Yeshiva to its new home in the United States. For all his efforts on behalf of his fellow Jews, and especially on behalf of his beloved yeshiva, Rabbi Avraham Kalmanowitz can be considered a giant of our times. His seal has been stamped securely on the souls of hundreds of Mirrer Yeshiva alumni – and on those of thousands of other Jews who owe their very lives to his endeavors – both in this country and around the world.

His seal has been stamped securely on the souls of thousands of Jews who owe him their very lives.

---

*Both episodes are excerpted from David Kranzler, **Thy Brother's Blood**, Mesorah Publications, New York, 1987, pgs. 36-38.

Rabbi Yaakov Kamenetsky

1891-1986

In Slobodka Yeshiva in Europe, one young man was known for his all-encompassing genius; his vast knowledge spanned history and astronomy, as well as an amazing proficiency in the entire *Shas* and *Poskim*, *Midrash* and *Aggadah*. Likewise, his all-embracing personality was able to relate to an endless array of Jews, and could connect with the greatest *gaonim* to the simplest of *baalei batim*. That man was Rabbi Yaakov Kamenetsky, whose synthesis of remarkable genius and sparkling character helped bridge the abyss-like gap between the destroyed world of the European yeshiva and the emerging contemporary Jewish life in the United States. In his all-inclusive cosmopolitan brilliance, highlighted by impeccable integrity, Rabbi Yaakov Kamenetsky has no peer. The quintessential mentor and counselor to the thousands of people who eagerly sought his advice, Reb Yaakov, the consummate *ba'al eitzah* (advisor) was a man even greater than the legends that are told about him to this day. His celebrated smile mirrored a heart filled

with boundless love for his fellow Jews. Rabbi Kamenetsky's impact touched the lives of leaders from every range of the Jewish spectrum. How else could the same man be visited by Israeli Prime Ministers on their trips to the United States to understand the position of the *chareidi* world, and also asked to speak at the erection of the Satmar *Rebbe's matzeiva*, thirty days after his passing?

Born near Dolhinov in 1891, Reb Yaakov moved to the larger town of Minsk, eventually studying with two men whose friendship and fellowship in Torah had a profound impact on his life – Rabbi Reuven Grozovsky and Rabbi Aharon Kotler. When Reb Yaakov was fifteen years old, he traveled to Slobodka, together with his younger friend, Rabbi Aharon Kotler, to study under the world-renowned *Alter* of Slobodka, Rabbi Nosson Tzvi Finkel. In particular, the *Alter* inculcated the young Reb Yaakov with a strong appreciation for *mussar*. The *Alter* even sent the young man to Slutzk to invigorate the yeshiva of

Bikur Cholim Shul, Seattle, WA.

Rabbi Isser Zalman Meltzer. Granted *semichah* at eighteen by a number of eminent Lithuanian rabbis, Reb Yaakov returned to Slobodka and married the daughter of Rabbi Dov Tzvi Heller, the yeshiva's *mashgiach*. Afterwards, Reb Yaakov spent a number of years in the Kovno *Kollel*. Rabbi Kamenetsky eventually became the *rav* in the tiny resort village of Tzitavyan, about twelve and one half miles from Kelm, his tenure spanning the years 1926 through 1937.

In 1937, the Kovno *Rav*, Rabbi Avrohom Shapira, asked Reb Yaakov to travel to America in order to collect funds for a certain yeshiva. However, shortly after he had assumed his position as solicitor, he discovered that there were certain business practices that were being conducted by that yeshiva's office that did not correspond with his idea of integrity. Reb Yaakov's outstanding honesty simply would not allow him to continue representing the yeshiva, even though by relinquishing his

Rabbi Yaakov Kamenetsky as a young man

position he was subjecting himself and his family to the rigors of abject poverty! Soon afterwards, a former colleague of his from Slobodka, Reb Alter Poplack, informed him of a six-month interim position as substitute rabbi for Rabbi Solomon Wohlgelernter, available in Seattle, Washington, at Congregation Bikur Cholim. Rabbi Kamenetsky was accepted for the position.

At the end of his tenure in Seattle, he learned that a position in the Torah Emes Shul in Toronto, Canada, had recently opened up, owing to the death of its spiritual leader, Rabbi Yehuda Leib Graubard. After obtaining the approval of the Kovno *Rav*, Reb Yaakov became the synagogue's new *rav*. His tenancy in Toronto was responsible for a literal makeover of the city, into the citadel of Torah that it is today. A generation of Toronto's *talmidei chachamim* owe their vast erudition in no small part to Reb Yaakov's herculean efforts in the field of Torah education.

A major turning point in Reb Yaakov's career came when he met Rabbi Shraga Feivel Mendlowitz at the dedication of a new building, at Yeshiva Ner Israel in Baltimore, Maryland. Politely refusing Rabbi Mendlowitz's offer to serve as head of his Aish Dos Teachers' Institute, he was taken aback when later Reb Shraga Feivel proposed that

R' Dov Tzvi (Ber Hirsch) Heller, Mashgiach, Slobodka

His tenancy in Toronto was responsible for a literal makeover of the city, into the citadel of Torah that it is today.

A man of sterling character traits, vast wisdom, and solid acumen like Rabbi Yaakov Kamenetsky was immediately implored to join the presidium of Agudath Israel, and later became a member of its prestigious Moetzes Gedolei HaTorah.

he give the daily *blatt shiur* at Mesivta Torah Vodaath – a discourse customarily given by one of the *roshei yeshiva*, Rabbi Shlomo Heiman, who was quite ill at the time. Afraid of hurting Rabbi Heiman's feelings, Reb Yaakov declined. However, after Rabbi Heiman's demise in 1944, Rabbi Kamenetsky did become a member of the Torah Vodaath faculty, where he eventually taught an advanced class leading to *semichah*. He also was responsible for the development of a high school, a post-high-school division, and a *kollel* at Mesivta Torah Vodaath.

A man of sterling character traits, vast wisdom, and solid acumen like Rabbi Yaakov Kamenetsky was immedi-

Rabbi Yaakov Kamenetsky

ately implored to join the presidium of Agudath Israel, and later became a member of its prestigious *Moetzes Gedolei HaTorah,* Council of Torah Sages. His close friends from Slobodka – the two well-known *roshei yeshiva*, Rabbi Reuven Grozovsky and Rabbi Aharon Kotler – were instrumental in involving Reb Yaakov in Agudath Israel. His influence on the other members of the presidium, as well as on the venerable sages in the *Moetzes Gedolei HaTorah*, was considerable – and often, a matter of public record. He also served on the Rabbinical Administrative Board of Torah Umesorah, where his was the voice of moderation and understanding. Reb Yaakov became the chairman after the passing of Rabbi Aharon Kotler.

As one of the two *Roshei HaYeshiva* of Mesivta Torah Vodaath appointed after the death of Rabbi Shraga Feivel Mendlowitz, Reb Yaakov made an everlasting impression on his *talmidim*, many of whom today are celebrated *talmidei chachamim* and *roshei yeshiva* in their own right. After his "retirement" from this exalted position in 1968, and his subsequent move to Monsey, New York, it might have been expected that he could finally rest from his frenetic schedule of activities. On the contrary, in Monsey, he was sought out by thousands of people for his sage advice and keen observa-

Class of Yeshiva Maharil Graubart, Toronto. (L-R, top): Shaya Zager, Avraham Atkin, Shmuel Kamenetsky (Reb Yaakov's Son), Moshe Goldberg, Moshe Knobel, Avraham Blumenfeld, (L-R, bottom): Joseph Horowitz, Avraham Leibtag, Rabbi Yaakov Kamenetsky, David Wohlgelernter, Joseph Goldwasser, Norman Horowitz.

(L-R): Rabbi Yaakov Ruderman, Rabbi Yaakov Kamenetsky, Rabbi Shimon Schwab

tions. Perhaps no other man had a hand in transforming Monsey into the famous *makom shel Torah* (bastion of Torah) for which it has become justifiably famous, as did Rabbi Yaakov Kamenetsky. His home was open to everyone. His advice was sought by every type of person imaginable – the gentile who was looking to convert; the child who wanted to ask a question on *Chumash*; the teacher who was seeking coun-

Rabbi Yaakov Kamenetsky signing a personal check for Agudah projects

sel on pedagogy; the rabbi who had a difficult congregation; the *Rosh Yeshiva* who needed sage guidance; the *askan* who was about to meet the President of the United States; the Senator who wanted to know how to react politically; the Israeli Prime Minister who wanted an understanding of the *chareidi* world.

One of the projects that Reb Yaakov considered a *chiyuv* (obliga-

He was sought out by thousands of people for his sage advice and keen observations. His was the voice of moderation and understanding.

Rabbi Yaakov Kamenetsky greeting a young Be'er HaGolah student; to his left, Rabbi Moshe Sherer

tion) that devolved on every principal and *rosh yeshiva* was the active support of the Yeshiva Be'er HaGolah for immigrants from the Soviet Union. Although already advanced in years, Reb Yaakov was able–solely through the force of his powerful Torah-laden personality – to demand nothing less than total agreement from educational leaders that

each yeshiva maintain at least one classroom filled with students from Yeshiva Be'er HaGolah. He became the chairman of the *Vaad HaChinuch*, the Board of Education, of this yeshiva. Although this was nothing new to a man who for years had been chairman of the Advisory Board of Torah Umesorah (The National Society of Hebrew Day Schools), Reb Yaakov was single-handedly responsible for the existence of Yeshiva Be'er HaGolah in the first place. His continuing supervision of its progress assured the Jewish world of a new generation of *talmidei chachamim* who, although they had grown up under the repressive Soviet regime, would be able to transmit Torah to

Rabbi Yaakov Kamenetsky conferring with members of the Moetzes Gedolei HaTorah. (L-R): Rabbi Yaakov Ruderman, Rabbi Yaakov Kamenetsky, Rabbi Moshe Feinstein, Rabbi Boruch Sorotzkin

Rabbi Yaakov Kamenetsky

thousands of their countrymen in the land of freedom, the United States of America.

With Reb Yaakov's passing in 1986, not long before his 96th birthday, *Yiddishkeit* lost a man of far-reaching capabilities, vast wisdom, and flawless character traits, who was certainly one of the greatest links to making "the world that is" as similar as possible to "the world that was."

With his passing, Yiddishkeit lost a man of far-reaching capabilities, vast wisdom, and flawless character traits, who was certainly one of the greatest links to making "the world that is" as similar as possible to "the world that was."

Rabbi Yaakov Yitzchok Ruderman with Rabbi Yaakov Kamenetsky

Rabbi Yaakov Kamenetsky walking with Rabbi Mordechai Gifter at a granddaughter's wedding.

❧ Rabbi Dr. Joseph Kaminetsky

1911-1999

Dr. Kaminetsky's goal was to have a day school in every Jewish community with over 5,000 people. Using his gift of oratory and persuasion, as well as his true love for every Jew, "Dr. Joe" made it happen.

Mention the name "Torah Umesorah," and automatically, Dr. Joseph Kaminetsky comes to mind. He joined the organization in 1946, and was actively involved for 35 years as its energetic and enterprising National Director. He served as a dynamic Director Emeritus for another six years. Dr. Kaminetsky was the key figure in the explosive growth of Orthodox day schools in the United States and Canada.

Joseph Kaminetsky was born in Brooklyn, New York in 1911. He attended Chaim Berlin, the Talmudical Academy (part of RIETS), and then became a member of the very first class of Yeshiva College, graduating in 1932. A man of tremendous idealism and energy, from the start Jewish education was his mission. He became the founding principal of the afternoon school of the Jewish Center of Manhattan, and later its assistant rabbi. Meanwhile, he earned his doctorate in education at Columbia University. Dr. Kaminetsky became the executive director of Manhattan Day School, and from there he joined the newly formed Torah Umesorah, as Educational Director.

When Dr. Kaminetsky became director of Torah Umesorah in 1948 (after the passing of Rabbi Shraga Feivel Mendlowitz), there were only 10,000 yeshiva day school students in just 49 schools in the entire United States, mainly in New York City. His mission was to create an organization that would persuade and encourage teachers and principals to travel to other cities and establish new day schools. In addition, he had to convince parents to enroll their children in these day schools instead of public school. It must be remembered that at the time even Torah-observant parents sent their children to public school, and many viewed a yeshiva education as "old-fashioned." Dr. Kaminetsky's goal was to have a day school in every Jewish community with over 5,000 people.

Most people thought his idea was ludicrous, that it would never happen. Using his gift of oratory and persuasion, as well as his true love for every

Dr. Joseph Kaminetsky

Jew, "Dr. Joe" made it happen. He was able to prevail upon teachers and principals to move to various cities throughout the United States to teach Jewish children. He trained them to be master teachers. Dr. Kaminetsky guided the educators through the early years of their careers, when they lacked confidence and made mistakes. His charisma, encouragement and know-how provided them with the necessary incentives. Dr. Joe realized that the stakes were enormous – it was a battle for the very survival of *Yiddishkeit* in America. Dr. Kaminetsky's magnetic personality helped convince parents to enroll their children in these day schools. His dedication, love, and personal example shaped countless lives and careers.

Dr. Kaminetsky developed an unusually close relationship with the *roshei yeshiva* in America. In his formative years, some of the greatest *gedolim* were his teachers and role models. He became their loyal servant, constantly seeking their advice and counsel on many halachic and hashkafic issues

regarding Jewish education. In addition, Dr. Joe kept in close contact with Rabbi Shraga Feivel Mendlowitz on many issues facing Torah Umesorah. The Rabbinical Administrative Board of Torah Umesorah set policy and was comprised of Rabbi Aharon Kotler, Rabbi Reuven Grozovsky, Rabbi Moshe Feinstein, Rabbi Yaakov Kamenetsky, Rabbi Yaakov Yitchak Ruderman, and Rabbi Yitzchak Hutner, who were all consulted on various matters confronting the organization. Each of these *gedolim*, in turn, respected and admired Dr. Kaminetsky.

JK (as he was fondly known) succeeded in obtaining financial support for these day schools, even from those who themselves were not Orthodox. At first, many of these people were quite hostile to him. With the passage of

His dedication, love, and personal example shaped countless lives and careers.

(L-R): Rabbi Yaakov Kamenetsky, Dr. Joseph Kaminetsky, Rabbi Shneur Kotler

time, however, they were so impressed by his idealism, convictions, and dynamic personality, that they agreed to support the day school in their communities.

No matter how much JK accomplished, he always gave the credit to others. Even when people criticized him for being too much of this or too little of that, he did not let this bother him. The only thing that truly mattered to him was ensuring a firm Torah-true education for more boys and girls. He never allowed personal feelings to enter into his dealings, even with those who disagreed with him. Grievance was not in his vocabulary. Bitterness was not something he could understand. Dr.

Kaminetsky related well to people and enveloped them with love.

After his retirement, Dr. Kaminetsky fulfilled a life-long dream and moved to *Eretz Yisrael*. There he dedicated the rest of his life to spiritual pursuits. He translated into English many of the lectures of one of his mentors, Rabbi Yitzchak Isaac Sher. Dr. Kaminetsky also wrote an autobiographical account of his life, *Memorable Encounters: A Torah Pioneer's Glimpses of Great Men and Years of Challenge* (Shaar Press). He spent most of his day learning Torah in a *beis medrash* near his apartment in Yerushalayim. During the last years of his life, Dr. Kaminetsky walked so slowly, it took him half an hour to walk to the *shul* next door to *daven*, yet

Dr. Joseph Kaminetsky addressing a Torah Umesorah Dinner

Dr. Joseph Kaminetsky

The American Torah community is still growing, and with it the yeshiva day schools, in large measure because of Dr. Kaminetsky's dedication to the mission that he set for himself.

he never missed a *minyan* and was always on time!

On March 17, 1999, Dr. Kaminetsky passed away at the age of 87. His funeral, attended by a large crowd of relatives, friends and admirers, took place outside the *beis medrash* where he studied Torah for the last ten years of his life. Years earlier, he had set a goal to establish a day school in every Jewish community of 5,000 people. At the time of his passing there were 600 Torah schools in America and Canada with 175,000 students. The American Torah community is still growing, and with it the yeshiva day schools, in large measure because of Dr. Kaminetsky's dedication to the mission that he set for himself. The American Jewish community will forever be in his debt.

Rebbetzin Vichna Kaplan

1913-1986

It all could have been forfeited by a lack of funds. Vichna Eisen, a young orphan, applied to the Bais Yaakov School in Crakow, but she did not have the money for tuition. However, she did not lack the motivation to earn a preparatory school diploma, which she also was missing at the time. But money was a different problem. To his credit, Dr. Leo Deutschlander, the administrator, obtained a scholarship for her, and her journey in *chinuch* began.

Rebbetzin Kaplan was born Vichna Eisen in 1913, in the Russian town of Slonim. She was orphaned at the young age of 11 and was raised by her uncle, the famous *mashgiach* of Baranovich, Rabbi Yaakov Yisroel Lubchansky. The "Enlightenment" movement was gathering momentum in those troubled times. Ladies and girls were drawn towards the freedom and fashions of the time, distancing themselves from the ways of their mothers and grandmothers. Families were being splintered as each pulled in opposite directions.

It was into the very vortex of the storm that the famed Sarah Schneirer

From the very outset her tremendous potential was sensed by the teachers and students of the Bais Yaakov of Crakow, the flagship of all Bais Yaakovs.

entered. She opened a seminary for girls, offering them an anchor and the stability to survive the storm, strengthened and firm in their *emunah*. It was to this island of sanctity and security that the young Vichna was drawn.

From the very outset, her tremendous potential was sensed by the teachers and students of the Bais Yaakov of Crakow, the flagship of all Bais Yaakovs. She was entrusted by Sarah Schneirer with responsibilities far beyond her years. Because of her abilities and character she became the closest student and confidante of Sarah Schneirer. At the tender age of 18, she was dispatched to the large city of Brisk to teach in the Bais Yaakov School. She was the school! Vichna Eisen was the only *limudei kodesh* teacher in the school, besides which she also tutored other girls in the evening. Once, she left for vacation and decided not to return. So great was her impact on the city's girls that they sent her a telegram in the Brisker Rav's name asking her to return. She had become quite close to the Brisker Rav while teaching in Brisk. Although she knew that the telegram was forged, she returned anyway, explaining, "If they had to go this far to keep me, they must be desperate, so how can I let them down?"

After a few years it was time for her to get married. She was introduced to an American *bachur*, a young man studying in Brisk, Boruch Kaplan. He was an excellent *bachur* with wonderful *middos*. Vichna Eisen came highly recommended – a letter sent to the Mirrer *Rosh HaYeshiva* said that "she is perfect, straight, good of heart, continuing to rise in attainment. She was created for greatness." They met, but Boruch had to return to America. They corresponded and finally became engaged, by mail, in 1936.

With the Brisker Rav's permission Vichna left for America. Before leaving, she requested and obtained permission from the Bais Yaakov offices to open a Bais Yaakov in America. With this endorsement a new era opened for Bais Yaakov and Rebbetzin Kaplan. She traveled to America and celebrated her wedding 11 days later. After their marriage, the couple settled in Williamsburg.

In 1938, Torah-observant schools for girls, such as Bais Yaakov, or European-style yeshivos for boys for that matter, hardly existed in America. No high school for girls was available at all. Rebbetzin Kaplan changed that. She started the first Bais Yaakov High School in New York with seven students around her own dining room table. Classes were held from 7-10 p.m. every night.

The Kaplans built the New York Bais Yaakov on love and *kavod habriyos,* respect for their fellow man. One time, a member of the adminstration came to Rabbi Boruch Kaplan complaining that some of the *talmidos*, were "hanging out" with *bachurim*. He responded, "Send the boys to the *Poilishe Shtibel* to learn. That will cure the problem." Similarly, Rebbetzin Kaplan would cross to the other side of the avenue to avoid embarrassing her *talmidos*. Once, while walking on Bedford Avenue, she suddenly told her daughter Miriam, "Let's cross the street, because I don't want to embarrass my *talmidos* who are socializing with boys." Such was her affection for and sensitivity to her students.

Rebbetzin Kaplan was loved by her *talmidos* because she lived "love." On the *yahrtzeit* of Sarah Schenirer, she would speak at an assembly to mark the occasion. And every year, when speaking about Sarah Schenirer, she would cry as if the loss was new and raw. Today, her *talmidos* feel the same way about her.

Rebbetzin Kaplan was a "lady" par-excellence. Although she had many children, she always was well groomed and came to school dressed impeccably. In addition, her honesty was unparalleled. When, for example, she was asked to send regards to another, she considered it a debt which had to be repaid immediately. Otherwise, she felt it was *geneivah* (theft).

Because of her great devotion to her students the program grew. Students from the entire spectrum of American Jewry joined the school. They were drawn by a desire to learn the words of Hashem. The remarkable pedagogue, Rebbetzin Kaplan, forged them together into a united body; united in purpose and spirit.

> The Kaplans built the New York Bais Yaakov on love and kavod habriyos, respect for their fellow man. Students from the entire spectrum of American Jewry joined the school.

Graduation Ceremony in the Bais Yaakov Auditorium

She was always available, and she listened – she listened to all that was on the girls' hearts and minds. She taught with love; she taught by example.

By 1944, a full-day high school was opened. It was not only subject matter that Rebbetzin Kaplan transmitted to her students. She inculcated them with the ideals and spirit of Jewish education and imbued them with the responsibility for the future of Torah on these shores. The students witnessed her devotion to them and to all *bnos Yisrael*. During the war years, the American Bais Yaakov absorbed and guaranteed more girls than any other similar institution. Rebbetzin Kaplan was a mother to all the girls, regardless of their background. She offered words of comfort and encouragement to the survivors, demonstrating endless patience for the students who were not on the level of the Bais Yaakov. Most of all, she was always available, and she listened – she **listened** to all that was on the girls' hearts and minds. She taught with love; she taught by example.

Her *kavod habriyos* (respect for every human being) was such that she placed the needs of others before her own. During her final illness, when she was very weak and bed-ridden, a *talmidah,* who was not aware of her condition, wanted to visit her. Her daughter Matty asked her what to do.

Her response was: "Of course she should come." Even her doctors realized that this was not an average person. During her last days, when they had to treat her for the pain she was suffering, they said: "You are a gem and we are just polishing up this precious stone."

It was from this single Bais Yaakov that the entire Bais Yaakov movement grew. Although they were all independent institutions, they each had their beginnings in Rebbetzin Kaplan's Bais Yaakov. To find teachers and obtain sage advice, they turned to the indefatigable Rebbetzin Kaplan. Her incomparable leadership changed and reshaped the horizons of American Jewry. Leading an army of dedicated women, these schools implanted true *Yiddishkeit* in the homes and hearts of their students. These mothers and teachers of the children – the future of *Klal Yisrael* – were, and still are, imbued with the love, appreciation, and dedication to their heritage generated by this remarkable woman. Rabbi Aharon Kotler claimed that Rebbetzin Kaplan was responsible for the *Kollel* and Torah movement in America, because she imbued her *talmidos* with a zealous

Rebbetzin Kaplan speaking at a gathering in memory of Sarah Schenirer

Rebbetzin Grunfeld (far right) next to Rebbetzin Vichna Kaplan

love for and commitment to Torah, preparing them for sharing their lives with bnei torah.

Rabbi and Rebbetzin Kaplan were wonderful parents to their own children. Consequently, they merited to raise sons who are *talmidei chachamim* and daughters who married outstanding *talmidei chachamim*. A number of her children are currently involved in the Bais Yaakov. Their daughters continue to direct Bais Yaakov and one son is responsible for the finances. In itself, this is a true testament to the ongoing legacy of Rebbetzin Kaplan.

Although she is not with us physically, she is perpetuated spiritually in every Bais Yaakov. Indeed, the Torah revolution with which we are blessed today is by no small means a result of Rebbetzin Vichna Kaplan's tremendous *mesiras nefesh* and devotion to the dissemination of Torah to women.

The Torah revolution with which we are blessed today is by no small means a result of Rebbetzin Vichna Kaplan's tremendous mesiras nefesh and devotion to the dissemination of Torah to women.

≈ Rabbi Chaim Mordechai Katz *1894-1964*

He could have said that he no longer had the strength to head an institution, but the strength of his conviction and his tremendous feeling of responsibility did not allow for this. Even before the loss of his family in the war and the decimation of his beloved yeshiva in Europe, he had suffered the loss of his first wife and young child. During the war, the Nazis murdered his second wife and ten children. He was the sole survivor of his immediate family. Reb Mottel, as he was affectionately called, began from scratch, rebuilding himself, a family and a yeshiva.

He was born in 1894, in the small village of Shadove. In his youth, he studied under Rabbi Yosef Leib Bloch, who was at the time *Rav* of Shadove. Though his family left Lithuania for South Africa, the budding scholar refused to accompany them, preferring to remain behind alone to continue his beloved studies. He continued studying Torah in Slobodka, Telshe, and Volozhin, where he was ordained by Rabbi Refael Shapiro, and he also studied in the yeshiva of the *Iluy* of Meichet. From his youth, his wholesome personality was obvious and all expected that he would achieve greatness.

He returned to Telshe in 1918. After a few years, he married the daughter of the *Rosh HaYeshiva*, Rabbi Yosef Leib Bloch. In Telshe, his pedagogic abilities helped him to guide the *Mechina* (preparatory school), and also were instrumental in the development of the Yavne School for girls, the first of its kind in Europe. His energy was not concentrated on the yeshiva alone. He soon became the *Rosh Kollel*, using his expertise to guide the young married scholars to higher levels of spiritual achievement and scholarship. He was a founding member of Pirchei Agudas Yisrael, and was an editor of the Agudah weekly, *Dos Yiddishe Leben*. Rabbi Katz was also a member of the Agudah's international committee. Even the passing of his wife and young child did not deter him in his dedication to fulfilling his responsibilities.

He married again, and together with his second wife he raised a large family. In the midst of the war,

From his youth, his wholesome personality was obvious and all expected that he would achieve greatness.

he and his brother-in-law, Rabbi Eliyahu Meir Bloch, were in America, investigating the possibility of establishing Telshe Yeshiva on American shores. The escalating war prevented their return to Europe. The tragic news of the destruction of Europe and the loss of his family did not crush his spirit completely. Together, he and Rabbi Bloch began to rebuild Yeshivas Telshe.

Rabbi Katz was described by his nephew and later *Rosh HaYeshiva* of Telshe, Rabbi Boruch Sorotzkin, as a visionary, albeit a very practical one. Although these characteristics may seem inconsistent – for one who dreams usually lacks the drive to see

his dream come to fruition – he not only had the vision, but he worked hard to actualize his dream.

The few *bachurim* who had made their way to Cleveland, Ohio, where he and Rabbi Bloch had decided to open the yeshiva, hardly replaced the student body that he had left behind. Both in spirit and depth, they were far below the level of European yeshiva students. Nevertheless, Reb Mottel was able to contain his brilliance and teach *shiurim* tailored to their level, without

Rabbi Yosef Leib Bloch

Telshe Yeshiva, Lithuania, faculty and student body, 1932: Roshei HaYeshiva, (L-R): Rabbi Chaim Mordechai Katz, Rabbi Zalman Bloch, Rabbi Avrohom Yitzchok Bloch, Rabbi Eliyahu Meir Bloch, Rabbi Ezriel Rabinowitz

Dedication of Telshe Yeshiva's new Wickliffe campus, 1956. (L-R): Rabbi Chaim Mordechai Katz, walking together with Rabbi Aharon Kotler and Rabbi Yaakov Yitzchok Ruderman

the notion that Torah could not take root in the heart of the American continent, outside New York. Together with his brother-in-law, Rabbi Eliyahu Meir Bloch, he raised the level of Torah scholarship in America. They were uncompromising, insisting that only Torah and not secular studies be taught on a *Bais Medrash/post-high school* level. To insure the purity of education in the local community, a day school was opened under the aegis of the yeshiva. The Hebrew Academy of Cleveland was, and remains, the flagship of the Day

compromising the quality of the lesson. Soon, the American boys developed into top-level yeshiva *bachurim*. They rose to the level that Reb Mottel expected of them.

Reb Mottel remarried a third time, and his new wife, *Rebbetzin* Esther Mindel, joined him in building a new generation of *bnei Torah*. Their own children and the yeshiva students were raised by their partnership. Although Reb Mottel was burdened with communal and yeshiva responsibilities, he always made time to converse with the *Rebbetzin* and involve himself with the education of their children.

He was a master pedagogue and successfully penetrated the minds and hearts of the American *bnei Torah*. It was not only information that he imparted to his students, he also molded and formed their personalities, replacing the American mindset with a Torah outlook on life.

The yeshiva flourished, dispelling

> He was a master pedagogue and successfully penetrated the minds and hearts of the American bnei Torah.

Rabbi Chaim Mordechai Katz listening to Chazaras HaShatz

Groundbreaking of the new Bais Hamedrash building.(L-R): Mr. Al Adelstein, Rabbi Boruch Sorotzkin, Rabbi Pinchas Teitz, Rabbi Chaim Mordechai Katz, Rabbi Yaakov Yitzchok Ruderman, Rabbi N.W. Dessler (speaking), Novominsker Rebbe, Rabbi Chaim Stein, Rabbi Shneur Kotler, Rabbi Mordechai Gifter, Rabbi Elozor Levi, Rabbi Pesach Stein, Rabbi Amram Blum, Rabbi Aizik Ausband, Rabbi Eliezer Sorotzkin.

School Movement. Reb Mottel headed the *Vaad HaChinuch* and took a daily interest in the school. The Dean, Rabbi Nochum Zev Dessler – himself an alumnus of the yeshiva in Lithuania – would confer with Reb Mottel on all matters pertaining to the educational development of the school. Later, a girls' high school and teachers' seminary were established.

Reb Mottel established and directed the *kollel* for advanced studies as part of the yeshiva. After their years of focused study, he encouraged every *kollel* fellow to seek a position in an area that would advance and enhance his achievements, following his tenure in the *kollel*. He felt that each *talmid* had a moral obligation to improve the

spiritual climate in this country through the dissemination of Torah. The existence of the *kollel* made a tremendous impact on the mindset of the American youth, who heretofore had viewed a college education as the key to a bright future.

He was committed to the service of the broader community and expected his *talmidim* to do likewise. Agudath Israel of America enjoyed his full support. He served as a senior member of its *Moetzes Gedolei HaTorah* (Council of Torah Sages). Rabbi Yaakov Kamenetsky said that when Reb Mottel attended a meeting one could be sure that a decision would be made and that action would be taken.

Reb Mottel was a builder. His entire life was spent building and rebuilding.

It was Reb Mottel who led the now homeless and saddened bachurim, infusing them with new life and vigor, to continue and intensify their avodas Hashem.

With the tremendous growth of the student body the yeshiva sought a new home. After numerous decisions, disappointments, and negotiations a large campus was purchased in the rural city of Wickliffe. The joy and celebration of laying the foundation-stone was marred with the passing of Rabbi Eliyahu Meir Bloch. Upon his demise, the leadership of the entire Yeshiva and its affiliates devolved upon Reb Mottel, who proved more than equal to the challenge.

It was during this trying period that the yeshiva answered the call of a group of *baalei batim* (lay leaders) in Chicago to open a yeshiva there. Undaunted by the opposition raised by some members of the Chicago community to the idea of a *yeshiva gedolah* opening in the city, Reb Mottel dispatched a core group of *bachurim*, under the leadership of

Rabbi Chaim Mordechai Katz

Rabbi Avraham Chaim Levin and Rabbi Chaim Schmelczer. Later, Rabbi Chaim Dov Keller joined the *hanhalah* of the yeshiva in Chicago. Together, they built a yeshiva high school, *beis medrash* and *kollel*, contributing greatly to the growth of Torah in America in general, and Chicago in particular.

Reb Mottel's leadership qualities were tested and confirmed by a tragic fire that consumed the dormitory building. Two young *bachurim* lost their lives in the conflagration. It was Reb Mottel who led the now homeless and saddened *bachurim*, infusing them with new life and vigor, to continue and intensify their *avodas Hashem*. The task of rebuilding the campus began. His vision gave birth to a new modern dormitory facility, as well as plans to build a spacious *beis medrash*, which was the largest one of its kind at that time. After the corner-

Rabbi Avraham Chaim Levin

Rabbi Chaim Schmelczer

Rabbi Chaim Dov Keller

*Rabbi Chaim Mordechai Katz
"living" a mussar shmuess*

stone was laid, Reb Mottel passed away, leaving the completion of the task to those

who survived him. In the *Rosh HaYeshiva's* will, he directed that the mantle of leadership should be conferred upon the *sheloshes ha'giborim* (three mighty leaders) – Rabbi Boruch Sorotzkin, Rabbi Mordechai Gifter and Rabbi Chaim Stein. Together with Rabbi Pesach Stein and Rabbi Aizik Ausband they built the Telshe Yeshiva in America into a premier *makom* Torah.

Reb Mottel was a builder. His entire life was spent building and rebuilding. His great mentors in Telshe, Lithuania, laid the foundation for his own personal formation. He persevered and realized his vision to establish a *makom Torah* in America. His *talmidim* are his legacy, and they aspire to emulate him as they continue to build in Hashem's honor.

He persevered and realized his vision to establish a makom Torah in America.

Roshei HaYeshiva / Telshe America

Rabbi Mordechai Gifter, zl

Rabbi Boruch Sorotzkin, zl

Rabbi Chaim Stein, Shlita

Rabbi Pesach Stein, zl

Rabbi Aizik Ausband, Shlita

Rabbi Dr. Hillel Klein

1849-1926

A lesser-known
personality who
greatly impacted
on the American
Torah scene in
the early 20th
century was
Rabbi Dr. Hillel
HaKohen Klein.

A lesser-known personality who greatly impacted on the American Torah scene in the early 20th century was Rabbi Dr. Hillel *HaKohen* Klein.

Born in Baratcka, Hungary, in 1849, Rabbi Klein was blessed with a prodigious mind. At age eleven, he already knew the entire *Tanach* by heart and was well versed in *Seder Nezikim* and commentaries. He became a *talmid* of the *Ksav Sofer* (Rabbi Avraham Shmuel Binyamin Sofer) at the Pressburg Yeshiva at the extremely young age of 12. Four years later, he went to Eisenstadt, Hungary, to become a *talmid* in Rabbi Ezriel Hildesheimer's Yeshiva – a unique place that taught secular studies in addition to *limudei kodesh*. In order to combat the spread of assimilation, Rabbi Hildesheimer wanted his students to have a basic knowledge of secular subjects.

Young Hillel Klein was teaching a *shiur* to thirty students before the end of the year, once his exceptional abilities were recognized. He left for Vienna two years later to enter the Gymnasium (high school) and then the University.

During that period, he was invited by Rabbi Zalman Spitzer to give a daily Gemara *shiur* in the famed Schiff Shul.

Rabbi Hildesheimer asked Reb Hillel to accompany him when he left Eisenstadt to establish the Hildesheimer Seminary in Berlin in 1869. In 1871, he received *semichah* from his *rebbe*, Rabbi Hildesheimer, and from Rabbi Binyamin Auerbach of Halberstadt, a foremost leader in the fight against the Reform movement. Rabbi Klein then received his doctorate from the University of Berlin in 1873.

Rabbi Klein moved to Kiev, in 1875, to tutor the son of Israel Brodsky, a millionaire and well-known religious industrialist who financially enabled the establishment of the Volozhiner Yeshiva *Kollel*. He remained there for five years, and was constantly in touch with the leading rabbis of Russia and Lithuania who frequented the Brodsky home.

In 1880, Rabbi Klein accepted the position of rabbi of Libau, Latvia. In Russia during that period, every Jewish community was served by two rabbis – an official crown rabbi, a government appointee who had graduated from a government seminary or European university, plus a true *rav,* who was responsible for the community's Torah institutions and answered *sh'eilos.* Rabbi Klein could serve in both capacities, which was unusual. In 1890, he was forced out of his position by the government, most likely because he would not promote assimilation as the government expected of its crown rabbis.

After two years on the job, the Chief Rabbi of New York, Rabbi Jacob Joseph, found his responsibilities overwhelming. He felt that Rabbi Klein possessed the unique attributes that the Jewish community of New York required. He suggested that Rabbi Klein be hired as the rabbi of Congregation Ohev Zedek on the Lower East Side. Rabbi Klein accepted the offer and arrived in New York in 1890, holding the position until his passing. Shortly afterwards, Rabbi Joseph appointed him as a *dayan* and he also became Rabbi Joseph's right hand man.

Rabbi Klein was very involved with Rabbi Joseph in his attempt to centralize *shechitah* and *kashrus* supervision in New York City. He was greatly concerned about the *shochtims'* welfare. Their working conditions were terrible and in 1892 they staged a strike. Rabbi Joseph and Rabbi Klein encouraged them to organize themselves to improve their situation. The outcome was a *shochtims'* organization called Meleches HaKodesh Society. Eventually, reforms were instituted. (Rabbi Klein also arbitrated and helped settle the matzah bakers' strike of 1911.) In addition, he was in charge of all the *Kehillah's* supervisory undertakings. After Rabbi Joseph's stroke, Rabbi Klein became the unofficial chief rabbi.

Together with Rev. Dr. Pereira

Rabbi Ezriel Hildesheimer

Mendes and Rabbi Bernard Drachman, the leaders of native American Orthodoxy, Rabbi Klein founded the Agudas Shomrei Shabbos in 1894, in an effort to further Shabbos observance. At that time Shabbos observance was a very serious problem because of the six-day work week. With few exceptions, most Jews succumbed and worked on Shabbos for fear of losing their jobs. Consequently, the younger generation was being raised in homes where there was no Shabbos observance. The organization approached manufacturers and stores to prevail upon them to close on Shabbos. Then they directed workers, who were, or wanted to be, *shomer Shabbos* to these employers. They also launched an educational campaign to convince the Jewish women not to shop on Shabbos, and the Jewish store owners to close on Shabbos. The organization advertised in the Yiddish press offering their

Rabbi Klein fought against Jewish secular movements in America, as he had in Europe. He particularly targeted the young people and tried to convince them of the authenticity of Torah Judaism to the exclusion of everything else.

The K'sav Sofer

An area of great concern to Rabbi Klein was Torah education.
He tried to help the only advanced Yeshiva/Beis Medrash in the U.S. at that time – Yeshiva Rabbi Yitzchok Elchanan, established 1896, on the Lower East Side.

assistance to all workers seeking *shomer Shabbos* employment. This effort helped alleviate the problem to some degree and gave religious Jews a place to turn to for assistance.

Rabbi Klein fought against Jewish secular movements in America, as he had in Europe. He particularly targeted the young people and tried to convince them of the authenticity of Torah Judaism to the exclusion of everything else. After the passing of Rabbi Joseph, Rabbi Klein retained the *hashgachah* of a number of cattle *shechitah* houses. In 1914, Judah Magnes and others tried to establish a central New York *kehillah*. They asked Rabbi Klein to help with *kashrus* supervision. The hope was that the *kehillah* would unite all the Jews into one organization. It would be comprised of several divisions – *kashrus*, education, and *tzedakah*. The *kashrus* division would try to eliminate unreliable *shochtim* and *mashgichim* by licensing only those who were fit for the job. Also, a *beis din* for *kashrus* matters was to be established for all areas of the city.

This plan never became completely operational. Naturally, there were objections from all those with vested interests in retaining the status quo. Unfortunately, the entire *kehillah* concept failed when funds and encouragement were exhausted at the end of World War I.

An area of great concern to Rabbi Klein was Torah education. He tried to

help the only advanced Yeshiva/*Beis Medrash* in the U.S. at that time – Yeshiva Rabbi Yitzchok Elchanan, established 1896 on the Lower East Side. A major goal of the yeshiva was that the *talmidim* who were European immigrants would eventually receive *semichah* and become rabbis and serve their communities. However, the yeshiva was in great financial straits, because the only potential supporters were the immigrants whose means were limited. Consequently, the yeshiva did not even have a permanent building and moved from place to place. Rabbi Klein agreed to become president in 1902, and launched a building campaign. Two years later the yeshiva was able to purchase a building.

He also succeeded in finally educating the Jewish community as to the distinction between the yeshiva and the Jewish Theological Seminary, which was no longer an Orthodox institution as it had been at its inception. He formed a *Semichah* Board in 1906, to grant rabbinic ordination to worthy *talmidim* and assign them positions throughout the United States. Although he resigned as President of RIETS in 1908, he remained a supporter of the yeshiva until his death.

Another area of achievement was in the field of *tzedakah*. During World War I, the established European Jewish communities and yeshivos were uprooted and left without support – the very future of Torah learning was at stake. Together with other Orthodox rabbis and activists, Rabbi Klein approached the Orthodox Union and they organized the first relief organization, called the Central Relief Committee, to aid European Jews. Funds were raised and channeled to responsible *rabbanim* and community leaders in Europe to disburse to their communities and the yeshivos. Rabbi Klein remained active in the organization and ensured that the European yeshivos received aid for reconstruction. Without his help the existence of the yeshivos in Poland, Lithuania, Czechoslovakia, and Hungary would have been jeopardized.

Rabbi Klein also worked on behalf of the Old *Yishuv* in *Eretz Yisrael*. In addition, he helped found the organization Ezras Torah – a fund established to support Torah scholars in Europe during and after World War I. He served as treasurer for 10 years.

After the visits of two delegations from Europe representing Agudath Israel (1918-1920), Rabbi Klein was appointed president of the newly established American branch of Agudath Israel. However, it was not the right time for an American Agudah branch, and the attempt ended with his death. Rabbi Klein also served as a vice-president of the Orthodox Union.

On March 21, 1926, Rabbi Hillel Klein passed away. The man who preferred the title *"Hillel HaKohen"* had certainly accomplished a great deal in his 35 years in America. His brilliance and total commitment to *derech haTorah* empowered him in all his efforts to establish a Torah-true community in New York.

> *His brilliance and total commitment to derech haTorah empowered him in all his efforts to establish a Torah-true community in New York.*

Rabbi Aharon Kotler

1891-1962

Torah genius, personifier of outstanding *middos*, pre-eminent leader, unifier and master builder of Torah in America – all these and more describe Rabbi Aharon Kotler.

Reb Aharon was born in Sislovitz, White Russia, in 1891. His father, Reb Shneur Zalman, was the *Rav* of the city and young Aharon's first *rebbe*. His parents' untimely passing, when he was only ten years old, forced the young orphan to move to his uncle's home in Minsk. There, he persevered in his studies with continued vigor, amazing everyone with his achievements.

He was a mere eleven years old when his uncle enrolled him in the Yeshiva of Krinik, under the tuteluge of Rabbi Zalman Sender Shapiro. Here, too, he earned the admiration of the older students and was sent to a special group of *talmidim* called Pirchei Torah. Eventually, the name of this young renowned genius reached the ears of the "*Maskilim*," the self-proclaimed "enlightened," modern Jews of Minsk. They invested tremendous effort in their attempt to wean the young scholar from his studies. They even asked Aharon's sister to help convince him that a greater future lay in store for him at the university. With the support of his uncle, and his dear friend Rabbi Reuven Grozovsky, the young "*iluy*" remained steadfast in his dedication to Torah and did not succumb to their blandishments.

At thirteen, he was sent to Slobodka. Although younger than most of the student body, he was able to carve out a niche of his own at the great yeshiva. He also developed a close relationship with the *Alter*, who treated him as the apple of his eye. After spending seven fruitful years in Slobodka, he became the son-in-law of the Slutzker *Rosh HaYeshiva* – Rabbi Isser Zalman Meltzer. Together with his wife, Chana Perl, he made his home in Slutzk where he became an associate *Rosh Yeshiva* at twenty-two years old, making him the youngest *rosh yeshiva* at that time. After the communists took control of Russia, he fled to Kletzk

Torah genius, personifier of outstanding middos, pre-eminent leader, unifier and master builder of Torah in America – all these and more describe Rabbi Aharon Kotler.

where he established a yeshiva. It was in Kletzk that he gained international and eternal fame as the Kletzker *Rosh HaYeshiva*.

As *Rosh HaYeshiva* of Kletzk, it was necessary for him to travel to America to solicit funds for his yeshiva. During a visit in 1935, he encouraged Rabbi Shraga Feivel Mendlowitz to open a *kollel* in America. Much to his credit, Beis Medrash Elyon was opened in Spring Valley, New York. This was but the start of his involvement in building Torah in America. His real contribution was soon to be made. With the Russian occupation of Eastern Poland, as per the Russian-German non-aggression pact in 1939, the yeshiva was forced to escape the pending disaster that was about to befall European Jewry.

Via Siberia, Japan, and then San Francisco, Reb Aharon finally arrived in America. It was the great luminary, Rabbi Chaim Ozer Grodzenski of Vilna, who saw in Reb Aharon the future leader of *Klal Yisrael* – and so it was. Reb Aharon's energy and determination made that vision a reality. From the moment he met the small Orthodox

Rav Isser Zalman Meltzer, Rosh HaYeshiva in Slobodka

contingent at Pennsylvania Station, in New York City, he galvanized them into a force to be reckoned with. With the power of his personality, he forged a platform for the Orthodox viewpoint. Gone would be the days when only the secular-oriented Jews would expound the Jewish position on all matters in America.

Together with the Torah leadership of the time (under the auspices of Vaad Hatzala), he worked indefatigably to save the lives of the *bnei Torah* trapped in Europe. Not only did the Vaad Hatzala work towards freeing the *bnei Torah* and all European Jews, they also sent humanitarian aid to help them survive the war in the many far-flung places where they found themselves. He influenced rabbis, lay leaders, and government officials to recognize the vital need for *hatzalah* work. More importantly, he persuaded them to act on behalf of the beleaguered Jews of Europe. In the words of Rabbi Silver – "It was he [Reb Aharon] who was the

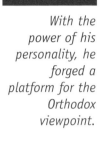

With the power of his personality, he forged a platform for the Orthodox viewpoint.

Inside the new Kletzk Beis Hamedrash, 1939

(L-R): Rabbi Elchonon Wasserman, Rabbi Aharon Kotler

The "Bendheim building," a remodeled apartment house on Sixth Street next to the original yeshiva building, used first for married scholars and later as a dormitory

Rabbi Aharon Kotler

From the shattered foundations of Lithuanian Jewry that survived, he began building Torah in America.

prime mover of all that we [the Vaad Hatzala] accomplished."

After the war, Reb Aharon turned to the task of building. From the shattered foundations of Lithuanian Jewry that survived, he began building Torah in America. Like his predecessors, he also faced ridicule and resistance. Undaunted, he battled on, first in White Plains, New York, and then in Lakewood, New Jersey. With fourteen European *bachurim,* Reb Aharon reopened his yeshiva. His goal was to

reestablish Kletzk in America. With time, American-born youths joined the yeshiva, later to become *roshei yeshiva* in their own right.

Reb Aharon, the *Rosh HaYeshiva,* was the paradigm of *roshei yeshiva.* He succeeded in transplanting the concept of *Torah lishmah,* Torah learning purely for its own sake, to an American yeshiva. Reb Aharon's goal was to produce *talmidei chachamim* who would dedicate their lives to Torah study. His brilliant *chiddushim* (novellae) and infinite flow of wisdom were shared constantly, at all hours of the day and night, with his students. But the lasting impact he had on his students stemmed from his personality. In Reb Aharon, they saw dedication to learning personified. His flashing blue eyes, burning with zeal and determination, his energy and concentration, all converged into his life's ambition – *ameilus baTorah,* toiling in Torah, learning Hashem's Word and living in accordance with His eternal Truth.

Rabbi Aharon Kotler visiting Eretz Yisrael

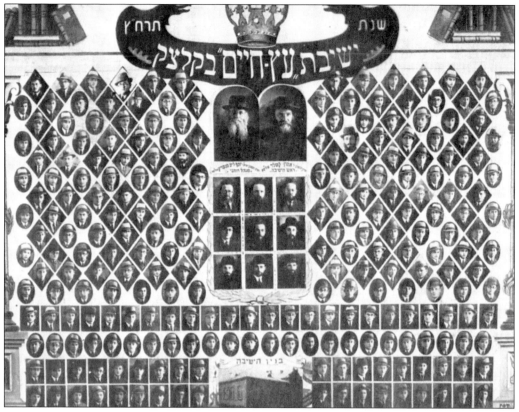

Faculty and student body of Yeshiva Eitz Chaim of Kletzk (1938)
Top box (L-R): Rabbi Yosef Leib Nendik (Menahel Ruchani), Rabbi Aharon Kotler (Rosh HaYeshiva)

Reb Aharon was the paradigm of roshei yeshiva. He succeeded in transplanting the concept of Torah lishmah, Torah learning purely for its own sake, to an American yeshiva.

His love for his students is legend. Every student can recall an instance when Reb Aharon placed the *bachur's* needs over his own, or expressed a deep concern and consideration for the student's well-being. He lived his own life frugally, preferring to give the yeshiva any extra money he might have. His pious *Rebbetzin* lived happily within the constraints of their tight budget, in partnership with her great husband.

Bachurim were mesmerized by his total devotion and diligence to his learning. His *shiurim* were demonstrations of his love for Torah and teaching. Even students who were unable to comprehend his words were overwhelmed by his delivery. The sheer love that radiated from his entire person was tangible and left its mark on those who were present. Not only his *pilpul shiurim* edified his students but also his "*shmussen*," (ethical discourses). The ethics of the Torah are inseparable from the Torah itself. An often-discussed theme was the primacy of Torah in forming and shaping one's personality. He was a personal example of the effects of his

Groundbreaking for the new Beth Medrash Govoha in Lakewood, N.J.

His shiurim were demonstrations of his love for Torah and teaching...and left its mark on those who experienced then.

philosophy. The truth of his words and the conviction with which they were said molded his *talmidim* into true *bnei Torah*.

It was not only in Lakewood, which soon branched out to include many subsidiary yeshivos in its network, that his leadership was apparent. Torah Umesorah also embraced him as their mentor. Additionally, Reb Aharon played a leading role in Agudas HaRabbonim's battle with non-Torah-oriented institutions. He championed the cause of total separation from those streams in Judaism that stood in opposition to the Torah way of life. With the passing of his friend and colleague Rabbi Reuven Grozovsky, the leadership of the *Moetzes Gedolei HaTorah* was passed to Reb Aharon. With his powerful personality, he assigned a new importance to the *Moetzes*, which became the active board for all Agudath Israel-related campaigns and endeavors. Reb Aharon's respect for lay leaders was unique, as evidenced by his close relationship with Irving Bunim, Samuel Feuerstein, and Stephen Klein, during the Vaad Hatzala, Lakewood, Torah Umesorah, and Chinuch Atzmai years.

Those who challenged him did not intimidate him; he stood firmly behind his convictions. Yet he was not stubborn and when proven that there was a better way to proceed, he accepted that advice and followed it with the same zeal as if it were his own. When necessary, he even spoke out against those whom the yeshiva relied upon for financial support, refusing to fawn over anyone. Reb Aharon's sublime personality coupled with his integrity convinced many to change their positions and support his.

Reb Aharon's strong leadership and sagacious advice extended itself to Israel, where he joined the *Gedolei Yisrael* in their battle for Torah in the Holy Land. The deterioration of religious education in Israel gave rise to the independent school system called Chinuch Atzmai. Reb Aharon took a leading role in ensuring the effectiveness of the new system, as well as its financial viability. He called upon Stephen Klein to chair this trailblazing effort for Jewish education in *Eretz Yisrael*. Using his position in America, he was able to galvanize the local community to act on behalf of the Jews in the Holy Land. This affected the American community, giving them an appreciation of the total supremacy of Torah. In Reb Aharon, they saw the embodiment of *Torah lishmah* – the persona created by Torah, fulfilling the vision of Rabbi Chaim Brisker that "someday half of the world will rest on this boy's shoulders."

In the words of Rabbi Mordechai Gifter (eulogy published in *HaPardes*), Reb Aharon was like an angel sent from on High. His keen sense of *daas Torah* was honed to the extreme. He could intuitively perceive the inherent threat to the Torah position in any given issue, long before others realized it. Similar to an angel, he considered

(L-R): Rabbi Aharon Kotler with Rabbi Zalman Sorotzkin during his visit to Eretz Yisrael

Rabbi Aharon Kotler

ferred to allow others to accept the credit while he did much of the work.

The success of the Lakewood Yeshiva – Beth Medrash Govoha – and the impact that its illustrious alumni have made on the Jewish world and the multitudes of *shearis hapleitah* that he was instrumental in saving are all part of his accomplishments. His legacy of Torah scholarship and leadership still illuminates the path of countless rabbinic and lay leaders, myriad *talmidim,* and the various institutions opened in the sacred tradition to which Reb Aharon dedicated his life.

Thousands petitioned him for advice on matters pertaining to the entire gamut of life. He never turned anyone away – in his mind he belonged to the Klal.

himself merely an agent, not an independent leader, always taking into account the true needs of *Klal Yisrael.*

His home was open to all. Thousands petitioned him for advice on matters pertaining to the entire gamut of life. He never turned anyone away – in his mind he belonged to the *Klal.* Many yeshivos and organizations were nourished by his counsel – he never felt that other yeshivos were competitors, rather he viewed them as partners striving for the same ethical goal. All of his energies were concentrated on this goal. But his humility and self-efface- ment did not allow him to bask in the light of success. He pre-

Rabbi Aharon Kotler speaking at an Agudah convention. Seated (L-R): Rabbi Shimon Mordechovitz, Rabbi Chaim M. Katz, Rabbi David Ochs, Rabbi Meir Schwartzman, Rabbi Altusky, Rabbi Benjamin W. Hendeles, Rabbi Dovid Lifshitz, Rabbi Pinchas M. Teitz, Rabbi Moshe Feinstein, Rabbi Eliezer Silver, Rabbi Simcha Elberg, Rabbi Mendel Chodorov, Rabbi Moshe Sherer, Mike Tress

Rabbi Menachem Mendel Krawiec (Kravitz) *1907-1992*

A brilliant *talmid chacham, rosh yeshiva,* and *rav* who demonstrated wisdom, concern, and kindness to all, Rabbi Menachem Mendel Krawiec embodied the best of "the world that was." His personal example was a true *Kiddush Hashem* to those ideals.

Rabbi Menachem Mendel Krawiec was born in July 1907, in a little town, Shinafkeh, Lithuania, to his parents, Rabbi Avrohom Aron and Leah Malka. He was the youngest of a family of six. Not much is known about his early years, other than the fact that he was a brilliant child and at the age of 13, he was sent to study in Kletzk, at the yeshiva of Rabbi Aharon Kotler.

He was welcomed as a family member by the *Rosh HaYeshiva*, and lived with them for approximately 18 years. Indeed, he was considered by Reb Aharon's children as one of them. He also became very close to Rabbi Isser Zalman Meltzer, the father-in-law of the *Rosh HaYeshiva*, who came to Kletzk from Slutzk, where he had been the *rav* and *Rosh HaYeshiva*. He was forced to leave after the Communists closed down all the Jewish educational institutions.

The yeshiva in Kletzk was growing at that time and many outstanding *talmidim* attended. Rabbi Aharon Kotler was a giant among Torah scholars, a true genius, and his *shiurim*, were extremely difficult to follow, even for the most brilliant scholars. Reb Menachem Mendel was one of the very few who was able to comprehend them, and consequently was chosen to repeat the *Rosh HaYeshiva's shiurim* for the students in a more comprehensible manner. Reb Menachem Mendel was considered the *talmid muvhak* (primary student) of the *Rosh HaYeshiva,* who also asked him to study with his only son, Reb Shneur.

When Reb Aharon went on a fundraising mission to America, Rabbi Elazar Menachem Man Shach (who was then in Kletzk) considered it a good opportunity for Reb Menachem Mendel to take leave and study under the Brisker *Rav*, Rabbi Velvel Soloveitchik. Consequently, he left Kletzk for two years and went to learn in Brisk.

The two years in Brisk were a most rewarding experience in many ways. He became a very close *talmid* of the Brisker *Rav*, who taught him his *derech* (singular approach in learning). Reb Menachem Mendel gained tremendously from his *shiurim*. He also became close to the children of the *Rav*, a relationship which continued for many years. In fact, the Brisker *Rav* asked him to learn with his son, Reb Berel, and the two had a wonderful study partnership. Reb Berel eventually became the *Rosh Yeshiva* of Brisk in Yerushalayim. The Brisker *Rav's* other children have remained close with the Krawiec family to this very day. The experience in Brisk was a major part of his life and, even though it was only for a short time, it definitely helped shape his learning.

Rabbi Krawiec returned to Kletzk in 1938, at a time when changes loomed on the horizon for all the Lithuanian yeshivos. Many were compelled to leave their cities and flee to Vilna.

Rabbi Aharon Kotler was already a major leader in the Torah world. He often consulted the *gadol hador*, Rabbi Chaim Ozer Grodzenski. Rabbi Aron Berek served as a secretary of the *Vaad HaYeshivos,* which was headed by Reb Chaim Ozer, and was his personal secretary as well. The Bereks had a daughter who was a wonderful, intelligent young woman, and she was a constant household member in the home of Reb Chaim Ozer. The Berek home was open to great *Roshei Yeshiva* and *rabbanim*. Rabbi Aharon Kotler had a warm relationship with Reb Aron Berek and suggested his *talmid muvhak*, Reb Menachem Mendel, as a *shidduch* knowing that he would be able to continue his exceptional Torah study if they married.

They became engaged, but were soon caught up in the War. For five years they shared all the hardships endured by the Mirrer Yeshiva in Japan and then in Shanghai, China. They married in 1942,

in Shanghai, when things were somewhat more settled. Indeed, many others who were engaged earlier also married then.

The wedding was held without family and with little fanfare. Not much was available for the wedding *seudah*, but there was *simchah* and hope. The *Mashgiach,* Rabbi Yechezkel Levenstein, and the other great leaders in Shanghai were there for *chizuk* and served as family. Rabbi Avraham Kalmanowitz and Rabbi Aharon Kotler provided *divrei chizuk* and monies to the yeshiva community. Both these *roshei yeshiva* were also fully involved in facilitating everyone's departure from China when the War was over, and helped them settle either in *Eretz Yisrael* or in America.

Life in Shanghai was difficult, but they managed to endure the hardships mainly because of the support system provided by the entire *bnei Torah* community. Rabbi Krawiec was considered one of the outstanding young men in the Mirrer Yeshiva and became very close to the members of this exalted community.

Towards the end of the War, the Mirrer community found out about the Holocaust's horrific devastation inflicted on European Jewry. Everyone, including the Krawieces, suffered personal losses. It is difficult to imagine how all this news was received and absorbed, but most of them were determined to rebuild their lives.

In 1946, Rabbi Krawiec, his wife, and two very young children left China for America. After an

Rabbi Yitzchok Zev (Velvel) Soloveitchik

Rabbi Krawiec was considered one of the outstanding talmidim in the Kletzk Yeshiva and then in the Mirrer Yeshiva in Shanghai.

Rabbi Shnuer Kotler

Rabbi Aron Berek

Two years after arriving in America, he became Rosh Yeshiva of R.J.J. Teaching young American students was a challenge he met masterfully.

Rabbi Eliezer Menachem Man Shach

arduous journey they arrived in San Francisco and boarded a cross-country train to New York City. A relative found them an apartment in Seagate, a small community at the southern tip of Brooklyn, New York.

Life in Seagate was very different from anything they were accustomed to. There were many religious, cultural, and language barriers. With the support of family and old friends, they managed to settle in a tiny basement apartment. They made friends and integrated into the community and, eventually, Rabbi Krawiec assumed an important leadership role.

In the single Orthodox synagogue in Seagate, Rabbi Krawiec was offered the position of leading the *davening* in the basement *beis medrash* and teaching *Mishnayos*. He willingly undertook this position, even though it was a major adjustment for him. Ultimately, he established his own *beis medrash*, since there was a serious demand for such a place. Many wonderful families became part of this *beis medrash* and gained enormously from the experience. Rabbi Krawiec increased his *shiurim* and his involvement with his *mispallelim*. The summer visitors to Seagate, many of whom were chassidic, also joined the *shul* and formed a warm relationship with this Lithuanian scholar.

For the first two years after their arrival, Reb

Menachem Mendel studied at home. Rabbi Aharon Kotler was then instrumental in securing Rabbi Krawiec's appointment as the *Rosh HaYeshiva* of the Rabbi Jacob Joseph Yeshiva on the Lower East Side of Manhattan. It was a new challenge to teach young American yeshiva students to learn in the style of the European yeshivos and help them develop a life-long interest and love for studying Torah. His masterful *shiurim*, together with his patience and wisdom in dealing with his *talmidim*, made him highly respected, as well as beloved by all of them. Every *talmid* was treated as a son, as he helped each one develop his maximum potential in learning while broadening his scope of Torah knowledge. The *talmidim* wanted to learn and absorb everything that their great teacher had to offer and remained in his class for three to four years.

The schedule in R.J.J. was truly an arduous one. Rabbi Krawiec often gave two *shiurim* daily, in addition to "speaking in learning" and being available to answer questions and give advice.

Eventually, R.J.J. asked Rabbi Krawiec to prepare his students to receive *semichah*. It was a most successful program, which served as the catalyst for many *talmidim* to enter the rabbinate. Even those who entered other professions or the business world developed a life-long love of learning Gemara, Halachah, etc. and continued learning.

The *kollel* concept in America was in its infancy and Rabbi Aharon Kotler was anxious to bring to Lakewood, New Jersey, the best minds and the most motivated *talmidim* to build his yeshiva. Rabbi Krawiec sent him some of his best and brightest students, who were impelled to devote their lives to *Torah lishmah*. Among them were Rabbi Meir Hershkowitz, Rabbi Meir Stern, and

First Chag Hasemichah at R.J.J., June 1952.
(L-R): Rabbi Dr. Hillel Weiss, Rabbi Chaim Hyman,
Benjamin Koenigsberg, Rabbi Eric Schneider, (unidentified),
Rabbi David Hirshfeld, Rabbi Shmuel Dovid Warshavchik, Irving
Bunim, Rabbi Mendel Krawiec, Rabbi Mendel Hammer, Rabbi
Hershel Kurzrock, Rabbi Yitzchok M. Brun, Rabbi Irving Golombeck,
Rabbi Moshe Saks, (bottom left): Rebbetzin Bella Tendler

Rabbi Moshe Hirsch, all prominent Torah leaders today in their respective yeshivos.

The *talmidim* also turned to him for advice, guidance, and *chizuk*. Many of them visited with him on Purim and Chanukah in Seagate. Rabbi Krawiec became close to many of their parents and developed relationships that lasted his entire lifetime. After his passing, many former *talmidim* related how Reb Menachem Mendel had taken care of their personal material needs, obtaining clothing or other items, for them when necessary. It was all done in secrecy, without fanfare or publicity.

Rabbi Krawiec made *shemiras hamitzvos, mitzvah* observance, a priority in the community. By personal example, he taught them the practical application of the *mitzvos*.

Many well-meaning Jews who were somewhat intimidated by Rabbi Krawiec's adherence to and teaching of the "*shtetel*" way of life would often suggest that he change his lifestyle, his mode of dress, and become more Americanized. Notwithstanding these pressures, he remained steadfast in his European ways. Yet he was always friendly and warm to neighbors who could not understand his (and his family's) way of life.

Rabbi Krawiec was asked to publish his *shiurim* and with the able assistance of Rabbi Meir Hershkowitz, published his *sefer Chidushei Menachem Mendel* in 1985.

In 1973, after twenty-five years at R.J.J., Rabbi Krawiec was ready to retire. He hoped to achieve his life-long dream of settling in *Eretz Yisrael* and spending the rest of his life learning there. Soon after he and his wife moved there, he was invited to give *shiurim* in Yeshivas Stolin in Yerushalayim. When illness made it difficult to continue going to the yeshiva, the *talmidim* came to his apartment in Matersdorf.

Unfortunately, after two years, he was compelled to return to the U.S. because of his health. He lived in Miami Beach, Florida, during the winter months and in Boro Park during the summer. In Miami, he was asked to give a daily *shiur* which became very popular and drew many participants. His clarity of explanation, making Gemara and *Mishnayos* understandable to everyone, endeared him to many people.

Rabbi Krawiec was *niftar* on 25 *Iyar* 5753/1992 and was buried on *Har HaMenuchos*. His legacy is notable and enviable, carried on by his family and many *talmidim*.

His talmidim turned to him for advice, guidance, and chizuk... Rabbi Krawiec's legacy is notable and enviable, carried on by his family and many talmidim.

❦ Rabbi Dovid Leibowitz

1887-1941

"If Torah will possibly survive in America, it will be much to the credit of Rabbi Dovid Leibowitz." These impassioned words were spoken at his funeral. Reb Dovid came to the United States in 1926, before the arrival of the famous European *roshei yeshiva*. He brought with him the power and drive of Slobodka. Slobodka under the rulership of Rav Nosson Tzvi Finkel the *Alter (Elder)* was a foremost generator of Torah throughout the world. He came to raise needed funds for the Kovno Slobodka Kollel, and remained to give American *talmidim* a taste of the flavor of Torah learning that was the standard in Europe.

Rabbi Leibowitz was born in Zhetel, near Grodno. He studied at the Lomza Yeshiva during his early years. After a few years, his great-uncle, the famed Rabbi Yisrael Meir *HaKohen* Kagan of Radin known as the *Chofetz Chaim*, brought him to Radin. The *Chofetz Chaim* then personally monitored his progress and took him as a *chavrusa* when compiling *Hilchos Sukkah* in the *Mishnah Berurah*.

His teacher, Rabbi Naftoli Tropp, said of the teenager – "he is already a fine *lamdan*."

At 18, he transferred to Slobodka where he was eternally molded by the teachings of the *Alter*. He left Slobodka and married the daughter of Rabbi Chanoch Henoch Shereshevsky. With the passing of his father-in-law, Reb Dovid assumed his position as *Rav* of Sletchenk, a position he held for six years. He returned to Slobodka at the invitation of Rabbi Nosson Tzvi Finkel, to join the *Kollel* – a rare honor at the time. It was from there that he came to America.

His first position was as *Rosh HaYeshiva* in Mesivta Torah Vodaath. Even though it was a yeshiva of note, the method of learning and the direction of the students was not at all similar to its European counterparts. In America, learning in yeshiva meant preparation for a vocation as a rabbi. Long-term, in-depth learning for the sake of achieving Torah greatness was unknown. Reb Dovid challenged that view of Torah learning. He contended that the American youth could and would rise to the levels of

Rabbi Dovid Leibowitz with a group of students during the summer. Rabbi Pam, as a bachur, is third from right.

their European counterparts, they simply had to be offered the opportunity.

Reb Dovid's sterling character, as a *baal mussar* and *lamdan*, earned him the respect of all, his students and peers alike. But his style of teaching and insistence that high-level learning and *mussar* concepts must be taught even in America, did not concur with the direction of Torah Vodaath. The resulting contention led to his leaving the yeshiva. Penniless, but full of faith in Hashem, he founded his own yeshiva in 1933, named for his great uncle and mentor, Rabbi Yisrael Meir *HaKohen* – Yeshivas *Chofetz Chaim*.

It was in this yeshiva that he courageously began to teach, against the prevailing public opinion. He established this yeshiva to pass on his methodology in *mussar* (in the Slobodka tradition) to his students.

Reb Dovid was adored by his students, developing a deep and lasting relationship with them. They brought their personal problems and concerns to him. For each student, he had a sympathetic ear and room in his heart. Outside of the yeshiva, however, he was disparaged. Many could not fath-

om the wisdom of students devoting days and nights to studies that did not lead to a "contract," or money. Others challenged that every man was needed to bring Torah to the unaffiliated masses of American Jews. Reb Dovid was undaunted, responding that the *mitzvah* of *lilmod*, to learn, precedes the *mitzvah* of *lelamed*, to teach. With time, his students did indeed fill the ranks as educators, providing yeshivos and day schools with eminently qualified *bnei Torah*, bringing the "*geshmak*" of Torah to places where others had failed.

He taught his students to apply their learning to their daily life. Honesty and integrity were priorities

Rabbi Dovid Leibowitz with his first students

> Reb Dovid's sterling character, as a baal mussar and lamdan, earned him the respect of all: his students and peers alike.

(R-L): Rabbi Dovid Leibowitz (seated second from right) and Rabbi Chaim Pinchus Scheinberg (seated third from right) with the first semichah class

he demanded from his students. Reb Dovid believed that only internalized *frumkeit* would endure, whereas empty external expressions of piety would not.

Reb Dovid was not intimidated by those who challenged his approach. He would not deviate from the principles he had learned and internalized from his teachers in Slobodka. Lithuanian-style *mussar* and learning had not as yet achieved a foothold in America. Reb Dovid stood alone, against his own allies in the Orthodox world, fighting to plant the concept of *limud haTorah b'ameilus* (toiling in the study of Torah) on the fertile American continent. He paved the way for his friends and younger colleagues from Slobodka, such as Rabbi Y. Ruderman, Rabbi A. Kotler, Rabbi Y. Kamenetsky and Rabbi Y. Hutner. Although they also faced tremendous challenges and opposition in fulfilling their ambitions of building a strong yeshiva community, they did not have to introduce the concept to America. His direct influence was

While others came to seek their financial fortunes in America, he saw an opportunity to build Torah and achieve spirituality.

intensified by his *talmidim,* of whom the most famous are his son and spiritual heir, Rabbi A. Henach Leibowitz, Rabbi Gedaliah Schorr, and Rabbi Avrohom Pam.

Rabbi A. Henach Leibowitz

Rabbi Avrohom Pam

Rabbi Chaim Pinchus Scheinberg

In 1935, Rabbi Chaim Pinchas Scheinberg became the *mashgiach* of the yeshiva until 1960. Rabbi Scheinberg studied in America and received *semichah* from Rabbi Dr. Dov Revel. He then went to Mir, Poland where he later received *semichah* from Rabbi Avrohom Kamai, the Mirrer *Rav* and Rabbi Boruch Ber Leibowitz, the Kamenitzer *Rosh HaYeshiva*. Rabbi Scheinberg is probably the most prominent of the American students who were sent to Europe by the great *tzaddik* and Torah *askan*, communal worker, Rabbi Yaakov Yosef Herman, who later became his father-in-law.

Rabbi Leibowitz's view on America was typically the opposite of others – "There is no money here (in the USA), but if you want *ruchnius* you can grab it in fistfuls." While others came to seek their financial fortunes in America, he saw an opportunity to build Torah and achieve spirituality. For him it was a struggle, against tremendous odds.

The struggle ended with his passing at the young age of 54, but it could not extinguish his work. The yeshiva, headed by his son, Rabbi A. Henach Leibowitz, trained in the ways of his father, continues his legacy to this day.

Rabbi Yaakov Yosef Herman

He taught his students to apply their learning to their daily life. Honesty and integrity were priorities he demanded from them.

❧ Rabbi Yehuda Heschel Levenberg *1884-1938*

It took courage and resolution to establish a Lithuanian-type yeshiva gedolah in America in 1923 - but these were the qualities that Rabbi Yehuda Heschel Levenberg exemplified.

"It took courage and resolution to establish a Lithuanian-type *yeshiva gedolah* in America in 1923 – but these were the qualities that Rabbi Yehuda Heschel Levenberg exemplified. Rabbi Yehuda Heschel Levenberg was born in Pilten, Lithuania, on Chanukah, 1884. His father, Tzvi Halevi, was a great *talmid chacham* in his own right and the scion of an illustrious rabbinical family that had produced Jewish leaders and scholars for many generations. His devoted mother, Chaya Gela, was typical of many Lithuanian women of those times, whose only ambition for their children was that they grow up to become *talmidei chachamim* and *yarei Shamayim*, G-d-fearing Torah scholars.

At a young age, Yudel's family moved to Toltchin where his brilliance, outstanding *middos* and *hasmadah* were immediately recognized, even as a young *cheder* child. Before his *bar mitzvah,* he was sent to study in Maltch, under one of the greatest scholars of the generation, Rabbi Zalman Sender Kahana Shapiro, who immediately recognized his new student's virtuosity and phenomenal memory and predicted that he would one day become a true *gadol b'Yisrael*.

While still a teenager, Yudel was accepted into the famous Yeshiva of Slobodka where he developed a close relationship with Rabbi Noson Tzvi Finkel, the *Alter* of Slobodka. "Yudel Toltchiner," as he was fondly called by his fellow students and teachers, continued to excel in all areas of Torah study. He also immersed himself in the *mussar* classics and became a devotee and proponent of the *Derech HaMussar* of Rabbi Yisrael Salanter. This was a time of great turmoil in the yeshiva, where intense debate prevailed between the *mussar* school and a very strong and vociferous anti-*mussar* movement. Reb Yudel entered the fray and thus gained first-hand experience in fighting opposing forces; this would serve him well in his later battles against those attempting to destroy Torah *Yiddishkeit* at the turn of the last century.

Rabbi Levenberg was destined to carry on this struggle, through a lifetime of public battles and personal tragedy, against the forces of compromise and erosion of religious values on the shores of the New World.

At the age of twenty, he received *semichah* from his beloved *Rosh HaYeshiva,* Rabbi Moshe Mordechai Epstein; Rabbi Aharon Walkin, the famous author of *Bais Aharon*; and the *"Revid HaZahav,"* Rabbi Zev Wolf Avreich. During the same year, 1904, he married Devorah Edelshtein of Vindova, where the couple settled for ten years, as Rabbi Levenberg continued to immerse himself totally in his Torah studies. Throughout these years of spiritual growth, he maintained his close bond with his *Rosh Yeshiva,* as well as the *Alter.*

The Lithuanian yeshivos were in dire straits in those years, as the political winds of change swept throughout the European continent and created overwhelming poverty all over the Jewish world. In the meantime, Rabbi Levenberg had gained a widespread reputation as an orator and world-class *talmid chacham,* as well as a *baal mussar* par excellence and *yarei shamayim.* His *Rosh Yeshiva,* Rabbi Epstein, turned to him in this time of great crisis and asked him to travel to America, in order to raise much-needed funds for the yeshiva. There was also a great concern among the Torah leaders of Europe regarding the religious anarchy that was rampant in the American Jewish community. Rabbi Epstein hoped that his illustrious student would have an impact on the American scene and restore *Torah Yiddishkeit* to the masses of immigrants.

He left Vindova for America at the end of June 1910, and stopped in England for over two months, speaking in the major synagogues of London, Manchester, Liverpool, and Sunderland. He arrived in America in September of 1910, and shortly thereafter was invited to become the spiritual leader and Chief Rabbi of Jersey City, New Jersey. He then sent for his family to join him in this strange, wonderful, and forbidding land.

Jersey City was typical of the new "live-and-let-live Americanism"– it was traditional, but the people were ignorant in Torah learning. Many of their children were moving away from their religious heritage, customs, and traditions. They had many *shuls,* but they were lacking the communal institutions and organizations that were essential to the spiritual and social health of its Jewish community. Rabbi Levenberg immediately set himself to the task of organizing the community from the ground up. His boundless energy and devotion to his fellow Jews drove him, until his community became a model for others to follow. The local Talmud Torah was especially dear to his heart, for it was there that Jewish children went after a day at public school to learn Torah. The concept of a yeshiva day school was unheard of at this time, except for the Eitz

Rabbi Levenberg immediately set himself to the task of organizing the community from the ground up.

Rabbi Levenberg

Chaim, Rabbi Jacob Joseph, and Mesivta Tifereth Jerusalem yeshivos on New York's Lower East Side.

He was only twenty-six years old when he came to this country. But in the six and a half years spent in Jersey City, his great scholarship, masterful oratory, astounding organizational skills, and legendary acts of kindness made him one of the leading and most respected rabbinical figures in America. In 1917, with great reluctance, but also with great hope for improving the difficult situation of his fellow Jews, he accepted the position of Chief Rabbi of New Haven, Connecticut. It was there that Rabbi Levenberg was destined to write a glorious new chapter in the history of American Judaism.

For six years, he poured his heart and soul into his beloved new town, that prior to his arrival had been lacking the basic institutions that define a Jewish community. He became obsessed with the idea of creating a *mussar* yeshiva on these shores, built on the model of his beloved alma mater, Slobodka. For five years, he struggled and campaigned against the skeptics and opponents who said that such an institution could not become a reality in America.

With the blessings of his *rebbeim*, Rabbi Epstein and the *Alter*, Rabbi Finkel, he hired Rabbi Moshe Don Scheinkopf to be the first *Rosh HaYeshiva*. In May of 1923, Rabbi Levenberg presented his idea to the national convention of the Agudas HaRabbonim of the United States and Canada in Lakewood, New Jersey. He received their resounding support.

The Yeshiva of New Haven received its charter and a short while later bought an 18-room house, officially opening its doors on August 12, 1923.

"Ben Yitzchok" wrote in *Der Yiddishe Licht* of March 14, 1924: "Rabbi Levenberg's dream of many years finally came to fruition. New Haven merited to have a "corner" of Torah built on the principles of the Slobodka Yeshiva: i.e., Torah, *mussar* (ethical studies), fear of Heaven, and serving G-d with great fire and enthusiasm, just as we were accustomed to seeing in "*der alte heim*" (the olden days in the old country)... It will surely become a model for other places in this country where they will hopefully establish more "Tents of Torah" such as this."

In keeping with the yeshiva's identification as a *mussar* yeshiva, Rabbi Levenberg brought a *Mashgiach* from Slutzk, Rabbi Sheftel Kramer, brother-in-law of his *Rosh HaYeshiva*, Rabbi Epstein. Rabbi Levenberg was literally "*moser nefesh,*" dedicating himself to the point of sacrifice, to raise the funds necessary to insure that the students had

For six years, he poured his heart and soul into his beloved new town, that prior to his arrival had been lacking the basic institutions that define a Jewish community.

Rabbi Nosson Tzvi Finkel

Rabbi Moshe Mordechai Epstein

Rabbi Moshe Don Scheinkopf (right) shaking the hand of Rabbi Isaac Herzog

all who had heard of his accomplishments in Jersey City and New Haven. Who better to organize the Cleveland Jewish community than Rabbi Levenberg himself? It was understood that where Rabbi Levenberg went, so too, went his yeshiva. Consequently, in December 1929, the yeshiva moved lock, stock, and barrel to Cleveland. Thousands of people greeted the yeshiva's arrival at the train station. A parade of cars escorted the leadership of the yeshiva and all of their *talmidim* to the Chibas Yerushalayim Shul, which would serve as the yeshiva's new *Beis Hamedrash* as well as Rabbi Levenberg's new pulpit. Upon coming to Cleveland, Rabbi Levenberg appointed an additional *Rosh Yeshiva* to the staff, Rabbi Samuel Belkin, the future head of Yeshiva University. In addition, Rabbi Kramer's son-in-law, Rabbi Yaakov Yitzchok Ruderman, also a *talmid* of Slobodka, had joined the yeshiva prior to its leaving New Haven and came to Cleveland in March of 1930.

Rabbi Levenberg was a man ahead of his time. America was not yet ready to concretize his vision. Whether in

everything they needed. He wanted to make certain that they could devote themselves, body and soul, to their Torah studies, just as he himself had done as a Slobodka *talmid*. The intensity and energy which he invested in this undertaking, which to him was more dear than life itself, resulted in his hospitalization before Purim of 1924.

Shortly after the yeshiva's first graduation on May 10, 1925, Rabbi Scheinkopf left the yeshiva to get married, and thereafter accepted the position of Rabbi of Waterbury, CT. Rabbi Kramer assumed responsibility for the learning program and daily guidance of the students.

The yeshiva continued to blossom until 1929, when the material situation of the yeshiva deteriorated. At this time, Rabbi Levenberg was brought to Clevland, Ohio, as part of a delegation of three *rabbanim* who were asked to bring some order to the chaos existing in the field of *kashrus* and rabbinic leadership. Pursuant to their recommendations, a group of lay leaders approached Rabbi Levenberg and asked him to assume the mantle of rabbinic leadership in Cleveland.

His reputation as an organizer, scholar, and diplomat was widely respected by

Rabbi Levenberg was literally "moser nefesh," dedicating himself to the point of sacrifice, to raise the funds necessary to insure that the students had everything they needed.

Rabbi Sheftel Kramer delivering a Shiur

Rabbi Levenberg giving a shiur

Rabbi Levenberg was a man ahead of his time. America was not yet ready to concretize his vision.

his attempt to create the first real European-style yeshiva, or to bring a measure of honesty and integrity to the *kashrus* market, or to demand rectitude and *yiras Shamayim* from his colleagues in the rabbinate, he encountered opposition at every step of the way. Sometimes the opposition was in the form of jealous individuals, other times in the form of "politics," but mostly in the form of a "*maaseh Satan,*" the forces of evil trying to prevent G-d's work from being accomplished.

When the yeshiva relocated, Rabbi Levenberg's wife was taken ill and was hospitalized, and therefore unable to join her husband at that time. By Pesach, her condition had deteriorated and Rabbi Levenberg had no choice but to move back to New Haven to be with his wife. The yeshiva was left in the hands of Rabbi Kramer and Rabbi Ruderman. Rabbi Belkin left soon thereafter, followed by eight of the best students who went to Europe to learn in the Mir Yeshiva.

During the next two years, the Cleveland Jewish community kept urging Rabbi Levenberg to return and lead them. The *Rebbitzen* slowly regained her strength and her health and on Friday, August 19, 1932, Rabbi Levenberg, his wife and children disembarked at the railroad station where they were greeted by a large delegation of rabbis, lay leaders, and his beloved yeshiva students. The excitement was immeasurable. The honor and respect accorded their beloved *Rav* was unlike any ever seen in Cleveland. But, unfortunately, the positive atmosphere would be short-lived, for Cleveland would hold nothing but grief and tragedy during the brief years of his sojourn there.

When Rabbi Levenberg attempted to take on the kosher meat industry and impose some halachic discipline, he was opposed by such interested parties as the slaughterhouse, the butchers, and some of the individuals who made their living from doubtful *hechsheirim*. One of the most infamous episodes in American Jewish history occurred when the *Rav* was framed by some of these individuals with vested interests, and jailed by the local authorities. The resulting demonstrations, outcry and anger resulted in the *Rav's* release, but the anguish he suffered from this incident remained with him for the rest of his life.

The yeshiva itself did not escape the intrigues and machinations of his opponents. The question of leadership of the yeshiva, after Rabbi Levenberg's protracted absence, became entangled with other community issues. The issues were eventually resolved through rabbinic arbitration and the yeshiva was able to continue training its students for a short while. Rabbi Ruderman left the yeshiva in 1933, to found Yeshivas Ner Israel in Baltimore, Maryland.

At that time, Rabbi Uri Meir Tzirlin was hired as *Rosh HaYeshiva,* and with the infusion of new *talmidim* the yeshiva began to bloom once more. But again, the pleasure Rabbi Levenberg took from his students was to be short-lived. In November of 1934, the community celebrated his fiftieth birthday with a great banquet in honor of the *Rav's* Jubilee Year. Shortly afterward, he showed major signs of weakness, which the doctors diagnosed as a cancerous brain tumor.

He went to Mount Sinai Hospital in New York for many months of treatments, not returning to Cleveland until Shavuos of the

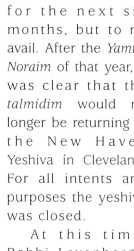

Rabbi Levenberg at work

following year. During his stay in New York, Reb Shraga Feivel Mendlowitz, the legendary *Menahel* of Mesivta Torah Vodaath, invited him to give *"mussar shmuessen"* to the students. *Rav* Mendlowitz had hoped that this opportunity to do what he knew best, educate Torah scholars in the ways of *mussar,* would give him strength and lift his spirits. The wars for Hashem and His Torah had indeed taken their toll.

Little by little his health returned, but in 1937, the yeshiva had another setback with the departure of Rabbi Tzirlin, whose health required that he take a position in Los Angeles to take advantage of the California climate.

Rabbi Levenberg refused to give up and on April 11, 1937, the yeshiva welcomed two new *Roshei Yeshiva* who, it was hoped, would be able to attract new blood to the school. Rabbi Moshe Feinstein and Rabbi Chaim Elazary made a valiant effort for the next six months, but to no avail. After the *Yamim Noraim* of that year, it was clear that the *talmidim* would no longer be returning to the New Haven Yeshiva in Cleveland. For all intents and purposes the yeshiva was closed.

At this time, Rabbi Levenberg's health deteriorated rapidly. He refused to take the medicines prescribed for his intense headaches, fearing that they would dull his mind and diminish his ability to think and learn Torah properly. During the last months of his life, he returned to New York for continued treatment and he gave a weekly *shiur on* Monday night, to his former *talmidim* of the New Haven Yeshiva. On *Shabbos Shirah,* January 15, 1938/13 Shevat, 5698, he returned his pure *neshamah* to his Maker. Rabbi Levenberg was an early twentieth-century visionary and trailblazer of Orthodoxy in America. His noble example helped set the standard for future *roshei yeshiva* and *rabbanim.*

Rabbi Levenberg was an early twentieth-century visionary and trailblazer of Orthodoxy in America. His noble example helped set the standard for future roshei yeshiva and rabbanim.

≈ Rabbi Yechezkel Levenstein* *1885-1974*

After World War I, with the break-up of the Austro-Hungarian Empire and the establishment of new national boundaries, a plethora of competing social-political ideologies caused traditional Torah observance in Eastern Europe to deteriorate.

In response to this tragic situation there were visionaries, such as Rabbi Ben Zion Halberstam of Bobov, who built a network of yeshivos throughout southern Poland in an attempt to stem the tide of assimilation and recapture the Jewish youth. Similarly, Frau Sarah Schneirer, rebounding from her initial failure to reclaim the older girls in Poland, who had been swept away by Polish Nationalism, began to reach out to the younger girls. In both cases, Hashem granted them success, albeit in limited numbers, but the foundation was laid for a future revival that transcended anyone's imagination. One such visionary whose actions were indispensable for the preservation of Torah was Rabbi Yechezkel HaLevi Levenstein, popularly known through his *sefarim* as the *Ohr Yechezkel*.

Rabbi Levenstein was born in Warsaw, Poland in 1885. His father, a businessman, was a Vorka *chassid*, while his mother's lineage included several chassidic *rebbeim*. The *Mashgiach*, as he later became known, was orphaned from his mother at age of five. Her final words to him served as a directive that would change his life, and, ultimately, help preserve Torah for all future generations. From her deathbed, she instructed the young Chatzkel to dedicate his life to Torah. Her pure words entered his young heart and the seed was sown for his future as one of the great leaders of *Klal Yisrael*.

Time passed and Mr. Levenstein expected that, at the appropriate age, Yechezkel would enter the family

One visionary whose actions were indispensable for the preservation of Torah was Rabbi Yechezkel HaLevi Levenstein.

---

*For a further depiction of this great Torah personality please refer to *The World That Was: Lithuania,* "Portrait of a Lithuanian Torah Personality" pgs. 106-111.

business and become a *frummer ba'al habayis*, a religious layman like himself, but it was not to be. Reb Chatzkel left home at 16 to fulfill his mother's dictate, first to study in a small yeshiva in Makova, Poland and then on to the Lomza Yeshiva, under Rabbi Yechiel M. Gordon. However, it was in the *Chofetz Chaim's* yeshiva in Radin that his future was decided. At that time, Rabbi Yerucham Levovitz served as *mashgiach* and it was not long before he realized the great *neshamah* that Heaven had entrusted to his keeping. Reb Chatzkel, in turn, was infused with a love of *mussar* after hearing only one of Reb Yerucham's *shmuessen* and from that moment on dedicated himself to *avodah*, perfection of character through introspection and total discipline. Before long, Reb Yerucham sent Reb Chatzkel to learn in the Kelm Talmud Torah, under the direction of Rabbi Tzvi Hersh Braude, the son-in-law of the *Alter* of Kelm. In the Kelmer tradition of *avodah*, the *Mashgiach* found the true expression of his soul. In 1935, after having served as *mashgiach* for a three-year period in both the Mir and Kletzk yeshivos, Reb Chatzkel left for Palestine to assume the position of *mashgiach* in Rabbi Reuven Katz's Lomza Yeshiva in Petach Tikva. When asked by Reb Yerucham why he would leave Mir, Reb Chatzkel responded that he felt that he could only perfect his *emunah* in the land of the *Avos*. Meanwhile, Reb Yerucham passed away in 1936; and in 1938, a telegram arrived asking Reb Chatzkel to return to assume the position of *mashgiach*

in the Mirrer Yeshiva in Europe. At that time, under the leadership of the *Chazon Ish*, Rabbi Avrohom Yeshayah Karelitz, the banner of Torah was again being raised in the Holy Land. Reb Chatzkel was in the process of developing many of the future Torah leaders in *Eretz Yisrael*. Rabbi Shmuel Rozovsky, popularly known throughout *Eretz Yisrael* as "the *Rosh HaYeshiva*," would often comment that he never would have become a *rosh yeshiva* and *marbitz Torah* without the *Mashgiach*, and this was true of many others as well. When word of Reb Chatzkel's imminent return to Europe became known, the *Chazon Ish* expressed his desire that the *Mashgiach* remain in *Eretz Yisrael*, for in Reb Chatzkel he saw one of the great Torah leaders of the generation and was loath to see him leave.

Rabbi Yerucham Levovitz

In the Kelmer tradition of avodah, the Mashgiach found the true expression of his soul.

The Chazon Ish

Rabbi Yechezkel Levenstein as a young man

The Mashgiach, with his iron will and Ruach HaKodesh, led the yeshiva during its miraculous escape from the destruction of Europe in 1940, to safety in Shanghai, China.

When the Mirrer Yeshiva evacuated to Vilna at the beginning of the War (along with many other yeshivos, under the unwavering supervision of Rabbi Chaim Ozer Grodzenski), the yeshiva came under the leadership of Reb Chatzkel and Rabbi Chaim Shmulevitz. Eventually, the yeshiva relocated to Keidan, deep into the heartland of Lithuania. When it was no longer safe in Keidan, the yeshiva divided up and went to four different towns: Krak, Krakinova, Shat and Ramigolah. While Reb Chaim oversaw the program of learning, the *Mashgiach* traveled from one village to another to be *mechazek* the *talmidim* with his *shmuessen*. Before the Mirrer *Rosh HaYeshiva*, Rabbi Eliezer Yehuda Finkel, left Lithuania for Palestine in 1940, he instructed the *talmidim* to be sure that Reb Chatzkel accompanied them wherever they traveled, until war's end and a safe haven had been reached. He said, "If Reb Chatzkel is with you, then the yeshiva will remain intact and survive. You must be sure that he remains with you the entire time."

Mir was the only yeshiva rescued in its entirety from the fires of destruction unleashed in Europe during World War II. The *Mashgiach*, with his iron will and *Ruach HaKodesh* led the yeshiva during its miraculous escape from the destruction of Europe in 1940, across Communist Russia and on to safety, first in Kobe, Japan, then for five years in Shanghai, China, and, finally, to the shores of America at war's end. Together with Reb Chaim, he rendered the life-and-death decisions that were contested (sometimes bitterly) at the time, but are now universally viewed as invariably correct. Reb Chatzkel toiled to maintain the spiritual well-being of the yeshiva student body, giving them the will to overcome the fearful tests they faced during their years of exile and separation from their families that, for the most part, no longer existed.

Talmidim from the Mirrer Yeshiva in Poland, 1938

In Shanghai, when presented with demands to alter the course he had charted for the yeshiva, the *Mashgiach* stood firm as a lion, refuting each argument with the soundest of logic, based on his vast knowledge of *Tanach* and *Chazal*. It was only after he thoroughly demonstrated the faulty underpinnings of the protestations presented to him that he revealed that his *rebbeim*, Rabbi Hirsch Braude and Rabbi Nochum Zev Ziv, had appeared to him in his dreams and revealed the course of action that he should take.

The Bais Yaakov Girls' School in Shanghai, established by the refugees

When information detailing the full extent of the destruction of European Jewry reached the *talmidim* in Shanghai, the *Mashgiach* was careful to look for any signs of emotional breakdown in his students. He went so far as to make sure that they bathed, brushed their teeth, and changed clothes regularly – all of the everyday behaviors indicative of a normal, emotionally balanced life had to be maintained. When the *talmidim* expressed the desire to learn one of the *Masechtos* in *Seder Kodashim* the *Mashgiach* refused their request. He told them that after the war, the Jewish People would have to be rebuilt. This would require Torah leaders familiar with the more basic tractates, *Nashim* and *Nezikim*. The *Mashgiach* remained unwavering in his resolve: "At such a time, we must be prepared to rebuild

The building in Shanghai which housed the talmidim of the Mirrer Yeshiva

what has been destroyed and to replant the song of Torah within the hearts of the next generation. Learn! Review! Create new *chiddushei Torah*! You will see that the new generation will be waiting for you, and through you Torah will again be returned to its splendor." And thus it was. Those who spent the war years with Reb Chatzkel testify that he was the *ruach chaim*, the driving and sustaining force, that upheld their spirits and fortified their *emunah* and *bitachon* during those awesome years.

When the Mirrer Yeshiva arrived in America and found its home in the East New York neighborhood of Brooklyn, New York, in 1947, the *Mashgiach* presided over a yeshiva whose *talmidim*, steeped in Torah and *yiras shamayim*, were at the forefront of the vanguard of those who would spread Torah across America and the world. Those who saw the Mirrer Yeshiva at that time – after five years of uninterrupted study

Reb Chatzkel toiled to maintain the spiritual well-being of the yeshiva students, giving them the will to overcome the fearful tests they faced during their years of exile and separation from family.

Rabbi Chaim Shmuelevitz

Ceremony at the City Hall of San Francisco in 1947, welcoming the refugees arriving from Shanghai, China. Rabbi Yechezkel Levenstein is in the center of the front row.

of Torah and *mussar* in Shanghai – witnessed a phenomenon never before experienced in America, remarking that it was a glimpse of Torah study in *Olam Haba*. Rabbi Avraham Kalmanowitz, *Rosh HaYeshiva* of the Mirrer Yeshiva of America, implored Reb Chatzkel to remain with the yeshiva to ensure that it was successfully replanted in America. Reb Chatzkel desired to leave immediately for *Eretz Yisrael*, but acquiesced to Rabbi Kalmanowitz's entreaties.

Reb Chatzkel only remained in America for two and a half years.

Rabbi Yechezkel Levenstein officiating at a wedding in Shanghai

The superficiality inherent in the materialistic American society was not for him – and this was in 1948. He used his *shmuessen* to protect his *talmidim* from the dangers of the American lifestyle. He perceived America as a land that "eats its inhabitants" (*Bamidbar* 13:32), by slowly numbing them to the pursuit of pure spiritual growth and replacing it with the desire for material acquisitions and physical pleasures. "What kind of society are we surrounded by . . .?" he protested. How distant, indeed, he must have felt from the consecrated environments of Kelm and the Mir.

Just before *Pesach* in 1949, Reb Chatzkel left America for *Eretz Yisrael*, where he rejoined the Mirrer Yeshiva

It was popular practice for people to come from all over Eretz Yisrael to Rabbi Levenstein's Purim seudah in Ponevezh for a berachah. Rabbi Chaim Ginsburg, Reb Chatzkel's grandson, is seated to his right.

one must jump into the fire...." he reflected. The Ponevezer *Rav*, Rabbi Yosef Kahaneman, referred to Reb Chatzkel as Hashem's special child of the generation, the one who lived and taught– in every deed, word and thought – the pathway to perfect belief and trust in the Creator. In truth, his life was one uninterrupted quest for *emes* and *deveikus* that will forever stand before us.

His life was one uninterrupted quest for emes and deveikus that will forever stand before us.

in Yerushalayim. (He later became *mashgiach* in Ponevezh Yeshiva.) He left behind a yeshiva – the sole remnant of the great yeshivos of Europe – that he had guided through the destruction of World War II and successfully replanted in America. From that nucleus, the Mirrer *talmidim* (and their students) have gone on to spread Torah throughout the world: There is no major Lithuanian yeshiva in America, or worldwide, that has not benefited from the *mesiras nefesh* of the *Mashgiach*.

In his later years, when asked how he merited to lead the Mir on its journeys during the War, Reb Chatzkel replied that one's personal considerations are nullified when weighed against the needs of a yeshiva, and the individual must respond to the greater responsibility of the *klal*. "Sometimes,

Rabbi Yechezkel Levenstein speaking from the lectern in the Ponevezh Yeshiva

✎ Rabbi Dovid Lifshitz

1906-1993

"ew *manhigei Yisrael* have had as profound an effect on the emerging American Torah-loyal rabbinate as did Rabbi Dovid Lifshitz, *Rosh HaYeshiva* of Yeshivas Rabbeinu Yitzchok Elchanan in New York City. A *talmid* of the venerable Rabbi Shimon Shkop, *Rosh HaYeshiva* of Yeshiva Shaar HaTorah in Grodno, Byelorussia, Rabbi Lifshitz internalized his *rebbe's* teachings and *middos,* which were to influence his own character and style of learning throughout his lifetime. He thus forged an important link between the old-time European rabbinate and the contemporary American rabbinate. Indeed, many of his students at Yeshivas Rabbeinu Yitzchok Elchanan became prominent rabbis whose major influence could accordingly be traced back to Rabbi Shkop through Rabbi Lifshitz.

Born in Minsk, in the first decade of the twentieth century, Rabbi Lifshitz was the grandson of the prominent *gaon* Rabbi Shlomo Zalman of Grodno,

author of *Olas Shlomo* on *Kodashim.* After he studied under Rabbi Shimon Shkop (to whom he would refer for the rest of his life as "my teacher and my *rav,* Reb Shimon"), he continued learning in the Mirrer Yeshiva, where he had the privilege of becoming a devoted student of both the celebrated *gaon* Rabbi Eliezer Yehudah Finkel and the *mashgiach* (spiritual mentor) of the yeshiva, Rabbi Yerucham Levovitz.

In 1933, he married the daughter of the Suvalker *Rav,* Rabbi Yosef Yoselovitch. In 1935, Rabbi Yoselovitch passed away, leaving a vacuum in the town of Suvalk. At the invitation of members of his father-in-law's *kehillah,* Rabbi Dovid Lifshitz became the new Suvalker *Rav,* a title he was to bear even when he resettled in the United States. After the outbreak of World War II and the Communist takeover of Suvalk, Rabbi Lifshitz and his family fled to Lithuania, only to discover that this nation too, was no haven for Jews. In 1941, he and his family escaped the clutches of the Nazis and traveled to Japan, from where he embarked on the final leg of his journey to the United States.

At first, Rabbi Lifshitz served as *Rosh HaYeshiva* of Beis Medrash L'Torah in Chicago, as well as assuming a rabbinical position in the same city. Simultaneously, he involved himself in the rescue work of the Vaad Hatzala. In 1943, both Rabbi Shraga Feivel Mendlowitz of Mesivta Torah Vodaath and Rabbi Samuel Belkin of Yeshivas Rabbeinu Yitzchok Elchanan offered Rabbi Lifshitz a teaching position at their respective institutions. He chose Yeshivas Rabbeinu Yitzchok Elchanan, joining the faculty in 1944.

What was Rabbi Lifshitz like as a *rebbe*? If you were to ask his students at Yeshivas Rabbeinu Yitzchok Elchanan, they would surely mention three aspects that distinguished their *Rosh*

(L-R): Rabbi Aharon Kotler, Rabbi Dovid Lifshitz

Yeshiva. First and foremost was his love for his students. The famous Chanukah and Purim get-togethers at his house were simple affairs full of warm spirit. He taught his American-born students the importance of using song as a medium for coming closer to G-d. He introduced them to the slow emotional rhythm of the great European dynasties, which he felt achieved the greatest results. His smile, penetrating first through a dark black beard and later through a long flowing white one, was extended to all. And the twinkle in his eye beckoned and drew close even the

First and foremost was his love for his students. His smile and the twinkle in his eye beckoned and drew close even the toughest student.

Rabbi Dovid Lifshitz and Rabbi Yosef Dov Soloveitchik, 1977

Rabbi Dovid Lifshitz saying Tehillim at the cemetery in Suvalk

Rabbi Dovid Lifshitz holding a grandchild

Israel and even allowed his name to be floated as a candidate for Chief Rabbi of a number of Israeli cities. He spoke a beautiful Hebrew at a time when many of the *shiurim* in the yeshiva were conducted in English or Yiddish. Indeed, even students with little Hebrew-speaking ability could easily participate in his *shiurim*.

Rabbi Lifshitz insisted that his students stay for at least two years, because he felt that relationships could not be nurtured in one short year. However, many remained for much longer, such was his influence. He

---

> *He was a tremendous "baal masbir" (possessing superior explanatory powers) and he loved to bring heavenly topics "down to earth."*

toughest student. Rabbi Lifshitz's second defining characteristic was his ability to make the most complicated subjects understandable. He was a tremendous *"baal masbir"* (possessing superior explanatory powers) and he loved to bring heavenly topics "down to earth."

Finally, there was his love for *Eretz Yisrael*. Rabbi Lifshitz traveled often to

Groundbreaking of Ezras Torah buildings

Meeting with the Mirrer Rosh Yeshiva on Rabbi Lifshitz's first visit to Eretz Yisrael.
Second from right, Rabbi Eliezer Yehuda Finkel; fourth from right, Rabbi Chaim Shmulevitz

(L-R): Rabbi Dovid Lifshitz speaking at an Ezras Torah meeting; on the left, Rabbi Y. Henkin

1976, succeeding Rabbis Naftoli Riff and Yosef Eliyahu Henkin, and re-mained as such until his death in 1993. The distinctive warmth and *ahavas Yisrael* which he had exhibited as a *rosh yeshiva* stood him in good stead in this important post, itself emblematic of genuine *chesed*.

As a bridge between two eras and two separate worlds,

Rabbi Dovid Lifshitz

taught his students about the *kol demama daka*, the still silent voice and the importance of merging the intellectual with the emotional in Judaism.

In addition to being the American rabbinate's *Rosh HaYeshiva* par excellence, Rabbi Lifshitz was a tireless communal activist. A dynamic member of the Agudas HaRabbonim (the Union of Orthodox Rabbis), he took over the helm of this organization after the passing of its previous leader, Rabbi Moshe Feinstein. He was also one of the founders of *Chinuch Atzmai / Torah Schools for Israel*. Rabbi Lifshitz is especially remembered for his role in Ezras Torah, the organization famous for its assistance and support of needy scholars. Indeed, he became its president in

Rabbi Dovid Lifshitz addressing a meeting in Eretz Yisrael

the Suvalker *Rav*, Rabbi Dovid Lifshitz, had an immense impact on today's American rabbinate – and that institution is so much the better for his influence and inspiration.

His distinctive warmth and ahavas Yisrael were fitting attributes for his role as president of Ezras Torah ... He bridged two eras, thereby linking the European and American rabbinates.

Rabbi Dovid Lifshitz arriving in Eretz Yisrael. At his right is Rabbi Simcha Elberg

Rabbi Tzvi Hirsch Meisels *1902-1974*

THE VEITZENER RAV

Rarely can one individual contribute so much to the spiritual development of a community as did Rabbi Tzvi Hirsch Meisels, the Veitzener Rav. But, then rarely do we come across an individual of such multi-faceted qualities and talents as Rabbi Meisels. Yet that alone would not have catalyzed Chicago's spiritual growth. It was *mesiras nefesh* of the highest order and uncompromising adherence to the Torah as seen through the eyes of *gedolei Yisrael* of yore. When one met the Veitzener Rav, he would be struck by his shining countenance which mirrored his inner sanctity. His warm smile was real, his kind words genuine, reflecting a love for all Jews, regardless of background or religious affiliation. Rabbi Meisels was a Torah genius who was revered for his ability to render the most difficult *halachic* decisions. An orator who mesmerized his audiences, he could speak on the most profound level, cap-

tivate a group of youngsters, or reach out and bring tears or laughter to the hearts and minds of the most unaffiliated Jews. Yet, with all these attributes he lived a simple life, after suffering through the infernos of the Holocaust.

With humility and faith his goal and purpose in life was to lead, to revive the culture that Hitler had destroyed. He hoped to reach out across the spiritual divide, fill the void imposed by American secularism, and bring back his brethren to serve Hashem as their parents, grandparents and ancestors did for thousands of years.

Rabbi Tzvi Hirsch Meisels was born in Ujhely, Hungary, in 1902. He was a scion of a chassidic dynasty which traces itself to the *Divrei Chaim*, the Sanzer Rav and the *Yetev Lev* of Sighet. His father, Rabbi Dovid Dov Meisels, was a brilliant scholar, *Rosh HaYeshiva* and *Rav* of Ujhely, and author of the *Binyan Dovid*, a respected halachic treatise. Even as a young boy, the Veitzener's fame as a diligent *iluy* spread. His ability to master the most difficult halachic problems and relate them to students helped him to secure his first rabbinic position in the Galician city of Neimark.

The five years that he spent in Neimark were the "best years of his life," as he was wont to say. Rabbi Meisels left a profound impression on the community and on the hundreds of students who flocked to his yeshiva. In 1930, he responded to a call from the community of Veitzen, a city known for its scholars, to be *Rav* and *Rosh HaYeshiva*. While at first they were taken aback by his chassidic garb, his captivating wit and warm personality soon overwhelmed them. During his tenure in Veitzen his fame spread, as he became known as a young scholar without peer. Rabbi Meisels published his first compendium of halachic responsa, entitled *Binyan Tzvi*. His proficiency as a *mohel* was also widely recognized.

But all this was to come to a bitter end. In 1944, Hitler's hordes deported the entire Jewish population to Auschwitz. It was in the inferno of the concentration camp that the Veitzener's heroism, his *mesiras nefesh* for *mitzvos* and his love for fellow Jews reached their zenith. There are countless stories describing these qualities in action and deed, and the Divine Providence by which he was spared from the clutches of death. His wife and seven of his children were not so fortunate. He was a wellspring of encouragement and hope to the embittered, brokenhearted Jewish inmates. He implored them not to give up their faith, regardless of the situation.

After his liberation from Auschwitz, the Veitzener became the Chief Rabbi of the Bergen-Belsen German/British

Veitzener Yeshiva in the Bergen-Belsen German/British section Center: Rabbi Tzvi Hirsch Meisels, Rabbi Zalman Leib Meisels, and his eldest son and present Veitzener Rav to his right

section. Once again, his unique personality and love for his fellow Jew shone. As a loving father, he restored faith; as a brilliant scholar, he addressed the many halachic questions regarding *agunos*, women whose husbands had disappeared and were presumed dead. Indeed, his responsa on the subject of *agunah* set the standard for guidelines used by the leading halachic authorities to formulate decisions on the subject.

In 1946, Rabbi Meisels came to America and began the daunting task of rebuilding the "world that was" – the chassidic culture of pre-World War II

> *Rabbi Meisels left a profound impression on the community and on the hundreds of students who flocked to his yeshiva.*

Student body of Yeshiva Shearis Yisrael, Bergen-Belsen, Germany

At the wedding of Rabbi Meisel's daughter.(R-L): Rabbi Dovid Meisels, Satmar Rav of Montreal as a young bachur, Rabbi Dovid Berish Meisels, Satmar Rav of Boro Park, unknown, Ujheler Rav, Rabbi Elimelech Paneth, Veitzener Rav, Bobover Rebbe, Urveyer Rav, Sorvisher Rav; back row, standing, third from right, Rabbi Eliezer Levin, Detroit.

Europe. His brother-in-law, the Bobover *Rebbe*, encouraged him to move to Chicago, a city that was a far cry from the European lifestyle that had been destroyed. This did not deter the *Rav*. He married again, to the daughter of the Deijer *Rebbe*. They were blessed with nine children, who have all followed in their illustrious father's footsteps. Rabbi Meisels' *shul*, Congregation Shearis Yisrael, by all appearances looked like a *shtibel*, but in reality it was an

(L-R): Rabbi Mordechai Gifter, Rabbi Meisels, Rabbi Chaim Dov Keller

Rabbi Meisels dancing at a mitzvah tantz

island of hope, a beacon of light, to all those who sought an ember of the fiery *chassidus* of the past. It was a *shul* that reflected the "*alter heim*," old home of Europe. Just by being there, they were transported from America to Veitzen, or any other European city.

The Veitzener took an interest in **every** facet of Jewish observance, ensuring that the standards were raised to accommodate **all** Jews. He succeeded in providing *chalav Yisrael* for the Chicago community, raising the standards of *mikveh* observance and initiating *Chevra Kadisha* practices in accordance with the strictest principle of Halachah. He focused on the city's educational system, establishing new primary and secondary schools. Rabbi Meisels inspired a generation of students who went on to become spiritual and lay leaders throughout today's Torah world.

(R-L): Rabbi Meisels, the Sighet-Satmar Rav, Bobover Rebbe.

While the spiritual growth of Chicago's Jewish community rests upon the shoulders of a unique group of lay and spiritual leadership, the Veitzener Rav was the catalyst for much of this development. He set a standard for others to emulate.

Rabbi Meisels inspired a generation of students who went on to become spiritual and lay leaders throughout today's Torah world.

At the dinner for Eidah Hachareidis – to the left of Rabbi Meisels is the Satmar Rav, Rabbi Yoel Teitelbaum

Rabbi Meisels with Rabbi Moshe Feinstein

Rabbi Meisels as sandek at a bris in 1972. Standing on left, giving the name, is Rabbi Chaim Schmelczer.

Rabbi Shraga Feivel Mendlowitz *1886-1948*

More than any other single person, Reb Shraga Feivel Mendlowitz caused the light of Torah to shine in America.

When Rabbi Yitzchak Isaac Sher, the Slobodka *Rosh Yeshiva*, met Reb Shraga Feivel during a visit to America, he greeted him by saying, "So you are the famous Rabbi Mendlowitz I have heard so much about." Taken aback, Reb Shraga Feivel replied, "I am not Rabbi Mendlowitz but Mister Mendlowitz." Responded Rabbi Sher, "Be that as it may, I have heard that you have accomplished more than any rabbi in Israel!"

Rabbi Moshe Feinstein said, "Were it not for him [Reb Shraga Feivel], there would be no study of Torah and no *yiras Shamayim* at all in America. As a result, he is the father of all the *bnei Torah* in America – those of our generation and those of future generations."

The Satmar *Rebbe* once commented, "Reb Shraga Feivel planted the first seed of Torah in America and from that seed grew everything that followed."

Rabbi Shneur Kotler once remarked that as a child in Europe, he remembers that his father, Rav Aharon, told him regarding Reb Shraga Feivel, "*Es is doh ah Yid, vos boit Torah in America* – There is a Jew that is building Torah in America."

Who was this man who in a mere 25 years of public life revitalized Yeshiva Torah Vodaath; built Mesivta Torah Vodaath; Bais Medrash Elyon; Torah Umesorah; Camp Mesivta; played a role in the formation of almost every major yeshiva in America; and helped the Satmar and Klausenberger *Rebbes*, as well as other chassidic *rebbes*, with moral and financial support when they arrived at these shores?

Born in Vilag, a small town near the border of Poland in what was then Austria-Hungary, to Reb Moshe and Bas Sheva Vilager, Reb Shraga Feivel was nurtured on Torah and acts of loving kindness. At the age of twelve, a short while after the death of his mother and remarriage of his father, he moved to the town of Mezo-Labortz, where he studied under Reb Aharon the *dayan* and, three years later, under the Chuster *Rav*, Rabbi Moshe Greenwald. Each of these *talmidei chachamim* was highly impressed with Shraga Feivel's outstanding mastery of Torah. At seventeen, he traveled to Hunzdorf, where he received *semichah* and continued his learning in Pressburg under the tutelage of the *Chasam Sofer's* grandson, Rabbi Simcha Bunim Schreiber.

After his marriage at age twenty-two, he settled in Humenne – and it was there that he began to study a conglomeration of Jewish writings, ranging from *Kabbalah* and *chassidus* to Jewish philosophy and history. In particular, Reb Shraga Feivel found himself drawn to the works of Rabbi Samson Raphael Hirsch, himself a Torah pioneer in nineteenth-century Germany. Rabbi Mendlowitz sought to emulate Rabbi Hirsch's ability to draw on the wellsprings of Torah, while concomitantly having philosophical and historical sources at his command, as weapons in the fight against the incursions of the Reform movement. This eclectic approach to disseminating Torah was to become Reb Shraga Feivel's hallmark throughout his professional career as both educator and *menahel*. Indeed, one of Reb Shraga Feivel's *talmidim*, Rabbi Avrohom Abba Freedman of Detroit, Michigan, once declared, "Rav Mendlowitz used to say that we in America should benefit from all the great *shitos* and *derachim* (philosophies and methodologies of learning) of the past. America should be a synthesis of all the best that the *galus* has produced."

In September 1913, Reb Shraga

Reb Shraga Feivel Mendlowitz as a young man in 1913

Feivel arrived alone in Philadelphia, having left behind his wife and children in Europe while he established himself on these shores. He settled in Scranton, Pennsylvania, where he lived for seven years, proving himself as a premier *mechanech,* even though he never became very fluent in English. Notwithstanding, the impression he made upon his students was indelible. One former *talmid* said to Reb Shraga Feivel's son many years later, "I have been taught by many great teachers and inspiring professors, but never did I have a teacher as exciting as your father! *Tanach* lived for us. Whatever *Yiddishkeit* I have today, I owe to your father!" Throughout this time – and during the rest of his life as well – he refused to be called "Rabbi Mendlowitz," insisting that he be called "Mr. Mendlowitz" instead. The *gedolei hador* (the great Torah sages of the generation) were not fooled, however. Indeed, when speaking of Reb Shraga Feivel, Rabbi Yosef Kahaneman, the Ponevezher *Rosh HaYeshiva*, said he should be called "*Nistar* (the hidden saint) Mendlowitz," rather than Mister Mendlowitz. When at long last (1920), Reb Shraga Feivel was able to bring over his family to the United States, he relocated to the Williamsburg section of Brooklyn. Just as he had

An uncompromising yet eclectic approach to disseminating Torah was to become Reb Shraga Feivel's hallmark throughout his professional career as both educator and menahel.

Rabbi Yosef Kahaneman (the Ponevezher Rav)

The first Mesivta building on Bedford Avenue

As principal of Yeshiva Torah Vodaath, he brought a freshness to the school's curriculum, while infusing it with that special brand of enthusiasm that was uniquely his.

done in Scranton for seven years, Reb Shraga Feivel assumed the role of master educator in his new neighborhood. But more than this position was in the offing for a man of his colossal talents. Reb Binyamin Wilhelm, one of the founders of Yeshiva Torah Vodaath and one of the staunchest supporters of Torah education in America, offered him the principalship of that school.

It was a match that was literally made in Heaven. Torah Vodaath needed Reb Shraga Feivel's uncompromising yet eclectic Torah outlook, and he in turn made the yeshiva the focus of his life's work. He brought a freshness to the school's curriculum, while infusing it with that special brand of enthusiasm that was uniquely his.

Notwithstanding all his success as principal of the elementary school, had Reb Shraga Feivel remained in that position it is probable that he and Torah Vodaath would be a mere historical footnote today. The forces pulling boys away from Jewish observance were too powerful to be resisted with an eighth grade Jewish education. The stage was set for the creation of a Mesivta.

With the opening of Mesivta Torah Vodaath in the fall of 1926, Reb Shraga Feivel sparked a revolution in Torah education in America. The magnitude of this innovation was evident from the difficulties he encoun-

A group of talmidim in the Mesivta in the 1930s

tered in selling the idea of the Mesivta, even to the religious public of that time – to everyone, from his own Board of Directors to parents of prospective students. No one imagined then (except Reb Shraga Feivel himself!) that the Mesivta would develop and produce generations of graduates, ranging from internationally renowned *talmidei chachamim* to religious *baalei batim* in the thousands.

Torah Vodaath became a center for Torah scholars who desired to partake of a smorgasbord of Jewish scholarship. Rabbi Freedman said, "How many places in the world were there... years ago where the *Ramban* (Nachmanides) was an esteemed and authoritative commentator as at Torah Vodaas? The *Sefer HaChinuch* received a new dimension there. The *sefarim* of the *monei hamitzvos* (those who reckoned the commandments) were reborn there. Reb Moshe Chaim Luzzato became

Parade for the Chanukas HaBayis of the Mesivta building

reacclaimed with his *Derech Hashem* and *Daas Tevunah* ... Rabbi Tzaddok HaKohen of Lublin received the preeminence that he deserved at Torah Vodaas. All the classic movements were not taught at the Mesivta (the high school) – they existed there as normal, integral parts of *Yiddishkeit*. The spirit of Rabbi Isaac Halevi and his *Doros Rishonim* ..., Reb Aharon Marcus and his *Der Chassidus*, Reb Isaac Breuer –[these were] also in the Mesivta."

It is obvious, then, that Reb Shraga Feivel had started a revolution of sorts – but in a Torah context.

There was another revolution that was rooted in

With the opening of Mesivta Torah Vodaath in the Fall of 1926, Reb Shraga Feivel sparked a revolution in Torah education in America.

The parade for the Chanukas HaBayis of the Mesivta building. Reb Shraga Feivel Mendlowitz is in the foreground. In the background (R-L): Rabbi Baruch Kaplan, Rabbi Shachne Zohn, Rabbi Gedaliah Schorr, and Rabbi Nesanel Quinn.

the leadership of Reb Shraga Feivel: he simply did not tolerate lateness to class. Having tried his hand at various business ventures while in Scranton and Williamsburg (even though these ventures were unsuccessful), he knew the importance of punctuality, and he insisted that his students recognize its importance to their learning. However, far more than a good business ethic was operative here. Rav Avrohom Pam, the most recent *Rosh HaYeshiva* of Torah Vodaath, pointed out that "lateness on the part of a student or a member of the faculty was not tolerated, not as a breach of Mesivta schedule, but as a sacrilege of time – that Divine dimension of action, accomplishments, creation."

However, his legacy is not limited only to Torah Vodaath. He never recognized any distinction between his yeshiva and others. Reb Shraga Feivel believed that one large yeshiva existed – the Yeshiva of the *Ribono shel Olam* – of which all yeshivos were branches. With such a mindset, we can understand why he was motivated to help other yeshivos in their formative years.

When Yeshiva Mesivta Chaim Berlin started out in Brownsville, New York, Reb Shraga Feivel sent boys who were already registered in Torah Vodaath to learn in Chaim Berlin. Later, he established a rule that any boy who lived closer to Chaim Berlin than to Torah Vodaath would not be accepted in the Mesivta.

In 1941, when Telshe Yeshiva opened in Cleveland, Reb Shraga Feivel sent *bachurim* there. In fact, he was the one who first suggested the establishment of Telshe in Cleveland to Rabbi Eliyahu Meir Bloch and Rabbi Mordechai Katz. At Reb Shraga Feivel's *levayah*, Rabbi Bloch told one of his students, "We are walking behind the *mitah* (bier) of one to whom Telshe Yeshiva owes its founding and continued existence."

Yeshiva Ner Yisrael was another of many such yeshivos that were helped in a similar fashion.

Soon after Rabbi Aharon Kotler's arrival in America, he expressed to Reb Shraga Feivel his desire to open a yeshiva in America like the one he had left behind in Kletzk. Without hesitation, Reb Shraga Feivel sent some of the Mesivta's best *talmidim* to Rav Aharon. The *Roshei Yeshiva* in Torah Vodaath were upset to lose such *talmidim*. Reb Shraga Feivel explained, "Our task is to cause Torah to flourish, and Reb Aharon cannot be a *rebbe* for students of a lower caliber." No wonder Reb Aharon said of Reb Shraga Feivel, "Who can compare to him? His every action is *l'shem Shamayim*."

He was no less generous with his financial resources. To help Chaim Berlin establish itself, he told some of his largest donors – including Mr. BenZion Eliyahu Fruchthandler, who lived closer to Chaim Berlin than to Torah Vodaath – to direct their support to Chaim Berlin. When Telshe Teshiva started, he urged the Spero brothers of Cleveland, who were among his supporters, to assist in building Telshe. When Rabbi Avraham Kalmanowitz opened Mirrer Yeshiva in Brooklyn, Reb Shraga Feivel offered him the names and addresses of all the supporters of Torah Vodaath. He also gave a considerable sum of money to both the Satmar and Klausenberger *Rebbes*, to help them in their work.

Reb Shraga Feivel's altruism and support was not limited to America, as illustrated by the following incident: *Erev Yom Kippur* 1942 found Reb Shraga

> *His legacy is not limited only to Torah Vodaath. He never recognized any distinction between his yeshiva and others. Reb Shraga Feivel believed that one large yeshiva existed – the Yeshiva of the Ribono shel Olam – of which all yeshivos were branches.*

Feivel visiting the great Sephardic *baal tzedakah*, Isaac Shalom, on behalf of Torah Vodaath. During their conversation, Mr. Shalom voiced his concern over the lack of Orthodox Jewish education in North Africa, Iraq, and Iran and the success the non-religious organizations were having in these countries. At the end of the conversation Mr. Shalom wrote a check for $5,000, but Reb Shraga Feivel refused to accept it. He told Mr. Shalom, "The Holocaust ended European Jewry. A new epoch is starting in which *Sephardim* will be at the center. You are the only one who understands this, so you must devote yourself to the *Sephardim*."

Reb Shraga Feivel's abilities also enabled him to reach out and affect others in ways that were generally not expected of *roshei yeshiva*. His experiences in the business world gave him the practical acumen to deal with laymen for whom the "bottom line" was the main criterion in measuring an endeavor's success. He was thus able to guide certain *bachurim* and send them into the business world, all the while maintaining a Torah perspective and a Torah orientation. Moreover, he was a skilled writer whose articles in *Dos Yiddishe Licht* (The Jewish Light), a weekly Jewish newspaper which he and famed cantor *Chazan* Yossele Rosenblatt co-published in the 20s, demanded action from American Jewish laymen, not just from rabbis.

In 1944, Reb Shraga Feivel drew on his wealth of talents, abilities, and sensitivities in founding Torah Umesorah, the famous umbrella institution for Jewish day-school education in America. Indeed, it was Torah Umesorah that he termed "*mein leibling* (my beloved)." Earlier (1941), he had founded a school for educators in Monsey, New York, called *Aish Dos* (Fire of Faith), to enable yeshiva graduates to develop and hone their skills in pedagogy and in *kiruv rechokim* (bringing unaffiliated American Jews closer to Torah Judaism). Unfortunately, the school was forced to

Reb Mendlowitz co-published the Dos Yiddishe Licht (The Jewish Light) with cantor Yossele Rosenblatt

Students in the Aish Dos program, summer 1943:
1. Heshy Mendlowitz (from Scranton) 2. Heshy Mashinsky 3. Avraham Abba Freedman
4. Meyer Lubin 5. Kestenbaum 6. Meyer Strassfeld 7. Rabbi Simchah Wasserman
8. Weinberger 9. Shalom Goldstein 10. Moshe Wolfson 11. Moshe Weitman 12. Eli Halberg

Primarily, what most of his students remember about Reb Shraga Feivel is his neshamah kedoshah burning with love for his Creator, for his people, and for his students.

close its doors after a short time. Reb Shraga Feivel then established Bais Medrash Elyon, which in its time was America's premier post-graduate yeshiva and *kollel*. Meanwhile, Torah Umesorah became a living, vibrant testimonial to a man who had become the pulse of the Jewish community and the conscience of its educational system.

Declaring, "In a few weeks of vacation one can lose all he gained in the year at the yeshiva," and anticipating the fate of many of his students during the summer months in New York City, Reb Shraga Feivel founded Camp Mesivta in 1931, the first summer camp of its kind in America in which a yeshiva lifestyle permeated the very atmosphere. First located in Mountaindale, New York, and later in Ferndale, New York, it became an oasis for thousands of yeshiva boys who might otherwise have wasted their summers. It also was a favorite retreat for *gedolim* like Rabbi Elchanan Wasserman, Rabbi Shlomo Heiman, and Rabbi Yaakov Kamenetsky.

Primarily, what most of his students remember about Reb Shraga

Feivel are not all these accomplishments – and many others which may not have been publicized. They recall a *neshamah kedoshah* burning with love for his Creator, for his people, and for his students. Rabbi Freedman states, "Who can forget the *Tanach* classes! Reb Mendlowitz [was] like the prophet himself, hammering away relentlessly, chapter after chapter. Who can forget how he occasionally lost the struggle to hide his emotions, and his voice became lost or choked in pain or ecstasy?" Rabbi Yitzchak Chinn, Rav of Mckeesport, Pennsylvania, writes that "he taught us how to sing a *niggun* and how to shed a tear, how to dance, and how to cry. He often remarked, 'If you can't dance on Simchas Torah with what you've got, you can't cry on *Yom Kippur* for what you're missing.' The incendiary character of his *rikud* forever seared its impression into the hearts of Reb Shraga Feivel's students."

During much of his adult life, Reb Shraga Feivel suffered from disease and pain caused by either tuberculosis or ulcers. He also was beset by a number of heart attacks, one of which he suffered while he was reciting *Kiddush* in Williamsburg, New York, at the same time that the Churvah Synagogue in the Old City of Jerusalem was being destroyed by bombs (during the State of Israel's War of Independence). Finally, on September 7, 1948, the classic educator who had said that "the Tree of Life is in the center of the garden"; who had insisted that "...no matter how far apart the ideas you learn may seem, they are different approaches to the *Eitz HaChayim* (the Tree of Life), to reach the Almighty," returned his soul to the Creator of all life. He encouraged and motivated a generation of Torah educators, who in turn inspired so many others. Indeed, we are all that much richer for his having lived.

Rabbi Aharon Kotler was heard to remark at Reb Shraga Feivel's funeral, "It will take 1,000 communal workers to replace him." The Klausenberger voiced the sentiments of countless others when he said, "Until the end of the generations, Jewry will be indebted to Reb Shraga Feivel."

Our Sages teach us that in recognition of the enormous contribution King Chizkiah made towards Torah study, they established a yeshiva near his grave. In fulfillment of this tribute, Reb Shraga Feivel's son, Rabbi Shmuel Mendlowitz, and his son-in-law, Rabbi Shia Shiff, founded Mesifta Beth Shraga in Monsey, in memory of the individual who exemplified Torah dissemination at its zenith.

Reb Shraga Feivel Mendlowitz singing a song of deveikus at his son's wedding

Reb Shraga Feivel Mendlowitz and Rabbi Aharon Kotler at the first Torah Umesorah Convention in Cleveland, Ohio, 1947

Rabbi Avraham Newhouse

1914-1972

The very future of Orthodox Judaism in America was at stake. Jewish daughters were being adversely affected by a secular society and their peers in public school, but there was no alternative. Enter Rabbi Avraham Newhouse – a man who dedicated his years in America to building Bais Yaakov, thereby ensuring the survival and growth of the Jewish family on these shores.

He was born in 1914, in Hechenberg, Germany, to Rabbi Eliezer and Yonina Newhouse. The Newhouse home was filled with Torah learning and exemplary *middos*. R' Eliezer had a *shul* and a *cheder* in their house, which was supported from his business. When Avraham was born, his parents decided to dedicate their son's life to Torah. Avraham was sent to Frankfurt to learn in the yeshiva of Rabbi Breuer. At the age of sixteen, he went to Lithuania to learn in the Telshe Yeshiva. There he forged a very close relationship with the *Rosh HaYeshiva*, Rabbi Eliyahu Meir Bloch. When Avraham

would return to Germany to visit his parents, he would travel throughout the country to give *shiurim* and *mussar* talks.

In 1937, he was appointed as principal of the Yavneh School for Girls in Kovno. This school was one of the first of its kind, and had been established to combat the secular schools that the girls would have been forced to attend had it not been for Yavneh. Rabbi Newhouse was so successful in this school that many great rabbis throughout Europe sent their daughters to Yavneh. He remained there until the school was closed by the government in 1940.

Since Rabbi Newhouse was a German citizen, he was able to obtain a visa for himself and his wife to come to America at the beginning of World War II. When they arrived, they helped establish the Telshe Yeshiva in America. Rabbi Newhouse was one of the people who traveled to different cities to determine where the Yeshiva could establish itself. The Yeshiva opened in Cleveland,

Rabbi Newhouse dedicated his years in America to building Bais Yaakov, thereby ensuring the survival and growth of the Jewish family on these shores.

Original building of Bais Yaakov of Williamsburg, 1945

The second Bais Yaakov of Williamsburg building purchased in 1950s (former public school building), currently Bais Rochel

Ohio, and at the beginning he was a *rebbe* there for a short time.

Rabbi Newhouse was very troubled that there were no Orthodox schools for girls in America. He left the Telshe Yeshiva and moved to New York to start a girls' school: At the time, parents had to send their daughters to public school, which was compulsory, and they received their religious education at home. Unfortunately, many girls were negatively influenced by their peers and were becoming irreligious. How could these girls be expected to marry yeshiva boys if they themselves were not educated in religious studies? This question greatly disturbed Rabbi Newhouse, and he was determined to do something about it. He set up a Bais Yaakov elementary school in New York in 1941, and worked with a few colleagues to establish an educational system for girls, as formulated by Sarah Schenirer in Europe. In order to

ensure that parents would send their daughters to the school, he did not charge tuition for those who could not afford it. After the War, he accepted all immigrant girls, even those who could not pay. Indeed, as the Newhouse family members recall, "It was a common

In front of Bais Yaakov, Division Avenue.

He worked tirelessly and with mesiras nefesh to establish a Bais Yaakov elementary school in New York with a strong educational program and consistent hashkafah.

Rabbi Newhouse, early 1950s

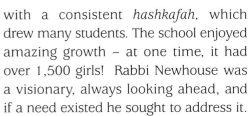

with a consistent *hashkafah*, which drew many students. The school enjoyed amazing growth – at one time, it had over 1,500 girls! Rabbi Newhouse was a visionary, always looking ahead, and if a need existed he sought to address it.

In 1944, he founded Camp Bais Yaakov in the Catskill Mountains, in New York. Today, there are many girls' summer camps, but at the time this was a unique concept. The counselors and other staff members were in a sense receiving their training to become teachers in the Bais Yaakov schools.

He envisioned the Bais Yaakov movement as a network of interrelated schools, an educational system requiring a council with central offices to coordinate it.

experience for all of us to hear the following: 'You are a Newhouse? When I first arrived in America, your father told me to pay what I could after I established myself.' "

Rabbi Newhouse continued working tirelessly and with *mesiras nefesh*, not resting on his laurels. The Bais Yaakov he built had a strong educational program

Giving the graduates their diplomas, 1950s

Rabbi Newhouse treated each of the girls in his school and camp as special individuals and was always available to speak to them when needed.

First graduating class

Camp, Main House building, 1963

New Camp, Main House building (in background), built 1963

He envisioned the Bais Yaakov movement as a network of interrelated schools, an educational system requiring a council with central offices to coordinate it. He created teachers' workshops, institutes, seminars, and conventions, before, during and after the summer months. Rabbi Newhouse would invite distinguished guests to speak at these events to guide the educators.

In the midst of planning and building for the future of girls' education in America, at the young age of 58, Rabbi Newhouse passed away. He was a true pioneer of American Jewry, and thousands of Jewish girls received their religious education and raised their families in the Torah way because of him. We are forever indebted to this noble individual.

He was a true pioneer of American Jewry, and thousands of Jewish girls received their religious education and raised their families in the Torah way because of him.

The original Camp, Main House

Rabbi Newhouse at Camp Bais Yaakov

Rabbi Dr. Dov Revel 1885-1940

From his early years in Kovno, Rabbi Dov Revel, the man who made a profound impact upon early American Orthodoxy, was a recognized *iluy*. His illustrious father taught him up until his untimely passing when Dov was only 12 years old. Wherever he went to learn he endeared himself to his mentors, among whom were the greatest minds of that generation, including Rabbi Yitzchok Elchanan Spector, the Kovno *Rav*; Rabbi Yoseph Z. Stern, the Shavler *Rav*; and Rabbi Yoseph Bloch, the Telzer *Rav*. The young student blossomed in learning, and decided to dedicate himself to studying and disseminating the Torah he held so dear.

His commitment to this ideal did not falter after his arrival in the United States in 1906. Already during his Kovno years he had acquainted himself with secular studies. Hoping to excel in both worlds, Rabbi Revel taught Talmud and *Mishnah* at the Mishkon Israel Yeshiva in Philadelphia, while simultaneously taking courses at Temple University. He continued his studies at Dropsie College, where he was awarded a doctorate in philosophy.

Rabbi Revel married Sarah Travis of Marietta, Ohio. After his marriage into the wealthy Travis family, Rabbi Revel spearheaded many successful business ventures in the oil market. All this was to change. In 1912, two yeshivos in New York, Eitz Chaim and Yeshiva Rabbi Yitzchok Elchanan, were combined. The directors sought a capable Orthodox scholar who could direct the new institution. Dov Revel, not yet 30 years old, was chosen. In 1915, he relocated his family to New York.

Rabbi Revel disregarded the notion then prevalent in the Orthodox world, that Torah would not thrive in America. The main obstacle preventing boys from continuing their yeshiva studies was the need to obtain a secular degree. To prevent the boys from falling prey to the world of spiritual indifference, he opened a mesivta high school. With strength and fortitude he forged ahead with his plans, even against the protests of those who felt that this was not in the spirit of the great yeshivos.

For the twenty-five years that he stood at the helm of RIETS, every aspect of the yeshiva was his domain. He tested the 500 students quarterly, delivered *shiurim,* and directed policies in all areas of the yeshiva's vast network. Fundraising and counseling graduate

For the twenty-five years that Rabbi Revel stood at the helm of RIETS, every aspect of the yeshiva was his domain.

Rabbi Shlomo Polatchek

Rabbi Moshe Soloveitchik

Rabbi Shimon Shkop

rabbis and lay leaders were all in a day's work. At first, he aligned himself with the Agudath Israel. Later, he shifted to the Mizrachi, preferring its stronger emphasis on Zionism.

Only the most eminently qualified *roshei yeshiva* were employed in the yeshiva, including Rabbi Shlomo Polatchek, Rabbi Moshe Soloveitchik, and, for a short while, Rabbi Shimon Shkop. In 1919, the first graduation of the Rabbinical College was celebrated. The five graduates were greeted as the hope of the future of American Jewry. Educated in the ways of Torah, as well as secular studies, they represented the spirit of the times.

Although he was an erudite *talmid chacham* in the traditional sense of the word, he appointed these great *roshei yeshiva* to lead the yeshiva in order to broaden the horizons of the students. Not only did Rabbi Revel share his place with these rabbis, he also invited visiting luminaries to address the yeshiva. He would go to great lengths to have an eminent rabbi speak to the yeshiva. This was an expression of his dedication to the students' education. His own needs and ego were secondary to the requirements of his students. Rabbi Revel would also offer vis-iting guests the hospitality of his own home. Consequently, his family was given the opportunity to interact with these great rabbis. Because of his self-lessness and dedication his fame spread far and wide.

Rabbi Revel was also actively involved in *hatzalah*. Through the yeshiva he was able to employ many scholars and students. Not only did he enroll the students in the yeshiva and employ new *roshei yeshiva*, he also sent funds to help those yeshiva students stranded in Siberia and elsewhere.

In 1919, Rabbi Revel conceived the idea of opening a college. His aim, as stated, was to offer his students the option of a strong yeshiva education and also a recognized secular degree. He felt that only if **both** avenues were open could the American Torah com-munity hold its own in the changing landscape of the New World. The tremendous fundraising campaign drew criticism from many quarters. What seemed to many an illusionary dream became a reality in 1928.

Rabbi Revel stood firm in the mission of Yeshiva College. He with-stood the attempts of the Reform element to amalgamate the yeshiva

Rabbi Revel was actively involved in hatzalah. Through the yeshiva, he employed many scholars and enrolled students. He also sent funds to help those yeshiva students stranded in Siberia and elsewhere.

His critical support and courage on behalf of Orthodoxy during its early years in America was crucial to its future growth.

with the Jewish Theological Seminary. He understood that such a move would undermine any Orthodox growth in the school. Rabbi Revel realized that his stand would jeopardize his base of financial support, but, nevertheless, he refused to compromise his principles. Rabbi Revel was a staunch activist on behalf of Orthodoxy and its concerns. He was an indefatigable fighter against those who attempted to dilute Judaism. His critical support and courage on behalf of Orthodoxy during its early years in America was crucial to its future growth.

His contention was that through the combined program of the Yeshiva College, all segments of Orthodoxy could be united. Every faction would be able to identify with one aspect of the total whole. The central and focal point would be the yeshiva, and the Torah studied therein. All else would align itself with the path forged by the yeshiva.

The graduates of the yeshiva would have the option of entering the rabbinate, having secured the necessary *semichah*, or the work force, having graduated from an accredited college. Both groups were essential to the development of a healthy and viable community. Educated laymen would provide the firm base upon which the Torah educators could function. Educators and teachers would emerge from the yeshiva to teach the future generations Torah and secular studies, all defined by the perspectives and convictions of the yeshiva. Through his involvement, Yeshiva graduates filled many pulpits across America. These educated leaders were able to infuse their congregations with new pride in traditional Orthodoxy.

His good intentions notwithstanding, the yeshiva received criticism from the mainstream Orthodox community. Rabbi Revel believed that the college existed in its own independent framework, and therefore did not adversely

Dignitaries at dedication of new building. Center, first row: (L-R) Rabbi Moses Margolies, Harry Fischel, behind them: Rabbi Shimon Shkop, Rabbi Revel (obscured); extreme right, Harris Selig.

Rabbi Revel in his office at Yeshiva College

affect the yeshiva, but rather complemented the total educational program offered by the institution. The inclusion of a Yeshiva College basketball team raised more than eyebrows. Yet Rabbi Revel stood firm, based on his conviction that American Judaism had to succeed on American terms.

He lived with these ideals and died with them. His last words to his *shiur* were – "Even if someone would deter you from the task I have set before you, tell him in my name that you must continue. The yeshiva is yours to build." And build he did during his quarter-of-a-century tenure at RIETS.

Rabbi Revel believed that the college existed in its own independent framework, and therefore did not adversely affect the yeshiva, but rather complemented the total educational program offered by the institution.

Rabbinical graduates, March 31, 1940, seated in middle of first row
(L-R): Rabbi Moshe Soloveitchik, Rabbi Dov Revel, and Rabbi Benjamin Aranowitz.

Rabbi Israel Rosenberg
1875-1956

Rabbi Israel Rosenberg was a European rabbi who bridged the diverse worlds of Europe and America. Acclimating himself to American culture and its attending challenges, he ministered to the spiritual and physical needs of his flock and instilled in them the desire to actively and materially support their brothers in Europe.

At the young age of 14, Israel Rosenberg was ready to leave his hometown of Lomza for the great Yeshiva of Slobodka. He was accompanied by a glowing letter of recommendation from the Lomza *Rav* and was accepted into the yeshiva. He continued his studies as a member of a select group of students in Malch. Upon leaving the group, much to their dismay, he went to Novardok where he was ordained by the famous author of the *Aruch HaShulchan*, Rabbi Yechiel Michel Epstein, in 1899.

He married the daughter of Rabbi Feivel Greenberg, a distinguished scholar and philanthropist, who undertook to support the young couple so that his brilliant son-in-law could achieve greater heights in Torah knowledge. Reb Yisrael would have preferred to dedicate his life to study, but that was not to be. His father-in-law suffered severe financial reversals and Reb Yisrael was forced to find a position in the rabbinate. It was this job search that brought him to America in 1902. The twenty-six-year-old Lithuanian rabbi made an immediate positive impression on Rabbi Dr. Hillel Klein, the most involved *rav* in New York at the .. suggestion that Rabbi Rosenberg assume the position of *rav* in Poughkeepsie, New York. His fame spread and after a short while, he was offered the pulpit in Bayonne, New Jersey, which he accepted.

As a Lithuanian yeshiva graduate, he was keenly aware of the needs of the Jewish community. Rabbi Rosenberg utilized his pulpit to open many Talmud Torahs for young children. But his major impact was made via the Agudas HaRabbonim. A retiring person by nature, his friends and admirers were the ones who propelled him to the helm of this organization. With his uplifting speeches, he was able to galvanize the members of the Agudas HaRabbonim to take action on many aspects of Jewish life in America. He was a firm believer in the power of

---

Rabbi Israel Rosenberg was a European rabbi who bridged the diverse worlds of Europe and America.

First Agudas Yisrael Dinner in America, Far Rockaway, New York, 1939. (L-R): Rabbi Berger, Rabbi Israel Rosenberg, Rabbi Silver, Rabbi Finkel (speaking), Rabbi Dr. Rosenberg, Rabbi Dachowitz

the rabbinate. Indeed, he felt that the *rabbanim* should involve themselves in every facet of the community. They should not wait to be asked; instead they should take the initiative and lead. Rabbi Rosenberg's position was that the Agudas HaRabbonim should be the focal point, the prime mover and innovater of everything Orthodox in America. They were the *daas Torah*, the expounders of the definitive Torah perspective in America. His rock of conviction braced the Orthodox rabbinate for the many clashes it encountered at present and would face in the future with other organizations that did not agree with its traditional stance.

Rabbi Rosenberg was not complacent with the Jewish status quo. After serving in Bayonne, he moved to Burlington, Vermont, where his financial remuneration was more than sufficient to support his material needs. It was his involvement with the Agudas HaRabbonim that precluded his stay in Burlington. His constant desire to be involved at the locus of the Jewish community, to feel the beating pulse of Judaism, necessitated a move closer to

New York. He assumed the pulpit in Paterson, New Jersey, followed a number of years later by his final *rabbanus* in Jersey City.

Rabbi Rosenberg felt that a rabbinical board was not sufficient to mend the breach in the Jewish community. Intermarriage was on the rise, and ignorance of basic Judaism was rampant. He assessed the situation and came up with a solution by taking an active role in the fledgling yeshiva – Rabbi Yitzchok Elchanan Theological Seminary. Rabbi Rosenberg understood that only by preparing and graduating qualified rabbis could the Jewish community survive. He became its first vice-president in 1904, and toiled tirelessly to recruit students and raise necessary funds for the yeshiva. For a number of years, he traveled all over the country during the summer months, spreading the words of Torah, inspiring the hearts and educating the minds of Jewish families.

All areas of Jewish life received his attention. He oversaw the creation of a *kashrus* organization, encouraging full inspection of cattle slaughtering and meatpacking. He was also an active participant in the establishment of the Central Relief Committee to assist European Jews who suffered during World War I.

World War I had created havoc for the Jewish communities of Poland and Russia. Hundreds of thousands of Jews were displaced and subject to abject poverty, disease and affliction. They had nowhere to turn. To this end, a number of prominent lay leaders

His rock of conviction braced the Orthodox rabbinate for the many clashes it encountered at present and would face in the future with other organizations that did not agree wtih its traditional stance.

Rabbi Rosenberg left a rich legacy of achievements encompassing a broad spectrum of endeavors.

together with the support of the Agudas HaRabbonim organized the Central Relief Committee whose goal was to provide relief and succor to the devastated Jews of Europe. Rabbi Rosenberg was asked to accept the position of vice-president, which he assumed with vigor and enthusiasm. The Central Relief Committee not only gave aid to thousands of Jewish families, it was also the catalyst for the creation of a number of charitable organizations.

A short while after the war, Rabbi Rosenberg led a mission of rabbis and distinguished lay leaders to assess the devastation of the once thriving European Jewish communities of pre-World War I. He met with a number of European *rabbanim*, led by Rabbi Chaim Ozer Grodzenski of Vilna and Rabbi Avrohom D. Shapiro of Kovno. This group of ded-

icated rabbis and laymen did whatever they could to help their European brethren. Indeed, through their exemplary efforts they were able to send fourteen million dollars to Europe!

Ezras Torah, an institution that supported rabbis throughout the world, was established and directed by the Agudas HaRabbonim shortly after the founding of the Central Relief Committee. It was recognized that while the Central Relief Committee was there to minister to the needs of *all* Jews of war-torn Europe, the specific needs of *rabbanim* and *roshei yeshiva* and their students throughout the world were not being met – even during the best of times their financial situation was deficient. Rabbi Rosenberg played a pivotal role in the success of Ezras Torah.

In 1918, the Agudas HaRabbonim decided to reprint the famous *Vilna Shas*. Rabbi Rosenberg became the Director of the Talmud Publications Society. Much toil was expended on his part to ensure that this major work come to fruition.

Rabbi Rosenberg was an active member of the Vaad Hatzala. He also supported the efforts of religious Zionists to settle Palestine and was a delegate of the Mizrachi Organization to the World Zionist Organization Congress in London in 1920 and 1929.

Rabbi Rosenberg passed away in Brooklyn in 1956, leaving a rich legacy of achievements encompassing a broad spectrum of endeavors.

At a dinner for the Jewish Educational Center in 1951. (L-R): Rabbi Binyamin Avraham Teitz, Rabbi Eliezer Silver, Rabbi Israel Rosenberg, a leader of Agudas HaRabbonim, the Central Relief Committee and Ezras Torah. Rabbi Pinchas Teitz is standing.

❧ Mr. Joseph Rosenberger

1911-1996

Mr. Joseph Rosenberger, or, as he was known to so many, "Mr. *Shatnez*," was a unique man who combined true piety and scientific genius. Born in Austria in 1911, he worked in his parents' clothing store until the Nazis seized it from his family and gave it to an Austrian. Yosef and his father were sent to Dachau in 1938. While in the concentration camp, he made a promise to Hashem that if he got out, he would dedicate his remaining years to rebuilding *Yiddishkeit*. In 1939, he arrived in America.

A few months after arriving in America, a friend, knowing that he was knowledgable about clothing, approached him to help him purchase *shatnez*-free* material for a suit. In Europe, people had their clothing made by Jewish tailors, who made every effort to obtain material which was *shatnez*-free. At his parents' store, when customers would inquire if a suit contained *shatnez* or not, Reb Yosef would obtain the necessary information from the suppliers of the material about their makeup. With the technological advances at the time and due to mass production of clothing, *shatnez* became a problem. Mr. Rosenberger asked several tailors how to obtain suitable material, but to no avail. Not only did they not know, they made fun of him for trying to find out. After this experience he came up with the idea of establishing a center where religious Jews could obtain reliable information regarding *shatnez*.

Mr. Rosenberger enrolled in Manhattan's Textile High School and took menial jobs in the garment industry, to learn all about the nature, characteristics, and chemical compositions of wool and linen. In addition, he learned about the production methods of the clothes manufacturing process, and the areas of the garment where linen materials, threads or fiber, could be used. Eventually, he developed a reliable, affordable test to analyze these materials. In 1941, the *Shatnez* Lab was officially opened under the aegis of Agudath Israel.

---

* According to Jewish law, one may not wear a garment made of *shatnez*, an admixture of wool and linen; a common occurrence in wool suits, in which the lining is made of linen.

Educating the American Jewish community about shatnez became his crusade. Reb Yosef developed a reliable, affordable test for shatnez and opened the Shatnez Lab in 1941.

Young Mr. Joseph Rosenberger as a young man

Mr. Rosenberger's trusted tools of the trade

Mr. Rosenberger went from *shul* to *shul* to announce the opening of the *Shatnez* Lab, and to discuss the importance of keeping this *mitzvah*. Most people just laughed at him, and did not take him seriously. Reb Yosef did not give up, nor did he pay heed to those who ridiculed him. "You wouldn't assume food in a store is kosher just because the man behind the counter has a beard and *payos*, would you? Clothing, like food, needs a *hashgacha*!" he would shout from the *bimah*.

His first major breakthrough came when Crawford's, a large men's department store, agreed to offer *shatnez* testing. Reb Yosef himself had to pay for advertising the service. Only a few customers came at first. Crawford's competitors, including Barney's, Chatham, Moe Ginsburg, Mays and others, were interested in offering the testing service as well. People started saying to themselves, "If all these stores are offering this service, I might as well take advantage of it. Maybe *shatnez* is important after all."

In the late 1940s Mr. Rosenberger moved into his home at the now famous address, 203 Lee Avenue. This was to become the *Shatnez* Laboratory's headquarters for the next

fifty years. His wife gladly helped him in his endeavor of *shatnez* checking. All the years, Reb Yosef only took a small fee. He limited the amount he took from the profits for himself, reinvesting the rest of the money into his *shatnez* projects.

Although awareness of *shatnez* had increased, it was still far from being as important as *kashrus* and Shabbos. Reb Yosef felt that in order to put *shatnez* at the forefront of *Yiddishkeit,* he had to reach out to the youth. Beginning in 1945 through the 1970s, Mr. Rosenberger would visit various yeshivos, discussing with the students the importance of having their clothing checked for *shatnez*. The students listened and went home to tell their parents to get their clothing checked for *shatnez*.

Mr. Rosenberger did not stop with the *mitzvah* of *shatnez*. He produced a magazine called "*Mitzvos ,*" which conveyed important halachos and homey anecdotes imparting *mitzvah* observance and *yiras Shamayim*. This magazine was distributed in many day schools in the New York area. Every edition featured a "coupon reward" program to be used by students each time they bought a suit and had it checked for *shatnez*. All they had to do was have it signed by the store clerk and send it to Mr. Rosenberger. For every coupon sent to him, he donated money to the yeshiva the student att-ended. Over the years, he contributed over $100,000 to various yeshivos.

Reb Yosef was also involved in many other community projects. He was one of the founders of *Hatzalah*, and served as a dispatcher. Many newcomers to America would stay in his house until they found a job or a place to live.

In the 1960s, "Mr. *Shatnez,*" as he became known, realized that *shatnez* testing should not be confined to New

York alone. He trained people in Lakewood, Philadelphia, and Detroit in *shatnez* testing. Complicated cases were sent to Mr. Rosenberger. Later, *shatnez* labs opened in Los Angeles, Baltimore, Toronto, Miami, Montreal, Boston, and Cleveland. By the 1980s, over one million garments had been checked for *shatnez*. Today, virtually every Jewish community in the United States, as well as many countries around the globe, provides *shatnez* testing.

Mr. Joseph Rosenberger at work in his Shatnez Laboratory

Mr. and Mrs. Joseph Rosenberger

Until the very end of his life, he carried on his crusade. Just a month before he passed away, he spent some time in Boro Park and made the rounds to various *shuls* to lecture on the importance of *shatnez* testing.

Mr. Joseph Rosenberger

On 7 *Cheshvan* 5757, Reb Yosef Rosenberger died at the age of 85. At his funeral, his son-in-law described Mr. Rosenberger as a man always on the move to do a *mitzvah*, whether it was the observance of *shatnez* or giving charity. Indeed, he fulfilled his promise and dedicated his life to promoting the observance of *mitzvos*.

Besides his unswerving dedication to the mitzvah of shatnez, he also was involved in acts of tzedakah, chesed and promoting mitzvah observance, serving the community all his life.

Rabbi Yaakov Yitzchok Ruderman *1900-1987*

"**D**o you doubt that we will have a yeshiva the size of Slobodka here?" These incredulous words of Rabbi Ruderman were spoken in the late '30s. At the time when yeshivos were yet to flourish, he saw a vision of a Slobodka in Baltimore, Maryland. With unwavering faith in Hashem, he fulfilled that vision. "Build – don't worry about finances." Build he did, and finances followed. The yeshiva grew and even those initially hostile to the yeshiva became loyal supporters and proud hosts of Ner Israel.

Rabbi Ruderman was born in 1900 in Dolhinov, near Vilna. His father, the local *melamed*, was his first *rebbe*. Young Yaakov Yitzchok's reputation as a child prodigy preceded him when he came to study at Slobodka Yeshiva, under the leadership of the *Alter*, Rabbi Nosson Tzvi Finkel. He studied diligently and his fame spread throughout Europe. So great was his scholarship that Rabbi Moshe Mordechai Epstein, Rabbi Isser Zalman Meltzer and Rabbi Meir Atlas granted him *semichah* at the age of 24.

He married Faige, the daughter of the legendary Rabbi Sheftel Kramer. Shortly afterwards, he immigrated to the United States. His first position in America was in Cleveland, Ohio. There, he joined his father-in-law in the New Haven Yeshiva which had relocated to Cleveland. In 1933, accompanied by five *talmidim,* he opened a yeshiva in the Tiferes Yisrael Shul in Baltimore, Maryland.

The *Rebbetzin* helped shoulder the responsibility of running the yeshiva. She marshaled the help of the local women. Parties were held to raise funds to supply the *bachurim* with linens and food. But her most important contribution was the constant support and encouragement that she offered the *Rosh HaYeshiva.* She never allowed him to despair. After several years, their son-in-law (the husband of their only daughter), Rabbi Yaakov Weinberg, joined him as assistant *Rosh Yeshiva.*

The yeshiva grew steadily, attracting *talmidim* from the South, West, and New York. Every *bachur* was welcome. Refugees, as well as local boys, found a home and place for spiritual growth

> *At the time when yeshivos were yet to flourish, he saw a vision of a Slobodka in Baltimore, Maryland. With unwavering faith in Hashem, he fullfilled that vision.*

*Rabbi and Rebbetzin Sheftel Kramer and their five daughters.
Girls (L-R): Rebbetzin Yehudis (Neuberger), Pasha (Shochatowitz
and later Heiman), Faige, (Ruderman), Leah (Skaist),
and Viola (Lewin)*

*Hurwitz Memorial Dining Hall – One of the yeshiva's earliest
buildings*

established the Ner Israel *Kollel*. With this venture, he was able to intensify his impact on the finest students who remained in the *Kollel*. He demanded total commitment from his students. Learning was to be their priority in life, much to his pleasure. Many of his *talmidim* entered the world of *chinuch*. Those who entered the world of commerce were exhorted to agree to study at least 2 hours a day. The thriving Torah community in Baltimore bears witness to his successes.

As the neighborhood changed, Rabbi Ruderman began a search for a suitable location for the yeshiva, which now numbered over 250 students. He led

His scholarship and personality left an indelible mark on each student – the thriving Torah community in Baltimore bears witness to his successes.

First European students arriving in America, many of whom later became prominent roshei yeshiva and rabbanim; far left, Rabbi Kowalski, one of the first rebbeim in the yeshiva

under the guidance of Rabbi Ruderman. He implemented the wealth of pedagogical skills he had learned as a student of the *Alter* of Slobodka, to infuse his *talmidim* with the priorities that would sustain them throughout their lives. His success as an educator attracted more and more *talmidim*. His scholarship and personality left an indelible mark on each student.

In the early '60s Rabbi Ruderman

Rabbi Yaakov Yitzchok Ruderman speaking at fifth semichah celebration, 1947

Ruchani. Although their personalities were different, Rabbi Ruderman was able to grant Reb Dovid latitude to function according to his own personality and perception. Other brilliant, young *talmidei chachamim* were included in the *hanhalah* of the yeshiva. This gave the students a wide spectrum of talented and different mentors to learn from. Rabbi Ruderman remained at the helm of the yeshiva, without losing any of his stature. *Bachurim* from various backgrounds joined the yeshiva, all finding a niche tailored to their own specific needs.

Not only learning and information were transmitted to his *talmidim*, but also the responsibility to build Torah, to share the wisdom that one had acquired with others. He encouraged his *talmidim* to undertake *klal* work on all levels, as *rabbanim, mechanchim, kiruv* and lay leaders. Indeed, the long-standing President of Agudath Israel, Rabbi Moshe Sherer, was a *talmid* of Rabbi Ruderman. With pride, he directed and delegated his students to positions all over the world. He expressed confidence in them and, in return, they put forth tremendous effort to succeed.

Not only learning and information were transmitted to his talmidim, but also the responsibility to build Torah, to share the wisdom that one had acquired with others.

the campaign to raise the funds to purchase a large campus in Pikesville. Rabbi Naftoli Neuberger, his brother-in-law and the yeshiva's executive director, assisted him each step of the way. Together they built the largest yeshiva campus in the world. Students continued to flock to Baltimore and many remained in the *Kollel.* Rabbi Ruderman's dream and vision were becoming a reality.

Rabbi Ruderman had the uncanny ability of delegating authority and creating a unified team to run the yeshiva. He invited Rabbi Dovid Kronglas, a *talmid chacham* of note, to become the *Mashgiach*

Rabbi Naftoli Neuberger

Rabbi Yaakov Yitzchok Ruderman

Sitting (L-R): *Rabbi Moshe Horowitz Bostoner Rebbe/New York, Rabbi Yaakov Kamenetsky,
Rabbi Yaakov Yitzchok Ruderman, Rabbi Moshe Feinstein*

(L-R): *Rabbi Dovid Kronglas, Rabbi Isser Yehuda Unterman,
former Chief Rabbi of Israel, Rabbi Blumenkrantz,
Rabbi Yaakov Yitzchok Ruderman standing by the podium,
Rabbi Shmuel Pliskin*

(L-R): *Rabbi Yaakov Weinberg
and Rabbi Naftoli Neuberger*

Rabbi Dovid Kronglas

It was his contention that dealing with *bachurim* was equivalent to dealing with *dinei nefashos* – matters of spiritual life and death. He demanded from his faculty the same sensitivity. Often, he would turn the tables on a *rebbe* who complained about a student, saying that perhaps with more patience he would do better. With patience and foresight, Rabbi Ruderman was able to generate self-confidence and self-esteem in students with personal problems. Rabbi Ruderman showed everyone courtesy and understanding.

He intervened on behalf of students who wanted to dedicate themselves to a life of learning against their parents' wishes. Many became teachers and *rabbanim* because of his encouragement.

Rabbi Ruderman was involved in *klal* work. He was a member of the rabbinic union of Agudas HaRabbonim and Ezras Torah, and served as a senior member of the Council of Torah Sages of Agudath Israel. His time was at a premium, but he gave of it unstintingly for the growth of Torah in America. He served on the Rabbinical Administrative Board of Torah Umesorah, recognizing and addressing the needs of the various day schools across the United States. He became its chairman after Rabbi Yaakov Kamenetsky retired from the position. It was his example that blazed the trail for his students to assume positions of prominence in the broader Jewish community.

(L-R): Rabbi Shmuel Kamenetsky, Rabbi Moshe Kulefsky, Rabbi Yaakov Yitzchok Ruderman, and Rabbi Yaakov Weinberg

In their great *rebbe*, students saw not only a brilliant scholar, fluent in all of *Shas*, but they also saw a vibrant Torah scholar, constantly striving towards higher levels and achievements. Even though he knew *Shas* verbatim, he studied it with a vitality and freshness that expressed his great love for the wisdom of Torah. He loved to hear new in-sights, from anyone, because not only was his *chiddush* important, but Torah was important. His students perceived and sensed this love and it entered their personalities by osmosis. When he entered the *Beis Hamedrash,* the entire student body spontaneously rose in his honor; his very presence commanded awe and respect. His constant toil in learning called for emulation, and his love for his *talmidim* demanded reciprocation. What better way to reciprocate his love than to learn with the same zest and enthusiasm as the *rebbe*. Learn they did, and the yeshiva soon achieved a position of Torah learning true to the vision of the *Rosh HaYeshiva*, Rabbi Ruderman.

Rabbi Yaakov Yitzchok Ruderman

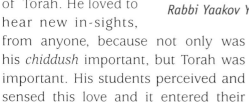

His constant toil in learning called for emulation, and his love for his talmidim demanded reciprocation.

Rabbi Yaakov Yitzchok Ruderman and Rabbi Yaakov Kamenetsky

Rabbi Yosef Yitzchak Schneerson *1880-1950*

THE LUBAVITCHER REBBE

> He viewed his arrival in America as more than an escape from the horrors of the Nazis – it was a Divine imperative to bring Yiddishkeit to these shores.

It was a balmy day in March 1940, the 9th of *Adar* 5700, when Rabbi Yosef Yitzchak Schneerson, the previous Lubavitcher *Rebbe,* arrived in New York Harbor, escaping the Nazi invasion of Poland. The thousands who greeted the *Rebbe* at the dock were not prepared for the *Rebbe's* new sweeping vision for American Jewry. He declared that "America must become a world center of Torah learning,…yeshivos and *chadarim* must be established."

Arriving a few hours later at the Greyston Hotel in New York, he called a meeting of his key supporters and *chassidim.* He drafted them to establish a new branch of the famed Lubavitcher Yeshiva, Tomchei Temimim, that had existed in Poland and Russia. He wanted it to be opened **immediately.** That night they agreed, and six days later studies began in Congregation Oneg Shabbos in Brooklyn. A few months later, the address that was to become synonymous with

Lubavitch, 770 Eastern Parkway was purchased. The *Rebbe* moved into the second floor and the yeshiva found a permanent home in the *Beis Hamedrash* on the ground floor. A new chapter had started in American Jewish life.

During the evening of his historic arrival, two of the *Rebbe's* closest supporters came to him. They each advised against the strident course of action that he was proposing. They told him that America was a country that devoured those who wanted to remake it; a country known for its insensitivity to traditional Judaism. It was a place where many *gedolei Yisrael* had come with ideas that had unfortunately resulted in failure.

These harsh words did not deter the *Rebbe.* Later that evening as he wrote of the advice of his close friends in his diary, he wept. He viewed his arrival in America as more than an escape from the horrors of the Nazis – a Divine Imperative to bring *Yiddishkeit* to these shores. He was

Escorted by an honor guard of the New York City Harbor Police, Rabbi Yosef Y. Schneerson arrives on his historic visit to the United States, September 17, 1929

determined to reinvigorate and remake Jewish life in the United States.

The *Rebbe* was born in Lubavitch, then part of Czarist Russia, in 5640/1880. He had studied under the tutelage of his father, the fifth Lubavitcher *Rebbe,* Rabbi Sholom Dov Ber. As his protégé, the young Yosef Yitchak entered community service at the age of fifteen, assisting his father as the prime leader of Russian Jewry. He undertook many crucial missions for the welfare of Russian Jewry and headed the famed Lubavitcher Yeshiva, Tomchei Temimim. His father passed away in 5680/1920 in Rostov, in Southern Russia, where he had escaped from the First World War. Immediately, Reb Yosef Yitzchak

assumed the position of *Rebbe,* the sixth leader of *Chabad Chassidus* since the *Alter Rebbe,* Rabbi Schnuer Zalmen of Liadi.

The *Rebbe's* arrival in 1940 was not his first visit to America. Just over a decade earlier, he had spent some ten months in the United States after escaping a death sentence from the Communists. That event occurred at the culmination of a Communist government campaign to wipe out Jewish observance. Spearheaded by the *Yevsektzia,* the Jewish communists, they wanted to destroy the Jewish underground by imprisoning its leader, the *Rebbe.* Jailed for months, he refused to capitulate. Finally, the Communists sentenced him to death. After much international political pressure, including that of the American government, his sentence was stayed and the *Rebbe* left Russia. From abroad, he continued supporting the secret network of *shuls,* yeshivos and *mikvaos,* which sustained the core of committed Jews in Russia until the fall of Communism.

Electrified by his courage against Communism, American Jews gave the *Rebbe* a hero's welcome in 1929. Prior to his return to Europe, President Hoover received him for a private meeting at the White House. The *Rebbe's* sojourn in America helped him gain a keen understanding of the challenges facing American Jewry. It set the stage for the revolution that he would launch just a decade later.

The establishment of the yeshiva, while the crown jewel of the *Rebbe's* efforts, was but his first step. The *Rebbe's* approach was different from others – he did not choose to simply establish a fortress of Torah. His agenda included the overall welfare of every Jew. He viewed the lack of Jewish edu-

His agenda included the overall welfare of every Jew. He viewed the lack of Jewish education as the prime cause for assimilation.

Rabbi Yosef Yitzchak Schneerson, the Lubavitcher Rebbe, upon his arrival in New York City in 1940

cation as the prime cause for assimilation. The *Rebbe's* goal was to remold communities and return them to the traditions of their parents and grandparents of Europe. His theme became "America is *nisht anderesh* – America in not different." Time and again he stated, "Just as *Yiddishkeit* flourished in Europe, so too, can it flourish in this continent."

In New York there were a few struggling yeshivos, while outside of the city almost none. In 1940, there were only three thousand children in the United States who were in day schools and yeshivos under Orthodox auspices. Other than one or two *talmidim* of the *Rebbe,* it was impossible to find a young man with a beard in Brooklyn. The Torah community was small, insecure, attempting to preserve itself.

A yeshiva student of the time explained the situation: "We, the few *bachurim* in one of the few New York yeshivos, felt like a wagon train on the prairie – isolated, surrounded by Indians, and holding on for dear life. The *Rebbe* arrived like the U.S. Calvary. He was not satisfied in fending off the Indians, protecting the wagons, and saving the settlers. He wanted to conquer the whole continent."

The *Rebbe* lost no time. While making every effort to save his *talmidim* in Poland, and continuing to help his *chassidim* in Russia, he began infusing new life into American Jewry. Within two years, he had laid the foundations for the renaissance of Jewish life. He opened fourteen yeshivos in the primary Jewish population centers of the United States and in Montreal, Canada; including Boston, Springfield and Worcester, Mass., New Haven, Conn., and Pittsburgh, Pa., one after another. He appointed his son-in-law, Rabbi Shammai Garry, as the director of the yeshivos. The *RaShag,* as he was known amongst the *Chassidim,* worked tirelessly, raising money, organizing new yeshivos and promoting Torah learning.

In 1941, the *Rebbe* established the organizations that were to have the broadest impact on Jewish life in the United States – *Merkos L'inyonei Chinuch*- The Central Organization for Jewish Education, and *Machne Israel. Merkoz's* mandate was Jewish education. *Machne* focused inwardly to the needs of the observant community. The *Rebbe* appointed his second son-in-law and eventual successor, Rabbi Menachem Mendel Schneerson, to head these organizations. The *Ramash,* as he was known amongst *chassidim* of the time, had escaped the horrors of Nazi-controlled France via Vichy, France, and Portugal, arriving in America in the spring of 1941.

Merkos undertook the development of Jewish education in the United States in a comprehensive fashion. It was the first organization dedicated to opening day schools throughout the United

States, as well as overseas. Within four years, 18 schools were already operating. During the early years, it primarily established girls' schools. The *shaliach*, emissary, sent by the *Rebbe* usually had to found two separate educational institutions, a yeshiva and a girls' school.

The schools were but one of the approaches of *Merkos*. Additionally, it launched a network of youth clubs, known as *Mesibos Shabbos*, where children would gather on Shabbos afternoon in a Torah atmosphere. Its division *Shalah*–The National Committee for the Furtherance of Jewish Education – pioneered release time at public schools throughout New York and other cities. *Merkos* also launched a publication division, *Kehot*, that eventually developed into the largest Jewish publisher in the United States. It also established a series of departments dealing with a wide variety of needs, such as the military, farmers, refugees, adult education, curriculum, and teacher training.

In 1943, *Merkos* initiated its summer outreach program, sending yeshiva students to visit Jewish communities outside of the New York area. The students went to the communities, evaluated their needs, supplied them with educational materials and initiated projects that raised the quality of Jewish life. The *Merkos Shlichus*, as it is commonly known, provided the *Rebbe* with "eyes and ears" in Jewish communities of all sizes and geographical locations. It infused many towns with new ideas and helped establish many schools, *shuls*, and, in later decades, *Chabad* Houses. [In the summer of 2000, some 500 yeshiva students visited hundreds of communities all over the world.]

The *Rebbe* sent his newfound American *talmidim*, as well as those who had escaped from Europe, to

(L-R): Rabbi Yosef Yitzchak Schneerson, the Lubavitcher Rebbe, Rabbi Eliezer Silver

establish the yeshivos and schools. He also had a unique base in the United States. There were approximately 80 Nusach Ari Synagogues, with about thirty percent in New York, set up by immigrants from Europe. Most were unlearned, but they had a connection with *Agudas Chassidei Chabad*, the central *Chabad* organization that had been established in 1924, in the United States.

The *Rebbe* seized any opportunity to develop new centers. The initial steps to open the first out-of-town yeshiva began on a wintry *Motzaei Shabbos* in December 1941. The *Rebbe* called in one of his *talmidim* from the yeshiva, Rabbi Mordechai Altien. The *Rebbe* told him that he had just received a letter from the Nusach Ari Shul in Pittsburgh with a request for a rabbi. Never one to delay, the *Rebbe* instructed him to go to Pittsburgh the next day to assume the position. A telegram sent to inform the *shul* of Rabbi Altien's arrival did not reach them in time and he received less than a cordial welcome from the *shul's* president.

The Rebbe established organizations that were to have the broadest impact on Jewish life in the U.S. Within a short time, he laid the foundation for the renaissance of Jewish communities across the country.

Rabbi Menachem M. Schneerson supporting his father-law, Rabbi Yosef Y. Schneerson, as he speaks at a Yeshiva Tomchei Temimim dinner, Sunday, June 14, 1942

No aspect of Jewish life in the United States was untouched by the Rebbe. Chabad's activities included the establishment of schools, shuls, mikvaos, adult education and teacher training.

Neither the hostility of the "Americanized" president, nor the apathy of the community, could repress the energy of the *Rebbe's talmid*. With the *Rebbe's* blessing, he began organizing a yeshiva that opened that winter. In 1999, it received a blue ribbon Presidential Award, as one of the outstanding schools in the United States. Pittsburgh was amongst the many communities that the *Rebbe's* pioneering vision helped transform.

The *Rebbe* himself opened many institutions, but he also played a crucial role in encouraging others to follow in his footsteps. Four years after his arrival, one of his *chassidim* brought him news that another Orthodox group had started an organization similar to *Merkoz,* called Torah Umesorah. Expecting the *Rebbe* to be upset by the competition, the *chassid* was surprised to hear of the *Rebbe's* joy with the new organization. "That's what I hoped they would do," the *Rebbe* remarked.

The *Rebbe's* correspondence from the last decade of his life reveals a remarkable breadth of interest: A *mikvah* in Washington Heights, a *shul* in Chicago, Torah study needs for young and old. No aspect of Jewish life in the United States was untouched by the *Rebbe*. When Mesivta Torah Vodaath faced a financial crisis, he quietly sent over a large sum of money to quell the emergency. He met with leaders of Young Israel, prodding them to open more *shuls*. From his home in Brooklyn, in a wheelchair, still suffering from the effects of his imprisonment years earlier, he was connected to all aspects of the Jewish community. News of a *chassid's* illness would bring him to tears, and information of the success of one of his *shlichim* enrolling a few more children in a yeshiva would cause his spirits to soar.

The *Rebbe* was a great *talmid chacham*, prolific writer, and teacher of Torah. Over fifty volumes of his deep insights into Torah have been published. His *Maamorim* and *Sichos* are studied today by thousands who wish to gain a deeper chassidic perspective into Torah. His writings provide a Torah viewpoint on all phases of Jewish learning.

In the years after the Second World War, in particular the last three years of his life, the *Rebbe* broadened his focus internationally. Many of his Russian *chassidim* escaped from the Soviet Union after the war and established a network of new *Chabad* centers. The *Rebbe* opened *Chabad* centers in Australia, France, England and other countries as well. In Israel, he set up Kfar Chabad, not far from Tel Aviv. He even sent a *shaliach* to Cuba in 1949, to revitalize *Yiddishkeit* in that small country. In each one of these locations, the *Rebbe* opened yeshivos, girls' schools, and built *mikvaos* and *shuls*. He instructed his newly appointed *shlichim* to make every effort to build *Yiddishkeit* from the ground up.

Just a week before his passing, on the tenth of *Shevat* in 5750/January 1950, he instructed his son-in-law, the *Ramash,* to send a *shaliach* to Northern Africa. He was deeply concerned with what he called, "*Acheinu Bnei Yisrael HaSefardim*, our brothers of the Sephardic Jewish community." There, hundreds of thousands of Jews received little Torah education. After the week of *shiva* had ended, the *Ramash* sent the first *shaliach*, Rabbi Michoel Lipsker, who established a network of schools and yeshivos that until today continue to imbue *Yiddishkeit* in the next generation of Moroccan Jews.

A year later, Rabbi Menachem Mendel Schneerson would formally accept the mantle of leadership as the successor of his father-in-law and become the seventh Lubavitcher *Rebbe*. In that gathering, the new *Rebbe* stated, "Three loves are intertwined: the love of G-d, the love of Torah, and the love of our fellow Jews. If you have only the love of G-d and not the love of your fellow, that is a sign that the love is lacking. The love of your fellow will bring you to the love of G-d and the love of Torah." The new *Rebbe* felt that his father-in-law had entrusted him with a mission to reach out to all Jews. In the years to come, he would be instrumental in transforming Lubavitch. It would leave its imprimatur on thousands of Jews worldwide with the massive outreach and educational projects that he would launch across the globe.

Rabbi Yosef Yitzchak Schneerson, the Lubavitcher Rebbe

Today, over 3,000 couples serve as *Shlichim* of Lubavitch in over 40 countries around the world.

The Lubavitcher *Rebbe,* Rabbi Yosef Yitzchak Schneerson, was a compassionate, dynamic individual. His influence on the development of post-war American Orthodoxy is enormous. The *Rebbe's* outreach programs to non-observant Jews was unique, and he was the first Jewish leader to implement *kiruv* work in America. Tens of thousands of observant Jews owe him immeasurable gratitude for bringing them back to their heritage. His great legacy continues to live on in his many *chassidim* throughout the world.

Rabbi Yosef Yitzchak Schneerson was a compassionate, dynamic individual. His influence on the development of post-war American Orthodoxy is enormous.

❧ Rabbi Gedaliah Schorr

1910~1979

The man considered to be the first American-raised *rosh yeshiva* was Rabbi Gedaliah Schorr. This outstanding *talmid chacham*, an exemplar of the finest *middos,* was a dedicated *rosh yeshiva*, completely involved in all aspects of the welfare of his *talmidim.* Although he was reticent to discuss his activities, it is known that he was very involved in *hatzalah* efforts during the war years. How does such a *gadol* emerge in the America of the early years of the 20th century?

Rabbi Gedaliah Schorr was born in 1910, in Istrick, a Galician hamlet. The Schorr family came to America when he was twelve years old, moving first to the Lower East Side of New York City, and then to Williamsburg, New York. Reb Gedaliah dedicated himself to learning Torah, with great love, at a very young age. At age fifteen, he spent a year in his room studying Torah without interruption. His mother brought him his meals so that he would not have to leave his studies. In his middle teens, he would stay up all Thursday night and Friday, then deliver a *shiur* at Zeirei Agudath Israel, and only afterwards go to sleep.

Rabbi Meir Shapiro, the *Rav* of Lublin, spent many months in the United States when Reb Gedaliah was almost twenty years old. The *Lubliner Rav* said of Gedaliah Schorr that he had the most brilliant mind he had encountered in America, and one of the most brilliant in the world. When he was only twenty-one, Rabbi Shraga Feivel Mendlowitz appointed him to deliver the highest *shiur* in Mesivta Torah Vodaath. Despite his acclaim as a great *talmid chacham* at such a young age, when his turn came to sweep and mop the floors of Zeirei Agudath Israel, he willingly performed the task.

Although he had achieved greatness and high stature in his youth, Reb Gedaliah desired to study under the *gedolim* in Europe, specifically Rabbi Aharon Kotler. In 1938, shortly after his marriage, he left Torah Vodaath to live in Kletzk and study under Reb Aharon. They developed a

Rabbi Gedaliah Schorr as a young mans

close relationship, and for the rest of his life he considered Reb Aharon his *rebbe*.

When World War II broke out, Reb Gedaliah returned to America and resumed teaching in Torah Vodaath. In addition to that position, he was the unofficial rabbi at Zeirei Agudath Israel. During the war years, Zeirei was at the forefront of *hatzalah* work. The leader of this movement was Elimelech "Mike" Tress, and Rabbi Schorr was its spiritual leader. Each Shabbos, Rabbi Schorr spoke of the importance of *hatzalah* work. From time to time, he would make appeals for the rescue and relief effort – even walking long distances on Shabbos.

Rabbi Schorr had only one precious possession, a *Vilna Shas,* purchased in Europe. He sold it for $80 (considered a large sum then), and donated the money to the *hatzalah* campaign. He did not like to discuss his wartime efforts with anyone, preferring to keep it a private matter.

Rabbi Schorr was appointed *menahel* of Torah Vodaath in 1948, and began serving as *Rosh HaYeshiva* in 1958. He felt that it was necessary to broaden the Torah understanding of his students, and made a point of teaching subjects that were outside of the typical yeshiva curriculum. He gave *shiurim* in those tractates of Gemara that were not often learned. His *shiurim* in *hashkafa* had a great impact on his students. Before every *Yom Tov*, Reb Gedaliah delivered dazzling *shiurim* pertaining to that holiday. Very often, as he was giving *shiurim* new ideas would come to him on the spot; consequently, his *shiurim* were a constant work in progress.

As a *Rosh HaYeshiva*, Rabbi Schorr was viewed as a father by many of his *talmidim*. His approach was informal and friendly, often using humor to get a message across to someone. Reb Gedaliah's humility, love and dedication to Torah and his students was unmatched. Scores of stories are told about his deep concern for every student and person who came to him for advice. Many of his checks from the yeshiva were not cashed, so that the yeshiva would have money to pay a stipend to someone in the *Kollel*. He would even borrow money to help support young men who were devoting their lives to learning. Most of his acts of kindness were done in secret. At times, the recipients never knew that Rabbi Schorr was their benefactor. One Torah leader said of Rabbi Schorr, "To say that he was a genius is to tell only part of the story. He was a Torah genius who combined everything that was needed to make life and death decisions."

Very often, as he was giving shiurim, new ideas would come to him on the spot; consequently, his shiurim were a constant work in progress.

At a meeting of rabbinical leaders listening to a report by Rabbi Moshe Sherer (L); at the head of the table are (R-L)Reb Moshe Feinstein, Reb Yaakov Kamenetsky and Rabbi Yaakov Yitzchak Ruderman; at the right are Rabbi Gedaliah Schorr and Rabbi Shraga Grosbard; at the left is Rabbi Boruch Sorotzkin.

His every action was based on Torah. Reb Gedaliah demonstrated compassion for every Jew, helping people in his capacity as a teacher, leader, parent, and member of *Klal Yisrael*. Rabbi Schorr would personally go with impoverished students to purchase suits and accessories for Pesach, or whenever the need arose. He felt strongly that a *rebbe* should tend to the personal needs of his *talmidim*.

When the cook of Bais Medrash Elyon passed away, Rabbi Schorr escorted the coffin to Kennedy Airport to be flown to Israel for burial. He was shocked to learn that the body would remain unattended on a cargo truck until it was put on the airplane. He asked for permission to stay with the truck, but was informed that airport security were instructed to shoot at anyone who did not have clearance. However, for a sizable "gift" the driver agreed to park the truck so that those remaining with the coffin would not be seen – but they had to lie down the

entire time. Reb Gedaliah, who was no longer young, climbed into the truck along with a few *talmidim*. He put aside his dignity as a *Rosh HaYeshiva* for the *mitzvah* of paying final homage to a man who had dedicated so many years to the yeshiva.

It was so important to Rabbi Schorr that every young man should be afforded the opportunity to learn, that he did whatever was necessary to keep a *talmid* in yeshiva. Many years before

The main building of Beth Medrash Elyon in Monsey, NY

His every action was based on Torah.
Reb Gedaliah demonstrated compassion for every Jew, helping people in his capacity as a teacher, leader, parent, and member of Klal Yisrael.

Rabbi Gedaliah Schorr (second from right), speaking to a former talmid at the Kosel.

In July 1979, Reb Gedaliah attended a *sheva berachos* of one of his students. After he spoke, he sat down, and it was obvious that he was not feeling well. Shortly afterwards, Reb Gedaliah's head fell forward, and he passed away. Thousands of current and former students, admirers, fellow *Roshei HaYeshiva*, family and friends attended his funeral.

his passing, a certain high school student wanted to continue learning in yeshiva, while his parents did not want him to stay. Rabbi Schorr recognized this *talmid's* great potential, but it could only be realized if he would remain in yeshiva. The *Rosh HaYeshiva* arranged for a prominent businessman (whom he felt would better be able to persuade the boy's parents) to happen to "pass by" the parents' store, and go in to speak to them. The discussion was successful and the young man went on to become an accomplished Torah educator. Rabbi Schorr had requested that the businessman not say anything about his involvement in the matter. Not until after his passing did the student find out who the real catalyst was for his remaining in yeshiva. Reb Gedaliah did not want or need the recognition for his achievements; rather, his only concern was for a positive outcome.

This first American-raised *Rosh Yeshiva* set the standard for dedication, leadership, and involvement within the yeshiva and the Jewish community at large. Rabbi Schorr's sterling *middos,* brilliant mind, love of Torah, and ability to relate and be concerned with every individual, are the paradigm of a true *gadol*.

Rabbi Schorr's sterling middos, brilliant mind, love of Torah, and ability to relate and be concerned with every individual, are the paradigm of a true gadol.

Rabbi Gedaliah Schorr (left) with Rabbi Yerachmiel Blumenfeld, who was Chief Rabbi of Brazil

Rabbi Avraham Nachman Schwartz

1872-1937

When considering the founders of Torah-Judaism in America, few people were more instrumental in its establishment outside of New York than Rabbi Avraham Nachman Schwartz.

Rabbi Schwartz was born in 1872, in Shidlov, Lithuania. He learned in the Telshe Yeshiva, as well as other Lithuanian yeshivos. He received *semichah* from Rabbi Yitzchok Elchanan Spector and Rabbi Refoel Shapiro. He was *Rosh Ha-Yeshiva* of the Yeshiva of Kruki, Lithuania, and later became Rabbi of Odessa, Ukraine. Due to horrible pogroms in Europe, Rabbi Schwartz immigrated to the United States in 1906.

Upon arriving in America, Rabbi Schwartz became the Rabbi of New London, Connecticut. Two years later, he moved to Baltimore to assume the position as Rabbi of Congregation Shomrei Mishmeres Hakodesh (The Lloyd Street Synagogue). His wife and family emigrated from Europe in 1911. The *shul* was open 24 hours a day.

Congregants would gather after their Friday night and *Yom Tov* meals for Torah discussions, to sing *zemiros*, and partake of refreshments at the Rabbi's home. He delivered a daily *Daf Yomi shiur* in his *shul* (today practically every *shul* has such *shiurim*, but then this was a rare occurrence). There was a *mikveh*, and matzah-baking facilities in his *shul* as well. Every year on Simchas Torah, his congregants would carry him on a chair through the streets from his home to the *shul*. The Schwartz home was always open, and they hosted many guests. Rabbis, politicians, and laymen of Baltimore turned to him for advice and counsel.

Rabbi Schwartz spent his years in Baltimore trying to build a meaningful Jewish life for himself and his community. At that time, the only way a Jewish boy received a Torah education was if he learned with his father after attending a full day of public school. In 1917, he founded the first boys' Jewish day-school in Baltimore (it was the first yeshiva day-school established outside of New York) – The Hebrew Parochial School. It initially opened with six students. Today, this elementary and high school yeshiva is known as Talmudic Academy – Yeshivas Chofetz Chaim of Baltimore, which has over 750 students and is a major force in the Baltimore community. His wife was one of the founders of Bais Yaakov of Baltimore.

Rabbi Schwartz was active in communal and civic affairs throughout his life. He helped establish the Union of Orthodox Rabbis of the United States and Canada, known as the Agudas HaRabbonim. Not wanting to be in-

from Vilna, he was instrumental in arranging for the first printing of the Gemara in the United States.

On February 5, 1937, at the age of sixty-five, Rabbi Avraham Nachman Schwartz passed away. The entire community of Baltimore mourned. Rabbis and *Roshei HaYeshiva* from New York, New Jersey, and throughout the country attended his funeral. Those who eulogized him spoke of his Torah scholarship, his gentle and kind demeanor, his warmth and hospitality, and how he was a model for all rabbis and leaders of Judaism. He generously spared time

Original building of Talmudic Academy, Yeshivas Chofetz Chaim

Today's modern campus of Talmudic Academy Yeshivas Chofetz Chaim of Baltimore

volved in organizational politics, he never became an officer of the organization. He was known as a fearless spokesman for the furtherance of Torah-true Judaism. Rabbi Schwartz contributed to leading rabbinical journals, and was recognized as a *posek.* Many rabbis from various communities would consult him regarding their halachic questions.

During World War I, when copies of the Gemara could not be exported

and energy to work for the advancement of Torah-true Judaism.

Today, Baltimore, Maryland, is a major thriving Jewish community, one of the largest in the United States. With scores of *shuls,* yeshivos for both boys and girls, *mikvaos,* and kosher shops, it is truly a bastion of Torah. In large measure this was made possible thanks to the vision and unstinting efforts of Rabbi Avraham Nachman Schwartz.

Noted for his Torah scholarship, his gentle and kind demeanor, his warmth and hospitality, Rabbi Schwartz was a wonderful role model. He worked tirelessly for the advancement of Torah-true Judaism.

Isaac Shalom 1885-1968

Some have called him the greatest leader of the Sephardic community of the twentieth century; others refer to him with awe and reverence. Regardless of the application, the name Isaac Shalom bespeaks a unique individual whose efforts on behalf of the American Syrian Jewish community, and as founder of the Otzar HaTorah schools for the Sephardic children of Israel, North Africa, and Europe are legend. His vision, dedication, and commitment to rebuilding Torah in communities that were hundreds of miles from Torah centers saved the spiritual lives of these children.

He was a humble man, never feeling it beneath his dignity to sleep on a simple cot in the dormitories of the Otzar HaTorah schools, among the children he had helped. Yet he was the one selected to plead the cause of East European Jewry before Secretary of State Cordell Hull. Guided by the inspiration and advice of Rabbi Avraham Kalmanowitz, Mr. Shalom met with the Secretary in the hope that he would influence President Roosevelt to help save Jewish lives.

Born in 1885 to Joseph and Nizha Shalom, he immigrated to New York in 1910. Starting out as a peddler, he established I. Shalom & Co, Inc. in 1919. The business soon expanded from a handkerchief supplier to a successful men's and ladies' accessories firm. For Isaac Shalom, material success meant very little. It was a means, a vehicle by which he could advance his spiritual goals.

Isaac Shalom became one of the most successful and affluent businessmen in the Syrian Jewish community. With material success came influence and respect. These attributes, in turn, catalyzed the realization of his spiritual visionary goals. Fully aware of the inadequacy of the afternoon Talmud Torah system for educating the Jewish youth, he helped found Yeshivah Magen David in Brooklyn in 1946. He encouraged friends and associates to remove their children from the public schools and enroll them in Magen David. At first, people were reluctant, but his charisma coupled with the deep

Some have called him the greatest leader of the Sephardic community of the twentieth century; others refer to him with awe and reverence.
His vision, dedication, and commitment to rebuilding Torah saved the spiritual lives of thousands of children.

reverence the community had for this special leader won them over. Today, Magen David Yeshivah is a major day school serving the religious needs of the greater Syrian Jewish community.

The synagogue was no less important. Mr. Shalom's leadership skills were instrumental in the development of the Magen David Synagogue and later Shaare Zion Synagogue in Brooklyn. He gave sage advice to both rabbis and laymen who turned to him for practical counsel and assistance. *Tzedakah* and *chesed* were his hallmark, as he reached out to minister to the financial needs of the members of his community. Indeed, as a result of his benevolence many of them achieved affluence and success. Following the example of their mentor, they in turn made significant contributions to sustain the growing spiritual network.

Mr. Shalom's support of *Eretz Yisrael* was inspirational. He invested in Amcor Ltd., which developed into one of Israel's major companies. The

Shaare Zion Synagogue

profits realized from this were used to further his commitment to the Land and its People. Mr. Shalom also supported Israel Bonds and the United Jewish Appeal. Sensitive to the spiritual void at the time, he was instrumental in building and sustaining a number of yeshivos, including Porat Yosef, the Yeshiva High School in Herzeliah, Yeshivah Nev'e Erez, and many others. Isaac Shalom was a model for others to emulate. He also made sure that the *rebbeim* who taught in the yeshivos were paid well, so that they could sanctify their efforts towards developing the next Torah generation. It was not a one-way street – he expected reciprocity from the *rebbeim,* in passion, devotion and commitment to their students.

A year after World War II ended, as a member of Vaad Hatzala, the committee for rescuing Jews from war-torn Europe, Isaac Shalom was deeply moved by reports concerning the plight of Sephardic Jews in far-flung communities. Although hundreds of years old, their isolation from the major Jewish centers precluded their religious observance and knowledge. He sought ways to respond to this

Isaac Shalom signing the mortgage for the Magen David Yeshivah

Tzedakah and chesed were his hallmark, as he reached out to minister to the financial needs of the members of his community.

Shaare Zion Synagogue, interior

ing and support of the venerable Mirrer *Rosh HaYeshiva*, Rabbi Avraham Kalmanowitz, he embarked on this enormous endeavor. Schools were established throughout Iran, Morocco, Tripoli and elsewhere.

The story is told that Isaac Shalom approached the Joint Distribution Committee and offered to construct the edifices which would serve Otzar HaTorah's school children, if the Joint would agree to provide the financial support for the overhead, i.e., teachers' salaries, maintenance, food, etc. Thinking that he would probably not construct more than one or two schools, the JDC accepted. We can well

serious problem. Not to act would permit a segment of the Jewish People to become spiritually extinct. His action resulted in the Otzar HaTorah network, providing Jewish education to the forgotten communities of North Africa. Indeed, the program was named "The Committee for the Forgotten Million." Receiving the spiritual bless-

1950s (L-R): Ralph S. Tawil, Rabbi A. Hecht, Isaac Shalom, Isaac Gindi, Mr. Hedaya, Joe Ashear, Abe Sultan, Norman Jemal, Morris Levy, Joe Tawil, and unknown

Isaac Shalom saved a generation of Sephardic children – thousands of *neshamos* – from spiritual extinction. He was admired and revered by the thousands of children and the educators who benefitted from his largesse. These young men and women carry the flame of Torah that was ignited in their souls through the efforts of this noble but modest man. Isaac Shalom never sought honor or acclaim for himself. His greatest reward was the knowledge that he had performed a *mitzvah* and brought more Jews under the banner of Torah.

Isaac Shalom was admired and revered by the thousands of children and the educators who benefitted from his largesse.

imagine their shock when in the short period of five years, the student population reached 10,000, with schools throughout North Africa! After a while, enrollment increased to 20,000 students. Today, many of their alumni reside in *Eretz Yisrael.*

Magen David Yeshivah - Isaac Shalom Elementary School

Rabbi Moshe Sherer *1922-1998*

One of the primary voices of Orthodox Judaism is Agudath Israel of America, and its major spokesman for over fifty years was Rabbi Moshe Sherer. He was a charismatic, articulate, poised leader who represented the Torah world to mayors, governors, senators, ambassadors, vice presidents, presidents and world leaders. He was a statesman, who represented and defended our principles, advocating for our welfare with dignity, class, responsibility, patience and tireless efforts.

Rabbi Sherer was born in New York City in 1921, the same year Zeirei Agudath Israel was founded in New York. He attended Yeshiva Torah Vodaath, and later Yeshiva Ner Yisrael in Baltimore. His mother's acts of *chesed* and love of Torah had a tremendous impact on him, and he would often quote her. As a young boy, walking to *shul* with his father on Shabbos, he saw men leaving the early *minyan* to go to work in the garment industry. Although he was young, the pain he saw on these people's faces remained with him.

As conditions grew worse in Europe during World War II, Zeirei Agudath Israel, under the leadership of Rabbi Sherer's cousin, Elimelech "Mike" Tress, launched a full-scale effort to do whatever they could to help save Jews. Recognizing his cousin's talents, Mike Tress asked his cousin to join him in the *hatzalah* work.

By early 1942, Rabbi Sherer became the Executive Director of the Youth Council. One of his first assignments was to attend a meeting of Orthodox groups dedicated to fostering Shabbos observance. When Reb Elimelech Tress became ill in the early 1960s, Rabbi Sherer assumed the role of president of Agudath Israel.

Rabbi Sherer was committed to making sure that Judaism was seen in the eyes of the world with the utmost respect and professionalism. He composed the Agudah's advertisements and press releases, ensuring that everything was skillfully and proficiently presented. He used to joke that he would drive the secretaries crazy, making certain the stamps on the envelopes were straight.

Rabbi Sherer deferred to the *gedolim* and turned to them for advice regarding the Agudah. His respect for them

---

One of the primary voices of Orthodox Judaism is Agudath Israel of America, and its major spokesman for over fifty years was Rabbi Moshe Sherer.

and their Torah was unparalleled. There were certain *gedolim* who had profound influence on him. When Rabbi Elchonon Wasserman came to America to raise money for his yeshiva, Moshe Sherer, then a yeshiva student, accompanied him. He was inspired by the wisdom, piety, and idealism of Rabbi Wasserman. Reb Elchonon encouraged him to devote his life to *Klal Yisrael*.

Another *gadol* who had a great effect on Rabbi Sherer was Rabbi Gedaliah Schorr, the *Rosh HaYeshiva* of Torah Vodaath. Aside from his Torah wisdom, Rabbi Schorr's tireless and heartfelt efforts expended in *hatzalah* work inspired Moshe Sherer.

The individual who had the most profound influence on Rabbi Sherer was Rabbi Aharon Kotler. Rabbi Kotler trained and guided him to be a leader. They spoke frequently, often several times a day. Reb Aharon was committed to the ideals and growth of the Agudah organization. From the beginning of their association, Rabbi Sherer kept the image of Reb Aharon before him.

Rabbi Sherer spoke of helping "*Klal Yisrael*" (the community) and "*Reb Yisrael*" (the individual). His countless personal acts of kindness were well known. Although he was a prominent figure, he was approachable, and people felt they could go to him for advice and help. He gave each person the time that was needed, and each one felt that he genuinely cared about them. No one will ever know how many people were helped through his interventions, advice, and influence. He would thank every person who did any act of kindness,

Rabbi Moshe Sherer addressing an Agudah dinner in 1943. Seated (L-R): Rabbi Michael Munk, Rabbi Yechiel Elbaum, Mike Tress

big or small, for him or the organization, with a phone call or thank-you note.

Rescue and relief work were a hallmark of the Agudah under his leadership. In 1956, the Agudah set up a center in Vienna for Jews fleeing Communism during the Hungarian Revolution. In the mid-1980s, the Agudah again opened a center in Vienna for Jews fleeing oppression in Iran. Additionally, hundreds of people were sent (sometimes secretly) to teach Torah to Jews in the former USSR.

In 1965, Rabbi Sherer testified before Congress on behalf of public aid to students attending non-public schools. He founded a committee of Orthodox lawyers to serve as advocates for Jewish rights. This committee eventually became COLPA (National Jewish Commission on Law and Public Affairs).

Within the Agudah itself, he established the Commission on Legislation

Moshe Sherer as a young man

His countless personal acts of kindness were well known. No one will ever know how many people were helped through his interventions, advice, and influence.

Rabbi Moshe Sherer receiving a Sefer Torah written in his honor at Agudath Israel's dinner. (L-R) Rabbi Paysach Krohn, Rabbi Shimshon Sherer, Mendel Berg, Rabbi Moshe Sherer, Louis Glueck

during his presidency was setting up the COPE Institute, a computer training facility which has provided livelihoods for thousands of families. Yet another network was created to help unemployed people find suitable jobs, and hundreds of families have benefited. The Southern Brooklyn Community Organization (SBCO) was formed, to build new housing and preserve neighborhoods in Brooklyn.

and Civil Action, which fought for the protection of Shabbos observers, kosher consumer laws, and the right of yeshivos to receive state funds. He also was instrumental in having the Mandated Services Law passed in New York, which gave state funds to yeshivos for state-required activities like testing and recording attendance.

Another major accomplishment

Rabbi Moshe Sherer davening in a shul in Moscow.

9th Siyum HaShas – "Hadran of Daf HaYomi"

One of Rabbi Sherer's most glorious achievements was the tremendous growth of *Daf Yomi* learning in the United States and throughout the world. The *Siyum HaShas* at the end of its seven-and-a-half-year cycle grew from a gathering of a few hundred people in Brooklyn, to the Manhattan Center, then the Felt Forum, and most recently Madison Square Garden, with satellite hook-ups throughout the country and world, with over 70,000 people in attendance.

Rabbi Moshe Sherer's father

Rabbi Moshe Sherer's mother

(least important to him) his own prestige.

Upon returning from this trip to Israel, Rabbi Sherer was hospitalized. He passed away a few months later. His funeral was attended by over 25,000 people, including *Roshei Yeshiva, rabbanim, admorim*, family, and friends, Jews and non-Jews alike. Many politicians and dignitaries attended the funeral because of their great respect for him. Rabbi Sherer spent his life working for the perpetuation of Judaism worldwide, on an individual and personal level. We are the fortunate beneficiaries of his many accomplishments. The *zechuyos* he merited are to be admired and emulated by us all.

Eretz Yisrael was foremost on his mind. He raised funds and assisted Chinuch Atzmai, the independent network of Torah Schools for Israel. Rabbi Sherer worked tirelessly to raise awareness and funds for *Shemittah* observance in Israel. He helped launch *Shuvu*, a fund for Torah education for immigrants to Israel from the former Soviet Union.

During the final months of his life, when illness was ravaging his body, he accomplished one of the greatest triumphs in his life. He created the *Am Echad* organization, a delegation to Israel to fight against Jewish Pluralism, and gained enormous respect for his cause, his message, and

Rabbi Moshe Sherer, keynote speaker at Motzaei Shabbos session at Agudath Israel Convention

RABBI MOSHE SHERER WITH TORAH LEADERS

1. *Rabbi Moshe Sherer with Vizhnitzer Rebbe, in Eretz Yisrael*

2. *Rabbi Moshe Sherer with Novominsker Rebbe (present Rosh Agudath Israel)*

3. *Rabbi Moshe Sherer with Rabbi Yaakov Kamenetsky*

4. *Rabbi Moshe Sherer with Rabbi Yitzchak Hutner*

5. *Rabbi Moshe Sherer with Rabbi Shlomo Z. Auerbach*

6. *Rabbi Moshe Sherer with Rabbi Eliezer M. Schach*

RABBI MOSHE SHERER WITH AMERICAN LEADERS

1. Rabbi Moshe Sherer with President George H. Bush

2. Rabbi Moshe Sherer with Nelson D. Rockefeller, Governor of New York

3. Rabbi Moshe Sherer with Rudolph Guliani, Mayor of New York City

4. Rabbi Moshe Sherer with President Lyndon Baines Johnson

5. Rabbi Moshe Sherer with President Jimmy Carter and Congressman Dennis Eckert of Ohio

6. Rabbi Moshe Sherer with President Ronald Reagan

❧ Rabbi Saul Silber *1881-1946*

Chicago today is the major Torah center of the Midwest, but this was not always so. At the turn of the century this city was struggling to develop its Jewish identity. Men of the caliber of Rabbi Saul Silber, visionaries whose passion for Judaism and the *Torah* way, coupled with a love for the Jewish People, were inspired to utilize their exceptional talents to develop the communities to which they came.

Rabbi Saul Silber was born in Lithuania on March 15, 1881. He demonstrated a surprising interest in learning at a young age. Unlike most boys his age, Saul Silber focused not only on the literal translation of the Talmud but also on the splendor of the ethical parables. In his quest for halachic learning, he did not abandon his inquisitiveness in Biblical literature. He therefore joined Rabbi Jacob Reines' yeshiva in Lida. Unlike most European yeshivos whose curriculum consisted of Talmud learning only, this yeshiva was famous for including Biblical and secular studies into the curriculum. Rabbi Reines believed that Jewish learning and secular knowledge accompanied each other. This ideology and way of learning later set the foundation of Rabbi Silber's yeshiva and developed it into the thriving school that it is today.

Rabbi Silber immigrated to the United States in 1900. After serving as Rabbi in Youngstown and Columbus, Ohio, he became the chief rabbi of Congregation Anshei Sholom in Chicago, one of the largest and most distinguished congregations in the United States at the time. People from far and wide would come to hear Rabbi Silber's inspirational lectures, ranging from topics such as the weekly *parashah*, the upcoming holidays, and the support of the *Yishuv*, the Jewish settlement in *Eretz Yisrael*. He instilled his congregants with a constant yearning for helping others in every possible way. Together with his congregation, Rabbi Silber established worldwide campaigns that aided thousands of people both spiritually and financially after the devastation of World War I. In contrast to many other rabbis, Rabbi Silber personally went from business to business, and from family to family, creating a close relationship with a multitude of supporters and friends who stood beside him

Rabbi Silber established worldwide campaigns that aided thousands of people both spiritually and financially after the devastation of World War I.

throughout all his endeavors. His actions resulted in the unanimous acceptance and support of numerous Jewish organizations, including charities, nursing homes, hospitals, orphanages and yeshivos across the world, as well as the Jewish Historical Society.

Recognized for his diplomacy, ingenuity, and progressive thinking, Rabbi Silber was elected as president of Hebrew Theological College of Chicago in 1922. The HTC Board believed Rabbi Silber would be the perfect candidate to represent and collect funds for their school. With his extensive friendships and connections, his systematic way of thinking, and his dynamic personality, Rabbi Silber attracted new students and followers to the school. In addition, he enhanced the reputation of HTC by attracting and employing highly esteemed and respected rabbis.

Under his reign, HTC distinguished itself from other yeshivos by mandating that students receive a B.A. degree in any subject of their choice while studying for their ordination. Rabbi Silber also hired a public speaking teacher and required the students to give lectures at community synagogues to prepare them for their ordination as *rabbanim*. He experienced one of his greatest feelings of success and accomplishment when his first ten students received *semichah* from the yeshiva, along with a separate ordination from the Gaon of Lomza, Rabbi Yeudah Leib Gordon, recognized as a preeminent halachic authority by the majority of the Chicago Jewish community. Indeed, he transformed a fledgling school into an institution of international scope and repute.

The Saul Silber Memorial Library of the Beth Medrash LaTorah, Hebrew

Rabbi Silber's dream: Hebrew Theological College Campus today

Theological College (HTC) of Skokie, Illinois, dedicated in memory of Rabbi Saul Silber, president of HTC from 1922–1946, is universally famous among rabbis and yeshiva students. Its 62,000-volume compilation consists of current as well as historic Judaica and Hebrew books, microfilms, audio and videotapes. The rare book collection includes manuscripts, autographed books, and Hebrew books dated back to the late 1700s. The HTC library is a continuous reminder of the man who supported countless organizations and transformed a once struggling yeshiva into one of the most legendary schools in the United States.

Rabbi Silber established a yeshiva brilliantly encompassing the traditions and customs of a European yeshiva together with contemporary American thought and study. He was a father to all his students and was the moving force behind HTC, as well as numerous schools and organizations. Rabbi Silber lived in a period that witnessed many hardships, but he always knew the true direction of life. He dedicated his life to helping others and ensuring the education of future rabbis. Rabbi Silber's sense of commitment to his community and to *Klal Yisrael* serves as an inspiration to the generations of students whose spiritual growth he affected.

He was a father to all his students and was the moving force behind HTC, as well as numerous schools and organizations.

Rabbi Eliezer Silver *1882-1968*

Cincinnati! Say this name to different groups and you get pictures as disparate as the Equator or the North Pole of the prototype Midwestern-American Jewish community.

To one group, the name "Cincinnati" is tantamount to speaking of the original Reform movement, since its seminary is located there. Moreover, the founder of American Reformism, Isaac Mayer Wise, chose Cincinnati as his "capital."

But to Orthodox Jewry, the Ohio city called Cincinnati will always suggest the *gedolim*, the truly great Torah scholars and activists, who lived and worked there, all the while proving to be formidable opponents to the Reformers in their own "capital." In particular, there are three Cincinnati *gedolim* who must be mentioned in any account of the history of the Jewish community of Cincinnati: Rabbi Yissachar Dov Illowy, famous student of the *Chasam Sofer*; Rabbi Avrohom Lesser, and, most prominent of all, Rabbi Eliezer Silver.

It is no mere accident that Rabbi Silver is never referred to as "Reb Eliezer" or as "Reb Lazer" in any of the accounts written about him. After all,

how could anyone refer that way to the President of the Agudas HaRabbonim, the chief of the Union of Orthodox Rabbis of America (and of Canada, as Rabbi Silver would often remind his listeners!)? He was a man so singular, so iconoclastic, so outspoken that no human being could ever put him at a loss for words – or action.

Truly, Rabbi Silver was the kind of Torah scholar and activist who synthesized the total commitment of the European rabbis of old with the toughness demanded of a New World firebrand.

Born in 1882, in Abel, Lithuania, Rabbi Silver had a distinguished roster of Talmud instructors, the first being his father, Rabbi Bunim Tzemach. He also learned with the *Ohr Sameach* (Rabbi Meir Simcha of Dvinsk) and with the famed *Rogatchover Gaon* (Rabbi Yosef Rosen). At age twenty-four, Rabbi Silver was ordained by a number of rabbis, chief among them Rabbi Chaim Ozer Grodzenski. The bond between Rabbi Silver and Reb Chaim Ozer was exceedingly strong, lasting throughout the latter's lifetime.

Arriving with his young wife in the United States in 1907, at the age of

He was a man so singular, so iconoclastic, so outspoken that no human being could ever put him at a loss for words - or action.

twenty-five, Rabbi Silver spent a short time in New York City and Philadelphia before deciding upon Harrisburg, Pennsylvania, as his center of activities. Harrisburg was, in turn, followed by Springfield, Massachusetts, and by Cincinnati, Ohio – the last achieving "capital" status, as it were, in his career. It is almost superfluous to add that in each city, Rabbi Silver bequeathed a lasting legacy in the areas of vastly

Installation of Rabbi Eliezer Silver in Springfield, Massachusetts, in 1925. Front Row (L-R): unidentified, Rabbis Samuel Friedman, Bernard Revel, Israel Rosenberg, Moses Z. Margolies, Eliezer Silver, Bernard Levinthal, Sheftel Kramer, Baruch Epstein (author of Torah Temima); between Rabbi Rosenberg and Rabbi Margolies is Rabbi Meyer Berlin; between Rabbi Levinthal and Rabbi Kramer is Rabbi Yehuda Levenberg. In the back row, at the extreme right, is Rabbi Shlomo Polatchek, with Rabbi Judah Forer to his right.

improved *kashrus* standards and heightened *taharas hamishpachah* and the establishment of proper *mikvaos* observance. Moreover, in Harrisburg and Cincinnati, he was successful in helping to initiate local day school education.

Rabbi Silver became active in the Agudas HaRabbonim, an organization founded in 1902 to provide Torah-loyal leadership and guidance to the Orthodox congregations of North America. In 1923, he became one of the three members of its presidium, and in 1929, its sole president. Additionally, in 1915, Rabbi Silver participated in the founding of Ezras Torah, the world-renowned *tzedakah* fund for indigent scholars that later was headed by Rabbi Yosef Eliyahu Henkin, of blessed memory, from 1925 until his passing in 1973.

Through Agudas HaRabbonim and its activist arm, the Vaad Hatzala for War-Torn Yeshivos, thousands of people

Rabbi Silver participated in the founding of Ezras Torah, the world-renowned tzedakah fund for indigent scholars

Rabbi Yissachar
Dov Illowy
*Famous Student of
the Chasam Sofer*

Ohr Sameach
Rabbi Meir Simcha
of Dvinsk

Rogatchover Gaon
Rabbi Yosef Rosen
of Dvinsk

Agudas HaRabbonim convention in 1926. (L-R): Rabbis Eliezer Silver; Israel Rosenberg; Moses Z. Margolies; Ezekiel Lifshitz of Kalish, Poland; Bernard Levinthal; Isaac Siegel; Joseph Konvitz

Rabbi Silver brought material sustenance and spiritual solace to those in the DP camps...

were saved from extermination in the Holocaust. Although it was generally referred to by its shorter name, Vaad Hatzala, it was the only rescue organization totally dedicated to providing rescue, relief and, later, rehabilitation to *roshei yeshiva* and *talmidei chachamim*. The list of *chassidic* rabbis and leading yeshiva figures that the Vaad had a hand in saving is impressive indeed: Rabbi Aharon Kotler, founder of Beis Medrash Govoha in

Lakewood, New Jersey; the Lutzker *Rav*, Rabbi Zalman Sorotzkin; Rabbi Elya Chazan of the Mirrer Yeshiva; the *Gerrer Rebbe*, Rabbi Avrohom Mordechai Alter; and many others. Furthermore, the Vaad played a major role in keeping alive those yeshiva refugees who had been exiled to Siberia by the Soviet government. The Vaad assumed responsibility for sustaining the refugees who, having traveled across Siberia, were living as exiles in Kobe, Japan. Indeed, an entire institution – the Mirrer Yeshiva under its world-renowned *Rosh HaYeshiva*, Rabbi Chaim Shmuelevitz – was able to continue functioning, owing to aid that the Vaad funneled to it. As president of the Vaad, Rabbi Silver became a master at dealing with a basically intransigent and often hostile State Department – and frequently, with equally unyielding Jewish groups that opposed the Vaad's rescue activities as "dealing with the enemy."

After the war, the Vaad continued its work in the area of rescue, and it was officially recognized by UNRRA

Vaad Hatzala committee that went to assist the war refugees in Oswego, New York, August, 1944. (L-R): Yitzchak Furstenberg, Irving Bunim, Rabbi Eliezer Silver, (unidentified), Rabbi Mosco Czechoval, Dr. Isaac Lewin.

(the United Nations Relief and Rehabilitation Administration). As the Vaad's representative and dressed in the uniform of an American Army officer, Rabbi Silver brought material sustenance and spiritual solace to those in the DP (displaced persons) camps, who had technically survived the war, but might not withstand the peace. When it came to saving Jewish lives, Rabbi Silver had no compunction about how to do so. Discussing the requisite means of saving Jews from the Holocaust inferno, he wrote the following:

"We are ready to pay ransom for Jews and deliver them from con-centration camps with the help of forged passports. For this purpose, we do not hesitate to deal with counterfeiters and passport thieves! We are ready to smuggle Jewish children over the borders, and to engage expert smugglers for this purpose, rogues whose profession this is! We are ready to smuggle money ille-gally into enemy territory, in order to bribe as many as necessary of the killers of the Jewish people, those dregs of humanity!"

In truth, after the war, Rabbi Silver was compelled to follow the same philosophy, both in trying to rescue Jewish youngsters from Christian homes and convents where they were hidden during wartime, or in providing money to the DP camp refugees. Rabbi Shlomo

Pappenheim, who has actively been engaged in rehabilitating distressed Jewish girls at Jerusalem's *Bayit L'pletot* (Home for Refugee Girls) and whose wife had suffered in the camps, told the following story about Rabbi Silver:

"When it came to saving lives, Rabbi Silver was not averse to using whatever method worked. Once, when the rabbi arrived at a DP camp, an American guard demanded to frisk him to ascertain that he was not carrying

Rabbi Eliezer Silver and Yitzchok Sternbuch with rescue activists in Czechoslovakia. Identified (R-L): Herman Landau, Israel Goldstein, Joseph Goodman, Eliezer Gips, Rabbi Silver, Mr. Sternbuch and Meir Shenkolewski

contraband – which indeed he was: $10,000 to help the downtrodden Jewish refugees there. The money, in small bills, was taped to the inside of his U.S. Army jacket. At first, Rabbi Silver demurred, asking in astonish-ment, You're going to check *me* – Rabbi Silver?! The guard answered, Sorry, Rabbi, but orders are orders. So, Rabbi Silver opened his uniform jacket and thrust the main part behind him [here, the gold-robed *chassid* demonstrated how Rabbi Silver must have done it], and declared, OK, check! Of course, the guard was unaware that what was

When it came to saving Jewish lives, Rabbi Silver had no compunction about how to do so.

then considered an exorbitant amount of money was located right behind the rabbi – and literally, right under his nose!"

The major purpose of the Vaad Hatzala had been completed by the end of the '40s, but not before it had succeeded in literally establishing a new and vibrant Orthodoxy on the shores of America, a nation that many European Jews had considered for so many decades to be the archetypal *treife medina* (unkosher country). Perhaps this is its most enduring legacy.

Rabbi Silver was a fundraiser par excellence. Oftentimes, he was so moved by the causes he was called upon to aid that he himself contributed beyond his means. When funds were not available, he would borrow from the bank, or mortgage his home, not

Rabbi Avraham DovBer Kahane Shapiro, the Kovno Rav, and Rabbi Eliezer Silver

knowing from where he would get the funds to repay the loans. The list of his beneficiaries reads like the "Who's Who" of the yeshiva world. He was responsible for helping Rabbi Yosef Kahaneman, the Ponovezer *Rav,* establish his yeshiva. Merkaz Horav Yaakov Kook received its initial aid from him. Rabbi Yosef Yitzchak Schneerson, the Lubavitcher *Rebbe,* turned to him to rescue religious Jewry under communist dominion. The plight of refugee rabbis in *Eretz Yisrael* did not escape him, as he raised the necessary funds to sustain them. He assisted a number of *rabbanim* in the printing and dissemination of their treatises on Jewish law and philosophy. Among the more prominent ones were, the *Dvar Avraham*, by Rabbi Avraham DovBer Kahane Shapiro, the Kovno *Rav* and Rabbi Avraham Zelig Reuven Bengis, head of the *Beis Din* of the Eidah HaChareidis, author of seven volumes of discourses on the Talmud entitled *Liflagos Reuven.* Indeed, during his tenure, Rabbi Silver was involved in every area of Jewish life.

While Rabbi Silver's activities on behalf of the Vaad Hatzala were probably the most rewarding of his life, giving full vent to his endless energy, unique personality, and youthful enthusiasm, he nonetheless remained the dedicated yeshiva *bachur* throughout his life. He was a *masmid*, diligent and studious, to the fullest extent of the word. His learning was done primarily in the wee hours of the morning and late into the night. He would usually retire at two a.m. and rise by six a.m. Slight in build, he possessed boundless energy for his *klal* work. He was rarely fatigued at the end of the day, at a time when most people fell asleep from sheer exhaustion, and he would then begin to learn his daily *seder* of Torah study. Possessing a brilliant mind, he was constantly writing new interpretations and explanations. He published articles in numerous periodicals. Because of his hectic schedule, he did not have the time to organize his writings and publish them. Finally, in the last decade of his life, he began publishing his novellae. Following his demise, thirty notebooks were discovered in his desk; they were filled with brilliant rabbinic elucidations, in his handwriting and that of his father.

Rabbi Eliezer Silver

His memory was remarkable, instantly recalling almost everything he had ever studied or wrote. Once, while studying with a young man he later ordained, Rabbi Silver requested that the student bring him a volume from his library. He commented that some thirty years earlier he had written novellae in the margin on a certain page. Sure enough, the interpretation was there. Thirty years had gone by, but his memory remained as fresh and vibrant as before!

Rabbi Silver was the quintessential scholar. His novellae, *Anfei Erez* and *Tzemach Erez,* give us some indication of how much he could have accomplished just in the world of scholarship alone. But first and foremost, Rabbi Silver was the consummate Jewish activist, and the deep imprint that he has left on Cincinnati (in fact, the first Torah Umesorah SEED program in 1974 was held in his old *shul*, Knesseth Israel, and was called "Yad Eliezer" after him; today it hosts a flourishing *kollel*), the United States, and the world at large has not diminished in the decades since his death in 1968. A reporter once wrote of him, "Quicksilver. That is the word which sticks to my mind when I think of him. … He can keep no specific office hours because 24 hours a day are simply inadequate for the complete performance of all his duties." But then, Rabbi Eliezer Silver was an American colossus – a man who had no peer!

Possessing a brilliant mind, he was constantly writing new interpretations and explanations.

Dais at Agudath Israel Dinner (L-R): Rabbi Eliezer Silver, Rabbi Aharon Kotler, Rabbi Moshe Feinstein, Boyaner Rebbe, Novominsker Rebbe, Bluzhever Rebbe

Rav Zelig Reuven Bengis

Rabbi Dr. Yosef Dov Soloveitchik *1903-1993*

It was the third of *Shevat* and the lecture hall at Yeshiva University was filled to capacity. Those who arrived early were fortunate to find seats, while others crammed themselves into any available space, including the hallway. Over a thousand people from all walks of life gathered – students and rabbis, young and old, some with black hats and others with leather *yarmulkes*. They all came together on this long-awaited evening to hear the inspiring words of a unique individual, who had the ability to captivate his audience for hours at a time. Then a hush fell over the crowd, and everyone rose as the *"Rav,"* Rabbi Yosef Dov Soloveitchik, entered the room to deliver a *yahrtzeit shiur* in memory of his father.

Rabbi Yosef Dov Soloveitchik, known as "the *Rav*" to his students, was born in Pruzhan, Poland, on February 27, 1903, to Rabbi Moshe and *Rebbetzin* Pesia, daughter of Rabbi Eliyahu Feinstein, spiritual leader of Pruzhan, and the author of *Halichos Eliyahu*. His mother was a first cousin of Rabbi Moshe Feinstein, who later

became the leading *posek* of American Jewry. His formative years were spent in Khaslavitchy, White Russia, where his father took the position of *Rav*. At the local *cheder,* he came under the influence of a charismatic and gifted *rebbe*, who was a Lubavitcher *chassid*. During that year, Yosef Dov delved into the *Tanya*, the focal classic of *Chabad* chassidic literature. The lessons inspired the young student for decades to come. It introduced him to the disciplines of *chassidic* thought and philosophy.

His paternal grandfather, Rabbi Chaim Soloveitchik (popularly known as Reb Chaim Brisker), instituted a new system for Talmudic study, termed "the Brisker Method." Emphasizing in-depth analysis, exact definition, and precise classification, this method focused on the *Rambam's Mishnah Torah* as a pivotal source of study and research. Yosef Dov was first introduced to this technique as a young boy. From the very beginning, he prodigiously developed innovative approaches and original interpretations for various complex passages. His father, Reb Moshe, was so impressed with his son's insights, that he compiled them into a notebook and sent them to his father, Reb Chaim. After reading his grandson's *chiddushei Torah* Reb Chaim proudly predicted that the young boy would surely emerge as a prominent Torah leader for future generations.

Unlike other boys of that time, Yosef Dov studied a wide range of secular subjects. He possessed a keen interest in math, physics, and philosophy, and excelled in these areas. In 1931, he received his doctorate in philosophy from the University of Berlin. His later synthesis of secular education and Torah teachings established the

Rabbi Eliyahu Feinstein

Rabbi Chaim Soloveitchik

Rav as a renowned thinker of his era.

Rabbi Soloveitchik, together with his wife and firstborn child, immigrated to the United States in 1932, and settled in Boston where he became its Chief Rabbi. Coming from the European *shtetel* steeped in tradition, Rabbi Soloveitchik was shaken by the lack of Jewish knowledge within the Boston community. Consequently, he embarked on a pedagogical mission to raise the spiritual level of the community to its highest potential. Several years later, starting with only six students, Rabbi Soloveitchik opened the Maimonides School, the first Jewish Day School in

...he persevered and by investing his heart and soul into the school, it became the center of Jewish education in the Boston area.

RIETS Faculty, c. 1944. Standing (L-R): Rabbi Joseph Arnest, Rabbi Ephraim Steinberg, Samuel Sar, Rabbi Samuel Volk, Rabbi Joseph Weiss, Norman Abrams.
Sitting (L-R): Judah Levine, Rabbi Aaron Burack, Rabbi Isaac Rubenstein, Rabbi Abraham Selmanowitz, Rabbi Yosef Soloveitchik, Rabbi Moshe Shatzkes, Rabbi Samuel Belkin, Rabbi Judah Weil, Rabbi Samuel Gerstenfeld, Rabbi Moses Poleyeff, Rabbi Chaim Shunfenthal.

*Rabbi
Soloveitchik
had the
distinction of
being the first
to ordain more
than two
thousand
rabbis...*

the New England area. The school faced much opposition from many members of the community, who feared that a Jewish Day School meant returning to the Old World. During its first years, the school struggled through many adversities, and, often, Rabbi Soloveitchik was forced to hold class in his own living room. However, he persevered and by investing his heart and soul into the school, it became the center of Jewish education in the Boston area.

After the death of his father, Rabbi Soloveitchik succeeded him as the *Rosh HaYeshiva* of the Rabbi Isaac Elchanan Theological Seminary / RIETS at Yeshiva University. For the next forty years, Rabbi Soloveitchik left a lifelong impression on the faculty and students

Rabbi Yosef D. Soloveitchik, c. 1940

alike. He was known not only for his brilliance and vast knowledge, but also for integrating his grandfather's method of Talmudic study into the modern-day teaching of Talmud, successfully translating the Brisker terminology into the English vernacular. Rabbi Soloveitchik firmly believed that American rabbis should be conversant in secular knowledge, in order to gain the respect of secularly educated Jews and convince them of the primacy of Torah study and halachic observance. This approach generated extensive controversy, but as a maverick, Rabbi Soloveitchik was not intimidated. He adhered to his convictions and did not concede.

More than two generations of students considered Rabbi Soloveitchik as their "*rebbe muvhak*" (primary Torah teacher). His students admired his intelligence and feared his criticism. The *Rav's* teaching led his students on a breathtaking journey, deep into the mystics and passages of the Talmud. "These were magical times for us," said one of his former students. He taught that the crucial responsibility of a rabbi is to "redress the grievances of those who are abandoned and alone, to pro-

Rabbi Yosef Soloveitchik with his son-in-law, Rabbi Aharon Lichtenstein, March 6, 1983

tect the dignity of the poor, to save the oppressed from the hands of the oppressor." All were welcome in Rabbi Soloveitchik's classroom and lectures. He had the ability to look deep inside each student, recognizing his potential, regardless of his background.

Rabbi Soloveitchik had the distinction of being the first to ordain more than two thousand rabbis. Besides mentoring students, people from far and wide sought his guidance and advice. His association with the Rabbinical Council of America played a pivotal role in the organization's growth and influence. His presence and guidance provided encouragement and hope for its rabbis, caught up in the difficulty of representing and disseminating Torah to American Jewry, especially during the mid-20th century. Although he was hesitant to become an authority in halachic topics, Rabbi Soloveitchik became the head of the Halachah Commission of the Rabbinical Council of America. Rabbis from all over the world consulted him on both halachic and personal issues. The *Rav's* writings

Rabbi Soloveitchik lecturing at Yeshiva University, 1960

eloquently transmitted his thoughts and ideologies to the world. They include, among others, *Ish Ha-Halachah, Kol Dodi Dofek,* and *The Lonely Man of Faith.* His prolific writings, like his lectures, revealed a distinctive combination of both contemporary and deep-rooted Jewish thought. However, his foremost objective was the study and teaching of the Talmud and Jewish literature. In 1974, Yeshiva University published *Shiurei HaRav, A Conspectus of the Public Lectures of Rabbi Yosef Dov Soloveitchik,* which was reprinted in 1994 because of popular demand.

Rabbi Soloveitchik was not one to involve himself in politics or political issues. Originally, he was a member of

Besides mentoring students, people from far and wide sought his guidance and advice.

(L-R): Rabbi Shneur Kotler, Rabbi Yosef Soloveitchik and Rabbi Moshe Feinstein

His prolific writings, like his lectures, revealed a distinctive combination of contemporary and deep-rooted Jewish thought.

the Agudath Israel of America, which was reconstituted in 1939. While there were a number of attempts to organize the Agudah at earlier intervals, it was only with the influx of Eastern European refugees that the American division took hold. The *Rav* soon became chairman of its national executive committee and a member of the newly formed American Council of Torah Sages. Although he later left Agudath Israel, he became a staunch supporter of the Chinuch Atzmai independent school system, which the Agudah had subsequently established in Israel. At the invitation of Rabbi Aharon Kotler, the *Rav* delivered the keynote address at the Chinuch Atzmai dinner on January 11, 1956. In his address, the *Rav* paid tribute to the chairman, Stephen Klein, and the venerable *Rosh HaYeshiva* and founder of Beth Medrash Govoha in Lakewood, New Jersey, "Reb Aharon, the great

Rosh Yeshiva, has no cold light in him; it is hot, it kindles. And as you approach him, you, in turn, become enkindled. And if there is one single individual who has warmed me toward Chinuch Atzmai, it is the senior *Rosh Yeshiva*, Reb Aharon, to whom I pay homage."

As the tragedy of the Holocaust became apparent, the *Rav* became a member of the Mizrachi movement. From 1946 until his death, he served as its honorary president. He continually urged the leaders of Israel's Mizrachi political party to emphasize religious education, not only religious legislation. As a result of his identification with religious Zionism, many of his students chose to make *aliyah*. He refused to accept the position of Chief Rabbi of Israel, because he feared becoming an officer of the State. He felt that the mere fact that, from time to time, halachic problems were addressed as political issues, constituted an infringement on the sovereignty of the rabbinate.

Rabbi Soloveitchik eventually took his place as leader and mentor of the growing "Modern Orthodox" movement in North America. Nevertheless, he was never totally at ease in this milieu. He felt that Modern Orthodoxy lacked a deep emotional foundation and self-effacing commitment. In his view, Modern Orthodoxy "lacks the wings to soar to the heavens and is bereft of its roots to

(L-R): Rabbi Dovid Lifshitz, Rabbi Zevulun Charlop (Dean of RIETS), Rabbi Yosef Soloveitchik, c. 1977

The Rav delivering the Yahrtzeit Shiur

truly penetrate the depth of religious experience."

Rabbi Soloveitchik passed away on April 8, 1993, at the age of ninety, and was deeply mourned throughout the world. Rabbi Hillel Goldberg, editor of the Denver Intermountain Jewish News, wrote, "What a link he was to so many strands of the covenantal people, to everything from the particular genius of his grandfather, originator of the "Brisker Method" of Talmudic analysis, to the world of Eastern European Jewry that is destroyed; to the "anonymous Jew" of the centuries with whom Rabbi Soloveitchik had so much sympathy; to the world of the Patriarchs and Matriarchs, with whom Rabbi Soloveitchik seemed to be on such intimate terms. And now he leaves a void." This is a moving testimony to the legacy of Rabbi Soloveitchik, his perspective and achievements.

Rabbi Moshe Feinstein greeting Rabbi Aharon Kotler at a Chinuch Atzmai dinner; in the center is Rabbi Yosef Dov Soloveitchik.

Rabbi Yisroel Spira 1889-1989

THE BLUZHEVER REBBE

A man of sensitivity and great insight, the Bluzhever *Rebbe*, Rabbi Yisroel Spira, instilled spiritual courage in so many suffering Jews imprisoned in the Nazi death camps. Despite enduring incomprehensible personal anguish, he helped whomever he could, and came to America prepared to rebuild. He actively assisted countless people who sought his advice and *berachos*, always demonstrating warmth and wisdom. The Bluzhever *Rebbe* was one of the most beloved Torah leaders of our time.

Rabbi Yisroel Spira was born in 1889, in the city of Bluzhev, Galicia. His father, Reb Yehoshua, was the *Rav* of Ribitchie and renowned both for his piety and Torah scholarship. He served as his son's primary teacher of Torah. Reb Yehoshua traveled frequently to Bluzhev to visit his father, the *Rav* of Bluzhev, and young Yisroel would accompany him. As a result of these visits, he became the apple of his grandfather's eye. When he was a teenager, Yisroel lived primarily with his grandfather.

At age sixteen, Yisroel received semichah from Rabbi Meir Arik of Tarnow, a renowned Torah figure at that time. That same year, Reb Yisroel married the daughter of Rabbi Shalom Dovid Unger, the Szabne *Rav*. At age nineteen, he became Rav of Prochnik. In 1924, his grandfather passed away, and his father Reb Yehoshua became the new Bluzhever *Rebbe*.

In 1932, Reb Yisroel's father passed away. His will stated that his son, Yisroel, should become the next *Rebbe*. Since he had an older brother, Reb Yisroel was uncomfortable accepting the position. He decided to become the *Rebbe* in Istrik and his older brother would serve as *Av Beis Din* in Bluzhev, while their father's *Beis Medrash* would function on its own. Reb Yisroel was very active in community work. He was a member of Agudath Israel of Galicia, and attended the first *Knessiah Gedolah* in 1923.

Reb Yisroel's five years under the Nazi regime were fraught with tragedy and loss. Two of his three daughters died before World War II. At the outbreak of the War, Reb Yisroel fled with his family from Istrik to Lemberg.

There, his daughter, son-in-law, and only grand-child were killed. Reb Yisroel and his wife were taken from Lemberg to the Belzec death camp. At the *Selektion* the able-bodied men were separated, while the others were sent to another line, soon to meet their end. The officer in charge called out, "Which men are under

Bluzhever Rebbe as young man

at Bergen-Belsen, where he spent the latter part of the War, Reb Yisroel, who was now referred to as the Bluzhever *Rebbe,* was the spiritual leader of his fellow prisoners. *Chassidim, Litvaks* and even non-observant Jews turned to him for comfort, support, and advice during those horrible years. He was an encouraging and inspiring figure to many fellow prisoners.

One year, before Chanukah, shoe dye was smuggled out of the camp factory by the women inmates. Threads were pulled from sweaters by the women and spun into wicks. Scores of Jews, risking discovery, came to hear the *Rebbe* recite the *berachos*

Bluzhever Rebbe visiting Zeirei's rescue operations after his arrival in America. Seated to his right is Rabbi Herbert S. Goldstein. Standing on the left is Mike Tress, to his left are Moshe Dyckman and Rabbi Chaim Uri Lipshitz. Third from right in Nathan Hausman, at far right is Rabbi Moshe Sherer.

fifty?" Realizing that these men would be saved, his wife called out, "My husband is forty-five." Reb Yisroel did not want to be separated from his wife, and truthfully said, " No, I am fifty-two, you do not want me." The Nazi officer believed his wife, and moved him to the line of those who would work. She was killed a short while later.

Many great miracles happened to him while he was in the camps. While

on the Chanukah lights. A non-believing Jew asked Reb Yisroel how could he make the *berachah* of *Shehechiyanu,* which thanks G-d for keeping us alive and sustaining us. "How can you offer thanks when we are being tortured and killed; aren't you mocking our suffering?" Reb Yisroel replied, that he, too, was wondering how he could joyfully make this *berachah.* However, when he saw how many Jews gathered

At Bergen-Belsen, the Bluzhever Rebbe was the spiritual leader of his fellow prisoners – encouraging, advising and comforting them.

Bluzhever Rebbe with Kopyczinitzer Rebbe

(L-R): Reb Shia Bertram, Reb Moshe Bertram, Rabbi Yaakov Horowitz, Bluzhever Rebbe

The Rebbe said, "We Jews never give up; for centuries people have tried to destroy us, and we are living proof that we always try to rebuild."

to participate in this *mitzvah* despite their suffering and at risk to their lives, he realized that he was witnessing great courage and faith, and for that alone we must thank G-d. He continued, "We Jews never give up; for centuries people have tried to destroy us, and we are living proof that we always try to rebuild." This is just one example of how Reb Yisroel encouraged others in the camps.

Reb Yisroel arrived in America after the war, in 1946. Chassidic Jews were anxious to speak with the first *Rebbe* who had survived the concentration camps. As is the custom when

someone visits a *Rebbe*, a sum of money was left for him. Every penny he received was sent abroad to help the survivors. Eventually he set up a *Beis Medrash* in Williamsburg, NY, and immediately drew a large crowd.

The Bluzhever *Rebbe* became involved in community work as soon as he settled in America. He served as a member of *Agudas HaAdmorim*, an organization of chassidic *Rebbes*. He also was active in various aspects of *hatzalah* work, helping other *rebbes*

Bluzhever Rebbe greeting Rabbi Moshe Feinstein

Bluzhever Rebbe acting as sandek at a bris

Bluzhever Rebbe

Reb Yisroel was extremely involved in Agudath Israel, whose presidium looked to him for guidance and support. Many people turned to the *Rebbe* for advice and Torah knowledge – his simplified approach was very appealing.

The Bluzhever *Rebbe* lived to be 100 years old. His funeral was attended by thousands of his *chassidim* and admirers. Many years earlier, as he was being dragged away from his wife at the camps, she called out to him, "The world still needs you. May this knowledge give you strength." For the Bluzhever the four decades after the war were one great expression of inner strength, an unyielding faith and love of G-d, so that his mission in life could be fulfilled. How true were the words of his wife – the world really needed him.

The four decades after the war were one great expression of inner strength, an unyielding faith and love of G-d, so that his mission in life could be fulfilled.

who came from the camps reestablish their communities, as well as aiding all survivors who came to America.

(L-R): Boyaner Rebbe, Novominsker Rebbe, Bluzhever Rebbe

(I-R): Rabbi Elya Svei, (standing at table) Rabbi Moshe Sherer, Bluzhever Rebbe, Rabbi Yaakov Yitzchok Ruderman, (far right) Rabbi Mordechai Gifter

Rabbi Yoel Teitelbaum *1887–1979*

SATMAR RAV

It was 1928 when the small town of Satmar installed a new *Rav*, Rabbi Yoel Teitelbaum, the second son of the famous Sigheter *Rav*, a scion of the Ujel-Sighet dynasty founded by the *Yismach Moshe*. Although he was still a young man, Reb Yoel had already achieved fame as the *Rav* of Muzheyer and Krule; but it was in Satmar that he became famous in the *chassidic* world. Prior to his arrival, the town of Satmar (Satu-Mare) was relatively unknown, and because of Reb Yoel's personality and strength of character, he was able to unite the community – both *chassidim* and *misnagdim* – into an integrated *kehillah* dedicated to Hashem and His service.

From his youth, he was known as a prodigy both in scholarship and piety. Stories are legion about the young "Yoilish." The *Rebbe*, however, did not rely on his brilliant acumen; rather, he exerted himself, often to the limits of human endurance. For a period of almost forty years, starting at his *bar mitzvah* until the outbreak of the war, he never slept on a bed, except on Shabbos. He spent his days and nights delving into the sea of Talmud. So vast was his scholarship that on a visit to Telshe Yeshiva in his later years, he delivered a brilliant impromptu *shiur* on the Gemara being studied in the yeshiva, having been informed of the topic only moments before. His scholarship was rivaled only by his immense demonstration of *Ahavas haTorah*. This legacy remains for generations to come, in his series of sefarim entitled *Divrei Yoel*.

One Shabbos morning in tranquil prewar Satmar, the *Rebbe* awoke, trembling with fear. During the night, he had a dream that he was presiding over his tisch – in America. Concerned, as to what ominous reason would cause him to relocate, the *Rebbe* fasted on Shabbos, as prescribed by the *Halachah*.

Years passed and Satmar, together with many other Hungarian cities, were trampled by the jackboot of Nazi terrorism. The *Rebbe* and his commu-

The Satmar Rebbe as a young man

nity were deported to the infamous Bergen-Belsen concentration camp. Even under the horrific conditions there, the *Rebbe* refused to compromise his fastidious levels of *mitzvah* observance. Undaunted by the fear of punishment, he hid his beard and *peyos* under bandages and avoided all food that was unkosher or contaminated. He had been saved from certain death by being included in the Kastner train (Rudolph Kastner was president of the Hungarian Zionist Movement), which transported 1600 Hungarian Jews to Bergen-Belsen instead of Aushwitz. After several months in the camp, they were freed and transported to Switzerland, as a result of negotiations between Kastner and Eichmann. After a brief stay in Switzerland, in 1946, he took up residence in the Williamsburg section of Brooklyn.

Even under the horrific conditions in Bergen-Belsen, the Rebbe refused to compromise his fastidious levels of mitzvah observance.

(L-R): Bobover Rebbe with Satmar Rebbe

The Satmar Yeshiva building in Williamsburg

several newcomers, attached themselves to him. With great determination, the *Rebbe* set about rebuilding the community destroyed by the War. The *Rebbe* was the focal point and the driving force of the emerging community. Even after being weakened by a stroke, he continued to lead his community. The Satmar community was based on his convictions that only total isolation from all foreign encroachments could ensure its purity. He therefore saw to it that the community provided itself with all the necessary religious institutions – *shuls,* yeshivos and *mikvaos* were built and maintained under the *Rebbe*'s constant direction. *Kashrus* supervision, includ-

The *Rebbe*'s radiant personality, full of faith and hope, infused new life into the survivors who came to America. Soon a group of *chassidim*, including

> *The Rebbe's radiant personality, full of faith and hope, infused new life into the survivors who came to America.*

Satmar Rebbe walking in Yerushalayim

Satmar Rebbe in Yerushalayim

encouraged material growth, urging his *chassidim* to succeed as businessmen so they could help their brethren. Every decision in business, no matter how mundane, included the *Rebbe* in the decision-making process.

With the foresight of a great leader, the *Rebbe* ensured that the successful *chassidim* employ their brethren. Strict adherence to the laws of modesty, which are common in Satmar places of business, allowed Satmar young women to avail themselves of a sheltered environment to earn a livelihood. The Bais Rochel girls' school also prepared girls with job-oriented skills. With the increased job opportunities in *shomer Shabbos* businesses, the challenges facing new immigrants was minimized.

Built with the generosity and financial success of a number of Satmar *chassidim,* multiple *chesed* institutions were established. *Bikur Cholim* of

The Rebbe built the Satmar community based on his convictions that only total isolation from all foreign encroachments could ensure its purity.

ing *shechitah* and bakeries, were added to the infrastructure of the Williamsburg community.

Limited in their secular education by the Satmar school system, the young men of Williamsburg entered the business and trade world. The *Rebbe* was rigidly opposed to any secular studies beyond those related to the immediate pursuit of a livelihood. He

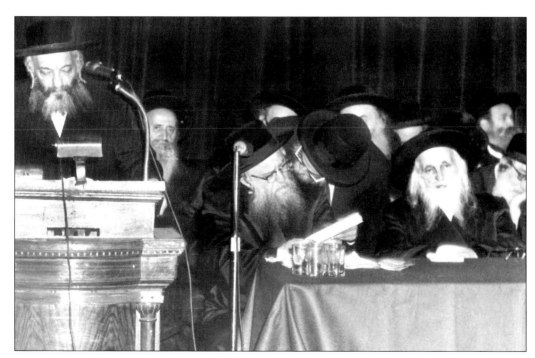

Pupa Rav speaking at podium. Seated, Voidislaver Rav, Satmar Rebbe

(L-R): Sighet-Satmar Rav, Satmar Rebbe, Rabbi Avraham Kalmanowitz

Understanding the allure of the American lifestyle, the Rebbe realized that the community must offer a viable standard of living, comparable to that of the general society, to neutralize the threat of defection to the outside world.

Williamsburg developed into the flagship of all other *Bikur Cholim* organizations. The *Rebbe*, with his characteristic insight, encouraged his *chassidim* to spend their money on themselves also. Beautifully appointed homes, inside and outside, abound in Williamsburg. Understanding the allure of the American lifestyle, the *Rebbe* realized that the community must offer a viable standard of living, comparable to that of the general society, to neutralize the threat of defection to the outside world.

Only after the community had achieved financial stability did the *Rebbe* allow the opening of a *kollel*. Previously, the *Rebbe* had encouraged his *chassidim* to join the work force, but with the growing need for *rabbanim* and *dayanim*, coupled with the financial wherewithal of the community, it was time to establish a *kollel*. The *Rebbe* interviewed the prospective *talmidei chachamim*. Among the questions that he asked them was the cost of their weddings and furnishings. If the amount seemed excessive to the

Rebbe, they were disqualified. The *Rebbe* explained that the community is not obliged to support an excessive lifestyle. In the *Kollel*, practical Halachah was stressed. Graduating *rebbeim* insured a constant source of *rabbanim* and *poskim* for the growing Satmar community in Williamsburg, and the new Satmar communities that were blossoming in other cities.

The *Rebbe* committed himself to building the Satmar *Kehillah* on the American landscape. Strict adherence to the customs of old was a benchmark of Satmar. The distinctive dress was retained, as was the unshorn beards and *peyos*. This was not a yearning for a long-lost past, but an end in itself. Distinction in all areas of life, both physical and spiritual, is demanded of the Torah Jew. Changes of location must not and do not determine the application and practice of Torah and *mitzvos*. Rather, in every circumstance, the Torah Jew must transcend his environment and remain totally faithful to the eternal ideals of the Torah. Many have said that because Satmar was prepared to stand at the extreme, the rest of the Jewish community was able to survive, even with their lenient attitude to dress and fashion.

Central to Satmar philosophy is their staunch anti-Zionism. This philosophy aligned with the *Neturei Karta* of Yerushalayim of that time, who appointed the Satmar *Rebbe* as their spiritual mentor. Whereas many felt the need to join the government under the aegis of Agudath Israel, the *Rebbe* refused to involve himself in any way with the secular Israel government. The *Rebbe* was firm in his stand, not for political concerns but for halachic reasons. His position was firmly founded on the words of *Chazal*, as detailed in his numerous halachic works. Because this philosophy was based on *Chazal*, it was immutable. As a man of integrity and honesty, nothing could alter his point of view and what he felt was propounded in Halachah.

It was this integrity that earned him the respect of all, even his opponents, for they knew that his stand was not self-serving but a part of his total dedication to Halachah. Although he forbade his followers to take money from the Israeli government, he took it upon himself to support institutions in *Eretz Yisrael*, knowing fully well the vital purpose they served. His solidarity with the Torah leadership on communal issues and their mutual respect was obvious to all.

With his passing, the Torah world lost a great and dynamic leader – a leader described by a foremost *Rosh HaYeshiva* (Rabbi Mordechai Gifter) as one whom the generations awe. When the Satmar *Rav* lived amongst us, his perception of truth and his integrity demanded from everyone that they

Satmar Rebbe on the ship traveling to Eretz Yisrael

consider their positions honestly, for any deviation from Torah would result in an immediate response from the Satmar *Rav*.

Satmar Rebbe

Strict adherence to the customs of old was a benchmark of Satmar. In every circumstance, the Torah Jew must transcend his environment and remain totally faithful to the eternal ideals of the Torah.

❧ Rabbi Mordechai Pinchas Teitz *1908-1995*

The architect of an American Jewish community was a European rabbi who came here in the mid-1930s. Rabbi Mordechai Pinchas Teitz built a complete Torah community in Elizabeth, New Jersey, and innovated projects that have global repercussions. He focused his brilliant mind and sparkling personality on one goal: teaching Torah. More hazardous to our people's vitality than any outside threat, he believed, is the danger of ignorance within. Only Torah knowledge can guarantee our future.

Born on the eighth of Tammuz 5668, corresponding to July 7, 1908, in Subat, Latvia, to Rabbi Binyamin Avraham and *Rebbetzin* Shaina Sira Rabinovich, his father adopted the Teitz surname to avoid conscription in the army. Rabbi Teitz was descended from an illustrious family, going back more than 300 years, and included such Torah giants as the *Levush* and the *Maharshal*. His forebears taught him the vital qualities of courage, fidelity to Halachah, and responsibility for the Jewish People.

He focused his brilliant mind and sparkling personality on one goal: teaching Torah.

In 1914, the family escaped from the battlefront in Latvia to Poltava. In 1921, when the Communists came to power, the Teitzes returned to Latvia, where Rabbi Binyamin Teitz became *rav* in Ribinizik. One year later, they moved to Livenhof, at the urging of a community that had four chassidic *shuls* but wanted him, a *misnagid*, to lead them.

After learning in Ponevezh and Riga, Rabbi M. Pinchas Teitz studied for six years in Slobodka, where he enjoyed a warm relationship with Rabbi Moshe Mordechai Epstein and his son-in-law, the *Yerushalmi*, Rabbi Yosef Zusmanovich. A lifelong friendship with Rabbi Yaakov Kamenetsky began during their years at Slobodka.

When he had to take time off to recuperate from an appendectomy, he decided to learn *Yoreh Dei'ah* and visit with the *Rogatchover Gaon* nearby in Dvinsk. A month's convalescence turned into a year of spending every weekday with the *Gaon*. The insights he gained were written up almost forty years later in an introduction to the volumes that he published of the *Tzofnas Pane'ach*.

Rabbi Teitz worked in Riga with Rabbi Mordechai Dubin and Shimon Wittenberg, both representatives in the Latvian parliament; Avigdor Balshanek, the head of Agudah in Latvia; and Rabbi Chaim Hodokov, who was in charge of Jewish education. He also served as a *rav*, an officer of Agudah, editor of *Unzer Shtimme, (Our Voice)*, and a leader in the movement to boycott Germany.

His learning, speaking and organizational gifts prompted Rabbi Avraham Yitzchak Bloch of Telshe to ask him to travel to North America with Rabbi Eliyahu Meir Bloch. Rabbi Teitz spent the *Elul Zeman* at Telshe to acquaint himself with the yeshiva he would represent. Between November 1933 and December 1934 Rabbi Teitz and Rabbi Bloch gave *shiurim* in every major Jewish community in the United States and Canada. A testimony to the Jewish People's love for Torah was the large attendance at these *shiurim* and the money American Jews generously gave for a Lithuanian yeshiva, even during the Depression. Rabbi Teitz found great Torah scholars in the United States who, for lack of English, could not share their knowledge with their communities. He also noted that in almost every city the Reform congregation was in the richest neighborhood, the Conservative one in the middle-class area, while the Orthodox *shul* was in the poorest area of town, contributing to a fear that *Yiddishkeit* was played out.

A young man who chauffeured Rabbi Teitz and Rabbi Bloch during their stay in his city wanted to express friendship when they parted. Since he did not know Yiddish, he shook their hands and said the only phrase he knew, "*Mazel Tov!*" Rabbi Teitz heard

(L-R): Rabbi Aharon Kotler, Rabbi Cywiak, Rabbi Teitz

in that "*mazel tov*" the longing for closeness to Torah. At an Agudas HaRabbonim convention when he was asked to speak on conditions across America, he reported that we were losing our younger people because of the language barrier. Consequently, he felt that every *rav* must learn English to communicate with them.

In January 1935, he married Basya Preil and became the successor to her father, Rabbi Elazar Mayer Preil, a Torah scholar and rabbinic leader, in Elizabeth, New Jersey. He wrote a pamphlet in Yiddish ("*Urah!*") which he translated into English (Awaken!) calling for action and trust in Hashem to build Torah education and Torah life in the modern world. Rabbi

Rabbi Elazar Mayer Preil

Rabbi Teitz united the private Hebrew classes in Elizabeth into an organized, communal Talmud Torah...

Teitz united the private Hebrew classes in Elizabeth into an organized, communal Talmud Torah; built a *mikveh*; and in 1940, he re-opened the yeshiva day school which Rabbi Preil had started in 1920 and 1930. Each of the earlier schools had lasted three years, but on this third attempt the yeshiva flourished. Finally, in 1951, he erected a large modern building that became a model school in the most desirable neighborhood. Yeshivos opened in a number of cities, but it is difficult to document them since those that did not succeed closed and their records were lost. The schools that did survive in the 1930s and 40s in Baltimore, Boston, Chicago, Elizabeth, Jersey City, Cleveland and several other places proved that a yeshiva could exist outside New York. Elizabeth, New Jersey, verified that a Jewish population of ten thousand could sustain a school. When World War II ended, rabbis and laypeople were ready to heed Rabbi Shraga Feivel Mendlowitz's call and establish day schools across the continent.

Rabbi Teitz, who was active in Vaad Hatzala during the war, went to Europe to rescue people from DP (Displaced Persons) Camps in the autumn of 1945.

Rabbi Teitz built *shuls* in the two best neighborhoods of Elizabeth and created a *kehillah*, caring for everyone in the classic Jewish way. He expanded the yeshiva to include a junior high school, then added a boys' Mesivta in 1955, followed by a girls' high school, Bruriah, in 1963. In the early 1970s, when a modern building for

For thirty-six years, from post-Sukkos in October until pre-Shavuos in May, Rabbi Teitz taught a page of Talmud every Saturday night, broadcast from the radio station in Manhattan or pre-recorded at his studio in Elizabeth. He always wrote insights on the border of the page of his gemara, but otherwise did not use a script.

Bruriah went up on its own campus, a mile away from the Mesivta, he moved the junior high school classes for girls to Bruriah. He always arranged many adult education courses, particularly, "Learn to Read Hebrew" and "The Geography of the *Siddur*," as well as advanced Talmud classes. He wanted to empower *every* Jew with literacy and knowledge.

In 1953, he founded the *Daf Ha-Shavua*, the "Talmudic Seminar of the Air," teaching the Talmud on the radio on Saturday nights in the New York - New Jersey area. Tapes of the program were broadcast in Boston, Chicago, Los Angeles, Miami, Montreal, and Philadelphia, and led to the renaissance of *Daf Yomi* learning in the United States. He taught Gemara on long-playing records called *Bas Kol*, with the lesson on one side in Yiddish and on the other side in English. Although Torah tapes and *Dial-a-Daf*

Rabbi Teitz held the annual celebration of the Daf HaShavua in a different neighborhood every year to spread the enthusiasm for learning Torah.

are now widely accepted, at the time some people criticized using a new means to teach Torah. Rabbi Moshe Feinstein, Rabbi Isaac Halevi Herzog, Rabbi Yosef Kahaneman (Ponovezer *Rav*), Rabbi Aharon Kotler, Rabbi

A historic moment: launching Torah on the radio. Pictured here, Rabbi Teitz preparing for the first broadcast of Daf HaShavua in 1953.

In 1953, he founded the Daf HaShavua, the "Talmudic Seminar of the Air," teaching the Talmud on the radio on Saturday nights.

Rabbi Eliezer Silver and Rabbi Teitz worked to rescue Jews through Vaad Hatzala. They were among the rabbis who went to Washington to see President Roosevelt, but were rebuffed.

Menachem Mendel Schneerson (Lubavitcher *Rebbe*) and Rabbi Yechiel Yaakov Weinberg (author of *Seridei Aish*) all approved and encouraged Rabbi Teitz's innovation. Rabbi Feinstein,

Rabbi Kahaneman and Rabbi Kotler showed their support by attending the first annual *Daf HaShavua* celebration; the other *rabbanim* sent *Daf HaShavua* messages and halachic analyses.

Rabbi Teitz defended *shechitah*, from legislative attacks on the state and federal levels. He and *Rebbetzin* Teitz and their daughters made twenty-two trips to the USSR in the 1960s and 70s. Because he was a naturalized American citizen from a country under Russian domination, he had to travel each time with a family member who was born in America to protect himself against arrest. He brought all the necessities of Jewish life to communities across Europe and Asia – providing *siddurim* and teaching materials for the youth. Rabbi Teitz saved Jewish cemeteries from destruction; restored gravestones and built a protective *ohel* for the

*Rabbi Teitz said, "The Torah speaks the language of tomorrow...The mitzvos apply in **every time** and **every place.**"*

(L-R): Rabbi Yaakov Kamenetsky and Rabbi Teitz. They began their life-long friendship at the Slobodka Yeshiva.

graves of many *gedolim*. Additionally, he dispatched *gittin* between husbands and wives who had chosen to live on different sides of the Iron Curtain. Because Rabbi Teitz did not want anyone caught in the vast prison system of Communist domination to suffer, he did not speak about his work. After his passing, Rabbi Yitzchak Yosef Zilber and Rabbi Eliyahu Essas gave some details of what the *rav* they called a *held*, a hero, had done.

Rabbi Teitz appreciated everyone's efforts for Torah. He understood the courage it took for *rabbanim* and laymen across the country to sustain day schools against all odds. He knew what commitment it took to be observant from the 1930s through the 1970s, when the turn-about occurred for Orthodoxy and instead of being derided, it became respected and even admired.

Rabbi Teitz said, "The Torah speaks the language of tomorrow." Although people in America protested that only "angels in heaven could keep the

Rabbi Teitz listening to Rabbi Moshe Feinstein

mitzvos," or that, "across the ocean, in Europe, you could be observant, but not on this side of the Atlantic," he did not agree. He maintained that the Torah anticipated these objections: the *mitzvos* apply in **every time** and **every place**; externals don't matter; what is in your mouth and in your heart should determine your actions (see *Devarim* 30:11-14). "Don't adapt the Torah to modern life"; he said, "adapt modern life to the Torah."

Rabbi Teitz served on the presidium of Agudas HaRabbonim for 12 years, working closely with Rabbi Feinstein, Rabbi Kamenetsky, Rabbi Kotler, Rabbi David Lifshitz and Rabbi Eliezer Silver. He was Treasurer of Ezras Torah for close to 40 years and a good friend of Rabbi Yosef Eliyahu Henkin throughout.

Rabbi Teitz passed away on the fourth of *Teves* 5756, December 26, 1995. He fulfilled "the three L's of Judaism" that he listed on his Jewish Educational Center postmark: "**L**earn Torah, **L**ove Torah, **L**ive Torah." He also accomplished a fourth imperative as well: Share Torah. His legacy is multi-dimensional, and the recipients of his achievements will always be grateful.

Rabbi Mordechai Pinchas Teitz

He fulfilled "the three L's of Judaism that he listed on his Jewish Educational Center Postmark: "Learn Torah, Love Torah, Live Torah."

Reb Elimelech Gavriel (Mike) Tress *1909-1967*

Reb Elimelech Gavriel "Mike" Tress (he was always referred to as Mike) was a pioneer and unrelenting warrior for Judaism in America. He was a courageous individual who gave up a thriving career, using his personal fortune and plunging himself and his family into poverty, while he transformed and inspired all those around him to help in the salvation of Jews both during and after World War II. Although he did not have a yeshiva education, he had a tremendous respect for *Yiddishkeit* and *gedolim.* R'Elimelech understood the vital role yeshiva education played in the perpetuation of *Yiddishkeit* in America. He also realized that Jewry must play a vital role in the preservation of human freedom and dignity.

In 1933, Mr. Tress was elected president of the Williamsburg branch of Zeirei Agudath Israel, which at the time was little more than a Jewish club for young men. Under his leadership, it grew into a national movement with branches around the country, its own newspaper, a Jewish Serviceman's Bureau, and a refugee home. The Agudah established summer camps for boys and girls, which were unique in their time as being the only Jewish summer camps with learning groups twice a day. As a result of attending these summer camps many boys and girls went on to attend yeshivos and Bais Yaakovs. He was a charismatic leader, who was able to relate to everyone in the organization. All those who came in contact with him, young and old, felt he was their friend. It was through the influence of Bnos (the girls division of Agudah) and Mike's persistence that New York's first two Bais Yaakovs grew in size.

There were a few major influences on Mr. Tress, which propelled him to give up everything in his life to help his brethren in Europe. Rabbi Elchonon Wasserman came to America to raise money for his yeshiva in Baranovich. No matter how much people tried to dissuade him from returning to war-ravaged Europe, Rabbi Elchonon was not swayed. As he was boarding the boat he said, "Stop pleading with me. I have to go back to my students and share with them what G-d has in store for us. But you here in America have a tremendous challenge, come what may. This is not a time to live for yourselves. You must act now. G-d will be with you." These words had such an impact on Mike that they mobilized him into action and motivated everything he accomplished.

There were others who also had a tremendous effect on Mr. Tress. Reb Shraga Feivel Mendlowitz, who gave a *shiur* at Zeirei and worked for the advancement of Torah education in America, forged a very close relationship with Mike. They worked together on many projects throughout the 1930s, during World War II, and afterward as well.

The unofficial rabbi of Zeirei was Rabbi Gedaliah Schorr, who

Reb Elimelech Gavriel Tress

later became the *Rosh HaYeshiva* of Torah Vodaath. Rabbi Schorr gave *shiurim* at Zeirei and answered all the questions that arose in the organization. Mike and Rabbi Schorr enjoyed an extremely close relationship. Mr. Tress would consult him on a myriad of issues facing the Agudah and world Jewry. After Rabbi Aharon Kotler arrived in America, the two shared an unusually close relationship, working tirelessly on behalf of *Yiddishkeit*.

As World War II began, Mike saw that American Jewry was in a position to help in many ways. He set up an office at the Zeirei headquarters in Williamsburg (616 Bedford Ave) for rescue operations. Using his business contacts, charisma, and sheer persistence, he convinced many volunteers to help in this effort.

During World War II, Mike and the Agudah were at the forefront of *hatzalah* work. They sent food packages to Jewish men in the armed service, who otherwise would not have had kosher food. He personally wrote letters of encouragement to many servicemen, and dedicated many pages of the Agudah newspaper to covering stories and information pertaining to them. He worked with a group of young volunteers day and night to save Jews from the War. Affidavits were obtained and visa applications were processed (by hand) through the Immigration Division of the Agudath Israel Youth

Using his business contacts, charisma, and sheer persistence, he convinced many volunteers to help in hatzalah work.

Rabbi Elchonon Wasserman

Mike Tress and family (L-R): Mrs. Tress, in the background, Mike's mother

Camp Agudah, Highmount, NY, 1952

the War, food packages were also sent via the American Red Cross into the concentration camps.

Once the War ended, Mike continued to raise money and send food, clothing, supplies, and religious articles to the Displaced Persons Camps. In fact, the Agudah packages reached the DP camps before the Joint Distribution Committee's relief arrived. The Agudah compiled lists of survivors and scrutinized them to see if families already in America had any surviving relatives. In 1945, Mike traveled to Europe and spent a month in various Displaced Persons Camps throughout Europe. He actually slept among the survivors, spending hours listening to their stories and encouraging them to continue living and build a new life. Throughout his stay, he would jot down notes about what he saw and heard. (For complete details of the Agudah's rescue/relief efforts, see chapter III on Zeirei Agudath Israel.)

Once the War ended, Mike continued to raise money and send food, clothing, supplies, and religious articles to the Displaced Persons Camps.

Council, which saved thousands of lives. He had daily contact with the State Department, and traveled to Washington regularly. Mike personally played a major role in obtaining special emergency visitors' visas for 70 European Torah scholars and their families. The postwar growth of yeshivos in America would have been unimaginable without the rescue of these scholars. In addition, he raised funds to send food packages to Jews trapped in the various ghettos in Poland, as well as to the city of Vienna. Toward the end of

Mike Tress speaking at an Agudah event

Thanking U.S. Postmaster General Albert Goldman for his assistance in bringing children from concentration camps to Camp Agudah. (L-R): Mike Tress, Louis S. Septimus, Albert Goldman, unidentified, Rabbi Moshe Sherer

Mike and the Agudah raised funds to erect schools, housing, and trade schools for survivors who emigrated to Israel.

Upon his return, Mike gave many speeches detailing what he had seen firsthand in the DP camps. He described the horrible conditions many survivors still had to endure, and impressed upon the crowd how much work still had to be done. His purpose was not to make those in attendance feel guilty, but rather to motivate them to donate money, clothing, and religious articles, or to volunteer to help in relief efforts. Those who knew Mike well stated that he was never the same after he returned from the DP camps.

In addition, the Save A Child Foundation was established to help rescue children who had been left either in monasteries or gentile homes before the War, and to return them to their families. Although only 100 or so children were actually saved, it was not due to a lack of funds and manpower on the part of the Agudah. Rather, it was because of the unwillingness of those who raised these children and, at times, the children themselves.

Many survivors of World War II emigrated to *Eretz Yisrael*. Mike and the Agudah raised funds to erect schools, housing, and trade schools for them. Many socialist and non-religious organizations expended major efforts

Bobover Rebbe and Mike Tress

A Jewish girl, hidden during the Holocaust in a Christian home, returned to her grandparents by Agudah emissaries

to convince orphaned children newly arrived in *Eretz Yisrael* to reject religion. This made the effort to raise money for schools of utmost importance. During the early 1950s, Chinuch Atzmai – or Torah Schools for Israel, as it was known in America – was estab-

Mike speaking at the Agudah dinner honoring Rabbi Eliezer Silver. Seated in front row, (L-R): Rabbi Yaakov Kamenetsky, Rabbi Aharon Kotler, Rabbi Eliezer Silver, and Rabbi Moshe Sherer

lished under the leadership of Rav Aharon Kotler and Stephen Klein. The Israeli government covered 60% of a yeshiva's budget, and the other 40% had to be raised through contributions. Once again, Mike used his contacts to help raise the needed funds. Even after Chinuch Atzmai became a separate organization, Mr. Tress continued to speak on their behalf, and helped them make influential contacts.

In 1956, fighting broke out throughout Hungary between the Soviet Union, which was in power at the time, and those seeking an independent Hungary. During the chaos of the revolution, 20,000 Jews fled the country to Austria. Though the Soviet Union regained power, the unstable conditions made it possible to smuggle Jews out. Mike saw the opportunity to free Jews, who until then were locked behind the Iron Curtain. The Agudah sent thousands of dollars to aid in the smuggling effort. Mike traveled to Austria to help organize the rescue effort. He obtained visas for many of these people to come to America, and helped them find homes and jobs once they arrived.

From 1961 until 1967, Mike suffered from coronary disease that made it increasingly difficult for him to work. For a man who was used to working around the clock, the frustration of not being able to contribute was the worst of all. His tremendous *bitachon* protected him from bitterness and kept him going in those last years. In 1967, Mike's doctors told him that his condition had deteriorated to the point that the only option was heart by-pass surgery. At that time, this procedure was still in its infancy stage and very expensive. Insurance did not cover such experimental procedures and Mike did not have the money to pay for it. Coincidentally, just at that time his daughter noticed in the newspaper that Esquire Shoe Polish had been sold for $3,000,000. One third of that would have been Mike's had he not sold the stock (to pay for *hatzalah* work). "Just think," his daughter said, "Everything would be different had you not sold those shares." Mike's only reply was, *"Baruch Hashem* how different."

Somehow, the Kopyczinitzer *Rebbe* heard of his plight and gave Mike the

The Kopyczinitzer Rebbe, Rabbi Avraham Yehoshua Heschel

Mike Tress speaking at Agudah Dinner (L-R): Mike Tress, Rabbi Eliezer Silver, Rabbi Moshe Sherer, Rabbi Gedaliah Schorr, Louis Septimus

sum needed for the surgery. He told the *Rebbe* that he would be repaid. The *Rebbe* replied, "No, it is you who will be repaid," meaning G-d would repay him for all he had done. Mike was confident the surgery would be a success. The surgery was a success, and for six months he regained some of his former strength. Tragically, medicine prescribed for a relatively minor condition caused him to have a stroke. The following week, R' Elimelech Gavriel Tress passed away.

Jews from all walks of life attended his funeral, including many *rabbanim* and *roshei yeshiva*. It can be said that almost everyone in attendance felt a personal closeness to him. Mike Tress is an example of what an individual can accomplish with conviction, drive, and complete faith – the consummate *moser nefesh*. Even today, we are all recipients of his selflessness.

Mike Tress is an example of what an individual can accomplish with conviction, drive, and complete faith - the consummate moser nefesh.

Rabbi Yakov Yosef Twersky

1899~1968
THE SKVERER REBBE

In 1899, a new link in the chain of the great Chernobyl chassidic dynasty was forged. Yakov Yosef, as the baby was named, was wrought of different steel than the others. This link would join the European roots of Chernobyl to America.

Reb Yakov Yosef spent his early years in Skvira, Ukraine, under the tutelage of his father, Reb Dovid, who was the *Rebbe* of Skver. His mother was Rebbetzin Tziporah, the daughter of the *Rebbe* of Ostroh. The family had moved from the Ukraine because of the dangerous situation that prevailed there after the Bolshevik Revolution. Following the *petirah* of his father, the members of the family who were miraculously spared found safe haven in Kishenev, Romania. It was there that Reb Yakov Yosef wed Rebbetzin Trana, the daughter of Reb Pinchas of Ostilla.

The young couple settled in Ostilla, where Reb Yakov Yosef was offered the position of *Rav*. However, he turned it down, explaining that none of his ancestors had been *rabbanim*. Two years later, he returned to Romania.

The *chassidim* of Skver, who for years made their home in Kalarash, appointed him as their *Rebbe*, and thus began his lifelong service to *Klal Yisrael*.

He relocated to the city of Yas, where eventually he and his flock would suffer the pain and sorrow of the Second World War. The *Rebbe* miraculously survived the war and moved to Bucharest, Romania for three years. His home was the address for spiritual and physical sustenance for the survivors of the Nazi destruction. In early winter of 1948, he began the long and arduous journey to America. With stops in Budapest, Hungary; Prague; Poland; Antwerp, Belgium; and London, England, he finally arrived in New York in Adar 1948. Immediately upon his arrival, he began to build a chassidic court in Boro Park, New York. He later moved to Williamsburg, where he attracted thousands of *chassidim* in a relatively short time.

Despite the *Rebbe's* overwhelming success in Williamsburg, he still had a

Rabbi Yakov Yosef Twersky, a link in the chain of the Skverer chassidic dynasty, joined the European roots of Chernobyl to America.

The Skverer Rebbe with survivors in Bucharest, Romania. To the Rebbe's right is Reb Menashe Zundel Koenig

vision to establish a community far from the metropolis of New York — distant not in miles but in *hashkafah*. He longed for a place removed from the influences of American society, where the unadulterated chassidic lifestyle of Europe could prevail. His dream became a reality with the establishment of New Square, (Skver Town) in Nissan 1957.

For eleven years, he dedicated himself to the spiritual and physical needs of his flock. He was felicitous to the traditions of his predecessors – the path of the Baal Shem Tov. No compromises were tolerated in Skver Town. With his immense *ahavas haTorah* and *yiras Shamayim*, he guided his chassidim through the struggles of acclimating to the American spiritual wasteland, without losing the purity of their own spirituality. The *Rebbe* exemplified *kedushah*, in its most pristine and exalted form. This was a virtue he strove to imbue in his *chassidim*.

The force of his personality was the prime factor that caused his influence and fame to overflow the boundaries of Skver Town and inundate the entire Jewish community. Many turned to

him for advice, advice that was totally objective and honest. Most important, though, was his non-partisan stand on all issues. He avoided *machlokes*, controversy, at all costs. The Kopyczinitzer *Rebbe* lauded his achievements with individuals and institutions as follows: "No one invested more *emunah* in America than the Skverer *Rebbe!*"

The great *Rosh HaYeshiva*, Rabbi Aharon Kotler, frequently sought the *Rebbe's* advice. Reb Aharon felt that the *Rebbe's* keen understanding of human nature was unparalleled, and when problems arose regarding individual *bachurim*, he would consult with the *Rebbe*. A famous incident that displayed the *Rebbe's* spiritual prowess is often retold: An excellent *bachur* in Lakewood suddenly found himself confronted by questions in *emunah*. Reb Aharon called the *Rebbe*. The surprising response was, "How does he set his watch?" After inquiring, it was discovered that the *bachur* set his watch according to the chiming of the bells of the local church. As soon as he stopped this practice, the questions dissipated.

The Skverer Rebbe in Eretz Yisrael. In the background is Rabbi Yehudah Horowitz of Dzikov.

With his immense ahavas haTorah and yiras Shamayim, he guided his chassidim through the struggles of acclimating to America, without losing the purity of their own spirituality.

Ahavas Yisrael was the focal points of his life's philosophy.

Skverer Rebbe in Eretz Yisrael. On his right is Rabbi Meir Brandsdorfer of the Eidah Hachareidis.

His soft heart was open to all; at times, he would actually lose sleep over the problems of others. It made no difference if the petitioner was young or old; everyone received his full attention and concern. His joy on hearing good news was tangible. People who reported good news to him actually felt as if they had done him the greatest favor. From this heart overflowing with empathy and caring, blessings emanated. Many who received these blessings saw immediate improvements in their situation.

Ahavas Yisrael was the focal point of his life's philosophy. On occasion when he heard someone talk disparagingly of another Jew, the *Rebbe* was aghast — he could not fathom speaking this way about a

Skverer Rebbe speaking with a chassid

Skverer Rebbe walking in Skver Town. On his right is Reb Moshe Eisenbach, on his left is Rabbi Zalka Korn, Menahel of the Skverer Kollelim.

fellow Jew! The fact that that same person had attempted to prevent the *Rebbe* from receiving a building permit to build Skver Town made no difference – a Jew is a Jew.

With his sharp eye and concern for the spiritual health of his *chassidim* and all observant Jews, the *Rebbe* was constantly seeking ways to improve their lot. He initiated a campaign to provide a private bus line from Williamsburg to Manhattan, alleviating the need for observant businessmen to use public transportation. At his behest many other aspects of behavior in businesses were improved, bringing modesty and integrity to the workplace.

Although he was always careful to follow the path set by his ancestors, the *Rebbe* found areas in which he could be innovative. His was the first *chassidus* to encourage and then open a *kollel* for young married men. When a *chassan* would come to him seeking his blessing prior to his wedding, the *Rebbe* would demand of him that he set aside at least one year for full-time Torah study. He was of the opinion that if one did not study for at least two years after his wedding, he would "never open a *sefer*," and would not

daven, properly. After debates with other *rebbeim*, they eventually followed suit. His goal, however, was not the same as others who opened *kollelim*. His aim was not only to produce great scholars, but also to imbue the love of Torah study into "*Yiddishe shteiber*," Jewish homes. In the end, he achieved both of these goals.

For eleven years, the *Rebbe* toiled to build the community of Skver Town. At his passing on the 2nd of Nissan 1968, he bequeathed a thriving community and a vibrant *chassidus* to his son. The new link in the Skverer chassidic chain had indeed demonstrated and proved its strength and endurance.

The force of his personality was the prime factor that caused his influence and fame to inundate the entire Jewish community.

Present Skverer Rebbe, Rabbi Dovid Twersky in Yerushalyim, reading from the Likutei Tzvi prior to tearing kriah at the Kosel HaMaaravi

❧ Rabbi Simcha Wasserman *1902-1992*

"In the event that I will return my soul to its Creator during the lifetime of my wife, may she live on, and she will be present at my funeral, I hereby request to be eulogized only by one individual. Also, no praise be mentioned, except that on most occasions when I taught students I tried to make them comprehend the words of the Torah according to their abilities. Also that, blessed be G-d, I have indirectly influenced a few people to become observant Jews. Otherwise, no other praise should be said. Should my wife, may she live on for many good years, not be present at my funeral, I request that there should be no eulogy at all."

This was the Last Will and Testament of Rabbi Elazar Simcha Wasserman. Presenting a comprehensively accurate biography of his life's accomplishments is a challenging undertaking, because of Rabbi Wasserman's humility. For every act that is known to us, there are countless others that will remain unknown. This quality of *anivus* was one of the explanations for Rabbi Wasserman's success. Comfortable with anonymity, he did not take credit for himself.

Growing up, Reb Simcha was surrounded by many of the Torah leaders of the generation. His father was the great Rabbi Elchonon Wasserman, *Rosh HaYeshiva* in Baranowitz, and his uncle was Rabbi Chaim Ozer Grodzenski. He was fortunate to study in the foremost European yeshivos and became close with the *Roshei HaYeshiva* in each one. He studied in Novardok for some years after his *bar mitzvah*. While attending the yeshiva in Radin, he lived at the home of Rabbi Moshe Landinsky, the *Rosh HaYeshiva*. He also benefited from his association with his father's *rebbe*, the *Chofetz Chaim*. He studied under Rabbi Shimon Shkop in Grodna and Rabbi Chaim Soloveitchik in Brisk, and the *Alter* of Slobodka.

A product of many European yeshivos, Rabbi Wasserman's *hashkafah* was a blend of both the *mussar* of Novardok and the intellectual mastery of the Lithuanian yeshivos. This combination contributed to Rabbi Wasserman's effectiveness as he taught Torah. His broad comprehension of Halachah gave him the ability to explain its minutiae with clarity. He was a European-trained, "old world"-style *Rosh HaYeshiva* who could speak to anyone on any level, intellectually or personally.

At an early age, Rabbi Wasserman began his career as a traveling "truth salesman," Under the *Alter* of Novardok's guidance, he journeyed through Eastern Europe teaching Torah and establishing learning facilities. However, the Russian Revolution had just ended and travel was dangerous. Once, he was caught without a travel permit and was sentenced to labor in a work camp. Despite the other prisoners' harassment during the first week, he received permission to remain at camp on Shabbos to avoid desecrating the holy day. The work crew never came back that night. They were all shot as punishment for another prisoner's escape. Soon, he was released from the camp by a Jewish commissar who had hidden his faith from his supervisors. He arrived home after several torturous weeks, experiencing many ordeals including being beaten many times and being jailed.

Rabbi Wasserman was in Radin in 1933. Prior to leaving he went to say good-bye to the *Chofetz Chaim,* for what would be the last time. The *Chofetz Chaim* implied to Rabbi Wasserman that he should teach and disseminate Torah in places throughout the world where it was lacking. The first place he went was Strasbourg, France, where he established the only yeshiva in France at the time. He planted the seed that provided a continuity of Torah learning in France, which has allowed Judaism to flourish there to this very day.

When he was 24, he married Faige Rochel Abowitz, the daughter of the *Av*

Beis Din of Novardok. Five years later, he received *semichah* from Rabbi Isser Zalman Meltzer. In 1938, he left Europe to teach Torah in what was then known as a Torah wilderness, America. His first position was teaching in Mesivta Torah Vodaath, where he became close to Rabbi Shraga Feivel Mendlowitz. At that time there was limited Torah leadership and very few people were able to teach Torah and impart its values to the next generation. Rabbi Mendlowitz created a retreat called "Aish Dos," in 1941, where aspiring teachers spent the summer developing and refining their pedagogic skills. Rabbi Wasserman taught Talmud and outreach skills to the group. These young men became the first teachers and principals in yeshivos established in places where, previously, real Torah learning had been thought an impossibility.

With the outbreak of World War II and the ensuing Holocaust, Rabbi Wasserman threw his energy into the Vaad Hatzala. He worked closely with Rabbi Aharon Kotler, Rabbi Eliezer Silver and Mr. Irving Bunim. He went back to Europe to arrange transportation and safe havens and thereby saved many Jewish lives. The whole experience was extremely painful for Rabbi Wasserman. Many times, he would book tickets to safety only to have them canceled before departure. Wealthy "donors" mocked the organization by contributing tiny sums of money. Some people even slandered the volunteers by reporting back to America that the volunteers in Europe were living in luxury and ignoring the terrible situation. After the Holocaust ended, Rabbi Wasserman traveled across Europe searching for Jewish adults and children, and he attempted

With the outbreak of World War II and the ensuing Holocaust, Rabbi Wasserman threw his energy into the Vaad Hatzala.

Many Jews fled to Rio de Janeiro, Brazil, during the war and Rabbi Wasserman became their leader on the road back to Yiddishkeit.

to reunite them with their families and their Judaism. Rabbi Simcha Wasserman himself had lost almost his entire family in the war, including his beloved father. Trying to put the sadness behind him, he worked hard to build for the future. As his *Rebbetzin* said, "He has a *name* to live up to."

His next journey brought him back to America, this time to Detroit. There, he built a day school and an institution for adult Jewish education. It was in Detroit that he began to work with *baalei teshuvah*, a movement which was not to gain popularity until more than 20 years later.

He took a year's leave of absence from Detroit to go to England, where he worked with Rabbi Herzog to save

Rabbi Simcha Wasserman speaking with Rabbi Mordechai Gifter

hundreds of Jewish children from monasteries.

After leaving England, he settled in South America, in Rio de Janeiro,

Brazil. Many Jews had fled there during the war and Rabbi Wasserman became their leader on the road back to *Yiddishkeit*. He traveled the length of Latin America, through Mexico, Central and South America, helping people and teaching Torah wherever he went.

Los Angeles became the last stop of his American journey; there he founded Yeshivas Ohr Elchonon in the early 1950s. By then, Judaism had taken root and was flourishing on the East Coast, but the West Coast was still lacking Jewish leadership, institutions, and people dedicated to living true Torah lives. The yeshiva was the center for Torah and attracted many searching individuals. The three goals of the yeshiva were to teach the students, involve their parents, and reach out to Jews who were ignorant of their heritage. Rabbi Wasserman, his wife, and students traveled throughout California searching for such people. They would tell them about the yeshiva, or just share a little Torah, hoping to somehow spark an interest. The Wassermans and the yeshiva had to deal with many challenges, including the strong and so-called Jewish movements that had major followings in the west.

Rabbi Simcha Wasserman leading a discussion on issues in Jewish education in the library of the Hebrew Academy of Cleveland (L-R): Rabbi Meir Eisemann, Rabbi Abraham Bruckenstein, Rabbi Simcha Wasserman and Rabbi Nochum Zev Dessler

Rabbi Wasserman's sincerity and naturalness drew people to him, even before they were influenced by his teachings. He accepted people at face value and helped them understand themselves. He did not want his students to imitate him, rather he addressed each student on his own level, and treated them like his own children. He was truly interested in the other person and helped each one develop on the path that Hashem had already placed him.

Finally, in 1979, the Wassermans moved to *Eretz Yisrael,* as they had always hoped. Rabbi Simcha Wasserman set to work on establishing Yeshivas Ohr Elchonon in Jerusalem. When they outgrew the building they were occupying, Rabbi Wasserman, then almost 90 years old, took upon himself an international travel itinerary to raise money for his yeshiva's new building. He also helped found another branch in Tiberias. He continued to help Jewish people of the next generation return to their heritage. The Wassermans always had many guests at their Shabbos and *Yom Tov* meals. He also conducted question-and answer sessions at various yeshivos specializing in Jewish outreach.

In late 1992, just after his Jerusalem yeshiva moved into their new building, Rabbi Simcha Wasserman entered the next world. His wife followed him a week later. Although they left behind no biological children, they did leave thousands of spiritual offspring all over the world: generations of Torah observant Jews exist to a large degree because of his selfless devotion and magnanimous efforts.

Generations of Torah-observant Jews exist to a large degree because of his selfless devotion and magnanimous efforts.

❧ Rabbi Michoel Ber Weissmandl *1903-1957*

The child destined to be the conscience of world Jewry was born in Tyrnau, Slovakia, in 1903. Young Michoel Ber was a diligent and bright student. He matured under the guidance and tutelage of his teachers in various *yeshivos*. His main teacher and mentor was Rabbi Samuel David Ungar, the *Rav* of Tyrnau. When the latter moved to Nitra, his dedicated student, an accomplished rabbi in his own right, moved with him. Thus, in 1931, began his lifelong affiliation with Nitra Yeshiva. He soon became his *Rebbe's* son-in-law.

Rabbi Weissmandl's spectrum of expertise encompassed many complicated areas of Halachah, and he also had a penchant for manuscripts. Addi-tionally, he inno-vated various inventions and hoped to support him-self from them. In this capacity of fundraiser, he utilized his oratorical skills to encourage the alumni of Nitra Yeshiva to assist in covering the financial burden. Rabbi Weissmandl also taught in the yeshiva.

In 1938, Nazi anti-Semitism shattered the placid life of Slovakian Jewry. Rabbi Weissmandl immediately acted on behalf of his fellow Jews, informing government leaders of their perilous circumstances. In 1944, he was included in a transport to Auschwitz. He managed to jump off the train and encouraged others to do the same, thus begining his role as the prime mover in all *hatzalah* efforts. It was Rabbi Weissmandl who alerted the free world to the plight of the Jews, but to his dismay no one heeded his urgent call.

After the war, having lost most of his family and his community, Rabbi Weissmandl returned to Nitra, where the yeshiva had been reestablished. Although he mourned deeply and profusely for the lost members of his family and for all of the Jews martyred during the war, Rabbi Weissmandl sufficiently overcame his grief to rebuild the destroyed glory of Hashem's people. The dedication of the Nitra students to their learning and their yeshiva, which had been the last beacon of Torah during the war in Eastern Europe, was reignited after the war. In the post-war period, people visited Nitra and were deeply impressed with the intensity

The child destined to be the conscience of world Jewry was born in Tyrnau, Slovakia, in 1903. He alerted the free world to the plight of the Jews, but to his dismay no one heeded his urgent call.

Rabbi Samuel David Ungar

and dedication of the *rebbeim* and students.

Europe, however, was no longer a hospitable location for a yeshiva, and plans were made to transfer it to a different place. Of the three alternatives, Palestine, Tangiers and America, the latter was deemed the only solution. In 1946, Rabbi Weissmandl traveled to the United States and, with the help of Rabbi Shraga Feivel Mendlowitz, he succeeded in securing eighty visas for the rabbis, their families, and the students.

Orthodox Jewry in America at the time was still in the early stages of development and Rabbi Weissmandl sensed the people's inability, and perhaps indifference, to helping him rebuild his yeshiva. With determination and trust in Hashem, and the help of former *talmidim* and friends, Rabbi Weissmandl rented a building in the vacation town of Somerville, New Jersey, intending to eventually open the

yeshiva there. In the winter of 1946, with about sixty students, survivors of the Holocaust, Nitra Yeshiva was reborn on the American continent.

Nitra Yeshiva was unique. Rabbi Weissmandl's vision was to build a combination school and agricultural settlement. He realized that Somerville was not the appropriate place for the yeshiva, and after an eight-month search the Mount Kisco location was purchased. With obvious Divine Providence the $100,000 that was needed was raised. It was not without tribulations that the yeshiva took root. The local inhabitants of the township attempted to have the yeshiva closed. Rabbi Weissmandl, at the helm of the yeshiva, successfully guided it around all the obstacles, including protracted legal battles.

By building the yeshiva in tandem with an agricultural settlement, Rabbi Weissmandl sought to establish a firm financial base for the yeshiva. The agricultural settlement would be manned by graduates of the yeshiva, thus retaining its religious nature, while it supported those students who were to spend the entire day studying. Only the most dedicated students would continue to learn full time after their marriage, while the rest would work.

The rural setting of Mount Kisco in Westchester County, New York, was specifically chosen because it was removed from metropolitan New York City. Rabbi Weissmandl believed that life in the big cities created too many temptations and distractions. On their estate, the villagers and the workers would grow vegetables and fruit, and raise cattle and chickens. Rabbi Weissmandl also installed a printing press, and channeled his love and

Rabbi Weissmandl's spectrum of expertise encompassed many complicated areas of Halachah, and also a penchant for manuscripts. His lifelong affiliation with Nitra Yeshiva was manifest in his untiring efforts on its behalf.

The courtyard of the Nitra Yeshiva. Rabbi Ungar (in foreground),
Rabbi Weissmandl behind him.

As an educator, Rabbi Weissmandl was concerned with every aspect of his students' growth.
He taught about ethics, and always referred to the tragedy of the Holocaust.

experience with ancient manuscripts into it. He also planned various industrial projects.

As an educator, Rabbi Weissmandl was concerned with **every** aspect of his students' growth. He designated four years as the amount of time they were to study prior to their marriage. The requisite amount of sleep was six hours, and so forth, regarding all other aspects of their daily life. Older students were obligated to help the younger students. The villagers were required to reserve at least four hours a day for study. At the end of every Gemara class, Rabbi Weissmandl spoke to his students about ethics, and always referred to the tragedy of the Holocaust.

Perhaps the most telling clause in the Yeshiva settlement's constitution was that if a person was caught in a lie three times after having been warned, he was expelled! Rabbi Weissmandl was a man of truth and conviction. With his total being he abhorred falsehood and complacency. Whether it

was the falsehood of the so-called Jewish leaders who had interfered and sabotaged the negotiations to save European Jews during the war, or those who attempted to stop the development of the Orthodox community, Rabbi Weissmandl stood up against them boldly. At times, his was a solitary voice, but it shook many out of their complacency, and to his credit many survived the Holocaust and rebuilt their lives in the free world.

Although the Holocaust had left a deep and searing scar on his life, Rabbi Weissmandl realized the need of the hour and rose to the challenge. He remarried; his second wife was Leah Teitelbaum, sister-in-law of Rabbi Shalom Ungar. He and his wife raised five sons and a daughter. In his writings, he reveals his positive, almost prophetic, hopes for a better and more vibrant future for world Jewry, an optimism not readily shared by all.

Besides administering the yeshiva, Rabbi Weissmandl was indefatigable in his efforts to gather documentation of the Holocaust. For the rest of his life, he never let others forget how his appeals for help during the Holocaust were ignored, and the great number of Jews that could have been saved. His famous book, *Min Ha'meitzar,* includes a wealth of documents and letters detailing the frantic attempts of Slovakian Jewry to save themselves against all odds, and the overwhelming despair when their cries fell on deaf ears. He also authored a book entitled *Toras Chemed*, a brilliant anthology of letters and *remazim*, allusions, which he deduced by virtually counting the letters of the Torah and deriving signifi-

Rabbi Michoel Ber Weissmandl

cant lessons from their juxtaposition to each other.

Throughout his life, Rabbi Weissmandl suffered from heart problems. In 1957, he was stricken by a severe heart attack. Even in his weakened state, he still worked on behalf of the yeshiva. However, his condition deteriorated and on *Erev Shabbos,* Kislev 6, 1957, while learning *Rabbeinu Bachya's* commentary on the Torah, a treasured volume from his grandfather had bought in honor of his *bar mitzvah*, his sensitive yet bold *neshamah* was returned to its Maker.

> With his total being he abhorred falsehood and complacency. At times, his was a solitary voice, but it shook many out of their complacency, and to his credit many survived the Holocaust and rebuilt their lives in the free world.

⁓ Reb Binyomin Wilhelm

1886-1972

History is not only made up of major events. At times, a seemingly inconsequential action of a seemingly undistinguished individual can have great impact. In a prosperous paper and twine store in the Lower East Side of New York, Leibel Dershowitz challenged the proprietor to open a yeshiva in the up-and-coming neighborhood of Williamsburg (c. 1917). Binyomin Wilhelm accepted the challenge – and this yeshiva was the forerunner of Mesivta Torah Vodaath.

Binyomin Wilhelm was neither a *rav* nor a *Rosh Yeshiva*; he was not a scion of a chassidic dynasty; he was a regular *baal habayis*, layman. He was a businessman who realized, at a time when many others did not, that a neighborhood without a yeshiva is not the place to raise a family. A family needs more than space and modern conveniences. It needs a yeshiva. Even a *shul* or a *shtibel* is not enough. Reb Binyomin was one of the few dedicated individuals who refused to capitulate to the mores of American

society. His dedication to Torah and Torah education contributed immensely to the burgeoning of Torah in America.

Binyomin Wilhelm was born in 1886 to a chassidic family in Lodz. At the tender age of 12, his mother died. After his father remarried, the young Binyomin left the household. He lived for a while with various members of his extended family until he embarked on his fateful journey to America. Already on the boat, where he had purchased his passage by working as the *mashgiach* Binyomin came face to face with the tragedy of "American" Judaism. People who were observant in Europe, already frequented the "other" dining room. Although young in years, Binyomin encouraged them to eat only kosher and to remain faithful to the traditions that they had ob-served in Europe.

Upon his arrival in New York, Binyomin joined a group, Adas Bnei Yisrael, a fraternity of young immigrants who had committed themselves to remain faithful to the Torah under all circumstances. They studied together, *davened* together, and faced poverty and adversity together, and *baruch Hashem* they persevered and succeeded. Like many others, young Binyomin worked from a pushcart from the time he arrived, at the age of seventeen, until he was able to rent a store of his own.

From the age of twenty until he was twenty-five, he managed his store, which prospered and grew. It was then that he began his search for a wife. He had already endeared himself to the legendary Torah activist Moshe Weberman, and his search for a *shidduch* brought him even closer. Blima, Mr. Weberman's daughter, was a fitting *shidduch* for Reb Binyomin. Mr. Weberman, who had arrived in America right after the Civil War, had remained faithful to Torah, notwithstanding the enticements of the American culture. In 1911, they

married and laid the foundation of their family in the Lower East Side of New York.

As the Wilhelm family grew, the shortage of space became acute. A move to the new neighborhood of Williamsburg was not a consideration, since that bustling Jewish community was not home to any yeshivos. It was then that Leibel Dershowitz issued his challenge. The 30-year-old Wilhelm rose to the challenge. He recorded in his diary his futile attempts to rally support for the yeshiva. All he encountered was apathy and despair. He wrote how the observant Jews had created a new reality; they felt that tradition was for the older generation, but for the youth it was useless.

A young Reb Binyomin Wilhelm

He recorded in his diary his futile attempts to rally support for the yeshiva. All he encountered was apathy and despair.

50th wedding anniversary celebration, 1927, of (L-R): Pinchas Aharon Bruder, Moshe Weberman, Tzurtel Weberman, Bracha Bruder

Tzurtel Weberman with her children.
Front row, second from left, is Blima, who
became Mrs. Binyomin Wilhelm

In the *shtibel* where he *davened,* people vacillated between pity and contempt when he made his proposal, but he persevered. Soon, many of his adversaries became his ardent supporters. He went from *shul* to *shul, shtible* to *shtible,* podium to podium, speaking, cajoling and convincing. The odds were stacked against him. In desperation, on *Hoshanah Rabbah* night, he delayed the services and refused to budge until they allowed him to make his point. His dynamic and heartfelt words that night broke the final barriers, and checks to the tune of $15,000 a huge sum of money in those days, were collected. Next, he formed a committee. Success brought success in its wake, and many important figures joined the committee. Now he needed the most important component – students.

It was not an easy ride. Every time the committee flagged, Reb Binyomin ignited their spirits, again and again. But students were not to be found. The parents would say, "We don't want our children to be 'bahnk kvetchers'" (bench pressers – a derogatory name for yeshiva students). "In America, we want baseball players who will go to college and become lawyers and doctors." There was even religious opposition: "What? A yeshiva combined with secular studies? That is sacreligious!"

Many, including his own father-in-law, agreed that a yeshiva was in the best interests of the community and aligned themselves with it. Reb Binyomin was strong-minded and assertive and the committee that he had formed tried to exclude him from meetings. They had grandiose ideas for the opening of the yeshiva. Mr. Wilhelm felt that all those plans would delay the actual opening of the yeshiva, which was the real issue and of paramount importance, not the unrealistic plans and visions of grandeur. He wanted a school immediately.

Reb Binyomin did not relent. Finally, the opening was set for the

Blima Weberman Wilhelm
engagement picture

Reb Binyomin Wilhelm holding American flag at Mesivta dedication parade, 1941. Foreground (L-R): Reb Shraga Feivel Mendlowitz; behind him, second from right is Rabbi Avrohom Pam

Shavuos party, Bais Yaakov, 1942

coming school year. A banquet was prepared to announce the event. The summer was spent recruiting students. The frenzied efforts resulted in a paltry 45 students, from grades 1-7. Again there were meetings, and the committee decided that it was not financially viable to start a school with so few stu-

(L-R): Reb Binyomin Wilhelm, Rabbi Yaakov Kamenetsky, Rabbi Yisroel Belsky

dents. Mr. Wilhelm did not rest; he prevailed on them not to cancel the opening. After all, how could they disband a yeshiva between Rosh Hashanah and Yom Kippur?

Yom Kippur started early that year for Binyomin Wilhelm. He spent the day going from *shul* to *shul*, mounting podiums and shaking Jews out of their slumber. His persistence and determination were incredible. After *Neilah*, exhausted and on the verge of collapse, Mr. Wilhelm entered the emergency meeting and announced, "The school can go on. We now have 90 students!" To cut costs, the board wanted a principal/ teacher and also a secretary/teacher. Reb Binyomin would not hear of it – the principal would be a principal *only* and the secretary would be a secretary. In the end, all of his demands were

Reb Binyomin did not relent. His persistence and determination were incredible. He expended super-human effort to open the school, and he succeeded.

(L-R): Moshe Fensterheim, Frank Neuman, Berel Belsky, Rabbi Herschel Leiman, Rabbi Gedaliah Schorr at Berel Belsky's chassan tisch

Even after the school was operational, he continued to be actively involved.

met. With one class per teacher, Reb Mordechai Eliyahu Finkelstein as principal, and a full staff of highly competent and qualified teachers, the school year began. It was a difficult start; many parents did not send their children at first, but with time the school was functioning well.

Within four short years, when the enrollment swelled to over 1000 students, the yeshiva outgrew its building and moved to a larger one. Even after the school was operational, Reb Binyomin continued to be actively involved. He recruited many students, including a young boy named Berel Belsky. Berel continued his studies under the *Chofetz Chaim* in the yeshiva in Radin. Upon his return, he married Chana Wilhelm, and became the Wilhelm's son-in-law. Today, Berel Belsky's son, Rabbi Yisroel Belsky, is a *Rosh Yeshiva* in Mesivta Torah Vodaath.

(L-R): Rabbi Leibel Goldenberg, Rabbi Yaakov Shurkin, Rabbi Sender Linchner, Berel Belsky at Yeshiva Radin, Poland, 1932

Perhaps the most significant action that Mr. Wilhelm took was the appointment of "Mister" (as he preferred to be called) Shraga Feivel Mendlowitz, as principal of the yeshiva. Reb Shraga Feivel's imprimatur is indelibly stamped on much of American Orthodoxy to this very day. His breadth of knowledge and wisdom won over the hearts of the teachers, parents and, most of all, the students. This occurred in America in the year 1923! It is to the credit of Binyomin Wilhelm that he was perceptive enough to bring Reb Shraga Feivel out of the business world and into the world of Torah *chinuch*.

Binyomin Wilhelm and Torah Vodaath remained inseparable. He was one of the *ba'alei tefilah* on the *Yamim Noraim,* and he also served as surrogate host to the many guests who came to participate in the services at the yeshiva. His store was a veritable branch of the yeshiva office. Indeed, many of the fundraising campaigns

Reb Binyomin Wilhelm and his wife walking down at the wedding of their first grandchild

were initiated there. His family continued in his footsteps, involving themselves in the yeshiva as students, members of the faculty and supporters.

Mr. Wilhelm did not limit his concern for *chinuch* to the yeshiva. In the
late 30s he was a central figure in
the founding of the Bais Yaakov of
Williamsburg, the first successful elementary school of its kind in America.
After retiring to Jerusalem, he continued to work for *Klal Yisrael*. He established an organization for Sephardic
youths, to help them retain the fervor
of their rich heritage. He named the
organization Mifal Torah Vodaath,

*Rabbi Yisroel Belsky at the bris of his nephew
Yisrael Barkin in Cleveland, Ohio, 1986*

because all that he did was inextricably
connected to the yeshiva.

In his final months, he was physically feeble but his mind remained
alert and active. Two days before his
passing, he quipped to his grandson
after having been offered a cup of tea,
"In America they call it tea. *Tee*! Never
forget–*tee*." (*Tee* means *to do* in Polish
Yiddish.) His large family, children and
grandchildren are a tribute and a living
legacy to his dedication to *chinuch* and
Yiddishkeit. The multitude of students
and graduates of Torah Vodaath bear
testimony to the words of Rabbi
Yaakov Kamenetsky, "We can thank
Reb Binyomin Wilhelm for two-thirds
of the Torah in America."

Succah party, 1948

*Binyomin
Wilhelm and
Torah Vodaath
were inextricably
connected...
his family
continued in
his footsteps,
involving
themselves in
the yeshiva
in various
capacities.
They are a
living legacy to
his dedication
to chinuch and
Yiddishkeit.*

Diversity in Pioneering Torah

A pioneer courageously dares to go where others fear to tread. He prepares and cultivates what is barren and void, transforming it into a vibrant and flourishing entity. He is relentless in his commitment, working tirelessly to achieve results, as he confronts many hardships.

This section provides three first-person accounts of Torah pioneers in America in the 1940s-50s. They were students of Rabbi Shlomo Heiman, *Rosh Yeshiva* of Torah Vodaath in the late 1930s and early 40s. In addition to Rabbi Heiman's imprimatur, they were also influenced and shaped by the legendary Reb Shraga Feivel Mendlowitz, *menahel* of Torah Vodaath and founder of Torah Umesorah. Reb Shraga Feivel directed young *musmachim*, rabbis (who were also his students), as to what *derech* they should follow, based on their individual strengths. He encouraged these three men to pursue the fields of Jewish education and the rabbinate. The influence of their *Rosh Yeshiva* guided them on the difficult and challenging odyssey upon which each one embarked 60 years ago. It was a journey that required *mesiras nefesh*, hard work, and the ability to stand up and fight for a Torah way of life. These men represent what Reb Shraga Feivel meant when he charged his students with the dictum to go out and build Torah in an *"eretz lo zeruah"* – places that were unsown and religiously barren.

Rabbi Dessler, a Telzer *talmid*, spent his first months in America as a student in Mesivta Torah Vodaath. He subsequently went to the midwest, to an area then considered desolate, to assist his *rebbeim* in the building of Telshe Yeshiva and the Hebrew Academy of Cleveland, which later served as a model for future day schools. It continues to play a vital role in Torah *chinuch* through the many curricula it has designed, which are used by schools throughout the country. Cleveland has developed into a leading Torah community in the midwest, in large measure because of his unremitting efforts.

Rabbi Binyomin Goldenberg, one of the pioneers of Torah Umesorah, demonstrated incredible self-sacrifice and determination as he traveled across America obeying the charge of Reb Shraga Feivel. He established numerous day schools, which in turn helped build the Jewish communities where they were located.

Rabbi Pelcovitz, a pulpit rabbi was – like his two colleagues – willing to heed Reb Shraga Feivel's call and go to uncultivated areas of the country and build Torah. In each community that he served, Rabbi Pelcovitz brought the people closer to a Torah way of life. His relentless pursuit of establishing a firm Torah foundation made it possible for today's *shuls, yeshivos, kollelim* and all aspects of an Orthodox Jewish life to flourish in Far Rockaway, N.Y., where he was *rav* for 50 years. Far Rockaway is considered one of the premier Orthodox Jewish communities in the United States.

It cannot be emphasized enough that the Torah communities and institutions we have today are built upon the foundation they established. They were the pioneers who led the way, paving the road, so that the many outstanding Torah communities which we presently enjoy could be established. Indeed, we stand upon their shoulders.

≫ Rabbi Nochum Zev Dessler

"From Kelm to Cleveland"

"Why did we survive?" asked Rabbi Eliyahu E. Dessler, author of the classic *Michtav M'Eliyahu*, following the unspeakable atrocities of the Holocaust. More than anything else, Rabbi Dessler focused on the mission of those who survived. It was clear to him that the destruction of European Jewry presented a new sense of urgency, and Rabbi Dessler summed it up in a letter to his only son, Rabbi Nochum Zev Dessler: "After what was destroyed, our obligation is to build; to rebuild what was destroyed and to restore what was lost."

Perhaps it was this sense of mission that motivated a determined Rabbi Nochum Zev Dessler to persevere and to establish and to achieve lofty goals. Those goals would ultimately change the face of Cleveland's Jewish community. A man of impeccable character, Rabbi Dessler epitomizes the finest qualities and ideals of a pre-Holocaust Lithuanian Torah personality. Yet, possessing a keen insight of modern American society, Rabbi Dessler has successfully empathized with, educated and inspired generations of Americans, both young and old. His lifetime achievements are inspirational. His profound impact upon the world of Torah *chinuch* are immeasurable.

Can a Jewish child who was born and raised in America truly appreciate the long and lonely journey from Kelm, Lithuania, to Cleveland, Ohio, USA? It was not just a journey in distance; it was also a journey in time, and culture. Having been raised in a family where *caring for the other person* was paramount, where *what you were* was far more valuable than what you owned, and knowing that your behavior had to mirror these values – arriving in this country some sixty years ago was a most challenging experience. Rabbi N.Z. Dessler, Dean of the Hebrew Academy of Cleveland and one of the pioneers of Torah *chinuch* in America, looks back on the years of turmoil and upheaval, and the faith and courage it took to build Torah on these shores. How evident was Hashem's Providence!

It was a long lonely journey from Kelm, Lithuania, to Cleveland, Ohio – not just a journey in distance, but a journey in time, and culture.

Without His *siyata d'Shmaya*, it would have been impossible to transplant what was lost, so great were the challenges they encountered every step of the long road to mere survival.

In contemporary society, we hear much about "relationships." Indeed, the relationship between parent and child is considered to be one of the primary factors that influence a child's educational development. At times, parents must make the ultimate sacrifice – for the benefit of their child. With this in mind, we can only imagine what it must have meant to Rabbi Dessler's parents to send their *ben yachid*, only son, across the ocean to a distant yeshiva for his adolescent and young adult years – so that he not be influenced by the frivolous values and morals of London at the time.

A scion of an illustrious lineage, Rabbi Dessler was born in Kelm and lived there until age nine when the family moved to London, where his father, the renowned *mussar* personality, Rabbi Eliyahu Eliezer Dessler, founder of the Gateshead Kollel and *Mashgiach* of the Ponevezh Yeshiva, served as *rav*. Two and a half years later, he was sent to learn in Vilkomir, and then Telshe, Lithuania. Today, we would be hard-pressed to relate to the danger and physical deprivation that accompanied Rabbi Dessler, and so many others, as he fled the Nazi onslaught in 1940, by traveling the breadth of Russia, across the Sea of Japan to Yokohama and Kobe, Japan.

Can we visualize and comprehend the loneliness of a foreign-born *bachur* in Mesivta Torah Vodaath; and the difficulty of being a pioneer in the nascent Torah-education movement; the rebuffs and disbelief which con-

Telshe Yeshiva Building in Lithuania. Rabbi N.Z. Dessler in black coat on left

fronted Rabbi Dessler and his *rebbeim*, the Telshe *Roshei Yeshiva*, as they endeavored to re-establish Telshe Yeshiva, that great Lithuanian institution, here in America? He was destined and fortunate to be among the first few, who, like Nachshon ben Aminadav, took that inspiring leap. That plunge was the beginning of a story that should, and *must*, be told!

Growing up in Kelm meant learning night *seder* by candlelight in the *Beis Medrash* of the *Yeshiva Ketana*. It meant living in an exclusively Jewish neighborhood: indeed, for all intents and purposes, the town itself was Jewish! Moreover, in Rabbi Dessler's home, adherence to proper *derech eretz* – sensitivity and concern for other people – was the norm, as well as a great respect for learning.

"I remember once walking with my maternal grandmother on the street of the Talmud Torah Hagadol. As we made our way down the sidewalk (which was made of two wood planks), my grandmother suggested that we cross to the other side.

Growing up in Kelm meant learning night seder by candlelight in the Beis Medrash of the Yeshiva Ketana.

Rabbi Reuven Dov Dessler,
paternal grandfather

Rabbi Nochum Zev Ziev,
maternal grandfather

they enjoyed a brief respite from tending customers. Today, our students learn about the sacredness of private property and possessions when they study Tractate *Bava Metzia*; Rabbi Dessler observed firsthand the many instances of utmost caution and care which people exercised when they happened upon the possessions of their fellow man.

"A relative who spoke at my *bar mitzvah* in Kelm related that he had last been there for my *bris*. At that time, he had left his cane in the *Talmud Torah*. Thirteen years later, when he returned for the *bar mitzvah*, he went directly to the spot where he had left the cane, and there it was! That in itself was not remarkable. People did not touch the possessions of others. What impressed him was that, over the years, it had been taken from its place, dusted, cleaned, and then returned exactly where he left it."[**]

In Kelm, even the most common men - wagon drivers and water carriers alike - were involved in a daily regimen of learning, many of them while they enjoyed a brief respite from tending customers.

She remarked that the people from the Talmud Torah have great *derech eretz* for others and if we are walking on the same side of the street, they will step off the planks into the dirt and mud to make room for us. By doing this, we would be inconveniencing *bnei Torah*. She urged me to remember never to inconvenience someone who learns Torah. Thus, we crossed the street and walked on the other side."[*]

In Kelm, even the most common men – wagon drivers and water carriers alike – were involved in a daily regimen of learning, many of them while

When the storm clouds of war threatened to engulf Europe, Rabbi Dessler was already a "veteran" in Telshe Yeshiva, located in the city of Telshe, Lithuania, where he had started at age 15. He was just entering the third *shiur*,

Rabbi Tzvi Hirsh Braude, Menahel of the Talmud Torah of Kelm, son-in-law and nephew of the Alter of Kelm

Rabbi Eliyahu Eliezer Dessler, father of Rabbi N.Z. Dessler and author of the Michtav M'Eliyahu

---

[*] Refer to Rabbi N.Z. Dessler's story in **The World That Was: Lithuania**, The Living Memorial Publications, Cleveland, Ohio, 1996, pg. 58

[**] Ibid., pg. 59

when the world as he knew it collapsed. During the months of *Av* and *Elul* of 5699 (August and September, 1940), the Russians were in full control of Lithuania. Consequently, anyone who wanted to leave had to procure an exit visa from them – except, of course, for Lithuanian citizens, who were denied that "privilege." Ironically, in order to receive a visa, one first had to be interogated by the N.K.V.D. – the dreaded Russian secret police. Moreover, without a ticket to the final destination, a person could not get a visa either. Almost all the tickets were sent from America, either by family, friends, or the Vaad Hatzala. If one did manage to obtain a visa, it was usually to the Dutch West Indies by way of Japan (for which a transit visa was also needed).

Rabbi Dessler managed to leave Lithuania by train – on the famous Trans-Siberian railroad. First, however, he had to journey to Moscow and stay

Three generations of the Dessler family (1892):
Rabbi Eliyahu Eliezer Dessler as an infant with parents
Rabbi Reuven Dov Dessler and his rebbetzin, and his grandparents,
Rabbi Yisrael Dovid Dessler and his rebbetzin

there for days in order to get the train. This was only the beginning. Once the group began the six-to-seven thousand kilometer journey through Siberia

Rabbi Dessler's escape route from Telz to Yokohama, Japan

At a family Simcha. (R-L): Rabbi Shmuel Brudny (a mechutan of the Dessler's), Rabbi Shneur Kotler, Rabbi Mordechai Gifter, Rabbi Boruch Sorotzkin, Rabbi N.Z. Dessler, Reb Leibish Rapaport.

Today, we would be hard-pressed to relate to the danger and physical deprivation that accompanied Rabbi Dessler, and so many others, as he fled the Nazi onslaught in 1940.

across the Soviet Union, they were compelled to remain on the train the entire 11 days, except for obtaining hot water at a few of the stations along the way. Whatever little food they were able to bring along helped sustain them during the long and arduous journey. The final stop was Vladivostock, where they traveled in a small fishing boat to Japan, and then traveled to Yokohama, which is on the outskirts of Tokyo.

Rabbi Dessler remembers those times and the important Jewish personalities whose paths he crossed. *Rosh Hashanah* was spent in Yokohama, together with the Modzitzer *Rebbe*, Rabbi Shaul Yedidia Taub, and the Telshe *Roshei HaYeshiva*, Rabbi Eliyahu Meir Bloch and Rabbi Chaim Mordechai Katz, who had arrived earlier.

Rabbi N.Z. Dessler in the early 1940s

On the first day of the *Yamim Noraim*, the *Rebbe* led *Shacharis*, and Reb Eliyahu Meir, *Mussaf*; on the morrow, the order was reversed. On *Yom Kippur*, Rabbi Dessler was on a boat called the *President Cleveland* bound for San Francisco, where he arrived on *Simchas Torah*, 5700. A delegation that included Rabbi Gershon Katzman, *rav* of San Francisco, met them at the pier in the afternoon to greet them. That *Simchas Torah* burns brightly in Rabbi Dessler's memory. Three of his fellow passengers, who were Lubavitcher *chassidim* (including a *rosh yeshiva*) were in his cabin in the hold of the ship. He drank a *l'chaim* with them – as did two Chinese gentiles who also shared the cabin!

From San Francisco, Rabbi Dessler

made the wearying cross-country train ride to New York City. Rabbi and *Rebbetzin* Naftoli Carlebach (the former *rav* of Baden-Baden – and the father of Rabbis Shlomo and Eliyahu Chaim Carlebach) spoke with the famed Rabbi Shraga Feivel Mendlowitz of Mesivta Torah Vodaath and obtained a student visa for him, and financed a ticket as well. Years before, Rabbi Dessler had first met them in London and showed them around the city. They reciprocated by welcoming Rabbi Dessler into their home when he first arrived in New York City.

"In today's day and age, in which communications are almost immediate and a phone call across the world is a common occurrence, it might seem strange that during this entire period, including my years of study in Telshe, I never once called my father

> "I never once called my father by telephone, since doing so was frightfully expensive...my only contact was by letter through the mail."

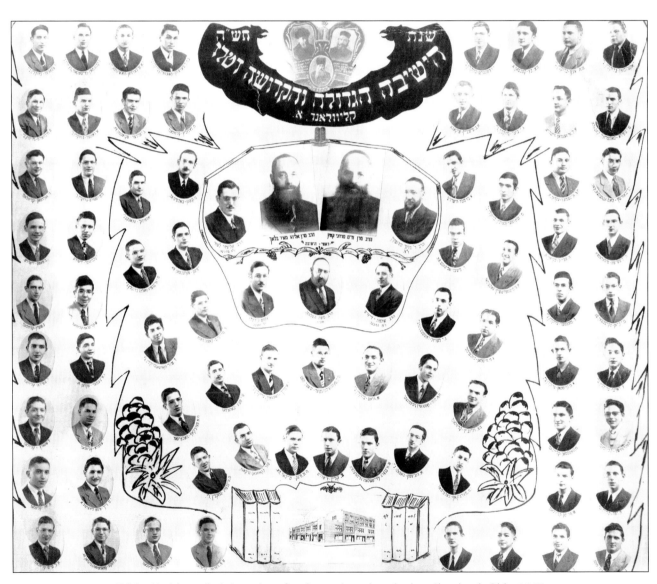

Telshe Yeshiva administration, faculty and student body - Cleveland, Ohio 1945.
Middle box, first row (L-R): Rabbi Elozor Levi, Rabbi Eliyahu Meir Bloch, Rabbi Chaim Mordechai Katz, Rabbi Boruch Sorotzkin. Second row (L-R): Rabbi N.Z. Dessler, Rabbi Moshe Helfan, Rabbi Shlomo Davis

Rabbi N.Z. Dessler with Dr. Joseph Kaminetsky, National Director of Torah Umesorah

In Torah Vodaath, Rabbi Dessler flourished under the tutelage of the Rosh HaYeshiva, Rabbi Shlomo Heiman, and under the influence of his chaburah.

by telephone, as doing so was frightfully expensive. In fact, I was also not in touch by phone with my mother and sister in Lithuania. They had gone to visit my grandmother in Kelm (whom the Nazi beasts eventually murdered) and had later escaped to Australia. My father was in London and Gateshead, England. Indeed, I had not seen my father for many years. My only contact was regularly through the mail."

Upon his arrival in the States, Rabbi Dessler entered Mesivta Torah Vodaath as a *talmid* where he studied for eight months. Rabbi Dessler left for Cleveland on the sixth of *Cheshvan* 5701, the eve of the *yahrtzeit* of the *Alter Telzer Rav*, Rabbi Yoseph Leib Bloch. In Torah Vodaath, Rabbi Dessler flourished under the tutelage of the *Rosh HaYeshiva*, Rabbi Shlomo Heiman, and under the influence of his *chaburah* at that time, Rabbi Eliyahu Moshe Shisgal, *zl*, Rabbi Shraga Moshe Kalmanowitz, *zl*, and *ylt*, Rabbi Simcha Schustal and Rabbi Don Ungarisher. Although his physical accommodations were far from comfortable, he was fortunate to have Rabbi Yisroel Kanarek as his roommate in a makeshift "dormitory" consisting of two adjoining houses near the yeshiva's new location on South Third Street. These men all became outstanding Jewish personalities and *roshei yeshiva* in their own right.

Although there was a kitchen in the basement of Torah Vodaath on Wilson St. there was no cook in attendance – except, of course, for the *bachurim* themselves. Eating arrangements were meager and left much to be desired.

"I basically managed somehow. However, when Rabbi Shraga Feivel Mendlowitz was apprised of my "finicky" appetite, he came up with a novel solution: he claimed that I was needed to be a *chavrusa* for a big *talmid chacham*– and included in this arrangement was sharing meals with him. Such was the saintliness and wisdom of Reb Shraga Feivel!"

Indeed, Reb Shraga Feivel played an integral role in Rabbi Dessler's life in other ways. After studying a few months at Mesivta Torah Vodaath, he spent his first summer at Camp Torah Vodaath in Ferndale, New York, where Rabbi Sender Linchner was head counselor. Both Reb Shraga Feivel and

Rabbi Nesanel Quinn

Rabbi N.Z. Dessler addressing Telshe Yeshiva Dinner. Rabbi Mordechai Gifter is seated at the left

Rabbi Shlomo Davis

Rabbi Moshe Helfan

Rabbi Yitzchok Sheiner

Rabbi Nesanel Quinn spent their summers there as well. As always, Rabbi Mendlowitz continued to be most thoughtful and concerned about Rabbi Dessler's personal welfare.

"Needless to say, I arrived penniless when I entered the yeshiva. Accordingly, Reb Shraga Feivel devised a stratagem whereby Rabbi Quinn would put a dollar (donated by Reb Shraga Feivel) into my pocket every week."

Eventually, Reb Shraga Feivel arranged for him to tutor another student for which, he was paid the munificent sum (for those days) of ten dollars. Unfortunately, the job lasted only a few weeks. Afterwards, Rabbi Mendlowitz arranged a weekend job for him in Riverdale, New York. Rabbi Dessler's duties included spending Shabbos, helping out a nascent *minyan*, *leining* the weekly *parasha* for the congregants, and learning with the boys of a distinguished Swiss family.

The father of this family had already died by the time Rabbi Dessler made their acquaintance. The father had become quite wealthy after successfully investing in real estate, but his untimely death prevented him from experiencing fully the *nachas* that a parent receives

when he sees his children advancing in Torah study. Rabbi Dessler learned with the sons and, eventually, one continued his studies in Telshe Yeshiva.

"An interesting anecdote reveals the saintliness of Rabbi Mendlowitz. When it came time to go to Cleveland to establish the Telshe Yeshiva, before departing I went to say goodbye to the *Roshei Yeshiva* of Torah Vodaath. Seemingly disconcerted by my intention to brave this new frontier, the *Rosh Yeshiva* said, 'You are going to Cleveland, a place of desolation? Don't go!' I responded, 'We're going to build!' At that moment, Reb Shraga Feivel declared to the *Rosh Yeshiva* in Yiddish, 'Let him go, and be successful. Give him a *berachah*!' And so he did."

Rabbi Dessler did not travel to the Midwest alone. He was accompanied by his good friend Rabbi Binyomin Goldenberg from Torah Vodaath. Later other distinguished young men would join them in Cleveland – Rabbi Hillel Bodek, *zl*, and still later, Rabbi Yitzchok Sheiner, today the *Rosh Yeshiva* of Kaminetz in Yerushalayim.

Rabbi Dessler was privileged to be able to participate in a crucial episode in the history of Torah Jewry in

...most bnei Torah know of the role that Zeirei Agudath Israel played in saving tens of thousands of Jewish lives.

Back Row (L-R): Rabbi N.Z. Dessler, Israel Comet, Rabbi Aaron Paperman, Irving Stone. Front Row (L-R): Jacob Sapirstein, Rabbi Chaim Mordechai Katz, Isaac Bruder

"I remember how impressed I was with the campaign that this organization initiated in preparing affidavits of support and sending packages to our starving brethren."

America. By now, most *bnei Torah* know of the role that Zeirei Agudath Israel played in saving tens of thousands of Jewish lives. Following are some of his recollections:

"I remember how impressed I was with the campaign that this organization initiated in preparing affidavits of support, and sending packages to our starving brethren. How can I ever forget my first view of their office at 616 Bedford Ave, in Williamsburg? People were sitting on the floor with their typewriters, as they sought to move the political powers-that-be to come to the aid of the masses of European Jewry that were threatened with extinction. Since I had just arrived from Europe, the members of Zeirei Agudath Israel were eager for me to describe the devastation and hardships that I had witnessed."

The story of how Cleveland, Ohio, was chosen to be the new location of the Telshe Yeshiva is most fascinating. Rabbi Eliyahu Meir Bloch and Rabbi Chaim Mordechai Katz, *Roshei HaYeshiva* of the Telshe Yeshiva in Lithuania, arrived in New York City in the spring of 1941. At the first meeting, these great leaders asked Rabbi Dessler to call together other alumni of Telshe Yeshiva. Rabbi Dessler contacted Rabbi Elozor Levi (later *Rosh Mechina* of Telshe Yeshiva), Rabbi Avraham Newhouse (later principal of Bais Yaakov Elementary School in Williamsburg), and Rabbi Shlomo Davis (later *Maggid Shiur* in the Telshe *Mechina*), who was in Baltimore. At this meeting it was decided to break into groups and travel to various cities, to reconnoiter a location that would be as close to the ideal as possible for the re-establishment of their great institution on the shores of America.

At that all-important first organizational meeting, it was decided who would travel to which city. Rabbi Dessler and Rabbi Avraham Newhouse were asked to travel to a midsize Northeastern Jewish community. It was there that they got a taste of the bitter pill that would be foisted upon them on any number of occasions – not only by the *baalei batim*, but often by the *rabbanim* of the various towns that they visited. Though there were rabbis who were enthusiastic about the re-establishment of the famed Telshe Yeshiva on the shores of America, there were others who were either undecided, or

Mr. and Mrs. Feigenbaum

vehemently opposed.

"In this fine community, where we spent a few days at the home of a great *talmid chacham*, we met with the local *rabbanim*, whose chairman declared that since he himself had been unable to establish a yeshiva in fifty years in America, we obviously would not succeed either."

At that original organizational meeting, two other young men were directed to travel to communities in the Midwest, two to the Northeast, and two to Cleveland, Ohio. Likewise, the *shluchim* (emissaries) who traveled to other communities on the Eastern seaboard did not find the Jews of those cities receptive to the idea. Cleveland, however, was quite different.

The representatives, the *Rosh HaYeshiva*, Rabbi Chaim Mordechai Katz, and secretary, Rabbi Moshe Helfan, traveled to Cleveland for Succos. Like so many before them, Rabbis Katz and Helfan were hosted by the magnanimous Reb Yitzchok Feigenbaum, who, upon hearing the news of the possibility of establishing

First home of the Telshe Yeshiva, and subsequently the Hebrew Academy of Cleveland

the new Telshe Yeshiva in Cleveland, was both enthusiastic and encouraging. Indeed, at a meeting with the local *rabbanim*, these spiritual leaders echoed Mr. Feigenbaum's fervor. Mr. and Mrs. Feigenbaum had always provided lodging for the *roshei yeshiva* and *rabbanim*, traveling charity collectors, and anyone who might need a

First Hebrew Academy of Cleveland School Bus

Telshe Yeshiva Today

place to stay. In
fact, most people
who visited
Cleveland and
needed lodging
came to their home!
He was one of the
very few people
at that time who
had constructed a *succah* outside in
his yard. And what a *succah* it was!
Constructed entirely of glass – except
for the roof, of course – like a green-
house, it was aesthetically pleasing, as
well as crucial for Torah-observant
Jews. Moreover, Mr. Feigenbaum customarily hosted Shabbos *Minchah*
services – and provided *Shalosh Seudos*
for the group as well. He kept a *Sefer
Torah* in his living room.

It was Mr. Feigenbaum who charac-
teristically offered his house as the first
edifice to be known as Telshe Yeshiva;
and for a while he and his wife
remained in the same house as the
yeshiva. They later purchased a house
down the street and moved out, leaving their house to the yeshiva as its first
full-time structure. When the yeshiva
moved two years later, they turned the
home over to the Hebrew Academy.

*Rabbi N.Z. Dessler accepting award at Torah
Umesorah dinner. (L-R): Rabbi Amos Bunim,
Rabbi N.Z. Dessler, and Moses Feuerstein*

This very special family, like so many
others at the time, were responsible for
laying the foundation for Torah in their
respective communities.

Rabbi Dessler spoke to Rabbi
Shlomo Davis about joining the new
yeshiva. They had studied together
in Yeshivas Eitz Chaim in England
and Telshe Yeshiva in Lithuania. At the
time, he was residing in Baltimore,
practicing *shechitah*. He was also an
accomplished *baal koreh*. Little persuasion was necessary and soon Rabbi
Davis moved to Cleveland. He later
married and became a valuable asset
to the growing staff. A *talmid* of the
Telshe Yeshiva in Europe, Reb Yitzchok
Chinn also joined them. He later
became a *shochet* in Philadelphia.

At the *Chanukas Habayis* in 5702,
Rabbi Yitzchok Siegal from Chicago, a
student of the original Telshe Yeshiva,
was the guest speaker. During his
address, the reality of the miracle of
the re-establishment of the Telshe
Yeshiva in America, despite the most
formidable odds, must have overwhelmed him, and he broke down in
tears, asking plaintively, *"A kleiner*

Rabbi Elozor Menachem Man Shach speaking with Rabbi N.Z. Dessler

tzimmer, un dos iz Telzer Yeshiva?" ("A small room – and this is Telshe Yeshiva?") He added his fervent wish that "we should see it grow!" Reb Eliyahu Meir, the *Rosh HaYeshiva*, also addressed the assemblage, and he enthusiastically declared: "וְהָיָה רֵאשִׁיתְךָ מִצְעָר וְאַחֲרִיתְךָ יִשְׂגֶּה מְאֹד", "Then, though your beginning was insignificant, your end will flourish exceedingly" (*Iyov* 8:7).

They soon realized that to entertain any real hope for the future of the Telshe Yeshiva, they would have to establish a system of Jewish education that would begin at the roots – with the youngest students – and that a grass-roots appeal would have to be made to the *baalei batim* themselves. Consequently, Rabbi Dessler and Rabbi Elozor Levi spent two months during the summer of 1943 canvassing potential students for a brand-new concept in Jewish education – a Jewish day school. Nothing quite like it had ever existed before in Cleveland. Usually, youngsters from observant homes were sent to New York City when they reached a certain age. Moreover, there was a part-time afternoon school known as Yeshivas Adas, in which many of the children studied four hours a day, five days a week – after first attending public school.

They were successful in attracting eleven children for kindergarten and first grade. The students were drawn primarily from *shomrei Shabbos* Young Israel families. As they went from house to house in search of children, they were less than satisfied with the skepticism displayed by many.

Afterwards, the nascent Hebrew Academy moved to 105th Street, using two rooms in the basement of the Jewish Center located there.

Rabbi Shlomo Weissman was the first principal. When he became ill, Rabbi Dessler traveled to New York and brought in another talented individual, Rabbi Leon Machlis, a classmate of his from Torah Vodaath.

Rabbi Dessler was drafted, and reluctantly gave up his position as a *maggid shiur* in the Telshe Yeshiva Mechina, to become the official principal of the new Hebrew Academy of Cleveland in the fall of 1944. By this time there were approximately fifty children enrolled in the school.

The contemporary American mind-set might find it difficult to appreciate the extraordinary conditions – the *bitachon* and the *mesiras nefesh* – under which these individuals labored. They did not take salaries. The *Roshei Yeshiva* of the newly established Telshe Yeshiva, Rabbi Eliyahu Meir Bloch and Rabbi Chaim Mordechai Katz, were thoroughly involved in every aspect of the Hebrew Academy. They would sign every page of the minutes of the *Vaad HaChinuch*, overseeing the Education Council meetings. Moreover, the Telshe Yeshiva agreed to match the Academy's income dollar for dollar, since it was perceived to be an integral part of the

They soon realized that to entertain any real hope for the future of the Telshe Yeshiva, they would have to establish a system of Jewish education that would begin at the roots with the youngest students.

Rabbi N.Z. Dessler with Rabbi Avraham Pam

Rabbi N.Z. Dessler with Rabbi Yaakov Kamenetsky

Hebrew Academy were founded by pioneers who planted the enduring seeds of Jewish education, succeeding far more than anyone thought possible. It was they who, at tremendous self-sacrifice, did not heed the cynical naysayers who were skeptical of their attempts. These individuals were true pioneers – who overcame challenges, surmounted obstacles, and lived with the loneliness that invariably accompanies breaking ground in a new terrain. The pursuit of the goal of *harbatzas Torah* was not merely an opportunity; it was a glorious mission.

Today, the Jewish community of Cleveland has grown beyond anyone's expectations. Graduates of the Telshe Yeshiva and alumni of the Hebrew Academy have settled in communities and assumed positions of leadership both in a spiritual and lay capacity, here and around the globe. Rabbi Dessler started with a fledgling school more than half a century ago. Today, Rabbi Dessler enjoys the ultimate *nachas* of seeing a school that has grown in quantity to number 700 students and, in quality, providing an

> **Telshe Yeshiva and the Hebrew Academy were founded by pioneers who planted the enduring seeds of Jewish education, succeeding far more than anyone thought possible.**

yeshiva. The girls' high school, called Yavne, was established in the 1950s to fulfill a need for an ongoing girls' school that would provide a viable continuing Jewish education. Yavne's first principal was Rabbi Chaim Tzvi Katz, who was a pioneer and innovator in so many critical and constructive ways, and a highly dedicated individual.

Interestingly enough, once these institutions established a foothold, they continued to develop further. Taking note of and appreciating the school's "products," people enthusiastically began to send their children to the Hebrew Academy/Yavne Schools. Mr. Irving Stone*, a lifelong and dear friend of Rabbi Dessler, expended Herculean efforts on behalf of Jewish education and opened many doors for the Hebrew Academy, and eventually for other day schools as well.

In retrospect, Telshe Yeshiva and the

Yavne Principal Rabbi Chaim Tzvi Katz with students

---

* Refer to the biography of Mr. Irving Stone, pg. 436

excellent education. Setting the standard for Torah *chinuch* in North America, the Hebrew Academy of Cleveland is a flagship day school of Torah Umesorah, providing curricula,

Rabbi Dessler with the Novominsker Rebbe, Rabbi Yaakov Perlow, Rosh of Agudath Israel of America

text books, and study aids to yeshiva day schools in the U.S. and overseas as well. Its 5000-plus alumni have made major contributions towards the development of Torah in the world. Nachshon ben Aminadav took the first plunge and others followed suit. This has been the scenario throughout the country as yeshivos and day schools have mushroomed – thanks to the dedication, perseverance, and self-sacrifice of the early pioneers. Rabbi N.Z. Dessler and the Hebrew Academy of Cleveland have together written a unique chapter in the chronicles of Torah *chinuch* in this country.

Rabbi Dessler with Rabbi Chaim Stein, Rosh Yeshiva Telshe

Hebrew Academy of Cleveland Building

The Jacob Sapirstein Campus, Boys Junior High and Yeshiva High School

The new Beatrice J. Stone Yavne High School

This has been the scenario throughout the country as yeshivos and day schools have mushroomed - thanks to the dedication, perseverance, and self-sacrifice of the early pioneers.

≈ Rabbi Binyomin Goldenberg

TRAILBLAZING TORAH CHINUCH IN AMERICA
- An Insider's View

On June 6, 1944, *The New York Times* – one of America's major newspapers – had the following eight-column banner headline:

Allied Armies Land in France
Great Invasion Is Underway

In a special box to the right of the papers name was the timely note: "6 A.M. Extra."

On Wednesday, June 8th, the eight-column headline in *The New York Times* read as follows:

Hitler's Wall Is Breached
New Allied Landings Are Made

At that very period in history another major news story was unfolding. Understandably, this story was nowhere to be found, even though this newspaper prides itself on being a "newspaper of record" and trumpets on its front page's daily legend: "All the news that's fit to print."

It was then – at that time and in those days – that Torah Umesorah, the National Society for Hebrew Day Schools, was launched.* And it was then that the great Torah revolution –

the yeshiva and the Hebrew day school movement – began in North America.

An idea, the dream of its legendary founder, Rabbi Shraga Feivel Mendlowitz, Torah Umesorah began its first hesitant steps in 1944. The dream haltingly became a reality and, in time, the idea took on a vibrant life of its own. Joining Rabbi Mendlowitz were the leading *roshei yeshiva* who were then in America, and Rabbi Aharon Kotler, founder of Beth Medrash Govoha in Lakewood, New Jersey, was chosen as the first chairman of Torah Umesorah's Rabbinical Administrative Board.

From the very start, one family, known for its outstanding record of lay leadership, became closely identified with Torah Umesorah. At the invitation of Rabbi Shraga Feivel Mendlowitz, Mr. Samuel C. Feuerstein, of Brookline, Massachusetts, became Torah Umesorah's founding President, a position which he honored with

Torah Umesorah began its first hesitant steps in 1944. The dream haltingly became a reality and, in time, the idea took on a vibrant life of its own.

---

*Please refer to Chapter on Torah Umesorah, pg. 58

many years of creative involvement. His son, Moses I. Feuerstein, soon thereafter became a most active chairman of the Torah Umesorah Board of Directors.

When the Hebrew Day School movement was launched in 1944, there were only 30 schools in America, 27 in New York and 3 outside of New York, with a total of 7000 students.

Today, almost sixty years later, Torah Umesorah boasts a Hebrew day school movement comprising over 600 schools in the United States (and Canada), with an enrollment of over 180,000 pupils.

THE JEWISH COMMUNITY IN AMERICA IN 1944

What was it like in those days? How receptive was the American Jewish community to the idea of a Hebrew day school in its midst? What were the tools used to gain acceptance? Who were friends and supporters, and who were not? What were the fears and the suspicions about the Hebrew day school when the idea was first launched within the American Jewish community?

In retrospect, and in terms of historical facts, we can thankfully note the dynamics of the Hebrew day school movement. Zeal permeated it and inventiveness was the hallmark of its first-generation leaders and workers. These, indeed, were the factors which overcame the apathy, battled the prevailing negativity wherever it was present, and paved the way for the

(L-R): Rabbi Dr. Leo Jung, Samuel Feuerstein, Rabbi Aharon Kotler speaking, Moses Feuerstein, Rabbi Yitzchak Hutner

miraculous birth of a Torah world across America and its subsequent flourishing.

Yes, all this is retrospect, but looking back, what was it like in those days almost sixty years ago? Be it from the perspective of sociology, history, or cultura anthropology, words alone may not be sufficiently descriptive. Perhaps an anecdote, a personal recollection, may suffice to shed some light and open the curtain on a revealing scene – a scene which will realistically highlight the factors at play when one undertakes the establishment of a Hebrew day school in a setting outside of a large metropolitan area, such as New York City.

Within a year or so of Torah Umesorah's establishment, and due in part to an advertisement which appeared in a Yiddish newspaper and some brief news stories in a few Anglo-Jewish weeklies, interest was sparked among five people in a small Jewish

At its inception, zeal permeated the dynamics of the Hebrew day school movement. Inventiveness was the hallmark of its first-generation leaders and workers.

How receptive was the American Jewish Community to the idea of a Hebrew Day School in its midst? Apathy and negativity prevailed and had to be overcome. Slowly, interest was sparked.

community located in upstate New York. These few were eager to discuss the possibility of a Hebrew day school in their community. The prospect, the group thought, was remote. "How do we go about doing it?" they asked. "We don't really know what to do. Is there a handbook that tells one how to launch a Hebrew day school in an out-of-town community"? Obviously not. And so, a Torah Umesorah representative went there to meet with this group. It was decided to call a meeting in the local Jewish Community Center to discuss the Hebrew day school idea for this community.

The evening of the meeting, about 25 people showed up. The few initiators felt that attendance-wise it was a fair showing. Without much fanfare, it was decided that the chairman would deliver a few opening remarks and then introduce the Torah Umesorah representative, who would explain the Hebrew day school concept briefly and then ask for a general discussion of the project.

As the chairman was introducing the Torah Umesorah speaker, a women entered the room from the back. Naturally, eyes turned to the visitor, followed by lots of whispering, head-turning, and agitated conversation. The women, aristocratic in bearing, looking neither to the right nor the left, marched straight down the aisle and took a seat in the front row facing the speaker, while the whispering continued. The chairman, a bit agitated, quickly finished his remarks and briefly introduced the Torah Umesorah representative, who hesitantly, nervously, mystified, walked over to the podium.

No sooner did he start to speak, than the aristocratic women immedi-

ately rose to her feet, pointed her finger at the speaker and in a clear, resolute voice shouted out, "Get out of my town. Get out of my town! You Jew, you...You New Yorker...You East-Sider... You, get out of my town!"

Bedlam ensued. The speaker, flustered, did not continue. The meeting broke up. The women purposefully turned around and slowly strode out.

No Hebrew day school was started that night, nor that year, nor for a few years afterwards.

After the women left, the group informed the Torah Umesorah representative why there was so much whispering when she had initially arrived. She was the last person in that community who was expected to attend the Hebrew day school meeting. A Vassar College graduate, her father was the prime builder of the local community center and her husband was a leader of the local Reform Temple.

This is the recollection of the Torah Umesorah representative. This is the memory of what it was like then. How receptive was the Jewish community to the Hebrew day school idea in the forties and continuing, to some extent as well, into the fifties? Granted that the above incident was an extreme case, accentuated by local color. But generally speaking, what was the reception? What was the mood? What were the fears and suspicions?

Most important, what did the parents think? How ready were they (who did not live in New York) to trust their children to a new idea in their community? This was the ground that had to be sowed. These were the real people who had to be faced. What did they think? What did they say, and more important, what didn't they say?

THE WORK BEGINS

I was privileged to travel extensively throughout the United States during Torah Umesorah's early tentative years, helping to establish Hebrew Day Schools in various communities. Not always was the opposition expressed so vociferously as in the upstate community I had visited. Not always, but in one form or another there was opposition, expressed or muted. And always there were the doubts, the fears, the suspicion. And at times a pervasive opposition, a sense of "You people really don't belong here. Aren't you really a European *shtetel* transplant? This, of course, is Middle America."

Sometimes, we had to contend with the opposition of establishment figures. Sometimes, we had to cross swords with Federation heads and, at times, argue our "raison d'etre" with sincere Jews. There were times when local Talmud Torahs were fearful of competition. This was revealed as a silent opposition, so to speak, shared with key players in the community.

But above all, and of greatest importance, was the real target audience which we faced. The parents of young children, a group of native-born Americans, graduates of public schools and colleges, GI's, who had returned after the wars and raised families. These were the people we really needed, the people we really wanted. They didn't shout, "You Jew, you, get out of my town!" But they had their honest doubts, and wanted reassurances. They had their suspicions and wanted to be told the truth, since they knew so little about this new educational venture. Without a personal background or experience in a Hebrew day school setting, they felt somewhat uncomfortable

(L-R): Rabbi Dr. Joseph Kaminetsky, Rabbi Binyomin Goldenberg

and were not overeager to line up immediately as fervent parents and supporters – not yet, not yet.

WE TALK AND TALK – AND GET TO KNOW EACH OTHER

In many instances, it was a meeting with prospective parents that spelled success or failure. Having an honest and frank discussion with such parents often turned the tide. It cannot be said that overnight these parents became enthusiastic Hebrew day school patriots and fervent Hebrew day school ideologues. But it is fair, upon recollection, to say that at least they were ready to give it a try. They didn't all think that somewhere, somehow, the Hebrew day school proponents had a hidden agenda. The key always was to engage in an honest and frank discussion. We said, in effect, tell us what you think, what you fear, and we in turn will tell you who we really are and what we really think. Such meetings required

The people we really needed – parents of young children – had their honest doubts, and wanted reassurances. Without personal background or experience in a Hebrew day school, they were not overeager to immediately become fervent supporters.

The key always was to engage in an honest and frank discussion. Such meetings required certain skills in terms of presentation, an aura of genuine sincerity, and a good dose of shared concern.

certain skills in terms of presentation, an aura of genuine sincerity, and a good dose of shared concern.

During Torah Umesorah's early years, in the first decade, there was a feeling of, "Yes, we are strangers, but let's get to know each other." I had many such encounters. In due time, I came to know the doubts parents had and the questions they harbored and expressed, and consequently was able to deal with them honestly.

At one point, I recalled these experiences and made a list of the key questions and the pressing fears of prospective Hebrew day school parents. Borrowing an idea from social psychologists, I then decided to create a four-page enrollment brochure, listing all the questions, fears and suspicions on the front page. On the inside pages, the questions were repeated and the relevant answers given, short and to the point.

The enrollment brochure was called "Basic Questions People Ask About the Hebrew Day School." A large question mark was printed on the entire front page. These are the questions:

But it is a ghetto, isn't it?
But we are not observant?
Can you really teach two programs in one school day?

Will my child be able to mix with other people? Can he get along?

Is a Hebrew Day School really American?

Don't Secular Studies suffer in a Hebrew Day School?

This really was the face of the American Jewish community in the forties and fifties, as Torah Umesorah initiated its heroic program to establish Hebrew day school in the American setting.

In due time, it should be noted, Torah Umesorah acquired additional enrollment materials, reprints of articles, an enrollment slide show, advertisements, brochures, etc. However, the enrollment brochure was a most successful weapon in Torah Umesorah's arsenal to launch a Torah education revolution in the American Jewish community.

Furthermore, to know the face of America then, to realize the challenges confronted, to appreciate, indeed, which barricades had to be surmounted, it is worthwhile to look again at the above questions. It helps one to understand the sincerity and honesty which permeated the above-mentioned coping arena.

"YIRMIYAHU" IS DRAFTED – THE "SILENT" FULL PAGE ADVERTISEMENT AND THE ELOQUENT LAST LINE

Memory, a gift of G-d, is a precious commodity. One gets older, events and faces fade. Yet certain memories persist and stay with a person for years and decades, while so many others disappear from the memory treasure house.

One such treasure, one such gem, is an advertisement. Yes, a full-page advertisement which appeared on Friday, August 10th, in the year 1945. It was printed in the widely read newspaper called *Der Yiddisher Morgen Journal*. It was written mainly by Rabbi Shraga Feivel Mendlowitz. I had the privilege of working together with Reb Shraga Feivel in preparing the copy of the advertisement. It was late Thursday afternoon when work was finished. I recall taking this advertisement down to the newspaper office building, which was then located, if my memory serves me, on Bowery Street in Manhattan.

Why the advertisement? Why the

care and concern for the right kind of message? Rabbi Mendlowitz wanted this to be the first public announcement of the birth of Torah Umesorah, the first words that would shout out to the world the urgency of such an agency. It was also the first attempt to spell out the heart and soul of a Torah Umesorah program, as the start of a critical dialogue with the American Jewish community.

Briefly, here is what the advertisement proclaimed:

כי לא ימושו מפיך ומפי זרעך זרעך ומפי זרע זרעך אמר ה' מעתה ועד עולם – ["*My spirit ...My words] will not be removed from your mouth, nor from the mouth of your offspring, nor from the mouth of your offspring's offspring, said Hashem, from now and forever*" (Yeshaya 59:21).

"At this moment we already know the truth of the Holocaust and the destruction of Europe and its Torah institutions. Is it enough to cry, sigh, and despair? Can we say with a clear conscience that we really did enough? Can we do nothing to rebuild Jewish life in the free America – the life which has been totally and brutally destroyed? Surely, future generations will blame us for our apathy as we watched the physical destruction of European Jewry. Should we also then do nothing to rebuild the spiritual life here in America? Are we ready just to sit by with folded hands? Are we to allow the golden Torah chain from Sinai to be abruptly cut off here in America?

"The future is now in the hands of American Jewry. For every Torah institution destroyed there, let us build one here in America. There should not be one city, one community, without a Torah educational institution for the young generation. It is our task to continue the *shalsheles hazahav* (the gold-

Rabbi Mendlowitz famous advertisment for Torah Umesorah

en chain) now that there is no Poland, Lithuania, Hungary and other Torah centers.

"We now carry the responsibility not only for ourselves but for world Jewry. We have to build a network of educational institutions. We have to create a revolution in our thinking concerning our future. We can't be satisfied with a school in one city or one neighborhood. We must reach out to America from coast to coast.

"American Jews, our program is ambitious, because the times decree an ambitious program. Our aim is far-reaching, because the hour now demands a far-reaching program. Our

Rabbi Mendlowitz took out a full-page ad in the popular newspaper Morgen Journal. It was to be the first public announcement of the birth of Torah Umesorah.

program is of historic importance, because the moment now is of historic importance."

The above paragraph was the last paragraph in the full-page advertisement. That's it. Nothing else. A reader may wonder, what is "our program," who is "our aim," which party or institution is behind this ad?

But wait, wait. At the very bottom in very small letters there appeared the following lines in parenthesis:

(דאס רעדט צו אייך א איד וועמעס
הארץ וייטאגט פאר דעם חורבן
פון אונזער אומה און וועלכער האפט
אז סוועט נאך קומען די צייט אז תורה
וועט אין אמעריקע אויפגעבוט ווערען
ברוח תורה ומסורה)

This is a Jew talking to you whose heart hurts for the [physical and spiritual] destruction of our people, and who hopes that the time will yet come when Torah in America will be built up in the spirit of Torah and Mesorah.

Nothing more. One sentence, on the bottom of the page, in very, very small letters.

Think hard, and think creatively. An institution or an agency is announcing its birth and agenda, using an advertisement to proclaim its cause. Such an advertisement would at least have its name, address, and phone number printed in the ad. Furthermore, such an advertisement would solicit support and financial help. It would seek membership, ask you to come to a dinner, a meeting, or some similar event, all to help a worthy purpose. This is standard, and seeking public support is expected. No such solicitation appeared in this advertisement, however.

Furthermore, such an advertisement would surely list names – the name of its leader, president, chairmen, members of the board of directors, the name of the founder or founders, etc.

The idea and much of the copy was the thought, vision, and work of Rabbi Shraga Feivel Mendlowitz. The concept of no name, no solicitation, etc. was all his idea. However, the last line in very small letters, written in parenthesis, was a most telling indication of the man and the concept.

"This is a Jew talking to you whose heart hurts for the destruction of our people, and who hopes that the time will yet come when Torah in America will be built up in the spirit of Torah and *Mesorah.*"

POSTSCRIPT REACTION; HISTORY IS MADE

What is a Jew to do when he reads this advertisement? Send money, come to a dinner, attend a meeting, discuss with his friends the members and leaders of this new agency. But there is not even a name, address, or telephone number. Who is behind this? "Since there is no information perhaps we can

This ad was also the first attempt to spell out the heart and soul of a Torah Umesorah program, as the start of a critical dialogue with the American Jewish Community.

Torah Umesorah Dinner, 1985

just ignore it," might be people's reaction. Of course, people were curious. What did they think? How will they react? Will they want to do anything, and if so what? As the cliché says, "Now that the flag has been raised, how many will salute, if any?"

And so, a Jew in St. Paul, Minnesota, reads this. He is active in the local afternoon Talmud Torah – a good school, as such schools go, but he is not satisfied. Possibly there can be a better school for his community, a Hebrew day school, a *yeshiva ketana*. But, who? What? There is no name or number.

In the weeks following the publication of the ad Rabbi Shraga Feivel Mendlowitz visited the offices of Torah Umesorah, as usual. Generally, he would take the bus near City Hall to return to Brooklyn, and I would frequently accompany him to discuss some Torah Umesorah matters. I asked him if there was any reaction to the advertisement.

He pulled out a crumpled letter written in Yiddish. The man had obtained the address by contacting the newspaper. The writer indicated that he had read the advertisement of Torah Umesorah's plans for building new Hebrew day schools outside of New York. Since he lived in St. Paul and was somewhat active in the local afternoon school, the Talmud Torah, he wanted someone to come out to Minnesota and establish a Hebrew day school.

Rabbi Shraga Feivel Mendlowitz turned to me and quietly suggested that I pack up in a day or so and go to Minnesota.

At a Torah Umesorah Dinner. Front dais, (L-R): Rabbi Aharon Schechter, Rabbi Elya Svei, Mr. David Singer, Rabbi Bernard Goldenberg. Rabbi Yaakov Perlow (Novominsker Rebbe) is speaking.

A flurry of thoughts hit me at that moment, none of which now seem very rational. I said to myself, "It's cold enough in New York, let alone in Minnesota! And how would I get there?" I was not a very sophisticated traveler at this point. Furthermore, in those early years, for many reasons, one didn't travel that far away from New York City.

When I haltingly offered the objection that I had no idea how to get to Minnesota, Rabbi Shraga Feivel Mendlowitz demolished it with a quip: "You are not too lazy to find out, are you?"

Still, I was not very eager to undertake such a mission in the winter of 1945. I told him what was really bothering me. "Rabbi," I asked in all sincerity, "What do I do when I get to St. Paul? How does one start a Hebrew day school so far away from the New York area?"

To which he answered quickly, "Talk to the Jew who wrote this letter. Here is his address."

Our conversation continued; I don't remember **exactly** what we said during the next several minutes. I do remember that two busses passed. Reb Shraga

"How did people react to the ad? One Jew from Minnesota contacted Reb Shraga Feivel and he wanted to send me there to establish a day school."

Feivel wasn't boarding and I still wasn't saying yes. I was troubled primarily by the idea of starting from scratch in such a faraway place; I had no idea how to go about opening a school or where I could get help.

Still another bus passed. With a tiny bit of resignation and a smile, Reb Shraga Feivel turned to me and said, "Hopefully, the day will yet come when they will say about you what Yirmiyahu the *Navi* said."

I asked him not to get on the bus. I was curious, very curious. I wanted to know what the *Navi* Yirmiyahu had said, which might have something to do with me.

Rabbi Mendlowitz's smile grew bigger as he replied,"*Yirmiyahu hut gizogt* (said; *Yirmiyahu* 2:2) זכרתי לך חסד נעוריך לכתך אחרי במדבר בארץ לא זרועה, 'I will remember the kindness of your youth … when you followed Me in the wilderness, in a land that was not sown.'" He repeated the last phrase – "*B'eretz lo zerua*, in a land that was not sown" – and then, placing his hand on my shoulder and interpreting the verse homiletically, he said, "Go to Minnesota – to a land where the negativism, the disbelief, the '*lo*', is sown. Go to that wilderness and start a school."

I went. Better still, we went – a small handful of Torah Umesorah people who worked in that tiny office on Nassau Street. That pioneering group, included Dr. Joseph Kaminetsky, Torah Umesorah's first national director, whose great leadership launched so many crucial and vital pro-

In those days, traveling far away from New York City was uncommon. Reb Shraga Feivel, in his own inimitable manner, discussed the importance of our mission and convinced me to go and succeed.

jects; and Rabbi Alexander (Sender) Gross, a colleague and fellow *talmid* of Reb Shraga Feivel, whose ebullience, imagination, and vision spurred all of us in the right direction.

We trekked through that "desert" together and went to a land where disbelief was deeply rooted, and we built a school, and then another and then another. We hoped fervently that the Almighty will remember the affection of a new generation of Jews who followed Him into the wilderness.

As has been mentioned before, memories have their own life. The advertisement, the efforts spent working with Rabbi Shraga Feivel Mendlowitz on this advertisement and, essentially, the conversation with my mentor and rabbi near Manhattan's City Hall, while the busses whizzed by, are as clear in my mind today as if they had happened yesterday. That rendezvous, that conversation, has now aged nearly six decades. But frankly, it hasn't. It is still fresh and treasured.

THE ORIGINALS – THE DYNAMICS OF THE PHENOMENON

If all the above is a retelling of a story and a reviewing of a definitive

Rabbi Binyomin Goldenberg speaking at a dinner

period in the history of the American Jewish community, note should be taken that the teller is a primary source for both the story and its relevant history. Historians are careful to point out that in history there are primary sources as well as secondary sources.

Primary sources can easily say, "My eyes have seen this and my ears have heard this"; whereas secondary sources merely report what the eyes of others have seen, and what the ears of others have heard.

With this in mind, perhaps we should mention the initial group of people who made up the staff of Torah Umesorah; those students of Rabbi Shraga Feivel Mendlowitz who were devoted to launching his vision and actualizing his ideas. This, in fairness, should include non-staff members who visited community after community as canvassers for pupils to enroll in the prospective Hebrew day schools.

When I said to my mentor Rabbi Shraga Feivel Mendlowitz that I didn't know how to go to St. Paul, Minnesota I was telling the truth. When I said that I didn't want to go to a strange city because I didn't know what to do there, I wasn't just making an excuse. It was neither a lie nor an excuse when I asked Reb Shraga Feivel, "And what do I do when I get there?" It was fear that motivated that question. I was scared. Yes, in the forties and early fifties, there was no handbook, "How to Start a Hebrew day school in Minnesota or in Mississippi." Without a handbook, there had to be faith in the Al-Mighty, belief in your mission, zeal in your endeavor and a soldier's spirit to follow your mentor and your teacher, i.e. Rabbi Shraga Feivel Mendlowitz and the *Roshei Yeshiva* who guided Torah

Umesorah, known as the Rabbinical Administrative Board.

Such was the venue, such was the spirit, and such was the frame of reference in which the Hebrew day school movement began and flourished. If your arrival in a town or community meant that you were the recipient of brickbats and unkind criticism from communal leaders, so be it. If your initial appearance called forth an experience similar to being "tarred and feathered," again, so be it. And, on a personal note, if it meant being away from your family for weeks on end, or traveling by busses rather than planes and the like, who said you were created for a life of pleasure?

And if you were hoping that the initial meeting to discuss the possibility of a Hebrew day school in the community would bring out some 50 people and only 3 showed up, there was always the verse from *Yirmiyahu* as interpreted by my mentor, with his hand on my shoulder, as he let the busses go by on a street in Manhattan.

We knew negativism, we saw disbelief all around us, but we were also energized by the ideal, the vision, and the guidance we received from the words of *Yirmiyahu*, "I will remember the kindness of your youth...when you followed Me in the wilderness, in a land that was not sown." We knew of the wilderness, we didn't have to imagine it. But we also felt that America was destined for greatness. We know the promise of נצח ישראל לא ישקר, (the Glory of Israel will not fail) (*Shmuel* I 15:29). And we prayed that somehow Torah Umesorah would be the agency that would take the first hesitant but giant steps towards that goal.

And so we tried and tried again.

Without a handbook, there had to be faith in the Al-Mighty, belief in your mission, zeal in your endeavor and a soldier's spirit to follow your mentor and your teacher, i.e. Rabbi Shraga Feivel Mendlowitz and the roshei yeshiva who guided Torah Umesorah.

But above all, we went. We arrived and arrived again, in cities across America. We hoped and hoped again, that we would reach the heart and soul of the young generation of parents who hopefully would entrust their little children to us so that we could teach them to say the *Shema*, for starters. Didn't Rabbi Shraga Feivel Mendlowitz once say that if we teach a young boy or girl in Kansas to say the *Shema*, it would all be worthwhile?

A CONVERSATION ON A DOORSTEP

A measure of the worth of Torah Umesorah – its importance at this stage of American Jewish history – is a description, or rather a memory, of an encounter on the doorstep of a Jewish home in Providence, Rhode Island. It took place in the summer of 1945, when it was decided to send a small delegation from Torah Umesorah to lay the groundwork for a new Hebrew day school, a *yeshiva ketana* in that community. The delegation was to meet with local rabbis and some lay leaders, in order to create a greater degree of acceptance and support for the school scheduled to open in the fall.

The delegation was headed by Rabbi Reuven Grozovsky, who for more than a decade served as the *Rosh Yeshiva* of Mesivta Torah Vodaath and Beth Medrash Elyon of Monsey, New York. Reb Reuven was a member of Torah Umesorah's Rabbinical Administrative Board as well. A Torah Umesorah staff member also accompanied the delegation, and his assignment included canvassing parents for the kindergarten and first grade of the projected new school. To test the waters, so to speak, Reb Reuven wanted to accompany the Torah Umesorah canvasser for a short period, to see what

We knew negativism, we saw disbelief all around us, but we were also energized by the ideal, the vision of Torah Umesorah.

the procedure was like and to hear the conversation that would ensue with the prospective parents. In a sense, this sage, scholar, and prominent *Rosh Yeshiva* was eager to personally play the role of a canvasser for the new Hebrew day school – for enrollment in the kindergarten and first grade!

Such was the scene as the canvasser rang the bell at the home of a family whose name had been suggested as prospective Hebrew Day School parents. A women opened the door, looked at the *Rosh Yeshiva* and said immediately, "My husband is not home." She looked again at the *Rosh Yeshiva* and said, "He will be home in the evening and you can discuss donations with him." Rabbi Grozovsky, who didn't speak English well, turned to the canvasser and said, "Tell her that, on the contrary, it's really her we want to see" ("זאָג איהר אַז מיר ווילען איר זעהן").

On the doorstep of this Providence home a short conversation ensued and the *Rosh Yeshiva* and Torah Umesorah canvasser were invited in. She asked them to be seated and the canvasser presented the advantages of a Hebrew day school for her child. The *Rosh Yeshiva* was actively involved, coaching the canvasser with relevant arguments and from time to time joining the conversation directly. Then the names of George Washington and Thomas Jefferson were mentioned and the conversation lasted about ten minutes. A short time later the *Rosh Yeshiva* was asked what he was doing as a canvasser. This is what he said.

"You ask what role does a *Rosh Yeshiva* have in the establishment of a kindergarten. Doesn't he have other things on his mind? But there is a long-standing rule in Torah that saving lives assumes a higher priority over everything else. Without Torah study, the children of this community are being buried alive. Without this kindergarten they will, of course, go to school and learn about Washington and Jefferson, but they will never know about Avraham, Yitzchak, and Yaakov, or Moshe *Rabbeinu*. Thus, the item of foremost priority on my agenda is to be here and ensure that these children will indeed live."

Thus the association of a sage, scholar, and *Rosh Yeshiva* with a new kindergarten. Thus the involvement of the members of Torah Umesorah's Rabbinical Administrative Board, who have guided Torah Umesorah from its inception until today.

HOW TO THINK COMPREHENSIVELY AND HOW TO OFFER GUIDANCE (*OLOMEINU, OUR WORLD*)

Rabbi Shraga Feivel Mendlowitz was a visionary. Torah Umesorah became the reality of his vision, though his actual life paralleled only the first four years of Torah Umesorah's history. His vision, however, went hand in hand with his pragmatism. His sense of reality demanded that his vision bear the kind of fruit which would develop his dream, totally subject to practical objectives. Herein lies the interesting story of *Olomeinu, Our World.*

One fall day in 1946, while walking with one of his students who was then a member of the original Torah Umesorah staff, Reb Shraga Feivel turned to him and said, "Are you giving any thought to all these Jewish children who are now being enrolled in all of the Hebrew day schools which Torah Umesorah has now established, with more yet to come, *im Yirtzeh Hashen* (please G-d?) Have you thought about the need to do something which will build on their

classroom experience and even expand their Jewish world, as it is being taught in the schools which they attend? We desperately need a Jewish magazine in English which will undertake this task. You are going to do it. We need a magazine to motivate Torah and *yiras Shamayim*. And you are going to do it."

The student stopped in his tracks and looked with total surprise at his *rebbe*. It was an incredible encounter and a totally surprising conversation. The student caught his breath, turned to his mentor and rabbi, quite flustered, and enumerated the reasons one by one:

"I don't know how to write fiction and non-fiction, neither for teenagers, nor for pre-teenagers. I never did it. I don't know how to deal with printers. I don't know how to put pages together. How do you get articles and illustrations together and what do we write about? I haven't the vaguest idea how to do it."

Rabbi Shraga Feivel Mendlowitz looked at his student, smiled, slapped him on his back, and said in Yiddish twice, "You will learn, you will learn" (״דו וועסט זיך אויסלערנין, דו וועסט זיך אויסלערנין.״)

Thus *Olomeinu, Our World,* was born. The first issue was a Chanukah issue, black and white, with few illustrations, and appeared on November 1, 1946, *Kislev* 5706. Today, *Olomeinu* is richly illustrated and has become the most popular English children's magazine in the Jewish world There were also editions published in Spanish, French and German.

The magazine circulation is above 20,000 and it is estimated that the readership is now over 75,000. *Olomeinu* reaches the entire spectrum of *yeshivos* and day schools, and it is read by par-

The pioneering staff of Torah Umesorah went to cities across America and confronted innumerable challenges. Yet, with Hashem's help, they established Hebrew day schools.

ents as well. Eight volumes of "The Best of *Olomeinu*" stories have been published by ArtScroll / Mesorah.

Rabbi Yaakov Fruchter, who serves as Director of Torah Umesorah's Department of Publications, has been responsible for its publication and growth for the past 40-odd years.

Olomeinu, indeed, has become a powerful tool, inculcating children with a love of Torah and a delight in *mitzvos*. Fifty-five years have passed since that talk between a Rabbi and his pupil, who was told that he would learn how to do it ("דו וועסט זיך אויסלערנין").

A SUMMARY STATEMENT - AN ACCOUNTING

Two weeks before his passing, Rabbi Shraga Feivel Mendlowitz told one of his devoted friends, "A person must make a *cheshbon hanefesh*, give an accounting of what he has accomplished during his lifetime. I am certain that I will receive rewards for my achieve-

> *Olomeinu, indeed, has become a powerful tool, inculcating children with a love of Torah and a delight in mitzvos.*

Rabbi Binyomin Goldenberg holding a volume of The Best of Olomeinu

ments in Yeshiva Torah Vodaath. However, it cannot be compared to the *sechar* I anticipate receiving for the establishment of Torah Umesorah."

This is what he said two days before he passed away. What shall we say 55 years since then? How can we appraise the day school movement which he created? How can we measure the generations of yeshiva and Hebrew day school graduates since then? How can we evaluate the children and the parents? How can we best describe the American Jewish community almost six decades after his dream was set in motion?

Perhaps this is best illustrated by a story related some years ago by one of his talmidim:

Rabbi Shraga Feivel Mendlowitz was sitting on a lawn chair near a rock garden. He asked one of his students to turn over one

Rabbi Dr. Joseph Kaminetsky, Mr. Berel Merling (designer of the original Olomeinu) and Rabbi Shlomo Zalmen Shragai, who was mayor of Jerusalem for a short while.

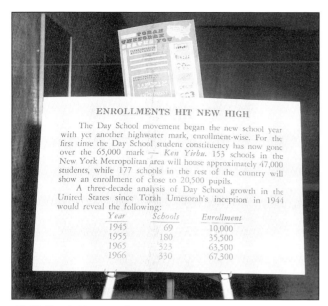

ENROLLMENTS HIT NEW HIGH

The Day School movement began the new school year with yet another highwater mark, enrollment-wise. For the first time the Day School student constituency has now gone over the 65,000 mark — *Ken Yirbu*. 153 schools in the New York Metropolitan area will house approximately 47,000 students, while 177 schools in the rest of the country will show an enrollment of close to 20,500 pupils.

A three-decade analysis of Day School growth in the United States since Torah Umesorah's inception in 1944 would reveal the following:

Year	Schools	Enrollment
1945	69	10,000
1955	180	35,500
1965	323	63,500
1966	330	67,300

1966 Torah Umesorah status report

of the large stones, that had obviously been in the ground for many years. When he did so, the student saw many, many insects swarming about. Rabbi Mendlowitz turned to his students and told them, "Look at these creatures. All their lives under that rock they believed the world to be a dark and dreary place. By turning over the rock, you revealed to them a whole new world of light and beauty. They now see the sun and the sky and have thus been given a new dimension of life. Your task is to remove the rocks from the Jewish souls and to allow the light of our heritage to 'illuminate their lives'".

A whole new world – one of light and beauty, of the sun and the sky.

Yes, he was convinced that it could be done, that the *neshamah* of the Jewish child could be reached by Torah. Thus his dream. Thus the history of the last six decades.

"Your task is to remove the rocks from the Jewish souls and to allow the light of our heritage to 'illuminate their lives'".

1966 display analyzing Torah Umesorah's success, along with an advertisement for Olomeinu

❧ Rabbi Raphael Pelcovitz

BUILDING THE TORAH COMMUNITY
- An American Rabbi's Retrospective

Instrumental in laying the foundation of the American Jewish Community in the 1940s and 50s was the pulpit rabbi. The dynamic leadership of a *rav* was essential to the growth and development of Orthodox Jewish communities across America, especially during that period. The rabbi of that era served in several capacities – he was rabbi of the *shul*, ministering to his congregant's spiritual and physical needs; a teacher; the director of the synagogue Talmud Torah, and all-around community developer and activist. Rabbi Raphael Pelcovitz, who has spent more than a half century in *rabbanus,* personifies this type of *rav.*

Born in Canton, Ohio, in 1921 to European parents, his father, Rabbi Ephraim Pelcovitz, was the rabbi of the *shul* in Canton and a foremost *talmid* of the Slobodka Yeshiva. The family moved to Bridgeport, CT, in 1928, a difficult time in America, just before the Depression. As was the norm, young Raphael attended public school and afternoon Talmud Torah.

"Walking there was an adventure –

the non-Jewish kids would lie in wait and you had to be a good runner! You felt very vulnerable."

The older Pelcovitz sons were sent away to yeshiva, and soon it was Raphael's turn. His father decided on a different course for his youngest child – he would go to *Eretz Yisrael* to learn, something that was unheard of in those days. There was another motivation for this decision – a suitable *shidduch* was needed for the eldest daughter.

Rebbetzin Pelcovitz traveled to *Eretz Yisrael* (then Palestine) with her daughters and the youngest son, Raphael, who was then 12 years old. It was a long trip by boat and train – two weeks. A wonderful *shidduch* was arranged with a *talmid* from Chevron Yeshiva, which had relocated to Jerusalem. Rabbi E. Pelcovitz traveled from America to attend the wedding and the family returned to the States, while young Raphael remained in *Eretz Yisrael* to attend Tiferes Tzvi, the *mechina* of Chevron Yeshiva. He stayed with his sister and brother-in-law while attending yeshiva. His parents were unable to return to Palestine to attend Raphael's *bar mitzvah*. After almost four years at Tiferes Tzvi, where he learned extremely well, Raphael returned to America because of the Arab unrest and riots.

The next stop in Raphael's education was Mesivta Torah Vodaath in Brooklyn, New York. There were no dormitories at that time and out-of-town students rented rooms in private homes. Generally, meals were not provided by the family and the *talmidim* ate in the yeshiva. Arrangements were made for Shabbos meals with different families for the out-of-towners. Occasionally, Raphael returned home, but the expense and time involved precluded this from occurring frequently.

It must be stated, once again, how important it is for us living comfortably in the twenty-first century to be aware of the tremendous *mesiras nefesh* involved in sending a child to yeshiva at that time (1930s-40s). There were very few yeshivos in America then and young boys had to be willing to essentially give up their families and live away from home in order to learn Torah. This sacrifice affected the entire family, but those who valued Torah learning appreciated what was at stake. This lifestyle fostered independence at a young age and a level of maturity not evident in most of today's youth. Such self-sacrifice is worthy of our admiration and respect.

"My *rebbe*, Rabbi Shlomo Heiman was a very outstanding individual. By nature humble and modest, he did not push himself into the public eye... Reb Shlomo taught his *talmidim* how to approach learning. He was a gifted *baal hasbarah* – he had a great ability to explain a *blatt Gemara.* I cannot overemphasize how very beneficial

this was – to know, simply, how to learn a *blatt*. The trouble, later on, was that *bachurim* would be involved in intricate *pilpul* and did not know how to learn a simple *blatt*. This was especially detrimental for *rabbanim* who had to know how to teach a *blatt* to *baalei batim,* but they didn't have the training. Reb Shlomo taught us how to present a *blatt* to others. In his case, it was the *amkus* of *pashtus* – he conveyed a depth perception to us that was deceptively simple, seemingly elementary, but it was far from elementary – it was clear and straight to the point.

"Rabbi Heiman was completely dedicated to his *talmidim* – he never had children of his own – he was extremely accessible, soft and kind. You felt you could go to him to discuss everything.

"In those days, not too many *talmidim* felt the need to be pampered or paid special attention. Then, at an early point in life, one stood on his own two feet – you did not have the dependency more evident today. You lived at a time when you were not spoon-fed in a material or spiritual sense; so you learned to cope yourself, with yourself and by yourself. As a result you did not have dependency on anyone, including your *rebbeim*." Although his father supported him by paying his tuition and board, Raphael earned expense money by teaching in Talmud Torah.

When he first arrived, Reb Shlomo gave a daily *blatt shiur*, but it was phased out after a while and the *Rosh Yeshiva* only gave a *shiur kelali* on Thursdays. All week the *talmidim* in the

Rabbi Ephraim Pelcovitz

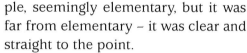

"My rebbe, Rabbi Shlomo Heiman, was a very outstanding individual. He was a gifted baal hasbarah – he had a great ability to explain a blatt Gemara. He taught us how to present a blatt to others."

higher *shiurim* learned with their *chavrusos* – such was the practice at that time.

Rabbi Shraga Feivel Mendlowitz, the *menahel* and unofficial *mashgiach*, knew the *talmidim* very well. While the *Rosh Yeshiva*, Rabbi Heiman, had tremendous impact on their learning, Reb Shraga Feivel impacted on their *hashkafa*, fundamental outlook on life. Reb Shraga Feivel gave *shiurim*

Raphael Pelcovitz as a young man

to a select group of *talmidim* (Rabbi Pelcovitz was among them), on *Ramban, Ramchal* and Rav S.R. Hirsch, whose philosophy greatly shaped his own *hashkafa*.

The *menahel* was not interested in Torah Vodaath being the type of yeshiva that just trained rabbis; to him that was incidental. He was more concerned with shaping Torah-oriented *baalei-batim*, but those who had an inclination and talent for *chinuch* and *rabbanus* were encouraged to pursue it. The yeshiva did not have a course of study for *rabbanus* per se. Reb Shraga Feivel arranged to have a *bochein* (one who administers tests) test those *talmidim* who wanted *semichah*. At that time, Torah Vodaath did not give *semichah*, since that was not the philosophy of the European yeshivos. The *bochein*, Rabbi Schneider, had a phenomenal memory and tested the prospective candidate for a few days. He then reported to the *Rosh Yeshiva*, Rabbi Heiman, who only granted *semichah* to those *talmidim* he personally knew and taught. Raphael Pelcovitz was awarded

"In those days... you did not have the dependency more evident today... you were not spoon-fed in a material or spiritual sense; so you learned to cope yourself, with yourself and by yourself."

semichah at a relatively young age by the *Rosh Yeshiva*.

Reb Shraga Feivel's policy at that time (late 30s - early 40s) was to permit certain *bachurim* to attend college at night – only those who were entering *rabbanus* or *chinuch* were allowed to go. Those *bachurim* that he felt were better suited to be diamond cutters (a trade that was becoming popular then), or work in other businesses, did not go to college – it was considered unnecessary. The yeshiva served supper early to accommodate those who attended college classes. The vast majority attended CCNY (City College of New York), which was considered a very good school, tuition-free; 95% of the student body was Jewish. Rabbi Pelcovitz was one of the *talmidim* who attended college at night.

It should be noted that during the early 40s a *bachur* had to have his own *parnassah* if he wanted to get married. The *kollel* as we know it today was not in existence then. Reb Shraga Feivel was perceptive enough to realize that professionally, college was necessary for those Torah Vodaath *talmidim* who wanted to become rabbis or teachers. He also helped those young men who were ready to leave the yeshiva and start working to find suitable jobs.

Rabbi Pelcovitz's first position was in *chinuch* – he became the principal of the fledgling day school in Hartford, CT., after being recommended by Reb Shraga Feivel. At that time (1942-44), the day school movement was in its infancy. It was an alien concept to the vast majority of Jews (even some religious ones), who felt that it was disloyal and un-American, since being an American meant being part of the mainstream. Establishing your own school (then called a parochial school) was considered isolationist and placed one's patriotism under a cloud. This was the prevailing attitude that confronted Rabbi Pelcovitz. Only a very small group of parents were supportive and interested in the day school. It was truly an uphill battle, in the face of apathy and even hostility. A few rabbis, lay leaders, and pioneering parents were the only supporters.

In the two years that he was in Hartford, Rabbi Pelcovitz managed to expand the school and recruit new students. In those days, the principal had to teach as well as administrate. The teachers in the Hebrew/religious studies department primarily came from Bais Medrash Le'morim and from some of the yeshivos. The experience was very worthwhile, but validated what Rabbi Pelcovitz already knew – that by upbringing and environment he was more suited to the rabbinate than *chinuch*.

Rabbi Pelcovitz received a call from Torah Vodaath to apply for the rabbinic position in Saratoga Springs, N.Y., if he was interested. It could not have come at a more opportune time. He applied and was chosen for the position of rabbi of the Orthodox *shul* (the only *shul* in town) and principal/teacher of the Talmud Torah.

Saratoga Springs was a typical small town, with one difference – it was a resort town offering mineral baths, spas, and healthful waters that attracted visitors during the season (Pesach -

Rabbi Pelcovitz and Rabbi Moshe Sherer

Labor Day), including Jews from New York. There were several kosher hotels and rooming houses. This influx of "big city Jews," who were more learned and sophisticated, presented a challenge for the young rabbi, because they attended his *shul*. Otherwise, the attendance was not that large – there was a small nucleus of European Jews and a segment comprised of American-born families who were respectful and retained loyalty to Orthodoxy in their own way. The younger group provided the leadership while the older members were the *daveners*. Only a handful were *shomer Shabbos*. Given the *shul's* make-up the *drashos* were delivered in Yiddish.

When Rabbi Pelcovitz first arrived there was only a *minyan* on Shabbos. He worked on expanding this to weekdays, at least on Mondays and Thursdays when the Torah is read. It was difficult to get people to come because of the harsh winters. During the Season, however, there was a large *minyan*.

Their attitude regarding the Talmud Torah was different – they **wanted** their children to learn. Nonetheless, it was relatively small and was comprised of

It should be noted that during the early 40s a bachur had to have his own parnassah if he wanted to get married. The Kollel as we know it today was not in existence then.

(L-R): Rabbi Raphael Pelcovitz with Dr. Joseph Kaminetsky at the 29th Annual Dinner of Torah Umesorah

The challenges faced by young pulpit rabbis at that time were many. The prevailing attitude of most people regarding religious matters was one of apathy and sometimes negativity.

children from many different grades. It was like a one-room schoolhouse and the rabbi had to accomplish as much as he could with each student.

Kashrus was another area of the rabbi's responsibilities. There was a local *shochet* for chickens and a kosher butcher, while kosher meat and many food items were imported from Albany or Schenectady. Rabbi Pelcovitz also instituted some adult classes. Considering everything, it was an excellent experience for a new rabbi. Saratoga Springs was always viewed by the *rabbanim* of that period as a stepping-stone position.

After two years, Rabbi Pelcovitz was offered a rabbinic position in Akron, Ohio. There were several advantages – it was a bigger community, the job did not involve teaching in the Talmud Torah and there were other *rabbanim*, hence colleagues, so more could be accomplished.

Unlike other places, in Akron there was a community Talmud Torah with a director and staff, instead of individual synagogue schools. Although the rabbis were involved in the Talmud Torah, they did not teach there. At that time,

there was no day school. However, during Rabbi Pelcovitz's tenure in Akron, the Conservative movement started making inroads and when they opened their own Talmud Torah, the community Talmud Torah was weakened. Their encroachment also affected the Orthodox *shul*. People left for business or social reasons; since their commitment was not very strong, the "defectors" did not feel it mattered where their shul affiliation was. This phenomenon was unfortunately occurring across America and presented a new challenge to the Orthodox rabbi.

"To a certain extent, the presence of a young Orthodox rabbi who is committed and able to reach people in itself was able to counteract this, but how much? You're swimming against the current. What kept you going were those who held fast and remained loyal. Then you felt you could hold the line until reinforcements would come."

Rabbi Pelcovitz's *shul,* Anshei Sfard, also called the Polishe Shul, had many European Jews, and they comprised the leadership. As time progressed, there was a shift in the power structure and the American-born members came to the fore. The European Jewish contingent gave the rabbi more problems than the American group. The reason was that they were enamored with the American milieu and were convinced that the **only** way to hold on to their children was to become more Americanized and more "modern" at the expense of religious observance. Although this was a misguided notion, it still prevailed and created serious problems for the Orthodox rabbi. In essence, this attitude meant that the backbone of the *shul*, those who came to *daven* and participate, were very attracted to modern approaches anti-

New building of Anshei Sfard, Akron, Ohio, 1951

thetical to Orthodoxy, and the rabbi had to contend with this very serious issue. Those who should have been the strongest supporters were in fact behaving like the weakest link.

On the other hand, the younger American congregants, who were not yeshiva educated and had very limited religious knowledge, could not provide the logistical support to the extent that was necessary. Consequently, the rabbi found himself quite isolated in principle and policy, since there was no group within the *shul* who understood, or were committed to sustaining the Orthodox spirit and ideology. True, there were loyalists to the *shul* and rabbi, but it was on a personal level. The rabbi had to be a strong leader in order to accomplish anything.

"That period (1945 – early 1950s), in out-of-town communities, you were dealing with *baalei batim* who were basically not learned, not observant, and not committed to Torah values, hence it was a difficult time for one in a leadership role. [As a] rabbi [you] had to be firm and convince them that you (a) are sincere, (b) have a position of authority, and (c) are unswerving – that you mean what you say. If you could do this, then the majority would follow you; most peo-

ple go with the current. The rabbi had to feel that there was hope of accomplishing what he set out to do and that he is not just spinning his wheels."

One of Rabbi Pelcovitz's major accomplishments in Akron was spearheading the erecting of a new *shul* building. The main issues of contention which confronted him in this venture was the *mechitzah* and the installation of a microphone. The primary reason *mechitzah* was such a problem for the membership was that they were exposed to the American concept that a house of worship is for families, hence there should not be separate seating. At countless meetings, as well as from the pulpit, Rabbi Pelcovitz tried to educate them on these issues. Although opposition was strong it was not militant and the rabbi prevailed – a *mechitzah* was built, and there was no microphone. "If you are strong and willing to do what is necessary, putting yourself on the line, 99% of the people will accept what you say."

Kashrus in Akron was on a communal level, overseen by the rabbis – there were *shochtim*, kosher butchers, and *mashgichim* who required supervision.

The greatest challenge was overcoming the lack of knowledge in Jewish learning, and especially its effects on the younger generation.

A misguided notion that created serious difficulties for the Orthodox rabbis was that many of the Jews in their communities were convinced that religious observance and being Americanized were mutually exclusive. Am ha'artzus was the biggest problem.

"You could count on the fingers of one hand those people who sent their children to yeshivos."

To combat this knowledge-gap, Rabbi Pelcovitz arranged several classes to teach his congregants and educate them in fundamental areas of *Yiddishkeit*. In addition, another venue utilized by the rabbi was personal friendships and teaching by example.

"It was not a conscious type of thing like today's *kiruv* work – there was no label associated with it then. You also could not allow numbers to measure your successes or failures. As the Chazon Ish said, 'The Mishnah does not say *harbei talmidim*, but *talmidim harbei* – the numerical quantity is not at issue; you work as hard as you can with what you have. You try to have a lasting impact on them, so they will continue to be your *talmidim* for years to come and become your supporters.

"In the rabbinate you never know how many people you affect or how. Years later, a person will come over to you and repeat something you said which you may not even remember, but to them it was important and made an impact.

"Just the rabbi's presence can have an effect. I learned this from a man in Saratoga Springs. He came over to me and said, 'I'm glad you're in town, because Pesach is coming and when a rabbi is in town I don't eat *chametz*. When there is no rabbi I feel differently.' Similarly, in Akron people would say, to me, 'Your presence has an impact.' Such remarks give you *chizuk*."

Akron was a typical out-of-town community in the late 1940s and early 50s. Apathy was the prevailing attitude regarding religious matters for most of the Jews. There was almost what could be characterized as a neutral spirit. It was dependent on the rabbi to take a position on important issues and be a leader, as well as educate the people. In this way he could make inroads and dispel some of the Jewish ignorance.

This period was also one of transition – there was no longer a strong presence of the European generation. They were dying out and those who remained had little energy or self-confidence. Additionally, they had provided little or no *chinuch* to their children, so even the younger generation was resigned to a low level of observance. Consequently, the rabbi had no strong nucleus to work with in order to accomplish anything exciting or innovative (i.e. day school).

"The rabbi tried to conserve what was there; he was "the keeper of the flame." The rabbi had to set the tone. Through persistence, he protected the status quo – the *shul, minyan, mikveh,* learning groups, *shochtim,* kosher markets. In a small town, if you lacked even a small nucleus of support you were, unfortunately, not in a position to do much... it was a challenge to preserve *Yiddishkeit.* You were like the *"neturei karta"* – the guardians of the city."

It must be noted that despite the limited level of Jewish knowledge and observance in a small town such as Akron, there was sufficient commitment to support the kosher butchers and bakers. Not only that, but the rate of intermarriage was surprisingly low. The answer may be, says Rabbi Pelcovitz, that:

"There was a certain stubbornness that they felt – the older generation was still around and the level of sophistication and higher education was moderate, because at that time their involvement in society at large was not as great as it later became... Assimilation and intermarriage accel-

In order to accomplish anything, the rabbi had to be a strong leader and educator, and convince the baalei batim that he was sincere and consistent in what he said and did.

erated with the degree of involvement in general society. The majority were plain people, who have a tendency to stick to the familiar. Not only that, but it also depends on what society accepts or frowns upon. At that time, intermarriage was not accepted, so it was minimal.

"If you were to ask me what was the greatest threat to *Yiddishkeit* at that time, I would say *am ha'artzus*, ignorance; and the deviation movements (Conservative and Reform) capitalized on this great ignorance of the Orthodox Jewish community, who did things by rote or because their parents did it, and they could not defend their position and commitment to their children."

The rabbinical position offered to him by the Far Rockaway, N.Y. *shul*, Knesseth Israel (a.k.a. The White Shul) had a strong nucleus of Torah-true Jews, as well as many other advantages.

"The Far Rockaway position offered a great opportunity – people were moving to this community who were *shomer Shabbos*, yeshiva educated and

committed Jews. It was a breath of fresh air. It was 1951, and the climate was such that there were only islands of Torah; there was a general lack of confidence in a Torah society and many *pesharos*, compromises, had to be made. Many rabbis found it hard to hold on and to take a position on issues of contention, such as *mechitzah* and microphone – it was easier to give in. Whoever dreamt of a maximal position? You were content with the minimal – you wouldn't talk about such things as T.V. in the house, wearing a *sheitel*, glatt kosher etc. – the majority were not on that level. Even though you, the rabbi, felt that Torah was primary and not *chochmas ha'umos,* you had to be careful expressing this. You had to choose your battles... The unsung heroes were those who preserved the little islands of Torah in the midst of an ocean that militated against *Yiddishkeit*."

Far Rockaway was a small community when Rabbi Pelcovitz arrived, but it was growing. Young families were mov-

"You had to choose your battles... The unsung heroes were those who preserved the little islands of Torah in the midst of an ocean that militated against Yiddishkeit."

Group picture of awardees at Israel Bonds dinner. (Seated far left): Rabbi Pelcovitz, center - Rabbi S. Goren and Rabbi Walkin

The original "White Shul" which stood on the corner of Nameoke and Dinsmore, 1925-1964

ing there who wanted to live in suburbia, in a place with all the necessary religious amenities and in commuting distance to their jobs in the city. Many were yeshiva educated and hailed from Brooklyn, Manhattan and the Bronx. Hence, they identified with the large Torah communities that were always strong in the large metropolitan cities like New York, Chicago, and Baltimore.

"A definite advantage of this was

that you were dealing with those who were receptive to what you wanted to present and accomplish... Even here, it was important to keep educating the people as to the importance of ongoing *talmud Torah* – that you have to have a *kevius*, an established time to learn, and improve your commitment and add to your knowledge. This had to be preached constantly.

"The climate of the community was such, and it was amazing to see, that as time passed there were social pressures to be <u>more</u> <u>observant</u>. For example, out-of-town, having a *succah* was an act of courage. In Far Rockaway, even in the 50s, it had reached a point in certain neighborhoods that if you did **not** have a *succah* you were ashamed. People built *succos* who were not even that *frum*. The benefit was that, eventually, some of these people became observant for the proper reason and not just "to keep up with the Joneses."

"It was also a time when you began to notice that some parents were less *frum* than their children. Religiously, the children were begin-

New building of the "White Shul," Knesseth Israel, in Far Rockaway, New York

Ponovezh Yeshiva Dinner - the Rav, Rabbi Yosef Kahaneman, is seated next to Charles Bendheim; Rabbi Pelcovitz is guest speaker.

In the 30s, 40s and 50s the definition of a frum Jew was different than today. It progressed... All these standards are still in a state of flux.

ning to outpace and surpass their parents – they also brought religious pressures on their parents."

In the 30s, 40s and 50s, the definition of a *frum* Jew was different than today. "Remember, the norm was not the same as it is today. It progressed. For example, how did one define a *frum* Jew? Then, it meant a person who was *shomer Shabbos* and learned (even a little), but it became more as time went on: Does this person keep glatt kosher, *chalav Yisrael*; does the woman cover her hair; do the children go to yeshiva? Then it progressed to another level – does he wear a black hat, learn in *kollel,* etc.? All these standards are still in a state of flux, but you have to have something to measure against.

"In those days there was nothing to measure against, so you had to create the standards. A combination of three forces – the family, *shul,* and yeshiva – and the leadership of parents, rabbi and *rosh yeshiva* created the standards. Then, there was a much

closer relationship between the rabbi and *rosh yeshiva*, but even then friction was emerging. What you did have at that time was a greater mutual *derech eretz.* Why? Even in the 50s you could see this. The *roshei yeshiva* felt, and they were probably right, that the conduct of the *shuls* and rabbis – especially out-of-town – was not according to the highest Torah standards. There was a breakdown in the reli-

Rabbi Yaakov Kamenetsky is delivering a message at the Dedication Ceremonies of the new "White Shul" building

Rabbi Pelcovitz delivering his address at the Dedication Ceremonies, June, 1964. Seated on the dais (R-L): Rabbi Yaakov Kamenetsky, Rabbi Benjamin Kamenetsky, and Emanuel Neustadter, President

Rabbi Pelcovitz was involved from the very outset in the development of the Far Rockaway Jewish community – kashrus, mikveh, yeshivos and day schools – as well as building up his own shul and its activities.

gious aspects of many communities, and the problems mentioned earlier of not making waves, taking a stand, and just going with the flow vis-à-vis religious matters. The focus in these places was more on organizational and community endeavors, so these rabbis became political figure-heads and social directors. Such rabbis lost the respect of the yeshivos and the serious-minded congregants. That's when the tendency began, and it was believed that *chinuch* was more the vehicle to strengthen and accomplish things in *Yiddishkeit* than *rabbanus*."

Rabbi Pelcovitz was involved from the very outset in the development of the Far Rockaway Jewish community – *kashrus, mikveh,* yeshivos and day schools – as well as building up his own *shul* and its activities. When he first came to Far Rockaway, there were only two Orthodox *shuls*: the White Shul, and Shaarei Tefilah – which was more "modern." There was only one day school – H.I.L.I. (Hebrew Institute of Long Island), which was co-ed at the time, as was the norm. The community rabbis were on the Board of Education and helped formulate policy. There was a mixed parent body, religiously speaking, but there were no alternative schools.

As time passed and the community grew, an all-boys' *yeshiva ketanah* opened and then an all-girls' school, as well as another day school, which was more modern and Zionistic. Eventually, a *mesivta* and *bais medrash* also opened. All of this was a natural type of growth, which transpires in every vibrant community. The *shul* Talmud Torah that was there when he came eventually closed (early 60s), because the membership sent their children to day school or yeshiva and no longer needed it.

As part of this evolutionary process, the *baalei batim* on the H.I.L.I. Board of Education phased out the participation of the community rabbis. As strong professional leadership was brought into the school, the lay leadership gained more confidence. They wanted to retain their own identity, so the rabbis lost their influence. This phenomenon did not occur everywhere across the United States, but depended on the community.

There was no *Vaad HaKashrus* when Rabbi Pelcovitz arrived. At that time, the *shamash* of the *shul* served as the *mashgiach* of the kosher butcher shop, and the butchers felt that they had their own *chezkas kashrus*, established claim of *kashrus*. There were no *shomer Shabbos* bakeries or take-home food establishments and pizza shops. As the community developed, these types of stores opened and a central *kashrus* organization was needed. Rabbi Pelcovitz, together with Rabbi Rackman of Shaarei Tefilah and Rabbi Berkowitz, established the *Vaad HaKashrus*, and as it slowly evolved additional *mashgichim* were hired as needed. It served Far Rockaway, the Five Towns and outlying communities.

(L-R) standing: Rabbi Dovid Lifshitz, seated: Rabbi S.M. Kalmanowitz, Rabbi Y. Gorelick, unknown, Rabbi E. Machlis, and Rabbi Pelcovitz

The *mikveh* serving Far Rockaway was then in Edgemere, a nearby community; it was very old and the growing Far Rockaway community wanted to build a modern facility in Far Rockaway. Rabbi Pelcovitz was very instrumental in making this dream a reality. One important area that was a potential minefield that he dealt with was satisfying the various factions of the community and addressing their different standards – after all, it was a *community mikveh*. Property was purchased and a new *mikveh* was built, serving not only Far Rockaway but the surrounding neighborhoods and communities.

Although there was a *Chevrah Kadisha* when Rabbi Pelcovitz arrived, only three men were involved. Rabbi Pelcovitz wanted to expand the *Chevrah Kadisha* and attract new members to this vital organization, especially the younger segment of the *shul*. He instituted a halachah class for them and designated the 7th of Adar as *Chevrah Kadisha* Day to give recognition, support, and honor to its members. Rabbi Pelcovitz also organized a women's *Chevrah*, with a nucleus formed from the experienced women who came from other communities. For many years this was the only women's *Chevrah* in the community. The veterans helped teach the new members, and the rabbi gave "refresher courses" on a regular basis, as the *Chevrah* grew into a large organization.

The newcomers to Far Rockaway, as well as a large segment of the *shul's* membership, were young families. A vibrant and strong youth activities program was important to them, and so was adult education. Rabbi Pelcovitz formed two committees to address these needs – a Youth Activities Committee and Adult Education Committee. The programming for

The newcomers to Far Rockaway, as well as a large segment of the shul's membership, were young families. Vibrant youth activities and adult education programs were important to them. The rabbi instituted and guided this programming.

(L-R): Rabbi Pelcovitz, Rabbi Moshe Feinstein

(Seated L): Rabbi Kahaneman, the Ponovezh Rav;
Rabbi Pelcovitz (standing on right).

An interesting phenomenon that existed in the White Shul, and was not that common in other communities, was that the establishment was not all that strong. Therefore, newcomers who wanted to play a role, were able to do so.

both was initiated, instituted and guided by the rabbi. When the Talmud Torah existed, they hired someone who could serve in two capacities – teacher and youth director, guided by the rabbi. After the Talmud Torah was discontinued, a professional youth director was hired. The youth leaders for the program came from the *shul.* A varied program was offered, primarily on Shabbos and Sunday. A youth *minyan* and junior congregation were instituted, as well as Shabbos afternoon *Oneg Shabbos* groups. Eventually, a teen *minyan* was added and classes were organized to teach *davening* and *leining.* Special events were arranged for *Yamim Tovim,* as well as *Chol Hamoed* trips. On Sundays, such activities as cooking, arts & crafts, and *bikur cholim* were offered in a club-like setting.

Adult classes were instituted by Rabbi Pelcovitz from the beginning of his tenure – for men, for women, and some co-ed. *Shiurim* in Gemara were offered on Shabbos and also during the week. At first the Gemara *Shiur* was given in *Yiddish,* but this changed. As the make-up of the *shul* became primarily young families, for whom Yiddish was not their mother tongue, the switch was made to English. The subject matter of the classes was varied – *Chumash, Nach, Hashkafa,* and specific halachah topics. Initially, it operated by trial and error, as the rabbi tried to ascertain what interested the people. The various classes had wide appeal and people attended from other *shuls* and communities.

The *Shul* Sisterhood was very weak when Rabbi Pelcovitz arrived. His *Rebbetzin* helped him revive it to become a meaningful and active group. In those days, most women did not work outside the home and it served as an important vehicle for their social needs. Special programs and activities were arranged – luncheons, family picnics, and, most important, fundraisers. The sisterhood raised a lot of money for the *shul* which helped to finance some of its programs. *Chesed* projects were instituted, as well as women's classes in *Chumash.*

An interesting phenomenon that existed in the White Shul, and was not as common in other communities, was that the establishment, the old guard of the *shul,* was not all that strong. True, there were a few who played a prominent role and were among the leadership, but by the time Rabbi Pelcovitz came, they had dwindled in number and strength. Besides getting older, their interests had changed and did not necessarily coincide with those of the new young families, who helped shape the programs.

"This may have been an attraction to new families. They could make a difference, because although there was an establishment, it was not that entrenched. The newcomers who wanted to play a role could do so and did not have to go up against the old guard who may have resisted.

"Similarly, in the early 60s when the building campaign for the new shul was launched, there was a broad base of donors, as opposed to a small group of major contributors. Consequently, the power generally associated with such a group was not a factor, and policy decisions were arrived at more equitably."

Over the course of half a century Rabbi Pelcovitz devotedly and indefatigably shaped and developed his *shul* and community. Today, Far Rockaway is one of the premier Orthodox Jewish communities in America.

We would be remiss if we did not mention the *Rebbetzins'* role. Every successful *rav* was supported and aided first and foremost by his wife, his *ezer k'negdo*. Without her personal *mesiras nefesh* – her willingness to move far and near, to start over again and again, not to mention often tending the family and home single-handedly to enable the rabbi to pursue all that he had to – much of what was accomplished never would have been realized. The active role these women played in building the *shuls*, along with their husbands, cannot be overlooked. These women truly personify the quintessential *eishes chayil*. Many a rabbi has echoed the words of Rabbi Akiva:

"All that is mine and yours is because of her" (*Kesubos* 63a).

Everything we have today and likely take for granted in the Jewish community – *kashrus, shuls,* yeshivos, and day schools, *shiurim, tzedaka, Chevra Kadisha, bikur cholim* etc. – began with the *rabbanim*. Do we even consider the difficulties and obstacles which they had to overcome? The *rabbanim* were the architects who helped lay the foundation and build the vibrant Orthodoxy that we have today.

"As my father said to one of the founders of his *shul* who complained that no one knows him, 'Look at the building – it stands on a foundation which can't be seen; it's in the ground. But the building can only be built if there's a strong foundation.'"

This is true of all areas in the development of the Jewish community. We may not "see" those who came first and toiled to cultivate the landscape that was the America of the 40s and 50s (and before), but these *rabbanim* helped lay the critical foundation, and then crafted the essential components that make for a dynamic community. Through their *mesiras nefesh*, hard work, creative talents, teaching abilities and personal example, they were instrumental in the regeneration and resurgence of Orthodoxy in America. The gratitude and respect we owe them is incalculable.

> *Through mesiras nefesh, hard work, creative talents, teaching abilities and personal example, the rabbanim were instrumental in the regeneration and resurgence of Orthodoxy in America.*

At bris of a great-grandson – 4 generations: Pictured, Rabbi Pelcovitz, infant Efraim and grandson Mordechai.

Torah Vanguards

A vanguard, by definition, is "at the forefront of a movement or field", he is a leader. The three individuals we have characterized as vanguards stood at the forefront, as lay leaders and advocates for Orthodoxy and Jewish education in their generation. Their *mesiras nefesh*, knowledge, and unfailing dedication enabled Torah life and Torah institutions to be built in America. They were actively involved in rescue and relief work, both during and after the war. In thought and deed, these men demonstrated that no action was too difficult and no sacrifice was too great when it came to saving their European brethren. These invaluable attributes were then applied to the awesome task of building Torah in America.

Mr. Irving Bunim, America's "*Shtadlan* for Torah," was at the forefront of transforming the fledgling Young Israel movement into a vital Orthodox organization. The challenges he encountered in this endeavor would have discouraged and dissuaded most people. But, Mr. Bunim was not "most people." The same qualities were brought to all of his undertakings for *Klal Yisrael*. His vital work and accomplishments for Vaad Hatzala are legendary. Similarly, he labored on behalf of yeshivos, as well as Torah Umesorah. We are the fortunate beneficiaries of his notable legacy.

Mr. Stephen Klein was the quintessential man of *chesed* and Jewish activism. A Holocaust survivor, he was committed body and soul to the rescue and relief work of Vaad Hatzala, and served as a chairman. He traveled to the DP camps to help the survivors rebuild their lives. As head of Rescue Children, Inc., he valiantly did everything possible to help the orphans of war. His efforts on their behalf were extraordinary, as well as renowned. He was relentless when it came to helping them, accepting no excuse. Stephen Klein's business was the first *shomer Shabbos* retail chain. The famous Barton's Bonbonniere advertisements appearing in the major newspapers, pertaining to Shabbos and *Yamim Tovim*, educated countless people about their heritage. His active involvement in Torah Umesorah and as a founder and generous supporter of yeshivos, girls schools, and major Jewish organizations is legend. His contribution to Torah *chinuch* in *Eretz Yisrael*, through his efforts as chairman of Chinuch Atzmai, has forever left an indelible impact. Mr. Klein's contributions to the annals of Orthodoxy in America are extraordinary, as well as enviable.

Mr. Irving Stone, "the architect of Torah philanthropy," is a name synonymous with *tzedakah* and Torah education. He was, indeed, a trailblazer in this country, recognizing how essential Jewish education is to the perpetuation of our people. Mr. Stone applied all of his brilliant business acumen to the field of *chinuch*, Jewish education. It is primarily to his credit that Jewish Federations throughout the United States support Jewish day schools. He impressed upon them that a people can only survive if it transmits its heritage from generation to generation. Truly, Irving Stone redefined philanthropy, creating a "Torah philanthropy." To make Torah accessible to all Jews, he undertook the vital task of having the *Chumash*, and the entire *Tanach* translated colloquially and annotated with commentaries from our greatest sages throughout the ages. These volumes are an invaluable contribution to transmitting Torah to Jews of all backgrounds, everywhere. Mr. Stone was the paradigm of what it means to be a philanthropist. His *tzedakah* and acts of *chesed* were of the highest level. Irving Stone's legacy is as enduring as his name.

These vanguards exemplify the *oskim betzarchei tzibur be'emunah*, "those who are involved faithfully in the needs of the community." The very essence of *Klal Yisrael* flowed through them. Our debt of gratitude to them is incalculable.

Irving M. Bunim 1901-1980

AMERICA'S SHTADLON FOR TORAH

Inevitably, there are a number of complex, unpredictable factors which combine to elicit greatness from a man. At times, uncontrollable historic events swirl around the casual observer, leaving him witness to events far beyond his ken. Another observer, with a more discerning eye, may perceive these forces as an incalculable challenge. Both history and challenge coalesced in the talented persona of Irving Bunim.

A Fire in His Soul, by Rabbi Amos Bunim, from the Introduction

Irving Bunim is one of the laymen most responsible for Torah in America, and worldwide, as we know it today.

It's a scene that's been repeated throughout history – sometimes in medicine, sometimes new technology, often on Wall Street and in industry. A novel idea–one that stands convention on its proverbial edge – lies infused within the mind, heart and soul of an individual of staunch resolve and, of course, must withstand a disbelieving public. Years later, our innovator is acclaimed for his brilliance while his peers lament, "Why didn't we think – or do – this? It seems so logical and obvious!" Einstein and his Theory of Relativity and Dr. Jonas Salk and the cure for polio; Alexander Graham Bell and his telephone and Thomas Edison and the light bulb – all provided contributions that have improved the quality of life for billions of people around the globe. These are true accomplishments for mankind – and they are great accomplishments, of a kind.

However, there are other accom-plishments that dwarf these, for not only are they accomplishments that benefit mankind, they are accomplishments that merit the continued existence of mankind. In a world of darkness, dedicated to the most vile idol worship, Avraham *Avinu* arose; when *Klal Yisrael* was sinking in the moral abyss of Egypt, almost to the point of no return, Moshe *Rabbeinu* was sent to herald the Exodus. At each turn in the history of *Klal Yisrael*, at the darkest and most foreboding moment, Hashem, in His mercy, dispatches His loyal servant–the one whose soul truly yearns for Hashem's glory, churning with a singular love for *Klal Yisrael* – to bring the light of redemption and dispel the darkness.

In the early years of the twentieth century in America, only the boldest could believe (much less give voice to the concept) that Torah Jewry would flourish in this country. As the years passed and the insidious trend of acculturation among the immigrants from Russia and Eastern Europe accelerated its frightening pace, almost no one thought *Yiddishkeit* could survive in the *Goldena Medina* – almost no one. At such a time, when, to all appearances, the light of Torah seemed destined to be extinguished in one country after another from indifference, poverty, pogroms, mass killings, gassing and the ovens – Hashem did not let His people drift into the darkness of oblivion. It was not to be. For He entrusted the future of His people to those whose souls burned for His glory. And, like Matisyahu and his sons, in the face of odds that defy rational explanation, the spirit of Torah Judaism was yet to be kindled in the darkness – the intransigent indifference – of all but the smallest minority of American Jewry.

Armed with an indomitable spirit and clarity of vision, Irving Bunim is one of the laymen most responsible for Torah in America, and worldwide, as we know it today. The man Rabbi Aharon Kotler called his partner in building Torah in America was the personality whose soul was ablaze with the fire of Torah. At present, each day brings new initiatives in Torah education and *chesed*, inspired by those who wish to ennoble the banner of Torah. The fire of their conviction was kindled by another, and he or she in turn, by yet another in an endless chain. In post-war America, when only disparate and feeble sparks of *Yiddishkeit* existed, Irving Bunim fanned them into

National Council of Young Israel shipping religious articles to the DP Camps via the Dutch consulate. (L-R): Royal Consul General of Holland Jonkheer G.C.G Van Swinderin and Irving Bunim.

a flame of Torah that was capable of sustaining future generations around the world. In truth, we cannot calculate the debt of appreciation and gratitude owed to this very singular man. How many look back with the hindsight of history, sigh and wonder, "Why didn't I do that?" Part of the answer is provided by Rabbi Amos Bunim, his son: "He lived knowing he would have to account for the way he used his life, his mind, his talents, his energy, his opportunities." Irving Bunim was a man in full realization of his purpose in this world, and strove to fulfill it in its entirety.

THE EARLY YEARS

Irving Bunim was born to Moshe and Esther Mina (Yoselofsky) Bunimowitz in 1901, in the Lithuanian city of Volozhin. Volozhin was renowned for the presence of the Volozhin Yeshiva, founded in 1802, by Rabbi Chaim Volozhiner, the foremost *talmid* of the *Gaon* of Vilna.

In America, when only disparate and feeble sparks of Yiddishkeit existed, Irving Bunim fanned them into a flame of Torah that was capable of sustaining future generations around the world.

Already imbued with the conviction that Torah *lishmah* was Judaism's highest goal, Bunim left Volozhin for New York at the age of nine. Young Irving was a product of the world that was, the *shtetel* that pulsated with Jewish tradition handed down from one generation to the next, even in the face of the terrible destruction caused by the Enlight-enment. So influential were the proponents of the Enlightenment that they were able to convince the Czar to close the Volozhin Yeshiva for refusing to introduce secular studies into its curriculum. The struggle between traditional Torah observance and the secular influences of the Enlightenment made a lasting impression on Irving, one that in future years would help him perceive alien attitudes assailing Torah Judaism where others saw no danger at all.

In 1905, due to a number of circumstances that compromised Jewish life in Volozhin, and coupled with the threat of the pogroms, Moshe Bunimowitz emigrated to America and settled in

Young Irving was a product of the world that was, the shtetel that pulsated with Jewish tradition handed down from one generation to the next.

Preparing a National Council of Young Israel shipment of religious articles to the refugees in Oswego, N.Y., 1942. (L-R): Irving Bunim, Israel Upbin (executive-vice president), Hon. Edward S. Silver

Bayonne, New Jersey. Like so many others, Sabbath observance was paramount to Reb Moshe and he suffered financially in order to uphold Shabbos. Finally, in 1910, he sent for Esther Mina and the children. From Bayonne, the family moved to the Lower East Side of New York where Esther Mina helped Reb Moshe bear the financial burden of the family. Her great fears about the impoverished state of *Yiddishkeit* were allayed when the boys were enrolled in the newly opened Rabbi Jacob Joseph School. In 1917, Reb Moshe assumed the position of *rebbe* in the new Mesivta Torah Vodaath in Brooklyn. He held this position until his death in 1935.

The human psyche is complicated beyond conception. The interplay of mind, memory, experience and emotion is the arena where men are made and destroyed. Each person has his particular challenges and the greatest challenge of all is to utilize the creative tension produced from deep within as the catalyst for accomplishment. For some, this challenge stands as a permanent obstruction, while for

Working for Vaad Hatzala, (L-R, standing): Irving Bunim, Rabbi Mordechai Kirshblum, Executive Vice-President of Mizrachi of America; Stephen Klein, Rabbi Pinchos Teitz, Rabbi Jacob Karlinsky

others this is the very conduit of accomplishment; the latter is true of Irving Bunim. Reared in the Lithuanian milieu where the intellect was revered and the emotions barely acknowledged, Irving, a sensitive youngster who sought his father's approval and direction, was hurt when they were not forthcoming. It was at this apex of inner tension that Bunim became mobilized to accomplish, and accomplish he did – focusing his intellect, emotional need for acceptance, his erudite and compelling oratorical ability and love for Torah to become Hashem's spokesman in a secular world.

In truth, the desire to please his father never really left him. That need to be loved, his family's poverty, and his love for Torah became the three forces that drove Bunim to prove himself, to accomplish things of great significance. (**A Fire in His Soul**, page 11)

In truth, there are two more elements that fueled Irving Bunim's soul and his desire to achieve – his parents' unconditional love for humanity, both Jew and gentile, and his unquenchable desire for *emes*. Many times we wonder why someone endowed with many talents and attributes never actualizes his full inherent potential. If that bothers and disturbs us, then Irving Bunim's manifest fulfillment of his potential should catapult us into action. Irving Bunim's son, Amos, comments that his father " . . . was a rare combination of event and personality; he was able to create so much because so much had to be created."

Irving Bunim's parents often . . . marveled at Irving's extraordinary religious convictions, his exceptional gifts of speech and memory, his energy, altruism and organizational skills. Modestly, they concluded that " . . . in some people the

National Council of Young Israel Annual Dinner, March 1951. (L-R): Meyer Weiner, Pinchas Iseson, Elijah Stein, Irving Bunim, Mayor Robert F. Wagner

flame of the soul burns more brightly for Torah than in others . . ," their son, indeed, was possessed of a unique neshamah. (**A Fire in His Soul**, page 14)

Irving Bunim:
A LEGACY OF ACCOMPLISHMENT

As history unfolds and events of life churn ever onward, the future is built upon a past whose singular details become increasingly unclear: individual achievement becomes blurred and absorbed in the greater brushstrokes of an "era." Nonetheless, the past is not one broad stroke; rather, it is composed of seemingly endless acts – great and small, intricate and obvious – threads of human activity that coalesce to form the tapestry of history. Some contribute a thread here and there, some more and some less, but there are few who actually define the events of an era and the "history" of future generations spawned by those events. Irving Bunim, then, is considered an architect of his era, of the future of Orthodox Jewry in America, and, by extension, throughout the world. Thus, it is impossible to recount all of his deeds, but it is necessary to know

...there are two more elements that fueled Irving Bunim's soul and his desire to achieve – his parents and his unquenchable desire for emes...

Irving Bunim is considered an architect of his era, of the future of Orthodox Jewry in America and, by extension, throughout the world.

and appreciate that he confronted the challenges Providence presented. With the destruction of European Jewry as the back-drop, he became a bridge from "what was" to "what will be," preserving the values of European Jewry while preparing a fertile environment for them to germinate and grow in a country where only few thought it possible.

YOUNG ISRAEL

In 1911, a group of young Orthodox activists were spurred into action to save Orthodox Jewish youth, upon hearing the news that Stephen Wise planned to open a branch of his Free Synagogue on the Lower East Side of Manhattan. Wise hoped to entice the Orthodox youth by offering his intellectual brand of Jewish observance in English, something not found in the *shtiblach* of their fathers. Choosing to negate the teachings of his ancestors, he presented Torah Judaism in a perverse manner. Because he was misguided, he was directly responsible for the fact that many Jews who could have been rescued during the Holocaust were not. By 1912, this neophyte activist movement became known as Young Israel [1], and it emerged at a time when Jewish youth were demanding greater participation within the synagogue structure and rituals.

These demands brought increased numbers of Jewish youth into active synagogue involvement, but after World War I a less religious element had become an entrenched part of the

National Council of Young Israel Dinner, Commodore Hotel, March 1972.
Presentation to Irving Bunim of a silver-covered copy of his book, 'Ethics from Sinai,'
(L-R): Nash Kestenbaum (national president), Irving Bunim, Rabbi Ephraim Sturm
(executive vice-president)

---

[1] Refer to the chapter on The Young Israel Movement, pg. 14

Young Israel movement. Even at this stage it must be emphasized, however, that without Young Israel, many American Jews may never have remained Torah observant, including his son's future father-in-law, Edward S. Silver, District Attorney of King's County, Brooklyn, New York, and judge of the Surrogate Court.

Yet Mr. Bunim had the prescience to know that a secularized presence would eventually devastate the hope for a strong Orthodoxy. In a brilliant move, using his hallmark clarity for the issues, sincere concern and respect for others, and power of persuasion, he decided that the best way to preserve the Young Israel movement was to work for change from *within*, resisting the dangerous lure of creating a new and separate entity. Entering into an arena of entrenched and disparate interests, Irving Bunim maneuvered issues and personalities with the precision of the most talented neurosurgeon, guided solely by his desire to see Young Israel remain an unadulterated Torah movement.

Pinchas Iseson, an important lay leader of Yeshiva Chaim Berlin, remembered Irving Bunim's lonely struggle, stating that, "Bunim single-handedly preserved Young Israel as a Torah movement . . ." Irving Bunim led the lonely and difficult battle to free the neophyte Young Israel movement from all influences other than those of Orthodoxy. In order to strengthen his position, he asked Dr. Bernard Revel, President of Yeshiva College, to help repel these forces. Dr. Revel called together the Young Israel leadership and, in unequivocal terms, clarified that a secularized approach to religion was totally antithetical to Torah and that the battle against this influence was one with no quarter.

Ultimately, Bunim successfully navigated issues and personalities, arriving at a resolution that completely removed the secular influence from within Young Israel. At the same time, he took steps to cement the spirit of Orthodoxy within Young Israel by inserting new requirements and standards into the Young Israel charter: all branches must have Shabbos and Yom Tov services, regular Torah learning, youth programs, *mechitzos* and Sabbath-observant officers. One can only imagine the lonely hours of mental anguish Bunim suffered as he worked tirelessly to secure Young Israel as a vital conduit for Torah observance in America. One need only consider the legions of young men and women studying in yeshivos, seminaries and *kollelim* around the globe to see that his vision was *lema'an Hashem*, for Hashem's sake. It is practically impossible to count how many of our finest Torah families are the direct product of – or were profoundly influenced by – Young Israel.

Rabbi Yosef Dov Soloveitchik reflected that, "Young Israel, led by Mr. Irving Bunim, did no less than save a whole generation of Jewish youth. Mr. Bunim never forgot that he lived in the United States, but he had a Torah *weltanschauung* in his mind and heart. He and his words radiated light – spiritually and physically. He worked for a great ideal and gave of himself completely, as a catalyst who guided a movement and was, in turn, guided by it. He never spoke of himself; he was humble, yet energetic and productive. He had a great sense of harmony and kindness and never tried to dominate a situation." Emotionally, Rabbi Soloveitchik once told Irving's son Amos that "every *gadol* who came from Europe had only one address in his pocket – the address of your father."

"Young Israel, led by Mr. Irving Bunim, did no less than save a whole generation of Jewish youth..."

CONNECTING WITH PEOPLE: TEACHER AND SPOKESMAN

One of Irving Bunim's most enduring accomplishments was his ability to connect with people. For 55 years, he taught *Pirkei Avos*, Ethics of the Fathers, both at the National Council of Young Israel and at Young Israel's annual mid-west conventions. His Torah lectures were filled with intellectualism, charm and humor. He employed his uncanny insight and understanding of others to attract them to Torah, in what can truly be called the beginning of the *baal teshuvah* movement in America. In each class, men and women were personally touched – an impact that changed the lives of many. Case in point: his classic, *Ethics From Sinai*, is in its 35th printing, having sold 100,000 sets, and it continues to influence the thoughts and practices of *baalei teshuvah* and traditionally Orthodox Jews today.

Irving Bunim served as President of the Rabbi Jacob Joseph School, transforming it from a small yeshiva into a major Torah center.

Rabbi Jacob Joseph School, Irving M. Bunim Mesifta, Edison, New Jersey

For three decades, through anguish and triumph, Irving Bunim served as President of the Rabbi Jacob Joseph School, transforming it from a small yeshiva into a major Torah center. During his tenure, the school's horizons expanded from day school to *mesivta* to rabbinic ordination, creating one of the finest contemporary Torah institutions in the country. Many of the students from these early years went on to become major Torah personalities in America and Israel.

Shortly after Irving Bunim became president, the New York State Board of Regents sought to revoke Rabbi Jacob Joseph School's accreditation (as well as that of Torah Vodaath, Tiferes Jerusalem, Crown Heights, Eitz Chaim and roughly two dozen other yeshivos) unless secular studies were taught in the morning hours. To this end the Board of Regents held a hearing in Albany, inviting the yeshiva representatives to attend.

As it turned out, the hearing took place on *Tishah B'Av*, the fast day commemorating (among other tragedies) the destruction of the First and Second Holy Temples. Thus, as Halachah requires, Bunim and his colleagues were unshaven and wearing sneakers. When the Board's attorney, Susan Brandeis, daughter of Supreme Court Justice Louis Brandeis, saw their unkempt appearance, she asked sharply, "Is this the way to come dressed to a Board of Regents hearing?" If her goal was to shock and unnerve the group, she only partially succeeded, never imagining the eloquence of the response she so rudely elicited. "Today is the anniversary of the destruction of the Temple in the year 70 of the Common Era. It is a law for Orthodox Jews to mourn and fast on this day. We are not permitted to eat, drink, shave or wear leather shoes for a period of 25 hours. It is a tragic and trying day for us, but due to our respect for this Board, we did not apply for a postponement." The room was still for a moment. Then Owen Young, Chairman of the Board of Regents and President of General Electric, said quietly, "Miss Brandeis, I think you owe these gentlemen an apology." She gave one.

Irving Bunim was one of the group's main spokesmen and he presented a most detailed case on behalf of the yeshivos. He offered statistics showing that despite years of secular studies in the afternoon, yeshiva students had collectively out-scored their non-yeshiva peers in Regents examinations. Duly weighing the evidence, the Board of Regents exempted the yeshivos from teaching secular subjects in the mornings.

Irving Bunim served as Vice-President of Torah Umesorah, the National Society for Hebrew Day Schools, from its inception until his death in 1980. His commitment, dedication and devotion to the building of day schools throughout the country was boundless. His leadership in Chinuch Atzmai, the religious school system in Israel, was an important dimension in the growth of the greatest network of Torah schools in the world.

RABBI AHARON KOTLER: A PARTNERSHIP ON BEHALF OF KLAL YISRAEL

The great Torah leader of the previous generation, Rabbi Aharon Kotler, spearheaded the rescue efforts of Vaad Hatzala[2] in which Irving Bunim served as chairman. Together, they worked with

Young Israel shipping packages of food and clothing to war refugees, 1945. (L-R): Hon. Edward S. Silver; top right, Irving Bunim, bottom right, Barry Berman

others to save and succor Europe's oppressed Jews. Irving Bunim fought valiantly against the secular Jewish establishment and their intransigent approach to rescue efforts. They felt that although human life was at stake, it was illegal to get involved with bribes, ransom and extralegal activities in order to save lives. The Vaad Hatzala, on the other hand, was deeply committed to Torah law and in matters of life and death Torah law states that *pekuach nefesh*, supersedes almost *all* law.

The secular establishment took their marching orders from Washington, while the Vaad Hatzala took theirs from Sinai. Rabbi Kotler, Rabbi Kalmanowitz

His commitment, dedication and devotion to the building of day schools throughout the country was boundless.

---

[2]Refer to the Chapter on the Vaad Hatzala, pg. 76

and Irving Bunim made many trips to Washington in order to obtain the assistance of the highest government officials in their rescue efforts. It must be stated that there were those in the Jewish (non-Orthodox) camp who actively sought to circumvent all salvation efforts, utilizing more than passive connections with like-minded individuals in the American government. Because of the Vaad's unrelenting efforts, Mr. Henry Morgenthau, Jr., the Secretary of the Treasury, became a strong ally and was helpful in opening the doors of many important officials[3], including Dean Acheson. This effort added a dimension to Bunim's dynamism that propelled him even further – stretching to the breaking point tight bonds of friendship, family and business. He had a remarkable and deeply held con-

Vaad Hatzala Testimonial Dinner honoring Hon. Henry Morgenthau Jr., Hon. William O'Dwyer and Hon. John Pehle at the Astor Hotel, December 1945. (L-R) : Irving Bunim, Hon. Henry Morgenthau, Jr., Hon. John Pehle, Hon. Herbert Tenzer

viction that every Jewish life in the world was as his own. His life and their lives were one and inseparable. When Jews suffered, Irving Bunim felt as if a piece of himself was dying. To this end, Bunim sacrificed with abandon his business and every personal comfort. This undaunted rescue effort by the few, against the wall of indifference and resistance of the many, was responsible for saving 100,000 Jewish lives.

Irving Bunim's relationship with Rabbi Aharon Kotler was historic and

---

[3]Bunim's belief in and subservience to *daas Torah* (viewpoints of the Torah leaders) and *emunas chachamim* (faith in the words of Torah leaders), is underscored in the following meeting with Henry Morgenthau, Jr., the Secretary of the Treasury of the United States. In February of 1945, Bunim, together with Rabbis Aharon Kotler and Avraham Kalmanowitz, met with Morgenthau to secure a deal with the infamous Heinrich Himmler, head of the German SS, to ransom thousands of Jews from Europe. The Vaad Hatzala was seeking government approval to transfer $937,000 to American agents in Switzerland, and Morgenthau was essential to gain this approval. Upon hearing Bunim's request, the secretary remarked, "Ransom! Surely you know that the motto of the United States is 'Millions for defense but not one cent for tribute.' We can't do it." Watching Bunim's face, Rabbi Kotler understood Morgenthau's response. In rapid-fire Yiddish, Rabbi Kotler told Bunim, "You tell him that if he cannot help rescue his fellow Jews at this time, then he is worth nothing, and his position is worth nothing, because one Jewish life is worth more than all the positions in Washington." Morgenthau did not understand Yiddish, but Reb Aharon's tone and intensity was unmistakable. Sensitive to the protocol involved in dealing with a man of Morgenthau's position, Bunim was attempting to formulate a properly worded response to relay Reb Aharon's words. When Reb Aharon saw Morgenthau's relieved look upon hearing Bunim's polite entreaty, Reb Aharon shot forth, "No! No! Bunim, tell him exactly what I said." Bunim knew that their chance to save thousands of lives came down to this one moment. Speaking deliberately, while never taking his eyes off of Morgenthau's face, Bunim delivered the message. Morgenthau looked from Bunim to Rabbis Kotler and Kalmanowitz. Then he sat down at his desk, his head resting on his folded arms. Many minutes passed by before he rose and stood directly in front of Reb Aharon, while telling Bunim to translate: "Tell the Rabbi that I am a Jew," Morgenthau said with great dignity and emotion. "Tell him that I'm willing to give up my life – not just my position – for my people."

First Chinuch Atzmai Dinner, January 1956. (L-R): Rabbi Yosef Dov Soloveitchik, Rabbi Aharon Kotler, Irving Bunim

legendary. Rabbi Kotler always referred to Bunim as his *shutaf*, partner, in building the greatest Torah institution in the world, Beth Medrash Govoha, in Lakewood, New Jersey. As a man endowed with many great attributes of character, a man of manifold accomplishments, originality and success, Irving Bunim's love, care and concern for this great *gadol* cannot be described adequately in words. Rabbi Kotler was truly the driving, motivating and most dynamic force in Irving. Bunim's life. *Reb* Aharon, as he is affectionately known, was Irving Bunim's *rebbe*, his mentor, his defender and his friend. In Rabbi Kotler, he saw a Torah giant who represented the total honesty and integrity of Torah. This was the most meaningful principle in Irving Bunim's life. As a consequence of this relationship, his life reached its zenith.

After Irving Bunim's death, Rabbi Yaakov Yitzchak Ruderman, *Rosh Yeshiva* of Yeshiva Ner Israel in Baltimore, Maryland, commented, "If not for Mr.

Bunim, Rabbi Kotler would not have succeeded in America." At that time, Rabbi Kotler's concept of young men studying Torah *lishmah* was totally unacceptable to the American Orthodox community, who viewed it as archaic and atavistic. He said, "Mr. Bunim opened all the closed doors for Rabbi Kotler and brought substantial support from the aristocracy of the American lay leaders."

Perhaps the single most sustained and eloquent *hesped* ever included in Beth Medrash Govoha's Annual Dinner Journal appeared shortly after Bunim's death. In part it read, "**Words fail us.**

"Mr. Bunim opened all the closed doors for Rabbi Kotler and brought substantial support from the aristocracy of the American lay leaders."

Presentation of Sefer Torah by Rabbi Moshe Feinstein to Irving Bunim, Chinuch Atzmai Dinner, June 1963. (L-R) Stephen Klein, Irving Bunim, Rabbi Moshe Feinstein, Zev Wolfson. (L-R, back) Rabbi Yaakov Yitzchak Ruderman, Rabbi Chaim Mordechai. Katz.

Our mind is numb, our heart is heavy, as we search for words to even briefly eulogize this master of eloquence whose words poured forth from the depths of a sensitive soul and was graced with a brilliant mind which had absorbed the teachings and wisdom of the luminaries of our time. Mr. Bunim was blessed with a broadly appealing eloquence. He never lost his common touch and his American background, as he warmly, strongly, brilliantly and majestically articulated the basic tenets, the laws, the ethics and *mussar* of our Prophets and Sages, as well as the words and wishes of the *gedolim* of our time.

"Mr. Bunim stood proud and unafraid on the podium or in private pleadings – for his golden tone only translated and reshaped the fire and the spirit, the heart and authenticity of a Rabbi Elchonon Wasserman, a Rabbi Meir Shapiro, a Rabbi Avraham Kalmanowitz and a Rabbi Aharon Kotler, who was his *rebbe muvhak*. Together, master and disciple, fiery spirit and talented layman, they forged a Vaad Hatzala, helped Rabbi Mendlowitz found Torah Umesorah

Beth Medrash Govoha, the jeweled crown of Rav Aharon, was Mr. Bunim's most beloved creation.

Rabbi Aharon Kotler speaking at a Torah Umesorah Dinner, 1956

and answered the call of Israeli *gedolim* to launch Chinuch Atzmai. However, Beth Medrash Govoha, the jeweled crown of Rav Aharon, was Mr. Bunim's most beloved creation. He chaired its Board and involved leading philanthropists in its endeavors."

When Rabbi Yosef Dov Soloveitchik came to be *menachem avel* he said to the Bunim family, "You should know that your father was a *malach* of *chesed* and a *gadol hador*." The great *posek* of our age, Rabbi Moshe Feinstein, said, "This great loss is not a private mourning, but, rather, a public mourning."

CONCLUSION:
THE LEGACY CONTINUES –
FROM FATHER TO SON

A number of years ago a well-known rabbi from Queens, New York, called Rabbi Amos Bunim to relate the following incident:

(L-R): Rabbi Shabse Frankel, Stephen Klein, Menashe Stein, and Irving Bunim with packages for overseas relief, shown at the Vaad Hatzala Warehouse (1946).

First aid extended by Vaad Hatzala through the synagogue ambulances

The Tel Aviv Hotel, on the corner of Forest Avenue and Seventh Street, was purchased and remodeled for an expanded beis medrash and additional dormitory rooms for Beth Medrash Govoha.

"A young woman confided in me that she was dating a certain young man from Argentina to whom she desired to become engaged. However, she was uncertain of his ancestry, and asked if I could research this for her. She agreed to bring her perspective husband to meet me and, in fact, we met a short time after this initial conversation. The young man made a pleasant impression, presenting himself as Juarez Bunim Sanchez. Piqued, my curiosity got the better of me and I asked the origin of his obviously inconsonant middle name. The young man explained that his parents, and hundreds of others, came to Argentina after surviving the Holocaust through the efforts of the Vaad Hatzala, and that the person most responsible for their being ransomed from the Germans during the war, and safe relocation afterwards, was Irving Bunim. In honor of his heroic efforts on their behalf, hundreds of children born to these survivors were given the middle name Bunim."

This sequel to the above vignette is supplied from a first-person experience that Rabbi Amos Bunim encountered on a trip to Cuba soon after his marriage:

"While touring the market area in the city we were visiting, I had the distinct feeling that a certain man was star-ing at me, and as we slowly made our way down the street, his gaze remained riveted upon me. Finally, I saw him leave his store and walk quickly in our direction. We were not in a hurry and he soon caught up with us. Politely, he asked if my name is Bunim. I nodded. He then asked if my first name was Irving and smiled broadly when I countered that it was Amos and that I was Irving's son. The man related that he was saved from the Holocaust and

In honor of his heroic efforts ... hundreds of children born to these survivors were given the middle name Bunim.

Irving Bunim making the appeal at a Beth Medrash Govoha Dinner, December 1959. (L-R): Irving Bunim, Rabbi Kotler, Hershel Rubinstein, Rabbi Leib Cywiak.

Ground-breaking ceremony of Beth Medrash Govoha, May 1963.
(L-R): Dr. Marvin Zuravin, Irving Bunim, Michael Gertner, Martin Klein.

provided with all necessary documents to rebuild his life in Cuba by the Vaad Hatzala. Before leaving Europe, he saw a newspaper published by a Jewish agency that chronicled his situation accompanied by a picture of Irving Bunim, the one most responsible for his group's visas and relocation. He remarked that when he saw me he was shaken by my similarity to my father and was moved by an overwhelming emotional wave of memories from what he endured in Europe; hence, the continual stare for which he apologized. Apology completed, however, he broke into a wide smile, took me by the arm and introduced me to the merchants up and down the street, quite a number of whom asked me to thank my father for his dedication on their behalf."

Irving Bunim speaking at the Chanukas Habayis for the new Beis Medrash building of Beth Medrash Govoha, May 1964. Among those present were: Charles Bendheim, Martin Klein, Samuel C. Feuerstein, Senator Harrison Williams (N.J.), Ludwig Jesselson, Moses Feuerstein, Moses Morgenstern, Jacob Cohen, Rabbi Dovid Lifshitz, Rabbi Zalman Reichman, Rabbi Moshe Feinstein, Rabbi Yaakov Kamenetsky, Kopyczinitzer Rebbe, Rabbi Joseph Baumol, Rabbi Pinchas Teitz, Rabbi Mordechai Gifter, Rabbi Simcha Zisel Broyde

Torah Umesorah Dinner, 1956. (L-R): Rabbi Amos Bunim, Irving Bunim, Rabbi Aharon Kotler

Rabbi Amos Bunim was raised in the shadow of his father's legendary deeds, and he accepted the challenge to fill the void left by his father's death. Though Amos has obscured his actions in unswerving dedication to his father's memory, he is, in every consideration, his father's son and successor. Confidant to the *Roshei Yeshiva* and reliable bearer of their directives, Amos had dedicated his life to the growth of Torah in *Eretz Yisrael* and America.

He continues to be involved in the growth and development of the very same organizations served by his father, allowing Amos to help provide the continuity and stability so fundamental to the success of these vital institutions. A private

man, Amos almost never speaks about himself, only his father. Thus, the greatest compliment one can pay to this man is that through his deeds his father's legacy continues.

Amos claims senators and federal judges among his admirers, and to them his word is the essence of truth. "Our mutual friend, Rabbi Amos Bunim, is, indeed, a remarkable man whose many outstanding contributions in the field of religious education of Jewish youth, both in Israel and in America, stand as an inspiration to all who have been fortunate enough to know him. He is one of the most dedicated men I have ever known." The pre-

Front Row (L-R): Irving Bunim, Rabbi Aharon Kotler, Rabbi Dovid Lifshitz. Behind them (L-R): Sarah Silver, Hon. Edward S. Silver, Rabbi Amos Bunim, Stanley Rudolf

Presentation of Sefer Torah to Irving Bunim at the Beth Medrash Govoha Dinner at the Hilton Hotel, December 1970. (L-R): Martin Klein, Rabbi Osher Katz, Rabbi Shneur Kotler (Rosh HaYeshiva), Irving Bunim, Rabbi Amos Bunim, Nash Kestenbaum, Rabbi Leib Cywiak, Ernst Bodenheimer, Hon. Herbert Tenzer.

Irving Bunim's great achievements and contributions for hatzalah and the growth of Torah in America serve as an inspiration to future generations.

ceding words were penned by U. S. Senator Richard Russel subsequent to a trip to Israel with Rabbi Amos Bunim.

It should be noted that through Amos' relationship with Senators Russel and Smathers and Congressman Passman – built upon their respect for his impeccable honesty and integrity – hundreds of millions of dollars in U.S. aid was made available for Torah vocational schools and social institutions in Israel, and for the *yeshivos gedolos* in America. These accomplishments are generally known; what is not known, however, is the crucial role Amos played in steering billions of dollars in U.S. aid and armaments to Israel in the months before the Six Day War in June, 1967, and during the Yom Kippur War in 1973. Nor did the individual Jew escape Amos' all encompassing attention. Many times the great *posek* of our generation, Rabbi Moshe Feinstein, *zl*, dispatched Amos to intercede for

Jews facing dire legal circumstances. One such mission earned him the everlasting friendship and respect of Federal Judge John D. Larkins of the Eastern District of North Carolina, who closed one of his letters to Amos regarding the successful resolve of a case Amos pleaded before him with the words, "All I can request, my friend, in closing, is that you continue to keep in touch with me in order that our friendship shall not soon perish. In fact, you have promised to revisit me on the occasion of my 80th birthday…"

Irving Bunim's great achievements and contributions for *hatzalah* and the growth of Torah in America serve as an inspiration to future generations. As he stood in his lifetime in total resolve for the honor of Hashem, so has Hashem bestowed eternal honor upon him in the minds and hearts of *Klal Yisrael*. Indeed, he fulfilled the mandate of Rabbi Rafael Shapiro, his *Rosh Yeshiva* in Volozhin so long ago, "to build Torah in America."

Postscript

While this article was in preparation, Amos' life partner, Mrs. Sarah Bunim, passed away suddenly. It should be noted that she was a dauntless partner in all of her husband's efforts on behalf of Torah and world Jewry. Mrs. Bunim was an eighth generation descendant of the *Vilna Gaon*. Rabbi Bunim expressed that the *Gaon's* words regarding his own wife so aptly fits his descendant: *"Ein erech v'ein temurah*, [her] value cannot be evaluated; there is no replacement."

Irving Bunim and his son Amos dancing at the 1963 Chinuch Atzmai Siyum haSefer.
In the background clapping is George Klein, Stephen Klein's son.

Stephen Klein 1907-1978

A MAN OF VISION AND ACTION

The Holocaust was proceeding in full, cruel, and evil force. The center of Jewish gravity was moving to America, a place where Torah education and Orthodox life only had a limited impact.

The challenges were manifold: How to save Jewish lives in Europe. Helping the surviving remnant rebuild their lives in countries where they would be welcome. Proving that a Torah-based society could live and thrive in the United States. Building yeshivos and girls' schools, and nurturing the growth of a generation that would make Jewish education its first priority. Creating advanced Torah institutions that could take the place of the Slobodkas and Pressburgs that were no more. Proving that Shabbos observance was not a ticket to poverty. Showing that even a big business could be closed on Shabbos and still win the patronage and respect of the broad American community.

In short – the challenge was to build a nation on the quicksand of death, pessimism, and precedent that pro-

claimed Ellis Island as the permanent barrier to "Old-World" Jewish life.

And if there was one man who embodied the answers to all these challenges – his name was Stephen Klein.

He combined family tradition, courage, vision and the audacity to defy the doomsayers who "knew" it couldn't be done. Instead, Stephen Klein plunged ahead and proved that it **should, could,** and **would** be done. Today's burgeoning Torah institutions and communities are his legacy.

Stephen Klein arrived in 1938 as a refugee from Nazi tyranny. Without resources, except for his incredible energy and dedication, he quickly founded a high-profile business, Barton's Bonbonniere, and played a leading role in saving Jewish lives and building major Torah institutions in America and Israel. Barton's was the only large-scale *shomer Shabbos* retailer in the country, an unprecedented *Kiddush Hashem*. Its sales campaigns for yeshivos and day schools were a mainstay of the annual fundraising for Jewish education. The full-page newspaper ads and candle lighting announcements sponsored by Barton's were the most far-reaching form of mass education and outreach to the broader Jewish community.

FAMILY AND BACKGROUND

The Klein family had a rich history of devotion to Torah and to the *gedolei Yisrael* spanning several generations. Stephen Klein's forebears accompanied the renowned Rabbi Shimon Sofer (grandson of the *Chasam Sofer*) when he left his post as rabbi of Mattersdorf in Burgenland (Austria) to become the chief rabbi of Cracow in Poland. The closeness between the *rav* and the Klein family was such that they could not think of letting him go to a large new community without loyal supporters. Reb Kalman Klein, Stephen Klein's grandfather, was a pillar of the Cracow community and one of the last in that glorious community to die peacefully, in August 1939, surrounded by his children and grandchildren, just before the Nazis invaded Poland in September 1939.

Reb Kalman's son, Reb Simcha Klein, moved from Cracow to Marienbad in 1916 and from there to Vienna. During World War I, large numbers of Galician Jews, including many of their *rabbanim* and chassidic *rebbes*, fled to Vienna to escape the battlefields where Austrian and Russian troops were engaged in lethal combat and civilians were caught in the crossfire. After the war, Vienna was host to more refugees from the carnage and destruction.

Some of the newcomers discarded their strictly Orthodox heritage. Reb Simcha Klein was one of those who looked for opportunities to strengthen *Yiddishkeit* and help develop Torah and *chesed* in his new home.

He was a follower of the Czortkover and Belzer *Rebbes,* and became *gabbai* of the synagogue of the Bikovsker *Rav,* Rabbi Chaim Pinter. He was also close with the Kopyczinitzer *Rebbe* in Vienna, and was frequently involved in his many efforts to help people in need. Reb Simcha's home was often the first address for newcomers from Galicia, for he and his wife always made room for guests.

Someone who personally experienced his hospitality told this anecdote:

"My father came to Vienna when he was diagnosed with a serious illness. The Klein family made him feel very much at home, and he stayed there while receiving medical treatment from one of Vienna's world-famous specialists. Sadly, although he received such kindness and the best treatment, the illness could not be cured and he died in Vienna. When I came to Vienna some months later, I was a young yeshiva graduate with little to my name other than my father's

Rabbi Shimon Sofer

Reb Simcha's home was often the first address for newcomers from Galicia, for he and his wife always made room for guests.

Reb Simcha Klein and his wife, Yachet

Stephen Klein never forgot the advice and wise words of the Chofetz Chaim. Much of his life's work reflected his determination to fulfill this charge.

reputation as a *talmid chacham*. I was still in shock over his death, for I had not even been able to come to Vienna to participate in his funeral. I had the address where my father had stayed, which happened to be the Klein home, and made my way there... hoping to meet someone who could tell me something of his last pain-wracked days. I turned into the street where he had spent his last weeks and as I looked up at the house, I burst into tears. All the feelings of grief and worry that I had held back suddenly burst forth like a torrent, for my loss, for my father dying so young, so alone, leaving all of his children without even having been able to say good-bye.

"I wept and wept, the tears dripping to the immaculate sidewalk of this elegant street. I do not know how long I stood there, but suddenly I felt a soft handkerchief of fine silk wiping the tears, and I heard a gentle voice whispering words of comfort. I opened my eyes and saw a dignified gentleman, trying to bring me out of my bitter grief. It was Reb Simcha Klein. He did not know me, he did not know why I was weeping, but he was a paragon of *chesed* delivered with uncommon sensitivity and delicacy."

Reb Simcha established a wholesale chocolate business and as his sons matured and joined him, the business grew into one of Vienna's largest commercial suppliers. His son Stephen, who was born in 1907, quickly became the major figure in the growth and development of the firm.

When the *Chofetz Chaim* visited Vienna in 1923, for the first Knessiah Gedolah of Agudath Israel, Reb Simcha Klein brought Stephen to him to receive his blessing. The saintly sage said to the young man, "May you be successful, and in all your endeavors, sanctify the Name of Hashem!" Stephen Klein never forgot those words. Much of his life's work reflected his determination to fulfull this charge.

ESCAPE FROM THE NAZIS

By the time the Nazis entered Austria in March 1938, after that country voted overwhelmingly to merge with Germany (the *Anschluss*), Stephen Klein was a rising young business leader. A friend alerted him to the fact that his main business competitor was a Nazi supporter, who was already making plans to ensure the prompt confiscation of the Klein company and Stephen's arrest as its principal executive.

Stephen Klein knew that hesitation could be fatal. Even though his wife, Regina, was expecting their third child, he left the country overnight, assuring his family that as soon as he got to Belgium he would find ways to bring them to safety. Working with his customary diligence, it took him only a few months to extricate his family and bring them to Belgium and from there to New York. His five brothers and two sisters fled to other countries and eventually, through his assistance, were all brought to America before the war. His father, however, who was in Cracow caring for his grandfather, was caught in a predicament which led to his death at the hands of the Nazis. Isaac, Stephen's youngest brother, stayed with his grandfather and was sent to Auschwitz. He was miraculously saved and later came to the United States.

BUILDING A BUSINESS IN AMERICA

Stephen Klein's business career in New York did not get off to an auspicious start. His savings, business connections, and familiar environment

Barton's store opening. (L-R): Stephen Klein, Martin Klein, unknown, and Herbert Tenzer

Crown Heights at that time was a prestigious address, a comfortable and affluent bastion of the American-Jewish middle class. Most of its Jews were members of large and flourishing non-Orthodox congregations. Rabbi Joseph Baumol, a *rav* who had recently arrived from Poland and who was a student of the famous Lubliner *Rav*, Rabbi Meir Shapiro, had been appointed in 1935, as rabbi of the local Orthodox synagogue. Rabbi Baumol, who knew the Kleins from Vienna, was to play a major role in introducing Stephen Klein to leading communal personalities, and helping him forge strategic partnerships in commercial and public affairs. As a result, Stephen Klein soon felt at home in his new community.

It was in the tiny and ill-equipped kitchen of Stephen Klein's first apartment that he embarked on his first chocolate-making venture in his new country.

were left behind in Europe. In New York, he had little more than his energy and ingenuity. The entire family, including four younger brothers and two sisters, lived in very modest apartments in Brooklyn.

It was in the tiny and ill-equipped kitchen of Stephen's first apartment that he embarked on his first chocolate-making venture in his new country.

Although unknown, and unfamiliar with the American business scene, Stephen Klein was a quick learner. Within weeks, he learned which recipes would be popular in the different ethnic neighborhoods of New York. Equally important, he acquired enough of a command of English to be an effective salesman from his attractively painted pushcart. Soon all the family members were drafted to help sell the chocolate delicacies. Armed with a small but steady home business, Stephen Klein felt confident moving from his first humble apartment to the vibrant Jewish community of Crown Heights.

Handing out dreidels at a Barton's store on Chanukah

Giving out Simchas Torah flags at a Barton's store

> "He had such a breadth of vision, although he had been in this country only a year or two – he already understood how American business works."

Before long he had plans for much larger ventures than a few pushcarts manned by family members. A New York candy manufacturer who lived in Crown Heights was impressed by the creative and talented young entrepreneur and offered him the opportunity of a joint venture. Although their partnership was a brief one, it introduced Stephen Klein to the world of American confectionery production and marketing.

It was then that he began to develop a plan – to match the quality and elegance of European confectioners with the large-scale marketing and distribution systems that dominated the United States' food business. However, there were two seemingly insurmountable obstacles which would have made anyone else give up the dream. First, who would trust a recent immigrant with the capital needed to open a factory and chain of retail stores? And second, how could anyone hope to succeed in operating large retail stores in New York that were closed on Shabbos, America's main shopping day?

A friend of his reminisced:

"The plan seemed so impossible that I asked him, 'Why don't you just look at the Jewish market? Produce some high-quality pareve chocolates for the observant community to serve for dessert at the Shabbos meals and give as gifts for special occasions.'

"With clarity and conviction, Stephen answered me: 'Why should someone swim in a pond, when he can swim in the ocean?'

"He had such a breadth of vision, that although he had been in this country only a year or two, he already understood how American business works. The Orthodox Jewish market was small, and he planned to launch a big venture, to have his stores on every major shopping thoroughfare in the region."

Unlikely though it seemed, he found a partner who was willing to help make his vision a reality. Herbert Tenzer was a young and promising attorney, an Orthodox Jew with a strong commitment to the community and a willingness to share in Stephen Klein's dream. Tenzer's capital and connections made it possible to create Barton's Bonbonniere – a business empire that would also be the cornerstone of many of the major Torah and *chesed* projects of the era.

One by one, he opened Barton's stores in prime locations throughout New York. He chose major shopping streets, where the sight of shutters rolled down at five o'clock on a Friday afternoon had never been seen before.

The existence of *shomer Shabbos* stores, selling the finest quality chocolates in the heart of the busiest shopping districts, inspired wonder and disbelief. Several newspapers ran articles about the strange phenomenon.

Years later, members of the Klein family still meet people who tell them that this public display of Shabbos observance gave their parents the courage to maintain Shabbos observance in their own livelihoods.

Within five years there were fifteen Barton's stores in prime retail locations in and around New York, designed by the finest architects and planners. Eventually, there were seventy-five Barton's stores in major city locations, all closed on Shabbos and *Yom Tov*. The Barton's factory employed over four hundred Jews, most of them survivors, who earned a decent living without compromising their observance of Torah and *mitzvos*.

From the very first production run of Barton's products for *Pesach*, these quality and novel products provided a fundraising opportunity for Torah institutions and Jewish organizations. Yeshiva students and parents took

Rabbi Kornmehl, brother-in-law of Stephen Klein and Chief Mashgiach at the Barton's Factory

orders for the Barton's products and the institutions received much-needed income from the sales. This was just one example of Stephen Klein's vision of business working for the Jewish community.

Stephen Klein insisted that Barton's products satisfy the most exacting *kashrus* standards. A suggestion was made that several innovative and desirable confections could be made if Barton's pioneered in producing kosher gelatin, a critical ingredient. Mr. Klein's older sister, Rosa, was married to a great *talmid chacham* and expert in

(R-L) Rabbi Aharon Kotler in discussion with the Mattersdorfer Rav, and Rabbi Nachum Kornmehl, brother-in-law of Stephen Klein.

The existence of shomer Shabbos stores selling the finest quality chocolates in the heart of the busiest shopping districts inspired wonder and disbelief.

kashrus – the *gaon* Rabbi Nachum Kornmehl. He had been ordained at the age of eighteen by the renowned Altstadter *Rav*, and had been appointed a *dayan* in Vienna, at the age of nineteen. Like Stephen Klein's other siblings, the Kornmehls had been brought to the United States by Stephen, and Rabbi Kornmehl was bound to Stephen by love and gratitude. In this country, he served as *rav* in Albany, New York, and later in Cedarhurst, and was a respected *posek*. He was consulted to resolve difficult *kashrus* issues for manufacturers throughout the country, including Barton's.

Naturally, when Barton's sought to develop a kosher gelatin, Rabbi Kornmehl was called upon to assure its *kashrus*. Working hand in hand with technical experts, they developed a method to produce kosher gelatin meeting the highest criteria for *kashrus*. But Stephen Klein would not sanction the production of this new form of gelatin without the approval of Rabbi Aharon Kotler, the great *rosh yeshiva* to whom he had become attached. Despite his enormous respect and admiration for his own brother-in-law, nothing would be permitted without the approval of Rav Aharon. Only when a written *teshuvah* from Rav Aharon was in his hands did Klein give the order to proceed with the production of kosher gelatin.[1]

> "Stephen Klein had a way of listening to people... it did not matter how busy he was; if he gave you an appointment he would ignore everything else and focus only on you."

ADVOCATE FOR TORAH AND *CHESED*

The rapidity of Stephen Klein's business success is a remarkable saga in its own right, but at the same time that he was creating an empire of enticing sweets, he was rapidly becoming a prominent figure in the Jewish community. Rabbi Joseph Baumol, in whose *shul* he *davened* recalled:

"Stephen Klein had a way of listening to people...it did not matter how busy he was: if he gave you an appointment he would ignore everything else and focus only on you. When someone came to him with a problem, regardless of who it was, he would listen to every word and genuinely try to help."

Stephen Klein was a philanthropist par excellence. He enjoyed a special relationship with many of the *roshei yeshiva* and Jewish lay leaders. However, his closest association was with the renowned Rabbi Aharon Kotler, *Rosh HaYeshiva* of Beth Medrash Govoha in Lakewood. A prominent

Vaad Hatzala delegation, with Stephen Klein and Herbert Tenzer in attendance.

---

1. Rabbi Henoch Cohen of Chinuch Atzmai, who brought the *teshuvah* from Rav Aharon's apartment in Boro Park to the Barton's Factory, is the source of this information.

contemporary community leader, Dr. Marvin Schick, who worked closely with both Rav Aharon and Mr. Klein, recalls:

"I never saw such a relationship of total devotion by a philanthropist and lay leader to a *rosh yeshiva*, as that of Stephen Klein to *HaGaon* Rav Aharon Kotler. He followed Rav Aharon's orders like a servant. He did not always agree with him, but he complied with his requests with all his heart and resources."

Together with his close friend Irving Bunim, Stephen Klein quickly became a major leader in Vaad Hatzala during and after World War II. Vaad Hatzala, the rescue committee of the Orthodox rabbinate and the *roshei yeshiva*, was founded at the behest of Rabbi Chaim Ozer Grodzenski of Vilna, to save the Torah leaders and students of Eastern Europe. As the war went on, the Vaad expanded its activities to general rescue work. More than once, he journeyed to Washington with Bunim and his business partner Herbert Tenzer, to accompany Rabbi Aharon Kotler and other rabbinic leaders to intercede with senior government officials. He brought to the team, practical skills as a business leader, immense energy, dedication and his personal familiarity with the plight of European Jewry. Unlike the other lay leaders, he had narrowly escaped the clutches of Nazi terror, and he had rescued many of his own kin in the nick of time. When he confronted power with truth, he could back his words with personal experience.

He used his contacts with civic and political leaders in New York and Washington on behalf of Vaad Hatzala. At his initiative, Mayor Paul O'Dwyer hosted fundraising meetings at Gracie Mansion, the official residence of the mayor of New York.

Stephen Klein at a Vaad Hatzala dinner, Paris, 1947

The Kleins were connected by marriage to the Reichmann family, which had managed to leave occupied Europe and find haven in the international city of Tangier, Morocco. In 1924, Tangier had come under the joint control of Britian, France, Italy and Spain. During World War II it was administered by Spain, which was a neutral country that had cordial relations with Germany. As a result, packages and mail could be sent from Tangier to Nazi-occupied countries and, with the assistance of Vaad Hatzala and Stephen Klein, the Reichmanns used their Tangier connection for communications and sending packages to the

As a member of the Vaad Hatzala delegations to Washington, he brought practical skills as a business leader, immense energy, dedication, and personal familiarity with the plight of European Jewry.

Chairman of Vaad committees, (L-R) standing: Nathan Hausman, Irving Bunim, Stephen Klein, Menashe Stein, Herbert Tenzer, Moe Rosenburg, Martin Lasher, Jacob Goodman. (L-R) sitting: Rabbi Simon Langer, Rabbi Shabse Frankel, Joseph Rosenzweig, Rabbi Simon Kornitzer, Rabbi Bernard Bergman

ghettos of Europe. Naturally, a popular component of many of these packages was Barton's chocolate, which the recipients could sell or barter for necessities of life.

When the war ended, the activities of Vaad Hatzala were expanded to encompass the survivors of the concentration camps; the Polish Jews in the Soviet Union awaiting repatriation; orphaned Jewish children, including those who had been placed with gentile families for safety; and stranded refugees in all corners of the globe. The Vaad had representatives and emissaries in many of these places, but not enough to meet the vast needs.

In 1946, Stephen Klein, chairman of the Immigration Committee of the Vaad Hatzala, volunteered to go to Europe as an accredited officer of the UNRRA (the United Nations Refugee and Rescue Authority) to spend six months working for the Jews in DP camps, opening yeshivos, arranging visas and supplying affidavits for thou-

In 1946, he volunteered to go to Europe as a UNRRA captain, and spent six months helping Jews in DP camps – a remarkable self-sacrifice.

(L-R): Saul Klein, Herbert Tenzer, Eli Klein, Stephen Klein, Martin Klein preparing candies to be shipped to Europe via Vaad Hatzala

sands of Jews to emigrate to the United States. For a man to leave his wife and young children, and the new business that was still growing under his leadership, was an extraordinary display of self-sacrifice.

His friends and associates arranged a dinner at an elegant Manhattan hotel to wish him success in his magnanimous undertaking. On behalf of the community, Rabbi Baumol quipped that he was personally looking forward to the trip because it would be a "vacation" for him, since when Stephen is in New York, he calls from his office at 6:00 AM with a stream of ideas and plans needing urgent action. To this, Irving Bunim, the master of ceremonies, responded: "Can you imagine what a vacation it will be for me? He normally calls me at five, because he's too respectful to wake the rabbi at that hour!" These good-natured gibes reflect clearly the incredible level of dedication and energy that Stephen Klein put into communal affairs.

When he returned from a grueling six months in Europe, wearing a captain's uniform of the United Nations Rescue and Relief Agency, Stephen Klein spoke with passion of the terrible

Stephen Klein as a UNRRA captain with orphaned children in Europe.

*Stephen Klein
presenting a Menorah
to L. Vasse,
of the
French Foreign Ministry,
in recognition of
his cooperation
with the
Vaad Hatzala program
(1947)*

deprivations he had seen and the urgent imperative for American Jewry to rally behind the European survivors.

In an interview with WEVD radio, he shared these comments:

"If you receive a letter saying that your relative is living in an apartment, don't think for a moment that he has two or three rooms to himself. I have seen large rooms divided among four couples! Each couple occupies one corner of the room, and there is no curtain to give them privacy! If there are children, they live in the corner with their parents. All the couples in the room share one stove!

"DPs receive two kinds of rations... they draw dry rations from the kitchen. At the present time, each person gets 1200 calories a day. How does that compare with what you eat? Just get yourself a calorie chart and add it up. You are probably eating three times as much. If you possibly can, please send our DPs 11-pound food packages to supplement their 1200-calorie diet. If you have discovered a relative in one of the camps, you have your own name and address

to whom to send food. If you have no one in particular to whom to send food, write me in care of the Vaad Hatzala Rescue Committee, 132 Nassau Street, and we will give you the addresses... Money does a man little good in Germany. Food, clothing and cigarettes have the greatest value.

"My job in Germany was to set up schools so that Jewishness could be

*(L-R): Miss Isabel Jacobs of Paris Vaad Emigration Office,
then working at Vaad office in Stuttgart; Mr. Weisenberg,
American Vice-Consul, Paris; Mr. L. Vasse, Mr. Levi,
"Captain" Stephen Klein, Dr. Samuel Schmidt, (unidentified)
Mr. Matthew Spoiffer and Rabbi Chodosh.*

saved in Europe. In every camp you will find children running around loose, with nothing to do, no toys to play with, no jobs to do around the house as in a normal household... While I was in Germany, the Vaad Hatzala set up 40 religious schools in the various D.P. camps.

Stephen Klein returned to the United States with a fiery drive to do everything possible for the tragic victims of Nazi persecution.

"As the major Jewish organization concerned with Jewish religious rehabilitation among European Jewry, it is part of Vaad Hatzala's duty to strengthen the religious life in the camps and provide them with the necessary ceremonial articles and the things which mean Jewish living to Orthodox Jews. The Vaad Hatzala provides the religious communities in Germany with *mikvaos*, religious slaughter knives, holy Torahs, prayer books, *taleisim, tefillin*, and *mezuzos*. It is very gratifying to know that there are many marriages in the camps, sometimes as many as five and more a week. The Vaad Hatzala provides the newlyweds with a dowry of $25 and two bed sheets...

(L-R, seated): Mr. Levi, Rabbi Morris Fischel of California, Mr. Stephen Klein, Mr. Isaac Sternbuch, Mr. Herman Landau, Miss Isabel Jacobs. (L-R, standing): Rabbi Chodosh of New York, Mr. Morris Unger, and Rabbi S. Wasserman of Detroit

"I'll never forget the mother in Munchenberg Camp who came to me with her child on her back...because the child had no shoes to wear. 'It's all very nice for Vaad Hatzala to make schools, but how is my child going to go to school if he has no shoes to wear?' So we had to give the child a pair of shoes...And so I am back to continue my work for the Vaad Hatzala. If we can help you, write us at 132 Nassau Street. We are ready to do everything we can for your loved ones overseas."

Stephen Klein returned to the United States with a fiery drive to do everything possible for the tragic survivors of the Holocaust, and determined to prevent bureaucratic delays. Factionalism and turf wars among the Jewish relief organizations distressed him greatly, and he resolved to overcome such obstacles. As he wrote in an impassioned letter in 1947 to Rabbi Israel Rosenberg, president of the Agudath HaRabbonim*:

Class in Rescue Children Inc. Center, Aix-les-Bains, France (1946)

---

* See complete copy of the letter on pg. 434

"How can I help but write this letter after realizing that it is already several months since the Evaluation Committee went to Europe; that they did not find time as yet to go to Germany, Austria or Poland where our Orthodox brethren are faced with grave problems, but instead the committee is still in Paris and one committee member even went to Palestine! How long should that committee stay in Europe and when will the next committee be going to Europe to bring back a report?

"Shall we wait again until it is too late and have more innocent lives on our conscience? Perhaps it is already too late.

"...I do not intend this letter to be a threat, but I beg you in the name of all the unfortunates to call me within 24 hours after you receive this letter...If you should fail to call me, ...I feel compelled to forward a copy of this letter to every rabbi in the country, to the members of the Union of Orthodox Rabbis, to the Rabbinical Council of America, to the Union of Orthodox Congregations and to warm-hearted Orthodox Jews who should be interested in this problem."

These words illustrate his passion for rescuing Holocaust survivors and his intolerance of organizational bureaucracy. His letters are full of the burning conviction that Torah life and study would flourish among the survivors of the Holocaust, if only their more fortunate co-religionists overseas would see to their material needs.

Several shorter visits to Europe followed, during which he helped both individuals and institutions, rushing from town to town in Czechoslovakia, Austria, Germany, France and Belgium. Typical of his approach is a letter to Rabbi Vorhand, the Chief Rabbi of Prague, in which he writes:

"It is with much regret that I had to forego the pleasure of seeing you while I was in Europe. As you can very well understand, there were innumerable matters that had to be attended to and my time was terribly limited. However, I expect to visit Europe again shortly, and at that time, I expect to have more assistants with me and will definitely take time to visit you personally... O.H. has a student's affidavit as well as a passport. Please go over to the consul with him and do whatever is necessary in this direction. Spare no expense, as I will be only too happy to reimburse you."

The minutes of a Vaad Hatzala meeting provide further evidence of his altruism:

"We are not involved in rescuing our own relatives or looking for ways to help personal friends. Stephen Klein's own family members are still in DP

His letters are full of the burning conviction that Torah life and study would flourish among the survivors of the Holocaust, if only their more fortunate co-religionists overseas would provide help for their material needs.

Stephen Klein with refugee children

camps and he won't let them be pushed ahead of the others..."

When Stephen Klein passed away, the Telshe *Rosh Yeshiva*, Rabbi Aizik Ausband, recalled that he had visited the small remnant of Telshe Yeshiva after they were able to leave Russia and were in France awaiting visas to the United States. American consular officials were reluctant, for various reasons, to give priority to yeshiva students. The refugees were crushed by years of deprivation in Siberia and the difficulties of crossing Europe. The thought that it might take years before they could rejoin their yeshiva in the United States was more than they could bear. Stephen Klein went to the consulate personally. His charm and conviction, and an oversized box of Barton's chocolates, worked wonders. The visas were expedited.

After the war, it soon became clear that one of the biggest problems was what to do with the many orphaned children. Often there was not a single surviving relative to care for them.

> Stephen Klein's remarkable commitment to come to the aid of people in need was his hallmark. No challenge was insurmountable if a Jew was in distress.

Stephen Klein addressing Agudath Israel leaders

Some of these children had been in hiding, or placed with non-Jewish families during the Nazi occupation, and now they needed a great deal of special attention to help them re-acclimate to normal Jewish life. Vaad Hatzala created an independent entity, Rescue Children Inc., to operate homes and schools for these children. Herbert Tenzer was the head of Rescue Children. His partner and friend, Stephen Klein, and Rabbi William Novick were his associates and major supporters.

IMMIGRATION AND ASSISTANCE

Stephen Klein's hallmark was his remarkable commitment to people in need. No challenge was insurmountable if a Jew was in distress. Before granting a visa, the United States required an affidavit that the person would not become dependent on government assistance. Most survivors had to wait a long time for an organization such as HIAS (Hebrew Immigration Aid Society) to provide such a document. Stephen Klein, however, personally provided affidavits for thousands of survivors!

Once they arrived in the United States, he would help them find work and a place to live, and often continued for years to be concerned for their welfare.

Rabbi Abraham Kelman, a Viennese refugee, was in Canada and eager to

Kesser Torah awards presented to Stephen Klein and Irving Maidman at Chinuch Atzmai Dinner, June 1963. (L-R): Hon. Edward S. Silver, Irving M. Bunim, Rabbi Amos Bunim, Stephen Klein, Irving Maidman.

Chinuch Atzmai Dinner: The rabbanim on dais (L-R): Rabbi Gedaliah Schorr, Rabbi Shneur Kotler, Rabbi Boruch Sorotzkin, Rabbi Yaakov Kamenetsky, Rabbi Dovid Lifshitz.
Front dais (L-R): Stephen Klein, Chairman, speaking, Rabbi Yaakov Ruderman and Rabbi Moshe Feinstein.

Many of those who came to this country with his affidavit were also the beneficiaries of his assistance once they arrived in the United States.

come to the United States. Stephen Klein enabled him to come to New York, and when Rabbi Kelman decided to start a school for girls, Stephen Klein helped him raise the necessary funds and served as the founding president of the school. Thanks to Stephen Klein's faith and generosity, The Prospect Park School for Girls became a major institution.

CHINUCH ATZMAI/TORAH SCHOOLS FOR ISRAEL

In 1948, when the State of Israel was founded, the government agreed to provide free education for all. Even the strictly Orthodox would have their needs met by the so-called *Zerem Revii* Fourth Stream, a network of traditional Jewish schools for both boys and girls. By 1953, it became clear that the government would not keep its commitment, and the *Gedolei Yisrael* in Israel and the United States concluded that these schools would have to become independent. From that time on, the Orthodox boys and girls schools, en-

compassing 46,000 children, became known as Chinuch Atzmai, Torah Schools for Israel. Only part of their budget came from the government; for the balance they would have to rely on the generosity of world Jewry.

Rabbi Aharon Kotler immediately took upon himself the responsibility for

Chinuch Atzmai Dinner, January 1956. (L-R): Rabbi Mordechai Gifter, Rabbi Yosef Dov Soloveitchik, Stephen Klein, Rabbi Aharon Kotler.

Dr. Joseph Kaminetsky presenting the Torah Umesorah Jewish Heritage Award to Mr. Stephen Klein

It was to his loyal friend Stephen Klein that Rabbi Aharon Kotler turned to chair the new critical project — Chinuch Atzmai.

Chinuch Atzmai, and set about establishing proper channels of support for the schools in the United States. It was to his loyal friend Stephen Klein that he turned to chair this new critical project. Reportedly, Rav Aharon walked into Mr. Klein's office and said, "I have to inform you that you are now the Chairman of the Board of Chinuch Atzmai."

At that time, Vaad Hatzala's operations were winding down and Stephen Klein threw himself into his new cause. He was determined not to let down the Torah-true school system of Israel. He also believed that it was possible to unite all elements of American Orthodoxy to support Chinuch Atzmai. To that end, he encouraged Rav Aharon to seek the support of Rabbi Yosef Dov Soloveitchik of Boston and Yeshivas Rabbi Yitzchak Elchanan, who was revered by the broader Jewish community. Stephen Klein's charm and dedication won Rabbi Soloveitchik's heartfelt support, and for the rest of his life Rabbi Soloveitchik served as Chinuch Atzmai's honorary president and spoke at numerous events on its behalf.

A meeting of prominent Jewish leaders was arranged at the Klein residence on Maple St. in Crown Heights, with Rabbi Soloveitchik as the guest speaker. His superb oratory could not fail to inspire the guests, but the best-laid plans sometimes fall victim to the weather. There was a blinding snowstorm. One could hardly walk more than a few blocks and there were no taxis or buses. To Stephen Klein's chagrin, only seven people showed up.

Somehow, Rabbi Soloveitchik managed to get to Brooklyn despite the weather. He looked around the table, saw the sadness of his host, and changed the theme of his speech. He quoted the *Midrash* that Hashem weeps in secret for the pain of *Klal Yisrael*: "*Bamistarim tivkeh nafshi,* My soul will cry in its hidden chambers." (*Yirmiyahu* 13:17). So too, said Rabbi Soloveitchik, this endeavor is close to Hashem, for it is also a scene of *bamistarim tivkeh nafshi.*

Stephen Klein was extremely generous to Chinuch Atzmai from his own funds, and treated it as a favorite child until the end of his life. Even today, his legacy as chairman for over 20 years lives on in the hearts of more than 74,000 students studying in the hundreds of Torah schools throughout Israel.

CHAMPION OF JEWISH EDUCATION

Shabbos observance was just one area in which Stephen Klein used Barton's to foster awareness of Torah-oriented Judaism. He realized that when advertising his chocolates, he could publicize *mitzvos* at the same time. He found a young and talented creative advertising agency and explained his idea to them. From this brainstorm came a series of informative full page advertisements in The *New York Times* and other widely-read newspapers. Created by Bill Birnbach, with the assistance of the Merling-Marx advertising agency, the ads explained the laws and significance of Shabbos and the Jewish Festivals, describing their rituals and symbols and explaining their eternal message.

Reprints of these advertisements were made available to synagogues, schools and libraries throughout the world. The more popular themes, such as those about *Rosh Hashanah* and

Stephen Klein presented with a megillah by Rabbi Menachem Porush, Knesset member of Agudath Israel, on behalf of Chinuch Atzmai in Israel.

Pesach, had reprint runs of more than two million copies! These beautifully illustrated posters were a pioneering form of educational outreach to unaffiliated Jews at a time when large-scale *kiruv rechokim*, Jewish outreach, was not even a dream. Another Klein innovation was the space he reserved on the front page of every Friday's *New York Times* to announce Shabbos candle-lighting time.

The full-page advertisements were a stunning success. They made Barton's Bonbonniere a household name in Jewish homes, conveyed much information in an easy-to-absorb manner, and helped launch the career of a talented young man named Bill Birnbach, who became an advertising legend. His small agency, Doyle, Dane and Birnbach, would eventually become one of the world's largest, DDB Needham Worldwide. Bill Birnbach never forgot his first client, and when the agency published a commemorative volume about their greatest ads of all

time, those conceived by Stephen Klein were featured.

Stephen Klein was convinced that just as commerce thrives when it operates on a large scale, so too, Torah-oriented Judaism will thrive when one finds opportunities for extensive activities. He felt strongly that the future of the next generation depended on a yeshiva education for children, and he used the press to spread the message of Jewish education. He strongly supported the goal of Torah Umesorah, the National Society for Hebrew Day Schools, to establish a Jewish school in every neighborhood and community. With Moses Feuerstein of Boston and Dr. Joseph Kaminetsky, Torah Umesorah's National Director, he traveled throughout the country to open day schools. Every week, he wrote a column for Jewish newspapers in which he tirelessly appealed to parents not to be satisfied with a public school education

He was determined to do whatever was necessary not to let down the Torah-true school system of Eretz Yisrael.

Stephen Klein with Rabbi Yaakov Yitzchak Ruderman at Chinuch Atzmai dinner

Degel Yerushalayim, one of many organizations supported by the Klein Foundation

Stephen Klein was also extremely generous to Chinuch Atzmai from his own funds, and treated it as a favorite child until the end of his life.

supplemented by Hebrew school on Sundays or afternoons. He urged parents to give their children an intensive Jewish education, and begged each community to support its yeshivos.

In 1948, he founded and supported the development of Central Yeshiva High School for girls. This school was a pacesetter in the emerging system of Torah *chinuch* for teenage girls. In addition to Vaad Hatzala and Chinuch Atzmai, Stephen Klein's partnership with Rabbi Aharon Kotler included Beth Medrash Govohah, in Lakewood, New Jersey, which was to become the largest institution of its kind in the world. To found and maintain his great yeshiva, Rav Aharon needed dedicated lay leadership. Stephen Klein considered the *Rosh HaYeshiva* his *rebbe* and did everything within his power to assist in the early growth and development of the yeshiva. His brothers, Martin and Eli, also joined its leadership as presidents of the "Lakewood" Yeshiva. This legacy continues today with the broad involvement of Stephen's son, George, and the extended Klein family, in this home to over 5,000 students.

Near the end of his life, when he was already in poor health, he responded to the plea to rescue a struggling yeshiva in Brooklyn and single-handedly enabled it to survive. Thanks to his intervention, Yeshiva R'tzahd still serves Jewish children who would otherwise be in public school.

HIS PLACE IN HISTORY

Many names deserve to be remembered for their role in building the Torah community in America at a time when it was not a popular goal. All had the courage to stand up against the trends of the times and left a legacy of great accomplishments. Stephen Klein was in so many ways a singular example of a strictly Orthodox Jew who bridged the world of Torah observance with corporate America. His adherence to Halachah while building a large corporation; his view of himself as a *shlucha d'rabbanan* – a faithful emissary of the *gedolei HaTorah*; his generosity and kindness to individuals; his dedication to rescuing and sustaining his fellow

Rabbi Moshe Feinstein addressing the audience at a Chinuch Atzmai Dinner. Seated next to the podium is Stephen Klein.

Stephen Klein's son, George, addressing Chinuch Atzmai Dinner, 1988; Rabbi Avrohom Pam seated to his left

Part of the Klein family at the wedding of Mr. and Mrs. Stephen Klein's grandaughter

Jews; his commitment to Torah institutions in the United States and *Eretz Yisrael;* and his harnessing of the mass media to spread the word of Hashem, are all unforgettable lessons that inspire us to this very day. He was a man of vision and action, a leader and advocate of Torah and *chesed.* He fulfilled the words and blessings of the *Chofetz Chaim* to sanctify the Name of Hashem in all his endeavors.

The Talmud teaches us that saving the life of a Jew is tantamount to saving the entire world. This may well imply that a single human being has the potential to change the world, to elevate it, to accomplish things that will make the world a better place.

Today's Jewish world testifies that Stephen Klein was such a man.

He was in so many ways a singular example of a strictly Orthodox Jew who bridged the world of Torah observance with corporate America.

Postscript:

Shortly before the completion of this volume, Mrs. Regina Klein, Stephen Klein's life partner and matriarch of the Klein family, passed away. She was born in 1907, in Tarnov, Poland. Her father, Reb Avrohom Monheit, a Belzer *chassid,* imbued his family with a love for Torah and *mitzvos.* In 1932, she married Stephen Klein in Vienna and in 1938, they immigrated to America with their three children. Her father and most of her extended family were murdered by the Nazis in 1942 in the Tarnov Ghetto.

With selfless devotion, Mrs. Regina Klein assisted her husband in all his endeavors.

This quintessential *eishes chayil* enabled her husband to achieve his myriad accomplishments.

In his eulogy, her son George evoked the memory of his father, *zl,* by saying, "In Heaven, my father would surely be quoting Rabbi Akiva's singular tribute to his own wife –"*Sheli, v'shelachem, shelah hi,* All that is mine and yours, is hers."

Mrs. Klein, who was a woman of dignity and elegance, embodied the exemplary *eizer k'negdo,* helpmate. She saw her life's legacy fulfilled in the four generations she was privileged to build.

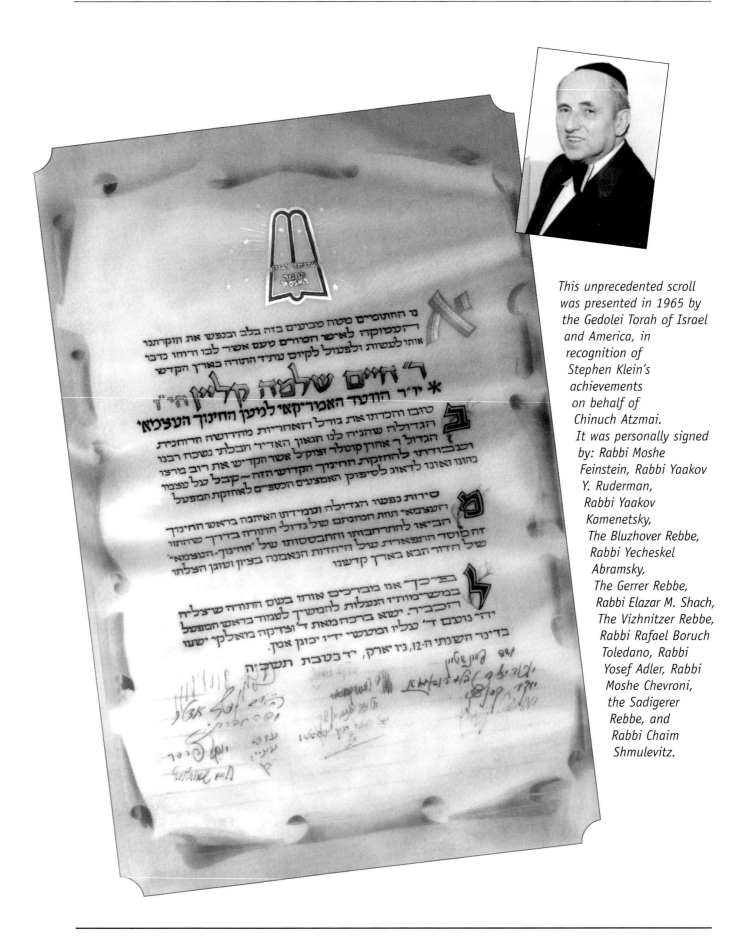

This unprecedented scroll was presented in 1965 by the Gedolei Torah of Israel and America, in recognition of Stephen Klein's achievements on behalf of Chinuch Atzmai.
It was personally signed by: Rabbi Moshe Feinstein, Rabbi Yaakov Y. Ruderman, Rabbi Yaakov Kamenetsky, The Bluzhover Rebbe, Rabbi Yecheskel Abramsky, The Gerrer Rebbe, Rabbi Elazar M. Shach, The Vizhnitzer Rebbe, Rabbi Rafael Boruch Toledano, Rabbi Yosef Adler, Rabbi Moshe Chevroni, the Sadigerer Rebbe, and Rabbi Chaim Shmulevitz.

Barton's Educational Advertisements

Rosh Hashanah 5716
ראש השנה תשט"ז

Sept. 17 & 18, 55. This is the Jewish New Year. Jews assemble in the synagogue to reaffirm their faith, examine their past conduct and pray for forgiveness. The Shofar (ram's horn) is blown to reawaken their responsibility to the Lord and call them to repentance.

TZOM G'DALYAH
צום גדליה

On this fast day, Jews mourn for G'dalyah, a Jew whom the conquering Babylonians temporarily appointed Governor of Palestine. The Jews saw in this a sign that their nation would rise again, but G'dalyah was ruthlessly assassinated.

YOM KIPPUR
יום כפור

On this Day of Atonement, the holiest day of the year, the Lord judges each individual. Jews fast all day, confess and repent, and ask pardon from the Lord and from their fellow men. In turn, they freely forgive their neighbors. At night, with a cleansed heart, they look forward to a good new life.

Sukkot
סכות

Oct. 1 thru 7, 55. The Feast of Tabernacles celebrates the ancient fruit harvest in the Holy Land. Jews everywhere build Sukkot (temporary booths) hung with fruits and flowers, remembering that the Israelites lived in flimsy booths during their desert wanderings—yet felt secure in the Lord's protection.

Sh'mini Atzeret
שמיני עצרת

Oct. 8, 55. This day is designated in the Bible as a day of Holy Assembly. Jews gather in the synagogue to celebrate this last festival of the harvest season, and to offer a fervent prayer for rain to bring full crops in the coming year.

Simchat Torah
שמחת תורה

Oct. 9, 55. The Torah (Five Books of Moses) is read in its entirety each year. On this happy day, the reading is completed and begun anew. The sacred scrolls are carried around the synagogue in procession. The children participate and receive gifts of sweets.

Chanukah
חנוכה

Dec. 10 thru 17, 55. On Chanukah the Maccabees freed the Temple from the Syrian conquerors. At its rededication only enough pure oil was found to light the Holy Lamp for one day. Miraculously it burned eight days. Thus, on the first day of Chanukah, Jews light one candle on the Menorah, adding another each day.

Asarah B'tevet
עשרה בטבת

Dec. 25, 55. This is the anniversary of the day the Babylonians began their siege of Jerusalem. Soon after, the city was taken, the Temple destroyed, and the first Hebrew Commonwealth was no more. Thus, Asarah B'tevet is a day of fasting and mourning.

At the beginning of this New Year we list for you

The 16 Jewish Holidays
and Fast Days
when they fall and what they mean

Chamisha Asar Bish'vat
חמשה עשר בשבט

Jan. 28, 56. On this Arbor Day Jews observe the Bible's commandment: "When ye shall come into the land ye shall plant all manner of trees." In Israel, children spend the day joyfully planting young trees. And because this is the 15th day of the Jewish month Sh'vat, Jews everywhere eat fifteen kinds of fruit.

Taanit Esther
תענית אסתר

Feb. 23, 56. The Megillah (Book of Esther) tells how the scheming Haman persuaded King Ahasuerus to destroy the Jews, and how Jewish Queen Esther and her people fasted three days before she dared to plead with the King to save them. This fast day, known as the Fast of Esther, commemorates her heroism.

Purim
פורים

Feb. 25, 56. This gayest of all Jewish holidays celebrates King Ahasuerus' decision to save the Jews and destroy their enemy Haman, instead. During the synagogue service the Book of Esther is read, and children twirl their gragers (noisemakers) every time Haman is mentioned, to drown out his name.

Pesach
פסח

Mar. 27 thru Apr. 3, 56. Pesach (Passover) recalls the deliverance of the Jews from Egyptian slavery. At the traditional Seder meal, Jewish families read the Haggadah (a book containing the story of the liberation) and eat Matzoh (unleavened bread) and other symbolic foods—thereby reliving their ancestors' experiences.

Lag B'omer
ל"ג בעמר

Apr. 29, 56. A plague among Rabbi Akiba's students ended on the 33rd day of "Counting the Omer," i.e. bringing an omer (measure) of new grain to the Temple. Jews happily recall this event, and honor the efforts of Rabbis Akiba and Bar Yochai and the brave Bar Kochba to re-establish the Jewish nation.

Shavuot
שבעות

May 16 & 17, 56. This holiday commemorates the sacred moment at Mount Sinai when Moses received from the Lord the Torah with its Ten Commandments. Shavuot also celebrates the early wheat harvest in Palestine. Jews throughout the world decorate their homes and synagogues with greens and flowers.

Shiv'ah Asar B'tammuz
שבעה עשר בתמוז

June 26, 56. On this day the Babylonian army made the first breach in the wall of Jerusalem. This led to the tragic end of the Jewish homeland and to exile for its people. Shiv'ah Asar B'tammuz is a fast day, followed by three weeks of mourning.

Tish'ah B'av
תשעה באב

July 17, 56. On this fast day, Jews grieve for the destruction of the first and second Temples. They mourn at the Wailing Wall in Jerusalem and in synagogues all over the world. Tish'ah B'av climaxes a nine-day period in which no meat may be eaten.

Barton's Educational Advertisements

HE BUSIEST STREET corner in the world was busier than ever. The grinning policeman in charge of traffic on this corner really had his hands full directing the busy flow of traffic this Saturday afternoon – to say nothing of the questions the visitors to New York asked of him every minute on the minute. Sometimes it seemed to him every New York visitor came to this most famous corner just to ask him their questions – such as where could they find their cousins who once lived in a brownstone house in Jamaica. By now no question could possibly surprise him any more.

That's what *he* thought. It all happened when the lights changed. There was this kindly old lady, crossing the street with hundreds of other pedestrians. "Officer," she said in a quiet voice, "how come this candy store across the street is closed now? Don't they care to do business on such a busy day?"

The officer scratched his head – stumped. The light changed again. He made sure the little old lady was right next to him. Couldn't take a chance with all this traffic coming through. "Gee, Lady," he finally said, "you got me there. I never really noticed it before." The lady left him when the light turned green again, but her question didn't. Funny, he thought, why should this candy store right here on the busiest corner of New York be closed during one of the busiest shopping days of the week?'

At four o'clock, the next shift came on and he left his traffic post. But before going home he made sure to go over to Barton's candy store. Everything looked

closed and under lock. Then his eyes caught sight of this sign on the door.

STORE HOURS
MONDAY–THURSDAY
8 a.m. – 10 p.m.
FRIDAY 8 a.m. - 4:15 p.m.
SATURDAY 5:15p.m.–10 p.m.
SUNDAY   9 a.m. – 7 p.m.

The next day that the store was open the officer made sure to go in and ask what the sign was all about. He then learned that all of Barton's 21 stores, located in New York City, are closed on Saturday – for the Barton chain is owned and operated by the four Klein brothers and Mr. Herbert Tenzer, who are all orthodox Jews – strict *Shomrei Shabbos*, and who have always occupied themselves with Yeshiva education and *tzedakah* (Jewish philanthropy).

The president of the company is Stephen Klein. He is well known for his work in Jewish education and in helping our brothers overseas. We were speaking

Mr. Stephen Klein

to Mr. Klein the other day and he told us that us that not only are all the 21 stores closed on Shabbos but the Barton factory, which employs 500 people, is also closed on the day of rest. Mr. Klein pointed out that not all the stores are located in Jewish neighborhoods. Quite a few of the stores are located in key shopping sections such as Times Square, 34th Street (near Macy's and Gimbel's) and downtown New York.

Yet, Mr. Klein told us his business has never suffered because of Sabbath observance.

"Our customers see the sign in our stores which tells them the exact time we close on Fridays and so they buy their chocolates before the Shabbos sets in. We have never had any adverse comment from non-Jews because we are closed on the Sabbath. If anything, they respect us for our religious convictions."

Very often pressure has been brought on the company's directors to drop this strict observance of Shabbos. "After all," some argued, "you are closed on what is perhaps the biggest day of the week. The 34th street store alone sells to 4,000 customers daily. The others also do a large business. We are a large outfit. We can't afford to lose all that business."

Arguments of this type, Mr. Klein usually answers by saying that "G-d did not see me and my brothers through the Nazi troubles so that I should now forget my faith and belief in the truth of Judaism. When you believe in all the principles of the Torah's way of life, it doesn't matter whether you own a small store in an honest-to-goodness Jewish section or a large store on Fifth Avenue and 42nd street."

THE JEWISH PRESS

THE LARGEST CIRCULATION OF ANY ANGLO-JEWISH WEEKLY NEWSPAPER IN THE WORLD
"Teach Me Thy Way, O L-rd, That I May Walk In Thy Truth"   Psalms 86:11

Copr. The JEWISH PRESS INC. 1977

REPRINTED FROM THE SEPT. 1, 1978 ISSUE

JEWISH PRESS • Page 36B

Friday, September 1, 1978

"Turn In Your Books And Get Out"

By Stephen Klein
Chairman of the Board
Barton's Candy Corporation

Several weeks ago I wrote an appeal to keep open the doors of R'Tzahd Yeshiva. The response was prompt and generous. Although we did not reach our goal, we were able to insure the opening of the school for the coming year. To our sorrow the R'Tzahd emergency is repeated far too often in yeshiva after yeshiva.year and year. It's time something was done about it. A Rosh Yeshiva once told me forty years ago. "Everybody talks about yeshivos, but nobody gets to the root of their problems". And so it's been with our yeshivos today. Everybody says that something should be done to eliminate the financial crises that burden our Torah institutions. but no one has come forth with an overall or long-lasting solution. How long can yeshivos survive conditions which hamper their operation, curtail their registration of new students and undermine the role of Torah education in the struggle to perpetuate Traditional Judaism?

I, for one. propose to stop talking about the problem. I mean to do something about it. I cannot and will not shirk the responsibility I took upon myself from long association with the great Rosehi Yeshiva of the past and present. The spark of Ahavas Torah which was implanted within me in my father's house, was fanned into a flame of dedication by such Torah greats. whom I knew personally, as the Chofetz Chaim, the Chazon Ish, the Gerer Rebbe, Rabbis Aharon Kotler, Eliezer Silver, Faivel Mendlowitz, and Zalman Sorotzkin, all of blessed memory. Among the present day Roshei Yeshiva who influenced me are Rabbis Moshe Feinstein, Yaakov Kamenetsky, Shneir Kotler, Yaakov Yitzchok Ruderman, Baruch Sorotzkin, Eliezer Menachem Schach, and others. All of these Gedolei Torah have, by their own dedication and self-sacrifice. set the goals that we must reach to insure the survival of Judaism. They didn't talk, they acted. We can do no less.

Let me illustrate the problem with a true story related to me just the other day by a young man applying for a job at Barton's. In his own words, this was his experience with a yeshiva:

"It was back in February of

MR. STEPHEN KLEIN

1967. I was in 5th grade and my brother in 7th grade in a well-known Day School. One morning I was summoned to the principal's office, without any prior indication as to the reason. When I arrived, I saw my brother backed up against the wall of the office, a look of bewilderment on his face. I stood beside him. Soon two members of the school's Board of Education entered the room and one of them said, "Your parents have failed to meet their financial obligations to the Yeshiva and you can't stay here anymore." My brother started to cry and said, "What do we do now?" "Go to your classroom, turn in your books, and get out." We did as we were told, and shortly thereafter my mother arrived. As soon as, she was notified of the situation she started screaming and pleading with the Rabbi who was principal of the school. She asked that he wait until April when a tax-refund check was expected from the government. Her words fell on deaf ears. There were more conversations later, between my father and the school officials, with negative results. After being out of school for over a week, we were transferred to another Yeshiva and continued our studies. But for my parents' persistence, we could well have ended up in public school." In the years that followed the young man went on to higher yeshivos and then spent one year at a yeshiva in Israel. He now has a B.B.A. from Baruch College and is studying for his Rabbinical Ordination examinations (Smicha). The young man's story is told for more than its human interest. It points up a shocking condition in the yeshiva world. Children are expelled and do not transfer to other yeshivos. Children are refused admission and do not persist in returning. We are losing manpower that we can ill afford to lose. I do not fault the

Yeshivos. They have real financial difficulties and can't cope. I do, however, find fault with the American Jewish Community which sits back and allows our future to be endangered. I therefore propose a solution which will eliminate crises in our yeshivos, and hopefully still forever the frantic cries for help.

I am working on this solution right now, and I hope to announce the details in the near future of the initiation of a $10 million Yeshiva Endowment Fund.

In the meantime, until the financial problems are solved, there is something that the Jews of America can do to insure the survival of the yeshiva method of education and of Torah Judaism. The two go hand in hand. Strengthen yeshivos and Judaism lives. Reb Aharon Kotler, ZTL, said to me over 35 years ago, "Our deficit is not money. Our deficit is children." It is our responsibility, aside from concern about lack of funds, to wage a relentless campaign against apathy and in favor of Yeshiva education. Parents give many reasons, or excuses, as to why they have not sent their children to Yeshivos.

"There is no Yeshiva in my community."

"I can't afford the tuition."

"I don't want my son to be a Rabbi."

"I don't want my son or daughter to be more religious than I am."

"I don't want my son or daughter to be religious."

And so on.. But these are not valid arguments. And besides, much can be done to eliminate these excuses. In the first place, parents with young children, or who are planning to have a family, should think seriously of the future. If they must relocate, for whatever reason, they should make certain there is a yeshiva in the area. Just as no one would consider settling in a city without a doctor, so should no Jewish parents live where there is no Yeshiva.

As to the fear of the student becoming a rabbi, this is not borne out by the facts. The truth is that the majority of yeshiva graduates in addition to becoming rabbis and teachers, go on to careers in medicine, law, science, social service, teaching and business. In addition, the yeshiva graduate is a better person for having experienced this special kind of education. He or she is a better American, a better citizen, a better Jew. And if the individual is religious, this is not anything for the non-religious parents to regret. Would they prefer hippies, pot smokers, cult followers? Our youth are looking for some

spiritual strength. Why, not give them their own heritage.

The yeshiva education campaign should involve every Jew. Rabbis should preach it, lecture about it, write about it. Laymen should stress it to their family, their neighbors, their friends and their own children. The R'Tzahd Yeshiva printed posters and placed them in store windows, on walls and on telephone poles. The result was a substantial increase in enrollment over the previous year. The same results can be achieved if similar action is taken by all yeshivos.

According to Torah Umesorah, a positive yeshiva campaign, spearheaded by them, was able to increase the number of Day Schools in North America from 78 in 1944 to over 510 in 1978 and from a meager few students to close to 100,000. And this has meant that synagogues do not have to go begging for a minyan weekdays or Saturdays, Kashruth is observed more widely, mikvas are built and supported. consumers look for kosher products, Hebrew is a live language, Israel has staunch supporters, aliyah is more than a dream. intermarriage is less frequent than it might otherwise be. and the future of yiddishkeit is brighter.

I believe that we can stimulate the further growth of yeshivos through my plan. Among other things. it will make scholarships available so that the yeshiva student body will grow by leaps and bounds. The plan will, in my estimation, increase yeshiva enrollment by 5000 students a year for the next 10 years. I am looking to the Jewish community to help me achieve this goal. I know it can be done. With your full cooperation it will be done.

One of Stephen Klein's many newspaper articles on behalf of Jewish education.

EXCERPTS FROM A TRIBUTE TO MR. STEPHEN KLEIN

By Rabbi Mordechai Gifter
Rosh HaYeshiva, Telshe Yeshiva

We are gathered here this evening, my friends, to pay tribute to an individual and to the cause which he has come to represent in the minds and hearts of all those who know him.

We have become accustomed to thinking of a gadol *only in terms of the great Torah scholar, one who represents Torah scholarship for his generation. As with many other terms in Jewish life, we are mistaken with understanding the title* gadol hador *also.* Chazal *define the* gadol hador *as being one who is not representative of* gadlus baTorah, *whose forte is not Torah scholarship.* Gedolei hador *are rather* anshei maasim v'tzaddikim – *men of righteous deeds – whose life is representative of never-ceasing action in carrying forth the dictates of the* gedolei haTorah *of all times.*

In this (the true) sense of gadol hador, *we have come here tonight to honor one who has justly earned the title 'gadol ish hamaaseh' in the highest sense of the word. His business gave to* shmiras Shabbos *and to Torah observance a special place of respect in the thinking of American Jewry. Down through the years he has been a leader in organizational work with a special emphasis on* chinuch – *Torah Jewish education. He has given of himself unstintingly in the area of Torah* chinuch *in the national day school movement. He is responsible for the establishment of high schools for boys and high schools for girls in New York and in other communities throughout the country. He has felt impelled as a* layman both to speak and write on the necessity of Torah chinuch.

In his activities in the heroic efforts of the Vaad Hatzala as Chairman of the Department of Immigration, he worked on special missions to bring bnei Torah *to the United States and to* Eretz Yisrael. *Many hundreds live today because of the blank affidavits signed by our guest of honor.*

In all his activities it was not his opinion which prevailed. He was always at the beck and call of the gedolei haTorah *in whom he found guidance through implicit faith – through* emunas chachamim.

He was privileged to be guided and inspired by that great luminary of our age, master architect of Torah in the post-war years, Rabbi Aharon Kotler. And when Reb Aharon called on him in 1953 to help give practical reality to Reb Aharon's master plan of Torah for Eretz Yisrael, *the Chinuch Atzmai, our guest of honor began to invest of himself in this great cause. His activities grew and the achievements of Chinuch Atzmai grew. So involved was he in the work as to become the National Chairman of Torah Schools for Israel. Reb Aharon in death has inspired him to such heights that he and the cause of Chinuch Atzmai have become synonomous. The man eats, drinks and breathes Chinuch Atzmai.*

My friends, our guest of honor is none other than Mr. Chinuch Atzmai, Reb Chaim Shlomo – Stephen Klein...

EXCERPTS OF STEPHEN KLEIN'S LETTERS (1947-1949) REGARDING VAAD HATZALA
TO RABBI ISRAEL ROSENBERG
PRESIDENT OF THE AGUDAS HARABBONIM

Dear Rabbi Rosenberg,

This is the third letter that I write on behalf of our unfortunate brethren in Europe since my return from Europe eight months ago. I shall try to call to your attention in this letter several salient facts which happened in the past eight months and in the period immediately prior, that concern rescue and Orthodox rehabilitation work.

It could be very easy for me to forget all the promises that you and your colleagues made to me concerning our unfortunate brethren. But in full knowledge of what happened to our brethren and being in Europe and personally having seen all the misery and misfortune and having committed myself on behalf of Vaad Hatzala for these unfortunates, my conscience bothers me day and night and I cannot let it go on promises alone without definite action on the part of your newly organized Central Committee. From letters that I receive and from representatives from overseas who visit me, constantly, I am daily asked, "Why is nothing being done to relieve our suffering and pain? Why are you asleep? How much longer will we have to suffer when actual help can and should be given by you?" Yeshiva scholars and rabbis escaping from Europe are asking why nothing is being done for their colleagues.

❧◆❧

Dear Rabbi Rosenberg,

You must forgive me for writing this letter and giving you the cold facts. You will then be able to show this letter to your colleagues – some of whom have misled you. You know that during all these years, since 1943 when I had the honor to work together with you on rescue and rehabilitation, I have had the greatest esteem and respect for you and I cannot believe even at this late date, if you had been aware of the outcome of this, that you would have sanctioned it. Please let me make this definite statement. "I have never underestimated the work that the Joint has done and is doing as a relief organization." I personally contribute large sums to the UJA (United Jewish Appeal). During my four month's stay in Europe, I saw the JDC work at close hand and I recognize its extreme value and the extensive scope of its job, but I wish to assure you that the work which the Vaad Hatzala has done could not have been done by the JDC (Joint Distribution Committee) and those people whom the Vaad Hatzala helped certainly did not get double portions. The Yeshivas, Torah institutions, kosher kitchens, Beth Jacob Schools, and other religious establishments which the Vaad Hatzala initiated would not be in existence today if it were not for the Vaad Hatzala.

Naturally I have no right to say anything, or perhaps give advice in spite of my many years in immigration, rescue and rehabilitation work, how your new Committee should be constituted, what they should do, or what type of representatives you should send to Europe, but after having had people coming from Europe tell me that they met with the representatives of this Committee and after telling these representatives of the sorrow and "tzores" the Jews must suffer and after being asked what they intended to do to help relieve their suffering, they were

answered by this Committee, "What are you worrying about, we have suffered for 2,000 years, we were born to suffer." How can I help but write this letter after realizing that it is already several months since the Committee went to Europe, that they did not find time as yet to go to Germany, Austria or Poland where our Orthodox Jews are faced with grave problems, but instead, the Committee is still in Paris and one Committee member even went to Palestine. How long should that Committee member stay in Europe and will the next Committee be going to Europe to bring back a report? What should be done for our unfortunate brethren in the meantime? Shall we again wait until it is too late and have more innocent lives on our conscience? Perhaps it is already too late. Besides, we already have all the information that is necessary. We know how many Orthodox institutions there are in Europe under the supervision of Vaad Hatzala; how many Yeshivas, how many kosher kitchens, how many mikvehs, how many Rabbis and Yeshiva scholars need our help. Again why did we not send men who have had the experience, who have been overseas, who know where to look and what to look for? Do you realize that the Committee that was sent, and for whom much money has been spent, did not know a thing about the inside of Germany except what they read in newspaper stories and reports?

Three months have passed since the Committee left and we have not heard from them but the complaints and requests for aid which come in daily, and nothing is being done. You asked me to step aside and I did so because I believed you, and I had the utmost faith in you. At this time I thought it would be an excellent idea if the Rabbis took such great interest in this vital problem and I was waiting patiently and did not do anything.

Please, Rabbi Rosenberg, forgive me for writing this letter and being frank and telling you what I think about this situation. It is only because I have suffered sleepless nights and see how much could be done for our people if the thing were not neglected. If someone is drowning they clutch at a straw with the hope that the straw will save their life. In this instance, because I feel that I know the situation overseas and know what the needs are, I would not do justice to the Shearith Haplaita if I do not write this letter.

I do not intend this letter to be a threat, but I beg you in the name of all the unfortunates to call me within 24 hours after you receive this letter for a conference with you and with your colleagues to discuss the following points that have to be taken care of immediately. I am only a messenger for the many people and it is not my request but their request. If you should, for any reason, fail to call me to such a conference, I have been asked by these people to call upon the whole rabbinate and all the important laymen in Jewish life in the United States and will request you to relieve the situation immediately. I therefore feel compelled, if I do not hear from you shortly, to forward a copy of this letter to every Rabbi in the country, to the members of the Union of Orthodox Rabbis, to the Rabbinical Council of America, to the Union of Orthodox Congregations and to warm-hearted Orthodox Jews who should be interested in this problem. Together with this letter I would send a copy of the agreement which was made between the Union of Orthodox Rabbis and

JDC. In my letter to them I would ask them to share this problem with me and to see what can be done immediately to take care of the following major problems:

1. The immediate establishment of an immigration office under the Vaad Hatzala in Austria, Poland, Italy and Czechoslovakia so that Rabbonim and Bnei Torah in these countries can be helped to migrate immediately.

2. We have approximately 1,200 outstanding contracts for Rabbis and students to go to this country from France and Germany. The immigration department of the Vaad Hatzala in this country and political division thereof would be strengthened immediately and should receive the necessary funds to carry on.

3. For ten months 650 ultra-Orthodox children in Romania have been prepared to transfer to other countries. Permission has been received from the Romanian Government for their exit and from the French Government for their entry. But nothing has been done and Vaad Hatzala hasn't the necessary funds. If the doors of Romania should be closed, these children will be lost to us forever.

4. The reports which we receive still advise us that thousands of children are still in the hands of gentiles, in convents and monasteries. These children must be redeemed and only an organization imbued with Torah spirit can do this work most effectively.

5. Our representatives in Germany and the Rabbinate there are begging us to establish more Yeshivas and Talmud Torahs and also establish Yeshivas in Austria and Italy since it becomes more evident as time goes on that they will have to remain there for some time until they migrate to other lands. Who is better equipped and who realizes the problem better than you and the other leaders of Vaad Hatzala? This means the preservation of our glorious heritage.

6. We have 700 visas for religious Jews who are now in Poland and something must be done to implement these visas so that these people may be able to leave. As mentioned before, we have 650 French visas for the children in Romania whom we must take out before it is too late.

7. The Jewish refugees in Sweden were helped by the Vaad Hatzala and Mr. Maurice Pineas made this statement in Johannesburg, "The Vaad Hatzala together with the Swedish section of the World Jewish Congress has done constructive work on behalf of the Displaced Persons in Sweden. Rav Aaron Price, the Chief Rabbi of Sweden, has done very little to alleviate the plight of the Jewish Displaced Persons." With the establishment of Talmud Torahs and Beth Jacob Schools and with financial assistance these D.P.s were enabled to observe the Sabbath, Kashruth and other traditions of our people. We did for them, Rabbi Rosenberg, what you and the Union of Orthodox Rabbis are trying to do for the Jews of America in your recent proclamation in the newspapers. But in recent months we were compelled to stop our assistance for lack of funds. Instead, we should be able to build more Talmud Torahs and Yeshivas in Sweden and give them more financial aid so that they can be saved and not become assimilated. The recent reports we have from there advise us that intermarriage with Christians is growing from day to day.

Dear Rabbi Rosenberg,

You know that I am the President of the Barton Candy Company which employs 450 people and which has, with the help of G-d, nineteen stores and a factory which is closed Shabbos and Jewish holidays. You know also that I sacrificed time from this business to go to Europe. While the Vaad Hatzala was functioning without disturbances, I was able with the help of the Almighty to establish contact with the Paris Consulate and government officials in Europe so that now close to 1000 Rabbis, scholars, students and religious Jews have been brought to this country. While in Europe I was able to help with the establishment of 65 Yeshivas, Talmud Torahs, Kosher Kitchens, Yeshiva Ketanos and Mikvehs in Germany and France. For more than a year this work has been going on, but recently the work has suffered, the immigration has slowed down, and the institutions which we established are in danger of closing their doors. You must realize that the only losers will be our Orthodox Jews, and Orthodoxy throughout the world will suffer. What we do not do today we certainly will not be able to do a half year later.

You should understand and realize that my work and my business occupies my time, but in spite of this great responsibility I am again willing to throw myself into the work of the Vaad Hatzala and help with time, energy and money to alleviate the suffering of our people. I know it helps because I had the great satisfaction of seeing some of these people receive their visas and I saw them on the boat and witnessed their arrival in the United States. These people add glory to Orthodoxy in the United States.

Dear Rabbi Rosenberg,

I am fully aware what it means to hold a position as great as yours and be the leader of the Rabbinate of America. As a simple Jew I know and understand what it means to respect the Rabbinate and the Torah which is represented by the Rabbinate. I have always had the greatest esteem for you and your colleagues and I shall continue to respect you in the future. But I feel sure that this respect will in no way be diminished if I write this letter and bring the facts to your attention so that you may take the necessary action. I also enclose a copy of the agreement that was made with the JDC and my remarks on each point and my reasoning. I am also enclosing a letter which I am sending to everyone who is to receive a copy of this letter I am sending to you.

I wish also to call your attention to the fact that when the Mizrachi came out in February 1947 with their campaign, you took a strong initiative and called upon all representatives of all organizations impressing upon them the importance of strengthening the Vaad Hatzala. After five months of strenuous work an agreement was reached and it was also decided that you would announce this agreement at the convention of the Agudas HaRabbonim. Instead, the Union of Orthodox Rabbis announced that they were going to make an agreement with the JDC. When I spoke to you about this agreement you promised me that the Vaad Hatzala would continue to function without any disturbances, but six months have passed and nothing has been done by the new Committee.

I am compelled again, Rabbi Rosenberg, to write these words to you and to advise you that if I do not hear from you I shall make this information public and request that immediate action be taken to help our unfortunate people. I look forward to hearing from you very shortly.

Respectfully yours,
Stephen Klein

⁓ Irving I. Stone *1909-2000*

ARCHITECT OF TORAH PHILANTHROPY

"Growing up in a home where Torah was precious and its study revered; imbued with his parents' philosophy that outstanding educators matter more than bricks and mortar; fired by the conviction that Jewish education means Jewish survival; firm in the belief that all segments of Jewry must support and benefit from Torah institutions – he became one of the monumental Torah pioneers and patrons of his time, in his native Cleveland, in Israel, and throughout America."

The Stone Edition of the ArtScroll Chumash

The name Irving I. Stone is synonymous with Torah education and Jewish life throughout the world. Irving's commitment to *tzedakah* and to *Klal Yisrael* is world-renowned, but he reserved his passion, vision, and energy for Jewish education. Irving Stone truly believed that a Jewish education is the key to Jewish survival. And throughout his life, Irving committed himself to developing a prototype of excellence in Jewish education for communities throughout the world to follow. The focus of his philanthropy was aimed at those organizations and institutions that promoted *achdus* among Jews. He was the dynamic chairman of American Greetings Corporation (founded 1906), a company he developed from a souvenir / postcard operation into the world industry leader that it is today – without compromising his *shemiras Shabbos*. Indeed, he might very well be considered the epitome of what a Torah businessman should be.

How did such an unusual man get his start?

The "family business" began in the living room of the Sapirstein home at 2169 East 70th Street in Cleveland, Ohio. At the age of five, Irving had the responsibility of stuffing the popular postcards into envelopes. In 1918, Irving was nine years old and a partner in the business, largely due to an influenza outbreak that left his father too weak to run the business himself. He delivered pots of his mother's chicken soup, as well as greeting cards, to his neighbors on 105th Street throughout the grueling winter months of 1918-1919.

"Everyone was close with each other in our neighborhood. It was a real shtetel. Nobody had a lot of money, but they had a lot of happiness.

Irving Stone truly believed that a Jewish education is the key to Jewish survival.

"My grandmother instilled in us the concept of caring for the needs of other people. Ever since I was a child, I was trained to be responsible for others. Anybody who came to the door and wanted help, we always helped. That was the way of living – the Jewish way of living. My father came here from Europe, a poor immigrant. He never forgot that when he was down and out the Joint Distribution Committee had helped him out.

"Now it is our responsibility to help others. We are all one people. I would rather give than have to receive. It is a responsibility we were taught as children.

"We were always very mindful of other people, and that the Al-mighty made us grow and do better. We share this with others. That was our way of living. We never said no to anything that came up. Anything worthwhile, we wanted to contribute. We always had the principle that the more you give, the more you'll make. The Al-mighty has been good to us. You can eat only three meals a day. I have indeed discovered that the more I give, the more I make."

There is little doubt, then, that a childhood filled with the teachings and admonitions of his elders to be deeply concerned with the welfare of others paid him big spiritual dividends. It is almost as though the young Irving Stone was apprenticed not in a manual trade, but in the noble arena of philanthropy!

However, as much as he was a pioneer in his philanthropic efforts, his success in creating a *shomer Shabbos* business helped to define him as a rugged Jewish individualist.

In a 1994 videotaped interview, Irving recalled, "We were able to build a

Jacob and Jennie Sapirstein with sons: (upper left) Irving, (bottom left) Harry, and Morris on his father's lap

big business without working on Shabbos. I did work on Sundays. In fact, as soon as Shabbos was over, I went down to work and stayed, often until midnight."

But even more important than his philanthropic endeavors and his establishment of one of the largest *shomer Shabbos* businesses in the entire world, Irving's main passion lay in actively promoting and furthering the Jewish education of the next generation. There is an interesting story that underscores the reasons for his almost superhuman devotion to Torah *chinuch*.

By 1921, Irving was twelve years old and was keeping the company's books. At this time, he and his father decided to take greeting cards to the people by making them available in corner drugstores, five-and-dimes, and other convenient places where people shopped. Nevertheless, waking early for school and working nights for his father's company left Irving little time

"We were always very mindful of other people, and that the Al-mighty made us grow and do better..."

A portrait of five generations: (Top L-R): Irving Stone, daughter, Hensha Gansbourg, (Bottom, L-R): Jacob Sapirstein, great-granddaughter Jodi Gottlieb and her daughter

---

"A people will not survive if they don't transmit their heritage from generation to generation."

to pursue religious study as a child. His mother, Jennie, insisted that Irving attend Hebrew school in the evenings.

"Every Shabbos, my dad would take out a Chumash and we would study it together. I loved to hear the stories and learn the history and the customs. That was a good way of life. *But as a youngster, I saw Jewish education as being shortchanged. People were not taking an interest.*

"When I married and had children, I remember that we had questions about their school. I was very unhappy that the schools were not up to the standards that they follow today. The teachers were never paid, and the community at that time was not sup-

porting Jewish day school education. I think we are suffering today because of the years back then, and because of the neglect of Jewish day school education. When my children had to go to school, I realized I didn't want them to go through the same thing I had to go through. I knew I had to train them. Otherwise, they were going to lose it. Of course, I couldn't do it myself; after all, I wasn't an educator. When you start the kids young with Jewish day school education, they never forget it.

"It goes without saying that I have a deep feeling for chinuch. It means a lot to me. A people will not survive if they don't transmit their heritage from generation to generation. I believe that if you're not going to transfer it, you will lose everything. I believe that Jewish education is our strongest guarantee for Jewish survival!"

Owing to this unbreakable bond with education, it was only natural that Irving Stone was one of the first pioneers to see the potential of the nascent Hebrew Academy of Cleveland in the 1940s: "We became involved with the opening of The Hebrew Academy of Cleveland, the first all-

Beatrice and Irving Stone

Jewish day-school in Cleveland. We became major supporters because we believed in it and it had a real meaning for us. When the Academy started, World War II had begun. Rabbi Bloch and Rabbi Katz, who were world renowned for promoting Jewish education, came to Cleveland looking to start a yeshiva. My father and a few others went to them and asked if they would help us open up a day school. Afterwards, what we did had a big impact on the community and on other communities all over the country. Day schools started to open up. However, it should be emphasized that Cleveland was really the first city to have a sizeable day school, run well, with top-notch teachers and a top-notch curriculum. Naturally, we insisted that it had to be top quality. It paid off. We came up with the money – it was really a struggle – but we achieved a new beginning. Although we started with but seventeen children, the school persevered as we did our part in shoring it up financially."

Indeed, Irving served as president of the Hebrew Academy of Cleveland from 1946 until 1976 and then served as board chairman until his death in 2000. He was considered a visionary on be.half of worldwide day school education. He was the first to successfully gain local Jewish Federation support for the Hebrew Academy of Cleveland, an example later followed by Federations across the country. Irving summed up his innovative approach toward working with Federation as follows:

"We had always been contributors to the Federation. Nonetheless, everybody fought with me about gaining Federation support for the Academy. The truth is, I was obstinate. I battled right through until I won! You should

Irving dancing with a Sefer Torah in honor of his 80th birthday

know that I had a big fight on my hands – even though we personally gave the Federation more money in those days than they ever gave the school."

As a consequence of his groundbreaking efforts in teaming up the Federation with the Hebrew Academy, and for the nationwide effects of such a *shidduch* Irving received the Charles Eisenman Award from the Jewish Community Federation of Cleveland in 1984. The Academy received this prestigious award in 1992.

Rabbi Nochum Zev Dessler, Dean of the Hebrew Academy of Cleveland, met Irving through his wife, Miriam, who had worked at American Greetings Corporation during 1941 and 1942.

The young couple invited Irving to their wedding in 1945, which was held at the Telshe Yeshiva.

Mrs. Dessler recalls her former boss being very impressed by the wedding:

"Mr. Stone was impressed with the whole experience. He danced with the *bachurim*. This was really not surprising – he was a *gutte neshama*, good soul."

Cleveland was really the first city to have a sizeable day school, run well, with top-notch teachers and a top-notch curriculum.

Soon afterwards, Rabbi Dessler introduced Irving to the Academy.

"I brought Irving in to visit the Academy. He had always had an interest in Jewish education, and he bemoaned the fact that he had never had the chance to attend a Jewish day school. He didn't feel he had learned much during his years in public school. He visited the Academy, and when I asked him to join us as a member of the board, he graciously accepted. He never missed a meeting, and he even came to some of our meetings with his father, J.S.

"I never asked Irving for money. I would take him around the school, and I would tell him what I thought our needs were at the time–and by the time we completed our visit, he would say, 'Well, we'll take care of all of that.' Big needs, small needs: it didn't make a difference.

(L-R): Rabbi Nochum Zev Dessler presenting award to Irving and Helen Stone.

"He was remarkable, of course, in his support of every Jewish endeavor. His generosity was without bounds, but it was coupled with and accompanied by a wonderful sense of humility and modesty. The more he did, the less he thought of himself as worthy. He was a remarkable person.

> *His generosity was without bounds, but it was coupled with and accompanied by a wonderful sense of humility and modesty.*

Irving Stone at the burning of the Young Israel mortgage

"He once told me, 'My dividends are the students learning at the Academy. And because I invest in them, those are the dividends that I possess, and those dividends will be with me forever.' His greatest pride were the graduates of our school. He treated them like his own children. He would often travel for business to countries as far away as Australia and South Africa and call me, just to tell me with pride that he found one of our alumni teaching at a yeshiva or holding a leading position in the community."

"Many years ago, our high school was located in the Young Israel building on Cedar Road. It was very crowded. It was a beautiful institution, but it was so limited in space. The next thing I know, Irving picked me up and took me to what is now the Mesivta grounds. He said, 'I like this area because it's secluded. Is it okay with you?' I said,

(L-R): Rabbi Shneur Kotler, Rabbi Moshe Feinstein, Irving Stone, Rabbi Henoch Cohen

'Sure.' His response was, 'You have it!' It cost him about $135,000 at the time. He had used his United Airlines stock to buy it – and you know what he told me? 'The more I give, the more I make!' " Even within the field of *chinuch*, Irving Stone was an innovator whose ideas continue to reverberate not just in Cleveland, but throughout

Even within the field of chinuch, Irving Stone was an innovator whose ideas continue to reverberate not just in Cleveland, but throughout the world as well.

Receiving an award at Chinuch Atzmai Dinner –
(L-R): Rabbi N.Z. Dessler, Rabbi Shraga Grossbard, Rabbi Henoch Cohen, Irving Stone, Rabbi Boruch Sorotzkin

the world as well. Rabbi Dessler reminds us that, "It was his idea to give scholarships to the graduates who went on to Israel for a year of study. In those years, $1000 was a lot of money. I would suggest to the graduates that they call Irving or visit him in person to say 'thank you,' but he never wanted them to know that the money came from him."

Mr. Stone applied his business techniques and strategies to providing for the furtherance of Jewish education. Rabbi Dessler attests, "Every year at banquet time, Irving and I would meet and go over the notes from the year before. He would make some phone calls for us and follow them up with a letter. The Academy still benefits from some of the men and women whom he had contacted on our behalf. People contributed to the Academy because of their respect for him. The Cleveland community identified the Hebrew Academy with Irving Stone. He was our president for over thirty years. I didn't want him to step down but he

> *Mr. Stone applied his business techniques and strategies to providing for the furtherance of Jewish education.*

said, 'No. We have to bring in other people. There are roles to fill, and we need to let some younger people come on board.' He became our chairman of the board. Irving saw to it that integrity and honesty should prevail in everything associated with the day school – both in its successes and in its failures."

He was also a major supporter of such educational institutions as Telshe Yeshiva in Wickliffe, Ohio, and Aish HaTorah, which offers adult Jewish education for those with either a secular or traditional background. He also served as president of the National Commission on Torah Education and as vice president of the American Association for Jewish Education. Regarding his efforts in this area, Rabbi Yehuda Appel, executive director of Aish HaTorah in Cleveland, asserts, "It was the area of Jewish education that was the most important of his charitable endeavors. Mr. Stone believed intensely that every Jewish child in Cleveland – regardless of need – should be able to have a Jewish education, and he was ready to pay for it. He truly believed that he had a G-d-given responsibility to do so – especially since G-d had blessed him greatly. He fulfilled this responsibility with wisdom, humility, and concern."

Lest one think that Irving Stone was concerned solely with the success of his hometown day school, the facts prove that he gladly extended his beneficence throughout the Jewish world. Rabbi Dessler relates, "Irving contributed to various yeshivos in *Eretz Yisrael*, in which our graduates had studied. We once went to Israel together so that he could see where his money was going. We toured the yeshivos together one day, and at the end of the day he turned to me and

(L-R): Stephen Klein, Irving Stone, Rabbi Fishel Gelernter, Irving Bunim

Family Portrait: (bottom L-R): Jeffrey Weiss, Jacob Sapirstein, Irving Stone; (top L-R): Morry Weiss, Gary Weiss, Elie Weiss, Zev Weiss

said, 'I'm glad I did it, but I'm not giving enough!'"

Irving's love of Torah and love of *Eretz Yisrael* soon manifested itself when he gave a substantial contribution to the Telshe Yeshiva to build a branch in the Holy Land. Soon thereafter, what became known as Kiryat Telshe-Stone began to take shape under the direction of Rabbi Eliezer Sorotzkin and guided by the venerable *Rosh HaYeshiva*, Rabbi Mordechai Gifter.

Irving's philanthropy was evident in several areas that, at first glance, do not seem to fall within the purview of Jewish education. One was care for the elderly, for which he felt a passionate commitment. Irving's generosity extended beyond bricks and mortar. Indicative of his commitment to the aged was his sponsorship of Stone Gardens, an Assisted Living Center and part of the Menorah Park geriatric complex. It serves as a lovely and serene setting where senior citizens can find respite and peace of mind in an independent setting. Regarding Menorah Park, one knowledgeable person has said: "When Irving Stone

It was the area of Jewish education that was the most important of his charitable endeavors.

Agudath Israel Dinner (L-R): Martin Klein, Rabbi Nathan Baruch, Irving Stone, Rabbi Moshe Sherer

sense of identity as religious Jews."

In keeping with his philosophy that Jewish learning knows no time or geographic boundaries, Irving could be seen helping everywhere – and at all times! Consequently, in 1993, he was honored by the Endowment for Democracy in Eastern Europe with the Founders' Award for his efforts to rekindle Jewish identity in Eastern Europe by helping to re-establish a Jewish day school in Budapest.

In his later years, when Irving found it hard to read the fine print in the *Chumash*, he commissioned a clearer, more modern edition of his own. In 1993, he sponsored the ArtScroll / Mesorah publication of *The Stone Chumash*, an unprecedented new English translation of the *Chumash*. *The Stone Chumash* contains an array of

---

"Irving Stone was a creative and resourceful visionary and activist whose idealism, strength, and determination built a new generation."

gave of himself, he gave with his heart and his soul. He was a friend and benefactor to our community and to many around the world. Without his vision and commitment, our community would certainly not have been the same. There are few individuals who have not been touched in some way by his generosity or by his love. And we are all the better for having known him."

Similarly, members of both the Orthodox Union and the National Conference of Synagogue Youth (N.C.S.Y.) attest that, "Irving Stone was a creative and resourceful visionary and activist whose idealism, strength, and determination built a new generation." Rabbi Pinchas Stolper, former senior executive of the Orthodox Union, said, "Mr. Stone knew the importance and the potential of N.C.S.Y. He saw that kids need a comfortable environment and a positive

Irving Stone at Yeshiva University Graduation

commentaries never before available in English versions of the classical Biblical text. As it is designed for year-round synagogue use, the *Stone Edition* also includes the *Five Megillos* and all the *Haftorahs*.

In 1998, Ohr Torah Institutions of Israel paid tribute to Irving for his generous support of their educational complex of high schools, college and graduate programs, and seminaries and yeshivos. The complex was re-named Ohr Torah Stone. Explains Rabbi Shlomo Riskin, chief Rabbi of Efrat and founding dean of Ohr Torah Stone: "Torah has kept the Jewish People alive for over 4000 years. Ohr is a light that illuminates, welcomes in, and unifies. In a similar vein, Ohr Torah Stone Institutions teach Torah, to Jewish men and women from all walks of life. The Ten Commandments were given on stone tablets. The Hebrew word for building [בנה] comes from the root word for 'stone [אבן].' 'Stone' in Hebrew is also related to the words for father and child [אב, בן] which together constitute the true building blocks of Jewish life and religion."

Is it any surprise, then, that every Friday afternoon, Irving called all his children and grandchildren to wish them a good Shabbos? "I call my children usually on Friday before the Sabbath, and say a few words and see how they are doing. It takes me a few hours, but I know that it's a worthwhile activity. I enjoy talking to them and hearing how they are all doing, **and I let them know that I love them.**"

The same may be said of Mr. Irving Stone's lifelong preoccupation with Jewish education, with the welfare of Jewish youth and Jewish seniors, and with his all-consuming love of Torah and his fellow-Jews. Rabbi Dessler has said it best – that when it comes to understanding Irving's love for Torah education and his affection for his family, **"Sometimes it wasn't easy to distinguish between the two. After all, he treated the Academy and its children and personnel just like his own family for over 50 years."**

Indeed, this statement may be made generally about Irving Stone and his relationship to his fellow Jews: he treated them *just like his own family his entire life!*

When it came to understanding Irving's love for Torah education and his affection for his family, "Sometimes it wasn't easy to distinguish between the two."

Entrance to Kiryat Telshe-Stone

✒ GLOSSARY OF TERMS

achdus– unity

agunah/agunos (pl)– women whose husband is missing with no evidence of his death

ahavas (ha)Torah– love for the Torah

aliyah– honor of being called to the Torah

Amen– word recited after a blessing to show one's acceptance of the truth of that blessing

Amora– Talmudic Sage who interpreted the words of the *Tannaim*

amud– lectern, platform

askan / askanim (pl)– communal worker

Av Beis Din– chief judge of the rabbinical court

aveilus– mourning

Avodas Hashem– Service of G-d

baal habayis / baalei batim (pl)– (lit,. head of a household) layman

baal (baalei, pl.) teshuvah– repentant or returnee to religious observance

bachur / bachurim (pl)– unmarried male student(s)

beheimah / beheimos (pl)– livestock

bein hasedarim– time between morning and afternoon study sessions

Beis Din– Jewish court

Beis HaMikdash– the Holy Temple in Jerusalem

beis (ha)medrash / battei medrash (pl)– study hall(s) of a yeshiva

bekisheh– black caftan

ben Torah / bnei Torah (pl.)– One who studies and adheres to the practices of the Torah

bentching– prayer after meals (Yiddish)

bentch licht– light [Shabbos/*Yom Tov*] candles (Yiddish)

bimah– podium upon which the Torah is placed and read in *shul*

bitachon– trust in G-d

blatt– folio page of Gemara

Boruch Hashem– thank G-d

berachah / berachos (pl)– blessing

bubby– grandmother (Yiddish)

chaburah / chaburos (pl)– organized learning group(s)

chacham / chachamim (pl)– sage

challah– special braided loaf of bread made for Shabbos and *Yom Tov*

chametz– leavening; substance forbidden on Pesach

chanukas habayis– dedication of a new house or building

chassan– groom

chassid / chassidim (pl)– follower of a chassidic movement

Chassidei Umos HaOlam– Righteous Gentiles of the World

chassidic– adhering to *Chassidism*

chasunah– wedding

chaver / chaveirim (pl)– friend

chavrusa– learning partner

Chazal– (acronym for **CH**achameinu **Z**ichronam **L**ivracha) the Sages from the time of the *Mishnah* and *Gemara*

chazan / chazzanim (pl)– leader of the prayer service; cantor

cheder / chadarim (pl)– Orthodox elementary school(s) (usually taught in Yiddish)

cherem– excommunication, ban

chesed– kindness

Cheshvan– the eighth Hebrew month

Chevra Shas– a group that learns Gemara

Chevrah Kadisha– burial society

chiddushei Torah– Torah novellae; original analyses and interpretations of difficult points of Torah topics

chillul– desecration

chinuch– Jewish education

chizuk– strength

chachmah– wisdom

chodesh– month

Chol Hamoed– intermediate days of Succos and Passover holidays

Chumash/Chumashim (pl)– the Five Books of Moses

chuppah– wedding canopy or ceremony

churban– destruction

daas Torah– Torah viewpoints

daven– pray (Yiddish)

dayan/dayanim (pl)– judge(s)

derech eretz– respect, proper manners

d'veikus– closeness to G-d

dikduk– Hebrew grammar

Din Torah– judicial case based on Torah law

divrei chizuk– words of encouragement

divrei Torah– Torah lectures (literally, words of Torah)

drashah / drashos (pl)– sermon

Elul– the sixth Hebrew month

emes– truth

emunah– faith in G-d

emunas chachamim– faith in the words of our Torah leaders

Eretz Yisrael– the land of Israel

erev– before, eve of...(erev Pesach, erev Shabbos)

erlicher– honest, moral (Yiddish)

esrog / esrogim(pl)– citron fruit (one of the four species used on Succos)

frum– religious (Yiddish)

frumer yid– a religious Jew (Yiddish)

gabbai/gabbaim (pl)– a) synagogue official b) *shamash*

gadol/gedolim (pl)– Torah leader of the generation

galus– exile, Diaspora

gaon/gaonim (pl)– genius; brilliant Torah scholar

gelt– money (Yiddish)

Gemara/Gemaros (pl)– book of the Talmud

get/gitten (pl)– Jewish divorce

geulah– redemption

goyim– gentiles

hakafah– circuit (with Torah scrolls on Simchas Torah)

halachah– Jewish law

Hallel– song of praise comprising certain chapters *Tehillim* written by King David

hanhalah– administration

Hashem– G-d, the creator (lit., "the Name")

Hashgachah Pratis– Divine Providence

hashkafah– religious outlook

hasmadah– diligence, perseverance

Haskalah– so-called Enlightenment movement, which disregarded many Torah laws and traditions

hatzalah– rescue

hatzlachah– success

Havdalah– ceremony at the conclusion of Shabbos and Festivals

hechsher/hechsheirim (pl)– kosher certification

heimishe– an Orthodox Jew of similar conviction and outlook usually a referance to a chassidic background. (Yiddish)

hesped/hespeidim (pl)– eulogy

heter– authoritative permission

hislahavus– enthusiasm, deep emotion

iluy– prodigy, genius

k'nas– fine

Kaddish– prayer recited by a mourner (or other individual) in honor of the deceased

kallah– bride

kana'i– zealot

Kaparos– atonement ritual performed before Yom Kippur

kapoteh– long day coat worn by Chassidic Jews (Yiddish)

kashrus– laws of keeping kosher

kavanah– thoughtful intent

Kedoshim– martyrs

kedushah– holiness

kehillah/kehillos (pl.)– community

kever– grave

Kiddush– prayer over wine made before eating on Sabbath and holidays

Kiddush Hashem– Sanctification of G-d's Name

kiruv– drawing near

Klal Yisrael– the Jewish Nation

kollel– Rabbinical Seminary; post-graduating yeshiva, usually for married men

korban/korbanos (pl)– sacrifice(s)

kvittel/kvitlach– notes with requests given to Chassidic *Rebbes* to include in their prayers on behalf of the petitioner

lamdan/lamdonim (pl)– accomplished scholar

lashon hara– gossip, slander

levayah– funeral

limud haTorah– Torah study

limudei kodesh– religious studies

lishmah– for its own sake

Ma'ariv– the evening prayer service

machlokes– controversy

machzor– special prayer book for High Holidays and Festivals

maggid/maggidim (pl)– preacher, lecturer

makom Torah– a place of Torah learning (and living)

malach– angel

malshin– slanderer, informer

mashgiach/mashgichim (pl)–
1. spiritual advisor and mentor of a yeshiva   2. supervisor of kosher food production

maskil/maskilim (pl)– follower of the "Enlightenment" movement

masmid– diligent student

Matan Torah– the giving of the Torah

matzeivah– memorial monument

matzliach– successful

maven– knowledgeable, expert

mechallel Shabbos– profaning the holiness of the Sabbath day

mechanech– teacher/educator

mechazek– give spiritual and moral strength

mechitzah– partition

mekubal/mekubalim (pl.)– mystic, student of Kabbalah

melamed/melamdim (pl)– Torah teacher (male)

Melaveh Malkah– meal eaten after *Havdalah* in honor of the departing Shabbos/festival

menachem avel– comfort a mourner

menahel– principal

menuchah– rest

mesader kiddushin– person officiating at a wedding ceremony

mesiras nefesh– self-sacrifice

mezuzah/mezuzos (pl)– small parchment with passages from the Torah, affixed to most doorposts of Jewish home

midah/midos (pl)– character trait

mikveh/mikvaos (pl)– ritual bath

Minchah– afternoon prayer service

minhag– custom

minyan/minyanim (pl)– quorum of 10 men necessary for conducting a prayer service

mischazeik– to be encouraged

mispallelim– worshippers

Mishnayos– books of the Oral Law

misnagid/misnagdim (pl)– opponent of the Chassidic movement

mitzvah/mitzvos (pl)– Torah commandment(s)

madreigah– level

Mora D'asra– Rabbi of a *shul* or city

Mashiach– the Redeemer, the Messiah

Motza'ei Shabbos– end of Shabbos (Saturday night)

Musaf– additional prayer service recited on Shabbos, Rosh Chodesh and festivals

mussar– study of ethical behavior

nedavah/nedavos (pl)– donation

nefesh/nefashos (pl)– soul

neshamah/neshamos (pl)– soul

niftar– (n.)the deceased; (v.) passed away

niggun– tune

nisayon– test

ohel– tent

Olam Haba– World to Come

Olam Hazeh– This World

oneg Shabbos– enjoyment of Shabbos

parnasah– income, livelihood

pasuk– verse

peyos– sidelocks (sideburns)

petirah– death

pikuach nefesh– saving an endangered life

posek / poskim (pl)– Rabbinic authority who decides Jewish law

psak halachah– final legal ruling

pushke– charity box (Yiddish)

rabbanus– rabbinate

rebbe– religious leader or teacher

rebbetzin– wife of a religious leader or teacher

Ribbono shel Olam– Master of the Universe

Rosh Chodesh– beginning of the Jewish month

Rosh Hashanah– the Jewish New Year

Rosh HaYeshiva/Roshei Yeshiva (pl)– dean of a yeshiva

Rav/rabbanim (pl)– rabbi of a congregation or community

ruach– spirit

ruchnius– spirituality

seder / sedarim (pl)– learning session

sefer / sefarim (pl)– religious book

seichel– understanding, common sense

semichah– rabbinic ordination

seudah– festive meal

seudah shlishis– the third Shabbos meal

Shacharis– morning prayer service

shadchan– matchmaker

sh'eilah / sh'eilos (pl)– question concerning Jewish law and practice

shamash– a) synagogue caretaker b) *Rebbe's* assistant or personal secretary

Shas– complete set of Talmud

Shechinah– Divine Presence

shechitah– ritual slaughter

shecht– to slaughter an animal according to Jewish law

sherayim– remainder of a *Rebbe's* meal, eaten by his chassidim

shidduch– marriage match

shiur / shiurim (pl)– 1. class 2. lesson

shiva– seven-day mourning period observed for the death of a close relative

shleimus– completeness, perfection

shliach mitzvah– emissary for a mitzvah

shliach tzibur– person leading the prayer service

shmues / shmuessen (pl)– lecture on ethics and proper conduct

shochet /shochtim (pl)– ritual slaughterer

Shomer Shabbos– Sabbath observer

shtetel / shtetlach (pl)– village (Yiddish)

shtibel / shtiblach (pl)– Chassidic *shul(s)* (Yiddish)

shtreimel– round fur hat worn by chassidic Jews (Yiddish)

shul– synagogue

sifrei kedushah– holy books

simchah / simchos (pl)– joy; joyous occasion

siyata d'Shemaya– G-d's help

Succos– the holiday of Tabernacles

siyum– completion (usually of a Talmudic tractate)

taharas hamishpachah– family purity

tallis/talleisim (pl.)– prayer shawl

talmid chacham/talmidei chachamim (pl)– Torah scholar

talmid / talmidim (pl)– yeshiva student

Talmud– explanation of the Oral Law (*Mishnah*)

talmud Torah– study of Torah

Tanach– books of the Torah, Prophets and Writings

Tanna– Authority quoted in the *Mishnah*

tefillah / tefillos (pl.)– prayer

tefillah b'tzibbur– public prayer with a *minyan*

tefillin– phylacteries

taharah– purification

Tehillim– the book of Psalms written by King David

teshuvah– 1. repentance, return 2. halachic ruling

tisch– (lit., table) chassidic Rebbe's meal at which he shares food, Torah thoughts and *zemiros*

Tishah B'Av– the 9th of Av, a fast day commemorating the destruction of the *Beis HaMikdash*

tzaddik / tzaddikim (pl)– righteous person

tzadeikes– righteous woman

tzaros– troubles

tzedakah– charity

tzenuah– modest woman

tzibur– community, congregation

tzidkus– righteousness

tznius– modesty

viduy– confession (recited on Yom Kippur and before death)

yahrtzeit– anniversary of a person's death

yahrtzeit shiur– a Torah lecture given on a yahrtzeit

yemach shemo– may his name be blotted out

Yamim Noraim– Days of Awe

yeshiva / yeshivos– school where Torah is taught

yeshiva gedolah– religious high school

yeshiva ketanah– religious elementary school

Yeshiva shel Maalah– Heavenly Torah academy, where the souls of the righteous dwell

yetzer hara– evil inclination

yichus– family lineage

Yid/Yidden (pl)– Yiddish word for a Jew

yirah– fear, usually associated with fear of Heaven

yiras Shamayim– fear of Heaven (G-d)

ylt – yibadel lechaim tovim– may he be singled-out for good life

Yom Kippur– Day of Atonement

yom tov– festival

zl– *zichrono livrachah* – may his memory be a blessing

z'man– specific amount of time; a semester

zechus– merit, privilege

zemiros– Sabbath songs

zocheh– to merit

≈ BIBLIOGRAPHY/ RECOMMENDED READING

AGUDATH ISRAEL ARCHIVES

Agudath Israel Of America, **Ashes to Renewal**, New York, NY 1997

Allswang, Dr. Benzion, **The Final Resolution**, Feldheim Publishers, New York, 1989

Araten, Rochel Sarna, **Michalina: Daughter of Israel**, Feldheim Publishers, Spring Valley, NY, 1986

Bais Esther LaBanos, *Shalsheles Bais Sanz*, Sanz, Klausenberg, Israel

Baumol, Rav Yehoshua, **A Blaze in the Darkening Gloom**, Feldheim Publishers, Spring Valley, NY, 1994

Benisch, Pearl, **To Vanquish the Dragon**, Feldheim Publishers, Spring Valley, NY, 1991

Bernstein, Saul, **The Orthodox Union Story**, Jason Aronson Inc., Northvale, NJ, 1997

Blau, Dr. Rivkah, **Learn Torah, Live Torah, Love Torah**, Ktav Publishing House, Hoboken, NJ, 2001

Bostoner Rebbe, **And the Angels Laughed**, Mesorah Publications, Brooklyn, NY, 1997

Brafman, Yaakov, and Tatz, Akiva, **Reb Simcha Speaks**, Mesorah Publications, Brooklyn, NY, 1994

Bromberg, Rabbi Y.A., **The Sanzer Rav and His Dynasty**, Mesorah Publications, Brooklyn, NY, 1986

Bunim, Rabbi Amos, **A Fire in His Soul**, Feldheim Publishers, Spring Valley, NY, 1989

Cohen, Israel I., **Destined to Survive**, Mesorah Publications, Brooklyn, NY, 2001

Dansky, Miriam, **Rebbetzin Grunfeld**, Mesorah Publications, Brooklyn, NY, 1994

Davidowicz, Lucy S., **The War Against The Jews: 1933-1945**, Holt, Rinehart and Winston, New York, NY, 1975

Dekelman Laura/Rebbetzin Chana Rubin, **The Final Solution Is Life**, Mesorah Publications, Brooklyn, NY, 2001

deSola Pool, David and Tamar, **An Old Faith in the New World**, Columbia University Press, NY, 1955

Encyclopedia Judaica, Keter Publishing, Jerusalem, Israel, 1978

Finkelman, Rabbi Shimon, **Reb Chaim Ozer – The Life and Ideals of Rabbi Chaim Ozer Grodzenski of Vilna**, Mesorah Publications, Brooklyn, NY, 1987

Finkelman, Rabbi Shimon / Scherman, Rabbi Nosson, **Reb Moshe**, Mesorah Publications, Brooklyn, NY, 1986

Fox, David, **Greatness in Our Midst**, Feldheim Publishers, New York, 1955

Friedenson, Joseph, **Dateline: Istanbul**, Mesorah Publications, Brooklyn, NY, 1993

Friedenson, J. and Kranzler, D., **Heroine of Rescue**, Mesorah Publications, Brooklyn, NY, 1984

Fuchs, Abraham, **The Unheeded Cry**, Mesorah Publications, Brooklyn, NY, 1986

Gilbert, Martin, **The Atlas of the Holocaust**, William Morrow, New York, NY, 1988

Granatstein, Yechiel, **One Jew's Power - One Jew's Glory**, Feldheim Publishers, Spring Valley, NY, 1991

Gevirtz, E. and Kranzler, D., **To Save a World, Volumes 1 & 2**, C.I.S. Publications, Lakewood, NJ, 1991

Grossman, Rav Reuven, **The Legacy of Slabodk**a, Feldheim, New York, 1989

Grossman, Rav Reuven, **The Rosh Yeshiva**, Feldheim, New York, 1988

Helmreich, William B., **The World of the Yeshiva**, Yale University Press, New Haven/London, 1982

Hertzman, Rabbi Elchonon, **The Mashgiach,** Jerusalem, Israel, 1981

Hoyt, Edwin P., **Hitler's War**, McGraw-Hill Publishing Co., New York, NY, 1988

Jackdaw Publications, **The Holocaust**, A Division of Golden Owl Publishing, Amawalk, NY

Kaminetsky, Dr. Joseph, **Memorable Encounters**, Shaar Press, NY, 1995

Kranzler, Dr. Gershon, **A Look Back**, Shaar Press, NY, 2001

Kranzler, David, **Thy Brother's Blood: The Orthodox Jewish Response During the Holocuast**, Mesorah Publications, Brooklyn, NY, 1987

Kranzler, Dr. David, **Rav Breuer: His Life Legacy**, Feldheim Publishers, NY, 1998

Kranzler, Gershon, **Williamsburg Memories**, C.I.S. Publications, Lakewood, NJ, 1988

Lamet, Rosalie, **City of Diamonds**, Feldheim Publishers, Spring Valley, NY, 1996

Leitner, Yecheskel, **Operation: Torah Rescue**, Feldheim Publishers, Spring Valley, NY,1987

Lev, Baruch, ***B'ikedushah Shel Maalah***, Machon Mishkenos Yaakov, Shikun Skvere, 2002

Levin, Nora, **The Holocaust**, Crowell Publishers, New York, 1968

Oshry, Rabbi Ephraim, **The Annihilation of Lithuanian Jewry**, Judaica Press, Brooklyn, NY, 1996

O.U. Centennial Booklet

Pekier, Alter, **From Kletzk to Siberia**, Mesorah Publications, Brooklyn, NY, 1985

Rabinowitz, Rabbi Tzvi, **Chassidic Rebbes**, Targum Press, NY, 1989

Rakeffet - Aaron Rothkoff , **Bernard Revel**, Feldheim Publishers, NY, 1972

Rakeffet - Rothkoff, **The Silver Era In American Orthodox Jewry: Rabbi Eliezer Silver and his Generation**, Feldheim Publishers, Spring Valley, NY, 1981

Rakeffet - Rothkoff, **Rabbi Dr. Joseph Soloveitchik**, Ktav Publishing House, Hoboken, NJ, 1999

Rosenblum, Yonasan, **Reb Shraga Feivel**, Mesorah Publications, Brooklyn, NY, 2001

Rosenblum, Yonasan, **Reb Yaakov**, Mesorah Publications, Brooklyn, NY, 1993

Rosenblum, Yonasan, **They Called Him Mike**, Mesorah Publications, Brooklyn, NY, 1995

Rosengarten, Judy, **Worlds Apart**, Targum/Feldheim, Spring Valley, NY, 1992

Rozman, Shlomo, **Roshei Golas Ariel**, Mifaal Zichron Kedoshim, Brooklyn, NY, 1975

Schiff, Rabbi Eliyakim, and G., **The Five Gates**, Feldheim Publishers, Spring Valley, NY, 1994

Schwartz, Rabbi Y. and Goldstein Y., **Shoah**, Mesorah Publications, Brooklyn, NY, 1990

Shain, Ruchoma, **All for the Boss**, Feldheim Publishers, Spring Valley, NY, 1984

Shapiro, Chaim, **Go, My Son**, Feldheim Publishers, Spring Valley, NY, 1989

Sherer, Rabbi Moshe, **Against All Odds**, Agudath Israel, New York, NY, 1997

Silber, Rabbi Dovid, **Noble Lives, Noble Deeds**, Mesorah Publications, Brooklyn, NY, 2002

Sinason, Jacob H., **Saba Marches On**, Feldheim Publishers, Spring Valley, NY, 1993

Sonnenfeld, Rabbi Sholom Zalman, **Guardian of Jerusalem**, Mesorah Publications, Brooklyn, NY, 1983

Sonnenfeld, S.Z., **Voices in the Silence**, Feldheim Publishers, Spring Valley, NY, 1992

Surasky, Aharon, **Giants Of Jewry**, Chinuch Publications, Lakewood, NJ, 1982

Surasky, Rabbi Aharon, **Reb Elchonon**, Mesorah Publications, Brooklyn, NY, 1982

Surasky, Rabbi Aharon, *Shlucha D'Rachmana*, Feldheim Publishers, Jerusalem, Israel, 1992

Surasky, Rabbi Aharon, *Tenuas HaMussar*, Jerusalem, Israel,

Stern, Rabbi Yechiel Michel, **The Mashgiach of Kamenitz**, Feldheim Publishers, Jerusalem, Israel, 1999

The Encyclopedia of the Holocaust, Macmillian Publishers, New York, NY, 1990

Wahrman, Rabbi Shlomo, **Lest We Forget**, Mesorah Publications, Brooklyn, NY, 1991

Wein, Berel, **Triumph of Survival**, Shaar Press, NY, 1990

Winston, Rabbi Pinchas, **The Unbroken Chain of Jewish Tradition**, CIS, Lakewood, NJ, 1986

Wolpin, Rabbi Nisson, **A Path Through the Ashes**, Mesorah Publications, Brooklyn, NY, 1986

Wolpin, Rabbi Nisson, **The Torah Personality**, Mesorah Publications, Brooklyn, NY, 1980

Wolpin, Rabbi Nisson, **The Torah Profile**, Mesorah Publications, Brooklyn, NY, 1988

Wolpin, Rabbi Nisson, **The Torah World**, Mesorah Publications, Brooklyn, NY, 1988

Wolpin, Rabbi Nisson, **Torah Lives**, Mesorah Publications, Brooklyn, NY, 1995

Wolpin, Rabbi Nisson, **Torah Luminaries**, Mesorah Publications, Brooklyn, NY, 1994

Wyman, David S., **The Abandonment of the Jews: America and the Holocaust 1941-45**, NY, 1984

Yoshor, Rabbi Moses M., **The Chafetz Chaim**, Vol. 1 & 2, Mesorah Publications, Brooklyn, NY 1985

YU Archives – Vaad Hatzala Collection

Zuroff, Efraim, **The Response of Orthodox Jewry in the United States to the Holocaust**, Yeshiva University Press, Ktav Publishing House, Hoboken, NJ, 2000